# Rational Choice
## in an
# Uncertain
## World

# 2
EDITION

# Rational Choice
## in an
# Uncertain
The Psychology of Judgment
and Decision Making
# World

EDITION

Reid Hastie
*University of Chicago*

Robyn M. Dawes
*Carnegie Mellon University*

Los Angeles | London | New Delhi
Singapore | Washington DC

*For information:*

SAGE Publications, Inc.
2455 Teller Road
Thousand Oaks,
   California 91320
E-mail: order@sagepub.com

SAGE Publications India Pvt. Ltd.
B 1/I 1 Mohan Cooperative
   Industrial Area
Mathura Road, New Delhi 110 044
India

SAGE Publications Ltd.
1 Oliver's Yard
55 City Road
London EC1Y 1SP
United Kingdom

SAGE Publications Asia-Pacific Pte. Ltd.
33 Pekin Street #02-01
Far East Square
Singapore 048763

Printed in the United States of America

*Library of Congress Cataloging-in-Publication Data*

Hastie, Reid.
Rational choice in an uncertain world: the psychology of judgment and decision making/Reid Hastie, Robyn M. Dawes. — 2nd ed.
   p. cm.
Includes bibliographical references and index.
ISBN 978-1-4129-5903-2 (pbk. : acid-free paper)
   1. Judgment. 2. Decision making. I. Dawes, Robyn M., 1936- II. Title.

BF447.H37 2010
153.8′3—dc22                                         2009033513

This book is printed on acid-free paper.

09   10   11   12   13   10   9   8   7   6   5   4   3   2   1

| | |
|---|---|
| *Acquisitions Editor:* | Lisa Cuevas Shaw |
| *Editorial Assistant:* | Sarita Sarak |
| *Production Editor:* | Karen Wiley |
| *Copy Editor:* | Teresa Herlinger |
| *Typesetter:* | C&M Digitals (P) Ltd. |
| *Proofreader:* | Scott Oney |
| *Indexer:* | Jeanne Busemeyer |
| *Cover Designer:* | Candice Harman |
| *Marketing Manager:* | Christy Guilbault |

# Contents

# Preface

*The greatest enemy of truth is very often not the lie—deliberate, contrived, and dishonest—but the myth—persistent, pervasive, and unrealistic.*

—John F. Kennedy

In this book, we present basic theories and research findings from the field of judgment and decision making in as nontechnical a way as possible. Students have liked this approach in the classroom, and we hope that readers of this book will like it, too. We have been teaching this material for more than 30 years to students at Carnegie Mellon University, University of Chicago, University of Colorado, University of Oregon, Northwestern University, and Harvard University. We have found that these courses are more popular with students than any of the other topics that we teach.

A primary motivation for writing this book was our belief that an understanding of the principles of rational decision making can help people improve the quality of their choices and, thus, their lives. The material is not only profound and fascinating; it is practically useful as well. Again, students recognize this and have frequently told us, years after they completed our courses, that what they learned has made a difference in their everyday lives (a greater difference than knowing that their anterior cingulate is part of the mesocortical system or that hebephrenic schizophrenics are the silly ones).

The book is divided into six sections. Chapters 1 and 2 provide some history and introduce the main themes of rational versus descriptive approaches to judgment and decision making. Chapters 3 through 7 review the psychology of judgment. Chapter 8 focuses on the accuracy and rationality of our habits of judgment. Chapters 9 and 10 review what we know about where our basic values come from and how we make choices when there is little uncertainty about obtaining outcomes, but often much uncertainty about how much we will like them. Chapters 11 and 12 review the major theory of rational decision making, subjective expected utility theory, and the major descriptive psychological theory, prospect theory. Chapter 13 takes a look at cutting-edge research directions in the field. The final chapter reviews our major themes and conclusions, with an exhortation to appreciate the positive aspects of living with uncertainty. Finally, the Appendix provides an introduction to the concepts from mathematical probability theory that we rely on throughout the book.

We compare basic principles of rationality with actual behavior in making decisions. There is a discrepancy. Moreover, this discrepancy is due not to random errors or mistakes but to automatic and deliberate thought processes that influence how decision problems are conceptualized and how future possibilities in life are evaluated. The overarching argument is that our thinking processes are limited in systematic ways, and we review extensive behavioral research to support this conclusion.

We attempt to present as clearly and forcefully as possible the implications of the research we describe. Subsequent research will doubtless show that some of the conclusions reached in this book are incorrect or that they require modification, but we take the position that research—not anecdotes, not "plausible beliefs," not common sense, and not our everyday experience—should be the basis for understanding and evaluating our decision-making achievements and defeats. Nevertheless, we have used anecdotes as a teaching device. Over a combined experience of more than 50 years of study and teaching, we have collected many anecdotes that illustrate how our thinking about decision problems systematically deviates from rationality.

The theme of limited cognitive capacity conflicts with our preconceptions about how smart we are. While many of us are willing to accept the idea that our unconscious (for Freud) or "animal" (for Plato and Aristotle) or "hotheaded" natures may interfere with our reasoning, the idea that thinking per se is a fundamentally flawed and limited process is an unpleasant one. Moreover, many people reject the view that thinking is flawed on the grounds that our dominant-species status on this planet is related to our cerebral capacity, and evidenced by our technologically advanced civilizations. This commonsense argument is flawed in several respects.

First, although evolution is often phrased in terms of the "survival of the fittest," its actual mechanism is better described as "survival of the *fitter*." Animals that have a higher probability than their competitors of surviving to adulthood and reproducing in a particular environment have a higher probability of dispersing their genes to future generations. Successful animals need not be optimal when compared with some physical or mathematical criterion of optimality, but only "one-up" on competing animals and their forebears. Even that comparative superiority is defined relative to the particular demands and survival tasks of a specific environment. If indeed the human cerebral cortex is responsible for our ascendance over competing species, that does not imply it is the optimal thinking device, just a slightly better one. Analogies between judgment and vision systems are instructive in this regard. The vision system is not designed to get the maximum amount of veridical information about the environment into our heads. It is designed to get the *right* amount of information into a mental representation to efficiently achieve our navigation goals for survival and reproduction.

Second, our technological development does not attest to the brilliance of our thinking as individual human beings. Rather, it is evidence for the human ability to communicate knowledge, within and across generations. A single human could not have created relativity theory, a symphony, or a hydrogen bomb without building on knowledge borrowed and inherited from living others and from the past. Such borrowing involves recognizing what is useful—but recognizing a valuable intellectual result is far easier than creating it. In contrast, when faced with an important decision in our lives, we are often "on our own" to think through what we might do and the probable consequences of the behaviors we might choose.

We must also counter the misconception that decision making is important simply because of the vastness of the choices with which we as individuals and as a species are faced today in the modern world. It is true that few of our great-grandparents seriously considered the option of divorce and that few of their political leaders considered risking the annihilation of the human race in order to achieve an international political objective. Nor were engineers of that day asked to produce energy by constructing complex power plants that could poison vast areas of the earth as a result of a single operator's bad judgments (as at Chernobyl). But despite the larger set of options available to us than to our ancestors, our decisions are probably not more difficult than were theirs. We adapt to whatever decisions must be made and to their consequences. Such adaptation is both a blessing (as when an individual in the worst prison camp can experience near ecstasy over eating a single crust of bread) and a curse (as when people who appear to "have it made" adapt to their riches and find themselves on an unsatisfying "hedonic treadmill"). The subjective weight of decision making has always been a heavy one. The new knowledge that underlies the field of decision making and this book is knowledge about simple principles that define rationality in decision making and scientific knowledge about our cognitive limits that lead us to not decide rationally.

Now we offer a word about format. We have avoided footnotes; subordinate explication and commentary has been incorporated into the text. For the most part, page number citations in the text are not necessary, as it is easy to identify the relevant material from the authors' names alone. We have attempted to rely on sources that discuss basic ideas in a nontechnical manner. When we refer to material that is presented elsewhere in this book, we provide section headings that point to a section within a chapter (e.g., a reference to Section 3.4 points to material in the fourth section within the third chapter).

We are intellectually and emotionally indebted to too many colleagues and friends to dare list their names, for we would surely neglect someone important and deserving. Our agent, Gerard McCauley, reluctantly accepted our plea for help in navigating the shoals of the textbook publishing business. We probably have no idea how much we owe to him. We would like to thank Andrew Hastie for his excellent work in constructing the graphics in this edition of the book and the Templeton Foundation for its financial support.

—*Reid Hastie and Robyn M. Dawes*

# 1

# Thinking and Deciding

*Life is the art of drawing sufficient conclusions from insufficient premises.*

—Samuel Butler

## 1.1 Decision Making Is a Skill

Humans today evolved from ancestors hundreds of thousands of years ago who lived in small groups and spent most of their waking hours foraging for sustenance. When we weren't searching for something to eat or drink, we were looking for safe places to live, choosing mates, and protecting our offspring. Our success in accomplishing these "survival tasks" arose not due to distinctively acute senses or especially powerful physical capacities. We dominate this planet today because of our distinctive capacity for good decision making. This same skill has allowed us to leave the planet, for brief periods; but, of course, the skill has allowed us to develop technologies and weapons that could render the planet uninhabitable if we make a few really bad decisions. Human beings have an exceptional ability to choose appropriate means to achieve their ends.

This book is about decision making, but it is not about *what* to choose; rather, it is about *how* we choose. Most of the conclusions in this book follow from research conducted by psychologists, economists, and biologists about how people actually make choices and decisions—people ranging from medical and financial experts to college student participants in psychological experiments. The important finding is that diverse people in very different situations often think about their decisions in the same way. We have a common set of cognitive skills that are reflected in similar decision habits. But we also bring with us a common set of limitations on our thinking skills that can make our choices far from optimal, limitations that are most obvious when we must make judgments and decisions that are not like those we were "selected" to make in the ancestral environments in which we evolved.

Our decision-making capacities are not simply "wired in," following some evolutionary design. Choosing wisely is a learned *skill*, which, like any other skill, can be improved with experience. An analogy can be drawn with swimming. When most of us enter the water for the first time, we do so with a set of muscular skills that we use to keep ourselves from drowning. We also have one important bias: We want to keep our heads above water. That bias leads us to assume a vertical position, which is one of the few possible ways to drown. Even if we know better, in moments of panic or confusion we attempt to keep our heads wholly free of the water, despite the obvious effort involved compared with that of lying flat in a "jellyfish float." The first step in helping people learn to swim, therefore, is to make them feel comfortable with their head under water. Anybody who has managed to overcome the head-up bias can survive for hours by simply lying face forward on the water with arms and legs dangling—and lifting the head only when it is necessary to breathe (provided, of course, the waves are not too strong or the water too cold). Ordinary skills can thus be modified to cope effectively with the situation by removing a pernicious bias.

This book describes and explains these self-defeating thinking habits, and then suggests other strategies that will improve the decision maker's skill. This approach reflects the spirit of Benjamin Franklin, whose letter of advice about a pressing decision to his friend Joseph Priestley (1772) began, "I cannot, for want of sufficient premises, advise you *what* to determine, but if you please, I will tell you *how.*" We will describe pernicious modes of thought in order to provide advice about how to improve choices. But we will not suggest what your goals, preferences, or aspirations ought to be when making these choices. The purpose of this book is not to improve tastes, or preferences, or ethics—nor to provide advice about how to implement decisions once they have been made. Likewise (unlike many other books written on this subject), this book does not offer advice about how to feel good about yourself. Rather, our purpose is to increase skill in thinking about decisions and choices. In addition, to better understand the decision process and to identify the situations in which our choices are less than optimal, we introduce a second perspective on decision making, namely analyses of the nature of rational decision processes by philosophers and mathematicians.

# 1.2 Thinking: Automatic and Controlled

What is thinking? Briefly, it is the creation of mental representations of what *is not* in the immediate environment. Seeing a green wall is not thinking; however, imagining what that wall would be like if it were repainted blue is. Noting that a patient is jaundiced is not thinking; hypothesizing that the patient may suffer from liver damage is. Noticing that a stock's price has dropped is not thinking, but inferring the causes of that drop and deciding to sell the stock is.

Sir Frederick Bartlett, whose work 50 years ago helped create much of what is now termed *cognitive psychology,* defined thinking as the *skill* of "filling gaps in evidence" (1958). Thinking is probably best conceived of as an *extension of perception*—an extension that allows us to fill in the gaps in the picture of the environment painted in our minds by our perceptual systems, and to infer causal relationships and other important "affordances" of those environments. (For example, Steven Pinker [1997] provides an instructive analysis of the assumptions that we *must* be using as "premises" to "infer" a mental model of our three-dimensional world based on our fragmentary two-dimensional visual percepts.)

To simplify, there are basically two types of thought processes: automatic and controlled. The terms themselves imply the difference. Pure association is the simplest type of automatic thinking. Something in the environment "brings an idea to mind," or one idea suggests another, or a memory. As the English philosopher John Locke (1632–1706) pointed out, much of our thinking is associational. At the other extreme is controlled thought, in which we deliberately hypothesize a class of objects or experiences and then view our experiences in terms of these hypothetical possibilities. Controlled thought is "what if" thinking. The French psychologist Jean Piaget (1896–1980) defined such thinking as "formal," in which "reality is viewed as secondary to possibility." Such formal thought is only one type of controlled thinking. Other types include visual imagination, creation, and scenario building.

To distinguish between these two broad categories of thinking, we can give an example. Many of our clinical colleagues who practice psychotherapy are convinced that *all* instances of child abuse, no matter how far in the distant past and no matter how safe the child is at the time of disclosure, should be reported, "because one thing we know about child abuse is that no child abusers stop on their own." How do they know that? They may have treated a number of child abusers, and of course none of those they have seen have stopped on their own. (Otherwise, our colleagues wouldn't be seeing them.) The image of what a child abuser is like is automatically associated with the abusers they have seen. These known abusers did not "stop on their own," so they conclude that all child abusers do not. The conclusion is automatic.

These colleagues do in fact have experience with abusers. The problem is that their experience is limited to those who have *not* stopped on their own, and since their experience is in treatment settings, these abusers cannot *by definition* stop without therapy. Abusers who have stopped on their own without therapy do not enter it and would be unlikely to identify themselves. They are systematically "*un*available." Or consider clinical psychologists and psychiatrists in private practice who maintain that low self-esteem "causes" negative social and individual behavior. But they see only people who are in therapy. People who engage in negative behaviors and don't feel bad about such behaviors don't voluntarily seek out therapists. (And therapists in coercive settings, such as residential treatment programs for severe juvenile delinquents, do not report that their clients have low self-esteem; in fact, it is often the opposite.) Thus, most people seen in voluntary treatment settings have engaged in negative behaviors *and* have a negative self-image. Therapists conclude that the self-image problem is at the basis of the behavior. It can just as easily be concluded, however, that the self-image problem leads people to therapy, or even that the negative self-image is *valuable* to these people because otherwise they would not be motivated to change their behaviors.

Controlled thinking indicates that the logic of this conclusion is flawed. A critic pointing out the flaw in his or her colleagues' reasoning does not do so on the basis of what comes to mind (the clients he or she is seeing), but quite literally *pauses* to ask "what if?" Such thinking corresponds to Piaget's definition of *formal*. The sample of people who are observed (child abusers who have not stopped on their own) is regarded as one of two possible sets, and the psychotherapist does not have the people in the other set available for observation. The playing field is not level when such logical specification of all possibilities is pitted against automatic thought. In these examples and many others that follow, the logical conclusion of "don't know" is supported, much to the distress of some readers. But it is better to know what we don't know and to deliberately seek more evidence on conclusions that are important, when we don't know.

The prototype of automatic thinking is the thinking involved when we drive a car. We respond to stimuli *not* present in the environment—for example, the expectation that the light will be red before we get to the intersection. Our thought processes are so automatic that we are usually unaware of them. We "steer the car" to reach a desired position without being aware that what we are doing is turning the steering wheel a certain amount so that the car will respond as we desire. It is only when we are learning to drive that we are aware of the thought processes involved, and in fact we have really learned to drive only when we cease being aware of them. While much of driving involves *motor programs* as opposed to *mental representations,* we nevertheless do "think." This thinking is so automatic, however, that we can carry on conversations at the same time, listen to music, or even create prose or music in other parts of our head. When automatic thinking occurs in less mundane areas, it is often termed *intuition* (e.g., we admire the intuitive wisdom of a respected physician, mechanic, or business leader).

In contrast, a prototype of controlled thought is scientific reasoning. While the original ideas may arise intuitively, they are subjected to rigorous investigation by consideration of *alternative explanations* of the phenomena the ideas seem to explain. (In fact, one way of characterizing Piaget's idea of formal thought is that it is scientific thinking applied to everyday situations.) *Plausible explanations* are considered, and most of them are systematically eliminated by observation, logical reasoning, or experimentation. (However, there are historical instances of ideas later regarded as correct being eliminated as a result of poor experimentation; Schroedinger's equations describing the behavior of the hydrogen atom are an example. The physicist Paul Dirac later commented that Schroedinger had paid too much attention to the experiments, and not enough to the intuition that his equations were "beautiful.")

Occasionally, the degree to which thinking is automatic rather than controlled is not clear until the process is examined carefully. The situation is made more complicated by the fact that any significant intellectual achievement is a mixture of both automatic and controlled thought processes. For example, business executives often claim their decisions are "intuitive," but when questioned reveal that they have systematically "thought through" the relevant alternatives quite deliberately before deciding which "intuition" to honor. At the other extreme, the thinking of chess grandmasters has been shown to be much more automatic than most of us novices believe it to be. When a grandmaster's visual search across the chess board is traced by an eye movement camera, it often shows that the grandmaster looks at the best move first. Then, the subsequent eye movement pattern indicates the grandmaster is checking out alternative possibilities—most often only to come back to the original and best one. Moreover, the grandmaster is not distinguished from the mere expert by the number of moves he or she "looks ahead"; the eye camera indicates that *both* experts and grandmasters look ahead only two or three moves, with a maximum of five. In addition, masters and grandmasters can look at a mid-game position in a typical chess match for 5 seconds and then reproduce it almost perfectly. But mere experts and novices cannot do that. (And no one who has been tested can do it for pieces randomly placed on the board, demonstrating that the ability is not due to a general skill for visual memory per se.) The conclusion is that grandmasters have a superior under-standing of the "meaning" of positions in sensible chess games, that in 5 sec-onds they can automatically encode entire patterns of pieces as being ones familiar to them, and that they know from experience (estimated to require at least 50,000 hours of practice for master-level players) what constitutes good and bad moves from such patterns. As Herbert Simon and William Chase (1973) summarized their findings, "The most important processes underlying chess mastery are . . . immediate visual-perceptive processes rather than the subsequent logical-deductive thinking processes." Such immediate processes are automatic, like the decision to brake to avoid a collision.

One fundamental point of this book is that we often think in automatic ways when making judgments and choices. These automatic thinking processes can be described by certain psychological rules (e.g., heuristics), and they can systematically lead us to make poorer judgments and choices than we would by thinking in a more controlled manner about our decisions. This is not to say that deliberate, controlled thought is always perfect, or even always better than intuitive thought. In fact, we hope the reader who finishes this book will have a heightened appreciation of the relative advan-tages of the two modes of thinking and when to trust one or the other.

## 1.3 The Computational Model of the Mind

There has been a modest revolution in the sciences of the mind during the past half-century. A new field has emerged, named *cognitive science,* with a new conceptual paradigm for theorizing about human thought and behavior (Gardner, 1985; Pinker, 1997). The computational model of the mind is based on the assumption that the essence of thinking can be captured by describing what the brain does as manipulating symbols. (Note that we say, "the *essence* of thinking." We do not mean to imply that the brain itself lit-erally manipulates symbols.) The computational model is obviously inspired by an analogy between the computing machine and the computing brain, but it is important to remember that it is an analogy. The two devices, brains and computers, perform similar functions, relating input information to output information (or actions) in an amazingly flexible manner, but their internal structures are quite different (most obviously, electronic circuits and biolog-ical neurons operate quite differently).

The central concept in the notion of a computational model is the manip-ulation of symbolic information. Perhaps the classic example of a cognitive process is the performance of a mental arithmetic task. Suppose we ask you to solve the following addition problem "in your head": $434 + 87 = ???$

If we asked you to think aloud, we might hear something like the following: "Okay, I gotta add those numbers up, uh . . . 4 + 7, that's 11 . . . write down the 1, and let's see, carry the 1 . . . ummmm . . . so 3 + 8 equals 11, again, but I gotta add the carry, so that's 12, and uhhhh . . . write down the 2 and I gotta carry a 1 again. Now 4, that's 4, but I have to add the carry, which was 1, so that's 5, write down the 5. So, that's 521. Does that look okay? Yeah, the answer is 521."

Another controlled, deliberate method that one of us (Dawes) uses is to "work down" from the highest multiples of 10, while making a list of "remainders" in "another part of the head." Thus, 434 + 87 is equal to 400, with 34 and 87 remaining. The 87, being larger, is attacked first as 100 minus 20, with a 7 left over. So we now have 400 + 100 − 20 = 480. We now attack the 34, which is larger than the other remainder of 7. It is basically 20 + 10, with a remainder of 4. Because we are already 20 short of 500, we reach it with a remainder of 10 + 4, to which we add the previous remainder of 7 to obtain 21. The answer is 521. While the second algorithm may appear complex upon first being stated, it has the advantage of avoiding silly errors that lead to large mistakes (e.g., as a result of not "aligning" what is to be "carried over"). But a little bit of practice can also lead to the type of speed that absolutely amazes people who don't know the method.

The point is that either of these computational strategies is a good illustration of what we mean by symbol processing: Information goes into your brain through the eyes (or another sense organ); it is converted to some kind of internal, symbolic code, that retains the essential information from the digits; and then we perform mental operations to compare, manipulate, and transform that information, including combining the information from the external problem with our knowledge of arithmetic facts and algorithms we have learned in school. When we believe we have achieved the goal we set for ourselves when we started thinking about the problem, we respond to report the answer. The "amazing flexibility" of thought processes is illustrated by the dramatic differences in the two sequences of thought, which solve the same problem and produce the same final response. (Without some measure of the interior cognitive processes, like the think-aloud reports, it would be impossible to distinguish between the two strategies. To a large extent, this is the primary task of cognitive psychological researchers— scientifically identifying the hidden thought processes that occur "under the hood," in our heads.)

It was tempting to try to create a theory of performance of cognitive tasks by summarizing the contents of think-aloud reports as a sequence of pieces of information (e.g., "the sum for the rightmost column is 11") and operations on that information to create new information (e.g., "plus" means looking up the sum of two digits in your long-term memory of arithmetic facts). However, such a theoretical endeavor was unsuccessful until we had an appropriate theoretical language in which to express all these complex representations and operations.

The "cognitive revolution" in psychology really got under way (in the 1960s) when the first computer programming languages were applied to the task of summarizing and mimicking the mental operations of people performing intellectual tasks like chess playing, logical deduction, and mental arithmetic. For example, the studies of grandmasters' chess-playing skills we mentioned above were part of a research program at Carnegie Mellon University aimed at describing human cognitive skills (including novice and expert levels) precisely enough so that computational models could be written in computer programming languages to simulate and compete with human players. As Newell and Simon (1972) put it,

> The programmed computer and the human problem solver are both species belonging to the genus "Information Processing System." . . . When we seek to explain the behavior of human problem solvers (or computers for that matter), we discover that their flexibility—their programmability—is the key to understanding them. Their viability depends upon their being able to behave adaptively in a wide range of environments. . . . If we carefully factor out the influences of the task environments from influences of the underlying hardware components and organization, we reveal the true simplicity of the adaptive system. For, as we have seen, we need to postulate only a very simple information processing system to account for human problem solving in such tasks as chess, logic, and cryptarithmetic. The apparently complex behavior of the information processing system in a given environment is produced by the interaction of the demands of that environment with a few basic parameters of the system, particularly characteristics of its memories. (p. 870)

Many aspects of human thinking, including judgment and decision making, can be captured with computational models. The essential parts of these models are symbols (e.g., a theoretical representation of the idea of "yellow," or "pawn," or "11") and operations that compare, combine, and record (in memory) the symbols. Thus, in the chess-playing example, symbols represent the board; the pieces; the rules; and at more complex levels, goals and strategies to win. One of the fundamental and ongoing research projects in cognitive science is to conduct an analysis of the contents of these representations, to describe the natural "mentalese" in which we think and to relate it to the biological substrate in which it must be implemented (e.g., Pinker, 1997, 2007). For purposes of the present book, we can rely on rudimentary descriptions of mental representations in order to characterize the "knowledge" part of cognitive models of decision processes.

The other half of the cognitive theory is a description of the elementary information processes that operate on the representations to store them, compare them, and transform them in productive thought. It is very important to recognize that most of these operations are unconscious. Although we are aware of (and can report on) some aspects of cognitive processing, mostly the symbolic products of hidden processes such as the digit ideas in mental arithmetic, most of the cognitive system is unconscious. So, the first insight from cognitive science is that we can think of intellectual achievements, like judging and deciding, as computation and that computation can be broken down into symbolic representations and operations on those representations. In addition, we emphasize that both automatic and controlled modes of thinking can be modeled as computations in this sense.

Another important insight from cognitive science concerns the nature of the mechanism (the brain) that performs the computations. Since about 1970, there has been increasing consensus on the nature of the "cognitive architecture" of the human mind. The early outlines of the cognitive system included three kinds of memory stores: sensory input buffers that hold and transform incoming sensory information over a span of a few seconds; a limited short-term working memory where most of conscious thinking occurs; and a capacious long-term memory where we store concepts, images, facts, and procedures. These models provided a good account of simple memory achievements, but were limited in their ability to describe more complex inference, judgment, and decision behaviors. Modern conceptions distinguish between several more processing modules and memory buffers, all linked to a central working memory (Figure 1.1, a good introduction to the modern computational approach is provided by John Anderson, 2000).

In the multi-module model, there are input and output modules, which encode information from each sensory system (relying on one or more memory buffers) and generate motor responses. A *Working Memory*, often analogized to the surface of a workbench on which projects (problems) are completed, is the central hub of the system, and it comprises a central executive processor, a goal stack that organizes processing, and at least two short-term memory buffers that hold visual and verbal information that is currently in use. The other major part of the system is a *Long-Term Memory* that contains all sorts of information including procedures for thinking and deciding. The details of this particular modular division of labor are justified by both behavioral results (e.g., systematic studies of mental arithmetic) and the results of hundreds of studies of brain functions. We will report on some of the more interesting results from neuroscientific analysis of decision processes in Chapter 13.

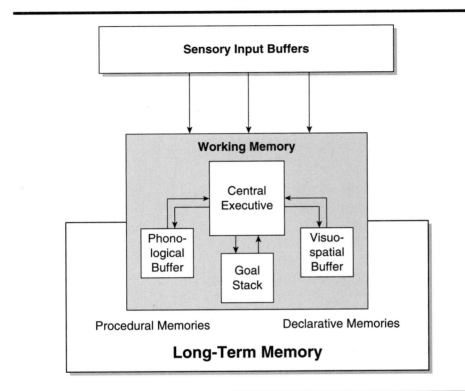

**Figure 1.1**    An overview of the human information-processing system (with arrows indicating the flow of information and control from one part of the system to another)

Two properties of the memory stores will play major roles in our explanations for judgment and decision-making phenomena. First, the limited capacity of Working Memory will be used to explain some departures from optimal, rational performance. As Newell and Simon (1972) said (see quote above), "The apparently complex behavior of the information processing system in a given environment is produced by the interaction of the demands of that environment with a few basic parameters of the system, *particularly characteristics of its memories*" (p. 870, emphasis added). James March and Herbert Simon (1958) introduced the concept of *bounded rationality* in decision making, by which they meant approximately optimal behavior, where the primary explanation for departures from optimal is that we simply don't have the capacity to compute the optimal solutions because our working memory imposes limits on how much information we can use. Second, we will often refer to the many facts and procedures that have been learned and stored in long-term memory. So, for example, we explain the differences between a grandmaster and a novice chess player with reference to stored knowledge about past chess games, good moves, and so forth, and with reference to special analytic skills (analogous to an educated person's knowledge of arithmetic algorithms), all stored almost permanently in long-term memory. (Remember we found that Working Memory differences could not explain the differences in chess skill as a function of expertise; research showed that novices and grandmasters had similar Working Memory capacities—both groups remembered the same number of chess pieces from a scrambled chess board. What the grandmasters seem to have that the novices lack is knowledge about chess stored in their long-term memories. This explains why experts remember so much more from a "meaningful" chess board.)

However, the sheer amount of information to consider—and the limits that Working Memory places on our ability to consider information—is not the only source of bounded rationality. For example, the type of automatic association discussed earlier can also provide impediments to rational thought in the simplest of situations (e.g., the automatic imputation of characteristics of child abusers seen in therapy to child abusers in general). "Information overload" is a sufficient condition for limited ("bounded") rationality, but it is not a necessary condition.

## 1.4 Through Darkest Psychoanalytic Theory and Behaviorism to Cognition

Most of the work discussed in this book has been done in the last half-century. Why? Because until the 1950s, psychology was dominated by two traditions: psychoanalytic theory and behaviorism. Neither of these traditions—which became preeminent in the early 1900s—treated thought as an important determinant of human behavior.

Unconscious needs and desires were the primary stuff of psychoanalytic theory; even defense mechanisms, by which these unconscious impulses could be channeled into socially acceptable—or neurotic—behaviors, were viewed as largely unconscious, and hence outside of the awareness of the individual. (People who claimed to be aware of their own defense mechanisms were said to be denying their problems through "intellectualization"; only the psychoanalyst could really understand them.)

Although dogmatic acceptance of psychoanalytic theory still lingers on in some settings, skepticism was enhanced by its failure to explain one of the most important psychopathologies of the 20th century, Nazism. A strong implication of the theory was that the Nazi leaders, who engaged in monstrous activities, *had* to be suffering from the types of pathologies postulated by the theory. Moreover, these pathologies had to be related to pathologies and traumas of childhood, which—according to the theory—are crucial to the development of adult disorders. As Wordsworth said, "The child is father to the man." In fact, a 1943 United States Office of Strategic Services report, by Walter C. Langer, was devoted to an analysis of Adolf Hitler and a prediction of his future actions based on his "psychosexual perversion," which was later found not to exist. Supposedly incapable of normal sexual intercourse, Hitler was believed to achieve sexual release through urinating and defecating on his mistress. Moreover, Langer (1943/1972) wrote that Hitler survived World War I by granting homosexual favors to his officers. There is no historical evidence of any such behaviors. In fact, applying Hitler's philosophy of the insignificance of the individual human life to his own life as well as to others, he served without hesitation in the particularly dangerous position of a battlefield messenger, declining promotion to a safer position.

Psychoanalytic interpretations made no mention of Hitler's basic cognitive assumptions about the world, his thinking style, the ways in which he framed problems, or the heuristics he used for solving them. Instead, his behavior was predicted on the basis of his conflicted hatred of his brutal father and his unconscious identification of Germany with his mother. Except for making the somewhat obvious prediction that Hitler wouldn't succeed, this psychoanalytic approach didn't work. Moreover, careful study of the defendants at the Nuremberg war crimes trials—complete with Rorschach inkblot tests—failed to reveal any extraordinary psychosexual disorders or childhood problems. These men and women were ordinary people, much too ordinary. Years later, studying Adolf Eichmann, the SS officer who served as the director of the Central Office for Jewish Emigration and was responsible for the deaths of millions of Jews under the Nazi regime, the philosopher Hannah Arendt (1963) coined the phrase "the banality of evil."

In 1963, Stanley Milgram published his striking experiments on "destructive obedience." In them, he demonstrated that *a variety* of people would administer extremely painful and potentially lethal shocks to strangers as part of a psychological experiment, provided that they were urged to do so by an authority figure who "took responsibility," and that the victim was physically distant from them. (The shocks were not actually administered to the stranger, but the experimental participants were led to believe that they were.) In effect, Milgram did not ask, "How were the Nazis different from us?" but rather, "How are we like the Nazis?" He was able to answer the latter question better than others had answered the former. Subsequent research has confirmed the general hypothesis of the banality of evil and the power of the immediate social situation to elicit remarkably cruel (or courageous) behavior from otherwise ordinary people (Ross & Nisbett, 1991; Zimbardo, 2007).

According to the behavioristic approach, in sharp contrast to psychoanalysis, the reinforcing properties of the rewards or punishments that follow a behavior determine whether the behavior will become habitual. Awareness is—as in the psychoanalytic tradition—unimportant; at most, it is an "epiphenomenon." B. F. Skinner, probably the most famous behaviorist of all time, put it this way: "The question is not whether machines think, but whether men do." Again, as with psychoanalytic theory, the failure of behaviorism can be attributed to its inability to account for important phenomena, rather than to any direct "disproofs." For example, there are no useful analyses of everyday speech and communication; intellectual achievements like "mental arithmetic" or chess playing; or behavior in modestly complicated gambling decisions from a behaviorist perspective. In fact, to address these phenomena, behaviorists have become so "cognitive" that it is difficult to separate them from psychologists who more comfortably march under the cognitive banner (Rachlin, 1989).

Accounts of even the most elementary learning processes seem to require more structure than is provided by basic behaviorism. For example, people and animals cannot be conditioned to avoid or fear just any food or danger. Children are distinctively nervous about snakes and spiders; rats (and children) are exceptionally sensitive to the pairing of smells and nausea (Garcia & Koelling, 1966; Mineka & Cook, 1993; Seligman, 1971). We are prepared (probably via some form of evolutionary selection) to learn certain associations, especially "causal" associations, and not others; the laws of behaviorist conditioning are not general across stimuli and responses. A related finding is that our conscious understanding of contingencies is a significant moderator, maybe even a necessary condition, for many forms of learning to occur. A number of ingenious experiments have demonstrated not only that awareness of "reinforcement contingencies" is important in determining whether behavior would be repeated, but also that in many areas—notably verbal behavior—such awareness was crucial (e.g., see Dulaney, 1968). This finding contradicted the general "law of effect," which maintains that the influence of consequences is automatic.

Ingenious experiments by Marvin Levine, Gordon Bower, Tom Trabasso, Jerome Bruner, and other early cognitive psychologists are one illustration of the necessity of postulating an active human mind in order to understand behavior (see Levine, 1975, for the history of this revolutionary research). The experiments involved a task termed *concept identification* in which participants are presented with stimuli that differ on many attributes—most often geometric figures that vary in size, shape, color, and various pattern characteristics. The participant's task is to sort these stimuli into two categories and by so doing, identify the rule (or "concept") that the experimenter has used as the basis for classification. For example, the rule may be that red patterns are to be placed on the left and green ones on the right. Participants are simply told "correct" or "incorrect" when they sort each stimulus, and they are judged to have identified the concept when their sortings are consistently correct (10 correct responses in a row).

Behavioral analyses of responses to this task focused purely on the reinforcement (being told "right" or "wrong") for each choice. Awareness, to the degree that it exists, was assumed not to affect sorting. Early results appeared to support such analyses. For example, some participants were able to achieve perfect sorting without being able to verbalize the experimenter's rule (although it turned out that they could if pressed, their earlier reluctance apparently resulting from being unsure of themselves), and in some tasks participants did not achieve the perfect learning that would be predicted from intellectual insight (but the experimenter's rules themselves may have been ambiguous). Moreover, average success in concept identification *across participants* appeared to increase gradually, much like the learning of an athletic skill.

However, clever follow-up experiments demonstrated that learning in such tasks was in fact not gradual but "all or none," the type of learning predicted on the basis of an active hypothesis-testing mind that continually searches for the correct rule whenever the experimenter indicates that an incorrect sorting has been made. First, these investigators analyzed each participant's responses separately and determined the pattern of correct and incorrect responses *prior to the last error*. If learning was gradual, as predicted by most reinforcement theories, the probability of a correct sort, within a single participant's learning trials, should increase gradually from .50 (the chance probability of being "correct"). Instead, it was *stationary* at .50. The gradual increase found earlier was an artifact of averaging across participants who had identified the correct concept at different points of time in the experiment. Moreover, patterns of sorting after each error were indistinguishable irrespective of the point in the experiment at which the error occurred. By making an error, the participant indicated that he or she "didn't get the concept"; hence, performance was at the chance level prior to each error. An error indicated that the participant had not yet had the insight into the experimenter's rule.

Marvin Levine (1975) demonstrated that participants' conscious beliefs were virtually perfect predictors of their responses, particular error patterns, and time it took to learn. In an especially ingenious demonstration, he showed that participants failed to learn very simple concepts (e.g., to sort all stimuli to the left), over hundreds of trials, if this concept was unexpected, or "absent from their hypothesis set." Bower and Trabasso (1968) devised a procedure they termed the *alternating reversal shift* procedure. Every *second* time the participant made an error, the rule was reversed. For example, participants who had initially been told "correct" when they placed red figures on the left and green ones on the right were told they were correct the second time they put a green figure on the left (or a red one on the right), and were subsequently told correct or incorrect according to this reversed rule—until they again made a second error, at which point the rule was reversed again. Except for participants lucky enough to identify the concept without making two errors, all participants would be "reinforced" a roughly equal number of times for placing red figures and green figures on the same side. If learning was a simple reinforcement process, participants should never identify the concept. But in fact they did. As a group, they identified the concept after being told they were incorrect (falsely called errors) roughly the same number of times as did those in comparison conditions where the rule was never reversed.

It is almost impossible to explain these results without postulating an active, hypothesis-testing mind mediating between the reinforcement provided by the experimenter and the behavior in the sorting task. Moreover, the mind we hypothesize is a limited mind. For example, participants who perfectly recalled all of their previous choices and the experimenter's responses to them would be totally confused by the alternating reversal shift procedure in the Bower and Trabasso experiments (and suspicious that the experimenter was doing something bizarre—because they were told they were wrong much less than half the time before identifying the concept). It is precisely such a limited, hypothesis-testing mind that this book is written about, and for.

Neither the psychoanalytic nor the behavioral tradition regarded people as decision makers who deliberately weighed the consequences of various courses of action and then chose from among them. Moreover, neither tradition has contributed useful explanations of decision-making behaviors. Most psychologists today accept the compelling assumption that ideas and beliefs cause behavior and that cognitive theories are the best route to understanding and improving important behaviors. If we want to understand why the juror said the defendant was a murderer, why the doctor diagnosed the patient with a blocked kidney duct, or why the pilot diverted to another airport for an unscheduled landing, the best way to proceed is to find out what they were thinking about before they made each of these decisions. This book uses such cognitive science concepts to better understand judgment and choice.

# 1.5 Quality of Choice: Rationality

If we aspire to give advice about how to make good decisions, we need to say something about what we mean by bad decisions. The quality of a decision cannot be determined unambiguously by its outcome. For example, most of us believe it would be foolish to accept an "even money" bet that the next time we throw a pair of dice we will roll "snake eyes." (The actual chance of throwing two ones, "snake eyes," is 1/36). Moreover, we would regard the person who accepted such a wager as a poor decision maker—even if he or she happened to roll snake eyes. On the other hand, if that person were in danger of physical harm or death at the hands of a loan shark, and that wager were the only way to raise enough money to avoid harm, then the person might not seem so foolish. What this example illustrates is that it is the potential outcomes, their probabilities, and their values to the decision maker *at the time the decision is made* that lead us to judge a particular choice to be wise or foolish. A general who is losing a war, for example, is much wiser to engage in a high-risk military venture than is a general who is winning a war. The failure of such a venture might not reflect unfavorably on the decision-making ability of the losing general; it is more "rational" for the losing general to take a risk.

So what is rationality? Often the term is used in a purely egocentric, evaluative sense: "Decisions I make are 'rational'; those of which I disapprove are not." Occasionally, we adopt a broader perspective, and judge rationality not just in terms of approval but in terms of the "best interests" *of the person making the decision*—although with "best interests" still defined egocentrically by *us*. As we said at the outset, good decisions are those that choose means, available in the circumstances, to achieve the decision maker's goals. Thus, for example, some of Adolf Hitler's decisions may be viewed as rational (and others as irrational), despite the fact that we disapprove of all of them.

In this book, *rationality* has a narrow technical meaning; it will nevertheless provide the criterion by which we will judge the wisdom of choices. A *rational choice* can be defined as one that meets four criteria:

1. It is based on the decision maker's current assets. Assets include not only money, but also physiological state, psychological capacities, social relationships, and feelings.

2. It is based on the possible consequences of the choice.

3. When these consequences are uncertain, their likelihood is evaluated according to the basic rules of probability theory.

4. It is a choice that is adaptive within the constraints of those probabilities and the values or satisfactions associated with each of the possible consequences of the choice.

Don't we make all our decisions like that? Definitely not. For example, Chapter 2 will detail how it is that we are affected not only by our present state but also by *how we got to it*—a clear violation of the first two criteria enunciated above. The past is over and cannot be changed, but we often let it influence our futures in an irrational manner. In Chapters 9 and 12, we will show how we are sensitive not just to the actual consequences of our decisions but also to the way in which we *frame* these consequences. Chapters 4 through 10 are devoted in large part to the cognitive heuristics (boundedly rational rules of thumb) we use to judge future likelihood— heuristics that systematically violate the rules of probability theory. Finally, Chapters 8 through 11 describe ways of making decisions that avoid the problems specified in the previous sections.

In fact, there are common decision-making procedures that have no direct relationship to these criteria of rationality. They include the following:

1. Habit, choosing what we have chosen before;

2. Conformity, making whatever choice (you think) most other people would make or imitating the choices of people you admire (Boyd and Richerson [1982] have pointed out that imitation of success can be adaptive in general, though not, for example, if it is imitation of the drug use of a particular rock star or professional athlete you admire for his or her professional achievements); and

3. Choosing on the basis of (your interpretation of) religious principles or cultural mandates.

The four criteria of rationality have a philosophical basis. If any are violated, the decision maker can reach contradictory conclusions about what to choose—even though the conclusions are based on the same preferences and the same knowledge. That is, the person violating these principles may decide that a course of action is simultaneously desirable and undesirable, or that choice A is preferable to choice B *and* that choice B is preferable to choice A. For example, a business executive who attends not just to the current assets of the company but also to the fact that they have been increasing or decreasing in the past could conclude that it is both wise and unwise to continue to finance a losing venture. A doctor whose probabilistic reasoning follows automatic thinking principles rather than the rules of probability could decide that a patient both should and should not have an operation; or a juror could decide that a defendant was both guilty and innocent. Because reality is not contradictory, contradictory thinking is irrational thinking. A proposition about reality cannot be both true and false.

## 1.6 The Invention of Modern Decision Theory

Where does this idea of rationality come from? It began in Renaissance Italy, for example, in the analysis of the practice of gambling by scholars such as Girolamo Cardano (1501–1576), a true Renaissance man who was simultaneously a mathematician, physician, accountant, and inveterate gambler. (He is also credited with inventing the combination lock.) In spite of his profound insights into risky decision making, he tended to lose, because his analyses of the numerical structure of random situations were accompanied by lousy arithmetic skills. The most recent impetus for the development of a rational decision theory, however, comes from a book published in 1947 entitled *Theory of Games and Economic Behavior* by mathematician John von Neumann and economist Oskar Morgenstern. (The first publication in 1944 omitted some of the most important analyses of decision making, so we cite the 1947 edition.) Von Neumann and Morgenstern provided a theory of decision making according to the principle of maximizing *expected utility*. The book does not discuss behavior per se; rather, it is a purely mathematical work that applies utility theory to optimal economic decisions. Its relevance to non-economic decisions was assured by basing the theoretical development on general *utility* (we prefer the term *personal value*), rather than solely on monetary outcomes.

This criterion of expected utility may most easily be understood by analyzing simple gambling situations. Because gambling situations are familiar and well-defined, we will rely on them heavily (as have most scholars in this area) to illustrate basic concepts, though we will try to provide a diverse collection of nonmonetary, everyday examples as well. Consider, for example, a choice between two gambles:

(a)  With probability .20 win $45, otherwise nothing.

(b)  With probability .25 win $30, otherwise nothing.

The *expected value* of each is equal to the probability of winning multiplied by the amount to be won. Thus, the expected value of gamble (a) is .20 × $45 = $9, while that of gamble (b) is .25 × $30 = $7.50. People need not, however, prefer gamble (a) simply because its expected value is higher. Depending upon their circumstances, they may find $30 to have more than four-fifths the *utility* of $45, in which case they would—according to the theory—choose gamble (b). For example, an individual may be out of money at the end of a week and simply desire to have enough money to eat until the following Monday. In that situation, the individual may find the difference in utility between $30 and $45 to be negligible compared with the difference between a one-fourth and a one-fifth chance of receiving any money at all.

Such a preference is represented in the von Neumann and Morgenstern theory by the conclusion that .25 times *that individual's utility* for $30 is greater than .20 times *that individual's utility* for $45. Let the utility of $30 be symbolized U($30) and the utility of $45 be symbolized U($45); then by simple algebra, $.25 \times U(\$30) > .20 \times U(\$45)$, which is true if and only if U($30)/U($45) > .20/.25 (which is equal to 4/5).

In point of fact, most people when asked prefer gamble (a). But when faced with the choice between the following two gambles, most prefer (b'), the one with the $30 payoff:

(a')  With probability .80 win $45, otherwise nothing.

(b')  Win $30 for sure.

An individual who preferred (a) to (b) yet (b') to (a') would *violate* the von Neumann and Morgenstern principle of choosing according to expected utility. Using the same algebraic symbolism as before, a choice of (a) over (b) implies that $.20 \times U(\$45) > .25 \times U(\$30)$, or U($45)/U($30) > .25/.20 = 5/4. But a choice of (b') over (a') implies that $.80 \ U(\$45) < U(\$30)$, or U($45)/U($30) < 1/.80 = 5/4. So, there is a logical (algebraic) contradiction between the two choices. This means the theory not only specifies what is rational, but it can also be compared against human choices to test if people are rational.

Another possible violation of expected utility theory would occur if a person were willing to pay more for one gamble than another, yet preferred the other gamble when given a choice between the two. For example, such a person might prefer the sure $30 of alternative (b'), yet—realizing that (a') has a higher expected value ($36 vs. $30)—be willing to pay more to play it than to play (b'). The theory equates the utility of each gamble with the utility of the maximal amount of money paid for playing each. The result is that by preferring the gamble for which he or she was willing to pay less, a person has implicitly indicated a preference for less money over more. Assuming any positive utility at all for money (a "no brainer" assumption), that is irrational—because the greatest amount of money is equal to the lesser amount plus some more. The conditions that lead to such contradictions will be discussed in Chapters 12 and 13.

What is important here, however, is not just that some choices can contradict expected utility theory, but that the four criteria of rationality listed above are *preconditions* for the development of expected utility theory. Thus, choices that violate expected utility theory can also violate very simple, fundamental, and plausible criteria for good decisions, criteria that almost all of us would say we would like to follow when we make important choices. Again, there is nothing in the theory that mandates what desires a decision maker should wish to satisfy—that is, the theory does not prescribe *what* the utilities for various outcomes should be. But the theory does imply fairly strong relationships between some choices and other preferences.

Von Neumann and Morgenstern's work *Theory of Games and Economic Behavior* (1947) inspired a lot of interest in utility theory; many mathematically oriented researchers worked to draw out consequences of maximizing expected utility that were not present in the initial formulation. Others suggested that the basic formulation might be in error, but they did not advocate abandoning the four criteria of rationality; instead, often supported by examples that were intuitively compelling, they suggested that rational decision makers might choose according to some rational principle other than maximizing expected utility. These initial works focused on the *normative* question of how decision makers *should* choose. Soon, however, people became interested in the *descriptive* question of how decision makers—people, groups, organizations, and governments—*actually* choose. Do actual choices conform to the principle of maximizing expected utility?

The answer to this question appears to depend in large part on the field of the person asking it. Traditional economists, looking at the aggregate behavior of many individual decision makers in broad economic contexts, are satisfied that the principle of maximizing expected utility does describe what happens. As Gary Becker (1976), Nobel Prize–winning behavioral scientist, puts it, "All human behavior can be viewed as involving participants who maximize their utility from a stable set of preferences and accumulate an optimal amount of information and other inputs from a variety of markets" (p. 14). Becker and many of his colleagues have taken this assertion seriously and have provided insightful analyses of nonfinancial, nonmarket behaviors including marriage, education, and murder.

There are good reasons to start with the optimistic hypothesis that the rational, expected utility theory and the descriptive—how people really behave—theories are the same. After all, our decision-making habits have been "designed" by millions of years of evolutionary selection and, if that weren't enough, have been shaped by a lifetime of adaptive learning experiences. Surely, truly maladaptive habits will have been eliminated by the pressures of evolution and learning and maybe, optimistically, only the rational tendencies are still intact.

In contrast, psychologists and behavioral economists studying the decision making of individuals and organizations tend to reach the opposite conclusion from that of traditional economists. Not only do the choices of individuals and social decision-making groups tend to violate the principle of maximizing expected utility; they are also often patently irrational. (Recall that irrationality as discussed here means that the chooser violates the rules of rational decision making and chooses contradictory courses of action. We are not talking about the nature of the *goals* of the decision maker; we are talking about the failure to pursue those goals coherently, whatever those goals might be for the individual.) What is of more interest is that people are not just irrational, but irrational in *systematic* ways—ways related to their automatic or "bounded" thinking habits. Chapters 4 through 10 of this book are devoted to a discussion of these systematic irrationalities.

Those behavioral scientists who conclude that the rational model is not a good descriptive model have also criticized the apparent descriptive successes of the rational model reported by Becker and others. The catch is that by specifying the theory in terms of utility rather than concrete values (like dollars), it is almost always possible to *assume* that some sort of maximization principle works and then, ex post, to define utilities accordingly. This is analogous to the assertion that all people are "selfish," by definition, because they do what they "want" to do. (As James Buchanan [1978] points out, many aspects of standard economic theory tend to be "vacuously true" when phrased in terms of utilities, but demonstratively false if money is substituted for utility. In addition, Herbert Simon [1959], defending his more psychological approach, has pointed out some of the explanatory contortions that are necessary to make expected utility theory work descriptively.) However, the best arguments that these principles do not work descriptively come from demonstrations of out-and-out irrationality in light of our four criteria for rational individual decision making (see above).

This book reflects the mixture of approaches to judgment and decision making that has characterized this complex field since its beginnings—the rational, normative hypotheses (often accompanied by the optimistic notion that we approximate the rational in our actual behavior) versus the cognitive, descriptive hypotheses about how we really behave. Both the top-down normative view and the bottom-up descriptive approach are necessary to understand the ideal of adaptive rationality and the reality of human decision-making processes. Moreover, important insights into human nature result from knowing when we do behave rationally, adaptively. Perhaps most important of all, knowing when human behavior departs from the rational model is the first step in designing improvements in our essential thinking skills.

# References

Anderson, J. R. (2000). *Cognitive psychology and its implications* (5th ed.). New York: Worth Publishers.

Anderson, J. R. (2007). *How can the human mind occur in the physical universe?* New York: Oxford University Press.

Arendt, H. (1963). *Eichmann in Jerusalem: A report on the banality of evil.* New York: Viking Press.

Bartlett, F. C. (1958). *Thinking: An experimental and social study.* New York: Basic Books.

Becker, G. (1976). *The economic approach to human behavior.* Chicago: University of Chicago Press.

Bigelow, J. (Ed.). (1887). *The complete works of Benjamin Franklin.* New York: Putnam.

Bower, G. H., & Trabasso, T. (1968). *Attention in learning.* New York: Wiley.

Boyd, R., & Richerson, P. J. (1982). Cultural transmission and the evolution of cooperative behavior. *Human Ecology, 10,* 325–351.

Buchanan, J. M. (1978). *Cost and choice: An inquiry in economic theory.* Chicago: University of Chicago Press.

Dulaney, D. E. (1968). Awareness, rules, and propositional control: A confrontation with S-R behavior theory. In T. R. Dixon & D.R. Horton (Eds.), *Verbal behavior and general behavior theory* (pp. 98–109). Englewood Cliffs, NJ: Prentice Hall.

Garcia, J., & Koelling, R. A. (1966). The relation of cue to consequence in avoidance learning. *Psychonomic Science, 4,* 123–124.

Gardner, H. (1985). *The mind's new science: A history of the cognitive revolution.* New York: Basic Books.

Langer, W. C. (1972). *Adolf Hitler: The secret wartime report.* New York: Basic Books. (Published version of Langer's 1943 *Wartime Report to O.S.S.*)

Levine, M. (1975). *A cognitive theory of learning.* Hillsdale, NJ: Laurence Erlbaum.

March, J. G., & Simon, H. A. (1958). *Organizations.* New York: Wiley.

Milgram, S. (1963). Behavioral study of obedience. *Journal of Abnormal and Social Psychology, 67,* 371–378.

Mineka, S., & Cook, M. (1993). Mechanisms involved in the observational conditions of fear. *Journal of Experimental Psychology, 122,* 23–38.

Newell, A., & Simon, H. A. (1972). *Human problem solving.* Englewood Cliffs, NJ: Prentice Hall.

Pinker, S. (1997). *How the mind works.* New York: Norton.

Pinker, S. (2007). *The stuff of thought: Language as a window into human nature.* New York: Viking.

Rachlin, H. (1989). *Judgment, decision, and choice.* New York: W. H. Freeman.

Ross, L., & Nisbett, R. E. (1991). *The person and the situation.* New York: McGraw-Hill.

Seligman, M. E. (1971). Phobias and preparedness. *Behavior Therapy, 2,* 307–320.

Simon, H. A. (1959). Theories of decision making in economics and behavioral science. *American Economic Review, 49,* 253–280.

Simon, H. A., & Chase, W. G. (1973). Skill in chess. *American Scientist, 61,* 394–403.

Von Neumann, J., & Morgenstern, O. (1947). *Theory of games and economic behavior* (2nd ed.). Princeton, NJ: Princeton University Press.

Zimbardo, P. (2007). *The Lucifer effect: Understanding how good people turn evil.* New York: Random House.

# 2

# What Is Decision Making?

*Reporter: Have you made up your mind yet?*

*Yogi Berra: Not that I know of.*

## 2.1 Definition of a Decision

A good image of what we mean by decision making is of a person pausing at a fork in the road, and then choosing one path—to reach a desired goal or to avoid an unpleasant outcome. The most important evolutionary situations that selected our basic decision-making capacities probably involved physical approach or avoidance—which waterhole, field, fruit tree, cave, stranger, mate, and so forth, to approach and which to avoid. In prehistoric times, bad decisions were punished in a dramatic manner; as the philosopher Willard van Orman Quine (1969) commented, "Creatures inveterately wrong in their inductions have a pathetic but praiseworthy tendency to die before reproducing their kind" (p. 126). In other words, animals, including humans, that make bad predictions of the future and consequently bad decisions tend to die before they can pass their genes on to the next generation; this is one reason that we, and other animals, are good at making survival decisions.

If we took a census of situations that we label *decisions* in the modern world, it would look quite different from the list of essential decisions in primordial environments. What college course should I enroll in next semester? Is the defendant innocent or guilty? Should I move my retirement investments from stocks to real estate? Which car should I purchase? Some, however, are still essential to survival and well-being: Should I marry my current partner? Should I have surgery or chemotherapy?

Table 2.1 is compiled from several surveys of examples of "decisions" reported by students, retired persons, academic historians, and decision textbook authors (see Allison, Jordan, & Yeatts, 1992, for a systematic study). (We present these examples exactly as they were stated by the sources—without any editorial changes.) It is worth noting that all of these decisions are deliberate, conscious accomplishments, although we probably want to call some highly automatic mental processes decisions as well. For example, it is useful to analyze automatic driving behaviors as a sequence of decisions, and a spate of scientific papers analyze the microsecond saccadic movements of the eyes as decisions (Newsome, 1997). However, for the most part we focus on more deliberate, controlled decision processes in this book. In addition, we briefly discuss the extended, long-term sequences of self-control behaviors that are often referred to as decisions, although only the initial events in those sequences could qualify as decision processes in the terms used in this book. For example, we might refer to the "decision" someone makes to lose weight, including long-term, persistent efforts as part of "the decision." But the self-control processes involved in implementation and adherence to such decisions lie outside of the scope of our discussion in this book.

A *decision*, in scientific terms, is a response in a situation that is composed of three parts: First, there is more than one possible course of action under consideration in the choice set (e.g., taking the right or the left path at a fork in the road). Second, the decision maker can form expectations concerning future events and outcomes following from each course of action, expectations that can be described in terms of degrees of belief or probabilities (e.g., the belief that the right-hand path becomes impassable a mile up the trail and that the left-hand path leads to a scenic lake with a good campsite). Third, the consequences associated with the possible outcomes can be assessed on an evaluative continuum determined by current goals and personal values.

The problem with this definition is that it includes so many situations that it could almost serve as a definition of *intentional behavior,* not just *decision behavior.* This is why we also rely on the collection of examples of decision behaviors to provide a more tangible sense of what counts as a decision for present purposes. The examples in Table 2.1 all fit the three-part definition: two or more courses of action, uncertainty about events that will affect the relevant outcomes, and positive-negative consequences contingent on the events. It is this integration of beliefs about objective events and our subjective evaluations of those events that is the essence of decision making.

| Table 2.1 | Examples of "Decisions" Generated by Four Samples of Respondents |
|---|---|

*Older Adults*

Whether to buy a new or used car

Whether to move into a retirement community or to live alone in my house

To retire early or to work for another 10 years

Whether to choose cremation or burial after death

Which heir to leave my money to

How much money to give to which charities

Whether to have a knee operation

Whether to travel by plane or bus

Which presidential candidate I should vote for

What church to join

Whether to get married

*College-Aged Adults*

To go to college

What career or job to choose

To work while my children were preschoolers

Whether to fix my car or "junk" it

To get a job vs. graduate school

Whether or not to have my tongue pierced

Religious preference

To vocally defend some of my controversial viewpoints or to just keep quiet

To abstain from all drugs

To have my dog put to sleep

To confront my father about his drinking

Which parent to live with after a divorce

Whether and when to sever a relationship

Which college courses to take

Where I want to live next year

To visit an old roommate or not

*(Continued)*

**Table 2.1** (Continued)

*Scholars' Examples of Significant 20th-Century Historical Decisions*

Johnson's decision to escalate involvement in Vietnam in the 1960s

Hitler's invasion of Russia (1941)

Supreme Court decision: *Brown v. Board of Education* in 1954 (desegregation of public schools)

Rosa Parks's decision not to give up her seat on the bus in 1956

Supreme Court decision: *Roe v. Wade* (to legalize abortion)

U.S. Public Health Service decision to put the birth control pill on the market, 1950s

King George's appointment of Churchill in 1940

U.S. election of Franklin Roosevelt (1932)

Truman's decision to support the Marshall Plan (1947)

Decision to establish the common market in Western Europe (1958)

Decisions of leaders to sign the Treaty of Versailles (1919)

Chamberlain's and Dadalier's decision at Munich to "appease" Hitler (1938)

*Decisions Appearing as Examples in a Popular Decision-Making Textbook*

Estimating the risks associated with nuclear war

Which medical treatment to use on a patient

Which lottery ticket to purchase

Which casino gamble to play

Whether to buy car insurance

Whether to support building a nuclear power plant

Deciding between two different financial (stock market) investments

Which classes to take

Which consumer product (e.g., television set) to buy or which apartment to rent

## 2.2 Picturing Decisions

We will use schematic "decision tree" diagrams to describe decision situations throughout this book. One of the major uses of these diagrams is to summarize the essential structures of personal or public decision situations in order to apply the principles of scientific decision theory to choose the best course of action. We will introduce this applied "decision analysis" approach in Chapter 11. But for the moment, we want to explain the method of constructing the diagrams so that we can use them to describe the tasks and situations that are important in research on decision-making behavior.

The conventions of the decision tree diagram are that the situation is represented as a hypothetical map of choice points and outcomes that lead to experienced consequences, like a roadmap representing forks in a road and the objects that are located along the road. For example, we might summarize a medical situation concerning a knee injury, as in Figure 2.1. On the left is a choice point—we use squares, □, to indicate "choice points" at which the decision maker chooses a course of action; the lines represent choices that lead to the outcomes that follow from choosing each course of action. In the medical example, we imagine two possible courses of action: have a knee operation or do not have the operation. Events that are out of the decision maker's control are indicated by circles (○) representing uncertain outcomes, sometimes the actions of a competitor or just another less-than-perfectly predictable human agent; we don't know for sure, nor can we control which path we will take *out* of a circle. In the medical example, the upper path ("do not operate") is associated with two possible outcomes: The knee improves on its own (it was "normal" in the first place) or the knee remains in bad shape (it was truly injured). The lower path, representing the "have the operation" course of action, is also associated with two outcome paths: The operation is successful (maybe the operation was necessary and fixed the problem, or maybe the operation was unnecessary) or the operation is a failure.

On the far right-hand side of the diagram, we list the consequences that are associated with choice points and events in the decision tree. We will often summarize the decision maker's evaluations of those outcomes (traditionally called "utilities," but we prefer to call them "personal values") with numbers. Sometimes a decision problem is stated with numbers associated with the consequences (e.g., money payoff gambles; life-and-death medical and policy problems, with "lives saved–lives lost" tabulations). In these problems, we may use the numbers in the problem statement as summaries of consequences—but keep in mind that the subjective personal values of quantities like dollars do not bear a direct, linear relationship to the predicted or experienced personal values. (We'll discuss the issues of valuation of such consequences in Chapters 9 and 10.) When the consequences are not already quantified, by convention we'll use a 0 (worst) to +100 (best) scale for simplicity. We will always assign a 0 to the worst outcome we can foresee (in the decision tree) and a +100 to the best. In the medical example, the worst outcome would be to "have the operation and the knee is still in bad shape" (0); the best outcome would be "no operation and the knee recovers" (+100). We might assign a +80 to the outcome "operation is a success" and +20 to "no operation and the knee is still in bad shape." (In this age of HMOs and various forms of governmental and private health insurance, the task of "scaling" the value of life under various medical conditions, e.g., as "quality-adjusted life years," is enormously important.)

We will also express the decision maker's degrees of uncertainty in judging the possible outcomes that occur at the event nodes in the diagram in numerical terms. Here we will use a probability scale (from 0.00, could not possibly occur, to 1.00, certain to occur; although we often talk about probability numbers on different scales, e.g., "There's a 70% chance the Bears will beat the Packers," it is important to use the 0.00–1.00 scale to make sure the arithmetic calculations are correct). For example, if the decision maker judges that the probability the knee will recover with no operation is .30, we would assign that number to the corresponding path from the event node. Thus, we would

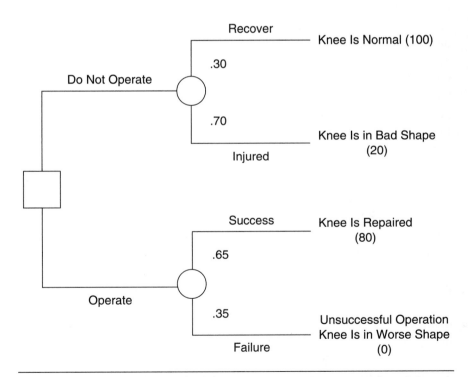

**Figure 2.1**    A hypothetical medical decision situation: An apparent knee injury requires a decision between whether to have an operation or not

assign .70 as the probability that the knee will remain in bad shape if there is no medical intervention. Since we expect that the chances of recovery would be higher if the patient has the operation, we might assign .65 as the probability the knee will recover if the patient decides to have an operation; thus, there is still a .35 probability of no recovery even after the operation.

We will use probabilities (in the range from 0 to 1) to represent beliefs about what will happen. Usually we mean to summarize people's *subjective beliefs* about those events. Although we use numbers that might be interpreted as formal probabilities by a mathematician, we do not assume that these numbers necessarily behave like true probabilities. In fact, one of the important discoveries of psychological research is that subjective probabilities are not always consistent with mathematical probabilities. (Chapters 7 and 8 summarize many of the ways in which our judgments under uncertainty violate rules of formal probability theory.) When we mean to refer to mathematical probabilities, we will make sure the context is clear. (The Appendix in this book introduces the mathematical laws of probability.)

We will not spend much time in this book on how these numbers summarizing consequence values and outcome uncertainties might be extracted from people's thoughts about decision situations, but psychologists and economists have developed many useful scaling methods to solve these measurement problems. To spare the reader a lot of technical detail, we will usually just present plausible numbers. The reader who wants to understand these methods can find this information in many other sources (e.g., Dawes & Smith, 1985).

We will often use simple gambles to illustrate decision-making principles and habits. Gambles are the most popular experimental stimulus in research on decision making, and they provide well-defined, easy-to-understand decision dilemmas in situations where we can be sure that our research participants want to "maximize" the amount of money they earn in the experiment. So, let's work through the representation of a typical experimental gamble in terms of the decision tree diagrams. Consider the choice between two gambles we described in Chapter 1:

(a)  With probability .20 win $45, otherwise nothing.

(b)  With probability .25 win $30, otherwise nothing.

Figure 2.2 summarizes this situation in a decision tree diagram—when the outcomes are naturally scaled with meaningful numbers like dollar amounts, we will just use those numbers for clarity (rather than the 0–100 scale we use for more subjective outcomes). An interesting question, which is of practical importance for judgment researchers, concerns the extent to which human

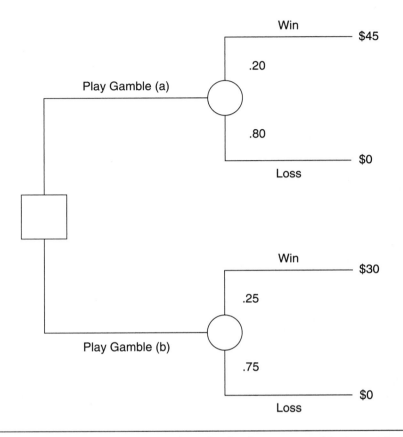

**Figure 2.2**    Decision tree representation of a simple money gamble that might be used as an experimental stimulus

thinking is the same both in crisp, well-defined gambles and in ambiguous everyday situations (like the knee operation; Lopes, 1994, provides a thoughtful discussion of this issue). We will frequently ask ourselves the following: Do the results from research in which people are asked to make choices among money gambles generalize to everyday decisions? If we know how a person chooses in an artificial gambling task, can we predict how that person will choose in an analogous naturally occurring decision situation?

## 2.3 Decision Quality, Revisited

The decision tree diagrams remind us that the crucial first step in understanding any decision is to describe the situation in which the decision occurs.

That step may sound trivial, but the attempt to construct a summary diagram forces us to answer difficult questions about what to include and, more difficult, what to exclude. Then the diagram prompts us to solve the challenging problem of *quantifying* the uncertainties and values that define the decision. Solving the problem of inferring how another person has conceptualized a decision situation is usually the toughest part of psychological research or applied decision analysis. (Much of the craft of research design involves creating experimental situations in which the researcher restricts the subject's thought processes and understands the effects of those restrictions on the subject's mental model of the experimental situation.)

If we believe that we have captured our subject's situation model in a decision tree diagram, it is relatively easy to calculate the decision that leads to the highest expected outcome by applying a rule that follows from decision theory (the four rational assumptions introduced in Chapter 1). This rule is called the *rational expectations principle,* and it is usually summarized as an equation:

$$\text{Utility} = \Sigma \, (\text{probability}_i \times \text{value}_i).$$

The equation prescribes that for each alternative course of action under consideration (each major branch of the decision tree), we need to weight each of the potential consequences by its probability of occurrence, and then add up all the component products to yield a summary evaluation called an *expected utility* for each alternative course of action (each initial left-hand branch). In our example medical decision (Figure 2.1), the calculations specify the expected utility for "have the operation" as +52 ([+80 × .65] + [0 × .35]) and for "do not operate" as +44 ([+100 × .30] + [+20 × .70]), implying that the rational decision would be to have the operation. In the case of the gamble (Figure 2.2), if we assume that the dollar values represent the decision maker's true personal values for those consequences (an assumption that needs to be carefully examined), the expected utility for gamble (a) is $9.00 ([$45 × .20] + [0 × .80]) and for gamble (b) is $7.50 ([$30 × .25] + [0 × .75]), implying the decision maker should choose to play gamble (a), if the expected value is the only consideration.

Note that these calculations assume we can describe the decision process in terms of numerical probabilities and values and that arithmetic operations (adding, multiplying) describe the decision maker's thought processes. The calculation also assumes that the decision maker thoroughly considers all (and only) the options, contingencies, and consequences in the decision tree model of the situation. As we will see, most everyday decisions are not as consistent or thorough as they would need to be to fit the rational expectations principle. However, the decision tree representation and calculations are a good place to start in creating a model to describe the decision thought process and, even if the representation is not descriptively accurate in all details, it may be useful as a model to analyze and improve our decision processes.

## 2.4 Incomplete Thinking: A Legal Example

Let's consider a complex decision that is made by many citizens of the United States, the acquit-convict decision that a criminal trial juror is asked to make. Figure 2.3 summarizes the contingencies and the consequences for a simple version of a juror's decision where there are only two possible verdicts, acquit or convict. (We'll ignore the possibility that the decision maker will "decide not to decide" and refuse to commit to a verdict, and we will avoid the complexities of multiple verdicts, e.g., innocent, or guilty of manslaughter, or guilty of second-degree murder, or guilty of first-degree murder.) According to decision theory, a rational juror should think through all four right-hand consequence terminals of the diagram, carefully assess his or her evaluation of each consequence, and then weight those consequences by their probabilities. In the diagram, we have inserted numbers to represent a juror's beliefs and feelings, and if we accept those numbers and perform a rational expectations principle calculation, this juror should conclude that the defendant is innocent and "acquit."

What is interesting is that people do not appear to engage in the thorough, consistent thought process that is demanded by the decision tree representation when they make these kinds of decisions in everyday life, even when they are in the jury box in a trial where their decision will have serious consequences. They do not appear to "think through" each of the options, to evaluate and weigh every one of the terminal consequence nodes in even a simple four-node tree like our example. Rather, people seem to focus on one or two nodes and reason extensively about those, but incompletely about the whole tree (Pennington & Hastie, 1991). Typically, people focus on the gains and losses associated with the decision they initially believe is most attractive, but ignore the gains and (especially) the losses associated with the other alternatives. Thus, jurors who form an early impression that the defendant is innocent usually evaluate only the consequences that might ensue if they make that decision.

This form of incomplete thinking is similar to the thinking of the clinician (discussed in Chapter 1) who was trying to assess the validity of the claim that child abusers never stop on their own. The clinician's thinking was dominated by his available experience. More generally, a decision maker's thoughts are dominated by his or her initial impression, a phenomenon referred to as a

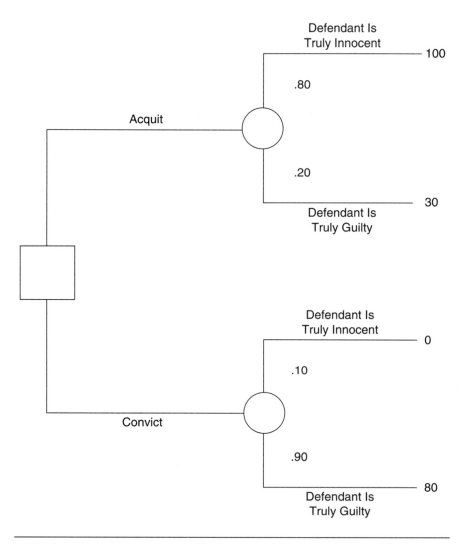

**Figure 2.3**    Decision tree for a stylized juror decision in a criminal trial

*primacy effect* or *confirmatory hypothesis testing* (Nickerson, 1998). Baruch Fischhoff (1996) reached a similar conclusion about people's thinking in more informal, everyday decisions such as teenagers' decisions about school, social, and family life (including some decisions about matters with serious consequences such as drug use, contraception, marriage, self-defense against criminal assaults, and career choices). Fischhoff observed a general tendency to focus on the few *most salient* possibilities and consequences and to ignore others, resulting in incomplete analysis (see also Galotti, 2002).

For the moment, we just want to make the point that people usually do not exhibit the systematic kind of reasoning demanded by decision theory and summarized in the decision tree representation. Although readers may have an initial reaction that many of the decision tree analyses seen in this book and elsewhere are oversimplified, the truth is that these trees are still more complex and balanced than our thoughts usually are, even in consequential situations. As researchers whose goals are to describe, predict, and enhance people's decision-making behavior, the critical first step in any psychological analysis will be to study how our subjects comprehend and represent the decision situation in their minds.

## 2.5 Over-Inclusive Thinking: Sunk Costs

Suppose that you and a companion have purchased discount ski tickets, rented skis, and driven to a resort. When you arrive, the conditions are rotten, it's cold, it's icy, and several of the best ski lifts are not operating because of the wind. In addition, both you and your companion feel lousy physically and out of sorts psychologically. *Your initial assessment of the situation is that you would have a much better day if you just turn around and drive home rather than stay and attempt to ski.* Your companion says it is too bad; you have already paid for the 1-day-only tickets and the nonrefundable ski rental—you both would much rather spend the time at home, but neither of you can afford to waste $90. You agree with this reasoning, so you decide to stay and ski.

But look at the problem another way. The moment you paid the $90, your net assets decreased by $90. That decrease occurred before your drive to the resort. Is the fact that your net assets have decreased by $90 sufficient reason for deciding to spend the day at a place you don't want to be? Still, you think that if you go home you will have *wasted* the $90; waste not, want not. Perhaps you are slightly overweight due to the same reasoning. Once you have paid for your food, you feel compelled to eat it all in order to avoid wasting it—even though the outcome of that particular policy is to decrease your dining pleasure *and* to make you fat.

The $90 you *have already paid* is technically termed a *sunk cost*. Rationally, sunk costs *should not affect decisions about the future*. If we draw a decision tree diagram, summarizing your situation as you stand in the ski resort parking lot wondering whether or not to use your lift ticket, we see that the $90 does not appear in your decision dilemma on the right side of the diagram (Figure 2.4). (Or you might include it in every consequence node, since it has already been spent; decision theorists [and most

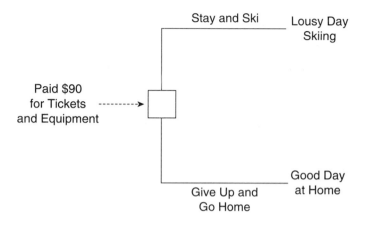

**Figure 2.4**    Decision tree for the ski trip sunk costs dilemma

people] agree that a consequence associated with every possible outcome is useless in discriminating between alternatives and therefore irrelevant to a decision.)

When we behave as if our nonrefundable expense is equivalent to a current investment, we are *honoring a sunk cost*. The diagram shows that at the decision point, the only choice available that avoids the contradictions specified earlier is the one you judge to be the more valuable—turning back. Honoring sunk costs is irrational. (We're excluding the possibility that you have motives *other* than personal enjoyment for going to the resort, or that you wish to create the impression you are at the resort when you actually are not. The information presented in the examples in this book is to be taken as the total information available to the decision maker. Naturally, if there is other information, or if there are other reasons for engaging in a behavior that are not specified in the examples, then the choices might be different.)

People honor sunk costs, as the examples below illustrate:

Finally, the day has finally come. You've got to think logically and realistically. Too much money's been spent, too many troops are over here, too many people had too many hard times not to kick somebody's ass. (Sergeant Robby Felton on the first day of the first Gulf War, January 16, 1991; and a more general remark attributed to proponents of continuing U.S. involvement in the 1960s war in Vietnam and the recent conflict in Iraq: ". . . our boys shall not have died in vain"; quoted in Dawkins & Carlisle, 1976)

Completing Tennessee-Tombigbee is not a waste of taxpayers' dollars. Terminating the project at this late stage of development would, however, represent a serious waste of funds already invested. (Senator James Sasser, arguing for further investment in an artificial waterway project that, if completed, would be worth less than the amount of money yet to be spent to complete it, November 4, 1981)

I have already invested so much in the Concorde airliner . . . that I cannot afford to scrap it now. (businessman quoted in Dawkins & Brockmann, 1980)

If these arguments are taken at face value, as compelling rationales for their conclusions (invade Iraq, invest further in the Tennessee-Tombigbee Waterway project, pay more to develop the Concorde airplane), the irrationalities are clear: Massive amounts of resources had been invested in mounting the war; therefore, we can't stop now, no matter what the current situation. Like lost lives, dollars must not be spent in vain. But limiting concern to the *future* consequences of choices, which is made clear when a decision tree is constructed, starting from the "present" on the left side and running to the future, is the best way to avoid honoring sunk costs. Conversely, honoring sunk costs violates the first criterion of rationality—that decisions should be based only on future consequences.

We should note that there is some ambiguity about the irrationality of these arguments for the speakers. Perhaps they are really rationalizations or are motivated by ulterior considerations: The soldier was quoted on the day the Gulf War started; he was about to risk his life anyway, with little choice about the matter. Why not think of a "logical and realistic" rationale for doing so? The senator was advocating further federal investment in his state, which would provide employment and other benefits to his constituents. Nonetheless, it is still puzzling that the speakers would expect others to find these sunk costs arguments convincing if they themselves did not accept their validity.

The descriptive, psychological point is that we have a habit of paying too much attention to past losses and costs when we make decisions about the future. Even in the context of our discussion of justifications of sunk cost thinking in terms of future consequences, there is ample evidence that we give too much weight to sunk costs in many practical decisions (Staw & Ross, 1989; Teger, 1980). With reference to self-improvement, we need to deal with the possibility of social disapproval as a potential future consequence of our decisions.

But consider some real-world *counter*examples: Hirohito, the Emperor of Japan, who on August 15, 1945, announced Japan's surrender at the end of World War Two by stating, "The war situation has developed not necessarily to Japan's advantage. . . . In order to avoid further bloodshed, perhaps even the extinction of human civilization, we shall have to endure the unendurable, to suffer the insufferable." He lived to see his country recover from the war to become one of the most prosperous nations in the world today. In another example, the Ford Motor Company wisely abandoned the Edsel as not suitable to American taste and later replaced it with the popular Mustang. During the 1964 presidential elections, the Republican candidate, Barry Goldwater, publicly chided Robert McNamara, the former president of Ford (then the secretary of defense), for having first promoted and then abandoned the Edsel—even though it could equally well be maintained that the Edsel venture provided Ford with invaluable information that led to the tremendous success of the Mustang. McNamara showed a much greater commitment to a sunk cost in Southeast Asia during the Vietnam War—as did the subsequent secretary of state, Henry Kissinger, who wrote, "We could not simply walk away from an enterprise involving two administrations, five allied countries, and thirty-one thousand dead as if we were switching off a television channel." The kindest interpretation of these commitments is that because the leaders of *other* nations honor sunk costs, the United States would have suffered a severe blow to its reputation as a wise world power had it failed to do so.

Another reason that some apparent sunk cost ventures may not be irrational is that the decision makers are choosing actions to project and preserve their reputations for being decisive or for not being wasteful. Just as the person who orders too much food might be labeled a poor judge of his or her own appetite and wasteful, these decision makers might be trying to protect their *future* reputations as morally consistent individuals or good decision makers. If, indeed, abandonment of a sunk cost negatively affects future reputation, then it may be wise not to do it. The auto maker who abandons the Edsel may be derided for making a "gutless" decision and lose future clout and actual power within his or her organization. The skier who gives up after having already paid $90 may be regarded not just as financially wasteful, but as confused or silly, and lose his or her friends' respect. Such future reputational costs are perfectly reasonable factors to consider in determining whether or not to abandon a particular course of action (see Figure 2.5). But the sunk cost *per se* should not be a factor. So long as other people believe in honoring sunk costs, the person who does not may be regarded as aberrant.

Some of these subtleties of interpretation were revealed in efforts to explain parental investment behaviors in human and nonhuman species. In a landmark, and still controversial, article on this topic, the anthropologist Robert Trivers (1972) defined parental investment as "any investment by the parent in an individual offspring that increases the offspring's chance of surviving (and hence reproductive success) at the cost of the parent's ability to

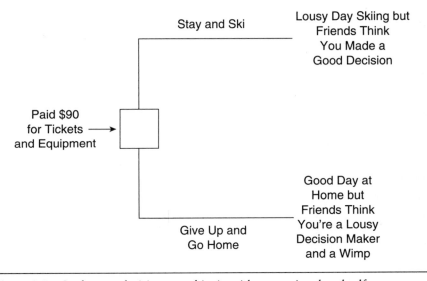

**Figure 2.5**    Sunk costs decision tree ski trip with reputational and self-concept costs included

invest in other offspring" (p. 139). Trivers used the concept of parental invest-ment (e.g., differential feeding of young, defense of a nest) to explain diverse phenomena such as differential mortality rates between males and females, promiscuity, competition for mates, and nurturing strategies. Trivers's origi-nal explanation for the tendency of males to be more likely to abandon their offspring and mates than females exhibits a true sunk costs fallacy:

> At any point in time the individual whose cumulative investment is exceeded by his partner's is theoretically tempted to desert, especially if the disparity is large. This temptation occurs because the deserter loses less than his partner if no offspring are raised and the partner would therefore be more strongly tempted to stay with the young. (p. 146)

However, later analyses by the biologists Richard Dawkins (famous for popularizing the "selfish gene" concept from evolutionary biology) and Thomas Carlisle (1976) showed that it was more plausible that the mate desertion phenomenon was explained by the deserter's sensitivity to *future* consequences (an explanation that Trivers later endorsed)—namely, that the offspring who had already received the greatest parental investment were the most likely to survive to future reproductive maturity and would also require less parental investment in the future.

Interestingly, there appear to be no known examples of sunk cost fallacies in the life-survival decisions of nonhuman animals. Evolution and learning provide extremely effective mechanisms for selecting adaptive, even optimal solutions for species survival decision problems. Hal Arkes and Peter Ayton (1999) point out that human examples of sunk cost reasoning may result from people's tendency to overgeneralize rules for conduct such as "waste not, want not." Further confirmation is provided by the finding that younger humans (who are less likely to have internalized everyday truisms like "waste not, want not") are less likely to demonstrate sunk cost behaviors than adults. As Arkes and Ayton conclude, maybe the human adults are "too smart for their own good."

The subtleties of the sunk cost phenomenon have another message for those of us who favor controlled experiments as a primary scientific method. As noted above, naturally occurring examples of sunk cost errors are very hard to "prove" because there are so often subtle future considerations that *might* explain why a rational decision maker would appear to be showing the sunk cost fallacy. But experiments allow us to create refined situations in which "other considerations" can be eliminated. Hal Arkes and Catherine Blumer (1985) arranged to have three different theater ticket subscriptions sold to people who bought season tickets to the Ohio University Theater series. The experimenters arranged it so that, randomly, one-third of the patrons paid the full $15 price for the tickets, one-third paid $13 for the same package, and one-third paid $8. Compared with those who paid full price, those who purchased at a discount attended fewer plays during the subsequent 6-month season. Those who "sunk" the most money into the tickets were most motivated to use them. The experimental demonstration eliminates the interpretive ambiguity that is present in the (also important) naturally occurring examples.

To conclude on a practical note, the social problems that arise after abandoning a sunk cost can be ameliorated by a type of conceptual framing. The framing consists of explaining that one is not forsaking a project or enterprise, but rather wisely refusing "to throw good money after bad." Rationally, that is exactly what is involved in abandoning a sunk cost, which involves terminating a project or enterprise. Using this phrase, moreover, tends to enhance the credibility of the speaker, who is then relieved of the necessity to explain the irrationality of honoring such sunk costs. This "good money after bad" framing focuses the listener's attention on the *present* as the status quo and phrases the abandonment of a sunk cost as the *avoidance* of a sure loss (which is good). In contrast, honoring a sunk cost involves framing a *past* state as the status quo and abandoning it as the *acceptance* of a sure loss (which is bad). The person who abandons a sunk cost benefits from behaving rationally, and if the present is effectively framed as the status quo, he or she also enjoys the approval of others. Remember that President Kennedy achieved the height of his popularity shortly after he abandoned the Bay of Pigs invasion.

## 2.6 The Rationality of Considering Only the Future

The notion of ignoring sunk costs has arisen only with modern decision theory, which in turn is based on probabilistic thinking that arose in the Italian Renaissance. This thinking is based on the idea that probabilities can be assessed properly only with reference to *future* events. For example, consider a fair coin that has been tossed four times and is to be tossed a fifth time. The probability of its landing heads is 1/2. The pattern of previous results is irrelevant because they have already occurred and do not affect the way in which the coin is handled when it is tossed for the fifth time. For example, four previous heads do not make a fifth head unlikely—even though, in general, "four heads and a tail" (in any order) is an outcome 5 times more likely than five heads.

That the idea of limiting such probability assessments to future possibilities was not intuitively obvious prior to the Italian Renaissance (and may not be obvious today to most people who do not understand probability theory) can be inferred from answers proposed to a famous problem in Fra Luca Pacioli's *Summa de Arithmetica, Geometrica, Proportioni e Proportionalita,* published in 1494 (see David, 1962, for a discussion of the history of this problem). The problem is this: "A and B are playing a fair game of *balla,* in which six goals are required to win (see Figure 2.6). The game actually stops when A has won five rounds and B three rounds. How should the stakes be divided?" Paccioli thought that "past accomplishments"—prior wins—should determine the division. Paccioli's answer: 5:3.

One objection to this answer—dividing the stake proportionally to the number of rounds already won, *in the past*—is that it implies A should get the same amount (the entire stake) whether he or she has won one, two, three, four, or five rounds in a row against no wins by B, although A clearly is in a much better position the more rounds he or she has won. Moreover, it implies that A is more deserving when ahead 2 to 1 than when ahead 5 to 3, even though it is clear that A has a much better chance of winning the six-goal game from the latter lead.

It was not until 64 years later that G. F. Peverone proposed a solution that doesn't have the problems listed above (or others) and is consistent with the principle of considering only future events. According to Peverone's solution, the more consecutive goals won, the higher the proportion of the stake, and a player ahead 5 to 3 should receive a higher proportion of the stake than a player who is ahead 2 to 1. Peverone's insight was that the division of the stake should depend on each player's *future* probability of winning the six-goal game.

The solution is based on two principles. First, where $p$ is the probability that A will be the first person to win six rounds *looking forward* from the current situation, $p$ is the proportion of the stake that should be given to A. Second, $p$ is computed by analyzing all of the possible rounds *remaining* (in the future) before A or B wins a total of six. The correct computation begins by noting that when A is ahead 5 to 3, the only way B can win six first is to win three consecutive rounds. Since the game is fair, that probability is $(1/2) \times (1/2) \times (1/2)$, or 1/8. (Regrettably, Peverone actually miscalculated $p$ in his original essay.) Hence, because B's probability of winning is 1/8 and A's probability is 7/8, the split should be 7:1 for A and B, respectively. Similar calculations can be used to determine A's proportion of the stake when A has won five consecutive rounds, when A is ahead 2 to 1, and so on. When A has won six, A has a probability of 1 of having won, and of course receives the whole stake.

In general, the past is relevant, but only for estimating *current probabilities* and the desirability of *future states*. It is rational to conclude that a coin that has landed heads in 19 of 20 previous flips is probably biased, and that therefore the probability it lands heads on the 21st flip is greater than 1/2. It is not rational to estimate the probability of landing heads on the 21st toss by assigning a probability to the entire pattern of results *including those that have already occurred*. (Again, the probability of five straight heads when tossing a fair coin is 1/32; and the probability of a fifth head *given four heads*

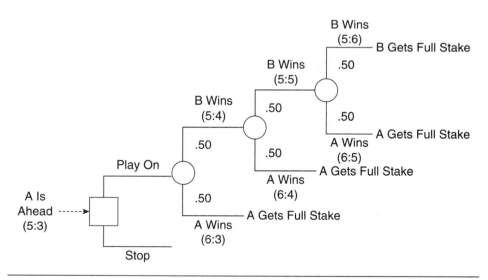

**Figure 2.6**   Decision tree for the game of balla

*in the past* is 1/2.) Rational estimation of probabilities and rational decision making resulting from this estimation are based on a very clear demarcation between the past and the future.

Rational decisions are based on a thorough assessment of future possibilities and consequences. The past is relevant only insofar as it provides information about possible and probable futures. Rational decision making demands the abandonment of sunk costs, unless such abandonment creates future problems outweighing the benefits of abandonment (e.g., the reputational costs discussed in the ski trip example). Today really *is* the first day of the rest of our lives.

## 2.7 The Rest of This Book

Two very general questions about decisions have dominated psychological research on this topic: What makes a decision good? And what makes a decision difficult? The answer to the first question has traditionally been with reference to principles of rationality: A decision is a good one if it follows the laws of logic and of probability theory, and their implications for behavior summarized in traditional decision theory. We will see that this standard is still the dominant one in professional evaluations of "goodness," although there has been a shift to include other measures of goodness. How robust is the decision process, and can it prevail over challenging conditions such as limited computational capacity ("brain power"); missing information; or in a chaotic, "nonstationary" environment? And how stable or "survivable" is the decision process in a competitive, "zero-sum" environment where it is pitted against other antagonistic decision strategies?

The second question is more psychological, and has achieved less consensus in behavioral research. But there are many intellectual aspects of a decision that will make it difficult: the number of alternatives under consideration; the potential for loss if a bad choice is made; the degree of uncertainty about the outcomes that will occur if different choices are made; and, especially, the number and difficulty of the trade-offs that must be made on the way to selecting one from many courses of action. There are more emotional aspects as well: the degree to which cherished values are involved and even threatened by the choice alternatives, the intensity of the emotions associated with the choice process or evoked when evaluating the possible consequences of the alternatives, and the presence of time pressure and other threats to a smooth decision process.

The rest of this book will present the best answers we know to these important questions. We will begin with a review of the psychology of the judgment process—the extensions of our perceptual systems that let us go beyond the information given to us through our senses (Chapters 3 through 8).

Then we will cover the rapidly advancing and still controversial subject area of the psychology of personal values and utilities (Chapters 9 and 10): How do we know and predict what we like? And we will conclude with an introduction to modern rational decision theory and some of its more psychologically valid modern descendants (Chapters 11 and 12).

# References

Allison, S. T., Jordan, A. M., & Yeatts, C. E. (1992). A cluster-analytic approach toward identifying the structure and content of human decision making. *Human Relations, 45,* 49–72.

Arkes, H. R., & Ayton, P. (1999). The sunk cost and Concorde effects: Are humans less rational than lower animals? *Psychological Bulletin, 125,* 591–600.

Arkes, H. R., & Blumer, C. (1985). The psychology of sunk cost. *Organizational Behavior and Human Performance, 35,* 129–140.

David, F. N. (1962). *Games, gods, and gambling: The origins and history of probability and statistical ideas from the earliest times to the Newtonian era.* New York: Hafner.

Dawes, R. M., & Smith, T. (1985). Attitude and opinion measurement. In G. Lindzey & E. Aronson (Eds.), *Handbook of social psychology* (3rd ed., pp. 509–566). New York: Random House.

Dawkins, R., & Brockmann, H. J. (1980). Do digger wasps commit the Concorde fallacy? *Animal Behavior, 28,* 892–896.

Dawkins, R., & Carlisle, T. R. (1976). Parental investment, mate desertion and a fallacy. *Nature, 262,* 131–133.

Fischhoff, B. (1996). The real world: What good is it? *Organizational Behavior and Human Decision Processes, 65,* 232–248.

Galotti, K. M. (2002). *Making decisions that matter: How people face important life choices.* Mahwah, NJ: Erlbaum.

Lopes, L. L. (1994). Psychology and economics: Perspectives on risk, cooperation, and the marketplace. *Annual Review of Psychology, 45,* 197–227.

Newsome, W. T. (1997). Deciding about motion: Linking perception to action. *Journal of Comparative Physiology, Series A, 181,* 5–12.

Nickerson, R. S. (1998). Confirmation bias: A ubiquitous phenomenon in many guises. *Review of General Psychology, 2,* 175–220.

Pennington, N., & Hastie, R. (1991). A cognitive theory of juror decision making: The story model. *Cardozo Law Review, 13,* 519–557.

Quine, W. O. (1969). Natural kinds. In W. O. Quine, *Ontological relativity and other essays* (6th ed., pp. 114–138). New York: Columbia University Press.

Staw, B. M., & Ross, J. (1989). Understanding behavior in escalation situations. *Science, 246,* 216–220.

Teger, A. I. (1980). *Too much invested to quit.* New York: Pergamon Press.

Trivers, R. L. (1972). Parental investment and sexual selection. In B. Campbell (Ed.), *Sexual selection and the descent of man* (pp. 1871–1971). Chicago: Aldine.

# 3

# A General
# Framework for Judgment

*Psychology has forgotten that it is a science of organism–environment relationships, and has become a science of the organism. This is somewhat reminiscent of the position taken by those inflatedly masculine medieval theologians who granted a soul to men but denied it to women.*

—Egon Brunswik

## 3.1 A Conceptual Framework for Judgment and Prediction

"The causes of the disaster are not due to faulty organization, but to misfortune in all risks which had to be undertaken. . . . We took risks, we knew we took them; things have come out against us, and therefore we have no cause for complaint, but bow to the will of Providence, determined still to do our best to the last." These were the last recorded words of British explorer Robert Scott, who lost the race to the South Pole and then perished from starvation and exhaustion only 11 miles from his return supply depot. Scott's eloquent message describes himself and his men as heroes defeated by the implacable, enigmatic natural world. But history has not been kind to Scott, and most commentators now attribute Scott's failure to repeated episodes of poor judgment as much as to unpredictable adverse events during his trek to and from the South Pole (Diamond, 1989; Huntford, 1999). It seems that Scott made many bad judgments, for example, about where to locate his supply base; about the endurance of his men, pack animals, and machines; and about numerous other details of his expedition.

This chapter is an introduction to the psychology of judgment, the human ability to infer, estimate, and predict the character of unknown events. Our judgment faculties are subject to certain systematic flaws, perhaps the most prominent of which is simple overconfidence.

The human mind has been designed by nature to go beyond the information given by our senses, and to go further beyond "the given" than does the nervous system of any other organism on this planet. Even the apparently effortless perception of a three-dimensional physical scene involves inferences that are mathematically impossible if based on only the information given to our retinas (Attneave, 1954; Pinker, 1997). Nonetheless, evolution has endowed us with a cognitive system that has the right assumptions built into it to do an excellent job of navigating through our three-dimensional environment without bumping into major landmarks. Our visual system is so good at making these unconscious inferences that it is impossible for us to figure out how we make them by examining our conscious experience. In some unusual cases of brain damage, a phenomenon called *blindsight* reveals that we are still able to make these judgments even when, due to damage to our primary visual cortex, we have no conscious awareness of the perceptual experience itself. This chapter is about the process of judgment, including a broad range of accomplishments, from the intuitive visual cognition involved in anticipating the path of a fly ball to the deliberate inferences of a physician trying to find out what is wrong with a patient's kidney.

For the moment, we will focus on the psychology of judgment processes where the goal of the judgment is to infer the nature of some condition that does or could exist in the external world (and ignore issues concerning judgments of internal mental events associated with evaluated consequences and personal values). Within psychology, a conceptual framework has been developed to deal with our judgments and expectations concerning events and outcomes of possible courses of action. The framework and its associated terminology may seem a little antiquated today, but the basic concepts still provide an excellent organizational scheme to summarize judgments made under *irreducible uncertainty,* meaning uncertainty that cannot be eliminated before a decision about what action to take must be made.

The framework is called the *Lens Model,* and it was invented by an Austrian-American psychologist named Egon Brunswik (Hammond &

Stewart, 2001). The model gets its name from the notion that we cannot make direct contact with the objects and events in the world outside our sense organs; we only perceive them indirectly through a "lens" of information that mediates between the external objects and our internal perceptions (Pepper, 1942). The framework is divided into two halves, one representing the psychological events inside the mind of the person making a judgment and the other representing events and relationships in the "real world" in which the person is situated. The framework forces us to recognize that a complete theory of judgment must include a representation of the environment in which the behavior occurs. We refer to it as a *framework*, because it is not a theory that describes the details of the judgment process; rather, it places the parts of the judgment situation into a conceptual template that is useful by itself and can be subjected to further theoretical analysis.

Let's take an example judgment and work our way through the conceptual diagram (Figure 3.1) for the Lens Model. Suppose we are trying to estimate the biological age of a man encountered on the street. (Judgments of the gender,

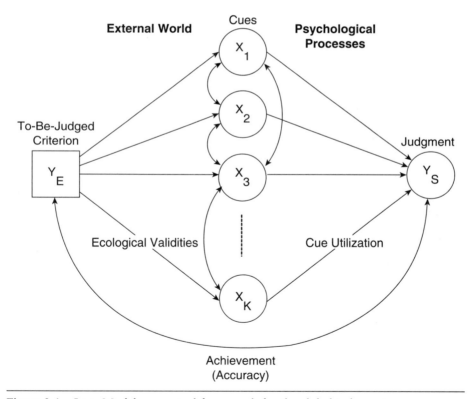

**Figure 3.1** Lens Model conceptual framework for the global judgment process

age, and ethnicity of other people are usually automatic.) The Lens Model frames this judgment as a process through which we, the judges, are trying to "see" a true state of the world (the person's age) through a proximal lens of items of information called *cues* that are available to us. In the case of an age judgment, we probably observe and rely on cues such as characteristics of the man's hair (Is it gray? Is he balding?), his skin quality (Wrinkled or smooth?), his body (How fit does he appear to be? Does he exhibit the gait and posture of a youthful or an aged man?), his clothes (Is he dressed like an older person or younger?), his voice (Is it childish, adolescent, harsh, faint?), and other signals that might support inferences about his age. Note that for an intuitive judgment (like age), even the person making the judgment will not be able to provide a report of the cues he or she is relying on.

The left side of the Lens Model diagram summarizes the relationships between the true, to-be-judged state of the world, called the *criterion* (the man's age), and the cues that may point to that state of the world. In the case of the age judgments, physical anthropological studies would address the relationships on the left-hand side of the diagram: What are the true relationships between biological age and the visible cues or signs it produces? Those relationships are often conceptualized as causal—the criterion state or outcome causes the cue, or maybe the criterion state produces or moderates the cue values where the relationships are not directly causal. In the middle of the diagram is the "lens" of cues that connect the judgment to the criterion or goal of the judgment. The vertical arrows connecting the cues ($X_1, X_2, \ldots$) represent the interdependencies or intercorrelations that usually exist between cues in most judgments. The right-hand side of the lens diagram is the psychological judgment process part of the framework. It refers to the inferences that a person makes to integrate information conveyed by the cues so as to form an estimate, prediction, or judgment of the value of the criterion. The overarching path in the diagram (labeled "achievement") represents the judge's ability to estimate the to-be-judged criterion accurately.

Using a statistical model to "capture" a person's *internal* psychological "judgment policy" (the right-hand side of the Lens Model) may seem odd to readers who are familiar with the common practice of modeling relationships between variables in the *external* world (the left-hand side of the Lens Model). To clarify the application of statistical modeling to analyze an internal psychological process, let us walk through a concrete example.

Several years ago, some students thought it would be interesting to capture one of the author's (Hastie's) judgment policy as he evaluated applicants to graduate studies in his PhD program. Every year about 125 written applications were received and he read all of them and assessed each applicant's qualifications for admission to the program. For purposes of the study, his students reviewed the contents of each application package and assigned quantitative scores to each of the 28 most obvious "cues" that Hastie might be relying on to make his judgments. Some of this information was already quantitative (e.g., the applicant's age, test scores, and grade point average), but much of it had to be "coded" into numbers by the students. For example, "college quality" was coded on a 4-point scale based on a popular national rating service and "warmth" of the recommendation letters was rated subjectively by the student researchers (with high inter-rater agreement).

Then Hastie reviewed the applications from two years of the admissions process and made a rating on a 10-point scale of "admissibility." The students took that matrix containing 28 items of information on 245 applications plus Hastie's 1-10 rating of admissibility and conducted a statistical analysis to determine the best-fitting linear model to predict Hastie's ratings from the 28 cues (see Freedman, Pisani, and Purves, 2007 or another good introduction to statistical modeling for the details of these analyses). Essentially, this approach provides a rough estimate of the average impact of the different items of information on Hastie's judgments across the 245 cases he judged. With due caution, we can say the statistical model is a summary of his policy for making admission judgments (the right-hand side of the Lens Model). In this case the equation was:

ADMISSIBILITY RATING = → + 0.012(VERBAL GRE TEST SCORE)

+ 0.015(QUANTITATIVE GRE TEST SCORE)

+ 0.250('WARMTH' OF RECOMMENDATIONS)

+ 0.410(COLLEGE QUALITY)

−13.280

What does this equation tell us about Hastie's judgment habits? First, he is reliably using only four items of information—two test scores, recommendation letters, and undergraduate college quality. Second, it's obvious he relies heavily on standardized aptitude test scores. The most remarkable result is how well the model does overall in predicting his behavior. The correlation between the model's predictions and his actual ratings was .90. To put that correlation in perspective, Hastie made repeated judgments on 50 cases, two weeks after he made the original judgments of all 245 cases. The reliability, measured by the correlation between his first round of judgments and the second round, was .88. In other words, the model was capturing every scrap of reliable predictive habits in his admissibility ratings!

Although the model does an excellent job of describing Hastie's behavior, it does not necessarily tell us how we should conduct admissions evaluations. To do that we would need an analysis of the cue-criterion relationships in the environment, on the left-hand side of the Lens Model (see Dawes, 1971, for such an analysis of graduate admissions).

## 3.2 Research With the Lens Model Framework

The Lens Model was invented by psychologists for use in research, so it can be interpreted as a blueprint for a method to analyze judgment processes. (Cooksey, 1996, provides a good introduction to the methodology and reviews results from this research paradigm.) Once a judgment has been selected for study, the first step for the researcher is to identify and measure the cues on which the judge relies. This is often a laborious task requiring several rounds of measurement and testing before all of the effective cues have been discovered. Obviously, this task is especially difficult for intuitive judgment processes, where the judge can't tell the researcher what cues are relied on (by the judge) to make the judgment. Often, this situation arises in important decisions made by experts. It is often very difficult for a physician, an engineer, or a financial analyst to "unpack" his or her highly practiced, automatic judgment process and to explain "how it's done." In the case of the age judgment, we would probably start out with our own intuitions, maybe consult with other people about how they make the judgment, maybe do a little research in the anthropometric literature on actuarial facts about human aging (a good first guess is that a human judge will adaptively use the scientifically correct cues to make any judgment), and come up with an initial set of candidate cues. Then we would conduct a study of the age judgment, and keep open the possibility that the initial cue set might need to be enhanced to include additional cues that are used by people to make the judgment.

The second step in the analysis is the creation of a model of the events on the left side of the diagram. Often, a linear regression model can be used to summarize the criterion–cue relationships in terms of the many correlations between the criterion and each of the cues that are related to it and might be used by a judge to infer the criterion (see a good elementary statistics text for an introduction to linear equations, e.g., Freedman, Pisani, Purves, & Adhikari, 1991, or Anderson, 2001). In this analysis, the correlation coefficient (or a related statistic) is used to summarize the strength of the relation between the criterion and a cue (the *ecological validity* of the cue) and between the cue and the judgment (the *cue utilization coefficient* or, more informally, the psychological impact of the cue on the judgment). Sometimes the modeler recognizes that the linear model is a simplified abbreviation of those "external environment" dynamics, although in many domains, linear equations provide a surprisingly complete summary of the environment. Our experienced world is dominated by approximately linear relationships.

The third step in research shifts over to the right-hand side of the diagram and involves inventing and testing models of the psychological process of cue utilization: How do people use the cues to make inferences about the criterion state? Here again, researchers have often found the linear statistical model to be a good description. The usual research tactic is to collect a sample of to-be-judged stimuli—for example, a sample of videotapes of men of various ages to present to an experimental subject for judgments of the age of each stimulus person. The judge's cue utilization habits are "captured" in an algebraic equation that relates the judgment to a weighted sum of the cue values. (Note that this analysis depends on the researcher's ability to measure the cue values on psychologically meaningful numerical scales.) Here the research literature is clear; the most general principle to describe cue utilization processes is the linear equation. For an amazing range of everyday and expert judgments, people seem to infer the implications of cue information as if it is measured on numerical scales, weight it, and add it up.

Imagine sitting in a doctor's office watching her diagnose patients. Each patient comes in, has an interview with the doctor, provides the history of a medical problem, and describes some symptoms. Usually, laboratory tests are made, and maybe some X-rays (or other "scans") are taken. Then, after reviewing all this material, the doctor makes a diagnostic decision about what is wrong with the patient. Consider recording these events for a few weeks to have a good sample of the cues (patient's history, symptoms, and test results) and diagnoses for this judgment task. Or transfer the same scenario to a busy college admissions office. Consider admissions officers reading applications—reviewing *objective* measures of achievement, like test scores and high school grades, and more *subjective* material such as letters of reference, lists of extracurricular activities, and a personal essay—and then making judgments about the admissibility of many applicants. Again, you observe until you have a sizable sample of cases (cues) and judgments.

The Lens Model approach analyzes the judgment by calculating an algebraic model to provide a summary of the weights placed on the cue values for each case so as to predict the judge's (physician's, admissions officer's) judgments. The weights are based on the correlation coefficients summarizing the linear dependency of the judgment of each cue; with everything else equal, the higher the correlation is, the greater the weight will be. The model can be extended to include nonlinear relationships (e.g., a U-shaped functional form with high judgments associated with extreme values on the cue dimension—for example, where both extremely thin and obese patients are at high risk of injury, while those of average body weight are at low risk; or perhaps an admissions officer who likes applicants who either participate in many extracurricular activities or have specialized in one activity, but does not like "average," 2–3 activity participators). The model can also represent *configural* relationships where the judgment depends on combinations of cues (e.g., high levels of a particular hormone in the blood are bad news for female patients, but uninformative for male patients; see discussion below of "interaction effects" in intervariable relationships). But again, the simple linear model is surprisingly successful in many applications. We say "surprisingly," because many judges claim that their mental processes are much more complex than the linear summary equation would suggest—although empirically, the equation does a remarkably good job of "capturing" their judgment habits.

If we had criterion values for our sample of judgments, we could also calculate a summary model for the left-hand side of the Lens Model diagram. In many applications to actual judgment tasks, however, it is difficult to obtain criterion values. In medical contexts, it is too time-consuming for a physician to track the history of patients to obtain final opinions about their presenting condition or outcomes of treatment; similarly, in the academic context, we have no access to values representing success in a college for students who were not admitted. But we are often interested in the psychology of the judgments, the right side of the lens diagram, not the complete environment-behavior system encompassed by the full framework.

Hundreds of studies have been conducted of judgments ranging from medical diagnosis to highway safety, from financial stock values to livestock quality (Brehmer & Joyce, 1988). There is great variety in patterns of results across judgment domains (i.e., weather forecasting is different from internal medicine, which is different from college admissions, which is different from livestock pricing) and across judges. (There are big individual differences in the weights placed on different types of informational cues—and there are some, but only a few, truly remarkably expert judges, while there are many so-called experts who are no better than complete novices; see, for example, Sherden, 1998.) At the risk of overgeneralization, here are some conclusions about typical judgment habits that are true of both amateur and expert judgment:

1.  Judges (even experts) tend to rely on relatively few cues (3–5). There are some exceptions to this generalization, for example, in very expert judgments of weather conditions and livestock quality. We believe that judgments are sensitive to more cue information in these exceptional domains because training for judgment involves immediate, precise feedback to the people learning to make the judgments (unlike, for example, training in medical diagnosis,

admissions decisions, or financial forecasting, where feedback is usually delayed and often never available to the person learning to judge).

2. Few judgment policies exhibit nonlinearity; most are additive and linear—again, contrary to many judges' own beliefs about their judgment processes.

3. Judges lack insight into their policies—they are unable to estimate their own relative "cue utilization weights" accurately—especially when they are expert and highly experienced.

4. Many studies (e.g., students' judgments of physical attractiveness, professors' graduate school admissions judgments, radiologists' judgments of tumor malignancy) reveal large individual differences in types of policies (patterns of cue utilization weights) across judges and low interjudge agreement on the judgments themselves. In important domains like medical diagnosis, this conclusion is disturbing, because we would like our medical experts to agree with one another (and with biological theory) when they make diagnoses and prescriptions. At a minimum, interjudge disagreements tell us someone is wrong, and undermine our confidence in all judgments.

5. When associated, but non-diagnostic, irrelevant information is presented to judges, they become more confident in the accuracy of their judgments, although true accuracy does not increase.

The picture of the expert, painted in broad brushstrokes by this research, is unflattering. However, the important message is that before we draw any conclusions about a judge's performance (whether it is the automatic acceptance of claims of wisdom and accuracy or the blanket assumption that all judges are inept), we need to take a careful look at that performance—and we should be prepared for surprises. Vaunted experts with extensive credentials and impressive demeanors may be no better than college sophomores at their specialty judgments, but then there are some true experts who are really worth heeding or hiring.

## 3.3 Capturing Judgment in Statistical Models

Historically, some of the earliest psychological research on judgment addressed the question of whether trained experts' predictions were better than statistically derived, weighted averages of the relevant predictors. Employing multiple regression analyses within the Lens Model framework in Figure 3.1, we can ask the following question: Which is better, a linear statistical model summarizing the left-hand side of the Lens Model diagram or the human judgment on the right-hand side of the diagram? This question has been studied extensively by psychologists and other behavioral scientists interested in predicting outcomes such as college success, parole violation, psychiatric diagnosis, medical diagnosis, investment values, and business success and failure. In the early studies, the information on which clinical experts based their predictions was the same as that used to construct linear models. Typically, this information consisted of test scores or biographical facts, but some studies included observer ratings of specific attributes as well. All of these variables could easily be represented by (coded as) numbers having positive or negative relationships to the criterion outcome to be predicted. (Higher test scores and grade point averages predict better performance in subsequent academic work; a higher leukocyte count predicts greater severity of Hodgkin's disease; more gray hair and more wrinkles predict more biological years, etc.)

In 1954, Paul Meehl published a highly influential book in which he reviewed approximately 20 such studies comparing the clinical judgments of people (expert psychologists and psychiatrists in his study) with the linear statistical model based only on relationships in the empirical data on the events of interest (the left side of the Lens Model). *In all studies evaluated, the statistical method provided more accurate predictions (or the two methods tied)*. Approximately 10 years later (1966), Jack Sawyer reviewed 45 studies comparing clinical and statistical prediction. Again, there was *not a single study* in which clinical global judgment was superior to the statistical prediction (termed "mechanical combination" by Sawyer). Unlike Meehl, Sawyer did not limit his review to studies in which the clinical judge's information was identical to that on which the statistical prediction was based; he even included two studies in which the clinical judge had access to *more* information (an interview with each person being judged) but still did *worse*. (In one of these, the performance of 37,500 sailors in World War II in U.S. Navy basic training was better predicted from past grades or test scores, alone or in combination, than from the ratings of judges who both interviewed the sailors and had access to the test and grade information used in the model.)

The near-total lack of validity of the *unstructured* interview as a predictive technique had been documented and discussed by E. Lowell Kelly in 1954 (see, more recently, Hunter & Hunter, 1984, and Wiesner & Cronshaw, 1988). There is no evidence that such interviews yield important information beyond that of past behavior—except whether the interviewer likes the interviewee, which is important in some contexts. (Some of our students maintain it is necessary to interview people to avoid admitting "nerds" to graduate study, but they cannot explain how they would spot one, or even what they mean by the term.)

A representative study of psychodiagnosis was reported by Lewis Goldberg (1968), a professor of psychology who was influential in the early history of the use of linear models to analyze judgment. Goldberg asked experienced clinical diagnosticians to distinguish between neurosis and psychosis on the basis of personality test scores (a decision that has important implications for treatment and for insurance coverage in psychotherapeutic practice). He constructed a simple linear decision rule (add the patient's scores on three scales together and subtract the scores on two other scales; if the result exceeds "45," diagnose the patient as psychotic). Starting with a new sample of patient cases and using the patients' discharge diagnoses as the to-be-predicted criterion value, "Goldberg's rule" achieved an accuracy rate of approximately 70%. The human judges, in comparison, performed at rates from slightly above chance (50%) to 67% correct. Not even the best human judge was better than the mechanical adding-and-subtracting rule.

Another study of clinical versus statistical prediction was conducted by Hillel Einhorn (1972). He studied predictions of the longevity of patients with Hodgkin's disease during an era when the disease was invariably fatal (prior to the 1970s). (Einhorn had a personal interest in the subject matter as he had just been diagnosed with the condition, which eventually took his life in 1987.) A world expert on Hodgkin's disease and two assistants rated nine characteristics of biopsies (cues) taken from patients and then made a global rating of the "overall severity" of the disease process for each patient. Upon the patients' deaths, Einhorn correlated the global ratings with their longevity. While a rating of overall severity is not precisely the same as a prediction of time until death, it should predict that. (At least, the world expert thought it would.) Einhorn found that it does not. In fact, the slight trend was in the wrong direction: higher severity ratings were associated with longer survival time. In contrast, a multiple regression analysis, based on the nine biopsy characteristics scaled by the doctors, was statistically reliable and significantly more accurate than the physicians' severity ratings.

Another striking example comes from a study by Robert Libby (1976). He asked 43 bank loan officers (some senior, in banks with assets up to $4 billion) to predict which 30 of 60 firms would go bankrupt within 3 years of a financial report. The loan officers requested and were provided with various financial ratios (cues)—for example, the ratio of liquid assets to total assets—in order to make their predictions. Their individual judgments were 75% correct, but a regression analysis based on the financial ratios themselves was 82% accurate. In fact, the ratio of assets to liabilities *alone* predicted 80% correctly.

The practical lesson from these studies is that in many judgment situations, we should ask the experts what cues to use, but let a mechanical model combine the information from those cues to make the judgment. The finding that linear combination is superior to global judgment is general; it has been replicated in diverse contexts. Not in psychology, but in some medical and business contexts, global judgment has been found to be superior; in those particular contexts, the people making the global judgments had access to "inside information" not available to the statistical model. A fair comparison would insist that both human experts and the models would have identical information. In at least one context, once this extra information was included in the statistical model, its predictions again became superior (in predicting 24-hour survival on an intensive care unit; see Knaus & Wagner, 1989). Meehl updated his classic review several times, and in 1996, he and a colleague concluded the following: "Empirical comparisons of the accuracy of the two methods (136 studies over a wide range of predictions) show that the mechanical method is almost invariably equal to or superior to the clinical method" (Grove & Meehl, 1996, p. 293).

## 3.4 How Do Statistical Models Beat Human Judgment?

Why is it that linear models predict better than clinical experts? We can explain this finding by hypothesizing a mathematical principle, a principle of "nature," and a psychological principle.

The mathematical principle is that both monotone relationships of individual variables and monotone ("ordinal") interactions are well approximated by linear models. Such interactions are illustrated in Figure 3.2. Two factors "interact" when their combined impact is greater than the sum of their separate impacts, but they do not interact in the sense that the *direction* in which one variable is related to the outcome is dependent upon the magnitude of the other variable. It is not, for example, true of monotone interactions that high-highs are similar to low-lows, but that high-highs (or low-lows) are much higher (or lower) than would be predicted by a separate analysis of each variable. If high-highs are similar to low-lows, the interaction is termed *crossed,* illustrated in Figure 3.2.

For example, a doctoral student of Dawes (Glass, 1967) subjected alcoholic and nonalcoholic prisoners to a benign or a stressful experience. He then had them spend 20 minutes in a waiting room before being interviewed by a psychologist about their experience. A nonalcoholic punch was available in the waiting room, and the behavior of interest was how much punch the prisoners consumed. The alcoholic and nonalcoholic prisoners drank virtually identical amounts after experiencing the benign situation. After the stressful situation, however, the alcoholic prisoners drank twice as much punch as the nonalcoholics did (see the middle two panels in Figure 3.2). Thus, a true

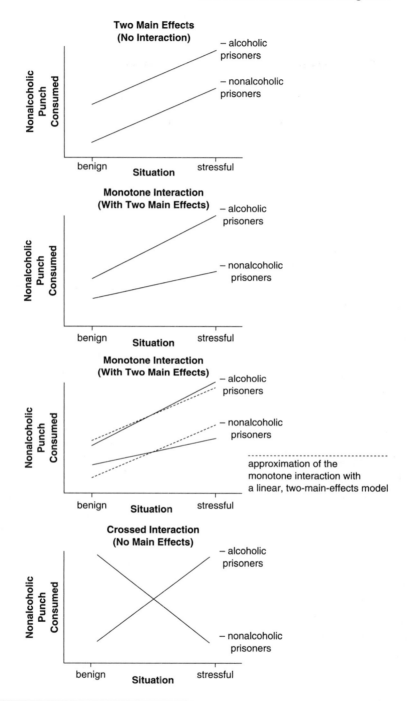

**Figure 3.2    Examples of crossed and non-crossed (monotone) interaction effects**

"monotone" interaction was found between stress and drinking behavior of diagnosed alcoholics: the amount of punch consumed could not be predicted by considering each factor independently; in the example, a distinctive prediction is made for the doubly potent alcoholism *plus* stress combination. However, the statistical analysis indicated that this interaction could be well approximated by the two independent main effects: One, alcoholics drank more punch, and two, all prisoners drank more punch after being stressed. A situation in which only main effects are present is truly linear.

To clarify our *mathematical principle*, consider the top panel in Figure 3.2; this depicts a pure main effects situation in which the two variables have simple, independent effects: Alcoholics drink more (no matter what), and prisoners in a stressful situation drink more (no matter what). A linear, weight-and-add model would fit these data perfectly. The bottom panel depicts the most complicated situation where we imagine a crossover interaction. In benign situations, alcoholics drink the least punch, but the pattern reverses in the stressful situation where alcoholics drink the most punch. No linear model can capture this pattern of effects, even approximately. However, true crossover patterns of causal relationships are very, very rare. And, as we just noted, the non-crossover relationships (which are much more prevalent) can be well approximated by linear relationships. (See the dotted lines in the lower "monotone interaction" panel of Figure 3.2. Also see any good introduction to statistics and data analysis for an exposition of the nature of interaction effects; e.g., Norman Anderson, 2001, is excellent, and Robert Abelson's insightful book, *Statistics as Principled Argument* [1995], contains an especially wise discussion of interactions and their interpretation in behavioral research.)

The *principle of nature* that partly explains the success of the linear statistical model is that most interactions that exist are, in fact, monotone. It is easy to hypothesize crossed interactions, but extraordinarily difficult to find them in everyday situations, especially in the areas of psychology and social interactions. Because the optimal amount of any variable does not usually depend upon the values of the others, what interactions there are tend to be monotone. Moreover, while a number of crossed interactions have been hypothesized in social interactions (e.g., authoritarian leadership is more effective in some types of situations, while libertarian leadership works better in others), they tend to be supported only by verbal claims and selective post hoc data analysis. In fact, interactions of *any* sort tend to be ephemeral, as was discovered by Goldberg (1972) in his analysis of how the "match" between teaching style and student characteristics predicts student success. Of 38 interactions he thought he had discovered in the first half of an extensive data set, only 24 "cross-validated" *in the right direction* in the second half (not significantly different from chance expectation of 19 cross-validations).

The *psychological principle* that might explain the predictive success of linear models is that people have a great deal of difficulty in attending to two or more noncomparable aspects of a stimulus or situation at once. ("Separable" and "incommensurate" are other technical labels for this relationship between stimulus dimensions.) Attention shifts from one cue to another and back again. For example, when Roger Shepard (1964) asked subjects to make similarity judgments between circles containing "spokes" at various angles (the stimuli looked like one-handed clock faces), the subjects attended to size of the circles *or* to angles of the spokes, but *not to both*. The experience of people evaluating academic applicants is similar. Often they anchor their judgment on a salient cue, such as a distinctively high or low grade point average or test score, and then adjust in light of less distinctive information in the applicant's folder. Sometimes the format of the information will determine the salient anchor value, as when a bias is introduced by placing one type of information (e.g., test scores) in a prominent location, such as first in a list of applicant information. Other people consistently start by attending to one cue, for example, a favored test score, then to a second priority cue (perhaps grade point average [GPA]), and then to tertiary information that they believe is less important. But notice that although the rough-and-ready, anchor-and-adjust judgment strategy provides for cognitively efficient integration of a considerable amount of information in a manner analogous to a linear statistical model, it is not optimal. In reality, how *could* an admissions committee member rationally integrate test information and GPA information without knowing something about the distribution and predictability of each student within the applicant pool? The need for such comparisons is one reason that a purely statistical integration will be superior to a global judgment. The statistical model will use valid, independent information from as many cues as convey such information, will be "calibrated" to the ranges of values on all the variables available in the situation, and will do so relentlessly and consistently.

Given that monotone interactions can be well approximated by linear models (a statistical fact), it follows that because most interactions that exist in nature are monotone *and* because people have difficulty integrating information from noncomparable dimensions, linear models will outperform clinical judgment. The only way to avoid this broad conclusion is to claim that training makes experts superior to other people at integrating information (as opposed, for example, to knowing what information to look at). But there is no evidence that experts *think differently* from others. (Remember the example of chess grandmasters from Chapter 1:

Grandmasters did *not* possess special visual or intellectual skills, but they knew much more than novices about "where to look," and they had much more knowledge in long-term memory about specific chess board positions and what to do in each situation.)

A further, more speculative conjecture is that not only is the experienced world fairly linear, but our judgment habits are also adaptively linear. So, the linear models, which are so popular to describe the right-hand, cue utilization side of the Lens Model diagram, convey a correct image of the human mind (see, for example, Anderson, 1996; Brehmer & Joyce, 1988). The mind is in many essential respects a linear weighting and adding device. In fact, much of what we know about the neural networks in the physical brain suggests that a natural computation for such a "machine" is weighting and adding, exactly the fundamental processes that are well described by linear equations. We explore some of the nuances of this very general judgment habit in the next chapter.

# 3.5 Practical Implications of the Surprising Success of the Linear Model

There is an enormous and almost unequivocal research literature that implies expert judgments are rarely impressively accurate and virtually never better than a mechanical judgment rule. As Meehl (1986) put it, 40 years after his "disturbing little book" was published, "There is no controversy in social science which shows such a large body of qualitatively diverse studies coming out so uniformly in the same direction as this one" (p. 373). The implication for practice seems clear: Whenever possible, human judges should be replaced by simple linear models. We put in the "whenever possible" qualification only because we also believe that some empirical tests should be done before any important decision is made in a new way. We do not advocate simply replacing all human judges without considering the specific circumstances of each judgment situation. There will always be special cases and changes in the nature of the task environment (perhaps a new diagnostic method is invented) that require oversight and adjustment. We do believe, however, that a substantial amount of time and other resources is squandered on expert judgments that could be made more equitably, more efficiently, and more accurately by the statistical models we humans construct than by we humans alone.

We advocate the broader use of actuarial, mechanical prediction methods. Research by one of the authors (Dawes, 1979) shows that it is not even necessary to use statistically optimal weights in linear models for them to outperform experts. For years, the nagging thought kept recurring: Maybe *any* linear model outperforms the experts. The possibility seemed absurd, but when a research assistant had some free time, Dawes asked him to go to several data sources and to construct linear models with weights "determined randomly except for sign." (It seemed reasonable that in any prediction context of interest, the direction in which each cue predicted the criterion would be known in advance.) After the first 100 such models outperformed human judges, Dawes constructed 20,000 such "random linear models"—10,000 by choosing coefficients at random from a normal distribution, and 10,000 by choosing coefficients at random from a rectangular distribution. Dawes used three data sets: (1) final diagnoses of neurosis versus psychosis of roughly 860 psychiatric inpatients, predicted from scores on the Minnesota Multiphasic Personality Inventory (the same set used by Goldberg in constructing his "add three, subtract two" rule); (2) first-year graduate school grade point averages of psychology students at the University of Illinois, predicted from 10 variables assessing academic aptitude prior to admission and personality characteristics assessed shortly thereafter; and (3) faculty ratings of performance of graduate students who had been at the University of Oregon for 2 to 5 years, predicted from undergraduate grade point averages, Graduate Record Examination (GRE) scores, and a measure of the selectivity of their undergraduate institutions. All three predictions had been made both by linear models and by human experts ranging from graduate students to eminent clinical psychologists. On the average, the random linear models accounted for 150% more variance between criteria and predictions than did the intuitive clinical evaluations of the trained judges. For mathematical reasons, *unit weighting* (that is, each variable is standardized and weighted +1 or −1 depending on direction) provided even better accountability, averaging 261% more variance. Unit or random linear models are termed *improper* because their coefficients (weights) are not based on statistical techniques that optimize prediction. The research indicates that such improper models are almost as good as proper ones. When it comes to the coefficients in a linear model, the signs on the coefficients are much more important than the specific numerical weights.

We would also point out that human judges relying on intuition are not very competent about adjusting for differences in the metrics of the scales that convey numerical information. If one type of information (e.g., test scores) is conveyed by numbers that range from 200 to 800 and another type (e.g., grades) is conveyed by numbers that range from 1 to 4, the human brain will be fooled into greater judgment adjustments based on the "larger quantities" on the first scale. The implication is that, when intuitive judgments are made, it's good practice to standardize the cue information scales. Another effective, though also "improper," approach is to fit a linear model to a large sample of a human judge's own judgments and then to use that model-of-the-judge instead of the original judge. This method is called *bootstrapping* (not to be confused with the "statistical bootstrap" introduced by Efron, 1988), and it almost invariably outperforms human experts, including the person who was used as the source of judgments for the original model. Again, there are several interpretations of the success of bootstrap models, including their reliability, imperturbability (the equations are not susceptible to bad moods or fatigue), and the fact that the abstracted judgment policy may better represent the human judge's true understanding of the process than either subjective reports or case-by-case explanations. But most of the success can probably be attributed to the remarkable robustness and power of (even improper) linear models that derive from their mathematical properties and their match to the underlying structure of the events in the to-be-judged environment.

## 3.6 Objections and Rebuttals

The conclusion that random or unit or "bootstrapped" weights outperform global judgments of trained experts is not a popular one with experts, or with people relying on them. All of these findings have had almost no effect on the *practice* of expert judgment. Meehl was elected president of the American Psychological Association at a young age, but the practical implications of his work were ignored by his fellow psychologists. States license psychologists, physicians, and psychiatrists to make (lucrative) global judgments of the form "It is my opinion that . . . ," in other words, to make judgments inferior to those that could be made by a layperson with a programmable calculator. People have transferred their confidence in their own global judgments to the global judgments of "experts," a confidence that is strong enough to dismiss an impressive body of research findings and to dominate predictions in our legal and medical systems.

There are many reasons for the resistance to actuarial, statistical judgment models. First of all, they are an affront to the narcissism (and a threat to the income) of many experts. One common defense of expert judgment is to challenge the expertise of the experts making the global predictions in the particular studies. "Minnesota clinicians!" snorted a professor of psychology at the University of Michigan. Little did he know that most of the Minnesota clinicians in the study had obtained their PhDs at Michigan. "Had you used Dr. X," the dean of a prestigious medical school informed one of us, "his judgments would have correlated with longevity." In fact, "Dr. X" was the subject of Einhorn's study of Hodgkin's disease predictions.

Another objection is to maintain that the outcomes better predicted by linear models are all short-term and trivial (like dying, ending up in jail, or flunking out of school?). The claim is made that "truly important long-term outcomes" can be predicted better by global judgments. But as Jay Russo (personal communication) points out, this objection implies that the long-term future can be predicted better than the short-term future. Such prediction is possible for variables like death (as we'll all be dead 100 years from now) and rabies (after the incubation period), but those variables, which are very rare, are *not* of the type predicted in these studies. Moreover, as we come to understand processes (e.g., the existence of the rabies or the AIDS virus in the blood), "incubation period" becomes nothing more than a figure of speech, and longevity is more readily predicted than death.

A final objection is the one that says, "10,000 Frenchmen can't be wrong." Experts have been revered—and well paid—for years for their "It is my opinion that . . ." judgments. As James March has stated, however, such reverence may serve a *purely social function*. People and organizations have to make decisions, often between alternatives that are almost equally good or bad. What better way to justify such decisions than to consult an expert, and the more money he or she charges, the better. "We paid for the best possible medical advice," can be a palliative for a fatal operation (or a losing legal defense), just as throwing the *I Ching* can relieve someone from regretting a bad marriage or a bad career choice. An expert who constructs a linear model is not as impressive as one who gives advice in a "burst" of intuition derived from "years of experience." (One highly paid business expert we know constructs linear models in secret.) So we value the global judgment of experts independently of its validity.

But there is also a situational reason for doubting the inferiority of global, intuitive judgment. It has to do with the biased availability of feedback. When we construct a linear model in a prediction situation, we know exactly how poorly it predicts. In contrast, our feedback about our own intuitive judgments is flawed. Not only do we selectively remember our successes, we often have *no knowledge* of our failures—and any knowledge we do have may serve to "explain" them (away). Who knows what happens to rejected graduate school applicants? Professors have access only to accepted ones, and if the professors are doing a good job, the accepted ones will likewise do well—reinforcing the impression of the professors' good judgment. What happens to people misdiagnosed as "psychotic"? If they are lucky, they will disappear from the sight of the authorities diagnosing them; if not, they are likely to be placed in an environment where they may soon *become* psychotic. Finally, therapy patients who commit suicide were too sick to begin with—as is easily supported by an ex post perusal of their files.

The feedback problem is illustrated by the opening example presented in Malcolm Gladwell's best seller *Blink: The Power of Thinking Without Thinking* (2005). Gladwell relates the story of the Getty Museum's acquisition of a classic marble statue of a young male nude from 4th-century BCE Greece, known as a *kouros*. The provenance of the statue was uncertain, so the museum hired an expert to perform scientific tests to determine if the composition of the stone and its surface was consistent with similar authentic kouroi. The expert was satisfied, and the museum went ahead with the purchase. However, when it was placed on display, several art historians had negative gut reactions when they first glimpsed the statue. Angelos Delivorrias, director of a renowned museum in Athens, said he felt a wave of "intuitive revulsion." Thomas Hoving (1996), perhaps the most famous museum director in the world, immediately felt the statue looked too "fresh," and commented, "I had dug in Sicily, where we found bits and pieces of these things. They just don't come out looking like that" (p. 315). (But note that the conclusion that the statue was a carefully constructed forgery is still controversial; Goulandris Foundation & J. Paul Getty Museum, 1993.)

What can we conclude from this apparent triumph of intuitive judgment over systematic analysis? First, it is likely that this was truly a case where chemistry was not the best way to detect fakery. If it is a fake, the forgers did their homework when selecting marble materials and "aging" the statue's surfaces. But without a prospective study (like the ones conducted to assess the linear models), we don't know how often the experts whose intuitions were right in this one instance would be right on a representative sample of fakes. How often had they been fooled in the past? We don't even know how many other experts' intuitions were wrong for this particular statue. If 36 people have an intuitive feeling that the next roll of the dice will be snake eyes and are willing to bet even odds on that hunch, on the average 1 will win. That person is the one most likely to come to our attention; for one thing, the other 35 probably won't talk about it much.

Another instructive example is provided by a "Dear Abby" letter published in 1975:

DEAR ABBY: While standing in a checkout line in a high-grade grocery store, I saw a woman directly in front of me frantically rummaging around in her purse, looking embarrassed. It seems her groceries had already been checked, and she was a dollar short. I felt sorry for her, so I handed her a dollar. She was very grateful, and insisted on writing my name and address on a loose piece of paper. She stuck it in her purse and said, "I promise I'll mail you a dollar tomorrow." Well, that was three weeks ago, and I still haven't heard from her! Abby, I think I'm a fairly good judge of character, and I just didn't peg her as the kind that would beat me out of a dollar. The small amount of money isn't important, but what it did to my faith in people is. I'd like your opinion.

—SHY ONE BUCK

Note that Shy One Buck did not lose faith in her ability to predict future behavior on the basis of almost no information whatsoever; she lost her faith in people. Shy One Buck still believes she is a "good judge of character." It is just that other people are no damn good.

Hillel Einhorn and Robin Hogarth (1978) examined availability of post-judgment information and demonstrated how feedback *systematically* operates to make intuitive judgment appear valid. Consider the example of a waiter who decides he can judge whether people tip well from the way they dress. A judgment that some people are poor tippers leads to inferior service, which in turn leads to poor tips—thereby "validating" the waiter's judgment. (Not all prophecies are self-fulfilling—there must be a mechanism, and intuitive judgment often provides one. Intuition is also a possible mechanism for some *self-negating* prophecies, such as the feeling that one is invulnerable no matter how many risks one takes while driving.)

In contrast, the systematic predictions of linear models yield data on just how poorly they predict. For example, in Einhorn's (1972) study, only 18% of the variance in longevity of Hodgkin's disease patients is predicted by the best linear model (see Section 3.3 of this chapter), but that is in comparison to 0% for the world's foremost authority. Such results bring us abruptly to an unsettling conclusion: A lot of outcomes about which we care deeply are not very predictable. For example, it is not comforting to members of a graduate school admissions committee to know that only 23% of the variance in later faculty ratings of a student can be predicted by a unit weighting of the student's undergraduate GPA, his or her GRE score, and a measure of the student's undergraduate institution selectivity—but that is in comparison to 4% based on those committee members' global ratings of the applicant. We *want* to predict outcomes that are important to us. It is only rational to conclude that if one method (a linear model) does not predict well, something else may do better. What is not rational—in fact, it's irrational—is to conclude that this "something else" necessarily exists and, in the absence of any positive supporting evidence, that it's intuitive global judgment.

One important lesson of the many studies of human judgment is that outcomes are not all that predictable; there is a great deal of "irreducible uncertainty" in the external world, on the left-hand side of the Lens Model diagram (Figure 3.1). Academic success, for example, is influenced by whom one shares an office with as a graduate student, by which professors happen to have positions available for research assistants, by the relative strengths of those with whom one competes for a first job (as judged by the professors who happen to be appointed to the "search committee"), and so on (Bandura, 1982). Moreover, there are clearly self-amplifying features to an academic career. A "little bit of luck" may lead a new PhD to obtain a position in an outstanding university (or an MD in an outstanding hospital or a JD in an outstanding law firm), and the consequent quality of colleagues may then significantly reinforce whatever talents the individual brings to the job. (Conversely, a little bit of bad luck may saddle the new PhD with a nine-course teaching load, inadequate institutional resources for scholarly productivity, and "burnt out" colleagues. Not many people move from a patent office to a full professorship after publishing a three-page paper, as Albert Einstein did.)

People find linear models of judgment particularly distasteful in assessing other people. Is it important, for example, to interview students applying for graduate school? In a word, "No." What can an interviewer learn in a half-hour that is not present in the applicant's lengthy past record? As Len Rorer (personal communication to Dawes) points out, belief that one's own interviewing skills provide access to such information is grandiose overconfidence. Moreover, even if the interviewer thinks he or she has picked up some highly positive or negative quality in the interview, is it really fair to judge applicants *on the impression they make in a single interview conducted by one interviewer*, as opposed to a record of actual accomplishment (or failure) over a 4-year college career? A GPA is a "mere number," but it represents the combined opinions of some 50 or so professors over several years; some professors may be biased for or against particular students, but surely a combined impression based on actual work over time is fairer than one based on a brief interaction with a single person (who has biases and unreliabilities, too). Furthermore, GPAs predict better than interviews: Is it fair to judge someone on the basis of an impression that does not work?

A colleague in medical decision making tells of an investigation he was asked to make by the dean of a large and prestigious medical school to try to determine why it was unsuccessful in recruiting female students. The decision-making researcher studied the problem statistically "from the outside" and identified a major source of the problem: One of the older professors had cut back on his practice to devote time to interviewing applicants to the school. He assessed such characteristics as "emotional maturity," "seriousness of interest in medicine," and "neuroticism." Whenever he interviewed an unmarried female applicant, he tended to conclude that she was "immature." When he interviewed a married one, he tended to conclude that she was "not sufficiently interested in medicine," and when he interviewed a divorced one, he tended to conclude that she was "neurotic." Not many women received positive evaluations from this interviewer, although *of course* his judgments had *nothing* to do with gender (sarcasm intended).

## 3.7 The Role of Judgment in Choices and Decisions

We have restricted our focus in this chapter to the judgment of events and outcomes, but the implications also apply to the larger framework of decision and choice between alternate courses of action. Linear models often provide a valid description of the psychological processes of judgment and they are pretty good rough-and-ready statistical tools to predict events in the external world. But, they also provide an effective method to predict our own evaluations and preferences, events in the "internal," subjective world. In a very real sense, making decisions requires us to predict what we will like in the future, often under conditions quite different from those at the time we must decide. Given that linear models predict better than intuitive judgment in situations where the accuracy of prediction can be checked, why not in situations where there is no clear criterion for truth as well? If we wish to make choices involving multiple factors, we would do well to construct *our own* (improper) linear models. This is, in essence, what Benjamin Franklin advised (discussed more fully in Chapter 10). His advice was to consider a course of action, to list the pros and cons, to weight them by apparent importance, and then to decide by adding up the weighted pros and cons to see which action had the highest total.

Thus, for practical advice about choosing, we rely on the robust beauty of even improper linear models. The philosophy presented in this chapter is based on the premise that "mere numbers" are in fact neither good nor bad. Just as numbers can be used to achieve either constructive or destructive goals in other contexts, they can be used for good or ill in decision making. Using them, however, requires us to overcome a view (*not* supported by the research) that the "mysteries of the human mind" allow us to reach superior conclusions without relying on deliberate, controlled thought processes. The mysteries are there, but not in this context. We are, all of us, overconfident in our abilities to judge. To do well by ourselves and to treat other persons fairly, we must overcome the attitude that leads us to reject adding numbers to make judgments, and we must experience no more shame when we do so than when we use numbers in determining how to construct a bridge that will not collapse.

# References

Abelson, R. P. (1995). *Statistics as principled argument.* Hillsdale, NJ: Lawrence Erlbaum.

Anderson, N. H. (1996). *A functional theory of cognition.* Mahwah, NJ: Lawrence Erlbaum.

Anderson, N. H. (2001). *Empirical direction in design and analysis.* Mahwah, NJ: Lawrence Erlbaum.

Attneave, F. (1954). Some informational aspects of visual perception. *Psychological Review, 61,* 183–193.

Bandura, A. (1982). The psychology of chance encounters and life paths. *American Psychologist, 37*(7), 747–755.

Brehmer, B., & Joyce, C. R. B. (1988). *Human judgment: The SJT view.* Amsterdam: North-Holland.

Cooksey, R. W. (1996). *Judgment analysis: Theory, methods, and applications.* San Diego: Academic Press.

Dawes, R. M. (1971). A case study in graduate admissions: Application of three principles of human decision making. *American Psychologist, 26,* 180–188.

Dawes, R. M. (1979). The robust beauty of improper linear models in decision making. *American Psychologist, 34,* 571–582.

Diamond, J. (1989, April). The price of human folly. *Discover,* 73–77.

Efron, B. (1988). Bootstrap confidence intervals: Good or bad? *Psychological Bulletin, 104,* 293–296.

Einhorn, H. J. (1972). Expert measurement and mechanical combination. *Organizational Behavior and Human Performance, 7,* 86–106.

Einhorn, H. J., & Hogarth, R. M. (1978). Confidence in judgment: The illusion of validity. *Psychological Review, 85,* 395–416.

Freedman, D., Pisani, R., & Purves, R. (2007). *Statistics* (4th ed.). New York: Norton.

Gladwell, M. (2005). *Blink: The power of thinking without thinking.* New York: Little, Brown.

Glass, L. B. (1967). *The generality of oral consumatory behavior of alcoholics under stress.* Unpublished doctoral dissertation, University of Michigan.

Goldberg, L. R. (1968). Simple models or simple processes? Some research on clinical judgments. *American Psychologist, 23,* 483–496.

Goldberg, L. R. (1972). Student personality characteristics and optimal college learning conditions: An extensive search for trait-by-treatment interaction effects. *Instructional Science, 1,* 153–210.

Goulandris Foundation & J. Paul Getty Museum. (1993). *The Getty Kouros Colloquium: Athens, 25–27 May, 1992.* Athens: Kapon Editions.

Grove, W. M., & Meehl, P. E. (1996). Comparative efficiency of informal (subjective, impressionistic) and formal (mechanical, algorithmic) prediction procedures: The clinical-statistical controversy. *Psychology, Public Policy, and Law, 2,* 293–323.

Hammond, K. R., & Stewart, T. R. (Eds.). (2001). *The essential Brunswik.* New York: Oxford University Press.

Hoving, T. (1996). *False impressions: The hunt for big-time art fakes.* New York: Simon & Schuster.

Hunter, J. E., & Hunter, R. F. (1984). Validity and utility of alternative predictors of job performance. *Psychological Bulletin, 96,* 72–98.

Huntford, R. (1999). *The last place on earth.* New York: Modern Library.

Kelly, E. L. (1954). Evaluation of the interview as a selection technique. In *Proceedings of the 1953 Invitational Conference on Testing Problems* (pp. 116–123). Princeton, NJ: Educational Testing Service.

Knaus, W. A., & Wagner, D. P. (1989). APACHE: A nonproprietary measure of severity of illness. *Annals of Internal Medicine, 110,* 327–328.

Libby, R. (1976). Man versus model of man: Some conflicting evidence. *Organizational Behavior and Human Performance, 16*(1), 1–12.

Meehl, P. E. (1954). *Clinical versus statistical prediction: A theoretical analysis and a review of the evidence.* Minneapolis: University of Minnesota Press.

Meehl, P. E. (1986). Causes and effects of my disturbing little book. *Journal of Personality Assessment, 50,* 370–375.

Pepper, S. C. (1942). *World hypotheses.* Berkeley: University of California Press.

Pinker, S. (1997). *How the mind works.* New York: Norton.

Sawyer, J. (1966). Measurement and prediction, clinical and statistical. *Psychological Bulletin, 66,* 178–200.

Shepard, R. N. (1964). Attention and the metric structure of the stimulus. *Journal of Mathematical Psychology, 1,* 54–87.

Sherden, W. A. (1998). *The fortune sellers: The big business of buying and selling predictions.* New York: Wiley.

Tversky, A., Sattah, S., & Slovic, P. (1988). Contingent weighting in judgment and choice. *Psychological Review, 95,* 371–384.

Wiesner, W. H., & Cronshaw, S. F. (1988). A meta-analytic investigation of the impact of interview format and degree of structure on the validity of the employment interview. *Journal of Occupational Psychology, 61,* 275–290.

# 4

# The Fundamental Judgment Strategy

## Anchoring and Adjustment

*Give me a firm place to stand, and I will move the world.*

—Archimedes of Syracuse

Our favored approach to understanding human judgment phenomena is through descriptions of the cognitive and emotional processes that intervene between the comprehension of a judgment task and the final impression, estimate, or choice. We have just shown how algebraic models can provide a good account for many judgments in which people combine several sources of information (cues) into a summary judgment. Thus, at one level, the algebraic model is a useful description of the process. In this chapter, we take a closer look at the underlying cognitive processes that were captured at a more general level by the additive linear equations from Chapter 3.

## 4.1 Salient Values

Often, our estimates of frequencies, probabilities, and even the desirability of consequences are vague. In ambiguous situations, an "anchor" that serves as a starting point for estimation can have dramatic effects. What happens is that people will adjust their estimates from this anchor but nevertheless remain too close to it. When we sequentially integrate information in this manner, we usually "underadjust." If we recall that a house sold for approximately $200,000, we start our efforts to infer a more exact estimate from that value and end up with estimates that are too close to the starting point. When we toss a coin, we expect 2 heads in 4 tosses (even though the probability of that particular occurrence is only 3/8). Sometimes even when we combine non-numerical information, we follow an anchor-and-adjust policy. If we know something about an individual professional football player, we expect other professional football players to be a lot like him. If we have had an exceptionally good meal in a particular restaurant, we expect the restaurant's other offerings to be equally tasty (and are often disappointed, due to regression effects; see Chapter 7).

Such anchors may be entirely arbitrary. For example, Amos Tversky and Daniel Kahneman (1974) asked students to estimate the percentage of African countries that were in the United Nations (the correct answer, in 1972 when they conducted the study, was 35%). Prior to making the estimates, however, the subjects were requested to make a simple binary judgment of whether this percentage was greater or less than a number determined by spinning a rigged wheel of fortune that contained numbers between 1 and 100. Subjects who first judged whether the percentage was greater or less than "10" selected by the spinner made an average estimate of 25%; those who first judged whether it was greater or less than "65" made an average estimate of 45%. Thus, 10 and 65 served as anchors for the estimates *even though those numbers were generated in a totally arbitrary manner.*

What happened is that the subjects' attention was focused on the anchor values at the start of the judgment process, and the final estimates were *insufficiently* adjusted away from these anchors. The finding of such insufficiency is general, and is related to the credibility of the original anchor and the amount of relevant information that the judge has *available* in memory or at hand. In Tversky and Kahneman's (1974) demonstration, the reader may question—as we do—whether even knowledgeable subjects could be expected to know that the actual percentage of United Nations members was as low as 35. For demonstration purposes, the situation was contrived to be one where the paucity of relevant information in estimators' memories would allow the arbitrary anchor leeway to exert a large effect on the estimate.

The anchor-and-adjust process appears in many judgments, and it is especially clear when the anchor selected is "obviously" arbitrary (as in the original Tversky and Kahneman wheel-of-fortune demonstration described above). Another example of an arbitrary anchor, this one implicit rather than explicit, comes from a study of mental calculation. Subjects were asked, again by Tversky and Kahneman (1974), to estimate the magnitude of "8 factorial," which means $1 \times 2 \times 3 \times 4 \times 5 \times 6 \times 7 \times 8$. The subjects did not know the answer, and the problem was presented in two different ways. Some subjects were asked to estimate the product $8 \times 7 \times 6 \times 5 \times 4 \times 3 \times 2 \times 1$, while others were asked to estimate the product $1 \times 2 \times 3 \times 4 \times 5 \times 6 \times 7 \times 8$. Tversky and Kahneman hypothesized that the first number presented would serve as an anchor (or perhaps the product of the first 3–4 numbers). Indeed, it appeared to do so. The median judgment of the subjects presented with the numbers in the ascending sequence $(1 \times 2 \times 3 \times \dots)$ was 512, whereas the median estimate for those presented with the descending sequence $(8 \times 7 \times 6 \dots)$ was 2,250. (Note that in both formats, people tended to underestimate the true factorial product, 40,320.)

## 4.2 Anchoring and (Insufficient) Adjustment

This serial judgment process is a natural result of our limited attention "channels" and the selective strategies we have developed to deal with that cognitive limit. Just as we can only focus on one location in a visual scene or listen to one conversation at a crowded cocktail party, we attend to one item of evidence at a time as we make estimates. We can summarize the judgment process with a flowchart diagram as in Figure 4.1.

The flowchart shows that the judgment process is complex and there are many places where biases might enter the system. The basic bias is that the process is prone to under-adjustments or *primacy effects*—information considered early in the judgment process tends to be overweighted in the final judgment. The anchor produces its bias through two cognitive routes. First, there is a *conservatism* in the adjustment process near the output end of the entire procedure (Epley & Gilovich, 2001). As the inclination to respond with higher or lower values occurs when new information is considered, it overweights what is already known. Perhaps this is simply an overweighting of the information considered most important, and naturally considered first. Second, there is a biasing effect of the anchor, more accurately the concepts associated with the anchor, on the kind of information that is considered second, third, and subsequently, especially when retrieving information from memory to make the judgment (Chapman & Johnson, 1994; Strack & Musweiler, 1997).

Nick Epley and Tom Gilovich (2001) propose that the true *under-adjustment* process plays a large role only when the person making the estimate selects his or her own anchor value. They conducted clever experiments using materials where the experimenter could be confident of the estimator's anchor.

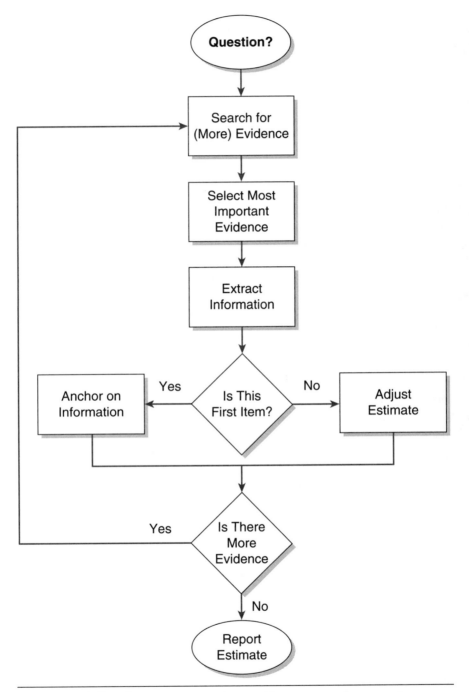

**Figure 4.1**    A flowchart representing the cognitive processes that occur in an anchor-and-adjust judgment

(For example, when asked, "When did the second European explorer, after Columbus, land in the West Indies?" every American college student is almost certain to self-anchor on "1492.") There was clear behavioral evidence that their participants were serially adjusting from the self-generated numerical values. But when control questions were asked ("What is the mean length of a blue whale's body?") and the experimenter provided anchor values, serial adjustment did not seem to occur. So, one indicator of sources of bias in the underlying cognitive process is the source of the anchor. More research needs to be done on these micro processes, but our hypothesis is that the more general principle is credibility—the more credible an anchor, the more influential it is in the estimation process (and a relevant value you have recalled yourself is going to be very credible).

The anchor and adjust process is the most common of the deliberate human information integration habits. The closely related *weighted averaging* process model is the most frequently identified descriptive model when algebraic models are fitted to human judgments (Anderson, 1996). And that equation is the basis of the statistical model most frequently used in the context of the very general Lens Model for judgment that we introduced in Chapter 3. Put more bluntly, we believe the extensive success of the additive linear equations to describe human judgments derives from the extensive role played by anchor-and-adjust information integration habits. When the time course of a judgment process can be mapped out, the most commonly observed sequential effect is a primacy effect, best interpreted as anchoring on the initial information considered and then under-adjusting for subsequent information. We suspect that there is something computationally simple, robust, and adaptive about the weighted average combination rule, especially when the computation is implemented in human neurons. In fact, the linear algebraic combination rule that is the heart of the anchor and adjustment process has remarkably robust mathematical estimation properties (see our discussion of the "robust beauty of [improper] *linear* models" in Chapter 3).

Even preposterously extreme anchor values are not ignored. Fritz Strack and Thomas Mussweiler (1997) asked college students if Mahatma Gandhi was more or less than 214 years old when he died (Mussweiler & Strack, 2001). This crazy anchor still influenced the estimates, though no one could have believed that "214" was a credible value. But anchors need not consist of extreme values. For example, people often use an average as an anchor. We all know such people, those habitual compromisers who always say "six" when one person says "one" and another says "eleven." In fact, such habits are illustrated in the behavior personally observed by a close colleague on a subcommittee for educational funding in a state legislature. No one at the meeting could remember exactly how much money the staff had recommended budgeting for continuing education. Two members had quite discrepant ideas about the amount, but neither was sure of the figure. These amounts were simply averaged, and the committee members proceeded to discuss whether or not the resulting figure should be raised or lowered.

The most common anchor, of course, is the status quo. While we are not constrained mentally—as we are physically—to begin a journey from where we are, we often do. Changes in existing plans or policies more readily come to mind than do wholly new ones, and even as new alternatives close to the status quo are considered, they, too, can become anchors. This generalization is true of organizations as well as of individuals. As Cyert and March (1963) write, firms "search in the neighborhood of the current alternative." Individuals and committees tend to rely on the last or current values of costs or time to complete projects to decide on the allocations of resources or time to those projects. Alas, these estimates are usually unrealistically optimistic, and anchoring on previous values yields underestimates—especially for money matters, time-to-complete problems, and athletic performances, where inflation, age, and regression processes play their relentless roles.

The "classic" and some of the most theoretically important studies on anchoring and adjustment were conducted using pricing versus choice to express preferences between gambles, by Paul Slovic, Baruch Fischhoff, and Sarah Lichtenstein (1982). They studied pricing and choice in two contexts: survey experiments in which college-student subjects made hypothetical choices and provided hypothetical monetary values for the gambles, and actual choices at a casino in Las Vegas in which gamblers played—bought or sold the gambles—for substantial amounts of real money. The results were the same; bids and bets were "attracted" to the most salient numerical values.

The gambles consisted simply of probabilities to win or lose certain amounts of money. Players were requested to respond to these gambles in one of two ways: Either they were asked how much money they would accept in lieu of playing the gamble (price), or they were asked which of two gambles they would prefer to play (choice). To encourage players to express the true personal worth of the gamble as their stated *selling price*, the experimenters used a device that determined a random *counterbid*. If this counterbid was lower than the stated selling price, the subject played the gamble; if it was higher, the subject was given the amount of the counterbid. Now consider any subjects who state a selling price that is *lower* than the true monetary value of the gamble to them. If the randomly determined counterbid falls *between* the stated selling price and the true monetary value, the subjects are given the amount of the counterbid when in fact they would prefer to play the gamble. Also consider subjects whose stated selling price is *higher* than the true monetary value to them. If the randomly determined counterbid falls between their true monetary value for the gamble and their stated selling price (which is then higher), these subjects would have to play a gamble when in fact they would prefer to receive the amount of the counterbid. Thus, subjects who state a selling price that is either too high or too low can be put in a position where they receive one alternative (the privilege of playing the gamble or the counterbid), although they would prefer the other. This valuation method was invented by Becker, DeGroot, and Marshak (1963) and, if clearly understood, it motivates a person to state the true monetary value of the option rather than over- or underbidding. This *sincere valuation* procedure was thoroughly explained to the subjects, and only when they understood its logic did the experiment commence.

Consider two such gambles. Gamble A has an 11/36 probability of winning $16 and a 25/36 probability of losing $1.50; gamble B has a 35/36 probability of winning $4 and a 1/36 probability of losing $1. (The expected values are both approximately $3.85; see Appendix.) Players asked for their selling prices produced a larger dollar equivalent for the first—after all, it has a higher payoff. But the same players, given the choice between these two gambles, had a strong tendency to choose the second, which has the higher probability of winning—after all, it is likelier to pay. The interpretation is that when people are asked to produce a monetary equivalent (through the selling price procedure), they *anchor on* the dollar amounts of the outcomes, and they insufficiently adjust, on the basis of the probabilities involved. But when the same people think of winning versus losing, they *anchor* on the probability of success; higher probabilities are more desirable. And then they insufficiently adjust their value judgment on the basis of the dollars to be won or lost. The result is that the very same player in different parts of the experiment or at the casino gaming table may prefer gamble B to gamble A, but state a higher selling price for gamble A.

This combination of anchor and adjust–based habits could turn a person into a "money pump." Suppose the experimenter "sells" the first gamble to the player for the amount specified. Then, given a choice between the two gambles and selecting the second, the player trades the second for the first. Now the experimenter buys back the second gamble for the selling price specified by the subject. Because this amount is less than the previous amount, the experimenter has made a profit—while the player is left with the original gamble. Hypothetically, the experimenter can repeat the sequence in order to "pump" the money out of the player's pockets; the experimenter can even begin by giving the subject one of the two gambles and still make an infinite profit (in theory, anyway). Interestingly, some people who have this pattern of preferences and selling prices will engage in this buying, choice, and selling procedure repeatedly—even though they realize while doing so that the experimenter is making a profit. Comments such as "I just can't help it," and "I know it's silly and you're taking advantage of me, but I really do prefer that one, although I can see how the other one might be more valuable," are common.

These subtle, but robust *preference reversals* also provide an instructive example of how the scale on which a response is made can bias people to choose one anchor over another (favoring dollar amounts, when the response is a price, but favoring probabilities, when the response is a choice). Furthermore, the results challenge standard economic theory, which equates the utility (personal value) of an object with the amount of money people are willing to pay for it. Two economists, David Grether and Charles Plott (1979), responded to the challenge of these demonstrations of irrational choice and pricing behavior by conducting a series of experiments using real monetary payoffs in which they examined every *artifactual* explanation for such reversals that they could imagine. (One example was this: Because the study was conducted by psychologists, the experimenters will be likely to lie and cheat when playing the gambles.) Nonetheless, they concluded that the original finding was robust; they found no artifacts.

Many important everyday financial situations are susceptible to anchor effects. These effects may be especially controlling in negotiations where two or more parties are trying to settle on a financial arrangement to share investments and profits. Greg Northcraft and Maggie Neale (1987) asked professional real estate agents to assess residential property values, a task that each had performed hundreds of times when helping clients bargain for a house. The agents were provided with detailed 10-page summaries of the characteristics of houses in the Tucson, Arizona, area, they visited the properties, and then they assessed *fair market values* and predicted selling prices—all part of their day-to-day jobs. The fair market price is supposed to be objective (often governed by explicit formulas based on the location, size, and condition of the property, with inputs for the recent actual sale prices of comparable properties). Northcraft and Neale manipulated one *irrelevant* variable, the original listing prices of the properties described in the written materials, across a range of ± 12% of the originally assessed fair market value. The listing price is chosen by the seller with subjective and strategic concerns in mind; although it is likely to bear an approximate relationship to the true market value, it may be higher or lower, depending on the seller's goals. The listing price manipulation had consistent and large effects on the agents' appraisals.

One of the most vivid demonstrations of financial anchoring was provided by Dan Ariely, George Loewenstein, and Drazen Prelec (2003), in a classroom auction of consumer products like bottles of wine, books, and luxury chocolates, with market values of about $70 on average. For each item, students were asked to look at the last two digits of their Social Security numbers and asked if they would pay that amount (or less) for the product. For example, if your last two digits were 85, would you pay $85 for a nice bottle of wine? After anchoring on their Social Security numbers, the students made actual willingness-to-pay bids for each product. The result of anchoring on the patently arbitrary Social Security number was a dramatic difference in serious bids. The average correlation between Social Security numbers and the final bids was approximately +.40; the highest Social Security numbers (80–99) bid $39 for the wine, while the lowest (00–19) bid $12. Ariely and colleagues dubbed this effect "arbitrary coherence," because the arbitrary Social Security number anchor set the global level of a person's bids, but within each person, there was a consistent ordering of products. (For this group, a cordless keyboard was consistently valued high and the luxury chocolates were valued low.) However, the numerical prices within that consistent ordering were heavily influenced by the arbitrary anchor.

This result—people rely on anchors—is not surprising, especially in the context of all of the other known anchoring effects. What is important, though, is that it appears in a consequential financial judgment, it occurs for professionals who have made the judgment many times, and it occurs in a non-laboratory setting in which the experts are provided with as much (actually, more) valid information than they would normally have to make these appraisals . . . and the anchor effects are still present and still large. Northcraft and Neale (1987) also observed that most of their experts said they would definitely notice any deviation in a listing price greater than 5% different from the true value of a property, but manipulations of ± 12% went unnoticed and had an impact on their appraisals.

Anchor and (insufficient) adjustment effects also play a role in many important legal judgments. For example, in civil tort lawsuits, the plaintiff usually requests specific dollar amounts in compensatory and sometimes punitive damages. In a realistic mock-jury experiment conducted by one of the authors (Reid Hastie, with David Schkade and John Payne, 1999), plaintiffs asserted either that "an award in the range from $15 million to $50 million" or "in the range from $50 to $150 million would be appropriate." (Attorneys often ask for a range rather than a single value, because they think this is an effective trial tactic—nudging the jurors' attention in the direction they want, but appearing to leave the final decision in the jury's hands.) Sure enough, the median awards were $15 million versus $50 million in the two conditions. This demonstration is especially interesting because it was observed after the judge clearly instructed the jurors that "the attorneys' recommendations are *not* evidence." Gretchen Chapman and Brian Bornstein (1996) summarized the results of these demonstrations with the phrase, "the more you ask for, the more you get."

A parallel sequence of judgments occurs on the criminal side in bail-setting and sentencing decisions. Like jurors, trial judges seem to be susceptible to anchor effects produced by attorney recommendations. For example, Ebbe Ebbesen and Vladimir Konecni (1975) sent their students into courtrooms to observe pretrial bail-setting hearings. They found that criminal court judges weighted the prosecuting attorney's recommendation for bail—the payment or financial commitment made by a defendant to guarantee appearance at a later trial—more heavily than any of the other information provided in probation reports; perhaps it is no accident that this anchor is the first piece of information presented to the judge. Gerd Gigerenzer and his colleagues have even proposed that under some conditions, people don't bother to adjust once they have an anchor. This so-called "take the best" judgment procedure terminates after only one persuasive salient cue value has been located. Mandeep Dhami and Peter Ayton found that magistrates setting bail in British criminal courts were best described as using only the prosecution's recommendation.

So, there are many important decisions that are influenced by salient or perceived-to-be-important numbers. This is probably no surprise to many experts. Experienced negotiators and salespeople know that a financial deal is often controlled by the party who establishes the early frame of reference for the exchange and makes the first offer. However, what is surprising is how blind we are to the effects of anchors on our own behaviors. As with so many influences on judgment, we can easily imagine how they affect "everyone else," but fail to draw the obvious conclusion that we are everyone else, too.

## 4.3 Anchoring on Ourselves

Some of the most important judgments we make all the time involve inferences about what other people like, think, and will do. How do we infer whether our friend will like a new movie? What proportion of our population has a college degree? What an auto worker will do, when she is laid off from her job? When we make judgments about someone we do not know well, we engage in an egocentric process that some researchers have called *projection*." As Nobel laureate Thomas Schelling (1966) once commented, "You can sit in your armchair and try to predict how people will behave by asking yourself how you would behave if you had your wits about you. You get, free of charge, lots of vicarious, empirical behavior." Schelling was talking about how some experts do behavioral science, but he was also describing how all of us make predictions about the behavior of other people. We "anchor" on our own attitude or behavior (or what we think we would do) and, when needed, adjust for aspects of the other person that are different from us or aspects of ourselves that we think are unusual.

Developmental psychologists (and virtually all parents) have observed that very young children view the world egocentrically, and it takes some significant experiences for them to learn that everyone does not like or know what they themselves like and know. But even adults still think egocentrically about others. For example, Nick Epley and his colleagues (Epley, Keysar, Van Boven, & Gilovich, 2004; Nickerson, 1999) asked people to communicate about a visual scene when viewing it from opposite perspectives. One player, the director, gave the other, the addressee, instructions about which object to pick up. The "trick" in this referential communication game was that the addressee could see several objects that were blocked from the perspective of the director (both could see which objects were occluded, but only one could tell the identity of the objects). In one case, the addressee could see three candles, while the director could see only two. This meant that if the director referred to the "smallest candle," the referent object would be different for the addressee. In this and in several other visual perspective tasks, participants had great difficulty avoiding egocentric reference pitfalls and failed to coordinate actions in intellectually simple object manipulation tasks. In later studies, Epley and his colleagues studied more subtle forms of miscommunication caused by differences in perspective. In one clever series, participants were asked to judge whether a phone message was sarcastic or not. Of course, sarcasm involves a discrepancy between the content of a verbal message, "The comedian was just hilarious," and the speaker's candid view of the situation (he actually found the comedian to be tedious and unfunny). In fact, we have all had the experience of being unsure whether someone we do not know well is being sincere or sarcastic. Epley et al. showed that this subtle social judgment begins with anchoring on the explicit contents of the message—we might call this the first interpretation—and only given the benefit of deeper thinking can that interpretation be adjusted away from the surface meaning to appreciate the true sarcastic message. This research is notable in that it carefully dissected the time course of reactions to the sarcastic messages, verifying that the comprehension process did anchor on the surface meaning and that appreciation of the deeper sarcastic meaning required adjustments away from the first interpretation.

Lee Ross and his students (Ross, Greene, & House, 1977) published a dramatic set of studies demonstrating what they dubbed the "false consensus effect." College students were asked if they would be willing to perform various outrageous acts on campus (e.g., walking around for 30 minutes wearing a large sandwich board that read "Repent!"), and then were asked what proportion of the rest of the student body would be willing to perform that act. Those who agreed to wear the "Repent!" sign thought 63% of their peers would comply; those who refused thought 23% would comply. There are now more than 100 studies demonstrating similar effects on predictions of peers' knowledge, attitudes, and actions. For example, there is a definite tendency to believe that a larger percentage of the voters prefer your favored candidate than actually favor that candidate (Granberg & Brent, 1983). The habit even includes beliefs about the candidates themselves, with voters thinking that their favored candidates are more like them than they actually are (Page & Jones, 1979). Another charming example is provided by an analysis of game show contestants' predictions of the trivia knowledge of audience members. Contestants consistently overestimated the numbers of knowledgeable audience members when they themselves knew the right answer; and the reverse occurred when they did not know the answer (Mullen, 1983).

Thus, the basic tendency to see ourselves in others is well established, and it is clear that an anchor-and-adjust process is responsible for many of these effects (see Krueger, 1998, and Nickerson, 1999, for more examples). But is the tendency a maladaptive judgment bias? In the absence of other information, egocentric projection is not a stupid heuristic for inferring what others think and will do. We share an enormous amount of "basic machinery" and experiences with other humans, so a good first approximation and a reasonable anchor for an inference about others is what "I think," "I want," or "I intend." For example, consider the extreme case where you did not know which pop song was favored by any individual, but you did know that there was universal consensus on the favorite. Under those conditions, it is obvious that your own preference would be a useful cue to the identity of the favorite. In more realistic situations where the correlation is less than 1.00 (say, consensus is 70%, not 100%), your own preference would still be a valid cue, just not perfect.

One of the authors of this volume pointed this out and noted that any study that wanted to establish a truly *false* consensus effect would have to show that the perceiver violated statistical rationality by putting too much weight on his or her own attribute over a series of judgments (Dawes, 1989). At a minimum, the study would have to show that the self was weighted more than another, randomly sampled individual. (Sherman, Presson, and Chassin [1984] are the only researchers to have done the analysis exactly right, in this respect, and they concluded no false consensus, except in domains that involved a threat to the person's ego.) Dawes looked carefully at the data from Ross et al.'s (1977) "Repent!" sign study and observed that the participants' estimates of 63% and 23% were very close to the proper Bayesian posterior probability estimates for the same quantities, given a sample of one sign-wearer or one non-cooperator. The point is not that people do not judge that others will be like themselves or that the cognitive process does not fit an anchor-and-adjust procedure, but rather that the conclusion is not necessarily irrational and maladaptive.

## 4.4 Anchoring the Past in the Present

Anchoring and adjustment can also severely affect our retrospective personal memory. While such memory is introspectively a process of "dredging up" *what actually happened,* it is to a large extent anchored by our current beliefs and feelings. This principle has been well established both in the psychological laboratory and in surveys. What we have at the time of recall is, after all, only our current state, which includes fragments (memory traces) of our past experience; these fragments are biased by what we now believe (or feel) to be true to an extent much greater than we know consciously. Moreover, the organization of these fragments of past experience into meaningful patterns is even more influenced by our current beliefs and moods— especially if we are particularly depressed or elated.

For example, Greg Markus (1986) studied stability and change in political attitudes between 1973 and 1982. Specifically, a national sample of 1,669 high school seniors in the graduating class of 1965, along with at least one parent in nearly every case, was surveyed in 1965, 1973, and 1982. A total of 57% of the parents (64% of those still living) and 68% of the students (70% of those living) were personally interviewed all three times. All subjects were asked to indicate on a 7-point scale (with verbal anchors at the end) their attitudes toward five issues: guaranteed jobs, rights of accused people, aid to minorities, legalization of marijuana, and equality for women. In addition, they were asked to characterize their political views as generally liberal or generally conservative. Most important for analysis of the retrospective bias, Markus asked the respondents in 1982 to indicate how they had responded to each scale in 1973. The results were quite striking. For their ratings on the overall liberal–conservative scale, the subjects' recall of their *1973* attitudes in 1982 was more closely related to their rated attitudes *in 1982* than to the attitudes they had *actually* expressed in 1973. Retrospecting, they believed that their attitudes 9 years previous were very close to their current ones, much closer than they in fact were. This bias was so strong that an equation set up to predict subjects' recall of their 1973 attitudes gives almost all weight to their 1982 attitudes, and virtually none at all to the attitudes they actually expressed in 1973 (with the important exception of the students' overall liberal versus conservative ratings). In addition, what discrepancy there was between 1982 attitudes and recall of 1973 attitudes could be explained in terms of stereotypic beliefs about how general attitudes in the culture had changed; the subjects believed that they had become more conservative in general, but that (again, in general) they have favored equality for women all along. Subjects whose attitude had changed in the direction counter to the general cultural change tended to be unaware of such change. Finally, the parent group attributed much more stability to their attitudes than did the student group, which is compatible with the belief that the attitudes of older people change less. In reality, however, the attitudes of the parent group were slightly *less* stable.

Attitudes are, of course, somewhat amorphous and difficult to determine. Linda Collins and her colleagues (Collins, Graham, Hansen, & Johnson, 1985) found quite similar results for actual behaviors when they surveyed high school students about their use of tobacco, alcohol, and illegal "recreational" drugs. They repeated the survey after 1 year and again after 2.5 years. At each repetition, the students (many of them then in college) were asked how much usage they had reported *on the original questionnaire.* (Collins and her colleagues had established strong rapport with this group and had reason to believe that their guarantees of confidentiality to the students, which they honored, were in fact believed.) Again, the subjects' belief in lack of change introduced severe retrospective bias. For example, the rating of past alcohol use for those subjects whose drinking had increased over the 2.5-year period was more highly related to their reported use *at the time of the current rating* than to the reports they had made 2.5 years earlier.

Thus, change can make us liars to ourselves. That generalization is not limited to change in an undesirable direction. As George Valliant (author of *Adaptation to Life,* 1977), who has studied the same individuals for many years throughout their adult lives, writes, "It is all too common for caterpillars to become butterflies and then to maintain that in their youth they had been little butterflies. Maturation makes liars of us all."

More generally, our first excursion into the realm of cognitive processes has explored the operation of one of the most ubiquitous human judgment habits: Start with the most salient or the most important facts and then adjust in the direction you think the truth lies. The anchor-and-adjust heuristic focuses on the manner in which we work with our limited attentional capacities by considering information item-by-item in sequence. Next, we will look at two other fundamental properties of the cognitive system: the manner in which our memory system affects judgments and the role of similarity—one of the most basic cognitive evaluations—in judgment.

# References

Anderson, N. H. (1996). *A functional theory of cognition.* Mahwah, NJ: Lawrence Erlbaum.

Ariely, D., Loewenstein, G., & Prelec, D. (2003). Coherent arbitrariness: Stable demand curves without stable preferences. *Quarterly Journal of Economics, 118,* 73–105.

Becker, G. M., DeGroot, M. H., & Marshak, J. (1963). Probabilities of choices between very similar objects. *Behavioral Science, 8,* 306–311.

Buehler, R., Griffin, D., & MacDonald, H. (1997). The role of motivated reasoning in optimistic time prediction. *Personality and Social Psychology Bulletin, 23,* 238–247.

Chapman, G. B., & Bornstein, B. H. (1996). The more you ask for, the more you get: Anchoring in personal injury verdicts. *Applied Cognitive Psychology, 10,* 519–540.

Chapman, G. B., & Johnson, E. J. (1994). The limits of anchoring. *Journal of Behavioral Decision Making, 7,* 223–242.

Collins, L. N., Graham, J. W., Hansen, W. B., & Johnson, C. A. (1985). Agreement between retrospective accounts of substance use and earlier reported substance use. *Applied Psychological Measurement, 9,* 301–309.

Cyert, R. M., & March, J. G. (1963). *A behavioral theory of the firm.* Englewood Cliffs, NJ: Prentice Hall.

Dawes, R. M. (1989). Statistical criteria for establishing a truly false consensus effect. *Journal of Experimental Social Psychology, 25,* 1–17.

Dhami, M. K., & Ayton, P. (2001). Jailing the fast and frugal way. *Journal of Behavioral Decision Making, 14,* 141–168.

Ebbesen, E. B., & Konecni, V. J. (1975). Decision making and information integration in the courts: The setting of bail. *Journal of Personality and Social Psychology, 32,* 805–821.

Epley, N., & Gilovich, T. (2001). Putting adjustment back in the anchoring and adjustment heuristic: Differential processing of self-generated and experimenter-provided anchors. *Psychological Science, 12,* 391–396.

Epley, N., Keysar, B., Van Boven, L., & Gilovich, T. (2004). Perspective taking as egocentric anchoring and adjustment. *Journal of Personality and Social Psychology, 87,* 327–339.

Gigerenzer, G., & Goldstein, D. G. (1996). Reasoning the fast and frugal way: Models of bounded rationality. *Psychological Review, 103,* 650–669.

Granberg, D., & Brent, E. (1983). When prophecy bends: The preference-expectation link in U.S. presidential elections, 1952–1980. *Journal of Personality and Social Psychology, 45,* 477–491.

Grether, D. M., & Plott, C. R. (1979). Economic theory of choice in the preference reversal phenomenon. *American Economic Review, 69,* 623–638.

Hastie, R., Schkade, D. A., & Payne, J. W. (1999). Juror judgments in civil cases: Effects of plaintiff's requests and plaintiff's identity on punitive damage awards. *Law and Human Behavior, 23,* 445–470.

Krueger, J. (1998). On the perception of social consensus. *Advances in Experimental Social Psychology, 30,* 163–240.

Markus, G. B. (1986). Stability and change in political attitudes: Observe, recall, and "explain." *Political Behavior, 8,* 21–44.

Mullen, B. (1983). Egocentric bias in estimates of consensus. *Journal of Social Psychology, 121,* 31–38.

Mussweiler, T., & Strack, F. (2001). Considering the impossible: Explaining the effects of implausible anchors. *Social Cognition, 19,* 145–160.

Nickerson, R. S. (1999). How we know—and sometimes misjudge—what others know: Imputing one's own knowledge to others. *Psychological Bulletin, 125,* 737–759.

Northcraft, G. B., & Neale, M. A. (1987). Experts, amateurs, and real estate: An anchoring-and-adjustment perspective on property pricing decisions. *Organizational Behavior & Human Decision Processes, 39,* 84–97.

Page, B. I., & Jones, C. C. (1979). Reciprocal effects of policy preferences, party loyalties, and the vote. *American Political Science Review, 73,* 1071–1089.

Quattrone, G. A., & Tversky, A. (1984). Causal versus diagnostic contingencies: On self-deception and the voter's illusion. *Journal of Personality and Social Psychology, 46,* 237–248.

Ross, L., Greene, D., & House, P. (1977). The "false consensus effect": An egocentric bias in social perception and attribution process. *Journal of Experimental Social Psychology, 13,* 279–301.

Schelling, T. (1966). *Arms and influence.* New Haven, CT: Yale University Press.

Sherman, S. J., Presson, C. C., & Chassin, L. (1984). Mechanisms underlying the false consensus effect: The special role of threats to the self. *Personality and Social Psychology Bulletin, 10,* 127–138.

Slovic, P., Fischhoff, B., & Lichtenstein, S. (1982). Responsibility, framing, and information-processing effects in risk assessment. In R. Hogarth (Ed.), *New directions for methodology of social and behavioral science: Question framing and response consistency* (Vol. 11, pp. 21–36). San Francisco: Jossey-Bass.

Strack, F., & Mussweiler, T. (1997). Explaining the enigmatic anchoring effect: Mechanisms of selective accessibility. *Journal of Personality and Social Psychology, 73,* 437–446.

Tversky, A., & Kahneman, D. (1974). Judgments under uncertainty: Heuristics and biases. *Science, 185,* 1124–1131.

Valliant, G. E. (1977). *Adaptation to life.* Boston: Little, Brown.

# 5

# Judging Heuristically

*We consider ourselves distinguished from the ape by the power of thought. We do not remember that it is like the power of walking in the one-year-old. We think, it is true, but we think so badly that I often feel it would be better if we did not.*

—Bertrand Russell

## 5.1 Going Beyond the Information Given

Our species has an unparalleled capacity to infer the characteristics of objects or events that are hidden or haven't yet occurred. This ability to "go beyond the information given to the senses" is a natural extension of our perceptual processes. In support of this judgment capacity, we have several fundamental, virtually automatic cognitive abilities: the ability to judge similarities between objects or events, the ability to recognize a previously experienced situation or individual, the ability to retrieve additional information about an object or situation once it has been recognized, and the ability to "see" causal relationships between events. These processes occur with little conscious effort and are "wired into" our brains so deeply that they do not change much across the healthy adult life span (Kahneman, 2003).

In this chapter, we provide more computational information processing models of the mental processes that link some specific types of cues to judgments (the cue utilization processes described by equations on the right side of the Lens Model diagram in Chapter 3). Following the insights of Amos Tversky and Daniel Kahneman (1974), we believe that a good account of many underlying cognitive judgment processes is provided by assuming that we have a *cognitive toolbox* of mental heuristics stored in long-term memory. Heuristics are efficient, but sometimes inaccurate procedures for solving a problem—in this case, providing rough-and-ready estimates of frequencies, probabilities, and magnitudes. The term comes from mathematics and computer science where a distinction is made between algorithms (often inefficient) that guarantee a solution for a specific problem type and heuristics that are efficient procedures to solve the same problems, but usually with some error in the answers. These heuristic mechanisms are usually constructed from more primitive mental capacities such as our similarity, memory, and causal judgment processes.

These *cognitive tools* are acquired over a lifetime of experience. They tell us what information to seek or select in the environment and how to integrate several sources of information to infer the characteristics of events that are not directly available to perception. We learn these cognitive tools from trial-and-error experience, as folklore from our family or peers, and through deliberate instruction. Some are controlled and deliberate (e.g., the algorithm we learned in school to do long division, the reasoning process to decide whether to bet or fold a poker hand), some are automatic and mostly implicit (e.g., the unconscious habits we use to judge whether another person is lying or how much salt to add to a dish we are cooking).

The notion is that when we encounter a situation in which a judgment is needed, we select a tool from our cognitive toolbox that is suited to the judgment. For many everyday judgments, we use heuristic strategies because they are relatively "cheap" in terms of mental effort and, under most everyday conditions, they provide good estimates. As Tversky and Kahneman (1974) wrote in their classic introduction to cognitive heuristics, "In general, these heuristics are quite useful, but sometimes they lead to severe and systematic errors" (p. 1124).

In this chapter, we will focus on two major judgment heuristics that depend on our basic, "wired-in" capacities for memory retrieval and similarity assessment. We will describe some of the situations in which they are used to make judgments, and point out systematic biases that are introduced into estimates and predictions when we rely on them. In essence, what happens is that we are called on to make a difficult frequency, magnitude, or probability judgment, and we substitute the assessment of an easier, more *automatic* attribute (such as ease of retrieval or similarity).

## 5.2 Estimating Frequencies and Probabilities

Consider our natural ability to estimate frequencies. Our perceptual and memory systems are "tuned" to automatically record the ambient frequencies of events as we experience them. Of course, many of these frequencies are of little use—for example, frequencies of individual letters in texts we read, the number of fast food restaurants we pass as we travel to work, the number of movies that have played on campus during the past semester. But others may be crucial for our survival, at least in some ancestral environments that were important in our evolution—for instance, it would have been essential to notice the quantities of edible plants in different parts of a forest, numbers of predators encountered at water holes, or the number of warriors in a competing tribe.

A single psychophysical function relating objective quantities to subjective estimates is characteristic of almost all memory-based frequency-of-occurrence estimates. At the low end of the objective frequency scale, estimates tend to be overestimates. As the number of to-be-estimated events increases, our subjective judgments err in the direction of underestimation. (This pattern of over- and then underestimation is called *regressive*, as it is similar to the flattened statistical regression curve.) The curve displayed in Figure 5.1 summarizes memory-based estimates of the frequencies of fatalities in various cause-of-death categories (e.g., heart attack, automobile accident, suicide). This same psychophysical curve has been observed in hundreds of other estimation situations, suggesting that we have some very general frequency estimation habits.

These psychophysical estimation curves are a bit different when the events are judged "online" while they are being perceived, rather than retrospectively based on memory retrieval. Under online conditions, small objective frequencies (1–5 events) are estimated with high accuracy. In fact, some of the earliest studies of short-term memory conducted by empiricist philosophers asked a person to estimate the number of pebbles in a handful thrown on a table and then quickly covered up. The almost perfect accuracy for estimates of up to five items was taken as a measure of the *scope of apprehension*. When the number of to-be-estimated events exceeds about 10 items, however, the tendency to underestimate the objective total appears as in the memory-based function. When there are more than about seven items (often cited as the capacity of short-term, conscious *working memory*), a more deliberate estimation strategy is used to make the judgment.

## 5.3 Availability of Memories

Many of the judgments we make are memory-based in the sense that we don't have the "data" necessary to make the judgment right in front of us, but we have learned information in the past, now stored in long-term memory, that is relevant to the judgments. This simple form of associative thinking is called the availability heuristic by researchers, and we rely on ease of retrieval to make a remarkable variety of judgments.

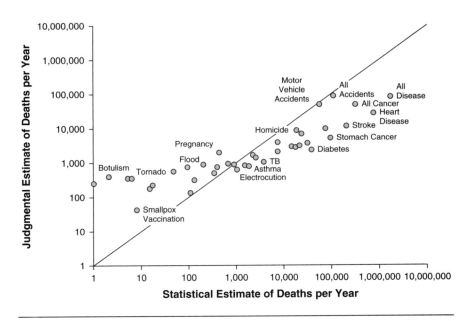

**Figure 5.1**    Frequency estimate curves for fatal risks (Note: The axes of the graph are on a logarithmic scale, to make the relationship more visible, but the basic pattern of overestimation of low frequencies and underestimation of high frequencies is clear.)

Sometimes all we do is rely on the ease (or fluency) with which information can be brought to mind to make judgments. We're planning a trip by air, the dramatic image of planes crashing into the World Trade Center comes to mind, and we have second thoughts. The number of airline passengers in the months immediately following the September 11, 2001, terrorist attacks dropped 20% (Gigerenzer, 2006). When no other information is available, people even rely on simple recognition to estimate magnitudes (Which has more inhabitants, Reno, Nevada, or Essen, Germany?) and values (Which stock is a better investment, Coco-Cola or Berkshire Hathaway?). We also rely on fluency when we make more deliberate efforts to retrieve data for judgments from memory. Norbert Schwarz and his colleagues asked college students to make judgments of their personal assertiveness (or lack of assertiveness; Schwarz et al., 1991). But first they were asked to recall instances in which their behavior exhibited the target trait. Half the respondents were instructed to recall 6 examples, an easy (fluent) task, and half attempted to recall 12, a difficult (disfluent) task. Self-ratings matched fluency of the retrieval task, implicating retrieval fluency as the mediating factor, even though the number of exemplars recalled was negatively correlated with self-rating between the two conditions. This effect has been demonstrated for judgments of risk of heart disease and inferences about personal preferences for various consumer goods (fluency also being a basis for liking; Schwarz, 2004).

Sometimes we rely on the number of items that come quickly to mind when we contemplate a judgment. Is the divorce rate increasing? Several vivid memories of acquaintances' divorces flash into our consciousness, and we judge the rate is high and increasing. We wonder if suicide or homicide is a greater threat to college students and can think of many more deaths due to homicide. Thus, we support increased investment in campus police, but not in the suicide hotline.

The operations of the availability heuristic can be broken down into seven subprocesses or subroutines (summarized in Figure 5.2): (i) the original acquisition or storage of relevant information in long-term memory; (ii) retention, including some forgetting, of the stored information; (iii) recognition of a situation in which stored information is relevant to making a judgment; (iv) probing or cueing memory for relevant information; (v) retrieval or activation of items that match or are associated with the memory probe; (vi) assessment of the ease of retrieval (perhaps based on the amount recalled, quickness of recall, or subjective vividness of the recalled information); and (vii) an estimate of the to-be-judged frequency or probability based on sensed ease of retrieval.

There are several points in the process at which biases might perturb the final judgment: The experienced sample of events stored in long-term memory (the information that is available to be remembered) might be biased, as in our example of suicide versus homicide estimates. The memory cue that is the basis for retrieval might be biased to produce a biased sample of remembered events, even if the population of

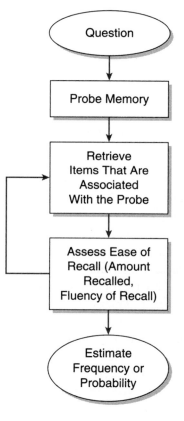

**Figure 5.2**  Flowchart summarizing the *availability heuristic* judgment process; arrows indicate the temporal sequence of substages in the global process

events in memory is not itself unrepresentative. Events may vary in their salience or vividness, so that some more salient events dominate the assessment of ease of retrieval. Any of these factors, individually or jointly, may introduce systematic biases into memory-based judgments.

## 5.4 Biased Samples in Memory

Statistics indicate that many more people commit suicide than are murdered (and the actuarial ratio is probably underestimated due to the tendency to err in the charitable direction of classifying ambiguous cases as "death by misadventure." How many deaths in single-car accidents are actually suicides? Such "accidents" are sometimes ascribed to alcohol, even when the drivers may have been drinking to "get up the guts" to kill themselves. Yet most people estimate that murder is more common. Why? The simplest explanation is that murders get more publicity. Whereas suicides of people who are not well-known are rarely reported in newspapers, murders are, irrespective of the identity of the victim. This explanation has been supported by the research findings of Barbara Combs and Paul Slovic showing people's estimates of frequency of causes of death (Figure 5.1 above) are correlated with the frequency with which causes are reported in newspapers independent of their actual frequency of occurrence. Thus, deaths due to plane crashes, shark attacks, tornadoes, terrorism, and other vivid and much-reported causes are overestimated, while deaths due to strokes, stomach cancer, household accidents, and lead paint poisoning are underestimated. The sample of experienced information (stored in memory and therefore "available" at the time of judgment) is biased in the first place.

What proportion of crimes are committed by ex–mental patients? By African Americans? When a former mental patient commits a crime—particularly a violent one—the fact that that person has been in a mental hospital is often mentioned by the news media. But when someone has never been in a mental hospital, that is never mentioned: "Archibald Smith, *who has never been in a mental hospital,* was convicted of the heinous crime of . . ." Not very likely. Systematic studies of media coverage show that the race of *minority* offenders, especially for violent crimes, is overreported ("the violent, scary world of local news" described by Franklin Gilliam, Shanto Iyengar, and their colleagues). Wendi Walsh, Mahzarin Banaji, and Tony Greenwald (cited in Park & Banaji, 2000) provided a demonstration of these memory biases by asking college students to circle the names on a list that they recognized as known criminals. Although none of the names on the list were in fact criminals, the students "remembered" almost twice as many African American names (e.g., "Tyrone Washington") as they did names characteristic of other ethnicities (e.g., "Adam McCarthy," "Wayne Chan"). These effects occurred even when the participants in the research were warned that "people who are racist identify more Black than White names; please do not use the race of the name in making your judgment."

Sociologist Barry Glassner (1999) has documented many of the biases introduced by "If it bleeds, it leads" news reporting, and by the strategic efforts of special interest groups to control the agenda of public fear of crime, disease, and other hazards. Is an increase of approximately 700 incidents in 50 states over 7 years an "epidemic" of road rage? Is it conceivable that there is (or ever was) a crisis in children's day care stemming from predatory satanic cults? In 1994, a research team funded by the U.S. government spent 4 years and $750,000 to reach the conclusion that the myth of satanic conspiracies in day care centers was totally unfounded; not a single verified instance was found (Goodman, Qin, Bottoms, & Shaver, 1994; Nathan & Snedeker, 1995). Are automatic-weapon-toting high school students really the first priority in youth safety? (In 1999, approximately 2,000 school-aged children were identified as murder victims; only 26 of those died in school settings, 14 of them in one tragic incident at Columbine High School in Littleton, Colorado.) The anthropologist Mary Douglas (Douglas & Wildavsky, 1982) pointed out that every culture has a store of exaggerated horrors, many of them promoted by special interest factions or to defend cultural ideologies. For example, impure water had been a hazard in 14th-century Europe, but only after Jews were accused of poisoning wells did the citizenry become preoccupied with it as a major problem (p. 7).

But the original news reports are not always ill-motivated. We all tend to code and mention characteristics that are unusual (that occur infrequently), and fewer people have been in mental hospitals than haven't, fewer people (in the United States) are black than white, and fewer are left-handed than right-handed. The result is that the frequencies of these distinctive characteristics, among the class of people considered, tend to be overestimated. The overwhelming majority of people on welfare are not "welfare queens" (those who abuse the system), but this leads to publicity for the rare welfare queens who are discovered, which produces a biased sample of welfare queens in our memories, which leads to subsequent overestimation of the number of people who are.

A single instance is a poor basis for a generalization, and it is a particularly poor basis when the instance is known to be atypical. Nevertheless, such generalization occurs—often with great ease. It is especially likely to occur when the instance is salient; for example, a non-Jew who believes that she has been cheated by one or two Jewish merchants may readily general-ize to form a negative view of all Jews:

> A young woman said to me: "I have had the most horrible experiences with furriers; they robbed me, they burned the fur I entrusted to them. Well, they were all Jews." But why did she choose to hate Jews rather than the furriers? (Sartre, 1948, pp. 11–12)

As Richard Nisbett and Lee Ross (1980) point out, rationally defensible deductive logic involves a *specification* from the universal to the particular ("*All* men are mortal, therefore Robyn Dawes is mortal."), but much less reliable inductive logic involves *generalization* from the particular to the universal ("This one Jewish merchant is dishonest, therefore *all* Jewish merchants are dishonest."). However, we are prone to do the exact opposite: we under-deduce and over-induce.

## 5.5 Biased Sampling From Memory

It is obvious that if the sample of information stored in memory is biased (per-haps because it is filtered through the popular media), subsequent memory-based judgments will be biased, too. But other aspects of the memory process can produce systematic biases as well.

> How many six-letter English words have the form
>
> _ _ _ _ n _?
>
> Not many? How many six-letter English words have the form
>
> _ _ _ ing? More?

When Tversky and Kahneman (1974) asked people to make such esti-mates, they judged words ending in -*ing* to be much more frequent than six-letter words with *n* in the fifth position. (There are, of course, more six-letter words with *n* in the fifth position than six-letter words ending in -*ing*. In fact, it is logically necessary that there be more, for every word ending in -*ing* has *n* in the fifth position, while there are additional six-letter words with *n* in the fifth position that do *not* end in -*ing*—for example, the word *absent.*) Of course, it is much easier to think of the six-letter words ending in -*ing*—for example, *ending;* it is even possible to go through the alphabet to readily find them: *aiming, boring, caring,* and so on. However, it is much more difficult to think of six-letter words with *n* in the fifth position (unless the ending -*ing* springs to mind). It is even possible intuitively to *estimate how difficult* it would be to generate six-letter words of the two different types.

Why do many people believe that they are particularly prone to getting into the slow checkout line at the supermarket when they are in a hurry, that it is more likely to rain if they do not carry an umbrella, and that sportscasters have "jinxed" athletes by praising them directly prior to an error? Given that there can be no logical connection among these events, such superstitious beliefs are based on summaries of experience. Those summaries, however, are *remembered* experience, and those instances of agitation in the checkout line, getting soaked, "jinxing," and other personally relevant coincidences are particularly available in our memories; we assume the other memories are in there, just not as easily retrieved. In fact, the common belief in psychic powers including clairvoyance is biased by our distinctively retrievable memories of coincidences, such as thinking about another person whom we haven't seen for years on the same day that we receive an unexpected telephone call from the person. The Nobel laureate Luis Alvarez (1965) provides an instructive analysis of just such a personal experience, showing the inevitability of coincidences occurring to someone somewhere. Although coincidences may be rare in each person's experience, we must remember they are "common" in a large population of individuals (Diaconis & Mosteller, 1989).

Robert Reyes, William Thompson, and Gordon Bower (1980) provide a controlled, experimental demonstration of the manner in which retrieval-biased availability affects a legal decision. They manipulated the presentation of materials in a drunk-driving case to make either the prosecution evidence or the defense evidence more vivid and more memorable. The verdict in the case hinged on whether the defendant was drunk when he ran into a garbage truck. Identically exonerating evidence about the difficulty of seeing the truck because it was gray in color was presented in either a pallid, forgettable version ("The owner of the garbage truck stated under cross-examination that his garbage truck was difficult to see at night because it was gray in color."), or in a vivid, memorable version ("The owner of the garbage truck stated that his garbage truck was difficult to see at night because it was gray in color. The owner remarked his trucks are gray 'Because it hides the dirt, it's a garbage truck. What do you want, I should paint 'em pink?'"). The same manipulation was performed on incriminating prosecution evidence—the pallid version ("On his way out of the door as he was leaving a party, the defendant staggered against a serving table knocking a bowl to the floor."), or vivid and memorable ("On his way out the door as he was leaving a party, the defendant staggered against a serving table, knocking a bowl of green guacamole dip onto the floor splattering guacamole on the expensive white shag carpet."). The side of the case favored by the more vivid evidence was the side that prevailed in mock jurors' verdicts; the vividness advantage was more pronounced when the verdicts were reported 48 hours after hearing the evidence—when a memory advantage would matter more.

Availability is exactly the bias that is capitalized on by trial lawyers who use *demonstrative evidence* to impress a jury. The attorney Melvin Belli once tried a personal injury case with a butcher paper–wrapped parcel on the table in front of him that was exactly the size of his client's missing limb, visible to the jury throughout the trial. No surprise that he won a record-setting award.

The emotion evoked by an event may have a further effect on memory and, hence, memory-based judgments: When we are in a particular emotional state, we have a tendency to remember events that are thematically congruent with that state. An early demonstration of the effects of emotion on risk judgments was provided in a laboratory experiment conducted by Eric Johnson and Amos Tversky (1983). They asked their experimental participants to make ratings of risks and accidents (like those estimated in Figure 5.1). At the same time, some of the participants were exposed to news stories on a radio playing in the background of the experimental waiting room that were designed to induce a feeling of anxiety and worry (stories about the death of another person similar to the participant). The negative emotion produced consistently higher ratings of the risks compared with ratings from participants who overheard happy or neutral news stories.

William Wright and Gordon Bower (1992) extended and replicated the above study with a stronger mood manipulation. Hypnosis was used to put experimental participants in a happy, neutral, or sad mood. The mood congruity effect was even more dramatic, such that participants rated events consistent with their mood as very likely to occur, and events inconsistent with their mood as unlikely to occur (Figure 5.3). Thus, a subject in a hypnotically induced happy mood gave high probability-of-occurrence estimates for "blessings" (e.g., world peace, discovery of cure for cancer), and low ratings to "disasters" (e.g., being injured in a car accident, major nuclear power plant accident).

Many more examples could be given. The principle is simple. When we have experience with a class of phenomena (objects, people, or events), those with a salient characteristic most readily come to mind when we think about that class. It follows that if we estimate the proportion of members of that class who have the distinctive characteristic, we tend to overestimate it. Our estimate will be higher than the one we would make if we deliberately coded whether each member of that class did or did not have that characteristic as we encountered it (e.g., by keeping a running tally with a mechanical counter). Selective retrieval from memory can produce large misestimates of proportions, leading to a misunderstanding of a serious social problem, and

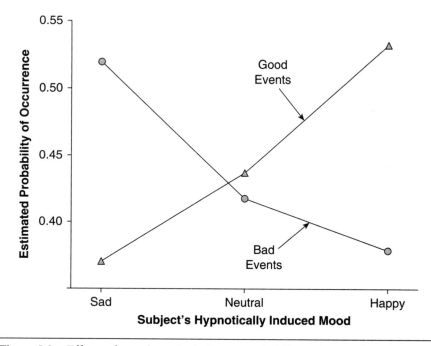

**Figure 5.3**    Effects of mood manipulation on probability estimates (based on experimental results reported by Wright & Bower, 1992)

finally to biases in important decisions like those required of voters, jurors, and policy makers.

## 5.6 Availability to the Imagination

Which is a greater threat to children, storing a gun in your home or installing a swimming pool? Even if you can't think of a single previous example, it's easy to *imagine* the child finding the weapon and injuring herself, but it's unlikely your first thought is of a lifeless body floating in the pool. Or imagine a group of 10 people. Make an intuitive estimate of the number of pairs of people—that is, "committees of two"—that can be formed from this group. Now make the same estimate of the number of "committees of eight" that can be formed. People estimate the former number, pairs, to be larger than the latter. It is much easier to *imagine* picking out pairs of people from the set of 10 than subgroups of eight. Once again, it is not necessary to form all such pairs mentally; we have an immediate impression of the ease of doing so without an exhaustive search, and in particular it *feels* easier to form pairs than to form committees of eight.

In fact, there is exactly the same number of committees of eight as committees of two. This conclusion can be reached by pure logic. Each time a unique pair is chosen from the group, a unique committee of eight remains. It follows that there is a one-to-one relationship between committees of two and committees of eight; it is not even necessary to use any formulas to conclude that their numbers are equal. Imagination is often deficient for judging the extent of mundane possibilities.

In these cases, availability *to the imagination* influences our estimates of frequency. The problem arises—just as with the availability of actual instances in our experience or availability of vicarious instances—in that this availability is determined by many factors other than actual frequency. It is clear that some types of thinking are easier than others and that some ideas come to mind more readily than others. Moreover, it is also clear that this difference is not based entirely upon past experience. (How many of us have had experience forming committees of two or eight?) The resultant ease of imagining biases our estimates of frequencies, and hence our judgments of probability based on such frequencies.

## 5.7 From Availability to Probability and Causality

A theoretically important availability effect occurs when people are asked to estimate frequencies or assess probabilities for sets of events that compose exhaustive, mutually exclusive complementary sets. Tversky and Kahneman, and their colleagues Donald Redelmeier and Varda Liberman, asked 52 physicians to provide probabilities for the outcomes to be experienced by hospitalized patients, based on the following descriptions of their cases:

- Dies during the present hospital admission
- Discharged alive, but dies within 1 year
- Lives more than 1 year, but less than 10 years
- Lives more than 10 years

Because the four events are exhaustive for the possible outcomes, the sum of their individual probabilities should equal 1. When the outcomes were assessed separately (one per physician), the mean sum of the four judgments was equal to 1.64—much too high, if the physicians were following the laws of probability theory that mandate the total probability allotted to a mutually exhaustive set of events is 1. The physicians were behaving according to the same rules as the baseball player Yogi Berra (famous for his malapropisms) when he told a reporter, "If there's a 50 percent chance we'll have a repeat American League winner, you gotta remember there's also a 75 percent chance we won't." Tversky and his colleagues explained this *subadditivity* of probabilities by proposing that support for each proposition was recruited from the physicians' imaginations. The complementary subevent descriptions provide effective cues to generate reasons for the specific outcomes. For example, the description "dies during the present hospital admission" suggests several concrete, vivid ways in which the patient might die in the hospital (surgical complications, anesthesiological mishap, postsurgical infection, etc.), while the implicit complementary event ("does not die during the present hospitalization") does not provide effective cues or associations for the imagination. Tversky and his student Derek Koehler (1994) have replicated this pattern of subadditivity for frequency estimates in many other domains including auto repair troubleshooting, weather forecasting, sports predictions, and so forth.

One of the authors of this book (Dawes) was interested in the presence of subadditivity in judgments of personal events, provoked by receiving an unsolicited report claiming that posttraumatic stress caused by the aftereffects of alien abductions is a significant mental health problem; the report alleged that at least 2% of the American population is affected by this problem (implying it should be ranked above homelessness on our national political agenda). As major support for the 2% conclusion, the authors of the report (Hopkins & Jacobs, 1992) cite the rate of affirmative responses to a recent Roper Poll question, "How often has this happened to you: Waking up paralyzed with a sense of a strange person or presence or something else in the room?"

Following up on Hopkins and Jacobs's (1992) preposterous conclusion, Dawes and a colleague, Matthew Mulford (Mulford & Dawes, 1999), asked a sample of respondents the same Roper Poll question. Remarkably, 40% of the people questioned about this bizarre experience answered that it had happened to them at least once. Comparable people in a (randomly) separate sample were simply asked how often they remembered "waking up paralyzed" (*without* asking about the "sense of an alien presence"). This time, only 14% responded affirmatively. Clearly, the more detailed description including the reference to a "strange person or presence" led the respondents to "recall cases that might otherwise slip their minds" (Tversky and Koehler's [1994] description of the underlying process).

Another, related example of subadditivity in judgments was studied by Michael Ross and his student Fiore Sicoley (1979). They asked the members of partnerships and teams to rate their proportional contributions to group efforts. Spouses, professor-student pairs, and basketball players all overestimated their individual contributions to group efforts; in every case, the sum of the individual ratings greatly exceeded the ceiling value of 100%. Perhaps most interesting was the finding that these overestimates occurred for both self-aggrandizing, *positive* contributions and for *negative* contributions ("causing arguments," "making errors in data analysis," "committing fouls"). The cognitive processes underlying these overestimates probably fall in the middle of the continuum from memory retrieval to imaginative generation, though retrieval is surely part of the explanation: Follow-up studies showed that these subadditive estimates were highly correlated with the respondents' ability to recall specific contributions, implying that memory availability was a component of the judgment process.

Tversky and Koehler (1994) refer to the re-description of a global event (car doesn't start, patient dies, economic recession, etc.) in an explicit disjunctive list of its component subevents as "unpacking" the global event (see also Rottenstreich & Tversky, 1997). Most studies find that subadditivity describes the relationship between the global event and its disjunctive, unpacked form ("car doesn't start" versus "out-of-gas, battery dead, ignition defective, etc."). However, there are examples of *superadditivity*, where the global whole is larger (on the probability measure) than its parts. This seems also to happen because of the nature of the underlying availability process: When the unpacked components are difficult to think about, to imagine and recall, then the components are judged (too) unlikely and the whole–part relationship is reversed, with the global event receiving more probability than its components. Laura Macchi, Daniel Osherson, and David Krantz have provided a technical demonstration of superadditivity in probability judgments that is best interpreted as a reverse difficulty-of-retrieval effect. In their studies, college students were queried about probabilities related to obscure scientific and almanac facts (Is the freezing point of gasoline greater than that of alcohol? Is the birthrate in Thailand less than that of Myanmar?). Here, the finding was that the component, unpacked probabilities added up to less than one.

Both the subadditive and the superadditive findings and other clever demonstrations of retrieval fluency verify the prominent role of availability as an underlying cognitive process. Some of the most important practical implications concern the manner in which citizens (and their political leaders) *set agendas* for the investment of public resources. The cognitive availability of alienated high school students, dishonest welfare recipients, pedophilic priests, faulty airplane wiring, wild-eyed terrorists, and many other exemplars in the public imagination has major consequences for where we spend our tax dollars and how we vote on relevant legislation (see John Kingdon's classic, *Agendas, Alternatives, and Public Policies* [1984], for the pioneering study of political agenda setting).

# 5.8 Judgment by Similarity: Same Old Things

The second elementary cognitive process that is often heuristically substituted for magnitude, frequency, and probability judgments is *similarity*. Many judgments are concerned with the proper category into which to classify an object or event. For example, we wonder whether the sore throat we've had for 2 weeks is just a simple cold, an allergy, or something worse like strep throat. We are looking for a low-sodium, low-fat item on the menu in a restaurant. We wonder if our new colleague is a behaviorist, a sports fan, depressive, or a born-again Christian.

Consider the following social category membership judgment:

> Penelope is a college student who is described by her friends as somewhat impractical, emotional, and sensitive. She has traveled extensively in Europe and speaks French and Italian fluently. She is unsure about what career she will pursue on graduation, but she has demonstrated high levels of talent and won prizes for her calligraphy. On her boyfriend's last birthday, she wrote him a sonnet as a present. What is Penelope's major field of study?

- Psychology
- Art History

Most readers doubtless believe, as we are tempted to, that Penelope is an art history student. She just seems to fit our *concept* of the kind of person who would study art history. But now consider the following question: In a typical university, suppose you pick a name at random from the student directory and look up that person's major field of study. Which of the fields of study mentioned in the question above is most popular? Which is least popular? What is the *probability* your random pick would be a psychology major? An art history major? (At a typical public university, recent statistics showed that approximately 2,300 students majored in psychology and 15 in art history, out of approximately 18,000 students; the *base rate probabilities* of these majors in the entire undergraduate student body are approximately .13 for psychology—the probability that a randomly selected student is a psych major—and .0008 for art history, or a ratio of 150 to 1! [If we restrict ourselves to females, the ratio is 140 to 1.]) After answering these latter questions, many people change their answers. They realize that the probability would be very low that anyone, no matter what their "personality sketch," would be 1 of the 15 (out of 18,000) Art History students. Moreover, some of those we questioned expressed embarrassment at their original answer. And a few expressed annoyance that they had been "tricked" by a description that sounded so much like someone who would major in an "extreme humanities" specialty—when they knew that they could not reasonably make this judgment given the brevity of the data and the tiny base rate of art history students.

This example illustrates the common tendency to make judgments and decisions about category membership based on similarity between our conception of the category and our impression of the to-be-classified object, situation, or event. As in the case of availability-based judgments, similarity slips into the judgment process automatically and dominates spontaneous judgments of category membership. The primary behavioral "signature" of relying on similarity is that people miss important statistical or logical structure in the situation and ignore relevant information (for example, the background, base rate frequencies, like the number of college majors in the Penelope problem above).

The Penelope problem intuitively demonstrates that we ignore a critical aspect of the situation. Let's look at another example where the error is more definitely proven. Tversky and Kahneman (1974) asked subjects to make probability judgments about the occupational categories of some men described by short personality sketches. Someone, for instance, who is described as being "unsociable, bored by politics, and devoted to working on his boat in his spare time" *sounds like* an engineer. In addition, the participants were given explicit base rate numbers: They were told the men being judged were either engineers or lawyers and drawn randomly from a pool of mostly engineers (70%) or mostly lawyers (70%). However, the results showed that the personality information completely overwhelmed the base rate percentages. The same probability judgment was made for a personality sketch whether the pool from which the man was drawn was 70% engineers or 70% lawyers. Even a bland, uninformative sketch ("has a wife and two children, promises to be successful in his field, and is well-liked by his friends") was judged as 50% likely to be a lawyer or engineer for either base rate, showing total base rate neglect. Only *when no description at all* was given did subjects correctly judge that someone drawn randomly from a pool of 70% engineers and 30% lawyers has a .70 probability of being an engineer (or someone from a 30% engineer versus 70% lawyer pool has a .30 probability).

Apparently, people relied completely on the similarity between their stereotypes of the occupational categories and the two-sentence sketch of the person's background. When the same subjects were asked to rate "resemblance" or "similarity" between the categories and the background sketches, they made the *same* judgments that they made when asked to assess probability— the similarity–probability correlations were all over +.95. This overreliance on similarity occurs even when people simultaneously acknowledge that the information they are using is unreliable, incomplete, and non-predictive.

Base rates are not the only relevant structural information that people miss when they make judgments based on similarity. Consider another example: Tversky and Kahneman (1983) asked college students to do the following:

> Linda is thirty-one years old, single, outspoken, and very bright. She majored in philosophy. As a student, she was deeply concerned with issues of discrimination and social justice and she also participated in anti-nuclear demonstrations. Please rank order by probability (highest to lowest) the following:
>
> - Linda is a teacher in an elementary school.
> - Linda works in a bookstore and takes yoga classes.
> - Linda is active in the feminist movement.
> - Linda is a psychiatric social worker.
> - Linda is a member of the League of Women Voters.
> - Linda is a bank teller.
> - Linda is an insurance salesperson.
> - Linda is a bank teller and is active in the feminist movement.

Fully 86% of undergraduates believed it more likely that Linda is a bank teller *and* active in the feminist movement than that Linda is a bank teller. The reason? Given the information about Linda, we can imagine her becoming a feminist bank teller, but it is hard to imagine her as merely an ordinary bank teller, even though feminism was not mentioned in the description of Linda. Even when the bank teller alternative was stated as "Linda is a bank teller *whether or not she is active in the feminist movement*," 57% of an additional 75 students still believed that "Linda is a bank teller *and* in the feminist movement" was more likely.

The logical error in this case involves missing the set relationships between bank teller and feminist bank teller. Feminist bank tellers form a subset of bank tellers, but surely there are many kinds of bank tellers: "traditional female role" bank tellers, Latter-day Saints bank tellers, anarchist bank tellers, and so forth. The set membership relations among these subsets may be unclear, but what is clear is that all are bank tellers (by definition) and some are not feminist bank tellers. So, how is it possible for it to be more likely that Linda is a feminist and a bank teller than a member of the larger category of all kinds of bank tellers, which includes feminist bank tellers? The answer is that it is not logically possible, and people (like us) who judge it is more likely she is a feminist bank teller than simply a bank teller are "missing" the logical structure of the judgment problem and over-relying on similarity of the description to our stereotypes of the social categories (the similarity–likelihood correlations were again over +.95).

Many of us are familiar with Venn diagrams (invented by the 19th-century mathematician and logician John Venn, who also wrote an important treatise on "The Logic of Chance") that use intersecting circles to represent sets of objects or events. The area of each circle represents the simple probability that an outcome is from it, and the overlap of the circles represents the probability that the outcome is from the corresponding compound event. A Venn diagram for the Linda problem makes it patently obvious that Linda cannot be more likely a feminist bank teller than a bank teller (of any kind; see Figure 5.4).

Tversky and Kahneman (1974) called these errors illusions, because like the many popular visual illusions, they persist even after we intellectually understand that they are incorrect. Steven Pinker (1997) reports that a student confronted with a series of such illusions stated that he was "ashamed of his species" (p. 344). And the evolutionary biologist Stephen J. Gould (1991) expressed the intuitive conflict that most of us experience: "I know that the conjunction is least probable, yet a little homunculus in my head continues to jump up and down, shouting at me—'but she can't be just a bank teller; read the description'" (p. 469). He concluded that "our minds are not built (for whatever reason) to work by the laws of probability." What our minds do seem to work by is a basic sense of similarity, as demonstrated by the almost perfect correlations between experimental participants' ratings of similarity and ratings of probability that the case descriptions belong to the relevant stereotyped categories.

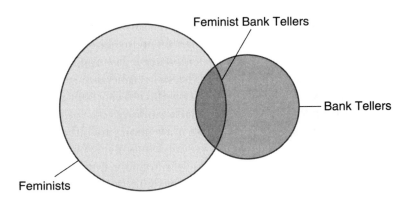

**Figure 5.4**    A Venn diagram showing the essential logical relationships underlying the Linda problem

# 5.9 Representative Thinking

The purpose of these examples was to demonstrate (1) that category membership judgments are usually based on the degree to which characteristics are *representative of* or *similar to* prototypical category exemplars, (2) that *representativeness* does not necessarily reflect an actual contingency, and (3) that probability estimates or confidence in judgments are related to similarity and not necessarily to the deeper structure of the situations about which we are making judgments. In the Penelope problem and the lawyers-engineers problem, people seem to forget about the background base rates of majors; in the Linda problem, people ignore the logical, set membership relation between bank teller and feminist bank teller. The overall similarity-based heuristic judgment process is summarized in Figure 5.5.

We find these early studies to be quite convincing on the point that people (over-)rely on similarity when making many probability judgments, perhaps because our own self-reflections when solving the original problems are completely consistent with the representativeness-similarity interpretation. A much more controversial issue concerns the *irrationality* of these judgments. Tversky and Kahneman (1974) designed the experimental dilemmas as concrete versions of textbook probability problems. Moreover, participants' responses were often *incorrect* in terms of the textbook answers. But the behavioral

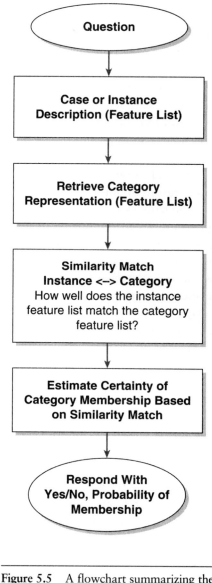

**Figure 5.5**    A flowchart summarizing the *representativeness* heuristic judgment processes

responses to similar problems are not perfectly consistent across all studies, the errors are not always as extreme as in the examples we presented, and there are rationales for even the apparently incorrect answers that many participants give (Birnbaum, 1983; Koehler, 1996). We'll return to the issue of whether these results prove people are irrational and make maladaptive everyday judgments in Chapter 8.

Modern psychologists hypothesize that our concepts of categories like bank tellers and feminists, and microcomputers, and skunks, and all kinds of things, are represented cognitively as the lists of attributes that we believe are defining and characteristic of those entities. This kind of conceptual representation is a very useful, but partly a fictional, simplification. Thus, if we ask someone to tell us what is meant by the category concept represented by the word *bird*, we usually get a list of the features associated with the label. If a thing is a bird, it flies, has feathers, lays eggs, eats bugs, and so forth; for *art history student*, features include sensitive, emotional, cultured, female, gentle, and so on. When we think about most everyday concepts, we think (and reason) about associated, characteristic, and correlated attributes, not just the truly essential defining attributes. And we often think about a category in terms of attributes ("flies" for birds, "cultured" for art history students) that we know do not apply to all members. Furthermore, we think about categories in terms of the *members* of the category that come to mind when we try to answer the "What does it mean?" question. So, there is even a role for memory availability in category concept representations.

The last piece of cognitive theory that we will need for our discussion of category classification is a model of the similarity judgment process. The most general model of this process is called the *contrast model,* and it says that we perceive similarity by making (very rapid) comparisons of the attributes of the two or more entities whose similarity is being evaluated. A useful model of this process is to suppose that our global impression of similarity arises from a quick tabulation of the number of attributes that "match" for two entities versus the number that "mismatch." The model includes provision for weighting the attribute match and mismatch pairs, to reflect our experience and beliefs about what is most important. So, for example, if we see a creature in the woods, the fact that it is not flying does not have as great an impact on our judgment about its "birdiness" as would the fact that it is covered with fur. In the Penelope judgment, there are so many "good matches" between attributes in the written description and in our stereotypes of art history major (retrieved from memory when we read the category name) that we respond "art history." In the Linda problem, there are more good matches for feminist (and bank teller) than for bank teller alone, between the sketch of Linda and the representations (stereotypes) evoked by the category labels.

In many cases, once an object is classified into a category, an association-based judgment is automatically made. In the case of skunks, the association provides a useful, quick message: Avoid this creature. But sometimes our associations with categories are morally troublesome or just flat-out irrational. The most carefully studied examples of this last type involve social stereotypes; our mental library of harmless stereotypes of art history students, bank tellers, and yoga teachers also includes some not-so-innocent stereotypes of socially significant groups. Perhaps the most troublesome characteristic of these racial, gender, and religious stereotypes is that they automatically evoke emotional reactions that affect our behavior toward members of the category. Once we've classified a person into a category with negative associations, we may not be able to help ourselves from reacting negatively to him or her. It is beyond the scope of this book, but the social psychology of stereotyped responding has revealed many uncontrolled properties of the automatic deductive and analogical inferences we make when social categories are activated and applied to people (Kunda, 1999; Wittenbrink & Schwarz, 2007). The many unconscious effects of stereotyped beliefs may even include rebound effects, where a well-intentioned effort to curtail stereotyped reaction is followed by an exaggerated application of the suppressed response in subsequent social interactions.

The following description of the decision process of a college admissions committee provides an example of an automatic, but logically dubious category association.

> The [Brown University] admissions committee scans applications from a small rural high school in the Southwest. It is searching for prized specimens known as neat small-town kids. Amy is near the top of her class, with mid-500 verbals, high-600 math and science. She is also poor, white, and geo— she would add to the geographic and economic diversity that saves Brown from becoming a postgraduate New England prep school. While just over 20% of the New York State applicants will get in, almost 40% will be admitted from Region 7—Oklahoma, Texas, Arkansas, and Louisiana. Amy's high school loves her, and she wants to study engineering. Brown needs engineering students; unfortunately, Amy spells engineering wrong. "Dyslexia," says Jimmy Wrenn, a linguistics professor. After some debate, the committee puts her on the waiting list.

What's wrong with making decisions on the basis of representative thinking? Once again, the problem is that similarity does not always reflect the underlying statistical and causal structure of the situation being judged. Misspelling *is* symptomatic of dyslexia. But, of course, there are many more of us who cannot spell well who are *not* dyslexic than who *are*. Nevertheless, the schema has been accessed and Amy has been pronounced dyslexic. It is neither relevant nor ethical to consider dyslexia in making such a decision, but as members of graduate admissions committees, both authors have observed many similar judgments in admissions and fellowship assignment committees.

When asked for "other information that the graduate admissions committee might find important," an applicant wrote that, "Being a Capricorn, I will be a careful experimenter." "We don't want any astrology nuts here!" one professor on the committee snorted, and the applicant—who ranked second out of more than 700 on a linear combination of GRE scores and GPA—was rejected. Of course, more applicants who knew their zodiac signs *were not* "astrology nuts" than *were,* but once again, the category schema ("astrology nut, therefore unreliable flake") was accessed.

The basic problem with making probability or confidence judgments on the basis of representative characteristics is that the schema accessed may in fact be *less* probable, given the characteristic, than one not accessed. This occurs when the schema *not accessed* has a much greater *extent* in the world than the accessed one. The categories "non-dyslexic" and "non-flake" are much larger in reality than those of "dyslexic" and "flake"; thus, the misspeller is more likely to be a non-dyslexic than a dyslexic, and the applicant who knew his zodiac sign more likely to be a non-flake than a flake. However, when the category schema is accessed automatically via similarity, its base rate is not. That requires a second, self-reflexive judgment: "How prevalent is this category?" (dyslexics or astrology-flakes or art history majors). Such a judgment invites the evaluation of base rates, *independent of the characteristic.* For example, the effect of the "think again" reminder about Penelope's major was to force the reader deliberately to consider the base rates of art history and psychology majors among college students. This failure to pay attention to the statistical structure of the situation and to ignore crucial information such as relevant base rates is a behavioral signature of judging by representativeness. But how should we properly use the base rate information when making judgments?

## 5.10 The Ratio Rule

In contrast to representative judgments, accurate judgments can be made by using the simplest rules of probability theory. Let $c$ stand for a characteristic and $S$ for a schema (category). The degree to which $c$ is representative of $S$ is indicated by the conditional probability $p(c|S)$—that is, the probability that members of $S$ have characteristic $c$. (In the present examples, this conditional probability is high.)

The probability that the characteristic $c$ implies membership in $S$, however, is given by the conditional probability $p(S|c)$, the probability that people with characteristic $c$ are members of $S$, which is the *inverse* of $p(c|S)$. Now, by the basic laws of probability theory,

$$p(c|S) = \frac{p(c \text{ and } S)}{p(S)}, \tag{5.1}$$

that is, the extent that $c$ and $S$ co-occur divided by the extent of $S$. Similarly,

$$p(S|c) = \frac{p(S \text{ and } c)}{p(c)}. \tag{5.2}$$

But $p(c \text{ and } S) = p(S \text{ and } c)$; it therefore follows that

$$p(c|S)/p(S|c) = \frac{p(c)}{p(S)}. \tag{5.3}$$

And, in general,

$$p(A|B)/p(B|A) = \frac{p(A)}{p(B)}. \tag{5.4}$$

This relationship is called the *ratio rule*—the ratio of inverse probabilities equals the ratio of simple probabilities.

In the present context of inferring category membership, this simple ratio rule provides a logically valid way of relating $p(c|S)$ to $p(S|c)$. To equate these two conditional probabilities in the absence of equating $p(c)$ and $p(S)$ is simply irrational. Representative thinking, however, does not reflect the difference between $p(c|S)$ and $p(S|c)$ and consequently introduces a symmetry in thought that does not exist in the world.

One of the most publicized misconceptions based on confusing inverse probabilities occurred in a televised statement by Harvard law professor Alan Dershowitz, a member of the defense "Dream Team" in the O. J. Simpson murder trial. The defense did not contest Simpson's prior history of spousal abuse of his deceased ex-wife Nichole Brown Simpson. Dershowitz said, "Among men who batter their wives, only one tenth of one percent go on to murder them" ($p$[husband-murders-wife|husband-battered-wife]). But, in a letter to the scientific journal *Nature*, the statistician I. J. Good (1995) pointed out that the relevant probability is conditioned on husbands who batter their wives *and* whose wives are subsequently murdered. Using Dershowitz's own assumptions, Good calculated the relevant probability, concluding that in one-half of such cases, the husbands are the murders: $p$(husband-murders-wife|husband-battered-wife *and* wife-was-murdered). (The simple actuarial probability seems to be about 1/3, although these statistics are uncertain because the category "battered wife" is difficult to define operationally.) Professor Good added, "Of course, this argument applies much more generally than to the O. J. Simpson trial. It shows once again, and dramatically, that the simple concept of [the] Bayes factor is basic for legal trials. It is also basic for medical diagnosis and for the philosophy of science. It should be taught at the pre-college level!" (p. 541).

Statements and beliefs about the relationship between pot smoking and hard drug addiction provide a rich source of such irrationality. For example, a headline in the *Redwood City* (California) *Tribune* of December 11, 1970, reads, "Most on Marijuana Using Other Drugs." The first line of the story that followed read, "Almost without exception, drugs are used by high schoolers in combination with marijuana when drugs are used at all, according to the findings." Whereas the text clearly states that of the students who use drugs, most use marijuana, *the headline asserts the reverse.*

The headline referred to the probability that a randomly chosen marijuana user ($M$) uses hard drugs ($H$), or "probability of uses hard drugs *given* uses marijuana," as estimated by the frequency of people who use both marijuana and hard drugs ($M$ and $H$), divided by the frequency of marijuana users ($M$):

$$p(H|M) = p(M \text{ and } H)/p(M) \qquad (5.5)$$

But the cited study was concerned with the probability that a randomly chosen hard drug user ($H$) uses marijuana ($M$), estimated by the frequency of people who use both marijuana and hard drugs ($M$ and $H$), divided by the frequency of hard drug users:

$$p(M|H) = p(M \text{ and } H)/p(H) \qquad (5.6)$$

The ratio of pot smoking given hard drug usage to hard drug usage given pot smoking is large because the ratio of smoking pot to hard drug usage is large, and these two ratios are equal (Equation 5.4). The survey found that the former conditional probability—smoking pot given hard drug use—is high, in accord with our everyday impressions. But that does not imply that the reverse is high also. The ratio rule indicates that the latter probability—of hard drug use given pot smoking—is much smaller than the former, so that a large value for the former does *not* indicate that "most on marijuana [are] using other [harder] drugs." Nevertheless, at about the time of this study, a

Democratic candidate for president, in response to an election-eve phone call, termed marijuana "what we in the pharmaceutical profession call a kicker."

Again, a Venn diagram makes it obvious that the inverse probabilities—$p$(pot smoker|hard drug user) and $p$(hard drug user|pot smoker)—are different. Clearly, being a pot smoker does not imply with high probability that a person is a hard drug user, but being a hard drug user does have such an implication for pot smoking.

In most writings about confusion of the inverse (also called the conditional probability fallacy), authors give funny examples. For instance, on August 27, 1967, *This Week* magazine published advice on how to stay alive in a car over Labor Day weekend (Barns, 1967). The author asserted that "the farther one drives from home the safer he is," because most deaths occur within 25 miles of home. This is a confusion of the probability of death given distance with the probability of distance given death; its invalidity becomes clear by invoking the ratio rule (Equation 5.4) and noting that the probability of driving close to home is *much* greater than the probability of being killed. It is easy to make fun of that confusion. By confusing the inverse, one might be tempted to tow one's car to the freeway. When, however, identical irrationality is used as a justification—or sometimes even as a reason—for enforcing harsh prohibitions against marijuana, the confusion is not so funny. For while an individual arrested may view the arrest as a natural consequence of government by the vindictive, uptight, and exploitive, many people approve of such arrests because they believe—along with the late Hubert Humphrey—that marijuana is "a kicker."

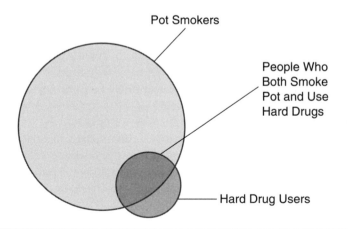

**Figure 5.6**   A Venn diagram summarizing the logical relationships between pot smoking and hard drug use

Occasionally, people assert dependency—and its direction—without considering either base rate (the background rates of occurrence of the characteristic, e.g., using marijuana, and the category, e.g., hard drug user). Consider the following item from *Management Focus*.

> Results of a recent survey of 74 chief executive officers indicate that there may be a link between childhood pet ownership and future career success. Fully 94% of the CEOs, all of them employed within Fortune 500 companies, had possessed a dog, a cat, or both, as youngsters.

The respondents asserted that pet ownership had helped them to develop many of the positive character traits that make them good managers today, including responsibility, empathy, respect for other living beings, generosity, and good communication skills. For all we know, *more* than 94% of children raised in the backgrounds from which chief executives come had pets, in which case the direction of dependency would be negative. Maybe executive success is really related to tooth brushing during childhood. Probably all chief executives brushed their teeth, at least occasionally, and we might imagine the self-discipline thus acquired led to their business success. That seems more reasonable than the speculation that "communication skills" gained through interacting with a childhood pet promote better relationships with other executives and employees.

Psychologists are not immune to such misjudgments. For example, Nathan Branden (1984) writes, "I cannot think of a single psychological problem—from anxiety and depression, to fear of intimacy or of success, to alcohol or drug abuse, to spouse battery or child molestation—that is not traceable to the problem of poor self-esteem." In other words, $p(c|S)$ is high, where $c$ refers to poor self-esteem and $S$ to problems. To state that these problems are "traceable" to poor self esteem, however, is to assert that $p(S|c)$ is high, which we do not know—*clients come to Branden because they have problems*. Branden's experience is with people who want help with their problems—his experience is conditional on $S$. Even if we found a high $p(S|c)$, we could not make a causal inference: People's self-esteem may be poor *because* they have the problems. Branden concludes the following:

> There is overwhelming evidence, including scientific findings, that the higher the level of an individual's self-esteem, the more likely that he or she will treat others with respect, kindness, and generosity. People who do not experience self-love have little or no capacity to love others. People who experience deep insecurities or self-doubts tend to experience other human beings as frightening and inimical. People who have little or no self-esteem have nothing to contribute to the world.

Following Branden's (1984) "I cannot think of" style, we cannot think of *any* scientific study in which the dependent variable was "nothing to contribute to the world." And it does *not* follow that since people with problems have (in Branden's experience) poor self-images, therefore, such problems have a high probability given "deep insecurities and self-doubts"—a characteristic that may not be that uncommon. While the word *deep* is sufficiently ambiguous that a clear statistical refutation of Branden's position is impossible, using representative thinking to communicate to a mass of people that they "have nothing to offer to the world" is intellectually irresponsible. In fact, Branden's observations are consistent with a conclusion that having low self-esteem is good for people who have problems (e.g., abuse children), for otherwise they wouldn't be motivated to seek change (e.g., enter therapy).

Fortunately, not everyone is prone to confuse inverse probabilities all of the time. For example, the great philosopher Bertrand Russell was not. His grandmother, in an effort to dissuade him from marrying his first wife, had impressed upon him how much insanity there was in his family. Nine years later, he was considering having children and consulted a doctor about the hereditary component of insanity. His biographer Clark (1976) writes the following:

> Four days later he saw his doctor, "who said it was my duty to run the risk of conception, the fear of heredity being grossly exaggerated. He says 50% of insane have alcoholic parentage, only 15% insane parentage. This seems to settle the matter." Settle, that is, until Russell, the potential parent, was overtaken by Russell the statistician; the footnote in his journal reads: "But he didn't say what proportion of the total population are insane and drunken respectively, so that his argument is formally worthless."

Even Russell, in this example, can be faulted for a degree of "mindlessness." Why, for instance, should he take the 50% and 15% figures so seriously at the outset? The problem is that to avoid such confusion, it is necessary to hypothesize classes of objects or events with which one has had little experience—for example, people with low self-esteem who nonetheless have a capacity to love others or who "have something to contribute to the world." Then, to estimate a conditional probability value, one must estimate the extent of this class, despite the lack of experience with its members. Doing so involves controlled "scientific" thinking—in Piaget's terms, regarding the actual (instances that *have been* observed) as a set of the possible (instances that *could* be observed) rather than vice versa.

Even ordinary people, not only great philosophers, utilize base rates more appropriately when we directly experience the events that compose the relevant categories, rather than learning about base rates by reading written summaries. When studies are conducted of physicians and accountants on the job, they seem to be tuned to the relevant base rates—for example, of local disease occurrence or of financial problem rates in different industries. This is somewhat reassuring, but there is still some base rate neglect in these noisy everyday situations. Laboratory studies of mock-medical diagnosis tasks have found that after substantial exposure to cases exhibiting distinct base rates (e.g., 25% of the cases turn out to be burlosis, 75% turn out to be coragia—fictitious diseases), participants are sensitive to the base rates— though, again, there are still experimental conditions under which base rates are neglected (Gluck & Bower, 1988; Goodie & Fantino, 1995, 1996).

Another situation in which we attend to base rates occurs if people ascribe some *causal* significance to discrepant rates. When they can see the causal relevance of the base rates, they often incorporate them into their reasoning. For example, the belief that one bus company has more accidents than another because its drivers are more poorly selected and trained will influence mock jurors to take this difference in accident rates into account in evaluating eyewitness testimony; but belief that a bus company has more accidents simply because it is larger will not. Study after study has shown that when these rates are merely statistical as opposed to causal, they tend to be ignored. Exactly the same effect seems to occur in real courtrooms; naked statistical evidence is notoriously unpersuasive—for example, the notable failure of the DNA evidence to persuade the jury of O. J. Simpson's guilt in his criminal trial for the murder of Nicole Brown Simpson and Ronald Goldman. Of course, *how* the $p(A)$'s and $p(B)$'s on the right-hand side of the ratio rule happened to come about is relevant; rationality demands their use (Koehler, 1997). But causal thinking has its own pitfalls, as we will see in the next chapter.

Finally, we seem to reason more competently in statistical problems of all types when we conceptualize the underlying relationships in terms of concrete numbers, *frequency formats,* rather than more abstract proportions and probabilities (see Barbey & Sloman, 2007, for a recent review). We'll return to this subject and provide some more advice on thinking correctly about conditional probabilistic relationships in Chapter 8.

Most of our thinking most of the time is governed by that ubiquitous law of thought, association, and hence we make representative connections, particularly when we assess probabilities. This chapter has emphasized informal observation and theory. In addition, a great deal of experimentation on representative thinking has been conducted (generally with college students as subjects), and it has consistently demonstrated the dominant roles of similarity and associations. Naive subjects do not distinguish between $p(A|B)$ and $p(B|A)$ in many circumstances, and when given one conditional probability, they infer the other without reference to the base rates $p(A)$ and $p(B)$, which must be considered according to the ratio rule. Our natural habit is to think associatively about what is salient to us in the immediate situation or what is immediately available from memory. It takes willpower and training to escape from the "dominance of the given" and to actually *think* about events and relationships that are not salient and explicit in our experience.

# References

Alvarez, L. W. (1965, June 18). A pseudo experience in parapsychology. *Science, 148*(3677), 1541.

Barbey, A. K., & Sloman, S. A. (2007). Base-rate respect: From ecological rationality to dual processes. *Brain and Behavioral Sciences, 30*, 241–297.

Barns, L. R. (1967, August 27). This quiz could save your life next weekend. *This Week*, 10–11.

Birnbaum, M. H. (1983). Base rates in Bayesian inference: Signal detection analysis of the cab problem. *American Journal of Psychology, 96*, 85–94.

Branden, N. (1984, August/September). In defense of self. *Association for Humanistic Psychology Perspectives*, 12–13.

Clark, R. W. (1976). *The life of Bertrand Russell*. New York: Knopf.

Combs, B., & Slovic, P. (1979). Newspaper coverage of causes of death. *Journalism Quarterly, 56*, 837–843.

Diaconis, P., & Mosteller, F. (1989). Methods for studying coincidences. *Journal of the American Statistical Association, 84*, 853–861.

Douglas, M., & Wildavsky, A. (1982). *Risk and culture: An essay on the selection of technical and cultural dangers*. Berkeley: University of California Press.

Gigerenzer, G. (2006). Out of the frying pan into the fire: Behavioral reactions to terrorist attacks. *Risk Analysis, 26*, 347–351.

Gilliam, F. D., Jr., Iyengar, S., Simon, A., & Wright, O. (1996). Crime in black and white: The violent, scary world of local news. *Harvard International Journal of Press/Politics, 1*, 6–23.

Glassner, B. (1999). *The culture of fear: Why Americans are afraid of the wrong things*. New York: Basic Books.

Gluck, M. A., & Bower, G. H. (1988). From conditioning to category learning: An adaptive network model. *Journal of Experimental Psychology: General, 117*, 227–247.

Good, I. J. (1995). When batterer turns murderer. *Nature, 375*, 541.

Goodie, A., & Fantino, E. (1995). An experientially derived base-rate error in humans. *Psychological Science, 6*, 101–106.

Goodie, A., & Fantino, E. (1996). Learning to commit or avoid the base-rate error. *Nature, 380*, 247–249.

Goodman, G. S., Qin, J., Bottoms, B. L., & Shaver, P. R. (1994). *Characteristics and sources of allegations of ritualistic child abuse*. Washington, DC: National Resource Center on Child Abuse and Neglect.

Gould, S. J. (1991). *Bully for brontosaurus: Reflections in natural history*. New York: Norton.

Hopkins, B., & Jacobs, D. M. (1992). How this survey was designed. In B. Hopkins, D. M. Jacobs, R. Westrum, J. E. Mack, J. S. Carpenter, & Roper Organization, *Unusual personal experiences: Analysis of the data from three major surveys conducted by the Roper Organization* (pp. 55–58). Las Vegas, NV: Bigelow Holding Company.

Johnson, E. J., & Tversky, A. (1983). Affect, generalization, and the perception of risk. *Journal of Personality and Social Psychology, 45*(1), 20–31.

Kahneman, D. (2003). A perspective on judgment and choice: Mapping bounded rationality. *American Psychologist, 58,* 697–720.

Kingdon, J. W. (1984). *Agendas, alternatives, and public policies.* Boston: HarperCollins.

Koehler, J. J. (1996). The base-rate fallacy reconsidered: Descriptive, normative, and methodological challenges. *Brain and Behavioral Sciences, 19,* 1–53.

Koehler, J. J. (1997). One in millions, billions, and trillions: Lessons from People v. Collins (1968) for People v. Simpson (1995). *Journal of Legal Education, 47,* 214–223.

Kunda, Z. (1999). *Social cognition: Making sense of people.* Cambridge: MIT Press.

Macchi, L., Osherson, D., & Krantz, D. H. (1999). A note on superadditive probability judgment. *Psychological Review, 106,* 210–214.

Mulford, M., & Dawes, R. M. (1999). Subadditivity in memory for personal events. *Psychological Science, 10,* 47–51.

Nathan, D., & Snedeker, M. (1995). *Satan's silence.* New York: Basic Books.

Nisbett, R. E., & Ross, L. (1980). *Human inference: Strategies and shortcomings of social judgment.* Englewood Cliffs, NJ: Prentice Hall.

Park, J., & Banaji, M. R. (2000). Mood and heuristics: The influence of happy and sad states on sensitivity and bias in stereotyping. *Journal of Personality and Social Psychology, 78,* 1005–1023.

Pinker, S. (1997). *How the mind works.* New York: Norton.

Redelmeier, D. A., Koehler, D. J., Liberman, V., & Tversky, A. (1995). Probability judgment in medicine: Discounting unspecified possibilities. *Medical Decision Making, 15,* 227–230.

Reyes, R. M., Thompson, W. C., & Bower, G. H. (1980). Judgmental biases resulting from differing availabilities of arguments. *Journal of Personality and Social Psychology, 39,* 2–12.

Ross, M., & Sicoly, F. (1979). Egocentric biases in availability and attribution. *Journal of Personality and Social Psychology, 37,* 322–336.

Rottenstreich, Y., & Tversky, A. (1997). Unpacking, repacking, and anchoring: Advances in support theory. *Psychological Review, 104,* 406–415.

Sartre, J. P. (1948). *Anti-semite and Jew* (G. F. Becker, Trans.). New York: Schocken Books.

Schwarz, N. (2004). Metacognitive experiences in consumer judgment and decision making. *Journal of Consumer Psychology, 14,* 332–348.

Schwarz, N., Bless, H., Strack, F., Klumpp, G., Rittenauer-Schatka, H., & Simons, A. (1991). Retrieval as information: Another look at the availability heuristic. *Journal of Personality and Social Psychology, 61,* 195–202.

Tversky, A., & Kahneman, D. (1974). Judgment under uncertainty: Heuristics and biases. *Science, 185,* 1124–1131.

Tversky, A., & Kahneman, D. (1983). Extensional versus intuitive reasoning: The conjunction fallacy in probability judgment. *Psychological Review, 90,* 293–315.

Tversky, A., & Koehler, D. J. (1994). Support theory: A nonextensional representation of subjective probability. *Psychological Review, 101,* 547–567.

Wittenbrink, B., & Schwarz, N. (2007). *Implicit measures of attitudes: Procedures and controversies.* New York: Guilford Press.

Wright, W. F., & Bower, G. H. (1992). Mood effects on subjective probability assessment. *Organizational Behavior and Human Decision Processes, 52*(2), 276–291.

# Explanation-Based Judgments

*For thousands, maybe millions of years, people have been telling stories to each other. They have told stories around the campfire; they have traveled from town to town telling stories to relate the news of the day; they have told stories transmitted by electronic means to passive audiences incapable of doing anything but listening (and watching). The reason that humans constantly relate stories to each other is that stories are all they have to relate.*

—Roger Schank and Robert P. Abelson, 1995

## 6.1 Everyone Likes a Good Story

Ask people how likely it is that an alcoholic tennis star who starts drinking a fifth a day will go on to win a major tournament 8 months later, and they will probably answer that it is extremely unlikely. Now ask other people how likely it is that an alcoholic tennis star who starts drinking a fifth a day will join Alcoholics Anonymous (AA) a month later, quit drinking, and win a major tournament 8 months later; to most people, that seems much more likely.

It is logically necessary, however, that the first outcome (winning the tournament) is more likely for the alcoholic star who starts drinking a fifth a day than is the second (joining AA *and* quitting *and* winning the tournament). The probability of three events must be less than the probability of one of them alone. A moment's thought tells us there are ways in which the star could win the tournament without joining AA (for instance, quitting drinking on his own, bribing the other players, maybe just being extraordinarily lucky).

Hence, winning the tournament must be more likely than winning it after the specific action of joining AA, which in turn is followed by the specific action of quitting. But joining AA links the parts of the story together into a plausible, coherent scenario, and scenarios are persuasive (Heath & Heath, 2007).

Human beings, perhaps uniquely among all animals, create mental models of the situations they are in, and those situation models often take the form of stories (the biologist Stephen Jay Gould once described humans as "the story-telling primate"). And, like every other fundamental characteristic of our minds, story construction plays a role in judgment and decision making. Scenarios, or narratives, are representations of temporally ordered sequences of events glued together by causal relationships—much of this "glue" is based on motives and intentions of goal-directed actors. Usually, narratives come in the form of simple linear causal chains—the missing nail caused the horse to throw a shoe, which caused the horse to go lame, which caused the message to arrive late, which caused the army to be unprepared, which caused the invader's victory, which caused the nation to lose the war, which caused the monarch to lose her throne . . .

## 6.2 The Conjunction Probability Error (Again)

Tversky and Kahneman (1983) term the belief that a specific combination of events can be more likely than parts of that combination the *conjunction fallacy.* A more precise designation is *conjunction probability error,* and we saw it earlier in the "Linda the feminist bank teller" representativeness-based error for category membership judgments. This same fallacy occurs in judgments of scenarios like the alcoholic tennis player scenario. Another example, in the context of scenario-based judgments, is provided by Tversky and Kahneman, again, who presented college students with the following:

> John P. is a meek man, 42 years old, married with two children. His neighbors describe him as mild-mannered but somewhat secretive. He owns an import-export company based in New York City, and he travels frequently to Europe and the Far East. Mr. P. was convicted once for smuggling precious stones and metals (including uranium) and received a suspended sentence of 6 months in jail and a large fine. Mr. P. is currently under police investigation.
>
> Please rank the following statements by the probability that they will be among the conclusions of the investigation. Remember that other possibilities exist and that more than one statement may be true. Use 1 for the most probable statement, 2 for the second, etc.
>
> - Mr. P. is a child molester.
> - Mr. P. is involved in espionage and the sale of secret documents.

- Mr. P. is a drug addict.
- Mr. P. killed one of his employees. (p. 306)

Eighty-six undergraduates ranked the events above; another sample of 86 students ranked a modified list with the last event replaced by "Mr. P. killed one of his employees to prevent him from talking to the police." Although the addition of the specific motive reduces the extent of the event (directly analogous to the case of Linda *the feminist bank teller* compared with Linda *the bank teller,* in Chapter 5), the mean rank of the conjunction event ("killed *to prevent him from talking*") was reliably higher (ranked at 2.90 on average) than the global "killed" (*for any reason*) event (ranked lower, at 3.17).

The statement that he killed an employee "in order to . . ." must be kept distinct from the "in order to" as a *reason* if we begin by *knowing* that he killed an employee. Because a combination of causes can yield an effect with higher probability than each cause alone, belief that an effect is "due to" a combination of things does not constitute a conjunction probability fallacy. For example, believing that someone was chilled *because* the person was outside and the temperature outside was below zero is more reasonable than believing that the person was chilled simply as a result of being outside (which would include being outside in the summer).

Tversky and Kahneman (1983) also discovered the conjunction probability fallacy when they asked medical internists questions about symptoms and diagnoses in an even more obviously "life and death" situation, detailed below.

A 55-year-old woman had a pulmonary embolism (blood clot in the lung). How likely is it that she also experiences the following?

- Dyspnea [shortness of breath] *and* hemiparesis [partial paralysis]
- Calf pain
- Pleuritic chest pain
- Syncope [fainting] *and* tachycardia [accelerated heart beat]
- Hemiparesis
- Hemoptysis [coughing blood] (Tversky & Kahneman, 1983, p. 301)

Of the 32 internists questioned, 91% believed that the combination of a probable symptom (in this case, dyspnea) and an improbable one (in this case, hemiparesis) was more likely than the improbable symptom alone. The combination of the two symptoms formed a coherent or good explanation in the minds of the medical experts.

## 6.3 Judging From Explanations

Conjunction probability violations of rationality are widespread. When we imagine the future, the content of our imagination tends to conform to our intellectual schemas. Thus, many of our scenarios are conjunctions of specific events that we believe are highly probable. Again, such belief is fairly automatic. Those of us whose thought processes are primarily visual tend to anticipate the future by "seeing" what we and others are likely to do, and our images will be quite concrete. Our knowledge that almost nothing turns out exactly the way we imagine does not stop us from imagining the future concretely by building vivid scenarios of sequences of likely events. It is only upon reflection that we attempt to assess the probability of events in isolation and thereby become less vulnerable to the conjunction probability fallacy. (The conclusion that the likelihood of events can better be considered by viewing them in isolation—rather than as part of a meaningful, holistic, apparently probable sequence—may be jarring to some readers.)

The scenario construction process and its consequences for judgment are summarized in Figure 6.1. Story construction, at least the perception of causal relationships between events, is so natural that we would list it as an automatic cognitive capacity along with our capacities for frequency registration, memory recognition, and similarity judgments. Roger Schank and Robert Abelson (1995) have made an interesting argument that virtually all of our everyday knowledge, from arithmetic skills to the fact that a whale is a mammal, is stored in narrative formats. This is probably going too far, but an enormous amount of knowledge in our memories is represented in or linked to stories. The essential cognitive function of maintaining a situation model that places us in our current context, prepared for action, is dominated by narrative formats. Experience is a temporal sequence of events, and that is the cognitive format we use to summarize the past and to project to the future.

Of course, it is no surprise that we look for good reasons for an event that we are predicting (or retrospectively diagnosing): The knowledge that a key player has been injured, that a company has a new CEO, or that a person is a drug addict is often enough cause to make a confident prediction, even if that is all we know about the situation. We humans have a compulsion to explain events in the world around us; this compulsion is part of a generally adaptive habit of maintaining useful mental models of our current situations, a habit with obvious survival value. Many prefabricated scenarios are available to our imaginations either because they correspond to stereotyped scripts or because they are available through particular past experiences. (Such availability need not be based on actual frequency, as pointed out at some length in Chapter 5.) Availability here, however, must refer to availability *to our imagination* rather than availability *in fact*—because it is logically impossible for us to experience conjunctions of events more frequently than we experience the individual components of these conjunctions. Nonetheless, imagination is an important determinant of feelings, thought, and action.

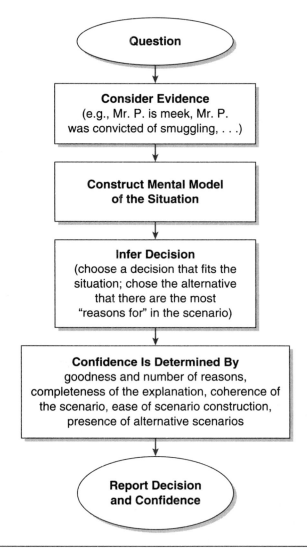

**Figure 6.1**    A summary of the explanation-construction process and its effects on judgments and decisions

Belief in the likelihood of scenarios is associated with belief in the likelihood of their components; believable components yield believable scenarios (and often vice versa as well). Complete stories, detailed stories, and sensible stories (with reference to other stories or to our general beliefs about human motivation and natural causality) are influential stories. It is somehow plausible to us that Cleopatra's physical charms could lead two of the most powerful men in the Classical world to behave like 15-year-olds, or that the sexual temptation of a 24-year-old intern could lead a U.S. president, one of the most powerful men in the modern world, to behave in the same manner.

Scenarios are even more believable if the components form a good gestalt because they fit into or exemplify some familiar narrative schema. For example, we might say the story of the alcoholic athlete who joins AA, is rehabilitated, and triumphs is a prototypical recovery narrative. Coherence leads to overestimation of the likelihood that a scenario is true or will occur; it is an overestimate for the following three reasons.

First, the combination of events may be improbable even though each event in it is probable; the probability of a combination of events 1, 2, . . . , $k$ is $p_1 \times p_2 \times \ldots \times p_k$, where $p_1$ is the probability of the first, $p_2$ is the probability of the second *given* the first, $p_3$ is the probability of the third given the first two, and so on ($p_1 \times p_2 \times \ldots \times p_k$ may be quite small, even though each $p_i$ in it is large—for example, $.90 \times .80 \times .85 \times .80 \times .85 \times .90 = .37$, even though .80 is the smallest number in this sequence). To estimate the probability of the sequence on the basis of its "typical" component probabilities (average = .85), as many people do, seriously overestimates this number. In fact, the probability of any conjunction of events, even if they don't compose a plausible narrative, is often overestimated—for example, the probability of getting four cherries on a casino slot machine. Painstaking behavioral studies suggest that this overestimation is usually the result of an anchor-and-adjust estimation strategy; people anchor on a typical component event probability (the probability of getting one cherry) and then under-adjust (see Chapter 4).

Second, the same cognitive factors—such as *imaginability*—that lead to an overestimation of the probability of a component may also lead to an overestimation of the probability of the scenario as a whole. In fact, the imaginability of the entire scenario may lead to greater belief in the likelihood of the whole than in one of its parts, as illustrated by the belief that Mr. P. being guilty of murder for a specific motive was more probable than his being guilty of murder for any reason.

And third, in many domains (e.g., sports, crime, health), when dramatic coincidences occur, composed of an unlikely combination of components, they tend to draw attention and are repeated and remembered, amplifying the basic conjunction overestimation effect through availability (see Chapter 5).

## 6.4 Legal Scenarios:
## The Best Story Wins in the Courtroom

In one of the most significant jury trials in recent history (*Silkwood v. Kerr-McGee Corp.*, 1984), the famous attorney Gerry Spence told jurors to think about the situation in terms of a zookeeper who carelessly left a cage door unlatched, allowing a ferocious lion to escape and attack a hapless woman who had the bad fortune to be in harm's way. The story about the negligent zookeeper "told" the jurors what to do about the corporation that had allegedly allowed employees to become contaminated with radioactive plutonium, and they found the company liable for $10 million in punitive damages. There seems to be little question that jurors' decisions are driven primarily by the stories they construct to comprehend and remember the evidence presented to them at trial.

Good trial attorneys know that good stories win cases. Another famous trial attorney, with the colorful nickname "Racehorse" Haynes, was quoted as saying, "The lawyer with the best story wins." He went on to advise (defense) attorneys, "The surest way to win a murder case is to convince the jury that the best ending for the story told by the evidence is that the decedent deserved to die." Anthony Amsterdam, another legendary attorney, has analyzed transcripts of attorneys' arguments to the jury to demonstrate that they often tell two kinds of stories: First are stories about the evidence, the "what happened" at the crime scene, and second are stories about the trial, with careful attention to the role that the attorney wants the jurors to play in that narrative (Amsterdam & Hertz, 1992). In the O. J. Simpson murder trial, Marcia Clark's closing argument as prosecutor included a detailed summary of the prosecution crime story, complete with a timeline; in contrast, the defense attorney, Johnnie Cochran, concluded by exhorting the jurors to accept the role, at trial, of protector, even avenger, of oppressed minority defendants (Hastie & Pennington, 1996).

The central cognitive process in juror decision making is *story construction*—the creation of a narrative summary of the events under dispute. Thus, the central claim of this hypothesis is that the story the juror constructs, often quite deliberately to "piece together the puzzle of historical truth," determines the juror's verdict. Ask any juror why he or she decided on a particular verdict, and you will more likely than not get an answer that begins, "Let me tell you what happened . . ." Using converging measures to "take cognitive snapshots" of the contents of several hundred mock jurors' thoughts, before and after rendering verdicts in a variety of cases, Nancy Pennington and Reid Hastie (1991) found that a narrative story structure was consistently the best summary of the jurors' memory structures. For example, when asked to decide a well-known civil case in which a mall employee (Kathleen Hughes) sued the mall owners (the Jardel Company) for damages after she was assaulted on her way to her car after work, the modal juror exhibited a cognitive representation of the evidence that looks like the network in Figure 6.2.

Note that the evidence at trial is almost never presented to the jurors in the chronological order of the events in the original crime, so the jurors must reorganize evidence, as they comprehend it, to produce memory structures that reflect the original chronological order of events depicted in Figure 6.2. This is a precedent-setting case of a lawsuit on behalf of the victim of a brutal assault as she left work at the Jardel-owned Blue Hen Shopping Mall. At issue in this complex trial was whether the mall owners were negligent in not providing more security guards to prevent incidents like Kathleen Hughes's assault. Mock jurors who heard the evidence as presented in the scrambled, nonchronological sequence from the original trial, all remembered it in the proper historical-temporal order.

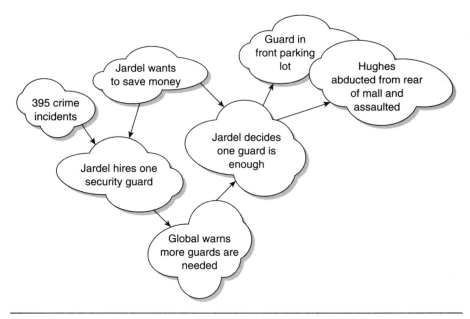

**Figure 6.2**   The schematic structure of a story constructed by a juror to comprehend (explain) the evidence in a civil lawsuit (*Jardel Co. v. Hughes,* 1987)

More important, though, is the finding that jurors who choose different verdicts have reliably different mental representations. Pennington and Hastie (1991) found that when jurors construct summaries of the evidence they are hearing and seeing in legal disputes, there are usually at least two competing interpretations (otherwise the dispute would not have gotten to court—over 90% of criminal cases and civil suits plea-bargain or settle before they get to court, presumably because one side or the other did not have the evidence to construct a plausible story). Different jurors are likely to construct different stories, and the stories lead to different verdicts. At least, after jurors reach different verdicts, they have different stories in mind. This situation is summarized in Figure 6.3 (for a criminal case): First, the juror constructs a story summary of the evidence (and there are usually only a few, two or three at most, alternate stories for any case); second, the juror learns something about the possible verdicts from the judge's instructions at the end of the trial; then the juror makes a decision by "classifying" the story into the best-fitting verdict category. Pennington and Hastie also found that jurors with more complete, more detailed, and more unique stories were more confident than those whose stories were less compelling.

An illustration of the power of story-based evidence summaries is provided by the dramatic differences between European American and African American citizens' reactions to the verdict in the O. J. Simpson murder trial. (There even appeared to be racial differences in response on the jury and within the defense team.) We believe that jurors' race made a difference in the acceptability of the defense story according to which a racist police detective (Mark Fuhrman) planted incriminating evidence. African Americans, compared with European Americans, have many more beliefs and experiences that support the plausibility of stories of police misconduct and police bigotry. Many African Americans and members of their immediate families have had negative, and probably racist, encounters with justice system authorities. African Americans know of many more stories of police racism and police brutality directed against members of their race (some apocryphal, some veridical) than do European Americans. This background of experience, beliefs, and relevant stories made it easy for African Americans to construct and believe a story in which a police officer manufactured and planted key incriminating evidence. (In an effort to find a European American version of the "racist cop" stereotyped scenario, one of the authors asked his colleagues if they knew, through personal experience, of any examples of biased or unfair authorities. The resounding answer? Internal Revenue Service officials! Almost everyone in his predominantly white, middle-class sample had had, or claimed to know someone who had, a bad experience with overzealous income tax auditors.)

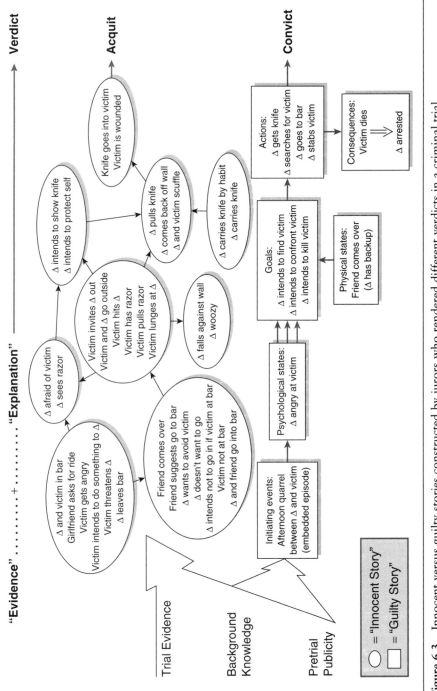

**Figure 6.3** Innocent versus guilty stories constructed by jurors who rendered different verdicts in a criminal trial

One of the most dramatic demonstrations that jurors' stories of the evidence cause their verdicts is a study by Nancy Pennington (Pennington & Hastie, 1991) of the effects of variations in the order of evidence presentation on judgments. Stories were expected to be easy to construct when the evidence was presented in a temporal sequence that matched the occurrence of the original events (Story Order). Stories would be more difficult to construct when the presentation order did not match the sequence of the original events. (This non-story Witness Order matched the sequence of evidence presented by witnesses in the original trial.) As predicted, jurors were likeliest to convict the defendant when the prosecution evidence was presented in Story Order and the defense evidence was presented in Witness Order (78% of the jurors judged the defendant guilty), and they were least likely to convict when the prosecution evidence was in Witness Order and the defense was in Story Order (31% said guilty). The difference in conviction rates is huge, over 40 percentage points. (We do not claim that the *order of proof* effect will be this large in actual trials, although we do believe the effect generalizes and advise attorneys to tell good stories, when they can, as do winning trial attorneys like Gerry Spence, "Racehorse" Haynes, and Johnnie Cochran.)

A more subtle aspect of scenario-based judgment occurs because stories tend to exist, *sui generis,* without multiple interpretations or versions. In the Pennington and Hastie (1988) studies of juror decision making, the perceived strength of one side of the case depended on the order of evidence both for that side *and for the other side* of the case. This finding implies that the jurors attempted to construct more than one story summary of the evidence and that the *uniqueness* or relative goodness of the best-fitting story is one basis for confidence in their judgment. The construction of multiple stories is almost forced on the decision maker by the traditions of our adversarial trial system. However, we suspect that in most everyday situations, when story construction is the basis for decisions, people stop after they have constructed one story.

During construction and evaluation of a story, people do consider alternative versions of *parts of* the stories. (This form of reasoning is called *counterfactual thinking,* because it involves imagining alternatives to "factual" reality that might have occurred—what we have referred to as Piagetian "scientific reasoning" elsewhere in this book.) For example, in the *Jardel Co. v. Hughes* case, the crucial inference that appeared to distinguish between jurors who decided the mall owners were liable versus those who concluded they were not liable involved the possible effects of adding extra patrol guards to the mall security staff. Jurors who reasoned, "If there had been more guards, the rape would have been prevented," went on to conclude the mall was liable. After all, if the owners had not been so greedy, if they'd paid a little more to add extra guards, then the assault would not have occurred. On the other hand, jurors who reasoned, "If there had been more guards, the rape would still have occurred" (i.e., in a large mall, full protection would require an impossibly large security force), concluded the owners were not liable. In legal contexts, this kind of reasoning is called the "but for" test of causality; a philosopher would probably describe it as testing if a candidate cause (few security guards) is a *necessary condition* for an effect (the assault on Kathleen Hughes) to occur. So, although there is a tendency for one story to dominate our mental representation of any situation, the construction of that story usually involves the consideration of alternative parts or episodes within the story. When there is uncertainty about those parts (e.g., a juror can't make up his or her mind about whether the rape would have been prevented by adding security guards), that local uncertainty is generalized to lower confidence in the whole story.

Follow-up research has addressed some practical questions about trial tactics in adversarial trials. For example, many criminal cases involve the presentation of only one story, by the prosecution, and the defense tactic is to "raise reasonable doubts" by attacking the plausibility of that story. (Some cynical attorneys describe this defense strategy as "creating a cloud of confusion in the juror's mind and then labeling that cloud 'reasonable doubt.'") In these one-sided cases, jurors construct only one story, and confidence in the verdict is determined by coherence and fit of that single story to the verdict category. In this situation, a weak defense story is worse than no story at all; in fact, a weak prosecution story is bolstered and more guilty verdicts are rendered when a weak defense story is presented. Again, this result implicates the importance of the comparative *uniqueness* factor when more than one story has been constructed.

Another observation, which reinforces the lore of trial tactics, is that when a narrative strategy is used to argue a case, the attorney should set up the story in his or her opening statement to the jury. The chance of obtaining a verdict consistent with a story is increased when the story is primed in advance and is ready in the juror's mind to interpret the evidence. But, as Gerry Spence (1994) warns, "When I make an opening statement, I always do it as a story. But, you'd better be able to prove your story, because if jurors who believed you find out you haven't told the whole story, then they turn against you."

## 6.5 Scenarios About Ourselves

It is widely believed among psychoanalytic clinicians that clients of Freudian analysts have Freudian dreams and clients of Jungian analysts have Jungian dreams (and clients of behavioral therapists have rapid eye movements, but nothing else worth mentioning). The extension that clients of Freudian and Jungian analysts have led Freudian and Jungian lives, respectively, is a bit more disconcerting, for it implies that the dearly gained insights of these clients may be joint inventions of the clients and analysts (inventions of unknown and unknowable validity). Research on the nature of retrospective and even allegedly repressed memory has reinforced this possibility, for the malleability of such memory implies that mere agreement with the therapist is a poor basis for judging accuracy (Campbell, 1998). Could the therapy process be partly, or even primarily, one of inventing a good story about the client's life? If so, could this "story" hinder as well as help to foster free and responsible choice?

This notion of *narrative truth* is consistent with the rationales behind many forms of psychotherapy. These therapies assume that clients' (narrative) representation of their lives is the key to understanding their maladaptive behaviors. The therapist's reconstruction of the client's life story into a more coherent and adaptive narrative is the primary goal of therapy. Freud himself originally believed that maladaptive behaviors were caused by actual events, but after discovering that several of his clients had manufactured memories that were impossible, he acknowledged that the crucial causal events might never have occurred. Thus, the goal of therapy is not solely to recall actual events, but to reconstruct a more adaptive life story, one that may not agree perfectly with actual, historical truth. These more adaptive life stories are aimed at helping the clients to accept their past distressed behavior as a normal consequence of what had previously occurred in order to make the decision to abandon this behavior. (Paul van den Broek and his colleague Richard Thurlow [1991] provide a thoughtful discussion of the role of narrative autobiographical reconstruction in psychotherapy from the point of view of laboratory-based cognitive psychology.)

The problem with therapies based on reconstructing life stories was pointed out by James March (1972), in discussing the problem with "discovering" that one's adult years flow naturally—as part of a good story—from childhood:

> [B]elief in the model seems likely to create a static basis in personal self-analysis. Individuals who believe the "formative years" hypothesis seem quite likely to consider the problem of personal identity to be a problem of "discovering" a pre-existing "real" self rather than of "creating" an "interesting" self. The notion of discovery is biased against adult change.

Such discoveries can become verbal straitjackets through the attributions they create—for example, "I have come to accept the fact that I suffer from a narcissistic character disorder" can lead to self-indulgence ("What can I do? After all, I'm a narcissist, and that's it.") and unrealistic projection onto others. The art of this form of cognitively oriented therapy is to construct *adaptive* life stories. (The psychotherapist who has developed this theme most fully is Donald Spence, whose book *Narrative Truth and Historical Truth* [1982] is a landmark in modern psychoanalytic theory.)

A hint of the potentially detrimental side effects of our habit of creating and reconstructing consistent life stories is given in studies of people's biased reconstruction of what they used to be like. As we will show at the end of this chapter, autobiographical memories tend to be dominated by our current attitudes, beliefs, and feelings about ourselves.

All of the elements needed for belief in the high probability of personal scenarios are there when we view our lives. These include stereotypes derived from family myths, cultural beliefs, literature, plays, movies, and television—and in the case of professional psychotherapists and psychiatrists, prototypical case histories communicated in textbooks or through contact with others who have an interest or a professional commitment. These sources all provide prepackaged, believable, complex sequences of events for our entertainment, education, *and use.* No wonder some pop psychologists have achieved great fame through arguing that we often act out preselected life scripts (e.g., Eric Berne's popular exegesis, *Games People Play* [1964]).

## 6.6 Scenarios About the Unthinkable

What do you think is the probability that there will be a massive flood somewhere in North America, in the next 12 months, in which more than 1,000 people drown? Now, what about the probability that there will be an earthquake in California, in the next 12 months, causing a flood in which more than 1,000 people drown? Or a tropical storm in the Gulf of Mexico, in the next 12 months, causing a flood on the Gulf Coast, in which more than 1,000 people drown? The more specific, causal stories somehow seem more compelling, and more likely. There are many reasons that a catastrophic flood could occur, but providing one vivid scenario ups the probability. But, of course, this is our old friend the conjunction error—a more specific category, that logically must have a smaller extent, is judged more probable than the larger, more abstract, and more likely class of events.

Several small countries are working on the development of nuclear weapons. Iran, North Korea, and Pakistan are obvious examples. One or more of these countries may be run by a fanatic who incites suicide missions such as the 9/11 terrorist attack on the World Trade Center. Given that H-bombs are now the size of a child's sled, it should be possible to smuggle one into New York or Los Angeles. Say that the suicidal fanatics all agree to die in the blast so that they cannot be traced. The city is annihilated, and there were no missiles, no early warning, no warning of any sort. The city is simply gone, and various terrorist groups claim responsibility. (The group actually responsible will make sure there are bogus calls as well.) The civil liberties of the U.S. citizens disappear soon after the city does, and international nuclear war is not far behind.

Vivid? Yes. The terrorists are thin, swarthy, excitable young men of Arab or Asian extraction, with moustaches. (Indeed, this scenario, originally sketched out by Dawes in 1988, in the first edition of this book, is also the basis for the screenplay of the 1998 movie *The Siege*.)

Likely? No, but not impossible. The point is that there are literally thousands of scenarios leading to nuclear destruction. The *real* availability, accuracy, and delivery speed of nuclear weapons increase year by year, yet we concentrate on a few scenarios. For example, roughly 60% of the university students in one of our decision-making classes believed it was "more likely that there would be a Mideast crisis leading to nuclear war between the United States and an Arab nation in the next 25 years than that such a war would occur for *any* reason." Furthermore, when we concentrate on a few scenarios, we develop a false sense of security by taking precautions against (only) them. If the first event of a scenario (perhaps an incident that leads to a confrontation between the United States and North Korea) does not occur, we believe the rest of the scenario will not occur either (just as we were [too] sure the tennis star must join Alcoholics Anonymous and quit drinking to win the tournament). Believing events such as nuclear war can occur only in the context of specific scenarios is thinking myopically and irrationally.

How high is the probability for a nuclear war each year? We are not claiming that it is a constant, merely that it can be approximated with a single value *given no additional information*. Let us suppose, for the sake of analysis, that the probability of nuclear destruction (which did not occur) between 1960 and 2000 was 1/3. That means, assuming a constant probability $p$ and independence between years (as rough approximations to reality), that $(1 - p)^n = 2/3$, or $p = .01$ per year. Thus, if $p$ remains constant, the probability of having a nuclear war sometime in the next century is 2/3 $(1 - .99^n)$. *But p does not remain constant.* If, for example, it were to become twice as likely in each of the next 40 years as the last—and if we accept the 1/3 figure—then the probability of surviving the next 40 years without a nuclear war is only .44.

The probabilistic approach to nuclear war also contains a positive message: *Whatever can decrease the probability of a war, by even a small amount, is valuable*. Assume, for example, the probability of .02 per year. As pointed out earlier, the probability of no war in the next 40 years is only .44 (assuming constancy and yearly independence). Now suppose some international agreement is reached that reduces that probability by 1/3—that is, to .0133. The probability of no war in the next 40 years would then be .58.

If that decrease does not appear important, consider this situation:

A barrel contains 100 balls, 44 of which are green, 14 of which are blue, and 42 of which are red. A single ball is drawn at random. Choose between two options:

- If a green ball is chosen, you receive $10,000. If a blue or red ball is chosen, you die.
- If a green or blue is chosen, you receive $10,000. If a red ball is chosen, you die.

Which option would you prefer? When the difference between .58 and .44 is viewed in this manner, the much greater desirability at .58 is evident. (Unfortunately, people tend to assess the magnitude of a probability difference in terms of *ratios*—for example, the "mortality ratio" for smokers versus nonsmokers—rather than in terms of actual differences.)

Our colleague Paul Slovic has emphasized the probabilistic approach to reducing the danger of nuclear war and other societal and personal risks. Small differences in probability for small intervals can yield large differences in broad ones. As Slovic points out, scenario thinking can once again get in the way of a probabilistic assessment. The desirable scenario for most of us would be an agreement among all countries capable of producing nuclear weapons resulting in technological control of such weapons to the point that they could not be used in haste or by accident. The least desirable scenario is an international confrontation followed by war. As mental images of what could occur in the next few decades, these scenarios are understandable, vivid, and compelling. Thus, we exaggerate the probability of confrontation and of total agreement while we neglect policies that would reduce the probability of nuclear war each year by some small amount.

The first step in resolving a problem is to think clearly about it. The big problem with scenario thinking is that it focuses the thinker on one, or a few, causal stories and diverts the decision maker from a broader, more systematic representation of the decision situation. Scenario thinking grossly overestimates the probability of the scenarios that come to mind and underestimates long-term probabilities of events occurring one way *or another*. Furthermore, there is a general tendency for memories and inferences to be biased so as to be consistent with the themes and theories underlying the scenarios. One of the main messages of this book is that rational analysis requires a systematic, comprehensive representation of situations and alternative outcomes, in order to assess the important underlying probabilities of events.

We believe that probabilities (and some other statistics) are the best tools our civilization has developed to deal with uncertainty and other sources of confusion in decision making. In contrast to immersion in the seductive details of a few vivid scenarios, probabilistic assessments tend to be more valid. Moreover, probabilistic thinking indicates that "small" changes in likelihood can have "large" long-term effects. For example, if we must continue to play nuclear Russian roulette, putting more empty chambers into the gun is preferable to trying to (vividly) imagine which chamber the bullet is in. In Chapter 8, we will return to the question of how to think more clearly and rationally in uncertain situations.

## 6.7 Hindsight: Reconstructing the Past

Memory for complex events is basically a reconstructive process. As the novelist Alain Robbe-Grillet put it, "Memory belongs to the imagination. Human memory is not like a computer which records things; it is part of the imaginative process, on the same terms as invention." Our recall is organized in ways that make sense of the present. We thus reinforce our belief in the conclusions we have reached about how the past has determined the present. We quite literally make up stories about our lives, the world, and reality in general. The fit between our memories and the stories we make up enhances our belief in them. Often, it is the story that creates the memory, rather than vice versa.

In a series of ingenious demonstrations, Baruch Fischhoff showed that people who know the nature of events *falsely* overestimate the probability with which they *would have* predicted them. (See Hawkins & Hastie, 1990, for a comprehensive review of the research on hindsight effects.) In his initial studies, Fischhoff simply asked people to predict what would happen before particular events occurred (e.g., U.S. President Nixon's visits to Russia and China in 1972) and then to later recall what they had predicted. Their recall was biased in the direction of having predicted what actually happened. It follows, as Fischhoff points out, that we are "insufficiently surprised" by experience. One result is that we do not learn effectively from it.

A study by David Wasserman, Richard Lempert, and Hastie demonstrates the role of causality in producing reconstructive hindsight effects. These researchers followed the Fischhoff procedure of comparing foresight judgments from one group of experimental participants with informed, *hindsightful* judgments from a second group. They presented their subjects with short vignettes describing historical or fictional events (the outcome of a military conflict between the British colonials and native Ghurkas in India, a gold-prospecting venture) and asked them to estimate the probability of various outcomes (British victory, success in the prospecting enterprise), either with or without knowledge of the "true" outcomes. (They employed an experimental method so that all possible outcomes could be presented as "true" to different groups of participants in the hindsight condition for purposes of experimental control.) Like Fischhoff, they obtained substantial hindsight effects, even when subjects were instructed to estimate the probabilities that would be given *by other people like themselves.* But, more important, Wasserman et al. manipulated the nature of the cause that was described as primarily responsible for the reported outcome. In half of the hindsight conditions, the outcome was attributed to a causally potent event (the better equipped and trained British troops, the superior knowledge of the battle terrain by indigenous guerrilla forces, etc.) or to a surprising "act of God" event (an unseasonal monsoon rainstorm disabled the British weapons and tactics, the rainstorm prevented the guerrilla forces from utilizing their superior knowledge of the terrain, etc.). The results were clear: Hindsight effects only occurred under conditions where persuasive causal explanations could be generated by the participants to "glue" the causes to the outcomes.

This hindsight bias is not always reducible to a knew-it-all-along attempt to appear more omniscient than we are. Sometimes motivational factors probably apply, as when that irritating friend claims to have predicted that the home team was going to lose the football game or that the dark horse candidate was going to win the election. But people actually *make mistakes* in their recall of what they thought would happen, even when they are motivated to be as accurate as possible. A classic example was provided by the natural experiment in which President Nixon's former aide John Dean attempted to recall, before congressional investigating committees, as truthfully as possible events that occurred during the Watergate scandal. (Dean tried to recall events that occurred between June of 1972 and March of 1973 in testimony given in June of 1973.) Dean exhibited detailed memory of countless events during meetings in which Nixon discussed the Watergate events and many other political matters. But subsequent to the testimony it was discovered that many of the same conversations had been secretly tape-recorded by the president. Comparisons between the Nixon tapes and Dean's testimony revealed his memory was exceptionally accurate, but the testimony was still peppered with memory errors and illusions, almost all biased to be consistent with Dean's knowledge of the situations *at the time he testified,* not at the time the original events occurred (Ulric Neisser [1981] conducted this analysis). "Creeping determinism"—to use Fischhoff's phrase—is well-documented, and the major determinant of hindsight effects is our proclivity to summarize experiences as coherent narratives, after we know how they turn out.

Sometimes, when we believe in change, we recall change even when it has not occurred. In order to make our recollection compatible with this belief, we resort (again not consciously) to changing our memory of the earlier state. We can, for example, reinforce our belief in a nonexistent change for the better by simply exaggerating how bad things were before the change. Certainly there have been times, for example, before a religious or psychiatric conversion, when a person was badly off (we all are at times), and memories of those periods persist; recall can be organized around the traces of these memories. A dieter who has not succeeded in losing a single pound can certainly recall periods of time prior to embarking on a diet when he or she was heavier than when the person completed the ineffective diet; by carefully not recording his or her weight before starting the diet, those times can be (mis-)recalled as evidence of its success.

Experimental evidence shows that when we believe a change has occurred, we are apt to distort the past to be consistent with the change. Michael Conway and Michael Ross (1984) randomly selected participants for a university program designed to improve study skills and created a control group of students who had volunteered for the program and were on the waiting list. Participants and controls were questioned before the study skills program began and at its conclusion. At both times, they were asked to assess their study skills (How much of your study time is well spent? How satisfactory are your note-taking skills?) and the amount of time they studied. At the second interview they were also asked to recall what they reported during the first session concerning their skills and study time.

At the initial interview, participants and controls did not differ significantly on any measure of skill, study time, or other variables. Both groups performed equally well and—most important to the study—the program itself was *not* found to improve study skills. Nor did it improve grades. When asked to recall their situations before the program started (or before they were put on the waiting list), however, the subjects did differ. There was no difference between the two groups in their memory of the amount of time they spent studying, but their recall of their skills was markedly different. Program participants recalled their study skills as being significantly *worse* than they had initially reported, while waiting-list control subjects recalled their skills as being approximately the same as they had reported initially. Thus, program participants exaggerated their improvement in a direction consistent with their beliefs of what *ought* to be (improved skills due to taking the course), not by exaggerating their current skills, but rather by reconstructing their memories to fit with the expectation that they should have improved. In short, they rewrote their autobiographical memories to be consistent with their current beliefs. There was not such distortion on the part of the subjects who had been put on the waiting list.

Moods also affect recall (see Chapter 5). Does the same principle apply to our recall of our own lives? It is a basic precept in many psychotherapies, from Freud on, that current misery is caused by unfortunate experiences in childhood, especially bad relationships with our parents. But what if current misery hindsightfully selects and reconstructs memories of childhood to be consistent with a miserable state today? Peter Lewinsohn and Michael Rosenbaum (1987) set out to answer this question with a rare prospective study of over a thousand citizen volunteers. The participants were recruited from the general population (not from a selected sample of clinical depressives) and asked to recall their parents' behavior. They were classified, during a 3-year follow-up, into four groups: nondepressives (people who had never been depressed), predepressives (people who were to become depressed during the 3-year study), acute depressives, and remitted depressives (that is, people who had once been depressed and were no longer). The researchers studied the relationship between current mood states and parental memories. Theories that say depression follows from childhood problems would predict that the childhoods of those of us who are depression-prone are different from those who are not and hence would be recalled differently, while theories about the effect of current mood on past recall predict that the difference in recall should be between people who are *currently* depressed and those who are not. Perhaps recollections of one's parents are influenced by a current state of depression or non-depression, or it could be that people who are prone to depression recall their parents differently from those who are not (the non-depressives). The results were consistent with the hypothesis that recollection of one's parents as rejecting and unloving is strongly influenced by current moods; negative recollections were not a stable characteristic of depression-prone people.

> Whereas the currently depressed subjects recalled their parents as having been more rejecting and as having used more negative control than the normal controls, the remitted depressives did not differ from the never depressed control in their recall of parental behavior. Similarly, the subjects who were about to become depressed shortly after the initial testing did not differ from the controls in their recollections of the degree to which their parents used negative control methods. (Lewinsohn & Rosenbaum, 1987, p. 617)

This study of depression is important in that it casts doubt on the degree to which adult problems are caused by childhood ones. Given a biasing effect of mood on memory, people who are distressed as adults tend to remember distressing incidents in their childhood. And, if a person also believes that current problems have their roots in early life (perhaps because their therapist told them so), this view itself may serve as an organizing principle to produce even greater distortion of recall (remember the Conway & Ross [1984] study above). Hindsightfully biased recollections reinforce the "child is father to the man" theory of life span development.

## 6.8 Sometimes It's Better to Forget

One primary function of our minds is to create a model of the current situation in which we are located. When a car changes lanes in front of us, we update our mental model of the traffic situation so as not to ram into it; when a person we once thought was reliable demonstrates that he or she is not, we adjust our mental model of that person and do not rely on him or her to come through for us in difficult circumstances. The maintenance of up-to-date situation models requires us to constantly refresh our beliefs about where we are and what is about to happen. This process is adaptive when we must make decisions about the future. Indeed, remember the fundamental tenet of decision theory that we should ignore *sunk costs* and focus only on future probabilities and utilities to make rational choices (see Chapter 1). But as we engage in this constant adjustment process, we lose the past and find it is difficult to recover what we used to think and sometimes even what we did. Usually, that's a good thing.

## References

Amsterdam, A. G., & Hertz, R. (1992). An analysis of closing arguments to a jury. *New York Law School Review, 37,* 55–122.

Berne, E. (1964). *Games people play: The psychology of human relationships.* New York: Grove Press.

Campbell, T. W. (1998). *Smoke and mirrors: The devastating effect of false sexual abuse claims.* New York: Plenum Press.

Conway, M., & Ross, M. (1984). Getting what you want by revising what you had. *Journal of Personality and Social Psychology, 47,* 738–748.

Fischhoff, B. (1975). Hindsight ≠ foresight: The effect of outcome knowledge on judgment under uncertainty. *Journal of Experimental Psychology: Human Perception and Performance, 1,* 288–299.

Hastie, R., & Pennington, N. (1996). The O. J. Simpson stories: Behavioral scientists look at *The People v. O. J. Simpson* trial. *University of Colorado Law Review, 67,* 957–976.

Hawkins, S. A., & Hastie, R. (1990). Hindsight: Biased judgments of past events after the outcomes are known. *Psychological Bulletin, 107,* 311–327.

Heath, C., & Heath, D. (2007). *Made to stick: Why some ideas survive and others die.* New York: Random House.

Jardel Co. v. Hughes, Del. Supr., 523 A.2d 518 (1987).

Lewinsohn, P. M., & Rosenbaum, M. (1987). Recall of parental behavior by acute depressives, remitted depressives, and nondepressives. *Journal of Personality and Social Psychology, 52,* 611–620.

March, J. G. (1972). Model bias in social action. *Review of Education Research, 42,* 413–429.

Neisser, U. (1981). John Dean's memory: A case study. *Cognition, 9,* 1–22.

Pennington, N., & Hastie, R. (1988). Explanation-based decision making: Effects of memory structure on judgment. *Journal of Experimental Psychology: Learning, Memory, and Cognition, 14,* 521–533.

Pennington, N., & Hastie, R. (1991). A cognitive theory of juror decision making: The story model. *Cardozo Law Review, 13,* 519–557.

Schank, R. C., & Abelson, R. P. (1995). Knowledge and memory: The real story. In R. Wyer, Jr. (Ed.), *Advances in social cognition* (Vol. 8, pp. 1–86). Hillsdale, NJ: Lawrence Erlbaum.

Silkwood v. Kerr-McGee Corp., 464 U.S. 238 (1984).

Spence, D. F. (1982). *Narrative truth and historical truth: Meaning and interpretation in psychoanalysis.* New York: Norton.

Spence, G. (1994, November 29). Winning attorneys. *New York Times,* p. E1.

Tversky, A., & Kahneman, D. (1983). Extensional versus intuitive reasoning: The conjunction fallacy in probability judgment. *Psychological Bulletin, 90,* 293–315.

Van den Broek, P., & Thurlow, R. (1991). The role and structure of personal narratives. *Journal of Cognitive Psychotherapy, 5,* 257–274.

Wasserman, D., Lempert, R. O., & Hastie, R. (1991). Hindsight and causality. *Personality and Social Psychology Bulletin, 17,* 30–35.

# 7

# Chance and Cause

*Say you're thinking about a plate of shrimp. Suddenly someone says plate, or shrimp, or plate of shrimp. Out of the blue. No use looking for one either. It's part of the lattice of coincidence that lays on top of everything.*

—From the film *Repo Man,* written and directed by Alex Cox, 1984

## 7.1 Misconceptions About Chance

On January 26, 1972, Vesna Vulovic, a 22-year-old Yugoslavian flight attendant, was serving drinks to passengers on JAT Flight 367 when the plane was demolished by a bomb planted by a Croatian nationalist group. Most people would think she was extremely unlucky—first, to be on a rare flight destroyed by a terrorist bomb and second, because of a name confusion, she had been assigned to work the wrong flight. Definitely the wrong flight. But there is a positive side to this story. Ms. Vulovic lived and now holds the world record for surviving the highest fall without a parachute—33,000 feet (10,000 meters). Just a little more than a year after the fall, she declared herself ready to return to work, a self-described "optimist" with a newfound belief in God. So, many people would describe her as exceptionally lucky. Ms. Vulovic goes with our first assessment, "I'm not lucky. Everybody thinks I am lucky, but they are mistaken. If I were lucky I would never have had this accident" (Bilefsky, 2008).

It is not surprising that people often think and talk about unexpected events in different, sometimes contradictory ways. After all, these events are unpredictable and by definition mysterious and poorly understood. But, even beyond that, our minds do not seem to be designed to reason systematically about chance and uncertainty. Perhaps for evolutionary reasons, we are inclined to over-explain uncertain events and, even when we recognize they are inherently unpredictable, we have some queer notions about how they behave, including many superstitious beliefs (Sagan, 1997). Because we have natural misconceptions about uncertainty and randomness, this is one case in which learning about the rudiments of a technical framework—probability theory—can make a big difference in how we see the world. But without special training, no one thinks about the world in terms of probabilities. Rather, the world seems to be a bunch of events and objects glued together by causal relationships, and most of us think about causation deterministically and in terms of degrees of causal force, but not in terms of probabilities.

We have been careful not to refer to the world as probabilistic or random. Probability theory is a language we can use to *describe* the world or, more precisely, to describe the relationships among our beliefs about the world. It is an unfamiliar language to most people, with a special symbolic vocabulary and rules of grammar (see the Appendix for an introduction to probability theory). As we noted earlier, probability theory was not invented until recently in the history of Western civilization, and words like *probability* don't seem to have entered the English lexicon until the 17th century. (Lexicographers believe it was derived from the expression "approvable," e.g., a *probable* husband was originally an acceptable or morally "approvable" husband.)

Sometimes we do talk about chance, luck, probability, or randomness in everyday events—we say, "she was lucky," "it happened by chance," "that was a random event." But the most sensible interpretation of these expressions is that they indicate the state of knowledge within the mind of the person speaking. Harking back to a very wise essay on the nature of chance by the philosopher Poincaré (1914/1952), the events that we refer to in everyday life are all brought about by deterministic, physical processes. What singles out the events that we refer to as random, chance, or probabilistic is that the causal context is hidden, complex, or unknown to the person who describes the event as such. We can't specify the physical events that occurred to preserve Vesna Vulovic's life, but we believe that she survived because of physical conditions that *could* be specified, if we had enough information. If we'd been able to observe her fall, including the minute details concerning her contact with the ground and her internal body state immediately before contact, we should be able to account for her remarkable escape from death in terms of physical causality.

For another example, we refer to the toss of a fair coin as a random process and assign the (ideal) probability value of .50 to the event of *heads*, although we believe that the hidden biological and physical events that *cause* the outcome of the toss are all deterministic. In fact, skilled sleight-of-hand magicians, like the mathematician Persi Diaconis, have developed their manual skills to the point where they can execute apparently uncontrolled coin tosses and reliably produce the desired result, heads or tails (Bayer & Diaconis, 1992; Diaconis, Holmes, & Montgomery, 2007). Of course, there are levels of physical analysis, for example, at the quantum level, where scientists do not believe causality maps directly onto the mechanical principles of causality we experience. But we do not experience the world at that level, and it is a rare conversation that refers to those events.

Of course, there are parts of our environment that approximate the idealized behavior of theoretical random processes; events in casinos and lotteries are "caused" by deterministic physical processes, but the causal mechanism is so complex and the determinants of the events are so subtle that the best way to think about these situations is in terms of probability theory. An important message of this book is that we should use probability theory to organize our thinking about all judgments under uncertainty, even where we know much more (or less) about the relevant causes than we do in a casino. But we tend to deny the random components even in trivial events that we *know* to be the result of chance. There is a wonderful story about the winner of a national lottery in Spain. When interviewed about how he won, the winner said that he had deliberately selected a ticket that ended with the numbers 4 and 8. He explained, "I dreamed of the number 7 for seven straight nights. And 7 times 7 is 48" (Meisler, 1977).

## 7.2 Illusions of Control

In a clever series of experiments, Ellen Langer (1975) of Harvard University demonstrated that—automatically, without any conscious awareness—we often treat chance events as if they involve skill and are hence controllable. For example, gamblers tend to throw dice with greater force when they are attempting to roll high numbers than when they are attempting to roll lower numbers. Langer conducted a lottery in which each participant was given a card containing the name and picture of a National Football League player; an identical card was put into a bag; and the person holding the card matching the one drawn from the bag won the lottery. In fact, Langer conducted two lotteries. In one, the participants chose which player would constitute their ticket; in the other, players were assigned to the participants by the experimenter. Of course, whether or not the entrants were able to choose their own players had no effect on the probability of their winning the lottery, because the winning cards were drawn at random from the bag. Nevertheless, when an experimenter approached the participants offering to buy their card, those who had chosen their own player on the average demanded *more than 4 times as much money* for their card as did those with randomly assigned cards. Upon questioning, no one claimed that being allowed to choose a player influenced his or her probability of winning. The participants just *behaved* as if it had.

In another striking experiment, Langer and Susan Roth (1975) were able to convince Yale undergraduates that they were better or worse than the average person at predicting the outcome of coin tosses. The subjects were given rigged feedback that indicated they did not perform any better than at a chance level—that they were correct on 15 of 30 trials. What the experimenters did was manipulate whether the subjects tended to be correct toward the beginning of the 30-trial sequence or toward the end. Consistent with a primacy effect (or anchoring-and-[insufficient]-adjustment), those subjects who tended to be correct toward the beginning were apt to think of themselves as "better than average" at predicting, while those who did not do well at the beginning judged themselves to be worse. (Of course, due to random fluctuations, the probability of success in predicting the outcome of coin tosses cannot be expected to be invariant across a sequence as short as 30 trials.) In addition, "over 25% of the subjects reported that performance would be hampered by distraction and 40% of all the subjects felt that performance would improve with practice." Thus, not only do people behave as if they can control random events; they also express the conscious belief that doing so is a skill, which, like other skills, is hampered by distractions and improves with practice. It is important to remember that these subjects were from one of the most elite universities in the world, yet they treated the prediction of coin tosses as if it involved some type of ability, not just dumb luck.

Moreover, as with most everyday applications of psychology, practitioners like the managers of casinos and lotteries already have an intuitive understanding of these principles. Commercial games of chance often contain deceptive skill elements, deliberately designed to confuse the players about the skill and opportunity for control involved in games of chance. In most states, lottery players can choose the numbers they bet their money on, and the lotteries often have skill-evoking cover stories: "Hit a home run and win Major League bucks," "Just by buying a Bowling for Bucks ticket, you're a winner."

A more serious consequence of the illusion of control is revealed in our preference for driving over flying. At least part of this irrational—from a survival point of view—habit is due to the fact that we "feel in control" when driving, but not when flying. The probability of dying in a cross-country flight is approximately equal to the probability of dying in a 12-mile drive—in many cases, the most dangerous part of the trip is over when you reach the airport (Sivak & Flannagan, 2003). Gerd Gigerenzer (2006) estimates that the post-9/11 shift from flying to driving in the United States resulted in an additional 1,500 deaths, beyond the original 3,000 immediate victims of the terrorist attacks.

One of the most compelling studies of the illusion of control demonstrated that it was related to consequential, poor performance in a real-world investment situation. Four British finance experts asked traders from four investment banks to play a computer game in which they attempted to influence the price of a fictional investment index (Fenton-O'Creevy, Nicholson, Sloane, & Willman, 2003). The movements of the index were completely independent of the actions by the trader-players—it was a random walk with a slight positive trend. The traders played the game for four rounds and rated their personal success in raising the index—because the index movements were independent of the actions of the traders, this is a measure of individual illusions of control. On average, the traders fell prey to the illusion that they had influenced the movement of the price index. More interesting, the level of individual illusions of control negatively predicted the traders' earnings and their managers' ratings of their talents and performance. Traders with a greater illusion of control earned substantially less than their more realistic peers ($100,000s); they contributed less to their bank's profits; and their managers rated them lower on risk management, analytical ability, and people skills.

## 7.3 Seeing Causal Structure Where It Isn't

A pernicious result of representative and scenario-based thinking is that they make us see structure (nonrandomness) where none exists. This occurs because our naïve conceptions of randomness involve *too much* variation—often to the point where we conclude that a generating process is *not* random, even when it represents an ideal random trial. Consider one of the simplest, most familiar processes we would describe as random, a coin toss. When asked to "behave like a coin" and to generate a sequence of heads and tails that would be typical of the behavior of a fairly tossed coin, most people produce too much alternation—nonrandomly too many heads–tails and tails–heads transitions. (They exhibit the same bias when shown sequences and asked to pick the "real coin" [Lopes, 1982].) Representativeness enters in because when we are faced with the task of distinguishing between random and nonrandom "generators" of events, we rely on our stereotype of a random process (analogous to our stereotype of a feminist or a bank teller or an art history major) and use *similarity* to judge or produce a sequence. Thus, when we encounter a truly random sequence, we are likely to decide it is *nonrandom* because it does not look haphazard enough—because it shows less alternation than our *incorrect* stereotype of a random sequence.

Suppose you're playing Langer and Roth's (1975) coin toss game with a fair coin (which you pulled out of your own pocket) and you are trying to predict the next outcome, heads or tails, after the coin has been tossed 8 times. Remarkably, the coin has come up heads on each toss, a run of 8 heads. If you're like most people, you'll have a feeling that tails is more likely on the ninth toss—you feel "it's due"—and you'd probably even bet some money on the prediction of tails. Another example of this feeling is the common, but incorrect advice about how to gamble: "When you're in Vegas and you see a roulette wheel come up with a run of three or more reds, bet black. You're sure to win." There is even a rationale for this belief: Nine heads (or reds) in a row is very rare; the odds are strongly against this happening ($[1/2]^9$ or $1/512$ or approximately $.002$ for the coin, less for the roulette wheel), so if you're looking at 8 in a row, it's very unlikely you'll get 9 in a row. This intuition and the rationale are an error called the *gambler's fallacy*—the notion that "chances of [independent, random] events mature" if they have not occurred for a while. Fair coins and roulette wheels have no memories; the chance of each event is independent of all the other events in a sequence, and the probability of tails or red is constant.

Many people believe airplane accidents happen in "bunches"—usually threes. (One clinical psychologist we know cites such coincidences as evidence for "Jungian synchronicity.") Russell Vaught and Dawes obtained data from the FAA describing all commercial airline crashes between 1950 and 1970. They examined the number of days between the occurrences of the crashes. A totally random model begins with the assumption that the probability of a crash on any given day is a constant, $p$. Hence, the probability of a crash occurring the day following another crash is $p$. The probability that the next crash occurs on the second day subsequent to a crash is $(1 - p)p$, because there must be no crash on the succeeding day and then a crash on the next one. (Note that $[1 - p]p$ is less than $p$, a result that some people find counterintuitive, perhaps analogous to "Linda the feminist bank teller" from Chapter 5.) Similarly, the probability that the next crash will occur on the third day following a crash is $(1 - p)(1 - p)p = (1 - p)^2p$, and in general the probability that the next crash will occur on the *n*th succeeding day is $(1 - p)^{n-1}p$.

Examining all crashes and fatal crashes separately, Vaught and Dawes (unpublished research) discovered that the fit to the theoretical random prediction based on a constant $p$ was almost perfect. Yet crashes seem to occur in "bunches." Why? Because $(1 - p)^j > (1 - p)^k\, p$ when $j < k$. Hence, truly random sequences actually contain "bunches" of events. The problem is that representative thinking leads us to conclude that such random patterns are *not* random. Instead, we hypothesize positive feedback mechanisms such as "momentum" to account for them. (Those of us hypothesizing "Jungian synchronicity" are in a minority.) While, for example, the maxim that "nothing succeeds like success or fails like failure" may be true, phony evidence for it can be found in the bunching of successes in patterns of people or organizations with high probabilities of success, and of failures in those with high probabilities of failure—even when the pattern is of independent events.

A well-defined situation in which people clearly see patterns that are not in the data is the *hot hand* phenomenon in basketball. The hot hand does not merely refer to the fact that some players are more accurate shooters than others, but to the (hypothetical) positive feedback performance process that makes players more likely to score after scoring and to miss after missing. (Note that the same term—a hot hand—is used to describe successful crap shooters, despite general acknowledgment that in well-run games, they cannot control the outcome of a roll.) Tom Gilovich, Robert Vallone, and Amos Tversky (1985) demonstrated empirically that the hot hand does not exist; that a success following a success is just as likely for an individual player as a success following a failure. At least, neither the floor shots of the Philadelphia '76ers, the free throws of the Boston Celtics, or the experimentally controlled floor shots of men and women on the Cornell varsity basketball teams showed evidence of a hot hand. But the players' *predictions* of their success showed a hot-hand effect, even though their performance did not. More than 90% of a sample of basketball players and sports reporters answered "yes" to the following question: Does a player have a better chance of making a shot after having just made his last two or three shots than he does after having just missed his last two or three shots?

Jay Koehler and Caryn Conley (2003) followed up the original studies with an analysis seeking nonrandom patterns in the NBA Long Distance Shootout Contest from 4 years of the competition. In this event, the best field goal shooters in the NBA attempt to score as often as possible within a 60-second time limit from the 3-point shot arc (the area of the court from which shots will count for 3 points instead of 2). Again, there was no evidence of nonrandomness. Even when the researchers conditioned their analysis on the announcers' assertions of "hotness," there were no patterns. It is notable that nonrandom streaks have been verified in other sports such as bowling, archery, billiards, and golf, suggesting that the statistics are sensitive enough to pick up patterns if they are there in the data. (It looks like there might be a bigger picture here: In nonreactive, uniform-playing-field sports, subtle sequential dependencies manifest themselves in performance; in chaotic, in-your-face, player-on-player reactive sports, there are no such patterns.)

These studies do not prove the *universal nonexistence* of the hot hand in basketball (which would be difficult to do, if you think about it), but their results imply that if it exists, it is small, unreliable, or very rare. The claim that any particular set of data is random is tenuous; it is more defensible to claim that a process that generates the data is random, in the sense that the observers of the data could not know the information necessary to predict the events in the data with any degree of specificity—that to these observers, the best description is a probabilistic or random process. The example of the hot hand in basketball is especially surprising because it is so easy to imagine a causal process that might generate the expected (but not observed) patterns. For example, one reply to Gilovich et al.'s (1985) and Tversky and Gilovich's (1989) original claim was that they had missed the true hot-hand pattern that was hidden in their data because they had ignored the timing of baskets. Patrick Larkey, Richard Smith, and Jay Kadane (1989) published a reanalysis consisting only of runs of shots occurring in close temporal proximity. They found one player, Vinnie "Microwave" Johnson of the Detroit Pistons, who departed from the random model. Microwave earned his nickname because of his reputation for streak shooting. However, Gilovich et al. (1985), in rebuttal, noted that the reanalysis found only one "hot" player, and that his statistically distinctive streakiness was due entirely to a single run of seven baskets. Then they pointed out that a review of the original game videotapes showed that the seven-basket run had *not* occurred. In fact, Microwave had a run of four baskets, missed a shot but scored on his own rebound, and then made one more score. After correcting for this data collection error, even Microwave did not depart from the random model.

Do 3 good weeks in a row indicate therapeutic success with a patient? Do 3 bad weeks indicate failure (or, more sanguinely, "coming to face problems")? Does losing three games in a row mean the coach should be fired? Or do three down quarters mean a CEO should be fined? No, no more than three heads in a row within a sequence of coin tosses indicate that the coin is biased. Yet, knowing the person's base rate for success—and expecting more alternation than in fact occurs if these weeks or quarters are totally *unrelated*—makes the temptation to impute causal factors to such strings almost overpowering, especially causal factors related to the actor's own behavior. (Another speculation is this: Could it be that the perceptual salience of "streaks" of hits and misses is the key temptation to see "hot" or "cold" patterns in performance? In professional basketball where fans talk avidly about "hot hands," the success rate for shots is well over 50%, and so, runs of "hits" would be common and violate our expectation for too many reversals [hit–miss and miss–hit transitions]. But consider baseball batting where the fans are likely to talk about "slumps" and where batting averages are all well below 50% so that runs of "misses" would be most salient.)

Why do we expect too much alternation? Tversky and Kahneman (1974) ascribe this expectation to the belief that even very small sequences must be representative of a population, that is, the proportion of events in a small frame must match—be representative of—the proportion in the population. When, for example, we are tossing a fair coin, we know that the entire population of possible sequences contains 50% heads; therefore, we expect 50% heads in a sample of four tosses. That requires more alternation than is found when each toss is independent. (At the extreme, 50% heads in a sequence of two tosses requires that each head is followed by a tail and vice versa.) Here, representative thinking takes us from schema to characteristic, rather than the reverse. Again, however, the basic belief is due to similarity matching—that is, to association. Moreover, the effect is compounded by our relatively brief span of attention—we want the short sequences *we can remember or imagine* to be representative (Kareev, 1992).

Consider the following question from a study by Tversky and Kahneman (1974):

All families of six children in a city were surveyed. In 72 families, the exact order of births of boys and girls was G B G B B G. What is your estimate of the number of families in which the exact order of births was B G B B B B? What about the number of families with the exact order B B B G G G?

Almost everyone (80% or more of respondents) judges the latter birth sequences to be less likely than the first. However, all exact sequences are equally likely (the probability of any exact sequence is simply $.5 \times .5 \times .5 \times .5 \times .5 \times .5$ or 0.015625, implying approximately 16 families out of a sample of 1,000 six-child families). Why do people have the strong intuition that G B G B B G is much more frequent? Because this short sequence captures all of our intuitions about what the result of a random process will look like: The sequence exhibits the correct proportion (half boys, half girls), it looks haphazard, and it has lots of alternation—in short, it looks "really random." (It is also the kind of sequence of hits and misses we would expect an ordinary basketball player to generate—too many short alternating runs, so that when we see a performance with longer runs, we are prone to say, "That can't be random. This player must really be 'hot.'") In contrast, the second sequence looks less likely because it violates *the law of small numbers* by having the wrong ratio of births (too many boys), while the third sequence is okay for proportion, but looks too orderly (three in a row, then three in a row).

Occasionally, this belief in alternation in random sequences (the gambler's fallacy that "red is due" because the last 6 outcomes on the roulette wheel were black) reaches ludicrous extremes. Consider, for example, the beginning of a "Dear Abby" letter:

> DEAR ABBY: My husband and I just had our eighth child. Another girl, and I am really one disappointed woman. I suppose I should thank God that she was healthy, but, Abby, this one was supposed to have been a boy. Even the doctor told me the law of averages were [sic] in our favor 100 to one.

A "graphic" example of the tendency to see patterns (and infer causes) where there surely weren't any occurred during the World War II bombing of London by German V-1 and V-2 missiles. London newspapers published maps of the missile impact sites (see Figure 7.1), and citizens immediately saw clusters of strikes and interpreted them with reference to the intentions of the hostile forces. What kind of stories did they tell to explain these patterns? The British citizens reasoned that the patterns they saw were the result of deliberate efforts to miss the areas of the city in which German spies lived. However, a classic probability modeling analysis demonstrated that the clusters were completely consistent with a random Poisson process–generating device, that there was no reason to infer a systematic motive or cause behind the patterns (see William Feller's classic textbook, *An Introduction to Probability Theory and Its Applications,* Vol. 1, pp. 160f, for a mathematical analysis).

A timely example of this tendency to infer causes for geographic patterns is part of the psychology of "cancer cluster" hysterias. During the past two decades, reports of communities in which there seem to be an unusual number of cancer incidents have soared (see Gawande, 1999). A community that notices an unusual number of cancers quite naturally looks for a cause in the environment—something in the water or the ground or the air. But investigating isolated neighborhood cancer clusters is almost always an exercise in futility. Public health agencies deploy thousands of "hot pursuit" studies every year in response to reports of raised local cancer rates. But Raymond Richard Neutra, California's chief environmental health investigator (in 1999), notes that among the hundreds of published reports of such investigations, *not one* has convincingly identified an environmental cause (cited in Gawande, 1999). And only one investigation resulted in the discovery of an unrecognized carcinogen. Neutra points out that in a typical Public Health Service registry of 80 different cancers, probability theory predicts you would expect to observe 2,750 of California's 5,000 census tracts to have statistically significant but random elevations of some form of cancer. So, if you check to see if your neighborhood has a statistically significant elevation in the rate of at least 1 of the 80 cancers, the chances are better than .50 it

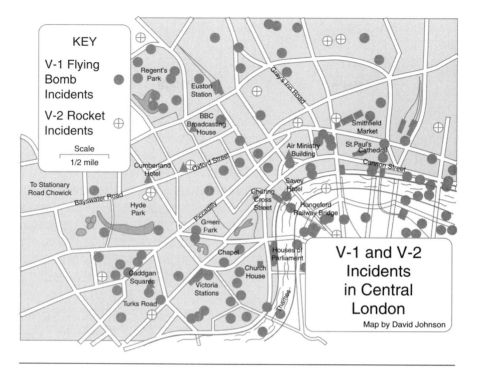

**Figure 7.1**    London V-1 and V-2 rocket impact pattern

will—but that discovery will be perfectly consistent with a random model of the distribution of incidences, assuming *no* environmental causes. Commenting on the hot-pursuit investigations that result from neighborhood cluster alarms, Alan Bender (quoted in Gawande, 1999), an epidemiologist in the Minnesota Department of Health, says, "The reality is they're a total waste of taxpayer dollars."

But what can we do to maintain public trust and to identify true environmental health hazards? The fact that a random probability theory model is *consistent with* the patterns does not prove that there are no causal effects— It's that "How do you prove it doesn't exist anywhere, ever?" problem again. But we are wasting a lot of public funds responding to emotionally and symbolically important events and discovering many false correlations between clusters and their contexts. The strategy of analyzing individual clusters and looking for correlations with some (any) environmental cause is called the *Texas sharpshooter fallacy* by epidemiologists, after the story about a rifleman who shoots a cluster of bullet holes in the side of a barn and then draws a bull's-eye around the holes. This is a case where we should go with the advice of statistically sophisticated experts and only respond when there are good a priori reasons to hypothesize an environmental cause, or there are truly extraordinary statistical patterns. The much-publicized case of the cancer cluster in Woburn, Massachusetts, described in the book and movie *A Civil Action,* was never resolved by the identification of a scientifically credible causal pathway relating the pollutants from the Riley Tannery to the incidences of cancer in the neighborhood surrounding the factory.

## 7.4 Regression Toward the Mean

A final problem with representative thinking about events with a random (unknown causes) component is that it leads to non-regressive predictions. To understand why, it is necessary first to understand regressive prediction.

Consider very tall fathers. On the average, their sons are tall, but about an inch shorter than their fathers. Also, the fathers of very tall sons are on the average shorter than their sons. Examine the vertical solid line representing Tall Fathers in Figure 7.2. The average son's height for tall fathers is indicated by tracing the horizontal broken line labeled "average for tall fathers" to the ordinate—the y-axis—in the graph. (The horizontal line is slightly higher than the midpoint of the vertical line between the top and bottom edges of the ellipse representing "the data" because the distribution of sons' heights on that vertical dimension is probably not exactly symmetric, but is likely to have a longer tail downward toward shorter sons' heights.) Tracing this path for a typical "Tall Father" simply works through the logic of identifying the mean height for sons of such fathers and shows that the mean "regresses"— that is, it is less extreme than the extreme father's height. The difference between D and d′ is an index of the degree of regression for this data set. Exactly the same abstract pattern in reverse is revealed if we work from Tall Sons, following the horizontal solid line for a typical Tall Son and tracing the vertical broken line path downward to the abscissa—the x-axis—for the average father's height for Tall Sons.

The British scientist Sir Francis Galton (1886) was the first to notice this relationship, which he labeled "filial regression towards mediocrity" (p. 246). At first, he thought the relationship was the result of some genetic process that made organisms shift toward average attributes, but after considering the reverse relationship (backward in time), he concluded it was a statistical property of all correlational relationships. The relationship is illustrated in Figure 7.2. What you see is a simple averaging effect. Because the heights of fathers and sons are not perfectly correlated (for whatever reasons), there is *regression*. *Non-regressive prediction* refers to people's tendency to miss the subtle regression relationship and to predict that extreme values will be associated with too-extreme values— as we will see in a moment.

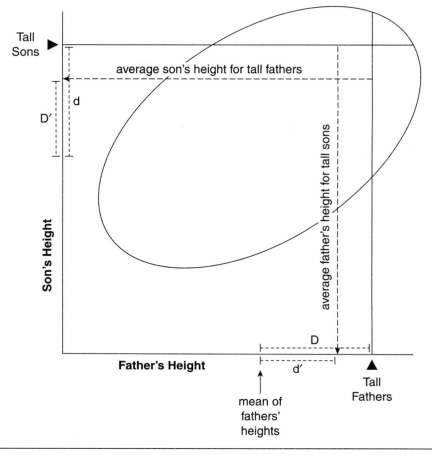

**Figure 7.2**    Illustration of statistical regression

Consider another example (based on the work of Quinn McNemar [1940], a psychologist who was one of the first to point out this statistical result and its implications for research on human behavior): Suppose that an intelligence test is administered to all the children in an orphanage on two occasions, a year apart. Assume, plausibly, that the group mean and standard deviation are the same on both tests; but that the correlation between scores on the two tests is not perfect (the actual correlation would be about +.80). Now consider only the children with the highest scores on the first test: Their scores on the second test will be on average lower. (Since the correlation is below +1.00, we expect some change; *since the two distributions of scores are the same,* the first test high scorers must get lower scores on average. The same was true for the children with the lowest scores: The average of the lowest-scoring children on the first test will be higher on the second. What if we reverse time and look backward from the second to the first test? The same relationships will apply: Extreme scores will be less extreme. Regression toward the mean is inevitable for scaled variables that are not perfectly correlated.

Perhaps it is easiest to understand regression by considering the extreme case in which we obtain perfect regression. Toss a fair coin 8 times; now toss it another 8 times. No matter how many heads are obtained in the first sequence of tosses, the expected (average) number of heads in the second sequence is 4. Because the coin is fair, the number of heads in the first sequence is totally uncorrelated with the number in the second—hence, average, of 4. That is total *regression to the mean.* As variables become more predictable from each other, there is less regression; for example, on average, the sons of very tall fathers are taller than the average person, but not as tall as their fathers. It is only when one variable is perfectly predictable from the other that there is no regression. In fact, the (squared value of the) standard correlation coefficient can be defined quite simply as the degree to which a linear prediction of one variable from another is not regressive. The technical definition of regression toward the mean is the difference between a perfect relationship (+/–1.00) and the linear correlation:

$$\text{regression} = \text{perfect relationship} - \text{correlation}$$

There are many examples of failure to appreciate regression toward the mean in everyday judgments. We are constantly surprised when an exceptional performance on Wall Street, a hit movie, a #1 pop song, or a sports achievement is followed by something more mediocre. The *Sports Illustrated cover jinx* is one of the classic examples. Readers noticed that when an athlete or a team was featured on the cover of *Sports Illustrated,* always for some exceptional achievement, the individual or team was likely to experience a slump in performance or some other misfortune afterward. Statistical analysis only served to reinforce the impression, and fans generated many plausible explanations for the phenomenon—the athlete became overconfident because of the publicity, the athlete was distracted by the media attention, and so forth. Of course, we know that most if not all of "the effect" was due to selecting extreme cases and observing regression toward the mean. No special explanation beyond noting "selection for exceptionality" is needed.

A classic academic example is provided by Horace Secrist's 1933 book, *The Triumph of Mediocrity in Business.* Secrist's thesis was that successful and unsuccessful businesses "tend towards mediocrity." The thesis is supported by hundreds of graphics showing that when businesses are selected in Year 1 for exceptional performance, on average the most successful become less successful and the least successful become more successful. Howard Hotelling, a prominent statistician, commented, "The seeming convergence is a statistical fallacy, resulting from the method of grouping. These diagrams really prove nothing more than that the ratios in question have a tendency to wander about." He points out that the true test of convergence toward mediocrity would be a consistent decrease in the variance among the groups over time—which was not observed. This same mistake was manifested in Tom Peters's and Robert Waterman's 1984 best-seller *In Search of Excellence*. These management consultants selected 43 exceptionally successful companies and reviewed the distinctive features that they believed made them "excellent." But, 5 years later, *Business Week*'s cover story, "Oops! Who's Excellent Now?" pointed out that over one-third of the original, sampled-because-they-were-extreme companies were in financial difficulty or bankrupt.

In many cases, we are interested in the effects of some treatment on performance—an educational enrichment treatment for low-performing school-children, bonuses for high-performing employees, a dietary supplement for the least healthy. Again, there is a problem of separating the true effects of a treatment, applied only to extreme cases, from simple regression. Some of the subsequent errors can be quite subtle. For example, when Daniel Kahneman (Tversky & Kahneman, 1974) was explaining to Israeli Defense Force flight instructors in the mid-1960s that reward is a better motivator than punishment, he was told by one instructor that he was wrong.

> With all due respect, Sir, what you are saying is literally for the birds. I've often praised people warmly for beautifully executed maneuvers, and the next time they almost always do worse. And I've screamed at pupils for badly executed maneuvers, and by and large, the next time they improve. Don't tell me that reward works and punishment doesn't. My experience contradicts it.

This flight instructor had witnessed a regression effect. People tend to do worse after a "beautifully executed maneuver" because performance at one time is not perfectly correlated with performance the next (again, for whatever reason). Performances also tend to improve each time after "badly executed maneuvers"—once more, simply because performance is not perfectly correlated from one occasion to the next. (The easiest way to obtain an award for "academic improvement" is to be right near the bottom of the class the semester prior to the one for which such awards are given, and the way to be labeled an "underachiever" is to score brilliantly on an aptitude test.) Unfortunately, as the flight instructor anecdote illustrates, teachers who do not understand regression effects may be systematically reinforced (by regression to better performance) for punishing students and disappointed (by regression to worse performance) for rewarding them. (Regression alone may be a sufficient explanation for some people's preference, like the flight instructor's, for punishment over reward as a means of behavior control.)

Another unhappy by-product of our ignorance of the inevitability of regression effects is our overconfidence in the success of interventions like firing coaches and CEOs. Consider the prototypical situation: A team performs poorly during the first half of the season. The owner reacts by firing the coach, and the team performs better during the second half of the season. Should we attribute the improvement to the firing and replacement of the coach or to simple regression effects? After all, mid-season firings are usually conditioned on an extreme, poor performance. Absent an experiment in which coaches are randomly fired, we cannot be sure (and such an experiment is unlikely to be performed). But careful statistical analyses consistently show that most of the improvement is due to regression (Koning, 2003), and the same is true for the firing of business executives. (The reality in sports is that, if a team performs extremely poorly during the first half of the season, it is likely to have been pitted against stronger teams, and the second half will involve weaker opponents, exaggerating the apparent success of the replacement coach even further.)

The rational way of dealing with regression effects is to "regress" when making predictions. Then, if there is some need or desire to evaluate discrepancy (e.g., to give awards for "overachievement" or therapy for "underachievement"), compare the actual value to the *predicted* value—not with the actual value of the variable used to make the prediction. For example, to determine patient "improvement" by comparing Minnesota Multiphasic Personality Inventory (MMPI) profiles at time 1 and time 2, first correlate the profiles to determine a (regressed) predicted score for each patient at time 2; then compare the actual profile with this predicted score, not with the score at time 1. Otherwise, patients who have high (pathological) profiles at time 1 may be mistakenly labeled "improved" ("they had nowhere to go but down"), while those with normal MMPI profiles may be mistakenly regarded as unresponsive to treatment. Representative thinking, in contrast, leads to comparing discrepancies without regressing first, and the results are predictable. For example, "Of particular significance was the fact that those scoring highest on symptom reductions . . . were those whose symptoms were initially more severe, and who were the less promising candidates for conventional types of therapy" (Dawes, 1986). (While Dawes was a clinical psychologist trainee, he asked the psychologists and psychiatrists at the hospital to dichotomize patients whose improvement was above average at discharge and those whose improvement was below average. Those they categorized as above average in improvement had higher scores on most of the MMPI scales on admission—significantly higher on the major clinical ones.)

Regression toward the mean is particularly insidious when we are trying to assess the success of some kind of intervention designed to improve the

state of affairs—like the flight instructor's efforts to improve student performance by intervening to punish poor performances. The worst case scenarios
for understanding the effects of interventions occur when the intervention is
introduced because "we've got a problem." For instance, it is almost impossible to accurately assess the causal effects of the introduction of a strict traffic enforcement program *after* a flurry of tragic traffic accidents, or the hiring
of a new CEO *after* several poor corporate performances, or the hiring of a
new coach after a losing streak. The chances are, the interventions are going
to show improvements, and it is almost certain that some or most of the effect
will be due to regression toward the mean.

## 7.5 Reflections on Our Inability to Accept Randomness

Some of the errors in judgment we have just described are probably not so
surprising. Why would we be smarter than casino operators who have spent
hundreds of years perfecting diabolical probability games to trap unwary
customers? Or why wouldn't sports fans confuse conditions under which
streaks do occur (in some sports events) with similar situations in which they
do not? But the pervasive tendency to see much more structure than is actually present and to imagine we have much more control over events than we
do in hundreds of important naturally occurring situations is still a puzzle.
In the next chapter, we'll introduce the best remedy we know for these hard-
to-eradicate bad habits—thinking like a probability theorist.

## References

Bayer, D., & Diaconis, P. (1992). Trailing the dovetail shuffle to its lair. *Annals of Applied Probability, 2,* 294–313.

Bilefsky, D. (2008, April 26). Serbia's most famous survivor fears that recent history will repeat itself. *New York Times.* Retrieved June 20, 2009, from http://www.nytimes .com/2008/04/26/world/europe/26vulovic.html

Dawes, R. M. (1986). Representative thinking in clinical judgment. *Clinical Psychology Review, 6,* 425–441.

Diaconis, P., Holmes, S., & Montgomery, R. (2007). Dynamical bias in the coin toss. *Society for Industrial and Applied Mathematics Review, 49,* 211–235.

Feller, W. (1968). *Introduction to probability theory and its applications* (3rd ed.). New York: Wiley.

Fenton-O'Creevy, M., Nicholson, N., Sloane, E., & Willman, P. (2003). Trading on illusions: Unrealistic perceptions of control and trading performance. *Journal of Occupational and Organizational Psychology, 76,* 53–68.

Galton, F. (1886). Regression towards mediocrity in hereditary stature. *Journal of the Anthropological Institute of Great Britain and Ireland, 15,* 246–263.

Gawande, A. (1999, February 8). The cancer-cluster myth. *New Yorker,* pp. 34–37.

Gigerenzer, G. (2006). Out of the frying pan into the fire: Behavioral reactions to terrorist attacks. *Risk Analysis, 26,* 347–351.

Gilovich, T., Vallone, R., & Tversky, A. (1985). The hot hand in basketball: On the misperception of random sequences. *Cognitive Psychology, 17,* 295–314.

Hotelling, H. (1933). Review of *The Triumph of Mediocrity in Business. Journal of the American Statistical Association, 28,* 463–465.

Kareev, Y. (1992). Not that bad after all: Generation of random sequences. *Journal of Experimental Psychology: Perception and Performance, 18,* 1189–1194.

Koehler, J. J., & Conley, C. A. (2003). The "hot hand" myth in professional basketball. *Journal of Sport & Exercise Psychology, 25,* 253–259.

Koning, R. (2003). An econometric evaluation of the effect of firing a coach on team performance. *Applied Economics, 35,* 555–564.

Langer, E. J. (1975). The illusion of control. *Journal of Personality and Social Psychology, 32,* 311–328.

Langer, E. J., & Roth, J. (1975). Heads I win, tails is chance: The illusion of control is a function of the sequence of outcomes in a purely chance task. *Journal of Personality and Social Psychology, 32,* 951–955.

Larkey, P. D., Smith, R. A., & Kadane, J. B. (1989). It's okay to believe in the "hot hand." *Chance, 2*(4), 22–30.

Lopes, L. L. (1982). Doing the impossible: A note on induction and the experience of randomness. *Journal of Experimental Psychology: Learning, Memory, and Cognition, 8,* 626–636.

McNamar, Q. (1940). A critical examination of the University of Iowa studies of environmental influences on IQ. *Psychological Bulletin, 18,* 63–92.

Meisler, S. (1977, December 30). Spain lottery—Not even war stops it. *Los Angeles Times,* p. D1.

Oops! Who's excellent now? (1984, November 5). *BusinessWeek,* 76–88.

Peters, T., & Waterman, R., Jr. (1984). *In search of excellence.* New York: Harper & Row.

Poincaré, H. (1952). *Science and method* (F. Maitland, Trans.). London: Dover. (Original work published 1914)

Sagan, C. (1997). *The demon-haunted world: Science as a candle in the dark.* New York: Ballantine.

Secrist, H. (1933). *The triumph of mediocrity in business.* Chicago: Bureau of Business Research, Northwestern University.

Sivak, M., & Flannagan, M. J. (2003). Flying and driving after the September 11 attacks. *American Scientist, 91,* 6–8.

Tversky, A., & Gilovich, T. (1989). The "hot hand": Statistical reality or cognitive illusion. *Chance, 2*(4), 31–34.

Tversky, A., & Kahneman, D. (1974). Judgment under uncertainty: Heuristics and biases. *Science, 185,* 1124–1131.

# 8

# Thinking Rationally About Uncertainty

*The actual science of logic is conversant at present only with things either certain, or impossible, or entirely doubtful, none of which (fortunately) we have to reason on. Therefore the true logic for this world is the Calculus of Probabilities, which takes account of the magnitude of the probability which is, or ought to be, in a reasonable man's mind.*

—James Clerk Maxwell

## 8.1 What to Do About the Biases

Ulysses wisely had himself chained to his ship's mast before coming within earshot of the Sirens. He did so not because he feared the Sirens per se, but because he feared his own reaction to their singing. In effect, he took a precaution against himself, because he knew what he would be likely to do if he heard the Sirens. Similarly, the cognitive biases of automatic thinking can lead us astray, in a predictable direction. We must take precautions to avoid the pitfalls of such unexamined judgment.

One of the goals of this book is to teach analytical thinking about judgment processes. The best way we know to think systematically about judgment is to learn the fundamentals of probability theory and statistics and to apply those concepts when making important judgments. Anyone who has taken or taught introductory probability theory realizes that Laplace's (1814/1951) famous dictum, that "the theory of probabilities is at bottom only common sense reduced to calculus" (p. 196), is certainly false. Probability theory was not invented until recent times, and our minds do not seem to be naturally "wired" to think according to its precepts. The first seven chapters in this book could be interpreted as a catalog of cognitive habits of thought that deviate, sometimes radically, from the laws of probability theory. We provide a summary of the basics of probability theory in the appendix of this book, but in the present chapter we will try to convey the essence of elementary probabilistic thinking illustrated with concrete examples.

Attempts to train people not to think representatively and not to be influenced by availability or other biases have been mostly unsuccessful. Associations are ubiquitous in our thinking processes (although perhaps they are not its sole "building blocks," as the English empiricists believed). Moreover, making judgments on the basis of one's experience is perfectly reasonable, and essential to our survival.

So, what is needed is some kind of alternative way of making these judgments, a method that "affirmatively" diverts us from relying on intuitions and associations and heuristics, at least when the judgments are important. One such precaution against our biases is the use of external aids. For example, a clinical psychologist can record instances (e.g., of suicide threats) on paper or in a computer file and then compile the data, using a symbolic formula or diagram, when he or she wishes to estimate the frequency. A simple charting of "good" and "bad" weeks can reveal a pattern—or the lack of one. Alternatively, even just writing down base rates and trying to apply the ratio rule can help us avoid irrational judgments.

The greatest obstacle to using external aids, such as the ones we will illustrate in this chapter, is the difficulty of convincing ourselves that we should take precautions against ourselves as Ulysses did. The idea that a self-imposed external constraint on action can actually enhance our freedom by releasing us from predictable and undesirable internal constraints is not an obvious one. It is hard to be Ulysses. The idea that such internal constraints can be cognitive, as well as emotional, is even less palatable. Thus, to allow our judgment to be constrained by the "mere numbers" or pictures or external aids offered by computer printouts is anathema to many people. In fact, there is even evidence that when such aids are offered, many experts attempt intuitively to improve upon these aids' predictions—and then they do worse than they would have had they "mindlessly" adhered to them. Estimating likelihood does in fact involve mere numbers, but as Paul Meehl (1986) pointed out, "When you come out of a supermarket, you don't eyeball a heap of purchases and say to the clerk, 'Well, it looks to me as if it's about $17.00 worth; what do you think?' No, you add it up" (p. 372). Adding, keeping track, and writing down the rules of probabilistic inference explicitly are of great help in overcoming the systematic errors introduced by representative thinking, availability, anchor-and-adjust, and other biases. If we do so, we might even be able to learn a little bit from experience.

## 8.2 Getting Started Thinking in Terms of Probabilities

Modern probability theory got its start when wealthy noblemen hired mathematicians to advise them on how to win games of chance at which they gambled with their acquaintances (as noted in Chapter 1, in Cardano's case, the advice was for himself). Perhaps the fundamental precept of probabilistic analysis is the exhortation to take a bird's-eye, distributional view of the situation under analysis (e.g., a dice game, the traffic in Boulder, crimes in Pittsburgh, the situation with that troublesome knee) and to define a sample space of *all* the possible events and their logical, set membership interrelations. This step is exactly where rational analysis and judgments based on availability, similarity, and scenario construction diverge: When we judge intuitively, the mind is drawn to a limited, systematically skewed subset of the possible events. In the case of scenario construction, for example, we are often caught in our detailed scenario—focused on just one preposterously specific outcome path.

Daniel Kahneman and Dan Lovallo (1993) note that decision makers are prone to treat each problem as unique and to take an "inside view." Their remedy, similar to ours, is to deliberately take an *outside view,* in other words, to think of the current problem as a member of a category of many similar problems and to apply the rules of probabilistic thinking. To illustrate the importance of the outside view, Kahneman tells the story of a project he was involved in to design a curriculum for a new course:

> When the project team had been in operation for about a year, with some significant achievements already to its credit, the discussion at one of the team meetings turned to the question of how long the project would take. To make the debate more useful, I asked everyone to indicate on a slip of paper their best estimate of the number of months that would be needed to bring the project to a well-defined stage of completion: a complete draft ready for submission to the Ministry of Education. The estimates, including my own, ranged from 18 to 30 months. At this point I had the idea of turning to one of our members, a distinguished expert on curriculum development, asking him a question phrased about as follows: "We are surely not the only team to have tried to develop a curriculum where none existed before. Please try to recall as many such cases as you can. Think of them as they were in a stage comparable to the one at present. How long did it take them to complete

their projects?" After a long silence, something like the following answer was given, with obvious signs of discomfort: "First, I should say that not all teams that I can think of in a comparable stage ever did complete their task. About 40% of them eventually gave up. Of the remaining, I cannot think of one that was completed in less than seven years, nor of any that took more than ten." In response to a further question, he answered: "No, I cannot think of any relevant factor that distinguishes us favorably from the teams I have been thinking about. Indeed, my impression is that we are slightly below average in terms of our resources and potential." (Kahneman & Lovallo, 1993, p. 24)

The point is that judgments are likely to be more accurate if the judge can step back, take an outside view, and think distributionally and probabilistically, even if the thought process is only qualitative. Judgments will be even better if they can be based on systematically collected data and follow the quantitative rules of probability theory.

Probability theory starts with a precise vocabulary with which to describe elementary events, sets of events, and the relationships between them. Let's start with the well-defined example of throwing two dice. First, there is the *simplest event,* a value on a single upper face of the die; for example, "I throw a 1." Second, there is a *conjunction* of two simple events; for example, "I throw a 1 *and* a 6" (in either order, on either die). Third, there is a *disjunction* of two simple events; for example, "I throw a 1 *or* a 6, *or both*" (sometimes called the "inclusive or"). Fourth, there are *conditional* events, the occurrence of one event, *given* that another has occurred; for example, "I throw a 1 (on either die) *given* that I threw a total of 7 on the two dice." In the case of perfect dice, we can systematically describe the entire *sample space* of 36 possible, equal-probability outcomes: You might throw the numbers 1 to 6 on the first die, and the same numbers 1 to 6 on the second; so there are $6 \times 6$ possible pairings or conjunction events.

For present purposes, once we have conceptualized the sample space of possible events, we want to assign frequencies and probabilities to the simple events and relational events in the space. In the case of idealized situations, we can reason logically about the kinds of events, their frequencies, and probabilities as dice, card games, and other honest gambling devices closely approximate these ideals. So, since there is 1 face out of 6 that matches the description "1 is thrown," we would say the probability of a 1 is 1/6. And there are two outcomes where a 1 and a 6 are thrown, out of 36, so we have a 2/36 probability of throwing that conjunction; and there are 20 outcomes out of 36 where a 1 or a 6 or both are thrown, so we have a 20/36 probability of the disjunction event. Finally, for the conditional event, "1 on either die given a total of 7," we focus only on the given "total = 7" and calculate the probability as 2/6, since there are six events where the total = 7 and for two of them a 1 is thrown on one of the dice.

Now, let's work through another, less precisely defined situation: Suppose we are interested in events that involve the characteristics of college students. If we pick a student at random from the college student body at the University of Chicago, what is the probability that student will be female? Out of the approximately 5,026 undergraduates at Chicago in 2008, a total of 2,513 were women; so the probability a randomly picked undergraduate is a woman is 2,513/5,026 or approximately .50. What about the probability of majoring in the physical sciences? A total of 815 students declared a physical science as their major, so the probability of a randomly sampled college student at Chicago being in the physical sciences is 815/5,026 or .16. Now, what is the probability of the conjunction event of being both female and a physical sciences major? A total of 211 students were both female and physical science majors, so the probability is 211/5,026 or .04. As for the disjunction, female or physical science major or both, 3,117 meet this description, so the probability is 3,117/5,026 or .62. And what about the conditional, "female *given* physical sciences major"? The probability is 211/815 or .26—we consider only students who are physical science majors (there are 815 of them) and then ask, What is the probability a physical science major is a woman? Here's another case where the categories or sets that define the events are well-defined (let's assume that femaleness and physical science major can be defined precisely), so we can count empirical frequencies to infer probabilities (not the idealized, logical frequencies of the dice game).

Notice that the inverse conditional probability, "physical science major *given female*," is *not* the same (211/2,513 or .08) as "female *given physical science major*" (211/815 or .26). In general, a conditional probability is not the same as its inverse, as illustrated by the ratio rule from Chapter 5—for example, $p$(female|physical science) $\neq$ $p$(physical science|female).

What about an even murkier situation, where we can define sets and categories but there are no obvious frequencies to count? Suppose we are trying to decide if a Republican will win the presidential election in the year 2012. As we wrote this book (in 2008), the lead candidate for the Democratic party would be Barack Obama (incumbent president), but there is massive ignorance about potential Republican nominees 4 years hence. Some names, mostly successful state governors, are in the air, such as Sarah Palin (Alaska), General David Petraeus (the most visible military leader at the moment), and Newt Gingrich (former congressman, now conservative pundit), but no one has a clue who might be electable in 4 years. Even

Obama's candidacy is uncertain, as his first 4 years in office are sure to be full of surprises. Nonetheless, the distributional approach is still the best method to analyze the situation and to make predictions. We can list most of the plausible outcome categories, starting with the slates of potential candidates for each party and the still uncertain events that are likely to have an impact on the party and electorate's votes (economic conditions, personal scandal, health problems, charisma factor, campaign funds, etc.). In a situation like this, the systematic listing is unlikely to make us confident about precise probabilities, but it will remind us just how uncertain that future is and keep us from myopically developing one scenario and then believing in it too much. Despite the murkiness, distributional representations and probabilistic analysis are a big improvement over spontaneous judgments. However, we are unlikely to rely primarily on relative frequencies about this saliently vivid, unique event—though, if we're really at a loss, we might resort to some statistics that *may* be relevant, for example, $p$(incumbent wins). However, even when we reason based on scenarios and "reasons for" the possible outcomes, a deliberate attempt to represent the problem systematically will improve the coherence and accuracy of our judgments.

Let's consider one more case: Will there be nuclear weapons deployed by one nation against another in the next decade? Here even the outcomes are poorly defined: Is it a nuclear deployment if terrorists (perhaps not even identified with a single nation) detonate a nuclear device in a Middle Eastern country? Our scenarios, really descriptions of concrete possible outcomes, are nebulous: "A minor skirmish between United Nations peacekeeping troops and an African Warlord escalates . . ."; "An assassination attempt on an Israeli leader fails, and the reprisal . . ." Now, it seems there are no relevant frequencies to count. The future situation will be different from any previous historical situation that comes to mind. But we still believe that the systematic distributional approach is the best method by which to make educated, though vastly uncertain, probability estimates. In fact, there is evidence from psychological studies conducted by Asher Koriat, Sarah Lichtenstein, and Baruch Fischhoff (1980) that simply spelling out many of the relevant events and systematically thinking through the "reasons for" and "reasons against" the occurrence of each event increase the quality of judgments under ignorance.

What points did we want to make with these examples? First, we introduced the basic set membership relationships that are used to describe events to which technical probabilities can be assigned. Second, we introduced four kinds of situations to which we might want to attach probabilities: (i) situations, like conventional games of chance (e.g., throwing dice), where idealized random devices provide good descriptions of the underlying structure and where logical analysis can be applied to deduce probabilities; (ii) well-defined "empirical" situations where statistical relative frequencies can be used to measure probabilities (e.g., our judgments about kinds of students at the University of Chicago); (iii) moderately well-defined situations, where we must reason about causation and propensities (rather than relative frequencies— e.g., predicting the outcome of the next U.S. presidential election), but where a fairly complete sample space of relevant events can be defined with a little thought; and (iv) situations of huge ignorance, where even a sample space of relevant events is difficult to construct, and where there seem to be no relevant frequencies (e.g., international conflict in the next decade?).

One of the remarkable characteristics of probability theory is that four simple axioms (see Appendix) provide the rules for how to reason rationally and probabilistically, even though there is massive disagreement about what the numbers refer to. Our four examples were chosen to give a feeling for the spectrum of interpretations of probabilities: as an extension of elementary deductive logic; as real numbers based on frequencies of events in the external world; or as indices of subjective confidence *in our heads,* but not in the external world.

Third, many errors in judging and reasoning about uncertainty stem from mistakes that are made at the very beginning of the process, when comprehending the to-be-judged situation. If people could generate veridical representations of the to-be-judged situations and then keep the (mostly) set membership relationships straight throughout their reasoning, many errors would be eliminated. Of course, there are also misconceptions about probabilities and about random processes, but many times judgments under uncertainty are already off-track even before a person has tried to integrate the uncertainties. Our primary advice about how to make better judgments under uncertainty is focused on creating effective external (diagrammatic and symbolic) representations of the situation being judged.

## 8.3 Comprehending the Situation Being Judged

It may seem difficult to start from a written description of a novel uncertain situation and to create a comprehensive representation of the situation, although it is probably even harder to create situation models from direct experience. Raymond Nickerson (1996) has cataloged many of the errors that occur at the comprehension stage in an essay that focuses on the ambiguities in verbal probability problems. Some of the best-known examples have been enshrined in the popular literature on brain teasers. Let's start with a simple problem that has been the subject of research on probabilistic reasoning (introduced to psychology by Maya Bar-Hillel and Ruma Falk, 1982, p. 119); play the game and make a personal estimate before you read on:

> Three cards are in a hat. One is red on both sides ("red-red"), one is white on both sides ("white-white"), and one is red on one side and white on the other ("red-white"). A single card is drawn at random and tossed into the air and lands red-side up. What is the probability that it is the "red-red" card?

A common response is "1/2" or ".50" (given by 66% to 79% of the participants in experiments conducted by Bar-Hillel). Interviews with participants revealed that a typical justification for this answer is, "Well, since the card landed red-side up, we know it's not the 'white-white' card. There are two cards left, so it's 50-50 whether it's the 'red-red' card." The implication is that the written problem led these subjects to create a "first three, then two cards remaining" problem representation. However, the (unambiguously) correct representation is in terms of the *sides* of the cards, not the whole cards (see probability tree representation in Figure 8.1; Brase, Cosmides, & Tooby, 1998, also make this point). The sample space for all outcomes comprises six events—one for each side of each card. And, after red is observed face up, there are three events in the "active sample space" where a red side ends facing up: "red-white" (red up), "$red_{side1}$-$red_{side2}$" ($red_{side1}$ up), or "$red_{side1}$-$red_{side2}$" ($red_{side2}$ up), so the correct answer is 2/3—in 2 of the 3 equally probable events, the card is truly "red-red."

A more complicated problem was published in the "Ask Marilyn" column of a popular magazine and received much attention because the answer is surprising to most people and subtle enough to provoke disagreements among some famous mathematicians (vos Savant, 1991; Deborah Bennett provides a good summary to this problem in her popular introduction to probability theory, *Randomness* [1998]):

> Suppose you're on a game show, and you're given a choice of three doors. Behind one door is a car; behind the others, goats. You pick a door—say No. 1—and the host, who knows what's behind the doors, opens another door—say No. 3—which has a goat. He says to you, "Do you want to pick Door No. 2?" Is it to your advantage to switch your choice? (vos Savant, 1991, p. 12)

The first difficulty with this brain teaser is the surprising complexity of the situation of "possible events" to which it refers. Try to diagram the situation by systematically listing each of the relevant events: There are three doors that the contestant could pick; there are three possibilities for where the car is located; there are several options for which door the host could open (and they differ in number depending on which of these nine "situations" is encountered). Then

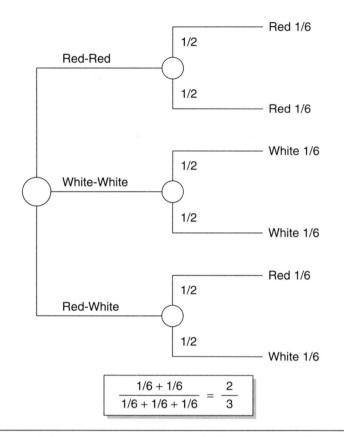

**Figure 8.1**    Probability tree representation of the Three Cards Problem

there is a further complexity created by which policy (stay or switch) is followed by the contestant; there are between 18 and 36 situations to keep in mind—*depending on which representation of the problem* a solver has settled on.

There is yet a further difficulty with this brain teaser because of the ambiguity of the written statement concerning the *host's rule for choosing a door to open;* unless this ambiguity is resolved, there is no unique sample space representation of the problem. There are at least three plausible interpretations of the host's rule given the problem statement. One rule is that the host always opens one of the non-chosen doors at random (e.g., by tossing a coin to choose Door No. 2 or Door No. 3 in the situation described in the written problem above). This means that he could open a door and reveal the car—presumably, then, he (and the audience) will just laugh at you for having chosen the wrong door and the game is over. But there is a second rule for the host, which is also consistent with the written problem statement:

Suppose the host always selects a door concealing a goat; never opens the door selected; and when the contestant has chosen the door concealing the car, the host picks a door at random. Now, there is a more complex dependency between the contestant's choice and the door opened by the host. An even more complex third rule has also been proposed: Suppose the host always selects a door concealing a goat; never opens the door selected by the contestant; and when the contestant has chosen door with the car behind it, the host has a bias to pick the remaining door with the lowest number (and there are other possible biases for this kind of rule). The underlying probabilities are different for each of these three rules—though all three are consistent with the original verbal problem statement.

The most popular representation to the problem is to interpret the problem statement to mean that the host always opens a door other than the one chosen originally by the contestant, and never opens a door revealing the car (i.e., follows Rule 2 above); then it is possible to say that the "switch doors" strategy may increase and will never decrease the probability of getting the car. So, under this representation of the problem, the answer is the contestant should switch. We provide an unambiguous representation of the problem in a probability tree format in Figure 8.2. The point is that representation is the essential, determinative first step in probabilistic reasoning. In the case of the Three Doors Problem, much confusion and controversy, and many academic journal articles, ensued from the ambiguity in the problem statement, though an unambiguous statement of the problem is complex and confusing in its own right. And real-world uncertainties and decisions are even more dauntingly ambiguous than probability word problems.

One major benefit of enrollment in probability and statistics courses is that it provides practice in translating situations into more precise and complete representations—or, in the case of real-world complexities, extracting the essential uncertainties and causal contingencies. We recommend the tables, probability (or decision) trees, and Venn diagrams that we use to illustrate most of the major judgment and decision situations described in this book. Unfortunately, the creation of appropriate and effective tables and diagrams is contingent on the specific problem being solved. We try the tree diagrams first, as they are the most generally effective, but sometimes one of the other formats is more illuminating. Fortunately, constructing these representations is a skill that any motivated student can learn with some practice. The first step is to study the examples in this book.

Furthermore, it is usually helpful to think about probabilities concretely in terms of *frequencies* of individuals in the relevant subgroups. People are much better able to keep track of the relationships between the partitions of the overall population when they imagine frequencies of individuals, objects, or events. In fact, some of the errors of judgment we presented in the previous chapters are

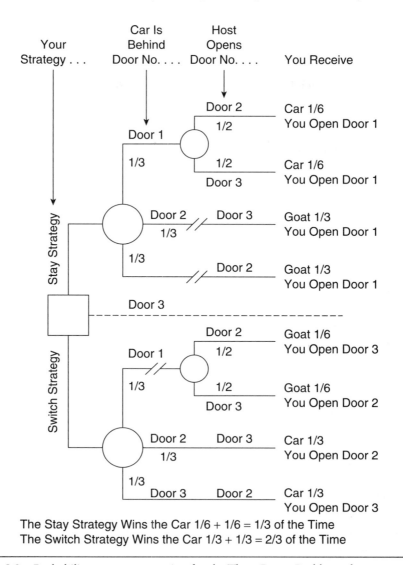

The Stay Strategy Wins the Car 1/6 + 1/6 = 1/3 of the Time
The Switch Strategy Wins the Car 1/3 + 1/3 = 2/3 of the Time

**Figure 8.2**    Probability tree representation for the Three Doors Problem when you choose Door No. 1 initially (This tree represents one-third of the possibilities—two more similar trees can be constructed for the cases where you choose Door No. 2 and Door No. 3, which exhausts the "sample space" of possibilities.)

reduced dramatically when people are encouraged to represent the situations in terms of frequencies instead of probabilities (e.g., Gigerenzer & Hoffrage, 1995; Sedlmeier & Betsch, 2002). Frequency formats are useful for preventing confusions of conditional probabilities (e.g., probability[cancer|positive test] versus probability [positive test|cancer]) and the conjunction error ("Linda is more likely to be a feminist bank teller than simply a bank teller of any kind.").

We will return to this theme of how to represent to-be-judged situations unambiguously and distributionally after we review the concept of rationality in judgments under uncertainty.

# 8.4 Testing for Rationality

In the first half of this book, we've provided many examples of judgments that are inaccurate or irrational. On what basis can we make such evaluations? The conditions necessary to conclude a judgment is *inaccurate* are relatively straightforward: (i) We need to have some measurable criterion event or condition in mind that is the target of the judgment; (ii) we need to be sure the person making the judgment is in agreement with us on the nature of the target and is trying to estimate, predict, or judge the same criterion value that we have in mind; and (iii) we also want to be sure that the judge is motivated to minimize error in the prediction and that the "costs" of errors are symmetric so the judge will not be biased to over- or underestimate the criterion. (For example, one of the authors of this book indicates that his judgments of acquaintances' ages [the criterion] are inaccurate and they tend to be systematically too low. But it is also important to know that this bias is partly deliberate to avoid offending people who are sensitive about being viewed as older than they really are.) This logic for assessing the quality of judgments has been dubbed the *correspondence framework* for accuracy, and it is the framework that underlies the Lens Model approach that we introduced in Chapter 3. (See Hammond, 1996, or Hastie & Rasinski, 1988, for further discussion.)

However, we also talk about irrationality or *incoherence* in judgments, when it is not obvious that a correspondence test can be applied. For example, we said that people who ranked "Linda is a feminist bank teller" as more probably true than "Linda is a bank teller" were irrational and made judgment errors, even though *there is no real Linda out there*, whose occupation and attitudes could serve as a criterion for a correspondence test of accuracy. In these cases, we are evaluating the quality of judgments, and we can only apply the approach to two or more judgments by considering their coherence or logical consistency with one another. We evaluate the judgments with reference to their consistency with the laws of logic and probability theory, which we accept as a standard of rational reasoning. By the way, if we are sure that a collection of judgments is incoherent, we can be sure that some are also inaccurate, though we often cannot say exactly which of the individual judgments are in error. (And, more generally, as noted in Chapter 2, that which is self-contradictory cannot constitute a true description of the world.)

Another convincing argument that the judgment errors we have identified are truly irrational is that experimental participants shown their own responses and told the rule they have violated often conclude, "I made a mistake," or even, "Boy, that was stupid, I'm embarrassed." Kahneman and Tversky (1982, 1996), who first identified many of the errors we discussed, label the these judgment errors *illusions,* because they are behavioral habits that we know are mistakes when we think carefully about them, but they still persist when we do not exercise deliberate self-control to counteract our intuitive tendencies—very much like the many familiar, but still irresistible optical illusions.

This dissociation of deliberate reasoning and mostly automatic behaviors is the basis for the separation of analytic versus intuitive reasoning and memory processes (Kahneman, 2003). Seymour Epstein and his students (Denes-Raj & Epstein, 1994) have reported several studies in which some of the errors demonstrated by Kahneman and Tversky, such as in the Linda problem in Chapter 5 and other probability brain teasers, were reduced or eliminated by simply instructing experimental participants to answer "how a completely logical person would respond." They aptly titled their paper, "When do people behave against their better judgment?" However, in general, simply instructing someone to "behave logically" is not sufficient to induce rational thinking.

Once we have committed ourselves to using logic, mathematics, and decision theory as the standards to evaluate rationality in judgments and choices, there is much more work to be done to evaluate rationality in practice. First, it is not always obvious how to represent a decision situation objectively so that rational principles can be applied. Even when we have clear verbal descriptions, as in the brain teasers described at the beginning of this chapter, there is still often incompleteness, ambiguity, and even contradiction in our knowledge about the to-be-analyzed situation. Furthermore, it is often difficult to specify exactly what an actor's goals are in a situation, and most rational analysis requires knowing what the actor is trying to "maximize" to define a rational standard for evaluation. So, even if we have a well-specified standard for rationality, there can be problems in deciding if and how a response is irrational.

Second, it is not always appropriate to focus on the short-run performance of a fully informed person with plenty of time to think in an ideally quiet environment. We should be more interested in performance in the long run over many judgments, made in noisy environments with distractions, interruptions, and missing information. It may well be that the optimal, ideally rational judgment calculation is not the *adaptively* best judgment process under more realistic conditions. This theme has been developed recently by researchers led by John Payne (Payne, Bettman, & Johnson,

1993), by Lola Lopes and Gregg Oden (1991), and by Gerd Gigerenzer (Gigerenzer, Todd, & the ABC Research Group, 1999). These groups of scientists have argued that "fast-and-frugal" algorithms or heuristics for judgments and choices may be more robust, sturdier, and have better survival value than optimal calculations that are superior only when lots of information, computational capacity, and time are available.

So far, we have presented the "behavioral side" of our story, illustrating these judgment errors in the last four chapters, organized according to the cognitive processes and heuristics that underlie these judgments and produce the errors. Now we will discuss the judgment errors with reference to the rules of probability and logic that are violated, with some advice about how to avoid these irrationalities. We should warn the reader that sometimes it is difficult to infer exactly which rule of probability theory was violated first in a person's judgment process. Because the rules are all inextricably interrelated, it is difficult to know for sure whether the primary error is a misrepresentation of the set membership relations among the events being judged, an error in assuming two different contingencies or probabilities are the same, the ignoring of a critical piece of judgment-relevant information such as a background base rate, or something else.

## 8.5 How to Think About Inverse Probabilities

We have given several examples of judgment errors that arise because people (including your authors) are not careful to keep separate the easily confusable inverse probabilities (see especially Section 5.10). Let's spend some time dissecting a detailed example (reported in a news article by Gay McGee, 1979).

> BAY CITY, MICHIGAN, 1979: A surgeon here is one of a handful in the country who is taking a pioneering approach to the treatment of breast cancer. Charles S. Rogers, M.D., is removing "high-risk" breasts before cancer has developed.
>
> The risk factor is determined by mammogram "patterns" of milk ducts and lobules, which show that just over half of the women in the highest-risk group are likely to develop cancer between the ages of 40 and 59. The mammogram patterns are the work of Detroit radiologist John N. Wolfe, M.D.
>
> The surgery, called prophylactic (preventive) mastectomy, involves removal of the breast tissue between the skin and the chest wall as well as the nipple.
>
> Reconstruction of the breast with the remaining skin is usually done at the time of the mastectomy. Silicone implants and replacement of the areola (the pigmented skin around the nipple) leave the patient "looking like a woman," according to the surgeon.

He has performed the surgical procedure on 90 women in two years.

The rationale for the procedure is found in the *surgeon's interpretation* of studies by the radiologist, Wolfe. The newspaper article continues:

In his research Wolfe found that one in thirteen women in the general population will develop breast cancer but that one in two or three DY (highest-risk) women *will develop it between the ages of 40 and 59.* [Italics added; Wolfe did *not* find that. What he discovered is explained in the next paragraph.]

The low-risk women (NI) account for 42 percent of the population, but only 7.5% of the carcinomas. By examining the DY women and those in the next-lower risk groups, P1 and P2, Wolfe felt that 93% of the breast cancers could be found in 57% of the population.

One remedy to these confusions is to shift to systematic symbolic representations. Translating each to-be-judged situation into probability theory notation and then carefully applying basic rules from probability theory can help. (See the discussion of the useful Ratio Rule in Section 5.10 and the more general discussion of Probability Theory in the Appendix.) Let's look at that approach and a probability tree representation applied to the Rogers example. Using Rogers's figures, it is possible to construct results for 1,000 "typical" women (see the table in Figure 8.3). No other numbers satisfy the constraints. Note that $499 + 71 = 570$, or 57% of the population, which is the stated proportion in the high-risk category. Also, $71/(71 + 6) = .92$. Thus, as stated, 92% of the cancers are discovered in 57% of the population. The overall breast cancer rate of the population is $(71 + 6)/1,000 = .077$, and so on.

To return to Rogers on breast cancer, while it is true that 92% of the cancers are found in the high-risk group, *the estimated probability that someone in this group will develop cancer is only 71/570 or .12.* (Remember, these calculations are based on Rogers's own proportions.)

The .12 figure can be determined even more easily by applying the ratio rule. According to Wolfe's figures, $p(\text{cancer}) = .075$, $p(\text{high risk}|\text{cancer}) = .93$, and $p(\text{high risk}) = .58$. Thus,

$$\frac{p(\text{cancer}|\text{high risk})}{.93} = \frac{.075}{.580} \text{; therefore,}$$

$$p(\text{cancer}|\text{high risk}) = .12.$$

The most informative statistic is negative—the estimated probability of developing breast cancer if the woman is from the low-risk group

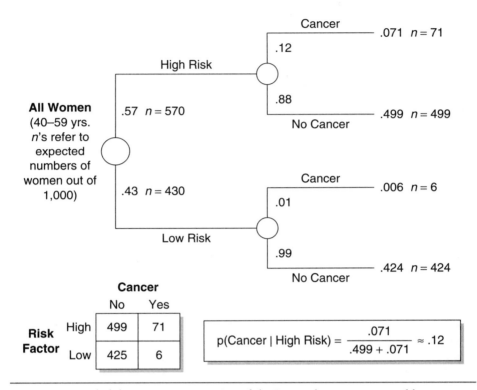

**Figure 8.3**    Probability tree representation of the Rogers breast cancer problem

being 6/(425 + 6), or .014. It is not possible based on the newspaper article to evaluate the claim about the very highest-risk group, DY.

Dr. Rogers does not stress the value of a negative inference. After urging *all women* over 30 to have an annual mammography examination, he is quoted as saying, "The greatest danger is in having a mammogram without a medical exam by a doctor. There are too many times when the surgeon feels a lesion that wasn't picked up on a mammogram. . . . This is definitely a case where one plus one equals more than three" (McGee, 1979).

Agreed. But, incidentally, his mammogram advice is also based on a confusion of inverse probabilities. Roughly 20% of cancers were not detected by mammography—that is, surgeons discovered a lesion "that wasn't picked up on a mammogram." But that is much different from the percentage of times women have cancer given a normal ("negative") mammogram result; $p$(cancer|negative) ≠ $p$(negative|cancer). In fact, this former figure at the time the article was written was approximately .5% (1 in 200) according to figures from the Hartford Insurance Project that had just been completed and published—which most of us would not regard as a "great danger." (In fairness to Rogers, it must be pointed out that the article did not specify how seriously high risk the "high-risk" patients would have to be before Rogers would operate. The point of the present critique is that his *reasoning* used to justify the procedure *at all* is, from a rational perspective, unpersuasive.)

In general, words are poor vehicles for thinking about inverse probabilities. It is clear that some verbal links are not symmetric; for example, "roses are red" does not mean that all red flowers are roses. Other verbal links, however, are symmetric; "dirigibles with hydrogen gas are the type that explode" also means that the type of dirigibles that explode are filled with hydrogen gas. It is easy to confuse symmetric and asymmetric verbal links. In fact, linguistic links are notorious for their ambiguity. (Does "the skies are not cloudy all day" mean that the skies are cloudy for only a portion of the day or never cloudy?) And it is possible to express sincere belief in a linguistic phrase without knowing what it means. (How many schoolchildren singing our national anthem know that *o'er* refers to "over" rather than "or"? Or when asked, "How many animals of each kind did Moses take on the Ark?" how many of us confidently answer, "two," without noticing that it was Noah, not Moses, who was supposed to have survived the Biblical flood on an ark.)

But it is difficult for many people to think without words. In fact, some eminent thinkers maintain that it is virtually impossible: "How do we know that there is a sky and that it is blue? Should we know of a sky if we had no name for it?" (Max Muller). "Language is generated by the intellect and generates intellect" (Abalard). "The essence of man is speech" (the Charodogya Upanishad). "In the beginning was the word" (Genesis 1:1). But perhaps the advice of the Lankavatara Sutra is more useful and correct: "Disciples should be on their guard against the seduction of words and sentences and their illusive meaning, for by them the ignorant and dull-witted become entangled and helpless as an elephant floundering around in deep mud." Or perhaps we should cultivate nonverbal thinking patterns such as those of Albert Einstein, who wrote, "The words or language, as they are written or spoken, do not seem to play any role in my mechanism of thought." But concrete, visual images are often no better than words, and images can still produce biased judgments.

Symbolic, especially algebraic representations are effective, but many people are not adept at algebra. Fortunately, graphical methods can be very helpful in representing probability problems and everyday situations. We have used Venn diagrams several times to clarify logical relationships, especially when conditional probabilities are involved. But for most problems we recommend decision trees and probability trees because they are more generally applicable and they are more useful for organizing numerical information relevant to decision problems.

## 8.6 Avoiding Subadditivity and Conjunction Errors

Another flagrant error we have described in judgments, especially those that depend on our sense of similarity and involve category memberships, is the habit of making estimates of several exclusive event probabilities that add up to more than 100%. For example, the probabilities that your car has failed to start because the battery is dead, or because a wire is loose, or because the gas line is plugged, or because the gas tank is empty, or because there is a seat-belt security bar on the ignition sum to 1.55. In its extreme form, subadditivity involves estimating that the probability of a subset, nested event is greater than the probability of a superset, superordinate event in which the subset event is nested (e.g., that Linda is more likely to be a feminist bank teller than any kind of bank teller at all). The problem is termed *subadditivity* because the probability of the whole is judged to be less than that of the sum of its parts—in the case of the conjuncture fallacy, less than that of a single part.

If we diagram the exclusive subset relations for "reasons our car didn't start," we are much less likely to distribute more than 100% of the probability space across the subset events, and we are also more sensible about estimating the basic probabilities of various failures (Figure 8.4). In fact, just reminding people verbally at the time they are making multiple subevent judgments that the sum of mutually exclusive events must not exceed 1.00, if they are using probability numbers correctly, is sufficient to produce more rational, comparative reasoning about event probabilities. Lori Van Wallendael and Hastie (1990) asked college students to solve some "whodunit" mysteries. Students who had not been reminded that the guilt judgments for different, mutually exclusive suspects needed to sum to unity, exhibited massive subadditivity. When they learned about new incriminating evidence, they increased their belief in the guilt of the most relevant suspect without reducing their suspicions about other suspects. However, when they were reminded of the "hydraulic" property of the mutually exclusive events, then they were more additive, and they traded off guilt and innocence judgments much more reasonably.

Representations like the probability tree or Venn diagram (see Figure 8.5) also reduce conjunction errors. In Section 5.8, we noted that if we draw a Venn diagram of the relationship between "bank tellers" and "bank tellers who are feminists," it is unlikely we will judge the probability (or frequency) of "feminist bank teller" to be higher than "bank teller." A probability tree

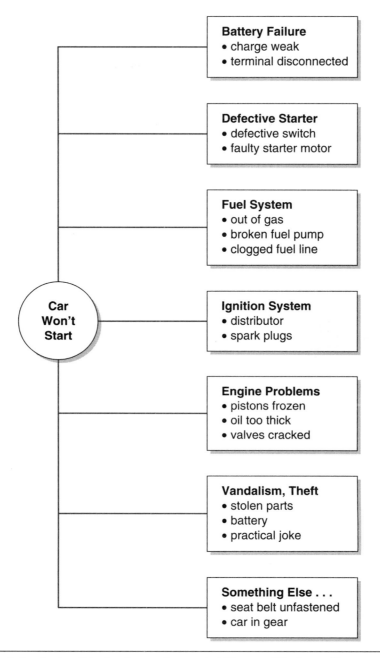

**Figure 8.4**    A plausible, but incomplete probability tree ("fault tree") to represent the reasons a car would not start

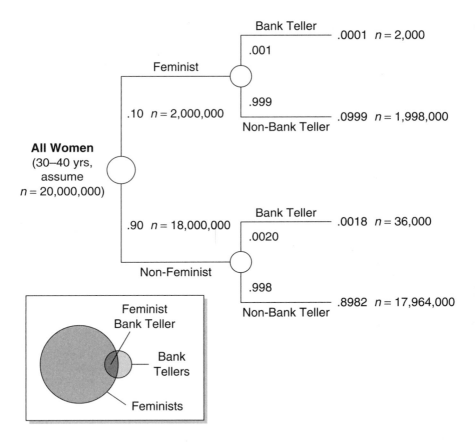

**Figure 8.5**    Probability tree and Venn diagram representations of the Linda the Feminist Bank Teller Problem (Some hypothetical assumptions about frequencies have been made to create plausible, but probably not exactly correct, frequencies: 20,000,000 women in the U.S. population in Linda's age cohort, 20 times more likely that a female bank teller is not a feminist than that she is a feminist, and 2 bank tellers out of every 1,000 women in the population.)

also protects us from this representative thinking error, and thinking about potential Lindas in terms of frequencies further de-biases our thinking. The conjunction error for the Linda the Feminist Bank Teller Problem was committed by 86% of the college students in the original probability format, but when Klaus Fiedler (1982) re-expressed the problem in a *frequency format*, the error rate dropped to about 20% (e.g., "Suppose that there are 100 people who fit Linda's description; how many of them are bank tellers? Bank tellers and active in the feminist movement?").

# 8.7 The Other Side of the Coin:
# The Probability of a Disjunction of Events

Consider a set of events 1, 2, . . . $k$. Suppose, moreover, that these events are *independent*—that is, whether or not one occurs has no effect on whether any of the others occurs, singly or in combination. (For a more precise definition of *independence*, see the Appendix.) Let the probabilities that the events occur be. $p_1 \times p_2 \times \ldots \times p_k$ What is the probability that *at least one* will occur? That is, what is the probability of the *disjunction* (as opposed to the conjunction) of these events? The probability of the disjunction is equal to 1 minus the probability that none will occur. But the probability that the first will *not* occur is $(1 - p_1)$, the probability that the second will not occur is $(1 - p_2)$, and so on. Hence, the probability that none will occur is $(1 - p_1) \times (1 - p_2) \times \ldots$ $(1 - p_k)$. (This also is explained in the Appendix.) The product may be quite small, even though each $(1 - p_i)$ is quite large, because each $p_i$ is small. For example, let the probabilities of six events be .10, .20, .15, .20, .15, and .10, respectively. Then the product of the $(1 - p_i)$'s is, once again, .90 × .80 × .85 × .80 × .85 × .90 = .37, so the probability that at least one of these events will occur is 1 − .37 = .63. The result occurs even though each separate event is quite improbable (the average being .15).

Just as we tend to overestimate the probability of conjunctions of events (to the point of committing the conjunction probability fallacy), we tend to *underestimate* the probability of disjunctions of events. There seem to be two reasons for this. First, our judgments tend to be made on the basis of the probabilities of individual components; as illustrated, even though those probabilities may be quite low, the probability of the disjunction may be quite high. We attribute this error primarily to the anchor-and-(under-) adjust estimation process. Second, any irrational factors that lead us to underestimate the probabilities of the component events—such as difficulty of imagining the event—may lead us to underestimate the probability of the disjunction as a whole. Occasionally, this underestimation problem is intuitively understood. For example, in their summations, lawyers avoid arguing from disjunctions in favor of conjunctions. (The great trial attorney, Richard "Racehorse" Haynes, illustrated the error of "arguing in the alternative" with the humorous example: "Say you sue me because you say my dog bit you. Well, now this is my defense: My dog doesn't bite. And, second, in the alternative, my dog was tied up that night. And, third, I don't believe you really got bit. And, fourth, I don't have a dog." Or more simply, Bart Simpson's famous defense: "I didn't do it; no one saw me do it; you can't prove anything.") Rationally, of course, disjunctions are *much* more probable than are conjunctions.

There is evidence for a *disjunction probability fallacy* comparable to the conjunction probability error—such a fallacy consisting of the belief that a disjunction of events is *less* probable than a single event comprising it (Bar-Hillel & Neter, 1993). But, of course, logically when the probability of A *and* B is higher than the probability of A alone (the conjunction fallacy), then the probability of not-A would be less than that of not-A *or* not-B. This is because the probability of not-A is 1 minus that of A and the probability of not-A or not-B is 1 minus that of A and B. So the former fallacy implies the latter. In fact, if we can arbitrarily decide what we call A and not-A (for example, call A not-being-a-feminist and not-A, being-a-feminist) and B and not-B (call B not-being-a-bank-teller and not-B, being-a-bank-teller), then aren't the two fallacious inequalities equivalent? Our answer is that they are logically equivalent, but not psychologically equivalent. We think in terms of categories, not their complements (negations). To a trained logician, not-A is as well-defined a category as A, but A's (which may have many associations) rather than not-A's (which tend to have few) crowd our minds. It takes a Sherlock Holmes to understand that the fact that the dog *did not bark* constitutes a crucial clue (implying that the dog was familiar with the criminal)—that is, to treat not-barking as an event.

## 8.8 Changing Our Minds: Bayes's Theorem

A very common judgment problem arises when we receive some new information about a hypothesis that we want to evaluate, and we need to update our judgment about the likelihood of the hypothesis. Consider a medical example that was introduced by physicians interested in how doctors and patients would interpret the new information provided by medical tests (Casscells, Schoenberger, & Graboys, 1978):

> The prevalence of breast cancer is 1% for women over age 40. A widely used test, mammography, gives a positive result in 10% of women without breast cancer, and in 80% of women with breast cancer. What is the probability that a woman in this age class who tests positive actually has breast cancer? (p. 999)

When David Eddy (1988) presented this problem to practicing physicians, an amazing 95 out of 100 responded with the answer, "About 75%." That estimate is dramatically incorrect—and in a context where these physicians deal with this type of judgment on a daily basis and where the numbers in the problem reflect the actual conditions surrounding mammography test results. What is the correct answer? About 7%—an order of magnitude lower than the physicians' modal answer!

One way to calculate the correct answer is symbolic, algebraic. If we study the rules of probability, it is not difficult to see that the following formula applies to this question (an informal derivation is provided in the Appendix, Section A.5):

$$p(\text{cancer}|\text{positive test}) = \frac{p(\text{cancer}_{\text{before the test}}) \times p(\text{positive test}|\text{cancer})}{p(\text{positive test}_{\text{with or without cancer}})}$$

The original problem statement gives us the probabilities we need to plug in on the right-hand side of the equation: $p(\text{cancer}_{\text{before the test}}) = .01$; $p(\text{positive test}|\text{cancer}) = .80$, and $p(\text{positive test}_{\text{with or without cancer}}) = .107$. The last term requires a little precalculation: If the person has cancer (1% of the women we are concerned with), the numerator gives us the probability .008 (= .01 × .80); if the person does *not* have cancer (99% of the women we are concerned with), we get the probability .099 (= .99 × .10); and since the only possibilities are having cancer or not having cancer, we add those two probabilities, .099 + .008 = .107. If we put all the numbers into the right-hand side of the equation, we get the following: (.01 × .80)/.107 or .075. That conclusion follows from the even simpler one, that $p(\text{cancer}|\text{positive test}) \times p(\text{positive test}) = p(\text{cancer}) \times p(\text{positive test}|\text{cancer})$.

The famous and useful formula for updating beliefs about a hypothesis (e.g., that an event is true or will occur) given evidence is called *Bayes' theorem* after Thomas Bayes, the British clergyman who derived it algebraically in his quest for a rational means to assess the probability that God exists *given* the (to him) abundant evidence of God's works. (Amazingly, almost any reader of this book can derive this profound theorem from the four basic principles of probability theory, once the derivation problem has been clearly stated; see the Appendix. The formula is also easily expressed as a probability tree; see Figure 8.6 for the application to the Eddy cancer diagnosis problem.)

$$p(\text{hypothesis}|\text{evidence}) = \frac{p(\text{evidence}|\text{hypothesis}) \times p(\text{hypothesis})}{p(\text{evidence})}$$

What systematic errors do people make as they try to update their beliefs about an event when they receive new information relevant to the judgment? We want to repeat our admonition that it is often difficult to figure out exactly which part of the judgment process is the fundamental error, and even harder to assign the error to a specific misconception or misapplication of probability theory. In the Eddy mammography example, we would describe the error as a failure to consider the alternative hypothesis, and to

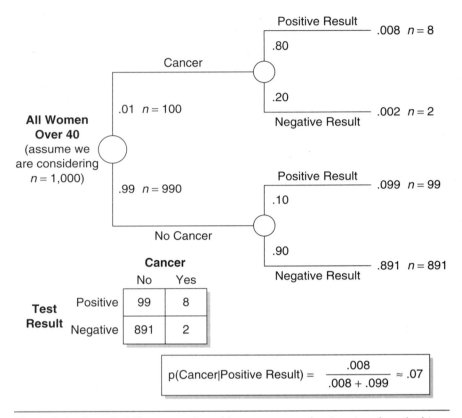

**Figure 8.6**    A probability tree and a table to represent the situation described in the Eddy cancer diagnosis problem

ignore the probability that the evidence would be observed even if the hypothesis is false—that is, what we symbolized as $p$(positive test|no cancer) in our example above is often ignored. This focus on the salient hypothesis is a general habit of our attention and reasoning systems; we might even attribute it to the general bias toward available, salient information, which we allow to dominate our judgments. (Nickerson, 1998, provides a thorough introduction to this *confirmation bias*.) A second error is to ignore the base rates of occurrence of simple events (e.g., to underweight the fact that only 1% of the patients walking into the clinic are going to have breast cancer—before we know the results of any test).

We've encountered the bad habit of ignoring base rates before, most obviously in Section 5.8 where we found that errors in judging Penelope's major field of study and errors in judging occupations of engineers versus lawyers were due to a reliance on similarity between personality sketches and social stereotypes. But conceptualizing the errors with reference to probability theory, instead of psychology, we would say people were under-using or ignoring background base rates. Here's another example judgment from Bar-Hillel (1980) in which it is obvious that base rates are being ignored (again, make your own judgment before you read our analysis):

> Two cab companies operate in River City, the Blue and the Green, named according to the colors of the cabs they run. [A total of] 85% of the cabs are Blue and the remaining 15% are Green.
>
> A cab was involved in a hit-and-run accident at night. An eyewitness later identified the cab as Green. The Court tested the witness's ability to distinguish between Blue and Green cabs under nighttime visibility conditions. It found the witness was able to identify each color correctly about 80% of the time, but he confused it with the other color about 20% of the time.
>
> What do you think is the probability that the cab in the accident was Green, as the witness claimed? (p. 211)

Let's represent the information of the problem in terms of Bayes' theorem: In this problem, the most relevant base rate corresponds to the proportions of green and blue cabs on the streets, and it should be used as the starting point for the judgment—the "prior probability" of green before any case-specific evidence (e.g., the witness's testimony) is heard. What Bar-Hillel (1980) found, when she presented the problem to a varied sample of people, was almost universal failure to consider the base rate; once they heard about the concrete, case-specific eyewitness testimony, the base rate faded into the background. Thus, Bar-Hillel found that the modal response was the eyewitness's accuracy rate (.80), with no adjustment for the base rate information. If we plug the numbers into the Bayes' theorem formula (see Figure 8.7), we get the correct answer: .41.

We should acknowledge here that there is ambiguity in the written problem statement: Is the witness accuracy already conditioned on the base rate of green cabs, a posterior probability, because the witness was tested under "15% green cabs" conditions? Moreover, there are other interpretations that depart from the information in the problem statement by assuming that readers import various kinds information into their problem representations from their background experiences with taxicabs or traffic accidents or eyewitnesses (see, for example, Birnbaum, 1983). However, there is no direct evidence that these alternative representations are conceived of by anyone except the experts intent on criticizing Bar-Hillel's conclusions by speculating about alternate representations. In fact, unpublished data collected by

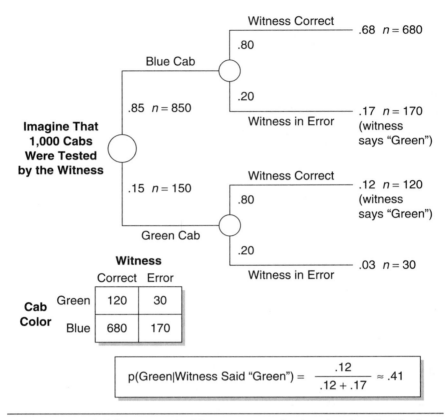

**Figure 8.7**    Probability tree and table to represent the situation described in the Cab identification problem

one of the authors (Hastie) is most consistent with Bar-Hillel's interpretation that college students comprehend the problem as in the Bayes formula format presented above, but ignore the base rate information.

How can these errors be remedied? First, we noted in Section 5.10 that when the problem statement links the base rate information more strongly to the outcomes in the situation, especially when causal relationships make the connection, people are more likely to incorporate the base rates into their judgments. Bar-Hillel (1980) created a version of the cab problem that stated, "Police statistics show that in 15% of traffic accidents involving taxi cabs, a Green cab was involved." With this causal connection, the majority of people presented with the problem used the base rate information to adjust down from the 80% value implied by the witness's testimony, though the adjustment (as we would expect) was insufficient. Perhaps this finding can be interpreted as a vote for the underlying rationality of our natural tendency to create and rely on situation models in the form of causal scenarios (see also Krynski & Tenenbaum, 2007). We speculate that causal scenario–based reasoning may be an intuitive way to keep track of the most important relationships among events—important when we need to make predictions, diagnoses, or just update our "situation models." However, spontaneous scenario-based reasoning cannot be sufficient by itself; most of the probability errors we have discussed are still prevalent when this mode of judgment is adopted.

Second, use of symbolic algebraic representations, like those we provide above, has a big impact on judgments. In medical diagnosis situations, there are now software decision aids that query physicians for relevant "prior probabilities" and "evidence diagnosticity" estimates and then compute the posterior probabilities. These systems improve performance in repeated clinical judgment situations, although there still seems to be a psychological mismatch between physicians' intuitive reasoning and the systems' response formats. People still have difficulty estimating the probability of observing the evidence (test result, witness testimony, symptom) *given* that the condition or disease was *not* present. But if a person making a judgment can deliberately spell out the problem in terms of the Bayes equation and then identify all the relevant information, performance improves. Even if the person only uses the formula to organize his or her thinking (but not to calculate), we expect improvements from (i) identification of incomplete and ambiguous descriptions of the judgment problem, (ii) consideration of nonobvious information necessary to make the calculation, and (iii) motivation to search for specific information and to think about focal hypothesis–disconfirming information (e.g., the probability that the witness says "green," *given* the cab was really blue; the probability that the test is positive, *given* that the patient did not have cancer; the probability of a DNA match, *even if* the defendant was not the criminal).

Third, and most helpful, we recommend the use of diagrams to represent the to-be-judged situation and to guide information search, inferences, and calculations as in Figures 8.6 and 8.7. Note that it is usually best to order the tree causally and temporally. In the mammogram diagnostic test situation, start with the fact that the prevalence of breast cancer is 1% for women over age 40. Then, consider the fact that the mammogram test is performed and it gives a positive result in 10% of women without breast cancer, and in 80% of women with breast cancer. What is the probability that a woman in this age class who tests positive actually has breast cancer? Finally, we recommend thinking about the situation in terms of frequencies; for example, imagine that 1,000 women are tested.

The task of reasoning coherently and rationally about probabilities is not a classroom homework problem anymore. All of us are more and more likely to encounter probabilistic evidence, presented as probability numbers in courtrooms and hospitals and financial investments. Consider the months of testimony and debate about DNA match and blood type evidence in the O. J. Simpson criminal and civil trials—or this woman reporter's story about a consultation with her physician after a mass was discovered in her breast (Kushner, 1976):

> "I'd like you to get a xero-mammogram. It's a new way to make mammograms—pictures of the breasts."
>
> "Is it accurate?"
>
> He shrugged, "Probably about as accurate as any picture can be. You know," he warned, "even if the reading is negative—which means the lump isn't malignant—the only way to be certain is to cut the thing out and to look at it under a microscope."

The woman then discussed the problem with her husband.

> "What did the doctor say?"
>
> "He wants to do a xero-mammogram. Then, whatever the result is, the lump will have to come out."
>
> "So why get the X-ray in the first place?"
>
> "It's something to go on, I guess. And our doctor says it's right about 85 percent of the time. . . . So, first I've scheduled an appointment to have a thermogram. If that's either positive or negative, and if it agrees with the Xerox pictures from the mammogram, the statistics say the diagnosis will be 95 percent reliable."

Is there any possibility that this patient will not have the tests? Or that she will decide not to get the lump biopsied *no matter what the test results?*

## 8.9 Statistical Decision Theory

Our discussion of estimates and judgments under uncertainty raises an important practical and theoretical question: How should we use judgments to decide whether or not to take consequential actions? The normative "should do" answer is provided by *statistical decision theory*. (We can only hint at the importance and sophistication of this area of theory; see also Macmillan & Creelman, 2004; Swets, Dawes, & Monahan, 2000). Let's consider a simple case where a physician assesses the probability that a patient has a serious condition like cancer and has to decide whether to operate or not. (Today, this is usually a joint physician–patient decision, although most patients want the physician to make the decision for them.) The bigger picture for this situation is provided by the scatterplot in Figure 8.8, representing this judgment being made for many similar patients. Millions of decisions can be summarized in this format, and the key question is, "How high does the probability have to be to take action?" Accept or reject, invest or don't invest, commit or withdraw, convict or acquit, evacuate or don't evacuate, retaliate or don't retaliate, and so on.

The answer to the "Should I take action?" question depends on these probabilities (relating your current knowledge and the true condition you're trying to infer) and how much you care about each of the four possible outcomes. (Note that in this simple but realistic example, if we knew for sure what the true condition was, we would know how to act; but since there's uncertainty, we face a tough decision.) More specifically, if we know how we value the outcomes, we can work backward and calculate the threshold probability that prescribes when we should shift from inaction to action, to maximize those values.

Figure 8.8 includes the popular labels for each of the four judgment-outcome possibilities: (a) a "hit" or "true positive" is when the judgment correctly identifies the focal target condition, for example, when the judgment correctly identifies the cancerous condition; (b) a "miss" or "false negative" is when the judgment incorrectly implies the patient does *not* have the condition; (c) a "false alarm" or "false positive" is when the judgment incorrectly implies the patient *does* have the condition; and (d) a "correct rejection" or "true negative" is when the judgment correctly indicates the patient does *not* have the condition. (The figure represents a situation in which 30 people truly have cancer and 170 are healthy out of 200, and where the correlation between the physician's judgment and the presence/absence of cancer is approximately +.65.)

One insight that immediately comes from the scatterplot is that we can control the rates at which the various judgment-outcome combinations occur by varying our threshold to decide to operate. If we set the *operate threshold* at the point where we judge the probability of cancer is .60, we see 15 hits, but also 15 misses (7.5% overall; 15 out of 30, or 50% of those with cancer), but we pay for quite a few false alarms (unnecessary operations—about 10% of all cases; 20 out of 35, or 57% of the operations performed). If we lower the threshold for treatment to judged *p*(cancer) of .50, we

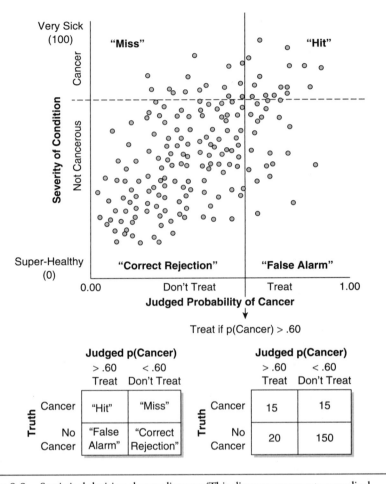

**Figure 8.8**     Statistical decision theory diagram (This diagram represents a medical
decision under uncertainty where a physician makes a judgment of the
probability that a patient has cancer and then acts to treat or not treat the
patient based on that assessment. The problem is represented as a
hypothetical series of judgments for 200 patients, who vary in health status.
The judgment is moderately accurate; $r = .65$ between judgment and true
health status. The judge is depicted as deciding to treat a patient if the judged
$p(\text{CANCER})$ is greater than .60; that set of judgments and outcomes for the
200 patients is summarized in the table at the bottom of the figure in terms
of the statistical decision theory concepts of "hit," "false alarm," "miss," and
"correct rejection." Warning: Different applications of statistical decision
theory may use different organizations of the summary table; the presentation
here is consistent with the conventions of psychological *signal detection
theory*, which is one useful version of statistical decision theory.)

increase hits to 20 (from 15) and reduce misses to 10, but pay for that with more false alarms (30, or 15% overall; 20 out of 35, or 57% of all operations, are on healthy patients).

This is a very important insight that seems to be ignored in many policy discussions: In many cases, more careful thought about what we care about, which errors we most want to avoid, can improve the decision. Often, we cannot increase the accuracy of a diagnosis or other judgment (in this example, we can't increase the diagnostic accuracy of the physician), but we can trade off the two types of errors (and "corrects," too). If misses are most costly, we can lower our threshold for action on the judgment dimension and reduce misses (but at the cost of more false alarms); if false alarms are the costly error, we can move the decision threshold up and reduce that error (trading it for more misses, of course). We often try to avoid these tragic trade-offs by increasing accuracy, so that there is less error of both types to trade off. Thus, we spend billions of dollars every year increasing the accuracy of medical, military, financial, and meteorological forecasts to accomplish just this. But there are very few policy situations in which we can abolish all uncertainty. In most circumstances, we should recognize we are stuck with trade-offs, proceed with a sensible discussion of what we value, and then set a decision threshold accordingly (Hammond, 1996).

If we do face these trade-offs, we need to try to value the various judgment-outcome combinations and then apply statistical decision theory to set a proper decision threshold. For example, suppose that the numbers +100, 0, +30, and +80 represent our values for each of the four outcome states (hit, miss, false alarm, and correct rejection; we stay with our convention of representing values on a 0–100 scale). Notice also that there may be significant disagreements between people about these values. A patient might place the highest value on a "hit" and lowest on a "miss" (as in our ordering on the value scale), while a policy maker might value "correct rejections" more highly and "false alarms" more negatively. To pursue our illustrative example, given a single numerical valuation, we can calculate the decision threshold that yields a maximum on the value function. In this example, the policy with the maximum overall value is attained by setting the decision threshold equal to a judged $p$(cancer) of approximately .55 (we omit the calculation because it involves calculus).

Thus, in many practical situations, we should be thinking harder about values, rather than accuracy. But the determination of values is itself a complex process, even when only one decision maker is involved (see the next two chapters), because everyday alternatives often have many attributes and serve multiple objectives. The task is even more daunting when we must perform an analysis across stakeholders with different personal values, as we must in any organizational or societal policy analysis.

However, these difficulties must not divert us from trying to think harder, more systematically, and from multiple perspectives about the unavoidable trade-offs.

## 8.10 Concluding Comment on Rationality

If a scientific theory cannot state when an event will occur, a skeptic might ask what good it is. In fact, a dedicated behaviorist (if any still exist) might critique this entire book on the grounds that since the phenomena discussed are not controllable, descriptions of them—and the mechanisms hypothesized—are of no scientific value. The answer is that insofar as we are dealing with mental events and decisions of real people in the booming, buzzing confusion of the real world, we can neither predict nor control them perfectly. The qualifier of *ceteris paribus* ("other things being equal") always applies to these phenomena. The uncertainty of predicting actual outcomes in the world is intrinsic to both the problem and the consequences of decision. Of course, it may be said that true scientists should not investigate such uncertain phenomena—that they should perhaps limit themselves to investigating the rate at which a rat presses a bar in an environment where the only moving part is the bar. (What, other than the consequences of manipulating the one thing that can be manipulated, could shape the rat's behavior?) But if all scientists followed this rule and stayed in their neat ivory towers, we would not have meteorology, agricultural science, genetic counseling, computer science, and many other useful applied sciences.

Of course, perfectly rational thought processes do not guarantee true conclusions. It is necessary to have realistic, valid inputs, too. When Hastie was teaching his judgment and decision making course for the first time, he encountered a middle-aged student in a class of 20-year-olds. After a few lectures, the older student introduced himself and explained why he was enrolled in the course. As the student told it, he had suffered a series of apparent misfortunes and was in the midst of a divorce and fighting his employer's efforts to fire him. He said that at first he was confused by the events that were happening to him, but that on reflection he realized that he was actually the subject of a huge "psychology experiment." (In fact, one reason he had come to Harvard to study was because he wanted to meet Professor B. F. Skinner, whom he believed was the experimenter who was manipulating his life.) He went on to cite dozens of instances of inexplicable behaviors and events that only made sense if the hypothesis that he was "in a psychology experiment" was true. Hastie asked for specific examples, but was not much impressed by the strength of the evidence for the student's hypothesis; most of the examples seemed at least as probable under the alternate hypothesis that the student was *not* in a psychology experiment (e.g., "I was interrupted by my wife, and she spoke exactly the words I was thinking, before I could say them myself"; "I was having a drink with a coworker after work, and he mentioned the company was laying off workers, and this happened only days before they told me I was fired"). The bright side of the student's delusional system was that he believed that eventually the experiment would be finished and publicized and that his demonstrated aptitude (for being controlled by the experimenter) would certify his qualities as a leader, who would be trustworthy and accountable in a high public office.

Perhaps the most fascinating part of this anecdote concerns the student's explanation for why he had approached Hastie: He was concerned that he not be irrationally deluded in his interpretation of these events. So, in order to ensure that he not reach a false conclusion, he was attempting to apply the instructor's advice as carefully as he could. After enrolling in Hastie's class, he realized that he needed to deliberately apply Bayes' theorem to evaluate the posterior probability of the hypothesis that "I am the subject of a huge, secret psychology experiment," with reference to the many items of evidence he had accumulated. He wanted help with his calculations to evaluate that hypothesis!

The story did not end that semester. A few months later, the student called on Hastie to testify on his behalf in his lawsuit to retain his job. Psychiatrists for his employer had asserted that he was suffering from massive paranoid delusions (which Hastie found plausible); that Bayes' theorem was part of his delusional system; and furthermore, that the Reverend Thomas Bayes was a figment of his schizophrenic imagination. (Hastie provided a deposition rebutting the psychiatrists' claims that Thomas Bayes was a delusion, although he noted that he was dubious of that posterior probability: $999,999/1,000,000$ and the conclusion that the student was the subject of a massive social experiment. Of course, the experience of producing the deposition also led Hastie to wonder why he was so confident in the existence of a vague historical figure whom he knew of only because a mathematical theorem was named after him.) "Delusions in, delusions out"—no matter how consistent the calculations connecting the two.

What we have attempted to do is to point out factors and thinking styles that lead us all to make irrational judgments and choices (based on those judgments). People will not necessarily engage in these thought processes, any more than a swimmer who panics necessarily attempts to keep his or her head above water. Like a swimmer with survival training, we can learn to counteract the intuitive response and to be more rational—but as with the swimming example, it takes knowledge, self-control, and effort. From a normative perspective, however, learning to specify conditions that facilitate or inhibit certain types of behavior, or to distinguish between productive and nonproductive ways of thinking, is quite an accomplishment for psychologists or other social scientists.

Finally, as will be pointed out in the concluding chapter, people who attempt to grasp the totality of situations in order to predict or control exactly what will happen seldom fare as well as those who seek the more modest goal of living with the uncertainty that is irreducible and determining what we can influence. A person who attempts to understand everything can easily end up understanding nothing. An understanding of irrational forms of thinking is not nothing, even though we cannot predict exactly when such irrationality will occur or always how to control it.

# References

Bar-Hillel, M. (1980). The base-rate fallacy in probability judgments. *Acta Psychologica, 44,* 211–233.

Bar-Hillel, M., & Falk, R. (1982). Some teasers concerning conditional probabilities. *Cognition, 11*(2), 109–122.

Bar-Hillel, M., & Neter, E. (1993). How alike is it versus how likely is it: A disjunction fallacy in probability judgments. *Journal of Personality and Social Psychology, 65,* 1119–1131.

Bennett, D. J. (1998). *Randomness.* Cambridge, MA: Harvard University Press.

Birnbaum, M. H. (1983). Base rates in Bayesian inference: Signal detection analysis of the cab problem. *American Journal of Psychology, 96,* 85–94.

Brase, G. L., Cosmides, L., & Tooby, J. (1998). Individuation, counting, and statistical inference: The role of frequency and whole-object representations in judgment under uncertainty. *Journal of Experimental Psychology: General, 127,* 3–21.

Casscells, W., Schoenberger, A., & Graboys, T. B. (1978). Interpretation by physicians of clinical laboratory results. *New England Journal of Medicine, 299*(18), 999–1001.

Denes-Raj, V., & Epstein, S. (1994). Conflict between intuitive and rational processes: When do people behave against their own better judgment. *Journal of Personality and Social Psychology, 66,* 819–829.

Eddy, D. (1988). Variations in physician practice: The role of uncertainty. In J. Dowie & A. S. Elstein (Eds.), *Professional judgment: A reader in clinical decision making* (pp. 200–211). Cambridge, UK: Cambridge University Press.

Fiedler, K. (1982). Causal schemata: Review and criticism of research on a popular construct. *Journal of Personality and Social Psychology, 42,* 1001–1013.

Gigerenzer, G., & Hoffrage, U. (1995). How to improve Bayesian reasoning without instruction: Frequency formats. *Psychological Review, 102,* 684–704.

Gigerenzer, G., Todd, P. M., & the ABC Research Group. (1999). *Simple heuristics that make us smart.* New York: Oxford University Press.

Hammond, K. R. (1996). *Human judgment and social policy: Irreducible uncertainty, inevitable error, unavoidable injustice.* New York: Oxford University Press.

Hastie, R., & Rasinski, K. A. (1988). The concept of accuracy in social judgment. In D. Bar-Tal & A. W. Kruglanski (Eds.), *The social psychology of knowledge* (pp. 193–208). Cambridge, UK: Cambridge University Press.

Kahneman, D. (2003). A perspective on judgment and choice: Mapping bounded rationality. *American Psychologist, 58,* 697–720.

Kahneman, D., & Lovallo, D. (1993). Timid choices and bold forecasts: A cognitive perspective on risk-taking. *Management Science, 39,* 17–31.

Kahneman, D., & Tversky, A. (1982). On the study of statistical intuitions. *Cognition, 11,* 123–141.

Kahneman, D., & Tversky, A. (1996). On the reality of cognitive illusions. *Psychological Review, 103,* 582–591.

Koriat, A., Lichtenstein, S., & Fischhoff, B. (1980). Reasons for confidence. *Journal of Experimental Psychology: Human Learning and Memory, 6,* 107–118.

Krynski, T. R., & Tenenbaum, J. B. (2007). The role of causality in judgment under uncertainty. *Journal of Experimental Psychology: General, 136,* 430–450.

Kushner, R. (1976, March 24). Breast cancer—the night I found out. *San Francisco Chronicle,* p. C1.

Laplace, P. S. (1951). *A philosophical essay on probabilities* (F. W. Truscott & F. L. Emory, Trans.). New York: Dover. (Original work published 1814)

Lopes, L. L., & Oden, G. D. (1991). The rationality of intelligence. In E. Eels & T. Maruszewski (Eds.), *Poznan studies in the philosophy of the sciences and humanities* (Vol. 21, pp. 225–249). Amsterdam: Rodopi.

Macmillan, N. A., & Creelman, C. D. (2004). *Detection theory: A user's guide* (2nd ed.). Mahwah, NJ: Lawrence Erlbaum.

McGee, G. (1979, February 6). Breast surgery before cancer. *Ann Arbor News,* p. B1 (reprinted from the *Bay City News*).

Meehl, P. E. (1986). Causes and effects of my disturbing little book. *Journal of Personality Assessment, 50,* 370–375.

Nickerson, R. S. (1996). Ambiguities and unstated assumptions in probabilistic reasoning. *Psychological Bulletin, 120,* 410–433.

Nickerson, R. S. (1998). Confirmation bias: A ubiquitous phenomenon in many guises. *Review of General Psychology, 2,* 175–220.

Payne, J. W., Bettman, J. R., & Johnson, E. J. (1993). *The adaptive decision maker.* New York: Cambridge University Press.

Sedlmeier, P. (1997). BasicBayes: A tutor system for simple Bayesian inference. *Behavior Research Methods, Instruments, & Computers, 29,* 328–336.

Sedlmeier, P., & Betsch, T. (2002). *Etc.: Frequency processing and cognition.* New York: Oxford University Press.

Swets, J. A., Dawes, R. M., & Monahan, J. (2000). Better decisions through science. *Scientific American, 283*(4), 70–75.

Van Wallendael, L. R., & Hastie, R. (1990). Tracing the footsteps of Sherlock Holmes: Cognitive representations of hypothesis testing. *Memory & Cognition, 18,* 240–250.

Vos Savant, M. (1991, February 17). Ask Marilyn. *Parade Magazine,* 12.

# 9

# Evaluating Consequences

---

## Fundamental Preferences

*De Gustibus Est Disputandum (You can account for taste.)*

—Anonymous

## 9.1 What Good Is Happiness?

The philosopher Jeremy Bentham (1789/1948) referred to pleasure and pain as the "sovereign masters" that "point out what we ought to do as well as determine what we shall do." Many people would say that *the* goal of decision making is to get outcomes that will make the decision maker happy. Moreover, the U.S. Declaration of Independence describes "the pursuit of happiness" as an "unalienable right." But when decisions are driven by the "pursuit of happiness," it is not the *experiences* of pleasure and pain that are most important. What is most important at the time of decision is our *predictions* and what will make us happy *after* we make a decision. Daniel Kahneman has called this anticipated satisfaction "decision utility," to contrast it with "experienced utility" (the "sovereign master" of behavior referred to by Bentham; Kahneman, Wakker, & Sarin, 1997). Most deliberate decisions involve the prediction of how we will feel about the outcomes that *we think* will occur if we choose one course of action or another. When we make a decision about what to study in school, we think about how we will enjoy the *future* experience and the opportunities we expect to follow;

when we decide to get married, we predict how much we will like spending the rest of our life with that partner; and when we choose a medical option, we evaluate how we will feel about living or dying with the results.

Psychologists are just beginning to uncover the processes that underlie subjective feelings of pleasure and pain, what we're calling *experienced utility*. These processes are mysterious because many evaluative reactions occur very rapidly, preceding full cognitive analysis. People often use the term *gut reaction* to describe an evaluative response, because they have difficulty explaining the basis of that response at a conscious level: "I just know what I will like." There is nothing uncognitive about this kind of unconscious response process. Any cognitive response that involves retrieval from memory or perceptual analysis will be partly implicit; this includes any response of interest to judgment and decision researchers.

Aristotle urged people to seek "the golden mean" between extremes, "moderation in all things" (which we interpret as including moderation in the pursuit of moderation). But why should this golden mean in general be desirable? Clyde Coombs and George Avrunin (1977) have enunciated a very simple principle that implies moderation: "Good things satiate and bad things escalate." This principle has reference to choosing between alternatives that *vary in amount*. Food is an obvious example. After deprivation, an individual derives both important nutritional value and pleasure from initial amounts of food. As the amount increases, however, nutritional importance decreases, and the pleasure in each mouthful decreases as well. These good things *satiate*. On the other hand, the possibly pernicious effects of calories, additives, processed sugars, fats, and so on, increase as food consumption continues. Moreover, the impact of these pernicious effects *escalates* and intensifies. For example, many of us believe that 500 extra calories per day are more than twice as bad for the eater as 250 extra calories per day (being 30% overweight is more than twice as bad as being 15% overweight).

Another of Coombs and Avrunin's (1977) examples is the length of a vacation. The first few days of getting away from it all are delightful. Soon, however, the vacationer begins to adapt to the new environment, and its positive qualities become less salient. The two-hundredth view of a mountain or a palace or a Rembrandt painting is less thrilling than the third. (There is an important exception to this over-general statement in that under some conditions, repeated exposure to subtle experiences—we're thinking about music, art, and literature here—can produce a deeper sense of appreciation and more satisfaction.) In addition, interesting challenges gradually become hassles. At the same time, the amount of drudgery upon returning home that is necessary to make up for lost time begins to mount. Because drudgery is an escalating phenomenon (2 hours devoted to drudgery is more than twice as bad as 1 hour), this bad characteristic of vacations also escalates with time (amount). The principle that "good things satiate and bad things escalate" can be visualized with the simple graph in Figure 9.1.

When the good, satiating characteristics (+) are added to the bad, escalating characteristics (−), the result is a *single-peaked function* that has a maximum value of a moderate amount (the dotted line in Figure 9.1). Net welfare (positive combined with negative) is maximized at moderate amounts. Coombs and Avrunin (1977) have proven that if (i) good characteristics satiate (the function relating goodness to amount having a slope that is positive and *decreasing*) and (ii) bad things escalate (the function relating bad characteristics to amount having a slope that is negative and decreasing—becoming more negative), and (iii) the negative function is more rapidly changing than the positive one, then (iv) the resulting sum of good and bad experiences (that is, the sum of the good characteristics function and the bad characteristics function) will *always* be single-peaked. In fact, a single-peaked function results from any additive combination where the sum starts off positive from 0,0 and the absolute value of the slope of the utility for bad characteristics is greater

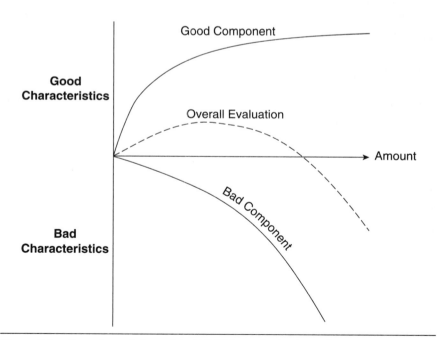

**Figure 9.1**   Coombs and Avrunin's (1977) hypothesis about the two components underlying single-peaked preference functions

everywhere than the absolute value for good characteristics. Furthermore, the "flat maximum" nature of this peak in Figure 9.1 is common. It is often very difficult to discriminate among the neighboring "good experiences."

The important point here is that many experiences exhibit a single-peaked preference function relating the amount of the experience (food consumed, days on vacation) to the associated pleasure (pain); in other words, we have personal "ideal points" on amount-of-experience dimensions. And notice that different people are likely to have different locations for that ideal peak: Ken doesn't like much sugar in his coffee at all, whereas Barbie likes a ton of sugar; 11 days vacation for Barbie, 3 days for Ken; 1 child is just right for Barbie, 4 is Ken's most preferred number; and so on.

Furthermore, many experiences can evoke positive evaluations and negative evaluations in parallel, followed by an integration of the two more primitive reactions, just as Coombs and Avrunin (1977) hypothesized. The evidence for this two-channel hypothesis comes from research conducted by Tiffany Ito and John Cacioppo (1999) in which they presented pictures of evaluatively evocative scenes to experimental participants while the researchers recorded their brain activity. Physiological studies had suggested pleasure and pain involve different neural circuits and different neurotransmitters (the family of dopamines associated with pleasure, the family of acetylcholine transmitters associated with pain). Consistent with this notion, Ito and Cacioppo found that some evaluative reactions are massively ambivalent (a recovering alcoholic's reactions to a glass of whiskey, a dieter's reaction to a rich dessert) and illustrate the workings of both channels simultaneously, independently, and in parallel.

Another discovery about evaluations of experience is that, even immediately after they occur, the sum of the momentary evaluations is not equal to the summary remembered from the experience. Donald Redelmeier and Daniel Kahneman (1996) asked people undergoing painful medical procedures (e.g., a colonoscopy, in which a medical instrument the size of a small baseball bat is inserted into the victim's rectum and moved through the large intestine) to report on their current levels of pain throughout the procedure. Then, immediately after, the researchers asked for a global rating of the painfulness of the whole experience. They found that a general *peak-end* evaluation rule applied to pain and pleasure experiences, such that only the level of the most intense part of the total experience and the final level of pain/pleasure needed to be considered to predict the summary evaluation.

An implication of the peak-end principle is *duration neglect*: People tend to be surprisingly insensitive to the length of the experience. Kahneman conducted a neat demonstration of the power of duration neglect and the "end" of the experience to determine overall evaluation. Experimental participants were exposed to two unpleasant ice-water immersion experiences: (a) immersion for 60 sec at 14 degrees Celsius and (b) immersion for 60 sec at 14 degrees with an unannounced shift to 30 more seconds at 15. When given a choice of which of the two unpleasant experiences to repeat, a majority (65%) of the participants chose the longer experience—without noticing that it must have been objectively worse than the shorter experience that was embedded in it!

Psychologists have designed programs intended to increase overall personal happiness (Diener & Biswas-Diener, 2008). The basic problem with this stems from the notion of *hedonic relativism*. As Philip Brickman and Donald Campbell (1971) put it, "How can we get off of the hedonic treadmill?" One psychologist, Allen Parducci (1995), has invented a "happiness game" in which players choose amounts of play money to receive and are taught, via feedback, to choose according to the author's range-frequency theory of happiness. However, given what we know about feelings of wellbeing in general, our best advice is not to overemphasize predicted happiness in making decisions, but rather deliberately to consider other aspects of decision alternatives and their consequences. (We give more advice on how to decide in Chapter 10.) For most people, an ambient sense of well-being is a moderately stable individual difference. Some people are usually a bit more optimistic and happy than others, and some are usually a bit below the norm, but for most of us there are modest perturbations up and down around a fairly stable "happiness set point"; in other words, global feelings of personal well-being seem to behave a lot like our body weight.

Sonja Lyubomirsky (2008) tells us that even though personal happiness set points have a big influence (she estimates 50%), we can still increase our capacity for happiness by working on it. She provides a set of exercises to increase happiness essentially by "counting our blessings" and improving our social relationships (e.g., by more frequently expressing our gratitude to others). Others prescribe ways to improve our choices by selecting options and experiences that we evaluate because of their inherent satisfactions and to which we do not adapt so quickly (e.g., Hsee, Xu, & Tang, 2008). And still others provide a catalog of "thieves of happiness" with recommendations on how to avoid them (Lykken, 1999).

It is important to realize that happiness and related feelings of well-being are not the only considerations in the evaluation of consequences. Many times we focus on other aspects of the expected consequences of our actions, and sometimes we appear to make decisions in a non-consequentialist manner: "I didn't decide to put my newspaper in the recycle basket; I'm just the kind of person who doesn't litter." "I didn't vote because I thought I would have an impact on the outcome of the election; I voted because I think every good citizen should do so." And, of course, impulsivity can play an important role in such decisions: "I didn't decide to tailgate the car in front of me; I was just try-ing to get to the airport in time for my flight." "I didn't decide to have sex; I did it because I could."

## 9.2 The Role of Emotions in Evaluations

Everyone knows that emotions play a significant role in decision making and choice. But it has been difficult to make progress in specifying that role. One obstacle to progress is that there is little consensus on a precise definition of the concept of emotion. Paul Ekman and Richard Davidson (1994) surveyed their colleagues' views in an attempt to identify points of consensus. They titled their concluding section, "What *Most* Students of Emotion Agree About" (emphasis added), and comment, "We originally did not include the word 'most' in the title of this section" (p. 412). They explain that they *could not find any topics* on which all agreed.

We don't hope to solve the problem of a universal definition of *emotion* in this book, but for present purposes, we think four concepts will be useful: emotions, feelings, moods, and evaluations. We define *emotion* as reactions to motivationally significant stimuli and situations, usually including three components: a cognitive appraisal, a "signature" physiological response, and phenomenal experiences. We would add that emotions usually occur in reaction to perceptions of *changes* in the current situation that have hedonic consequences. Second, we propose that the term *mood* be reserved for longer-duration background states of our physiological (autonomic) system and the accompanying conscious *feelings*. Note, the implication is that emo-tions and moods are not always conscious, and that the phenomenal experi-ence component is not a necessary element of an emotional reaction. Finally, we suggest that the word *evaluation* be used to refer to hedonic, pleasure-pain, good–bad judgments of consequences.

Judgment and decision-making researchers have only recently begun to study the distinctive role of emotions in decision-making processes. Decision making had long been viewed as a rational, cognitive process. Emotion, if considered at all, was just one more "input" into a global evaluation or util-ity. We would still assign a major role to anticipated emotional responses in the evaluation of the value or utility (either *decision utility* or *experienced utility*) of an outcome of a course of action; people usually try to predict how they will feel about an outcome and use that anticipated feeling to evaluate and then decide.

One way to avoid the confusions surrounding the concept of emotion is to study a simple situation in which operational definitions are generally accepted. Thus, some of the most illuminating research, especially on the relationships between behavioral and neural-physiological substrates, has been conducted in the well-defined fear conditioning paradigm with non-human subjects. The operational definition is with reference to a fear conditioning paradigm in which the experimental subject, usually a rat, is presented with a novel stimulus, usually a sound, paired with an unpleasant, mild electric shock. After the sound has been paired with the electric shock on several trials, so that the sound signals the shock, the sound alone produces a variety of fearful responses (freezing, defecating, suppression of pain responses, stress hormone release, and reflex potentiation). One of the strengths of the fear conditioning paradigm is the great diversity of reactions that are reliably produced in the animal, a diversity that is best explained by postulating a central "fear" response. Joseph LeDoux (1996), Edward Rolls (1999), and their colleagues have made impressive progress tracing out the neural and biochemical systems that underlie conditioned fear responses in rats and other animal models. These scientists have mapped the mostly non-cortical "circuits" and have assigned a central role to the amygdala in anxiety and fear responses.

One important message from this research is that the precursors of many emotional responses are unconscious and will be mysterious to the person experiencing them. How often do we become puzzled by an inexplicable reaction to a situation or person or even deny a strong emotional reaction that is obvious to everyone except ourselves: "I am *not* angry!" he screamed. The primary function assigned to the emotions by these researchers is that of a fast emergency response system. LeDoux (1996) writes that the subcortical fear system processes information more quickly than the conscious cerebral systems, and that this "quick and dirty pathway . . . allows us to begin to respond to potentially dangerous stimuli before we fully know what the stimulus is" (p. 274).

More generally, there seems to be agreement on the conclusion that an early, automatic reaction to almost any personally relevant object or event is a good–bad evaluation. Many behavioral scientists have concluded that an evaluation occurs very quickly and includes emotional feelings and distinctive somatic-physiological events. Robert Zajonc (1980) was one of the first to emphasize the theme that, in the words of the mathematician Blaise Pascal, "The heart has its reasons which reason knows nothing of." In support of his claims, Zajonc cited anecdotal and experimental evidence for a dissociation between analytic, cognitive responses and intuitive, emotional responses. He started with examples from memory-based judgments: How often have you been reminded of a book or a movie and know instantly that you liked it, a lot, but are unable to recall any specific details from it to explain your evaluation? In subsequent, experimental research studying online judgments, Zajonc demonstrated that evaluative reactions occur very quickly and often before or instead of cognitive recognition.

Cognitive neuroscientists have attempted to describe the properties of the neural-physiological processes that underlie these rapid evaluations. John Cacciopo, Tiffany Ito, and others have argued that there is a *bivariate* evaluative response system with two neurally independent circuits, one (dopamine-mediated) assessing positivity, one (acetylcholine-mediated) assessing negativity. Richard Davidson (1999) and his colleagues who study long-term individual differences in affective style (we would use the term *mood*) have found that people with relatively active right prefrontal hemispheric areas tend to exhibit more positive ambient moods and react more positively to stimulus events, while left prefrontal activation is associated with more negative moods and emotional reactions. Perhaps the most fascinating results concerning the role of emotion come from the laboratory of Antonio Damasio at the University of Iowa. Damasio (1994) argues that we humans, much like LeDoux's rats, have an emotional signaling system that helps us make quick decisions and decide when our slower deliberative cognitive systems are overwhelmed with too much information. (We'll review his work in detail in Chapter 13.) What's especially important here is the emphasis on the helpful, adaptive role of emotions—the claim is that without them, we'd make much worse decisions. This is a sharp contrast with the traditional emphasis in religion and Freudian psychology on the notion that emotions play a troublemaking role in decisions and interfere with clear, rational thinking processes. (Remember our discussion of visceral emotions in Section 9.1.)

Another recent conclusion is that experienced utility is intensified if it produces regret or rejoicing, and especially if it is a surprise. Barbara Mellers and her colleagues (Mellers, Schwartz, & Ritov, 1999) have designed a decision task to capture these reactions. In her experiments, subjects are either told or not told the payoffs returned by gambles they chose not to play, in addition to being given the outcomes from chosen gambles. This method allowed her to produce regret effects (e.g., when the non-chosen gamble pays off with a much better outcome than the chosen one, even more so if the payoff probability for the non-chosen gamble was low) and rejoicing effects (when the non-chosen gamble turned out much worse than the one chosen). However, it is not so clear under what conditions people actually infer and consider counterfactual emotions at the time they make the decisions—that is, under what conditions regret and rejoicing affect decision utility as well as experienced utility. Research on emotions and decision making is a fast-moving frontier in behavioral and neuroscience research with many new results every day (more on this subject in Chapter 13).

# 9.3 The Value of Money

In the 1923 edition of *Webster's International Dictionary*, the first definition of *value* is "a quality of a thing or activity according to which its worth or degree of worth is estimated"; subsequent definitions concern intrinsic desirability, and later ones talk about market equivalence in terms of money or goods. By the 1968 edition, in contrast, the first five definitions explicitly concern *monetary equivalents*: "1. A fair or proper equivalent in money . . . fair price. 2. The worth of a thing in matter of goods at a certain time; market price. 3. The equivalent (of something) in money. 4. Estimated or appraised worth or price. 5. Purchasing power." Only the sixth 1968 definition corresponds to the first 1923 definition. Hence, even in everyday usage, *value* has come to be almost synonymous with *monetary equivalent*. The more general concept of the degree of worth or desirability specific to the decision maker, as opposed to mere money, is better termed *utility*. Even that term is ambiguous, however, because the dictionary definition of *utility* is "immediate usefulness," and that is not what decision theorists have in mind when they discuss utility. Our own preferred term is *personal value—* to the decision maker. Nonetheless, most of the examples we discuss in this chapter involve personal value assigned to money, although the findings we describe apply to personal value more generally.

The standard account of valuation by economists and philosophers focuses on what a psychologist would call the psychophysical relationship between objective dimensions of experience and the subjective value derived from it. (Coombs's single-peaked curve [in Section 9.1] is in that tradition.) To understand the psychophysical approach to values and utilities, it may be helpful to take a brief historical excursion, going back to the 1850s. In that period, many psychologists asked a simple question: How much must the physical intensity of a stimulus be augmented for a person to notice the difference? For example, if a person is first given a 100-gram weight, how much heavier must another weight be for him or her to notice that it is in fact heavier? Psychologist Ernst Heinrich Weber (1795–1878) noted that, in general, the amount a stimulus must be incremented (or decremented) physically for people to notice a difference is proportional to the stimulus magnitude itself; that is, it must be incremented (or decremented) by a certain *fraction* of its physical intensity in order to achieve what is technically termed a *just noticeable difference*. (The standard procedure currently used for determining the just noticeable difference is to require people to judge which of two stimuli is more intense, and then to define this noticeable difference as occurring whenever the subjects are correct 75% of the time; that figure is chosen by defining the just noticeable difference as the intensity at which people can note a difference 50% of the time, and assuming that when they cannot note it they guess correctly 50% of the time; 50% + [50% of 50%] = 75%.)

The proportion that stimuli must be incremented or decremented to obtain a just noticeable difference in intensity has been termed a *Weber fraction*. The Weber fraction for lifted weights, for example, is approximately 1/30. The fact that this fraction is more or less constant for any particular type of sensory intensity has been termed *Weber's law*. It does not hold exactly over all dimensions and ranges of intensity, but it is useful in research and practice as a rough approximation.

In the 1880s, the psychologist Gustav Fechner (1801–1887) proposed that just noticeable differences could be conceptualized as units of *psychological intensity*, as opposed to physical intensity. This means that psychological intensity is a logarithm of physical intensity, and such a proposal became known as *Fechner's law*. Again, it does not hold over all dimensions and ranges of intensity, but it is a good approximate rule. In fact, it has been so well accepted that when the psychological intensity of noise was measured in bells and decibels, these units were defined as the logarithm of the physical amplitude. (A *bell* is a tenfold increase in physical amplitude, while a *decibel* is an increase of 1.26; $1.26^{10} = 10$; hence, the logarithm of $1.26^{10} =$ 10 times the logarithm of 1.26; that is, 10 decibels are equal to a bell.) This logarithmic function is illustrated in Figure 9.2.

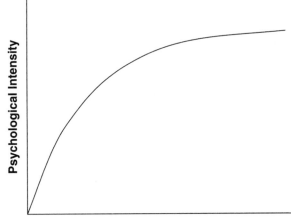

**Figure 9.2**    An illustration of the logarithmic functional relationship summarized in Fechner's law and later proposed by Daniel Bernoulli as a general value function relating objective outcomes like an amount of money to subjective satisfaction

The logarithmic function follows what may be termed the *law of diminishing returns,* or the *law of decreasing marginal returns.* Independently, economists have proposed that this law also describes not only sensory intensities, but also the *utility* (both decision utility and experienced utility) of money and possessions for individuals. Two million dollars would be worth less (have a lower personal value) than twice the value of $1 million to the reader of this book—even when these two amounts refer to money after taxes. This diminishing returns characteristic of what is termed the *utility function* for money need not yield a precise logarithmic pattern.

This function (Figure 9.2) was originally proposed by Daniel Bernoulli, a Swiss mathematician and physicist who lived in the 18th century. His proposal was the first clear statement of the principle that subjective satisfaction is not directly (linearly) related to objective amounts, and it is enormously appealing intuitively—who would disagree that the difference between nothing and $10 is much more salient, palpable, and pleasure-producing than the difference between $100 and $110 or between $1,000 and $1,010? It is tempting to try to relate this function to Coombs and Avrunin's (1977) derivation of the single-peaked preference curve. Certainly Coombs had the general principle of diminishing returns in mind when he proposed the "good things satiate" portion of his model. However, it is more correct to suppose that the Bernoullian utility function reflects both Coombs's positive and negative substrates and to imagine that it is single-peaked, too. This would mean that there is such a thing as too much money—a point at which harassment, social enmity, threats of kidnapping, and other anti-wealth or anti-celebrity actions would become so aversive that the curve would peak and more wealth would be less desirable.

The assumption of a diminishing marginal returns utility function relating dollar gains to utility has been a cliché in economic theorizing, and most research demonstrates that our evaluations of gains show a negatively accelerating, diminishing returns pattern. In the late 1970s, Kahneman and Tversky (1979) proposed what they termed *prospect theory* as a descriptive theory of decision behavior. A basic tenet of this theory is that the law of diminishing returns applies to good *and* bad objective consequences of decisions. There are many components of this theory, which we discuss extensively in Chapter 12, but only two of them need concern us here:

1. An individual views monetary consequences in terms of changes from a *reference level,* which is usually the individual's current reference point (usually the status quo). The values of the outcomes for both positive and negative consequences of the choice then have the diminishing-returns characteristic as they "move away" from that reference point.

2. The resulting value function is steeper for losses than for gains.

The addition of a moveable reference level is the major difference between prospect theory and traditional economic utility theories. Although in many situations it seems obvious how the context of a decision problem determines a reference point, the specification of behavioral principles to predict reference points is one of the most urgent research problems confronting modern prospect theory.

Consider the following choices: Imagine you have just received $200. Which of the following options would you prefer?

Option 1: You receive an additional $100.

Option 2: A fair coin is tossed. If it lands heads, you receive an additional $200; if it lands tails, you receive nothing more.

Most people prefer Option 1, the sure additional $100.

Now consider a variation on the first pair of options: Imagine you have just received $400, but there is a penalty attached. You must choose one of the two penalty options.

Penalty Option 1: You must give back $100.

Penalty Option 2: A fair coin is tossed. If it lands heads, you must give back $200; if it lands tails, you may keep all of the money ($400).

Now, presented with the penalty options, most people prefer the second alternative.

If we apply the prospect theory principles summarized above, we can see that a gain of $100 has, by the diminishing-returns characteristic of the value function, greater than half the value of a gain of $200; hence, people prefer the certainty of $100 to the 50% chance of $200. But at the same time, a loss of $100 is *more than half* as negative as the loss of $200, so people prefer a 50% chance of giving back $200 to a certainty of giving back $100. This pair of preferences is irrational; the irrationality enters because people do not look at the final outcomes of their choices, but rather allow the reference level to change and make judgments relative to that moving reference point. When they have been told they are given $200, they accept that status quo as their reference level; when they are told they have been given $400, they accept that as well. Thus, they make contradictory choices even though the final outcomes are identical in both problems ($300 profit for the Option 1 sure things, $300 expected value for the Option 2 gambles).

As Kahneman and Tversky (1979) point out, the psychological justification for viewing consequences in terms of the status quo can be found in the

more general principle of *adaptation* (also derived from historical developments in the study of sensory psychology). They write the following:

> Our perceptual apparatus is attuned to the evaluation of changes or differences
> rather than to the evaluation of absolute magnitudes. When we respond to
> attributes such as brightness, loudness, or temperature, the past and present
> context of experience defines an adaptation level, or reference point, and stim-
> uli are perceived in relation to this reference point. . . . Thus, an object at a
> given temperature may be experienced as hot or cold to the touch depending
> on the temperature to which one has adapted. The same principle applied to
> non-sensory attributes such as health, prestige, and wealth. The same level of
> wealth, for example, may imply abject poverty for one person and great riches
> for another—depending on their current assets. (p. 277)

The difference between prospect theory and the standard economic theory of
diminishing marginal utility is that the latter assumes that decision makers frame
their choices in terms of the *final* consequences of their decisions. The diminish-
ing-return shape of the utility function guarantees that *any gamble* between two
negative outcomes is *less* negative, worth more in terms of utility than the
corresponding certainty, and the utility for *any gamble* between the positive outcomes is worth less than the corresponding certain outcome. (Ironically, stock-
brokers often advise poor people to be conservative and wealthier ones to take
chances, which makes no sense at all from this framework—especially given that
poorer people who invest their money conservatively are virtually destined to
remain poor, while the wealthy have nowhere to go but down.)

The top half of Figure 9.3 presents the standard economic analysis, and the
bottom half illustrates the prospect theory analysis of the Option Choice
Problems. Recall that both choices are between a final outcome of $300 versus
a 50-50 chance of $200 or $400. These final outcomes form the basis of the
standard expected utility theory analysis. If there is marginal decreasing utility
for money, the average of the utility for $200 and the utility for $400 is less than
the utility for $300. This average is indicated by a point on the line connecting
the $200 point and the $400 point; the shape of the curve dictates that this line
will always lie entirely *beneath* it. If the decision maker has a positive asset level
that is added to the options in determining final consequences, the line connecting these points still lies entirely beneath the curve—the only change is that
they are moved to the right—so the certainty of $300 is still preferred. In fact,
a line connecting *any* two points will lie entirely beneath the curve, which in
general implies people will be "risk-averse" when thinking about gains.

Now consider the choice framed in terms of being given $200 and then
asked for a preference between $100 more for sure versus a 50-50 chance of
$200 more or nothing. According to prospect theory, the decision maker does

not look at the final outcomes ($300 versus a 50-50 chance of $200 or $400) but rather views each choice between options in terms of gains or losses from his or her status quo (reference level). The $200 has been incorporated into that reference level, and because the shape of the utility postulated by prospect theory is also marginally decreasing, the decision maker again opts for the additional certainty of $100. Like classic utility theory, prospect theory makes the general prediction that people will be risk-averse when thinking about gains.

Suppose now that the choice is framed in terms of being given $400 and being required to either give back $100 or take a 50-50 chance of giving back nothing or $200. The final outcomes remain the same. According to prospect theory, however, the decision maker analyzes the options in terms of losses from the status quo (the reference level having shifted to incorporate the $400). Given the (hypothesized) marginally decreasing utility function for losses as they get more severe (Figure 9.3, bottom half), the average of the disutility of –$200 and nothing is not as bad as the disutility of –$100. (This result is illustrated by the point on the line connecting the relevant outcomes; for losses, a marginally decreasing utility function will guarantee that the line connecting any two points lies wholly *above* the curve, which has the general implication that behavior will be "risk-seeking" for losses.) The prediction, according to prospect theory, is that people will choose the 50-50 risky gamble, and that is in fact the most common choice when people are presented with this problem.

Before discussing examples outside a gambling context, we will illustrate prospect theory predictions with the example used in Chapter 1 to illustrate expected utility theory. It involved choice between two pairs of gambles:

(a)  With probability .20 win $45, otherwise nothing, versus

(b)  With probability .25 win $30, otherwise nothing,

and

(a′)  With probability .80 win $45, otherwise nothing, versus

(b′)  Win $30 for sure.

As pointed out in Chapter 1, options (a) and (a′) have higher *expected values* than options (b) and (b′), respectively (e.g., the expected value of (a) is $9, while that of (b) is $7.50). Nevertheless, the marginally decreasing shape of an individual's utility function may lead to a choice of (b) and (b′). What is incompatible with classic utility theory is a choice of (a) and (b′) or of (b) and (a′). It is still possible, however, to choose (a) and (b′) or (b) and (a′) without violating the criteria of rationality presented in Section 1.5.

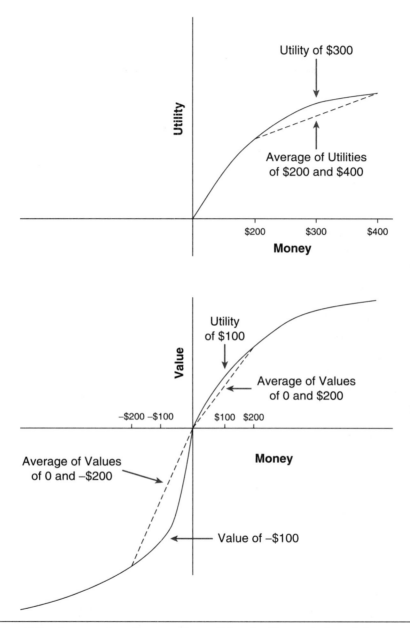

**Figure 9.3**   A comparison between the traditional utility analysis and the
prospect theory analysis of relationships between objective
consequences and experienced utility or value

Now consider a choice between two options:

(a″)  With probability .75 fail at Stage I of the gamble and receive nothing, but if Stage II is reached win $45 with probability .80, otherwise win nothing, versus

(b″)  With probability .75 fail at Stage I of the gamble and receive nothing, but if Stage II is reached receive $30.

If "Stage II" becomes a functional status quo, prospect theory predicts that (b″) may be chosen in preference to (a″) by subjects who would choose (b′) to (a′)—and in fact most subjects do. But (a″) is logically equivalent to (a) (because .25 × .80 = .20) and (b″) to (b) (because .25 × 1 = .25), so that a choice of (a) and (b″) or of (b) and (a″) is inconsistent and violates rationality. Such patterns of choice are common in research on preferences among gambles. This phenomenon has been labeled *pseudocertainty;* the prospect theory explanation is that the chooser adopts a particular stage in a probabilistic process as a psychological status quo and consequently becomes risk-averse for gains and risk-seeking for losses following it. If the stage is actually reached, there is nothing irrational about preferring the $30 certainty (b′ to a′) while, prior to reaching it, preferring the uncertain option with the higher expected value (a to b). But that violates classic utility theory. The irrationality here is that *pseudocertainty* leads to contradictory choice prior to knowledge of the outcome—depending upon whether the choice is viewed in its totality (which might lead to a choice of a in preference to b) or sequentially by components (which might lead to a choice of b″ in preference to a″). Notice that the pseudocertainty effect depends on the manner in which we reason about probabilities; it would occur for both raw dollar values or for subjective utility values.

Note that Coombs's "good things satiate, bad things escalate" (regarding amount) principle is in direct conflict with prospect theory, which includes (like Fechner's law and classic economics) a "decreasing marginal returns" principle for negative as well as positive outcomes. One possible resolution is that the moderation principle is a *realistic* generalization from past experienced utilities (although often an implicit one), while the framing effects of prospect theory involve *predictions* of future consequences (decision utility). A nuclear war that killed two-thirds of a population would be more than twice as bad as one that killed one-third, even though an individual decision maker in a particular crisis situation may choose a 50-50 risk of a nuclear war that would kill two-thirds in order to avoid losing one-third for sure. This interpretation is consistent with the irrationality of framing effects, in that a person choosing among alternatives that can equally well be framed positively or negatively cannot consistently frame them both ways. (For example, if a person normally sleeps 8 hours a night and regards the first

4 hours as the most important, then the last 4 hours of sleep lost must also be the most important; a *positively* accelerating function for the disutility of lost sleep is implied.) An alternative interpretation is that it is not true in many contexts that "bad things escalate." As pointed out earlier, this principle is *sufficient* for producing a single-peaked function, but it is not *necessary*.

Prospect theory is meant to *describe* behavior; thus, it predicts when irrationality may occur and even the direction in which the irrational response will deviate from the normative model. The theory describes choices made as the result of intuitive, automatic processes—for example, as the result of accepting our status quo as a basis for our choices, rather than framing them in terms of changes from our fixed global asset level. Of course, prospect theory does not describe everyone's decision-making behavior all the time; for example, some people some of the time will *not* make the contradictory choices resulting from the pseudocertainty effect. But it is the most successful, descriptive theory of decision making today (as we write this in 2009).

Classic economic utility theory, in contrast, is a *normative* theory of how we *should* choose, and only sometimes a description of how we *do* choose. A central thesis of this book is that our intuitive, automatic thinking processes can lead us to choose one alternative, while analytic, controlled thought leads us to choose another. If we could not choose differently "upon reflection," there would be little point in studying the normative theory of decision making. While we should not always be bound by the normative theory's implications, we should be aware of them and violate them only with self-awareness and for a compelling reason.

We have introduced prospect theory (and classic utility theory) in the context of the values we place on differing amounts of money. Obviously, it is easiest to measure amounts and calculate with theoretical equations when there are numerical scales easily at hand on both the objective (e.g., dollars) and subjective (values, utilities) sides of the conceptual framework. Moreover, most of the research on both theories involves monetary consequences. But both theories are meant to apply much more generally to all carriers of good and bad value—healthy lives, possessions, and pleasant and unpleasant experiences of all types. As we will see, both theories are intended to apply to experienced values and utilities, and predicted future experiences.

# 9.4 Decision Utility—Predicting What We Will Value

If the rational model of decision making is to be of any practical use, it must assume that tastes do not change often or capriciously and that decision makers have some capacity to predict what they will like and dislike when they experience them in the future. Ideally, preferences will be stable over time and there will be a good match between predicted, decision utilities and experienced, consumption utilities. Economists Gary Becker and George Stigler (1977) argued vociferously that tastes are stable and uniform—that there are few, if any, important variations in preferences that cannot be accounted for with reference to prices and incomes. In practice, when survey researchers or laboratory behavioral scientists attempt to measure their respondents' evaluations of everything from the quality of the air they breathe to support for the death penalty to strength of preference for a non-fat, skim, decaf latte, to desire to play a monetary gamble, they often find there is unreliability and apparent instability. Proponents of the *stable values* view explain these phenomena by asking if the respondents have been asked the right questions in a context in which sincere responding is encouraged. Proponents of the *unstable values* view conclude there is a basic unreliability in the mental process that underlies the generation of answers to the evaluative questions (Kahneman, Ritov, & Schkade, 1999). As it so often happens, we believe that both views have some parts of the explanation for why predictions of value are often wrong.

How do people predict, at the point of decision, what will make them happy or unhappy as a consequence of the actions they choose? We propose that a good account can be provided in terms of judgment strategies or heuristics that are employed to predict value. We call these *evaluation heuristics* by analogy with the *judgment heuristics* we introduced in Chapter 5. We propose three basic evaluation heuristics: predictions of value based on remembered past experiences, predictions based on simulating what the future experience will be like, and predictions based on deliberate calculations or inferential rules.

Past experience, learning, and memory play the dominant role in predictions of the future. If an outcome made us happy in the past, then we are likely to predict it will make us happy in the future and prefer to repeat the course of action that led to good outcomes in the past. So, remembered experienced pleasures and pains play a major role in choices that lead to future outcomes. Of course, another reason that memory for past pleasures and pain is important is because it is a contributor to our current feelings of satisfaction. These feelings in turn may have consequences for our behavior in social settings and as citizens who support or oppose their political leadership. When memory does not provide a clear answer, we have other judgment strategies that we use to predict our satisfaction with possible outcomes.

Daniel Gilbert and associates (Gilbert, Pinel, Wilson, Blumberg, & Wheatley, 1998) have identified a form of *non-regressive prediction* that occurs in judgments of future happiness/unhappiness. As noted by Richard

Harrison and Jim March (1984), if we do not appreciate regression effects (introduced in Chapter 7), we will systematically overestimate how positively we will feel about good consequences and overestimate the negativity of the bad consequences. Tim Wilson and Gilbert (1995) demonstrated this tendency to expect more extreme evaluative reactions and emotions than we actually experience. They asked people to predict how they would respond to personally important uncertain events that might occur in their near futures. For example, the researchers asked junior faculty members how they would react if their academic departments decided to deny or grant them promotion to senior, tenured faculty status. The respondents' predictions were much more extreme than their later, post-tenure ratings of specific and general well-being. In short, they expected to be elated or devastated, but a few months after the outcome, they felt pretty much the way they had felt before.

These same researchers created an experimental analogue to this situation by promising college students a desirable summer job, but then disappointing them. Hedonic reactions, like perceptual and cognitive responses, are very adaptive. These researchers labeled this adaptive habit *immune neglect*, by analogy with quickly adapting biological immune systems; the "neglect" refers to the tendency to neglect our adaptiveness when predicting future states. We believe that this habit of immune neglect is most likely to appear in predictions that rely on vicariously imagining how good or bad a future experience will be. We call this second strategy for judging future utilities the *simulation heuristic*.

When we rely on simulation, we are biased by our current emotional states. A very common and important judgment bias is associated with situations in which we exhibit *bounded self-control* (see the review by George Loewenstein, 1996). Contrary to the inspiring story of Ulysses' self-control tactics, most of us exhibit bounded self-control when we make decisions (not just *bounded rationality*). And, as the story of Ulysses suggests, the boundedness can be blamed on our failure to predict how we will react, later in time, when we are tempted. (Oscar Wilde encapsulated this insight in the aphorism "The only thing I cannot resist is temptation.") People underestimate the power of the situation, of immediately available gratification, to control their behavior. Consequently, people consistently mis-predict how they will behave in the future when they are sexually aroused, crave drugs, or are hungry. Loewenstein attributes this family of prediction errors to what he calls the "hot-cold empathy gap"—people cannot know what the effects of their feelings will be on their own behaviors when they are in different emotional states. They expect to be just as cool-headed and self-controlled when they are hungry, sexually aroused, and in the 20th mile of a marathon, as they are when they contemplate those situations from a distance. It is likely our predictions about behavior in social ("This time I'm really going to give my boss a piece of my mind.") and consumer ("I'll resist buying the expensive shoes.") situations are also subject to the illusion that we will choose according to our higher natures, and not succumb to our visceral desires. But the evidence is that these predictions are too optimistic, and we end up not using the condom, injecting the drug, and eating the unhealthy dessert when we are confronted by the actual choice situation.

Some surprising biases in evaluations occur as a result of *incidental emotions*—emotions experienced at the time a decision is made that have nothing to do with the decision itself, that is, they are involved in neither decision utility or experienced utility. The research of Jennifer Lerner and her colleagues (e.g., Han, Lerner, & Keltner, 2007) is especially informative on this point. Lerner has conducted many experiments in which participants' emotions are manipulated by an incidental, irrelevant-to-later-decisions exposure to a sad, happy, anger-provoking, scary, disgusting, or neutral film clip. Some incidental emotions have intuitively obvious effects: When you're scared, you're risk-averse. But others are much more subtle: sadness tells us, "Things aren't good. It's time to change your circumstances," leading to relatively high willingness to pay to get new possessions. Disgust tells us to "expel current possessions," leading to a willingness to sell current possessions for relatively low prices. Anger seems to tell us to take action to change a bad situation, which makes us bold and risk-seeking. The overarching point of Lerner's research is that emotions don't just signal "good or bad" messages to the decision maker; rather, individual emotions send very specific commands for behavior.

Finally, under many conditions we deliberately calculate how much we will like a future experience; we call this the *calculation heuristic* for evaluations. The *diversification bias* is an example of a systematic mis-prediction that occurs when we deliberately infer what we will like. Itmar Simonson (1990) asked students to choose 1 of 6 snacks to be consumed at each of three future class meetings. When the students made their choices by placing an order for all three snacks at one time in the first class meeting, they chose much more variety (from different snack categories) than when they chose sequentially at each class meeting. Furthermore, those who chose in advance and were then allowed to express their preferences at the later meetings (when they were already committed to a snack) showed considerable regret that they had not chosen more uniformly. This kind of study has been repeated with choices among other objects and experiences with similar results; people do not realize how similar their desires will be on different occasions. There is also a social version of the diversification effect: when we order out loud in a restaurant with a group of friends, we are much more likely to choose different options from the menu than when we order privately in writing, with the same group.

In our view, most of the apparent instabilities in value judgments can be accounted for with reference to several psychological considerations. First, there are simple changes in momentary goals. As noted above, when our current goals change, our evaluations change. Second, there is a gap between predicted satisfactions and experienced satisfactions, and researchers are developing a catalog of systematic biases in predictions of future satisfactions. Third, there will sometimes be shifts in value dependent on the changes in the evaluation heuristics that we rely on when we remember, simulate, or calculate future values.

## 9.5 Constructing Values

Survey researchers, with backgrounds in cognitive psychology, have proposed a general model that describes the processes that underlie remembered, simulated, and calculated values. Originally this *belief sampling model* was designed to explain instabilities in responses to general surveys. But we think the model can be applied usefully to explain unreliability in evaluations of many types. As the name suggests, the heart of the model is a (memory) sampling process. Thus, when, for example, a respondent is asked for an opinion about a political issue (e.g., the death penalty), about a political candidate (e.g., Barack Obama), or about a consumer product (e.g., Apple iPod), the label of the topic serves as a probe to retrieve information from the respondent's long-term memory. Many of the items of information retrieved from memory will be associated with or evoke molecular evaluative reactions of their own, and these elementary evaluations are integrated, on the fly, to yield a summary evaluation. The general properties of any cognitive memory system, namely fluctuations in the availability of information from memory, explain unreliability in the system. Human memory retrieval is highly context-dependent, and the specific information retrieved will fluctuate with small changes in the encoding of the retrieval probe and other changes in activation of parts of the system. For example, if a question about abortion or about Bill Clinton follows a question about individual freedom or about John F. Kennedy, the evaluation is likely to be different from what it would have been if the preceding context had activated ideas about family values or about Ronald Reagan.

Roger Tourangeau, Lance Rips, and Ken Rasinski (2000) have formalized this belief sampling process in an explicit model for survey responding that we summarize in Figure 9.4. They distinguish among four stages in the evaluation process: comprehension of the question, retrieval of value-laden information from

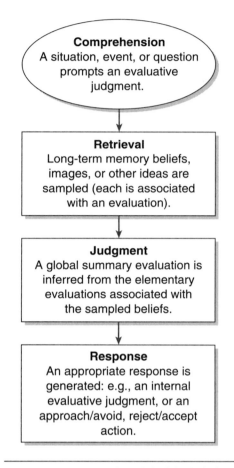

**Figure 9.4**    A general model of the belief sampling process for the construction of evaluations and attitudes for complex multifaceted objects, individuals, and attitudes (based on Tourangeau et al., 2000)

long-term memory, integration of the retrieved evaluations, and response generation. As we note, parts of the model are consistent with precepts from the articulated values position, especially its analysis of the important roles played by question comprehension and response generation. Other parts are consistent with the basic values position, especially the emphasis on variability in the memory sampling process. We would speculate that the retrieval and judgment stages of the model could be combined according to the anchor-and-adjust process model that we summarized in Figure 4.1. Tourangeau and his colleagues have assumed that the integration process can be described by the weighting-and-adding principle of a linear equation, and we pointed out in Chapter 4 that the anchor-and-adjust process is also essentially a weighted averaging operator (Section 4.2). The serial, integrate-one-retrieved-evaluation-at-a-time depiction of the anchor-and-adjust process is likely to describe the sampling and evaluation process in the model as well.

The notion that the memory sampling process is more like skimming the croutons off the surface of a bowl of boiling soup than like the orderly search for a location by address in a quadrilateral grid of city streets explains many of the troublesome phenomena that plague the important business of survey polling. Decades ago, the political scientist Philip Converse identified what he called "non-attitudes"—political issue and candidate evaluations that shifted unpredictably from one panel to the next when individual citizens were polled repeatedly. Such unpredictability would be a natural result of the unreliable memory retrieval process at the heart of the belief sampling model. The model can also account for context effects, *systematic* shifts in the evaluations when the prior question changes or when other factors that would impact memory retrieval vary (e.g., mood effects; Seymour Sudman, Norman Bradburn, & Norbert Schwarz, 1996, have identified and summarized many such effects). When the context or mood shifts from poll to poll, the information retrieved will change and so will the ultimate evaluation.

Research on the primitive sources of value judgments and the manner in which they are combined to evaluate realistically complex courses of action and other objects of choice is one of the fastest-moving subject areas of research in the behavioral sciences today. There are many apparent instabilities, inconsistencies, and just plain puzzling behaviors in this domain of research. Our view is that evaluations and the preferences based on them are not perfectly consistent or perfectly rational, but that for the most part people do a good job of choosing in a manner that will achieve their current goals.

# References

Becker, G., & Stigler, G. J. (1977). De gustibus non est disputandum. *American Economic Review, 67*(2), 76–90.

Bentham, J. (1948). *An introduction to the principles of morals and legislations.* Oxford, UK: Blackwell. (Original work published 1789)

Brickman, P., & Campbell, D. T. (1971). Hedonic relativism and the good society. In M. H. Appley (Ed.), *Adaptation-level theory: A symposium.* New York: Academic Press.

Coombs, C. H., & Avrunin, G. S. (1977). Single-peaked functions and the theory of preference. *Psychological Review, 84,* 216–230.

Damasio, A. R. (1994). *Descartes' error: Emotion, reason, and the human brain.* New York: Putnam.

Davidson, R. J. (1999). The neuroscience of affective style. In M. S. Gazzaniga (Ed.), *The new cognitive neurosciences* (pp. 1149–1159). Cambridge: MIT Press.

Diener, E., & Biswas-Diener, R. (2008). *Happiness: Unlocking the mysteries of psychological wealth.* New York: Wiley-Blackwell.

Ekman, P., & Davidson, R. J. (Eds.). (1994). *The nature of emotion: Fundamental questions.* New York: Oxford University Press.

Gilbert, D. T., Pinel, E., Wilson, T. D., Blumberg, S., & Wheatley, T. (1998). Immune neglect: A source of durability bias in affective forecasting. *Journal of Personality and Social Psychology, 75,* 617–638.

Han, S., Lerner, J. S., & Keltner, D. (2007). Feelings and consumer decision making: The appraisal-tendency framework. *Journal of Consumer Psychology, 17*(3), 158–168.

Harrison, J. R., & March, J. G. (1984). Decision making and postdecision surprises. *Administrative Science Quarterly, 29,* 26–42.

Hsee, C. K., Xu, F., & Tang, N. (2008). Two recommendations on the pursuit of happiness. *Journal of Legal Studies.*

Ito, T. A., & Cacioppo, J. T. (1999). The psychophysiology of utility appraisals. In D. Kahneman, E. Diener, & N. Schwarz (Eds.), *Well-being: The foundations of hedonic psychology* (pp. 470–488). New York: Russell Sage Foundation.

Kahneman, D., Ritov, I., & Schkade, D. (1999). Economic preferences or attitude expressions? An analysis of dollar responses to public issues. *Journal of Risk and Uncertainty, 19,* 220–242.

Kahneman, D., & Tversky, A. (1979). Prospect theory: An analysis of decision under risk. *Econometrica, 47,* 263–291.

Kahneman, D., Wakker, P. P., & Sarin, R. (1997). Back to Bentham? Explorations of experienced utility. *Quarterly Journal of Economics, 112,* 375–405.

LeDoux, J. E. (1996). *The emotional brain: The mysterious underpinnings of emotional life.* New York: Simon & Schuster.

Loewenstein, G. F. (1996). Out of control: Visceral influences on behavior. *Organizational Behavior and Human Decision Processes, 65,* 272–292.

Lykken, D. (1999). *Happiness: What studies on twins show us about nature-nurture, and the happiness set-point.* New York: Golden Books.

Lyubomirsky, S. (2008). *The how of happiness: A new approach to getting the life you want.* New York: Penguin.

Mellers, B., Schwartz, A., & Ritov, I. (1999). Emotion-based choice. *Journal of Experimental Psychology: General, 128,* 332–345.

Parducci, A. (1995). *Happiness, pleasure, and judgment: The contextual theory and its applications.* Mahwah, NJ: Lawrence Erlbaum.

Redelmeier, D., & Kahneman, D. (1996). Patients' memories of painful medical treatments: Real-time and retrospective evaluations of two minimally invasive procedures. *Pain, 116,* 3–8.

Rolls, E. T. (1999). *The brain and emotion.* New York: Oxford University Press.

Simonson, I. (1990). The effect of purchase quantity and timing on variety-seeking behavior. *Journal of Marketing Research, 27,* 150–162.

Sudman, S., Bradburn, N., & Schwarz, N. (1996). *Thinking about answers: The application of cognitive processes to survey methodology.* San Francisco: Jossey-Bass.

Tourangeau, R., Rips, L. J., & Rasinski, K. (2000). *The psychology of the survey response.* New York: Cambridge University Press.

Wilson, T. D., & Gilbert, D. T. (2005). Affective forecasting: Knowing what to want. *Current Directions in Psychological Science, 14*(3), 131–134.

Zajonc, R. B. (1980). Feeling and thinking: Preferences need no inferences. *American Psychologist, 35,* 151–175.

# 10

# From Preferences to Choices

*I don't know much about art, but I know what I like.*

—Anonymous

## 10.1 Deliberate Choices Among Complex Alternatives

A few years ago, at the upscale Draeger's Supermarket in Menlo Park, California, shoppers were confronted with a table displaying 24 exotic jams for sale—exotic meaning none of your run-of-the-mill flavors like strawberry or raspberry, but rather flavors like quince and kumquat. Customers were attracted to the display, and hundreds of them examined the jams and picked up the $1 discount coupons. But the jam promotion was not very successful. Customers said they were confused by the overwhelming display, and only about 3% went on to actually purchase one of the unusual jams. What is more interesting is that every hour the display was changed, and when 18 jams were removed, leaving only 6 on display, the response to this more modest promotion was surprising: There were fewer choice options, but now 30% of customers purchased 1 of the 6 options on display. This is surprising because if 30% of the customers found something good enough to buy in the choice set of 6 options, why wouldn't more customers find something enticing when 18 more options were added to the set? The customers' behavior seemed to contradict economic theory and common sense.

Many important choices don't involve split-second, visceral reactions or reasoning about quantities indexed on a single dimension of dollars, nor are they strictly memory-based. Many important choices are made more deliberately

217

from choice sets, available to inspection, that contain several complex, multi-attribute options. When we need to choose between apartments to rent, courses to enroll in, mountain bikes to purchase, vacations to commit to, or job offers to accept, we rely on *choice strategies* that are analogous to the judgment heuristics we studied in Chapter 5.

These choices are complex because they involve the integration of many small valuations into a global evaluation. For example, when considering an apartment to rent, each of its attribute values (the lousy location, the low rent, the remodeled kitchen, the noisy neighbors, etc.) are evaluated and then combined into a global assessment. The evaluation of individual attributes depends on current goals. If we are making choices to put together a softball team, form a software development team, or pick a roommate, an identical set of candidates with identical attributes will be valued differently. We will assume that the elementary evaluations have been made and the question we will address is, how are the pieces put together into a global evaluation?

What makes choices difficult is that often there are many alternatives to consider, and each alternative has many important, consequential attributes. The most difficult choices occur when there are *negative correlations* among the values of the attributes across the alternatives, forcing us to make difficult trade-offs because there is no perfect alternative: Cheap apartments are usually small, noisy, and poorly furnished; easy-to-reach vacation spots tend to be overrun with people; popular, useful courses are often crowded and "curved" so that it is hard to get a high grade. Perhaps this observation explains the puzzling behavior of Draeger's Supermarket customers: The large choice set was overwhelming and cognitively taxing, and choosing was an unpleasant experience, so the customers simply didn't.

John Payne and his colleagues Jim Bettman and Eric Johnson (1993) have conducted a systematic analysis of consumer choice strategies and compiled a catalog of the strategies in a typical shopper's "cognitive toolbox." Like judgment heuristics, some of these strategies are adaptive; they are robust when choices need to be made quickly under low and unreliable information conditions; they "work" even when the chooser is distracted by other cognitive tasks or by emotional stresses; and many of the strategies demand only modest amounts of attention and other cognitive resources. Gerd Gigerenzer labels some of the most common choice rules "fast and frugal heuristics," because they approach optimality, but are frugal, requiring the consideration of relatively little information about the alternatives, and hence are fast. Figure 10.1 (pp. 221–223) lists the most common strategies identified by behavioral researchers. The categories in this figure indicate some of the important dimensions along which the strategies differ from one another.

Imagine trying to decide which one of several available apartments to rent, and also suppose that the apartments are described by lists of their attributes (rent, location, size, furnishings, noisiness, etc.), as they often are in a rental property directory, in *Consumer Reports,* and on many commercial websites. Now imagine relying on one or another of the strategies listed in Figure 10.1 to understand some of the overarching dimensions that distinguish among the strategies.

The *amount of cognitive effort*—measured subjectively or objectively— varies across strategies. Effort also depends on the structure of the choice set. If the set is large, requires a lot of trade-offs across dimensions and across alternatives, lacks critical or reliable information, or includes a lot of similar alternatives, most of the strategies will demand a considerable effort. Research shows that people are sensible, perhaps exhibiting a kind of meta-rationality, about which choice strategies they use: If the choice is consequential— especially if the chooser is accountable to others—people rely on more thorough and demanding cognitive strategies, those that are also more likely to identify the best alternatives in the choice set.

Some strategies involve across-attribute compensatory trade-offs, while others do not. The good location of an apartment can *compensate* for the high rent and lead to an overall good evaluation; the reliability or safety of an automobile can compensate for its dumpy appearance. But some strategies, called *noncompensatory,* are unforgiving: If the rent is over $700 per month, the apartment is rejected, no matter how good its other features; if the automobile doesn't comfortably seat a family of four, it's not considered further. Such strategies usually demand less cognitive effort, and they often yield quick answers. However, these cognitive savings come at a cost. Non-compensatory strategies, especially, are likely to miss "balanced, all-around good" alternatives and sometimes terminate the search before a truly dominant "winner" is found.

Because our attention is limited, strategies tend to guide information search. A useful distinction is between *alternative-based* strategies and *attribute-based* ones. In alternative-based strategies, attention is focused on one alternative at a time, its attributes are reviewed, and a summary evaluation is performed of that item before attention is turned to another alternative. (The process is usually described by an "averaging model" like those reviewed in Chapter 4.) The contrasting organizational principle is a strategy based on attributes: An attribute (e.g., price, location) is selected and several alternatives are evaluated on that attribute. Then attention turns to the next attribute. Attribute-based strategies often stop with an "answer" after reviewing less information than alternative-based strategies; therefore, alternative-based strategies tend to be more cognitively demanding than those based on attributes.

Finally, although there is some dependence on the structure of the set of choice alternatives, the strategies differ in terms of the amount of information each is likely to consume in the choice process. Some are *exhaustive* and require perusal of all relevant information (and even deploy inference processes to fill in the gaps in information); others are likely to make a choice after a *small subset* of the total accessible information has been covered. Obviously, more information means more cognitive effort for most choice situations, and exhaustive strategies are exhausting. As noted above, non-compensatory, attribute-based strategies tend to be the most "cognitively frugal."

The most thorough, systematic, cognitively demanding choice strategy is the *multi-attribute utility theory* (MAUT) evaluation process that is essentially the linear weight-and-add, Lens Model judgment policy applied to valuation, rather than to estimating or forecasting "true states of the world" (i.e., applied to estimate our "internal" reaction to the object of choice). Most efforts to improve choice habits focus on inducing people to use strategies that are more like this method. For example, Benjamin Franklin (1772/1987) gave advice to his friend Joseph Priestley about how to make a difficult choice. Franklin wrote the following:

> When these difficult cases occur, they are difficult, chiefly because while we have them under consideration, all the reasons pro and con are not present to the mind at the same time; but sometimes one set present themselves, and at other times another, the first being out of sight. Hence the various purposes or inclinations that alternatively prevail, and the uncertainty that perplexes us. To get over this, my way is to divide half a sheet of paper by a line into two columns; writing over the one Pro, and over the other Con. Then, during three or four days consideration, I put down under the different heads short hints of the different motives, that at different times occur to me, for or against the measure. When I have thus got them all together in one view, I endeavor to estimate their respective weights; and where I find two, one on each side, that seem equal, I strike them both out. If I find a reason pro equal to some two reasons con, I strike out the three. If I judge some two reasons con, equal to some three reasons pro, I strike out the five; and thus proceeding I find at length where the balance lies; and if, after a day or two of further consideration, nothing new that is of importance occurs on either side, I come to a determination accordingly. And, though the weights or reasons cannot be taken with the precision of algebraic quantities, yet when each is thus considered, separately and comparatively, and the whole lies before me, I think I can judge better, and am less liable to make a rash step, and in fact I have found great advantage from this kind of equation, in what may be called moral or prudential algebra. (p. 522)

We'll return to the issue of advice on choosing wisely after we consider some implications of the fact that we often rely on frugal heuristic strategies when we choose, even when the choices are consequential.

| | Mental Effort | Compensatory vs. Non-compensatory? | Whole vs. Part? | Exhaustive |
|---|---|---|---|---|
| **DOMINANCE** | MEDIUM | NON-COMPENSATORY | ALTERNATIVE | YES |

Search for an alternative that is at least as good as every other alternative on all important attributes and choose it, *or* find an alternative that is worse than any other alternative on all attributes and throw that "worse" alternative out of the choice set. Consistent with prescriptions for rational choice, but will only "work" to select a unique best alternative if there is a "super-alternative" that beats all others in the choice set; *dominance* is often used as a first-stage strategy to weed out the weakest "dominated alternatives" in a large choice set.

| | | | | |
|---|---|---|---|---|
| **ADDITIVE LINEAR** | VERY HIGH | COMPENSATORY | ALTERNATIVE | YES |

Weight all the attributes by their importance (with reference to the current goals of the decision maker). Then consider each alternative one at a time and calculate a global utility by valuing each attribute, weighting it by its importance, and adding up the weighted values. This is a rigorous version of Benjamin Franklin's advice to a decision maker, and it is the strategy prescribed by economic theories for rational choice. It tends to find the uniquely "best all around" alternative in the choice set, but it requires a great deal of effort and time for complex choice sets.

| | | | | |
|---|---|---|---|---|
| **ADDITIVE DIFFERENCE** | VERY HIGH | COMPENSATORY | ATTRIBUTE | YES |

Consider two alternatives at a time; compare attribute-by-attribute, estimating the difference between the two alternatives, and sum up the differences across the attributes to provide a single overall difference score across all attributes for that pair. Carry the winner of this comparison over to the next viable alternative and make the same comparison. At the end of this process, the best alternative is the one that has "won" all the pairwise comparisons. (This strategy should pick the same ultimate winner as an *additive linear* or MAUT strategy, but the calculation process is different.) This strategy is commonly used in the final stages of everyday choices, e.g., among consumer goods. It often appears in a qualitative form, where the comparison only "counts" the number of winning attribute comparisons. In this form, it is sometimes called a "voting rule" for choice (in a pairwise comparison ["election"], each attribute pairing has one "vote"), and in the qualitative form, the order in which alternatives are

*(Continued)*

| | Mental Effort | Compensatory vs. Non-compensatory? | Whole vs. Part? | Exhaustive |
|---|---|---|---|---|
| (Continued) | | | | |

considered has a big impact on which is the ultimate winner. (This choice strategy is formally analogous to an election, and certain voting paradoxes known to happen in electorates occur when an individual makes a personal choice by following this strategy.)

| **"SATISFICING" (CONJUNCTIVE)** | LOW | NON-COMPENSATORY | ALTERNATIVE | NO |
|---|---|---|---|---|

First, set "acceptability" cutoff points on all important attributes; then look for the first alternative that is at least as good as the cutoff values on *all* important attributes; *or* use the strategy to select a set of good-enough alternatives (all above the cutoff points) for further consideration. *Satisficing* tends to select a homogeneous subset of "good" alternatives. It is often used as a first-stage strategy to screen out "losers" or in a general satisficing strategy to find the first alternative that is "good enough"—very common in consumer choice.

| **DISJUNCTIVE** | LOW | NON-COMPENSATORY | ALTERNATIVE | NO |
|---|---|---|---|---|

First, set "acceptability" cutoff points on the important attributes; then, look for the first alternative that is at least as good as the cutoff value on *any* attribute; *or* use the strategy to select a set of alternatives that are each very good on at least one dimension for further consideration. This strategy tends to select a heterogeneous subset of "specialists."

| **LEXICOGRAPHIC** | MEDIUM | NON-COMPENSATORY | ATTRIBUTE | NO |
|---|---|---|---|---|

First, review the attributes and pick the one most important attribute; then, choose the best alternative on that attribute. If there are several "winners" on the first attribute, go on to the next-most important attribute and pick the best remaining alternative(s) on that attribute (repeating until only one alternative is left)—common in everyday choices and can produce intransitivities (where the chooser makes a series of contradictory choices). Also, there is an opportunity for "manipulation" in that the order in which attributes are considered has a big effect on the final choice—there is often a possible attribute order that will result in choosing any option in the set. This strategy is very close to Gerd Gigerenzer's highly successful "take the best," fast-and-frugal heuristic (successful in choice and judgment environments that reflect the distributions of alternatives and attribute values in real, everyday environments). The only adjustment to our description would be to substitute the word *validity* (predictive accuracy) for *importance*, and order the attributes considered by their past validity in discriminating among good and bad alternatives.

| | Mental Effort | Compensatory vs. Non-compensatory? | Whole vs. Part? | Exhaustive |
|---|---|---|---|---|
| **ELIMINATION BY ASPECTS** | MEDIUM | NON-COMPENSATORY | ATTRIBUTE | NO |

Pick the first attribute that is salient and set a cutoff "acceptability" point on that attribute. Throw out all alternatives that are below the cutoff on that one attribute; then, pick the next most attention-getting attribute, set an acceptability cutoff on that attribute, and throw out all alternatives that are below the cutoff again (repeating until only one alternative is left)—often used to screen out "losers," the order of attributes considered (aspects) is heavily dependent on momentary salience, and there are the same possibilities for manipulation as in the lexicographic strategy (i.e., if you apply this strategy considering the attributes in one order, and then apply it again considering attributes in a different order, you are likely to end up choosing different alternatives).

| | Mental Effort | Compensatory vs. Non-compensatory? | Whole vs. Part? | Exhaustive |
|---|---|---|---|---|
| **RECOGNITION HEURISTIC** | LOW | NON-COMPENSATORY | ALTERNATIVE | NO |

In some choices, people are so poorly informed about the alternatives that they simply rely on *name recognition*; that is, they choose the first alternative that they recognize. Dan Goldstein and Gigerenzer (2002) have shown that in many realistic choices and judgments (choosing the city with a larger population, choosing the stock that is likeliest to increase in price, etc.), the fast-and-frugal recognition choice heuristic behaves surprisingly well.

**Figure 10.1**    A catalog of common choice strategies

## 10.2 Ordering Alternatives

Since we cannot think of all of our decision options—and their possible consequences—simultaneously, we must do so sequentially. (Notice how Benjamin Franklin's comments on difficulty in choosing agree with our discussion of bounded cognitive capacities, especially working memory limits.) The resulting order in which we consider options and consequences may have profound effects on decision making. Because many of the ways in which we order alternatives in our minds are automatic, irrational choices are common. Here's a simple example.

Richard Nisbett and Timothy Wilson (1977) asked people to state their preference from an array of merchandise (dresses and stockings). The items were arranged in a single row facing the subject. Nisbett and Wilson discovered that no matter where individual items were placed, the subjects tended to choose the item at the far right. The subjects were not aware that the positioning of the items had an effect on their choice, and certainly they would have rejected an explicit decision rule to "choose whatever happens to be on the far right." Similar *order effects on choice* have been observed for political voting (order of names on the ballot; Miller & Krosnick, 1998), evaluations of performances in the Eurovision Song Contests (talent shows similar to *American Idol* in the United States), classical music competitions, and sports competitions such as figure skating (de Bruin, 2005).

Nisbett and Wilson (1977) observed that most subjects scanned the products from left to right—a habit that may well be related to the fact that we read from left to right. (It would be interesting to repeat the experiment in Israel, where sentences are read from right to left.) Why did the subjects tend to prefer the product on the far right? One possibility is that each new product seen possesses desirable characteristics that the one previously scanned does not, but there is no product on the right of the one at the end of the row to bring attention to desirable characteristics that it lacks. (This interpretation is bolstered by the plausible assumption that any product must have a desirable characteristic that others don't in order to be on the market—for long, anyway.)

In Nisbett and Wilson's (1977) experiment, people looked at all the alternative choices. A severe problem with the ordering of alternatives is that it may *exclude* consideration of certain possibilities. Herbert Simon (1956) made a Nobel Prize winning contribution in the fields of individual and organizational decision making by demonstrating that, far from making optimal choices, individuals often search through the set of possible alternatives until they find one that satisfies an aspiration level, and then they terminate their search. Such a procedure yields a satisfactory decision but not necessarily an optimal one. Simon used the Scottish word *satisficing*—as opposed to *optimizing*—to describe this process.

The strategy of searching through possible alternatives only until the first satisfactory one is found has important implications in the study of the rationality of choice. It means the *order* in which people search may be of paramount importance, but order can be determined by many factors having very little to do with the consequences of choice (for example, left-to-right bias), or it can even be manipulated by a clever person with control of the agenda of a discussion. The strategy we are describing is not rational, because it operates independently of considerations of the desirability of the consequences of alternative choices. A search in one manner may lead to one decision, while a search in another may lead to a different decision.

Decisions that would be rational if they were not influenced by factors not directly tied to consequences—such as the order in which alternatives are considered—have been termed *bounded* by Simon (1956). Decision theorists now speak of "bounded rationality" to characterize a wide range of choice processes (most of the strategies in our Figure 10.1) that do not adhere strictly to principles of rationality, but may or may not approximate them. In later work, Simon has pointed out that such bounds on rationality are often the most important determinants of choice.

Bounded rationality can, nevertheless, have desirable consequences. First, there are situations in which it is not possible to specify all of the alternatives, their attributes, and their consequences in advance. In such a situation, a very reasonable strategy is to collect information in a predetermined manner over a specified period of time and then select the alternative that appears best up to that point. This strategy, however, is not as reasonable as one that constantly revises the manner and time frame of the search on the basis of information as it is gathered, although this is another form of bounded rationality that does not consider all the alternatives. Second, the consideration of all relevant possibilities and consequences involves *decision costs,* which are difficult to integrate with the costs and benefits of payoffs, because they are of a qualitatively different type. Let us give two examples— first, one of decision costs.

A visiting professor is contemplating three job offers of well-paying professorships, all of which would provide considerable time and support to do the research she loves. From the information she has gathered thus far, there is a clear ranking of how good the offers are, but she needs to collect more information. The situation is complicated by the fact that the offer that appears now to be best is one she must accept or reject within a month; she can postpone a choice between the other two (and any other alternatives that might appear in the meantime) for half a year. How much time should she spend collecting information, evaluating possible consequences and their probabilities, and attempting to integrate the information and potential results in order to reach a decision? There are other things she wishes to do with her time, and there is a deadline; moreover, such decision making is emotionally draining. Should she, as some friends have urged, begin by "bounding" her search by rejecting what appears to be the weakest offer? That clearly has the advantage of allowing her more time and energy to evaluate the other two, but it has the disadvantage of eliminating an option before it has been thoroughly evaluated. Should she make a higher-level decision about how to decide—for example, by adopting a criterion for the decision to reduce the set of three alternatives to two?

These questions are not as easily answered as are those in choices between gambles. What makes this choice particularly difficult, however, is the incomparability of the benefits and costs involved in making the decision with those involved in the jobs themselves. Given the professor's bounds on time and cognitive capacity, she cannot consider the decision costs in a fully rational manner—even if she had some way of integrating them with the consequences of the decision. And then, somewhat paradoxically, even if she could figure out a way to do that, she would have to take into account the probable time and effort involved in figuring it out in order to determine whether she should attempt to do so in the first place! The rationality of whatever decision she makes will be "bounded." Nonetheless, she must decide something.

An example of not considering all possibilities is that of someone hiring a secretary. In some areas of the United States it is not uncommon for as many as 100 applicants to apply for such a position. The decision is particularly difficult for someone who has only second-hand knowledge of what is required of secretaries and how to evaluate secretarial skills. Applications pour in over days. Should the employer wait until 100 applications have arrived and evaluate these in as thorough a manner as possible? That would require an enormous amount of time. Should the employer evaluate all 100 quickly in a superficial manner, and then evaluate 20 in depth? Could better information be gained by evaluating a few in depth? Let us suppose the employer uses a very bounded strategy: evaluate the first 20 applicants in depth and choose the one that appears to be best. How good or bad is this decision-making procedure relative to one of judging all 100 in depth?

We can evaluate one aspect of this strategy quite specifically. Let us suppose that the employer would be quite satisfied with any of the five best applicants. How likely is it that out of the potential 100 applicants, 1 of these 5 will appear in the first 20? Assuming the order of applications is random with respect to secretarial quality (that is, there is no systematic bias by which the better secretaries apply earlier or later), the probability is .68. In fact, there is a probability of slightly over one-half that 1 of these good secretaries will be among the first 15 applicants. So while the strategy of evaluating only the first 20 in depth does not satisfy the criterion of looking at all possible alternatives in terms of their consequences, it does not do badly—at least on the criterion of having access to a top-notch secretary. (Whether the employer will correctly judge the worth of one of these applicants is yet another matter.) The strategy has the advantage of cutting down on the decision time and effort, and it allows the employer to find out what the applicant pool is like in order to determine what qualities should be considered in evaluating applicants.

A similar procedure is to estimate the qualifications of a good candidate in this pool by sampling from it and using that information to set a criterion for a final choice. For example, suppose the employer examines 15 randomly chosen applicants and then continues the search until someone is found who is better than any of those. Doing so would result in a probability of .83 of picking 1 of the top 5, with an expected search length of 29 subsequent applicants. (It is a well-known mathematical result that if 37% [1/$e$] of candidates are randomly sampled from a pool and the search is continued until one better than any of these is chosen, the probability of choosing the best candidate is maximized; see Searle & Rapoport, 2000, for an introduction to this class of dynamic decision problems.) Or if the employer knew in advance how to judge the qualifications of potential secretaries, he or she could simply search until finding one in the top 5%. Then, an average of 17 applicants would have to be screened.

As pointed out by Amitai Etzioni (personal communication to Robyn Dawes, November 3, 1986), all three of the search procedures just described are "boundedly rational" or "satisficing." The first involves simply truncating the search, because there are too many alternatives to consider; the degree to which that procedure is desirable depends upon the degree of truncation, the trade-off between the costs of reaching the decision and the costs and benefits resulting from the decision itself, and the degree to which the chooser can avoid a pernicious bias in conducting the search. The second procedure involves using the first part of a search to determine what constitutes a desirable alternative, and the third involves a predetermined "aspiration level." The desirability of the latter two procedures is determined by the same three factors as that of the first one.

According to Richard Cyert and James March (1963), organizations as well as individuals often use bounded search procedures to arrive at satisfactory but not optimal solutions to many problems. Moreover, the characteristics that define the goodness of a solution may consist of a mix of those chosen at the beginning of the search and those that become more noticeable as it proceeds.

Another procedure for simplifying a search process involves concentrating on *aspects* of alternatives rather than on the alternatives themselves. For example, as Tversky (1972) has proposed, decision makers often *eliminate* alternatives by aspects. The *elimination by aspects* strategy involves choosing a desirable aspect, eliminating all alternatives that do not have it (or enough of it), then choosing another desirable aspect and eliminating all those alternatives not containing it, and so on, until either a single alternative is left or so few are left that they can be evaluated thoroughly. In the secretary choice, for example, word-processing skills and prior training with a particular software tool might be aspects by which to eliminate candidates.

If the aspects are considered in the same order as their desirability, this form of bounded rationality results in reasonably good choices—although it involves no compensatory mechanism. If the aspects are chosen probabilistically in proportion to their importance, the procedure is less successful. And, if they are chosen ad hoc on the basis of the ease with which they come to mind, it is a decidedly flawed procedure. Advertisers often try to manipulate the appeal of their products by highlighting specific aspects on which their product beats the competition, encouraging consumers to overweight those features or to eliminate options based on their product's best attributes.

Gigerenzer (Gigerenzer et al., 1999) has described a related choice strategy, *take the best,* in which the chooser searches through attributes starting with the most important (or valid, when making predictions), and *selecting* (rather than eliminating) the first option that is a clear winner on the most important attribute.

One of the most important insights provided by Payne et al.'s (1993) systematic analysis of the characteristics of the choice strategies was a test of the comparative success of each strategy under different constraining conditions. Even when there were no limits on computational resources or available information, many of the less cognitively demanding strategies did almost as well as the ideal multi-attribute utility evaluation (with reasonable choice sets and no missing information). When a choice deadline was imposed on the strategies, the MAUT strategy was prone to deadlock or "crash," while some of the other "quick and dirty" strategies still performed close to optimally. Gigerenzer (Gigerenzer et al., 1999) has conducted similar analyses of his *fast and frugal choice* algorithms and reached the same conclusions. For example, the recognition heuristic and the take-the-best heuristic can outperform much more cognitively demanding strategies under some realistic performance conditions. The implication is that these efficient, but nonoptimal strategies may even be adaptively optimal in noisy, stressful, and unforgiving environments.

Is there a contradiction between the bounded rationality of terminating searches and the findings of Nisbett and Wilson (1977)? No, because there is a crucial difference in the choice problems. In the Nisbett and Wilson study, the subjects were aware of all the choice options—the items were physically lined up in front of them. The problem with the satisficing procedure is that certain choices may not even be considered, including those that may be the best one or better ones for the decision maker (with greater or lesser probability depending on the situation).

# 10.3 Grouping Alternatives

Adaptation is one of the basic processes of human life. It affects judgment and decision making—for example, in framing alternatives relative to a status quo. Another basic phenomenon that affects judgment and decision making is sensitivity to *context effects*. Just as a particular visual stimulus (for example, a gray circle) appears different in different contexts (when surrounded by a yellow versus a blue background), a particular choice alternative may appear different to a decision maker when it is considered in different contexts. Specifically, it may be evaluated as more or less desirable when it appears in different choice sets. The more judgmental the evaluation, the greater is the importance of context effects. For example, despite the differences with which we perceive a color depending on the colors surrounding it, we experience a great deal more "color constancy" than would be expected from a simple analysis of reflected light frequency on an object and its surroundings; the light that illuminates an object does not have much effect on our perception of the object's color. When evaluating an alternative and its possible consequences, however, we often do not experience such constancy. In fact, the influence of competing alternatives can lead to a contradictory choice, even when the competing alternatives are never chosen.

One principle of rationality that most theorists accept is that choice should be *independent of irrelevant alternatives*. That is, if alternative A is preferred to alternative B when the two are considered alone, then A should be preferred to B when alternative C is considered along with them; the presence of alternative C should be irrelevant to the preference between A and B. Of course, if C is the preferred alternative in the set consisting of A, B, and C, we have no way of knowing whether its existence has reversed the preference for A over B, because C will be chosen. Hence, to demonstrate that choice may violate this principle of rationality, we must show that the choice of A over B is reversed in a situation where C is not chosen.

Can that happen? Yes, and its occurrence is due to context effects. Joel Huber and Christopher Puto (1983) asked people to make choices between consumer items like batteries, clothing, and beverages. Consider their example for calculator batteries:

Battery A lasts 22 hours and costs $1.80

Battery B lasts 28 hours and costs $2.10

Now add a third—Battery C lasts 14 hours and costs $1.50. No one chooses the third battery; it looks similar to Battery A, but inferior. Battery A lasts many more hours for a slight price increase. With Battery C in the set, most consumers prefer Battery A (more than 60%). Now consider A and B with a different third alternative, Battery D, which lasts 32 hours and costs $2.70. Battery B looks similar, but is a "better deal," and a majority (about 60% again) now prefer B to A. These *decoy alternative* effects are common in consumer choice, and in social choice and political election situations.

Tversky and Itamar Simonson (1992) describe another fascinating context effect in consumer choice. A mail-order kitchen supply store once offered a bread-making machine priced at $275. The item was very unpopular until the company added a second bread-making appliance that was slightly larger, but much more expensive, $429. The new appliance was also a sales failure, but sales of the original, smaller bread maker more than doubled. The contrast with the larger, overpriced machine made the smaller, cheaper machine seem like a good buy.

## 10.4 Choosing Unconsciously

Recently, there has been keen interest in the question of whether it is worth all the fuss to deconstruct the decision process (as we are doing in this book) and to try to discipline ourselves to make systematic, deliberate judgments and choices. Popular books like Malcolm Gladwell's best-seller *Blink* (2005) suggest that often fast, intuitive decision processes are more accurate and lead to more long-term satisfaction than careful, analytic processes. We find Gladwell's summary of scientific cases in favor of intuitive judgments and choices fairly unconvincing (see, for example, Hogarth & Schoemaker, 2005). But there are two research programs that do make a convincing case that intuition trumps analysis *under some conditions*.

It is important to begin this discussion by noting that all of the judgment and decision processes discussed in this book involve both conscious and unconscious elements. Furthermore, it is very difficult to determine the relative contributions of conscious and unconscious elements to the final judgment or choice. In fact, most cognitive researchers don't bother to specify which components of their models are consciously reportable and which are hidden in the unconscious. However, we can, at least intuitively, distinguish between judgments and choices that are more systematic and controlled and those that are more automatic and spontaneous. So, acknowledging that we won't be able to be as precise as we might want to be, we can compare more and less conscious processes or strategies.

Tim Wilson and his colleagues conducted several thought-provoking experiments in which participants chose jams, dorm-room posters, and psychology classes from choice sets of approximately 10 options (e.g., Wilson et al., 1993; Wilson & Schooler, 1991). They compared choices that were made with an instruction to state the reasons for the choice versus choices made with a simple "just choose" instruction. The poster choice study was the most convincing, though the results from all three experiments pointed to the superiority of the "just choose" process. In the case of the posters, they found that when participants "just chose," they were likelier to actually display the posters in their dorm rooms and to rate them as more satisfying 3 months after the original selection. Wilson and his colleagues' interpretation is that the automatic, uncontrolled choice process is closer to the evaluation that is performed when the chosen option is "consumed"— that stating reasons for the choice is unnatural and interferes with making an evaluation at the choice point that captures the attributes of the later consumption experience. This makes sense to us, especially for options like jams and posters that are "consumed" in a simple, automatic sensory manner. Overintellectualizing simple choices might well screw up the evaluations. We are a little surprised that the psychology course selection task also seemed to favor an unsystematic, intuitive choice process, but then the methods in that study did not prevent participants from thinking hard (and systematically) about the options in the "just choose" condition. The point we extract from these studies is that when choice options are simple and their "consumption" does not involve extensive cognitive analysis, simpler, more intuitive choice processes may produce better, more satisfying outcomes.

A second, much more provocative series of experiments has been reported by Ap Dijksterhuis and his colleagues (Dijksterhuis, Bos, Nordgren, & van Baaren, 2006). They studied mostly choices involving complex multi-attribute options like apartments to rent, cars, potential roommates, and so forth. In a typical experiment, the participant was asked to choose between four hypothetical cars, each described by 12 binary (high/low) attributes (e.g., cup holder/no cup holder, high mileage/low mileage). The attributes were presented rapidly, one at a time, in a randomly scrambled order. Then, participants were instructed either to think about their choice for 4 minutes and then choose, or to perform a distracting anagram problem-solving task and then chose. Thus, there were two choice conditions: *conscious thought* (think for 4 minutes) versus *unconscious thought* (distracted by the anagrams). One of the four cars had 9 out of 12 positive binary attributes, the others had 6 out of 12 positive, and choice quality was assessed by counting the number of participants who chose the best (9 positives) option. The surprising finding, replicated several times, is that the unconscious choice condition produces the most correct choices, 59% correct, while the conscious thought condition is essentially at chance levels, 22%. (In other experiments, a "choose immediately" condition was included, and it performed poorly, too.)

Dijksterhuis et al.'s interpretation is that there are two modes of thinking—unconscious versus conscious thought—and that the unconscious thought system has much greater computational capacity than the conscious system. They estimate that the conscious system processes a tiny amount of information per second (on the order of 2–3 bits per second, e.g., reading 5–7 words per second), while the unconscious system has a capacity of 11,200,000 bits per second. They attribute other differences to the two systems and conclude that for any complex intellectual task, the unconscious system should outperform the conscious system. This theoretical interpretation is highly speculative, but the more important products of the research program are the provocative behavioral results. In Dijksterhuis et al.'s tasks with their "number of positive attributes" criterion for choice quality, their distraction-based unconscious thought condition consistently beats conscious thought choices. These results are troubling to people, like the authors of this book, who believe that there are important advantages to systematic, controlled, deliberate, and relatively conscious choice strategies.

We would like to make some comments on the Dijksterhuis et al. results before we turn to a concluding section and recommend just the opposite of their unconscious thought strategy. First, we want to acknowledge the importance of the questions raised by Dijksterhuis et al.'s demonstrations. In fact, we cannot cite any research-based proofs that deliberate choice habits are better in practical affairs than going with your gut intuitions. Second, we would point out that the deliberate choice strategies we recommend (Section 10.5 below) are very different from Dijksterhuis et al.'s "think for 4 minutes" strategy. And third, we think there are some good reasons to believe that Dijksterhuis et al.'s conclusions are restricted to some very limited choice-task conditions. Note the unusual scrambled presentation of 48 binary facts, the requirement to "think for 4 minutes," and the fact that the conscious thought participants performed at chance levels of success. Furthermore, even under these odd conditions, other researchers have shown that when participants are instructed to "think about your choice as long as you want," performance is better than in Dijksterhuis et al.'s unconscious thought condition (Payne et al., 2008). So, it seems that within the conditions of Dijksterhuis et al.'s atypical choice task, they have created a low-performing version of conscious choice strategies. Contrary to Dijksterhuis and colleagues, we recommend a deliberate, controlled choice strategy for complex decisions, though our method, based on Benjamin Franklin's "prudential algebra," is very different from Dijksterhuis et al.'s experimental version of conscious thought.

# 10.5 How to Make Good Choices

Back to Ben Franklin (Bigelow, 1887; see also Clemen, 1996; Hammond, Keeney, & Raiffa, 1999, for introductions to personal and professional decision analysis), his advice is echoed in popular books on decision making that recommend the listing of possible consequences of choices, linking those to our personal values, and then choosing the alternative that has the highest summary value according to a simple weight-and-add rule. Another interesting but much simpler version of Franklin's method appears in Charles Darwin's (1887/1969) autobiographical summary of his decision processes when deciding whether to marry or not. Of course, there are problems. How do we determine and define the cue (value-carrying) variables? Might not many of them be interrelated? For example, in assessing a possible job, should we list salary, status, and autonomy as separate characteristics? How do we know they are important to us? Isn't it true that "high-level" jobs tend to be high on all three characteristics, while "low-level" jobs are low on all? If so, shouldn't we just list "job level" rather than its separate components?

The answer to the question of importance is rather easy: It is up to the decision maker. In constructing a weighting scheme, we should list the variables that are important to us, given our current goals. If, for example, we think of "job level" in a global and amorphous way, then we should list it. If, on the other hand, money, status, and autonomy each strike us as psychologically distinct and important, then we should list them separately. Franklin advised his friend not on *what to* decide, but *how to* decide it. When suggesting a list, he was not advising what should be on it, but rather suggesting how to become explicit about what is important to the decision maker. Research indicates that when specific variables are known, a linear model predicts better than global intuitive judgment. (In fact, simply determining the variables often makes the choice obvious.) Moreover, the weights assigned to the variables are those of the individual making the choice. If, for example, sexual compatibility is more important to a person choosing a mate than is character, altruism, or sanity, then there is no reason the person should not choose on that basis—and live with the consequences. Again, the point of this book is not what to decide, but how. Thus, the answer to the related variables question may be found in a distinction made by Wendell Garner and John Morton. The fact that two dimensions are correlated in nature (such as height and weight) does not imply that they are not psychologically distinct for the perceiver. If they are distinct to you, think about them as separate.

Once we have determined the variables, we face the problem of evaluating and weighting them. To do so, we must assume that we have some insight into our values and value systems—and in particular into how we compare and trade off conflicting values. Dawes's research on the robust beauty of (even improper) linear models has demonstrated that this insight need not be total or profound; evaluations and weights that are good, but not perfect, provide outcomes very close to those based on optimal ones (Section 3.5). Granted these assumptions, the decision is then *decomposed* so that each variable can be considered separately, and the results are combined according to a linear ("weight-and-add") scheme. The reason, once again, for believing that such decomposition can work well in a choice situation that lacks a criterion for evaluating the outcome, is that it works in situations where one is present.

Of course, it is not always a simple matter to determine values. In fact, there are cognitive biases in achieving a valid-deliberate decomposition, just as there are governing automatic choice. Thus, Tversky, Sattah, and Slovic (1988) have shown that when matching procedures are used to determine the relative importance of identified variables, the result is a systematic underestimation of the degree of discrepancy from choice situations. For example, most baseball experts consider batting average to be more important than home run hitting. Their implicit weighting of the two variables can be determined by asking them to match two players by assigning a value to one of the two variables so that the players are of equal value in their estimation. This could be done, for example, by deciding on the number of home runs a player with a batting average of .310 would have to hit per year to be of the same value as a player who has a .334 batting average and hits 15 home runs per year. But such matching judgments *systematically underestimate* the importance the judges ascribe to batting average relative to home runs when they are asked to choose the more valuable player among pairs.

Which procedure is better for determining true value? For that matter, what *is* such value? This chapter—and indeed this book—does not address those very difficult questions. What *can* be concluded is that the procedure of looking first *within* each variable and then comparing across by some weighting scheme is superior to that of making global intuitive judgments *across* variables regarding each choice in isolation.

# References

Bigelow, J. (Ed.). (1887). *The complete works of Benjamin Franklin*. New York: Putnam.

Clemen, R. T. (1996). *Making hard decisions: An introduction to decision analysis* (2nd ed.). Pacific Grove, CA: Duxbury Press.

Cyert, R. M., & March, J. G. (1963). *A behavioral theory of the firm.* Englewood Cliffs, NJ: Prentice Hall.

Darwin, C. (1969). *The autobiography of Charles Darwin, 1809–1892.* New York: Norton. (Original work published 1887)

De Bruin, W. B. (2005). Save the last dance for me: Unwanted serial position effects in jury evaluations. *Acta Psychologica, 118,* 245–260.

Dijksterhuis, A., Bos, M. W., Nordgren, L. F., & van Baaren, R. B. (2006). On making the right choice: The deliberation-without-attention effect. *Science, 311,* 1005–1007.

Franklin, B. (1987). *Writings.* New York: Library of America. (The original letter to Joseph Priestley was written on September 19, 1772.)

Garner, W. R., & Morton, J. (1969). Perceptual independence: Definitions, models, and experimental paradigms. *Psychological Bulletin, 72,* 233–259.

Gigerenzer, G., Todd, P. M., & the ABC Research Group. (1999). *Simple heuristics that make us smart.* New York: Oxford University Press.

Gladwell, M. (2005). *Blink: The power of thinking without thinking.* New York: Little, Brown.

Goldstein, D. G., & Gigerenzer, G. (2002). Models of ecological rationality: The recognition heuristic. *Psychological Review, 109,* 75–90.

Hammond, J. S., Keeney, R. L., & Raiffa, H. (1999). *Smart choices: A practical guide to making better decisions.* Cambridge, MA: Harvard Business School Press.

Hogarth, R. M., & Schoemaker, P. J. H. (2005). Beyond *Blink:* A challenge to behavioral decision making. *Journal of Behavioral Decision Making, 18,* 305–309.

Huber, J., & Puto, C. (1983). Market boundaries and product choice: Illustrating attraction and substitution effects. *Journal of Consumer Research, 10,* 31–44.

Miller, J. M., & Krosnick, J. A. (1998). The impact of candidate name order on election outcomes. *Public Opinion Quarterly, 62,* 291–330.

Nisbett, R. E., & Wilson, T. D. (1977). Telling more than we can know: Verbal reports on mental processes. *Psychological Review, 84,* 231–259.

Payne, J. W., Bettman, J. R., & Johnson, E. J. (1993). *The adaptive decision maker.* New York: Cambridge University Press.

Payne, J. W., Samper, A., Bettman, J. R., & Luce, M. F. (2008). Boundary conditions on unconscious thought in complex decision making. *Psychological Science, 19*(11), 1118–1123.

Searle, D. A., & Rapoport, A. (2000). Optional stopping behavior with relative ranks: The Secretary Problem with unknown population size. *Journal of Behavioral Decision Making, 13,* 391–411.

Simon, H. A. (1956). Rational choice and the structure of the environment. *Psychological Review, 63,* 129–138.

Simonson, I., & Tversky, A. (1992). Choice in context: Tradeoff contrast and extremeness aversion. *Journal of Marketing Research, 29,* 281–295.

Tversky, A. (1972). Elimination by aspects: A theory of choice. *Psychological Review, 79,* 281–299.

Tversky, A., Sattah, S., & Slovic, P. (1988). Contingent weighting in judgment and choice. *Psychological Review, 95,* 371–384.

Wilson, T. D., Lisle, D. J., Schooler, J. W., Hodges, S. D., Klaaren, K. J., & LaFleur, S. J. (1993). Introspecting about reasons can reduce post-choice satisfaction. *Personality and Social Psychology Bulletin, 19,* 331–339.

Wilson, T. D., & Schooler, J. W. (1991). Thinking too much: Introspection can reduce the quality of preferences and decisions. *Journal of Personality and Social Psychology, 60,* 181–192.

# 11

# A Rational Decision Theory

*There is nothing more profitable . . . than to take good counsel with [oneself]; for even if the event turns out contrary to one's hopes, still one's decision was right.*

—Herodotus

## 11.1 Formally Defining Rationality

We have made frequent references to rational choice processes. Now it's time to describe the reigning rational (normative) decision theory. Some experts have defined *rationality* in terms of compatibility between choice and value: Rational behavior is behavior that maximizes the value of consequences. But, as should be clear by now, the question of what constitutes a value is not easily answered, and we think that rationality of choice is a matter of the process of choosing, not of what is chosen. Nevertheless, some very important research in decision theory is concerned with the relationship between decisions and the values of the decision makers. This is the work of John von Neumann and Oskar Morgenstern (1947), in particular their classic analysis described in *Theory of Games and Economic Behavior*. Their *expected utility theory* is the most general and popular description of rational choice in the mathematical and behavioral sciences. We will introduce this framework and relate it to the psychology of decision making in this chapter.

We have mentioned, several times, that we (and most psychologists) believe rational theories are at best an approximate description of how humans really behave. While most people seem to realize that their actual behavior and rational standards diverge, they still want to make good decisions. They want to avoid contradictions in their reasoning and in their behavior; they usually want to behave consistently with the principles of rationality laid down in the expected utility theory we describe in this chapter. Just as with probability theory, as a species we are not endowed with a natural, intuitive sense of these principles. This lack of a clear intuition provides a good reason for an examination of the von Neumann and Morgenstern theory; it doesn't come naturally, so we need to study it to understand its implications for our behavior. To that end, we will also present a perspective on how expected utility theory can be used for *improving* the quality of decision making.

Von Neumann and Morgenstern's (1947) work was purely mathematical. They demonstrated that if a decision maker's choices follow certain (rational) rules ("the axioms"), it is possible to derive *utilities*—real numbers representing personal values—such that one alternative with probabilistic consequences is preferred to another if and only if its *expected utility* is greater than that of the other alternative. Let us break their argument up into a series of steps:

1. It begins by assuming that a decision maker's choices among alternatives with probabilistic consequences "satisfy the axioms" defining rational choice.

2. Then it is possible to associate a real number with each consequence that can be termed the *utility* of that consequence for that decision maker.

3. The *expected utility* of a particular alternative is the expectation of these numbers—that is, the sum of the numbers associated with each possible consequence weighted by the probability that each consequence will occur.

4. The conclusion is that a decision maker will prefer outcome X to outcome Y if and only if the expected utility (number) associated with X is greater than that associated with Y.

The axiomatic system achieves several important goals. First, it spells out succinctly and precisely a list of principles of rational decision making. Of course, even at the normative, philosophical level these principles are a hypothesis about the essence of rational decision making. Other philosophers and mathematicians have proposed alternative systems to prescribe rational decisions, although there is no question that the von Neumann and Morgenstern system is the current champion. Second, if the axioms are satisfied, then a scale of utilities can be constructed in which the real numbers represent the values of consequences in an orderly manner. In a moment, we will develop an analogy to scales for physical weight; it should be obvious how useful to progress in science and practical applications it is to have such a scale. (Imagine modern physics, chemistry, and engineering without numerical scales.) Third, although it is not specified in detail in the axioms, they provide a method to scale utilities, using human preferences for various outcomes as the inputs.

Many decision theorists who concentrate on the relationship between values and action define rationality as making choices that are consistent with these axioms, and they further hypothesize that real human choices are also described by the axioms. A rational decision maker would then be one who prefers alternative X to alternative Y whenever the expected utility of X is greater than that of Y. Of course, the system itself does not require a decision maker's choices to satisfy the axioms; the axioms are a hypothesis about ideal rational choices. In fact, much of the psychology of judgment and choice, already reviewed in the first 10 chapters of this book, implies that people do *not* satisfy the axioms in many decision-making contexts.

There is also nothing in von Neumann and Morgenstern's (1947) expected utility theory that states that the person making the decision has any insight into his or her utilities. The utilities are purely mathematical entities, and their existence is defined by the axioms—just as the lines and vertices of triangles we study in geometry are mathematical entities defined in terms of the axioms of that system. Nevertheless, just as we identify the abstract ideas of points and lines in geometry with the points and lines in the physical world—or on a piece of paper or pictured in our minds—these utilities are often identified with the personal values of the decision maker. Because humans are sentient, active agents (unlike the physical material to which geometry is relevant), there is a special confusion that arises between analytic and synthetic interpretations of the axioms. When expected utility theory is applied *analytically* (usually by economists), actual choices are interpreted as revealing preferences, and these revealed preferences are interpreted as implying utilities. The application has a *postdictive* flavor; as the psychologist Lola Lopes (1994) puts it, "In the modern [analytic] view, utility does not precede and cause preferences; it is instead merely a convenient fiction that can be used by the practitioner to summarize the preferences of those who, by choice or chance, follow the dictates of the von Neumann and Morgenstern axiom system" (p. 286).

In contrast, the theory can be applied *synthetically*. A person is asked first to make judgments about his or her utilities and probabilities, and then those judgments can be combined according to the axioms to predict that person's decisions. For most of us, this sequence makes the most sense: When we make a decision, we usually first try to figure out what we want and how to get it, and only then do we decide what action to take and what choice to make—first our goals and values are determined, then choices and actions. The analytic sequence—first we observe what we choose and then we infer what we must have wanted and expected—seems backward. However, there are some exceptions, as in psychoanalysis, where we attempt *analytically* to discover what our behavior implies about its precursors in desire and belief. And we must remember that the analytic interpretation of decisions is equally valid, and more popular than the synthetic interpretation, among the experts in economics and mathematics who are the primary users of the theory.

Nevertheless, as Tversky and Kahneman (1974) point out in a classic paper, even the probabilities are usually estimated first—and then "used" to make decisions. They write the following:

> It should perhaps be noted that, while subjective probabilities can sometimes be inferred from preferences among bets, they are normally not formed in this fashion. A person bets on team A rather than on team B because he believes that team A is more likely to win; he does not infer this belief from his betting preferences. Thus, in reality, subjective probabilities determine preferences among bets and are not derived from them, as in the axiomatic theory of rational decision. (p. 1130)

Early conceptions of utility in economics (e.g., Jeremy Bentham's [1789/1948] ideas) had a psychological quality, but modern utility theories have eliminated most of the psychology and retained only the behavioral principle that people choose what they prefer. However, there has been a major shift in the past decade with behavioral scientists like Daniel Kahneman, Colin Camerer, George Loewenstein, David Laibson, and others enriching the economic conceptualization with psychological content concerning the cognitive and emotional sources of value judgments.

When we talk about personal values, we have a far broader concept in mind than the concept of utility in the von Neumann-Morgenstern theoretical system. For example, we believe that people can verbalize some of their personal values or value systems; we do not infer these from behavior alone. Otherwise, our language system would not include such concepts as *hypocrisy,* which refers to a discrepancy between a stated value and a particular behavior. Moreover, we believe that values exist independently of both verbalization and behavior. In ordinary language, we regard values as an important existential dimension on which we can place objects, actions, and other phenomena. For example, we say, "He values freedom," as easily as we say, "He went to work yesterday." In fact, we often treat statements of value as if they were statements of fact, even though many philosophers make a very strong distinction between these two types of statements, and only after studying philosophy do most of us become confused by our own beliefs that we or others value certain objects or actions. (Some logical positivists have argued that statements that refer to values are arbitrary, or at least that such statements have no empirical referents.) Perhaps we should (another value!) be less cavalier in our everyday thinking and speaking. The research reviewed in Chapters 9 and 10 should warn us that many intuitive beliefs about our personal values are of dubious validity.

Another important characteristic of values is that they transcend particular situations. When we say we value something, we are referring to more than our behaviors, feelings, and beliefs in just one particular situation. "He values freedom," for example, refers to a general set of dispositions, actions, and beliefs, and once again, a set that a person can at least vaguely verbalize. In fact, there is a popular personality test, the Rokeach Values Inventory, that asks respondents to rank order the entries in a list of abstract value terms—equality, freedom, family security, wisdom, religious salvation—and then uses individual rankings to predict individual behaviors. For example, people who give the term *equality* a high ranking are likely also to support political policies such as school integration, affirmative action, and programs to benefit racial minority group members. Analogously, those ranking *salvation* highly are likely to be regular churchgoers. (We would speculate that the predictive power of the Rokeach test derives from the principles we discussed concerning the belief sampling model for the construction of summary values in Section 9.5. The value labels [e.g., "equality"] sample from the same pool of related, evaluatively loaded beliefs that are sampled when we are in relevant situations [e.g., have just been asked to sign a pro-affirmative action petition]; hence, the predictability stems from an overlap of memories retrieved with value-relevant cues.)

## 11.2. Making Theories Understandable—The Axiomatic Method

The Greek mathematician Euclid was the first we know of to summarize theories (geometry and number theory, in his case) as elegant, brief, axiomatic systems. The idea was that the essential assumptions of a theory would be extracted and written down in a precise notation, and then implications of the core theory (e.g., theorems) would be derived from those axioms. The benefits of such an approach to theoretical expression were numerous: Theorists could check for the completeness and consistency of the original theoretical statements. Scientists could focus on the essentials when applying, testing, and revising theories. And disagreements over what a theory assumed or what it implied could be resolved in a systematic and productive manner. However, axiomatization is far from universal in the sciences, and the method is even limited in mathematics. Utility theory is one of the behavioral science theories to have been axiomatized, and this has given it a great advantage in competition with less orderly formulations.

As an axiom system that leads to derivations of numerical utilities, the von Neumann-Morgenstern theory is of special interest to behavioral scientists because its conclusions have implications about decisions and values as we understand these terms in everyday language and life. Just as the conclusions of Euclidian geometry can be applied to real-world objects, we suppose the conclusions from expected utility theory describe or can be compared to human decision behavior—otherwise, they would simply be systems of rules for manipulating symbols and deriving numbers that would have little interest for most of us.

To explain the nature of a mathematical axiom system and how such a system can be related to real-world objects and phenomena, we will start with a system that is simpler and more concrete than von Neumann and Morgenstern's, but which has an analogous structure. Specifically, let us consider the weights of physical objects. Such weights are *positive real numbers;* they can be added together, as when a 137-gram weight and a 786-gram weight are put together on a scale to yield 923 grams. Such real numbers have important properties, eight of which are elaborated here.

> **Property 1. Comparability:** Given any two positive real numbers, one is larger than the other or they are equal. That may be expressed algebraically by letting $x$ and $y$ stand for the numbers. Then $x > y$, $y > x$, or $x = y$. To avoid expressing all of the following properties in terms of both inequality and equality, we will usually use the "weak" form of comparability: "greater than or equal to," symbolized $\geq$. Thus, we can express comparability as meaning that for any two real numbers $x$ and $y$, $x \geq y$, $y \geq x$, or both (in which case they are equal).

> **Property 2. Ordering:** The relationship "greater than or equal to" determines the transitive ordering of the numbers; that is, if $x \geq y$ and $y \geq z$, then $x \geq z$.

> **Property 3. Additive closure:** When we add two positive numbers, we get a third positive number; that is, if $x$ and $y$ are positive numbers, $z = x + y$ is a positive real number.

> **Property 4. Addition is associative:** The order in which we add numbers is unimportant; that is, $x + (y + z) = (x + y) + z$.

> **Property 5. Addition is symmetric:** The order in which two numbers are added is unimportant; that is, $x + y = y + x$).

> **Property 6. Cancellation:** When a third number is added to each of two numbers, the order of the two sums is the same as the order of the two original numbers; that is, $x + z \geq y + z$ if and only if $x \geq y$.

The next two properties are more mathematical in motivation. The *Archimedean* property (although it is credited to Eudoxus, circa 408–355 BCE) asserts that no positive real number is infinitely larger than any other; that is, no matter how much smaller one number is than a second number, there is some multiple of the first number that is larger than the second number.

**Property 7. The Archimedean property:** Given any two numbers, there always exists an integer-value multiple of one that is larger than the other; that is, if $x \geq y$, then there exists an $n$ such that $ny > x$. Here, $ny$ simply refers to $y$ added to itself $n$ times; this axiom does not involve the general concept of multiplication, since multiplication is unnecessary when we combine integers. (Note that the Archimedean property implies that there is no largest or smallest positive real number: Given any two numbers $x$ and $y$ with $x \geq y$, $x$ cannot be the largest number because there exists an $n$ such that $ny > x$. Similarly, $y$ cannot be the smallest, because $y > x/n$ with that same $n$.)

**Property 8. Solvability:** If $x \geq y$, there exists a $z$ such that $x < y + z$.

The German physicist and mathematician Hölder recognized that the way in which objects behave on a pan balance corresponds perfectly to the eight axioms of this system, where $x \ R \ y$ indicates that object $x$ outbalances object $y$ ($R$ can be thought of as a physical interpretation of the mathematical $>$ relationship), and the operation $O$ corresponds to placing two objects together on the same pan (*concatenating* them). Readers should confirm for themselves that the behavior of objects on a pan balance satisfies these eight properties restated as abstract axioms where $R$ refers to the tilt of the balance and $O$ refers to placing objects in the same pan. (This correspondence is *conceptual;* any particular pan balance may not be large enough to hold all objects that have weight or may be subject to errors in its actual operation.) Thus, Hölder demonstrated mathematically the correspondence between his axiom system and the positive real numbers, and noted the empirical correspondence between the axiom system and the behavior of objects on pan balances. The result is that the behavior of objects on pan balances may be used to assign them real-number measures, called *weights*.

Then, in 1901, Hölder demonstrated something quite profound. Using knowledge from a branch of mathematics called *measurement theory,* he showed that if a system has these eight properties ("the axioms are satisfied"), then real numbers can be associated with the elements of the system, and these real numbers are unique except for multiplication by a positive constant. (A measurement scale with these properties is technically called a *ratio scale.*) That is, he restated these eight properties in terms of axioms in which an abstract relationship $R$ replaced the $\geq$ and an abstract operation $O$ replaced addition. He subsequently demonstrated that if the elements of the system related by $R$ and combined by $O$ satisfy these eight axioms, then it is possible to associate a positive real number with each, such that (1) the real numbers associated with $x \geq y$ if and only if $x \ R \ y$, and (2) $z = x + y$ whenever

$z = x \ O \ y$. Moreover, any two sets of real numbers associated in this manner have the relationship that one set is a positive multiple of the other. For example, the number of kilograms assigned to an object is 1,000 times the number of grams. These numbers are termed *measures;* the measure associated with the entity $x$ is often symbolized $m(x)$. Just as a 1 is the unit of measurement in the real numbers, the *standard gram* or *standard ounce* is the unit of measurement for weights. Finally, the fact that we measure weights in grams or ounces—which are related multiplicatively—corresponds to the conclusion that two sets of measures assigned to the entities satisfying the axiom system are positive multiples of each other.

## 11.3 Defining Rationality: Expected Utility Theory

The axiomatic method, stating the essentials of a theory as an elegantly simple set of postulates that include all and only the necessary definitions and assumptions from which the entire theory can be derived, is a brilliant intellectual invention. Although the method is far from universal in the sciences, we believe it is reasonable to propose the axiomatic formulation as an eventual goal for the expression of all significant theories in any scientific discipline. Even where the theory is precisely stated in equations, a computer program simulation, or words, a summary of the essential principles is absolutely necessary for comprehension and evaluation of any theory (see, for example, Hastie & Stasser, 2000). There is not a unique axiomatization for each theory; usually different but logically equivalent axiom systems can be stated. Our choice of the particular eight properties of numbers, and hence the translation into the eight axioms of weight, is based on our judgment of which axioms readers will find easiest to understand. Other authors cite different systems, many of which are more elegant and may be easier for an expert to work with. In the case of the von Neumann and Morgenstern utility theory, there are many axiomatizations, and we have chosen the one that we believe is most comprehensible to an intelligent reader who is not an expert in mathematical logic.

The basic *entities* of the von Neumann-Morgenstern system can be conceptualized as *alternatives* to be evaluated or chosen between, consisting of probabilistic consequences—often referred to as *gambles.* The basic relationship is one of *preference,* which induces an order on the alternatives; we will settle for the *weak ordering,* $\geq$, which might be expressed as "is indifferent or preferred to" behaviorally. (Note that this expression is rough; a more precise interpretation of $\geq$ is "is not unpreferred to," because both $A \geq B$ and $B \geq A$ are possible, in which case $A \sim B$; however, that usage is quite awkward. To be technically precise, we should distinguish between strong preference (>) and weak preference (≥); the reader wishing such precision can translate by considering weak and strong preference separately.)

The basic *operation* for combining the alternatives (analogous to placing more than one object on a balance pan—the general term is *concatenation*) may be conceptualized as a *probability mixture* of alternatives. Thus, if $A$ and $B$ are alternatives, $ApB$ refers to receiving alternative $A$ with probability $p$ and alternative $B$ with probability $(1 - p)$. Note that the probability of receiving $B$ is implicit, and we will only consider binary, two-alternative gambles, so given the probability of $A$ (e.g., $p$), the probability of $B$ will be 1 minus that value $(1 - p)$ or the *complement*.

To illustrate some relationships that will be prescribed by the axioms, consider the evaluation of a complex, multistage gamble. The following results will be explicated when we discuss the interpretation of individual axioms (especially Axiom 3, "Closure," and Axiom 4, "Distribution of Probabilities"). Because the alternatives specify the consequences with particular probabilities, the probability mixture of alternatives is synonymous with a probability mixture of the consequences; that is, if alternative $A$ consists of consequence $x$ with probability $r$ and consequence $y$ with probability $(1 - r)$, whereas alternative $B$ consists of consequence $z$ with probability $s$ and alternative $w$ with probability $(1 - s)$, then $ApB$ consists of consequence $x$ with probability $rp$, consequence $y$ with probability $(1 - r)p$, consequence $z$ with probability $s(1 - p)$, and consequence $w$ with probability $(1 - s)(1 - p)$. An alternative with a single consequence is conceptualized as one in which the consequence occurs with a probability of 1.

We find it helpful to represent alternatives, consequences, and probability mixtures in the decision tree diagram format, as in Figure 11.1. These diagrams are useful when theoretical gambles are to be compared (e.g., to grasp the implications of the axioms or the structure of experimental stimulus gambles), and especially when the system is to be applied to analyze actual decisions.

What von Neumann and Morgenstern (1947) proved is that when their axioms are satisfied, a numerical measure can be associated with each consequence—termed a *utility* of that consequence (analogous to the numerical weight of a physical object)—and that the alternatives themselves can be ordered according to their expected utility. In other words, the basic result is that a preference between the alternatives can be represented by an ordering of their expected utilities. (Because a single consequence can be conceptualized as an alternative in which that consequence occurs with the probability of 1, and vice versa, the axioms can be stated in terms of either consequences or alternatives. We chose to present the axioms in

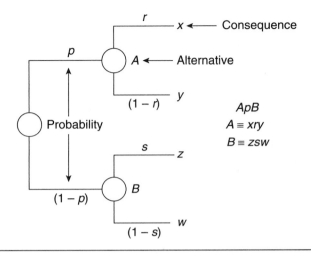

**Figure 11.1**    Example decision tree representation of a gamble that might be abbreviated in the von Neumann and Morgenstern axioms

terms of alternatives because we think they will be easier to understand in that form.)

We can summarize the analogy between the von Neumann and Morgenstern system and Hölder's axiomatization of physical weight as follows: Alternatives in a choice set are analogous physical objects to be weighed; weak preference is analogous to the "weighs the same as or more than" result from a pan balance test; and the "probability mixture" concatenation operation (mixing two alternatives together in a binary gamble) corresponds to placing more than one object on a pan at the same time. In both systems, if the axioms are satisfied, the result is a real-number scale, of utility or of physical weight.

Here, at last, are the von Neumann and Morgenstern axioms for expected utility theory:

**Axiom 1. Comparability:** If $A$ and $B$ are in the alternative set $S$, then either $A \gtrsim B$ or $B \gtrsim A$ or both, in which case $A \sim B$.

**Axiom 2. Transitivity:** If $A \gtrsim B$ and $B \gtrsim C$, then $A \gtrsim C$.

**Axiom 3. Closure:** If $A$ and $B$ are in alternative set $S$, then $ApB$ is as well.

**Axiom 4. Distribution of probabilities across alternatives:** If $A$ and $B$ are in $S$, then $[(ApB)qB] \sim (ApqB)$.

**Axiom 5. Independence:** If $A$, $B$, and $C$ are in $S$, $A \gtrsim B$ if and only if $(ApC) \gtrsim (BpC)$.

**Axiom 6. Consistency:** For all $A$ and $B$ in $S$, $A \geq B$ if and only if $A \geq (ApB) \geq B$.

**Axiom 7. Solvability:** For all $A$, $B$, and $C$ in $S$, if $A \gtrsim B \gtrsim C$, then there exists a probability $p$ such that $B \sim (ApC)$. (This axiom is crucial to the construction of the utility scale.)

If real numbers are substituted for the alternatives and probabilities for the $p$'s and $q$'s, then it is clear that these axioms are satisfied whenever the number associated with an alternative is equal to its expectation. What von Neumann and Morgenstern (1947) did was prove the converse: If these axioms are satisfied, then it is possible to construct a measure for each alternative equal to its expectation in such a way that the order of the alternatives corresponds to the order of the expectations. Moreover, the origin and units of these measures are arbitrary (as in the familiar scale of temperature). The number associated with an alternative is termed its *expected utility;* that number associated with a consequence, which is equivalent to an alternative that has that consequence with probability 1, is the utility of that consequence. Because only the origin and the unit of measurement are arbitrary in such utility assignments, any different assignments are related in a linear manner, meaning any two scales of utility across a set of alternatives will plot as a straight line in x-y graphic coordinates. Technically, this is called an *interval scale* because both the units of measurement and the "zero point" are arbitrary. (Remember that we called the weight scale a *ratio scale,* because the zero point was *not* arbitrary, although the units [e.g., grams, ounces] were.)

The arbitrary origin and unit of measurement allow us to use the solvability axiom to determine the utility of a third alternative whenever the utilities of two others are known. Suppose, for example, $A \gtrsim B \gtrsim C$. We can allow the utility of A to equal 100 and the utility of C to equal 0. Now, according to the solvability axiom, there exists a probability $p$ such that the utility of B is equal to the utility of $ApC$ that is simply $p$ times the utility of A plus $(1 - p)$ times the utility of C, which is $p100 + (1 - p)0$. Thus, as promised, the solvability axiom is crucial in determining the actual numerical values of these utilities. Because all possible scales and utilities are linear functions of each other, we can assign 100 as the utility of the most preferred alternative in each set $S$, and 0 as the utility of the least preferred alternative, and then solve for the utilities of all the remaining alternatives, locating their utilities in the 0–100 interval. Notice that the probability scale in the probability mixture operation is the means to scale the utilities. (The laws and scale of probability will be preserved in the decision maker's preferences *if* "the axioms are satisfied"—an assumption that may be hard to satisfy behaviorally, if the empirical results reported in Chapters 1–10 are valid.)

Von Neumann and Morgenstern's system is conceptually beautiful. At the risk of being repetitive, we state again that the *utilities* derived analytically from these axioms do not necessarily correspond to our intuitive or verbal notions of personal value, any more than the measures of weight derived from behavior of objects in pan balances necessarily correspond to our intuitive notions of weight. Nevertheless, just as a concept of weight that did not relate to our intuitions about which objects are heavier than which others would be a very strange notion indeed, the concept of utility is meant to have a relationship to subjective value. In fact, it is because the utilities derived according to the von Neumann and Morgenstern system *do* bear some relationship to our notions of personal value that they are of interest to psychologists. And this is the justification for our attempt to explain how they can be used to *improve* our decision-making capabilities at the end of this chapter. Most people, perhaps after some thought, acknowledge that each axiom individually seems to be acceptable as part of a general definition of rationality, and even as a prescription for how they wish they made their choices. Let's discuss each axiom in more detail.

**Axiom 1. Comparability:** If $A$ and $B$ are in the alternative set $S$, then either $A \geq B$ or $B \geq A$, or both, in which case $A \sim B$.

Axiom 1 states that when faced with two alternatives, the decision maker should have at least a weak preference. The strongest rationale for this axiom is the fact that a decision maker faced with alternatives must choose one of them. But it also equates inability to make such a choice with indifference. Is someone who maintains that he or she cannot choose between two alternatives necessarily indifferent? Consider, for example, the choice discussed in Chapter 10 of the professor trying to decide what job to take. If she were to conclude that she could not make a choice, would that really mean that she is indifferent, that she does not care? Jay Kadane, Mark Schervish, and Teddy Seidenfeld (1999), for example, maintain that not having a preference is *not* equivalent to being indifferent. And in some circumstances where "protected values" are perceived to be at stake, people refuse to make choices—which is, of course, a choice, too. Jonathan Baron and Mark Spranca (1997) cite situations in which many people refuse to choose. For example, when considering personal or policy alternatives where trade-offs between lives and money are demanded, many citizens appear to avert their gaze and "choose not to choose." But is it reasonable to say that these non-choices express a true indifference between 55 mph speed limits and inexpensive automobiles versus the deaths of approximately 50,000 fellow citizens from traffic accidents?

Apples and oranges are, however, both fruit, and if one must choose a fruit from a dish of apples and oranges, it will be either an apple or an orange. Could not the choice itself define the preference, analytically? Economists refer to such a choice as a *revealed preference*, and assume utility theory to infer that, for example, our highway safety preferences imply a dollar value of approximately $3,000,000 per human life. Moreover, isn't it true that when people say they have no idea why they made a choice, subsequent questioning often reveals that there really *is* a preference involved? For example, if the professor in Chapter 10 maintained that she really was incapable of choosing between jobs but "just happened to pick" one of them in order to be near (or away from) relatives, would not proximity to relatives be an important consideration in her choice? Perhaps she simply would be unaware of this factor at the time she made the choice—or perhaps embarrassed to discuss it, because she might not consider it a good reason for choosing one job over another. Our own position is that people really do have preferences, except in rare instances such as predicting the outcome of a coin toss, in which case they are truly indifferent. We do not, however, accept the revealed preference position—that the preference is inherent in the choice—for the reasons outlined in the previous chapters. Specifically, choice may be truly irrational, and hence, contradictory. Thus, it follows that there may be a discrepancy between choice in a particular situation and the preferences of the individual making the choice.

While revealed preference can be rejected on the basis of the cognitive difficulty of choice, the most common reason for rejecting the apparent evidence is that people sometimes do things they do not *want* to do; that is, they choose alternatives they do not prefer. For example, the psychologist and philosopher William James (1842–1910) noted that people with toothaches often prod the painful area of their mouth with their tongue, although they clearly prefer lack of pain to the pain that results from prodding.

The counterargument from the revealed preference theorist is that the very act of prodding the area of a toothache indicates that the individual has a greater positive value for the information gained that the tooth is still hurting than negative value for the pain experienced. Such values may appear "stupid," because toothaches tend not to go away on their own without treatment, and when a given part of our mouth is aching we can be more than reasonably sure that it will be more painful if we touch it with our tongue, *without* actually doing so. The revealed preference theorist, however, has the counterargument that *de gustibus non disputandum* ("There's no disputing matters of taste"). The fact that the sufferer prods the tooth reveals that even such redundant information is worth the pain.

Because what constitutes pleasure and pain to an individual cannot be known unambiguously, the argument that people often do what they really dislike doing is fairly ineffective against the revealed preference position. In contrast, knowing that the choices are often contradictory for *cognitive* reasons undermines this position.

## Axiom 2. Transitivity: If $A \geq B$ and $B \geq C$, then $A \geq C$.

The primary justification for Axiom 2 is that individuals who violate it can be turned into "money pumps." Suppose that John Dolt preferred alternative A to alternative B, alternative B to alternative C, and yet C to A. Assume, further, that he is not indifferent in his choice between any of these alternatives. Consequently, he should be willing to *pay something* to trade a less preferred alternative for a more preferred one. Now suppose John is given alternative C *as a gift*. Because he prefers alternative B to C, he should be willing to pay something to have B instead. Subsequently, John should be willing to pay something to have alternative A substituted for B, and finally to pay for the substitution of C for A. Then John will have paid three times for the privilege of ending up with the alternative he was given in the first place. By repeating this cycle indefinitely, John (hypothetically, anyway) would pay a lot of money to get nowhere.

The response to the money pump argument is that an individual with intransitive preferences would simply refuse to play that game. Choices are, after all, not made repeatedly, but in a particular context. A choice between two alternatives does not have to be one by which the individual is bound for all time and in all circumstances. One noted economist is quoted as saying that in a particular decision-making situation, most people will "satisfy their preferences and let the axioms satisfy themselves" (Paul Samuelson, quoted by Daniel Ellsberg, 1961). For example, consider the hiring of a new secretary. Suppose that the employer has three criteria for making a job offer: (1) clerical skills, (2) organizational ability, and (3) willingness to run errands and do other jobs not specifically in the position description. Suppose that the rank of three prospective secretaries (A, B, and C) on clerical skills is A, B, C; on organizational ability is B, C, A; and on willingness is C, A, B. Thus applicant A is superior to applicant B on two of these three dimensions (clerical skill and willingness), B is superior to C on two (clerical skill and organization), and C is superior to A on two (organization and willingness). A decision based on the principle that one applicant is preferred to another whenever that applicant is superior on two of three dimensions results in intransitivity. (This is the qualitative additive difference or *voting rule* choice strategy discussed in Chapter 10.) What will happen is that the *order* in which the applicants are considered will be crucial, with the applicant considered last being the one chosen.

Is this consequence necessarily a bad one? Even though the employer could in principle become a money pump, no one is going to make her one—by giving her one of the secretaries and then demanding payment for subsequent substitutions. But we suspect that many of our most frustrating decision experiences occur when we encounter alternatives that are important, and where each alternative has some good and some bad attributes, forcing us to consider compensatory trade-offs, and sometimes inducing intransitivity-producing strategies: "Okay, I'm going to take the high-paying job; but no, I don't want to give up the much more flexible vacation options in the second job; but wait, I don't want to live in the Midwest; but the chance for advancement is much better in the third job . . ." This sometimes produces great personal discomfort and leads to an inability to make a choice.

We believe that choices *should* be transitive. This idea is part of a general argument that choice is superior when it is made as if the decision maker *were* bound by that choice in a broader context and across time. This argument is from Immanuel Kant (1724–1804), who proposed that individuals should make choices as if they were formulating a *policy* for all people at all times. There is empirical evidence showing that when a criterion is available according to which we can decide whether choices are good or bad, choices made in accord with Kant's principle are in fact superior to those made in the narrower context of considering only the options immediately available.

**Axiom 3. Closure:** If *A* and *B* are in alternative set *S*, then *ApB* is as well.

Axiom 3 simply requires that the decision maker be capable of conceptualizing a probability mixture of alternatives as itself an alternative. If people were incapable of doing so, there would be little point in theorizing about decision making.

**Axiom 4. Distribution of probabilities across alternatives:** If *A* and *B* are in *S*, then *[(ApB)qB] ∼ (ApqB)*.

Basically, Axiom 4 requires that people follow the principles of probability theory (see Appendix). This axiom is illustrated in the decision trees in Figures 11.2 and 11.3; the two-stage gamble on the left must be treated as equivalent to the one-stage gamble on the right to satisfy the axiom.

Of course, people may violate it without disputing it; for example, it is violated by the person who reacts differently to a consequence of receiving $45 with probability .20 than to a two-stage consequence in which the person receives nothing with probability .75 in the first stage and then receives $45 with probability .80 if the second is reached. (Since $[1.00 - .75] \times .80 = .20$, the distribution axiom requires that the two lotteries be treated as identical.)

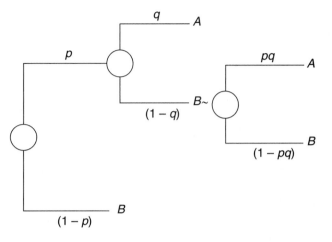

**Figure 11.2**   Decision tree representation of the two abstract lotteries mentioned in Axiom 4

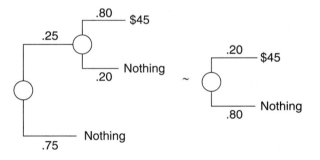

**Figure 11.3**   Decision tree representation of a concrete pair of gambles illustrating an equivalence implied by Axiom 4

Von Neumann and Morgenstern (1947) discuss probabilities as if they were objective. (Their $p$'s and $q$'s are supposed to be probabilities measured on an absolute scale, although the concept of accuracy or objectivity in probabilities is complex and controversial.) There are several decision theories in which this axiom is relaxed—most notably Ward Edwards's early proposal to shift from objective to subjective probabilities, creating an alternative rational decision theory. It is certainly possible to have a set of nonobjective probabilities that are internally coherent and consistent with the rules of probability theory (discussed at length in Chapter 9 and the Appendix). However, if the decision maker attempts to deal with future uncertainty by making probability assessments, these must be made according to rules of probability theory; otherwise, contradictory choices can result. In Chapter 12, we will explore prospect theory (introduced in Chapter 9), an axiomatic *non-expected utility theory* in which nonobjective and incoherent decision weights replace probabilities. Prospect theory is similar in overall structure to the von Neumann and Morgenstern theory, but it is meant to be descriptive of human decision behavior and *not* a model of rational choice.

**Axiom 5. Independence:** If *A, B,* and *C* are in *S*, $A \gtrsim B$ if and only if $(ApC) \gtrsim (BpC)$.

Axiom 5 is crucial. In fact, many decision theorists have investigated at length the effects of violating it, or of omitting it from a set of rules governing choice. At first reading, it appears innocuous: If one alternative is preferred to another, shouldn't that preference remain even though, with some specified probability, the decision maker receives neither, but a third instead? That is all this axiom states. Figure 11.4 summarizes the axiom graphically.

Warning: Some students are confused because they misread the axiom to refer to a situation as one of *joint receipt*—the chooser *receives* both A and C or *receives both*

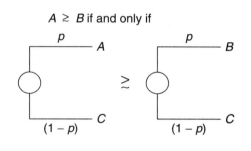

Figure 11.4    Decision tree representation of the situation described by Axiom 5

B and C—but the correct situation is a *probability mixture* of receiving A *or* B compared with a *probability mixture* of receiving B *or* C, where *or* is exclusive—meaning *not* both. If the situation was joint receipt, then the axiom wouldn't make much sense: Of course, we might have little desire to receive a right shoe *or* a left shoe, but to receive both a right shoe *and* a left shoe might be very attractive, depending on the shoes, of course.

Consider a pseudocertainty effect: Most people prefer a .20 probability of receiving $45 to a .25 probability of receiving $30 (Panel 1 in Figure 11.5), yet simultaneously they prefer $30 for sure to an .80 probability of receiving $45 (Panel 2). Now let *A* be the alternative of receiving $30 for sure and *B* be that of receiving $45 with the probability of .80. *A* is preferred to *B* (as in Panel 2). Let *C* be the alternative of receiving nothing. Now let *p* equal .25. Then (*A* .25 *C*)

Most people prefer the gamble on the left . . .

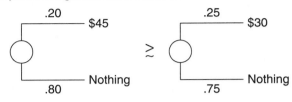

Most people also prefer the "sure thing" on the left in this pair. . .

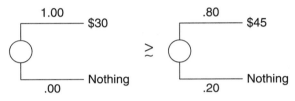

Axiom 5 ("Independence") implies the preference ordering for the prospects above applies to the corresponding prospects below . . .

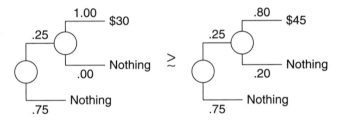

Axiom 4 (Probability Theory) implies the preference ordering on the simple gambles below, but this exactly contradicts the first preference ordering above.

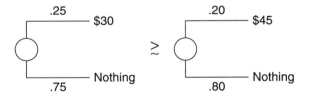

**Figure 11.5**    Illustration of the pseudocertainty effect that violates Axioms 4 and 5

is an alternative consisting of receiving $30 for sure with probability .25 versus receiving nothing with probability .75 (left-hand side of Panel 3), which—by the distribution of probabilities axiom—is just the alternative of receiving $30 with probability .25 (left-hand side of Panel 4). In contrast, (B .25 C) is the alternative consisting of a .25 probability of receiving $45 with probability

.80 and a .75 probability of receiving nothing (right-hand side of Panel 3)—that is, receiving $45 with probability .80 × .25 = .20 (right-hand side of Panel 4). Thus, the typical preferences summarized in Panel 1 imply the opposite ordering of that summarized in Panel 2. Therefore, anyone who has the Panel 1 and Panel 2 preferences (most people do) both exhibits the pseudocertainty effect and violates the independence axiom.

The pseudocertainty effect describes choices that are influenced by the way the consequences are framed, rather than solely by the consequences themselves. Is such irrationality the only reason for violating the independence axiom? There is another reason. Axiom 5 implies that the decision maker cannot be affected by the *skewness* of the consequences, which can be conceptualized as a probability distribution over personal values. Figure 11.6 shows the skewed distributions of two different alternatives. Both distributions have the same average, hence the same expected personal value, which

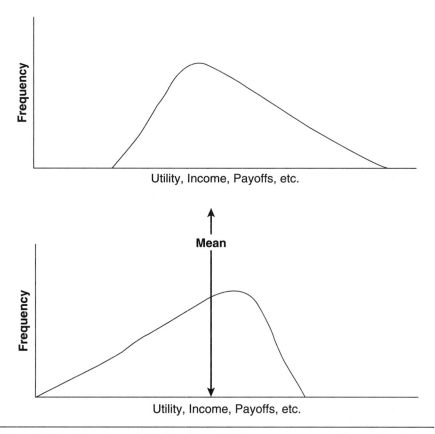

**Figure 11.6**   Two skewed distributions with the same average value and variance

is a criterion of choice implied by the axioms. These distributions also have the same variance. (For a description of the mean and variance of a probability distribution see a good introductory statistics text, e.g., *Statistics* by Freedman, Pisani, Purves, & Adhikari, 1991.)

If the distributions in Figure 11.6 were those of wealth in a society, most people would have a definite preference for the upper distribution; its positive skewness means that income can be increased from any point—an incentive for productive work—and incidentally it is the distribution that describes wealth in industrialized societies. Moreover, those people lowest in the distribution are not as distant from the average as in the lower distribution, where a large number of people are already earning a maximal amount of money, and there is a tail of people in the *negatively skewed* part of this distribution who are quite far below the average income. If we have such concerns about the distribution outcomes in society, why not about the consequences for choosing alternatives in our own lives? In fact, many of us do not like alternatives with large negative skews. Note also that popular lotteries, gambling devices, and competitive tournaments generally have positive skews (i.e., small probabilities of winning a lot). There are substantial individual differences in preferences for distributions of multi-outcome gambles or lotteries; in experimental studies in which money lotteries are evaluated, positive skewed lotteries (like the upper distribution in Figure 11.6) are the modal favorites for lotteries composed of both gains and losses (Lopes & Oden, 1999).

**Axiom 6. Consistency:** For all $A$ and $B$ in $S$, $A \geq B$ if and only if $A \geq (ApB) \geq B$.

Axiom 6 states that if we prefer one alternative to another, then we prefer at least some chance of receiving that alternative rather than the other one (see Figure 11.7). This axiom appears indisputable.

**Axiom 7. Solvability:** For all $A$, $B$, and $C$ in $S$, if $A \geq B \geq C$, then there exists a probability $p$ such that $B \sim (ApC)$.

Axiom 7 is similar to the Archimedean property in Hölder's axiom system for physical weights. What it states in effect is that no alternative is so much better or worse than another that some probability mixture of alternatives on either side is not regarded as equivalent to the original alternative. Consider, for example, three alternatives, $A$, $B$, and $C$, with the preference order $ABC$. The axiom states

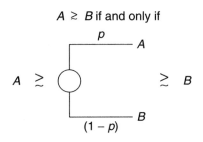

$A \geq B$ if and only if

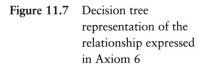

**Figure 11.7**   Decision tree representation of the relationship expressed in Axiom 6

that there will be *some* probabilistic way of combining $A$ and $C$ such that the individual is indifferent to choosing $B$ or this combination (see Figure 11.8).

Now, if $A$ were incomparably more attractive to the decision maker than any of the other alternatives, then *any* probability of receiving $A$ rather than $C$ might lead to a preference for $ApC$ over $B$. The same argument would hold *mutatis mutandis* (meaning "with the necessary changes") if alternative $C$ were incomparably worse than $B$. The axiom states that no such alternatives exist. Well, what about eternal bliss in Heaven? Or, conversely, sudden death? Would not any alternative involving even the slightest probability of eternal bliss be preferred to some other alternative with drabber consequences—so that

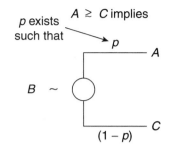

**Figure 11.8**  Decision tree representation of Axiom 7; the axiom implies there exists a probability *(p)* that satisfies the equivalence relationship between the "certainty equivalent" *(B)* and the gamble

the individual could never be indifferent in choosing between the drab alternative and a probability mixture involving such bliss? Or do we not eschew completely those alternatives involving some probability of death? (Perhaps we should not discuss eternal bliss, because we cannot even conceptualize it.) It is clear from our behavior that we dread death and attempt to avoid it, at least for as long as we have hope that the positive aspects of life and the future outweigh the negative. Do we not, then, avoid all alternatives that involve some probability of death? The answer is, "No." Everyday life involves some risk of death, even such trivial actions as crossing a street to buy a newspaper. Sometimes this probability is more salient than at other times—as when people who fear airplane trips still fly tens of thousands of miles a year. But it is always there. Even staying in bed all day to avoid what appears to be the risk of death would involve a risk of physical deterioration, perhaps leading to death. In addition, there are clear examples of thoughtful decisions that involve a high probability of death—for instance, a decision to join an underground resistance movement during a military occupation or the deliberate choice of a high-paying, but dangerous profession like industrial deep-sea diving.

All of the axioms appear quite reasonable. In fact, if we assume comparability, we can violate only the independence axiom without becoming outright irrational. The axioms, however, have strong implications, as do other mathematical results. Believing the Pythagorean theorem, for example, we anticipate the length of a third side of a right triangle when we know the length of two sides. If physical measurement does not confirm our expectations, we conclude that the triangle is not a right triangle; we rarely or never conclude that the theorem is true—that the triangle has a right angle and our measurements are correct—but that the logic of mathematical deduction just doesn't apply. The demanding aspect of the von Neumann and Morgenstern axioms is that if we accept them, we are bound to evaluate alternatives in a choice situation in terms of their expected utility. That is, numbers exist that describe the utility of each consequence of alternative choices. (Such numbers are, once again, those associated with alternatives that have that particular consequence with a probability of 1.) These numbers can be determined by some choices, using the solvability axiom; they then require that other choices as well be made in terms of the expected utilities computed. Other characteristics describing the distribution of consequences—for example, its skewness—are irrelevant.

The solvability axiom is especially useful if we want to design a method to scale a person's utilities for outcomes. A review of measurement and scaling methods is beyond the scope of this book (see Dawes & Smith, 1985, for an introduction), but here is an example to convey the basic method. For simplicity, consider three outcomes (which could be dollars, but let's consider something less quantitative): a 1-week vacation in the city of Boulder (Colorado), Pittsburgh (Pennsylvania), or Lubbock (Texas). Suppose further that our decision maker prefers them in that ordering, Boulder over Pittsburgh, Pittsburgh over Lubbock ($A \geq B \geq C$ as required by the solvability axiom). Now, where in the interval between Boulder and Lubbock is the decision maker's utility for Pittsburgh? Relying heavily on "solvability," we can assign the most favored and least favored options the values of 1.0 and 0.0 (or, for that matter, because the scale origin and units are arbitrary, 100 and 0) and present the decision maker with a series of gambles, mixing a trip to Boulder with a trip to Lubbock, until we find a gamble that is judged indifferent compared with the trip to Pittsburgh (the right-hand gamble in Figure 11.8). Then, if the axioms are satisfied we can use the probability mixture number from the gamble as a scale value for Pittsburgh's utility. For example, if a decision maker is indifferent between 1 week in Pittsburgh for sure and a .80 chance of ending up in Boulder mixed with a .20 chance of spending the week in Lubbock, we would scale the utility value for Pittsburgh at 80 on a 0–100 scale with Boulder and Lubbock as endpoints. This method can be generalized to scale any number of outcomes on an interval utility scale (and this method of eliciting *preference probabilities* is frequently used in applied decision analysis).

There are many studies in which utility functions are scaled, especially for the utilities of money. The forms of these functions are often used to interpret and even to predict the behavior of people from whom they've been derived. For example, a concave curve (negatively accelerating, with diminishing marginal returns) is sometimes interpreted as implying that the person who exhibits it is risk-averse in the domain of such a curve, while the reverse, convex curve is interpreted as implying a risk-seeking attitude. According to the theory, such curves summarize analytically and predict synthetically a person's behavior in choosing real-money gambles to play in the laboratory, and they are even associated with the occupational choices of business executives. Executives in financially volatile businesses are more likely to exhibit convexity in their utility curves than executives in more placid financial environments (MacCrimmon & Wehrung, 1986; see additional discussion of the interpretation of utility curves in Section 9.3).

## 11.4 Traditional Objections to the Axioms

The axioms were not presented as descriptions of actual behavior, but rather as conditions of *desirable* choices. Are they? After the publication of von Neumann and Morgenstern's (1947) book, several theorists suggested that the axioms placed unreasonable constraints on choice behavior and that they should *not* be satisfied. The best-known objections consisted of two paradoxes, originally stated as conceptual puzzles and later validated in experimental studies. One of these objections was raised by the Nobel laureate economist Maurice Allais and the other by the decision theorist Daniel Ellsberg (who achieved notoriety by releasing the *Pentagon Papers,* which exposed the United States government's secret objectives in the Vietnam War).

### The Allais Paradox

Maurice Allais won the Nobel Prize in Economics for his argument that the expected utility principle that results from the von Neumann-Morgenstern axiom system is too restrictive. Consider, for example, the choice between alternatives A and B involving millions of dollars:

**Alternative A:** Receive $1 million with probability 1.00 (i.e., for certain).

**Alternative B:** Receive $2.5 million with probability .10, $1 million with probability .89, and nothing with probability .01.

When presented with this (hypothetical) choice, most people choose alternative A. That means that if they abide by the axioms, it is possible to assign utilities to the consequences of receiving $1 million, $2.5 million, or nothing in such a way that the choice of A implies a higher expected utility for it than for B. Specifically,

U($1 million) > .10 U($2.5 million) + .89 U($1 million) + .01 U(nothing).

By the solvability axiom, we can set U($2.5 million) = 1.0 and U(nothing) = 0.0. The conclusion then is .11 U($1 million) > .10.

Now consider the choice between two different alternatives:

**Alternative A′:** $1 million with probability .11, otherwise nothing

**Alternative B′:** $2.5 million with probability .10, otherwise nothing

The expected utility of alternative A′ is .11, while that of alternative B′ is .10, because we have set the utility at $2.5 million equal to 1.0. Thus, the choice of A over B requires the choice of A′ over B′. Allais argued that it was nevertheless reasonable to choose A over B *and* B′ over A′, which is in fact the choice most people make when presented with this hypothetical pair of decisions. Why accept a 1/100 chance of receiving nothing when you can receive a million dollars for sure? Conversely, given that the most probable outcome in the second choice is to receive nothing at all, why not take a 1/100 risk of getting nothing in order to increase the potential payoff by a factor of 2.5 times?

The mathematician Leonard (Jimmy) Savage (1954) gave a compelling analysis of those questions. Consider his suggestion that the probabilities of the various outcomes are illustrated by randomly drawing a chip out of a bag containing 100 chips. Of these chips, 1 is black, 10 are blue, and 89 are red. Alternative A can then be conceptualized as paying out $1 million no matter which chip is drawn. In contrast, an individual choosing alternative B receives $1 million if a red chip is drawn, $2.5 million if a blue chip is drawn, and nothing if the black chip is drawn. Now it does not matter to the decision maker which alternative is chosen if a red chip is drawn, because in either case he or she receives a million dollars; hence, a choice of A over B implies that the possibility of receiving a million dollars rather than nothing if the black chip is drawn from the 11 chips that are not red is preferred to the possibility of receiving $2.5 million rather than nothing if one of the 10 blue chips is drawn. (Sometimes the choice is interpreted as a desire to avoid the potential regret of getting nothing: "Well, dear, I had a sure million dollars, but I decided to try to "maximize" my expected value and I gambled. Unfortunately, I lost. . . .") But that preference is violated if the individual also chooses B′ over A′. Once again, the outcome will be the same if a red chip is drawn, but the individual is now showing a preference for receiving $2.5 million if a blue chip is drawn and nothing if the black one is drawn over receiving $1 million if either a blue or black chip is drawn.

**Chips Drawn From a Bag of 100**

| | | 89 Red | 1 Black | 10 Blue |
|---|---|---|---|---|
| **CHOICE** | A | $1 million | $1 million | $1 million |
| | B | $1 million | nothing | $2.5 million |
| **CHOICE** | A′ | nothing | $1 million | $1 million |
| | B′ | nothing | nothing | $2.5 million |

**Figure 11.9**    Illustration of Savage's analysis of the Allais paradox

Savage's (1954) example is basically a restatement of the independence axiom in concrete terms; it makes this axiom quite compelling. Savage's argument is illustrated in Figure 11.9. In the figure, it is obvious that the event of drawing a red chip, with a constant .89 probability across the gambles, should be irrelevant to the choice, because its payoff is constant within each choice set pair.

## The Ellsberg Paradox

Ellsberg's (1961) problem focuses attention on the nature of the uncertainty presented by different gambles, but again it is an assault on the acceptability of the independence axiom. Imagine an urn containing 90 colored balls—30 red balls and 60 black and yellow balls. You do not know the exact proportion of blacks and yellows, only that there is a total of 60. One ball will be drawn at random from the urn. Which of the following gambles would you prefer?

**Alternative I:** Receive $100 if the ball drawn is red, nothing otherwise.

**Alternative II:** Receive $100 if the ball drawn is black, nothing otherwise.

Most people choose alternative I; the obvious interpretation is that they would rather bet on a precise, known probability of winning, than on an ambiguous uncertainty.

Now consider another pair of gambles. Again, which would you prefer?

**Alternative III:** Receive $100 if a red or a yellow ball is drawn, nothing if a black is drawn.

**Alternative IV:** Receive $100 if a black or a yellow ball is drawn, nothing if a red is drawn.

Now most people choose IV, again because they prefer the well-defined risk (60/90 balls) over the ambiguous uncertainty. (The chances of winning in alternative III could range from 31/90 to 89/90.)

The "catch" with this pattern of choices is that it violates the independence axiom, again. The table in Figure 11.10 makes this clear. The payoffs resulting from drawing a yellow ball are identical in each pair, so the preference should depend only on the pattern of payoffs for the red and black draws; the yellow outcome should be irrelevant. But the red and black patterns are identical across the two pairs, implying there should be no change in preferences from the first pair to the second. However, most people do exhibit strong preferences, but for reversed red-and-black patterns between the two pairs. Another way to express the contradiction is to note that in the first pair, the chooser prefers to bet *on* red, rather than black. But in the second pair, the chooser prefers to bet *against* red, rather than black. These

**BALLS IN THE URN**

|  |  | 30 | ⌐———— 60 ————⌐ | |
|  |  | Red | Black | Yellow |
| --- | --- | --- | --- | --- |
| **CHOICE** | I | $100 | nothing | nothing |
|  | II | nothing | $100 | nothing |
| **CHOICE** | III | $100 | nothing | $100 |
|  | IV | nothing | $100 | $100 |

**Figure 11.10**   The gambles presented in Ellsberg's paradox

choices imply that the chooser believes red is more likely than black *and* that not-red is more likely than not-black. Moreover, the chooser is acting as though *red or yellow* is less likely than *black or yellow*, but at the same time as though *red* is more likely than *black*. It is impossible to assign probabilities—numbers consistent with the principles of probability theory—to the outcomes given these choices.

## 11.5 The Shoulds and Dos of the System

Of course, people do not always choose in accord with von Neumann and Morgenstern's axioms, for several reasons, including the irrationalities of judgment and valuation that have been described in the previous chapters of this book. Daniel Ellsberg (1961) had an especially astute comment:

> There are those who do not violate the axioms, or say they won't; such subjects tend to apply the axioms rather than their intuition, and when in doubt to apply some form of the Principle of Insufficient Reason. Some violate the axioms cheerfully, even with gusto; others sadly but persistently, having looked into their hearts, and found conflicts with the axioms and decided, in Samuelson's phrase, to satisfy their preferences and let the axioms satisfy themselves. Still others tend, intuitively, to violate the axioms but feel guilty about it and go back into further analysis. (p. 655)

Should we make only choices satisfying the axioms of the system? Our answer to that question is a qualified "yes." The qualification is that although we should not be *bound* by the axioms, we should *consider* them when making choices. While it is difficult to determine whether a particular decision per se satisfies or violates an axiom or a set of axioms, the fact that the axioms are true if and only if choices are made according to expected utility provides a method for considering alternative decisions. For example, consider a husband and wife with children who decide to fly on separate airplanes. This indicates (according to the theory) that the couple felt that the death of both of them would be more than twice as bad as the death of either one alone. We will analyze this example within the von Neumann and Morgenstern framework.

There are three distinct consequences in this example: Both die, one dies and one lives, or neither dies. Because the assignment of two utility values is arbitrary (given that all utility scales are related to each other in a linear manner), we can arbitrarily assign the utility $-1$ to the consequence that both die and 0 to the consequence that neither dies. Now let $p$ be the probability that one airplane crashes; whether we estimate this probability objectively by looking at the airline's safety statistics or on the basis of our hunch, our conclusion is that the probability that both airplanes independently crash is $p \times p$ or $p^2$. This is the probability that both parents will die if they fly separately. In contrast, the probability that they both will die if they are in the same airplane is simply $p$. Now let the utility that *exactly one* of them dies be symbolized $x$ (which will be a *negative* number). The choice of flying separately is interpreted within the von Neumann and Morgenstern framework as

$$p(-1) < 2p(1 - p)x + p^2(-1).$$

The first term on the right half of the equation is $x$ times the probability that one parent will survive the trip and the other will not (which is equal to the probability that the first plane will crash and the second will not *plus* the probability that the first one will not and the second one will—that is, twice the probability that only one plane will crash). The second term is the probability that both will die on independent trips multiplied by $-1$, the arbitrarily assigned utility of the *both die* consequence.

Dividing by $p$ and rearranging terms yield $x > -\frac{1}{2}$. (After the $p$ is canceled out, move the remaining $-p$ on the right side to the left side, which yields $p - 1 < 2(1 - p)x$; dividing by $(1 - p)$ yields $-1 < 2x$. The $x > -\frac{1}{2}$ means that the death of exactly one has less than half the (negative) utility of both dying.

Our advice is that the couple might be well advised to consider whether the death of one of them is less than half as bad as the death of both. In this example, that would probably not change the decision; in fact, such consideration would most likely reinforce it. What we have done in this example is to assume that people have at least *partial* appreciation of the utility as specified by the framework. There is nothing in the framework itself that requires such insight—just as there is nothing in the physics framework for measuring the weight of objects that requires that the numbers obtained should correspond to our ideas of which objects are heavier than which. Nevertheless, just as weights measured by pan balances do correspond—at least partially—to our subjective experience of these weights, so might the utilities in the system correspond to our subjective conceptions of personal value. In fact, if there were no such correspondence in either case, there would be little reason to be interested in either axiom system.

Consider another example, this one from a medical context involving the diagnosis of a renal cyst versus a tumor on the basis of X-ray evidence. In his doctoral dissertation, Dennis Fryback studied decisions at a university hospital to test whether a kidney abnormality that appeared on an X-ray could be a cyst or a tumor (summarized in Fryback & Thornbury, 1976).

The standard procedure was for patients who appeared to be suffering from a kidney disorder to be X-rayed, and if an abnormality appeared, the radiologist interpreting the X-ray made a probability judgment about whether that abnormality was a cyst or a tumor. Then the patient would be tested directly by an invasive procedure. No procedure existed at that time, however, that tested for both a cyst and a tumor. Moreover, because there was always the possibility that an X-ray abnormality was a *normal variant,* a negative result on the test for one of these two pathologies required a subsequent test for the other. The decision Fryback studied was which test to do first. This decision was important to the patient, because the nature of each of the tests is quite different.

The test for a cyst is termed *aspiration.* It consists of inserting a large needle through the patient's back to the location of the abnormality and determining if fluid can be drawn from it; if fluid can be drawn, the abnormality is a cyst. The procedure can be accomplished in a doctor's office with a local anesthetic; the risk of a blood clot is very low; the cost is not great.

The test for a tumor is termed *arteriography.* A tube is inserted into the patient's leg artery and manipulated up to the kidney, at which point a device on the end of the tube removes a sample of tissue from the suspected spot; this tissue sample is then subjected to a biopsy. At the time of Fryback's study, this procedure required 1 day of hospitalization in preparation for the operation and at least 1 day's hospitalization after the operation. The probability that a blood clot would develop is approximately 10 times as great as that with the aspiration procedure; the patient experiences considerable discomfort in the days following the operation; and it is much more costly than the aspiration test.

Fryback found that in general the aspiration test was done first if the radiologist believed that the probability was greater than 1/2 that the abnormality was a cyst rather than a tumor; otherwise, the arteriography test was conducted. He also found that the patients, doctors, and potential patients from the general public he questioned all thought that the arteriography test was at least 10 times worse than the aspiration test. (Interestingly, discomfort, lost work days, and probability of formation of a blood clot were the major determinants of this judgment; cost was considered irrelevant—perhaps given the assumption that "insurance pays"—which is why we do not specify the cost difference in the above description.) Fryback then conducted an expected utility analysis on the assumption that the disutility of the arteriography test was 10 times that of the aspiration test. For the purposes of this analysis, we can conditionalize probabilities on the assumption that the patient has *either* a cyst or a tumor, even though the requirement that the second test be given if the first is negative arises because the patient may have *neither;* that is, we can let $p$ be the probability that the patient has a tumor *given* the abnormality is not a normal variant, and hence, $(1 - p)$ is the probability that the patient has a cyst given that the abnormality is not a normal variant. Again, we can arbitrarily set the utility of no test at all at 0; then, setting the utility of the aspiration test at –1, the utility of the arteriography test is –10, and hence the utility of doing both tests is approximately –11.

Let the probability that the radiologist interpreting the X-ray believes the problem to be that of a tumor be $p$. If the arteriography test is done first, the expected disutility of the entire testing procedure is

$$p(-10) + (1 - p)(-11).$$

The second term in the expression occurs because both tests are required if the abnormality is not a tumor. In contrast, the disutility of doing the aspiration test first is

$$(1-p)(-1) + p(-11).$$

The expected utility of doing the arteriography test first will be greater than that of doing the aspiration test first (i.e., the disutility will be *less negative*) whenever

$$-10p - 11(1 - p) > (1 - p) - 11p.$$

This is true if and only if

$$11p > 10 \text{ or}$$

$$p > 10/11.$$

In other words, doing the arteriography test first is better in an expected utility framework only under those conditions in which the probability of a tumor relative to that of a cyst is greater than 10/11—that is, when a tumor is 10 times more likely. Recall that the people questioned believed that the disutility of the arteriography test was *at least* 10 times that of the aspiration test; it follows that the 10/11 figure is a *lower bound*. Yet the procedure at the hospital was to test for arteriography *first* whenever the judged probability was greater than 1/2.

This example involved at least a partial equating of the utilities in the von Neumann and Morgenstern system with the personal values expressed by people when asked. Nevertheless, believing people can assess such utilities seems to be quite reasonable; in fact, when this conclusion was communicated to the hospital physicians, the procedure was changed. An interesting sidelight is that when the radiologists' probability judgments were checked against the actual frequencies with which cysts and tumors were found upon testing, these judgments turned out to be quite accurate. Simultaneously, however, the analysis indicated that they were also most usually irrelevant, because it implied that the aspiration tests should be done first, except in those rare cases in which the radiologist was at least 10 times more certain that the aberration was a tumor rather than a cyst.

The new (since 1970) field of applied decision analysis makes use of the von Neumann and Morgenstern approach in an attempt to aid decision makers in their choices (Clemen, 1996; Hammond, Keeney, & Raiffa, 1999). It is based on the premise that people do have some insight into their personal values, but that these values may not be reflected in single choices within a particular context—especially those that tend to be made automatically or according to a standard operating procedure. What the applied decision analyst does is question the decision maker at length about values and probabilities in hypothetical situations as well as the situation in which the choice of interest is to be made. After having done so, the analyst proposes an expected utility analysis that would allow the decision maker to systematize the alternatives in making subsequent choices. Such applications can have a profound effect, as when the hospital decided to change its order of tests.

Yet another example is provided by a man who owned a company in a small town and was considering automation. His family had owned the company for many years, and the factory provided employment to a substantial number of people in the community. After receiving an economic report on the probable increase in profits that would follow automation of many of the factory jobs, he was uneasy about implementing automation, but he was not sure why. He hired a consultant who worked as an applied decision analyst in such situations. After questioning the business owner at length, the consultant concluded that the owner's real utilities in running the business had very little to do with the profit he made. Instead, the owner derived great satisfaction from giving employment to so many people in the town; doing so provided him with status and a feeling of doing something important for the community. According to the consultant's analysis of expected utility, automation would be a very poor choice, one that would decrease rather than increase the utility this man derived from running his business. When the owner was presented with the results, his response was "aha!" He then understood that providing employment was exactly what he wanted to do. In fact, his reluctance to automate in the face of rather conclusive data that it would increase his profits was, he now understood, due to that desire. In addition to reinforcing his gut impression that something was amiss with the automation plan, the consultant's analysis gave him a rationale to use in explaining his refusal—both to himself and to those who might regard him as a poor businessperson for having bypassed the opportunity to increase his profits.

Such decision analysis is a form of psychotherapy because it helps people to change their behavior to be consistent with their personal values. The von Neumann and Morgenstern framework does not dictate what choice must be made, but it is an important tool for such therapy. Moreover, it can help prevent more basic irrationalities, because a decision made within this framework cannot be irrational. Consider, for example, an individual who is reluctant to abandon a sunk cost; because expected utility analysis concerns only the expectation of *future* consequences, sunk costs are not entered into the analysis. In effect, the individual who is tied to the sunk costs broadens his or her framework in such a way that the original motive—the perception of waste in abandoning the sunk costs—disappears when the person realizes that honoring sunk costs conflicts with the more important motive of behaving in an economically rational manner.

The decision analyst starts with the assumption that there are conflicts between a client's attitudes or dispositions to choose in certain ways in particular decision-making situations and more general dispositions. The analyst tries to identify, even quantify the conflicts, and then hopes that the client can resolve them in a manner more compatible with his or her "basic goals."

## 11.6 Some Bum Raps for Decision Analysis

A popular misconception is that decision analysis is unemotional, dehumanizing, and obsessive because it uses numbers and arithmetic in order to guide important life decisions. Isn't this turning over important human decisions "to a machine," sometimes literally a computer—which now picks our quarterbacks, our chief executive officers, and even our lovers? Aren't the "mathematicizers" of life, who admittedly have done well in the basic sciences, moving into a context where such uses of numbers are irrelevant and irreverent? Don't we suffer enough from the tyranny of numbers when our opportunities in life are controlled by numerical scores on aptitude tests and numbers entered on rating forms by interviewers and supervisors? In short, isn't the human spirit better expressed by intuitive choices than by analytic number crunching?

Our answer to all these concerns is an unqualified "no." There is absolutely nothing in the von Neumann and Morgenstern theory—or in this book—that requires the adoption of "inhumanly" stable or easily accessed values. In fact, the whole idea of utility is that it provides a measure of what is truly *personally* important to individuals reaching decisions. As presented here, the aim of analyzing expected utility is to help us achieve what is really important to us. As James March (1978) points out, one goal in life may be to discover what our values are. That goal might require action that is playful, or even arbitrary. Does such action violate the dictates of either rationality or expected utility theory? No. Upon examination, an individual valuing such an approach will be found to have a utility associated with the existential experimentation that follows from it. All that the decision analyst does is help to make this value explicit so that the individual can understand it and incorporate it into action in a noncontradictory manner.

Nor is decision analysis an obsessive, equivocating activity. In fact, some conclusions will mandate action rather than thought. For example, as mentioned earlier, there is a great deal more in von Neumann and Morgenstern's classic *Theory of Games and Economic Behavior* (1947) than has been presented here. One particularly intriguing section of that book concerns optimal play in poker games. There are 2,598,960 possible poker hands and, because no 2 of these hands are tied, drawing a particular hand is equivalent to drawing some number between 1 and 2,598,960. Since a hand is won by the person with the highest number, the question is what constitutes good betting strategy. Von Neumann and Morgenstern considered a simplified form of poker in which only two people play. Each person must ante, one person bets, and the other has the opportunity to either match the bet or raise it, at which point the first person may respond by matching the raise. What von Neumann and Morgenstern proved mathematically is that, according to the principle of maximizing expected utility, a player should either bet the maximum amount immediately or fold. (If the player is the first bettor, he or she may "check" or defer the bet until the other players act.) Our point is that this is a rigorous demonstration, within the context of the theory, that hesitant behavior is poor strategy. It implies the exact opposite of obsessing about a decision. In fact, the maximal strategy is to choose some number between 1 and 2,598,960 prior to looking at the value of the hand, bet the maximal amount if the value is above the chosen number, and otherwise not bet at all. In this context, dynamic decision making is supported. Absolutely nothing in the theory encourages people to obsess, procrastinate, or postpone.

# References

Baron, J. (1988). *Thinking and deciding.* New York: Cambridge University Press.

Baron, J., & Spranca, M. (1997). Protected values. *Organizational Behavior and Human Decision Processes, 70,* 1–16.

Bentham, J. (1948). *An introduction to the principles of morals and legislations.* Oxford, UK: Blackwell. (Original work published 1789)

Clemen, R. T. (1996). *Making hard decisions: An introduction to decision analysis* (2nd ed.). Pacific Grove, CA: Duxbury Press.

Dawes, R. M., & Smith, T. L. (1985). Attitude and opinion measurement. In G. Lindzey & E. Aronson (Eds.), *Handbook of social psychology* (Vol. 1, pp. 509–566). New York: Random House.

Ellsberg, D. (1961). Risk, ambiguity, and the Savage axioms. *Quarterly Journal of Economics, 75,* 643–669.

Freedman, D., Pisani, R., Purves, R., & Adhikari, A. (1991). *Statistics* (2nd ed.). New York: Norton.

Fryback, D. G., & Thornbury, J. R. (1976). Evaluation of a computerized Bayesian model for diagnosis of renal cysts versus tumor versus normal variant from exploratory urogram information. *Investigative Radiology, 11,* 102–111.

Hammond, J. S., Keeney, R. L., & Raiffa, H. (1999). *Smart choices: A practical guide to making better decisions.* Cambridge, MA: Harvard Business School Press.

Hastie, R., & Stasser, G. (2000). Computer simulation methods in social psychology. In C. M. Judd & H. Reis (Eds.), *Handbook of research methods in social psychology* (pp. 85–114). New York: Cambridge University Press.

Hölder, O. (1901). Die Axiome der Quantität und die Lehre vom Mass. *Reports on the negotiations of the Royal Saxon Society of Sciences, Mathematics and Physics Class, 53,* 1–64.

Kadane, J. B., Schervish, M. J., & Seidenfeld, T. (1999). *Rethinking the foundations of statistics.* Cambridge, UK: Cambridge University Press.

Lopes, L. L. (1994). Psychology and economics: Perspectives on risk, cooperation, and the marketplace. *Annual Review of Psychology, 45,* 197–227.

Lopes, L. L., & Oden, G. C. (1999). The role of aspiration level in risky choice: A comparison cumulative prospect theory and SP/A theory. *Journal of Mathematical Psychology, 43,* 286–313.

MacCrimmon, K. R., & Wehrung, D. A. (1986). *Taking risks: The management of uncertainty.* New York: Free Press.

March, J. G. (1978). Bounded rationality, ambiguity, and the engineering of choice. *Bell Journal of Economics, 9,* 587–608.

Neumann, J. von, & Morgenstern, O. (1947). *Theory of games and economic behavior* (2nd ed.). Princeton, NJ: Princeton University Press.

Savage, L. J. (1954). *The foundations of statistics.* New York: Wiley.

Tversky, A., & Kahneman, D. (1974). Judgment under uncertainty: Heuristics and biases. *Science, 185,* 1124–1131.

# 12

# A Descriptive Decision Theory

*In theory there is no difference between theory and practice. But in practice, there is.*

—Jan L. A. van de Snepscheut and others

## 12.1 Non-expected Utility Theories

Both the economists' paradoxes and psychologists' experiments have repeatedly shown that subjective expected utility theory is not a valid descriptive theory of human behavior. Most efforts to create a more adequate descriptive theory have the basic form of the rational expectations principle (Section 2.3). Thus, they are sometimes called *non*-expected utility theories as a reminder that they are derived from the expected utility framework.

But why should we work within the general expected utility framework? First, the framework includes the ingredients that our intuitions and experience tell us are essential to deliberate decision making. Second, the framework provides a roughly accurate descriptive account of decision behaviors in many situations; some economists call it a *positive theory* because it relates inputs and outputs (psychologists might say stimuli and responses) in decision behavior to one another approximately correctly. And third, the framework captures the essence of rationality (as best our culture can define it), and it is likely that we are adapted to be approximately rational in our behaviors; our optimistic hypothesis is that people are at least half-smart in achieving their personal goals.

However, as almost every paragraph in this book implies, human beings are far from the paragons of rationality and optimality demanded by fully rational behavior. So, a valid descriptive theory will not be exactly the same as the best normative theory. One response to the normative–descriptive discrepancy was to create theoretical variants on the normative formulation that accounted for the most reliable and important anomalies for the original theory. The most influential and successful of these non-expected utility theories is Kahneman and Tversky's prospect theory (1979; Tversky & Kahneman, 1992—we focus on the 1979 formulation "Original Prospect Theory" in this book). Like expected utility theory, prospect theory adopts an algebraic formulation to represent decision processes: A *prospect* is an alternative or course of action defined by one or more *outcomes* (i) that result in consequence *values* ($v_i$) that are weighted by *decision weights* ($\Pi_i$) that are related to the objective probabilities for each outcome's occurrence. The *overall value* (V) for that prospect is

$$V = \Sigma \ (\Pi_i \ v_i),$$

which is essentially the same equation as the rational expectations principle at the heart of all expected utility theories (Section 2.3).

There are two stages in the prospect theory decision process: *editing* the alternatives, which involves constructing a cognitive representation of the acts, contingencies, and outcomes relevant to the decision; and *evaluation*, in which the decision maker assesses the value of each prospect and chooses accordingly. The evaluation stage can be broken down, for clarity of exposition, into three steps for each prospect: (i) valuation, in which the value function is applied to each consequence associated with each outcome; (ii) decision weighting, in which each valued consequence is weighted for impact by a function based on its objective probability of occurrence; and (iii) integration, in which the weighted values across all the outcomes associated with a prospect are combined by adding them up. Let's look at each part of the process separately.

## Editing and Framing the Decision

Prospect theory goes beyond traditional decision theories to describe some of the cognitive processes involved when the decision maker comprehends a decision situation. Comprehension results in a cognitive representation that includes the prospects' outcomes, events, contingencies among them, associated values, a reference point, and perhaps links to other information (in long-term memory or in the immediate environment) relevant to the assessment of values or decision weights.

The first major editing operation that is hypothesized to occur is *setting a reference point* on the objective valuation scale. In the case of money and health, the current *status quo* is the most likely candidate for the reference point that will define zero on a personal gain–loss scale. The location of the reference point is central in explanations for many value-related phenomena, as it determines what is a gain and what is a loss, and it predicts where the decision maker will be most sensitive to changes in value (near the zero reference point). But the reference point is not always the status quo, as Tversky and Kahneman (1981) write: "A diversity of factors determine the reference outcome in everyday life. The reference outcome is usually a state to which one has adapted; it is sometimes set by social norms and expectations; it sometimes corresponds to a level of aspiration, which may or may not be realistic" (p. 456).

The most common reference point studied in psychology beyond the status quo is an *aspiration level*. This point not only defines success for many people—particularly those high in need for achievement—but is also often related to the length of time we search for alternatives yielding desirable outcomes. As we noted in Chapter 10, such satisficing strategies are not optimal, and we would expect aspiration level to interact with the order in which we encounter or consider prospects to determine how well the strategy works. An example of an aspiration-level effect is the observation that longshot bets are especially popular at the end of the day at racetracks—too much money is wagered on the horses that are objectively unlikely to win these late races. This phenomenon probably results from losing bettors' attempts to recoup their losses before they leave the track for the day. These bettors act and talk as though they have an aspiration level of "break even." Of course, this means that the higher-odds bets on favorites are a better value for those last races. Moreover, some bettors, casino players, and online stock investors of our acquaintance at least talk about quitting-point aspiration levels: "If I'm ahead $1,000, I quit for the day and go jogging."

The labile, adaptive reference point concept is troubling to many economists (though it was first proposed by an economist). Like all of the framing subprocesses proposed in prospect theory, it is not highly constrained, making it difficult to derive a priori predictions or to formally estimate post hoc parameters, such as the location of the reference point. Some progress has been made on these technical problems, however. Lopes and Oden (1999) conducted several incisive experiments studying participants' preferences for experimental lotteries, in which they have assessed the locations of special, sensitive points on the value continuum. For example, when asked to think aloud about their choices, the participants made remarks like the following:

> "The [riskless lottery] has a higher jackpot and greater chance of winning a larger amount under $100. I look at the highest amount I could lose rather than the highest amount I could win."

> "I picked the [riskless lottery] because both the minimum and the maximum amounts are more, and because for both there's a good chance of getting around $100."

> "I pick the [short-shot lottery] because the maximum loss is less and because you may be able to hit as low as a zero loss. No matter what, you lose $70 and possibly $200—too much risk." (p. 304)

Lopes and Oden (1999) concluded that three locations play key roles in people's evaluations of uncertain prospects: a reference point, an aspiration level ("What are the chances that I will achieve my goal of . . . ?"), and a security level ("What is the chance that I will lose . . . or more?"). Their interpretation is that there are individual differences in security-mindedness (analogous to risk-aversion) and potential-mindedness (analogous to risk-seeking). These individual differences are stable across time (e.g., from experimental session to experimental session), at least in the financial domain, and they may correspond to "cautious" or "risky" personality types. The aspiration level for an individual is hypothesized to be much more labile (unstable), and dependent on situational factors. Lopes and Oden interpret these individual "parameters," and indirect measures of attention deployment and eye movement measures confirm that they are related to perceptual orientation and information search in the experimental lottery choice tasks. (We recommend Lopes and Oden's SP/A theory as a strong competitor with prospect theory.)

March and Shapira (1987) find that business decision makers consider other critical amounts as well. They frequently refer to the *downside risk*, by which they mean the maximum amount that could be lost in a business venture. In addition, there are also discussions of *break-even points* and *survival points* (the amounts necessary to continue doing business). We suspect that careful studies of the behavior of these executives would reveal that they are especially sensitive to differences in financial values in the neighborhood of these attention-drawing reference points.

The second major editing operation hypothesized in prospect theory involves *combining or segregating* outcomes. It is hypothesized that people sometimes group gains and losses to increase their overall satisfaction. People certainly have beliefs about what will feel better or hurt more. For example, most people judge that they would gain more pleasure from receiving two separate money gifts than from receiving one lump sum gift; two separate tax refunds of $100 each would be more satisfying than one larger refund of $200. Likewise, most would rather take one big loss than several smaller losses; a single traffic fine of $200 hurts less than two $100 fines. These intuitions are consistent with the theoretical principle that we are most sensitive to gains and losses near our reference point (the status quo, in these examples)—two small movements, up or down from the zero point, on a diminishing returns value function would have a bigger impact on our satisfaction levels than one larger movement. Remember, the theory also assumes that the reference point shifts rapidly; otherwise, two small gains or losses in sequence would be no different from one large gain or loss. Richard Thaler has developed the implications of prospect theory for *mental accounting* to explain many anomalies in everyday consumer habits and financial markets (Thaler, 1999).

## Evaluation

The first step of the evaluation phase, *valuation,* involves inferring the personal values for the consequences attached to each outcome. The *value function* (see the lengthy discussion in Chapter 9, and Figure 12.1 below) summarizes prospect theory's assumptions about the translation of an objective measure of consequences into personal values for a typical person making a decision. The theory acknowledges that there will be individual differences in the basic function form and, sure enough, when the functions have been measured they do vary across individuals and across decisions, although there is considerable consistency, too. Each consequence is identified, as part of the framing process, and then translated into a personal value according to the value function. An illustrative equation for this function can be written as follows:

$$v(x) = \begin{cases} x^{\alpha} & \text{if } x \geq 0 \text{ (the "gains" portion of the function)} \\ -\lambda \, (-x)^{\beta} & \text{if } x < 0 \text{ (the "losses" portion of the function)} \end{cases}$$

This process has three major characteristics:

1. Reference-level dependence: An individual views consequences (monetary or other) in terms of changes from the *reference level*, which is usually that individual's *status quo* (the 0,0 coordinate on the value function graph).

2. Gains and losses satiate: The values of the outcomes for both positive and negative consequences of the choice have marginally diminishing returns. The

exponents, $\alpha$ and $\beta$, for the gain and loss portions of the value function are usually found to be less than 1.00—a value of 0.88 for both $\alpha$ and $\beta$ is a typical estimate (if the parameters were 1.00, the curves would be linear; if greater than 1.00, they would be positively accelerating).

3. Loss aversion: The resulting value function is steeper for losses than for gains; losing $100 produces more pain than gaining $100 produces pleasure. The coefficient $\lambda$ indexes the difference in slopes of the positive and negative arms of the value function. A typical estimate of $\lambda$ is 2.25, indicating that losses are approximately twice as painful as gains are pleasurable. (If $\lambda = 1.00$, the gains and losses would have equal slopes; if $\lambda < 1.00$, gains would weigh more heavily than losses.)

If we take this value function seriously, we can calculate predicted personal values for various options. For example, to understand loss aversion, we could calculate the prospect theory value for a sure gain of $100 and

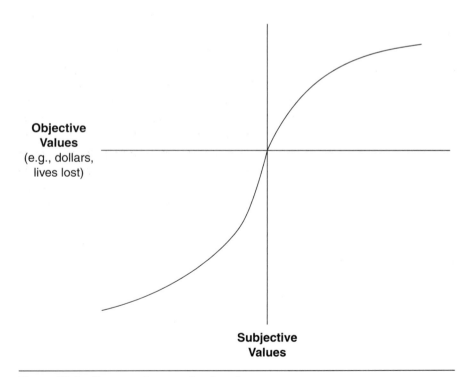

**Objective Values** (e.g., dollars, lives lost)

**Subjective Values**

**Figure 12.1**    Prospect theory value function

compare it with the value for a sure loss of $100: $V_{+\$100}$ = $100 = 57.54 versus $V_{-\$100}$ = –2.25(–$100) = –129.47. Obviously, the loss hurts much more than the gain pleasures. To understand the effects of segregating and aggregating consequences, we can calculate the personal value of receiving two gifts of $100 versus one gift of $200: $(V_{+\$100} + V_{+\$100})$ = 115.08 versus $V_{+\$200}$ = 105.90. And the same is true for losses: $(V_{-\$100} + V_{-\$100})$ = –258.94 versus $V_{-\$200}$ = –238.28. As noted above, the impact of segregated consequences is greater than the impact of a lump sum consequence, whether the outcomes are good or bad.

Prospect theory includes a decision weighting process, analogous to the weighting of outcomes by their probabilities of occurrence or expectations in expected utility theories. Again, prospect theory relies on another mathematical function to summarize the relationship between objective and subjective continua—translating probabilities into decision weights. In the case of well-defined gambles, the probability dimension is communicated to decision makers unequivocally as a numerical probability. However, it is tempting to think of applications of the theory beyond the domain of "risky gambles." Toward the end of his career, Tversky was working on a theory of "where the probabilities come from," named support theory. One might imagine that support theory (and what we know about heuristic judgment processes) could provide a connection to non-numerical ("non-risky" in technical terms) uncertainty situations; support theory would translate subjective uncertainty into numerical subjective probability on the x-axis of the decision weight function (see Fox & Tversky, 1998, for a first step in this development).

The modal decision weight function (again, typical for most individuals in most decision situations) looks like the backward S-shaped curve in Figure 12.2. A useful rule of thumb to interpret these psychophysical functions is that when the curve is steeper, it implies the decision maker will be more sensitive to differences on the objective dimension (x-axis): If the curve is steep, there is relatively more change in the psychological response to any difference on the objective dimension, as compared with where the curve is flatter. Several mechanisms have been postulated as explanations for the differences in steepness or slope—for example, differential attention, differences in sense organ sensitivity, and differences in the reactivity of neural-biochemical substrates.

An illustrative equation for this function can be written as follows:

$$\Pi(p) = \frac{p^\gamma}{(p^\gamma + (1 - p)^\gamma)^{1/\gamma}} \quad \text{(with a typical } \gamma = 0.64)$$

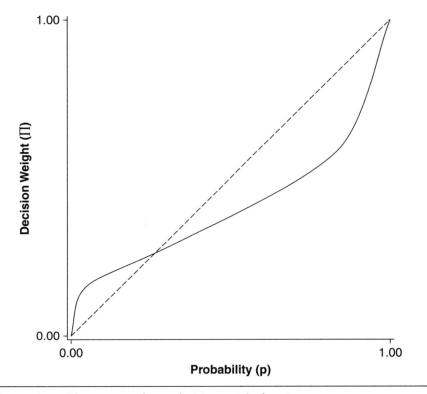

**Figure 12.2**    The prospect theory decision weight function

Let's walk through the characteristics of the decision weight function.

1. Near the zero point the curve is steep, implying that people are very sensitive to the difference between impossibility and "possibility-hood." This steepness is consistent with people's overreactions to small probability risks and is also part of the explanation for why people purchase incredibly long-shot lottery tickets. The business of industrial and governmental risk management is complicated by people's willingness to pay exorbitant amounts to completely eliminate low-probability threats. The Supreme Court justice Stephen Breyer (1993) refers to the "Unnecessary and unproductive attempt to remove the 'last 10 percent' of risk" from toxic spills, asbestos exposure, and disease susceptibility" (p. 75). Breyer quotes EPA administrators in support of the contention that about 95% of toxic material could be removed from almost all hazardous waste sites in a few months, but years are spent trying to remove the last little bit. Removing

that last little bit involves high cost, devotion of considerable societal resources, large legal fees, and endless argument. As a former trial judge, Breyer cites a memorable example from his own experience, arising out of a 10-year effort to force cleanup of a toxic waste dump in southern New Hampshire (*United States v. Ottatti & Goss,* 1990):

> The site was mostly cleaned up. All but one of the private parties had settled. The remaining private party litigated the cost of cleaning up the last little bit, a cost of about $9.3 million to remove a small amount of highly diluted PCBs and "volatile organic compounds" (benzene and gasoline components) by incinerating the dirt. How much extra safety did this $9.3 million buy? The forty-thousand page record of this ten-year effort indicated (and all parties seemed to agree) that, without the extra expenditure, the waste dump was clean enough for children playing on the site to eat small amounts of dirt daily for 70 days each year without significant harm. Burning the soil would have made it clean enough for the children to eat small amounts daily for 245 days per year without significant harm. But there were no dirt-eating children playing in the area, for it was a swamp. Nor were dirt-eating children likely to appear there, for future building seemed unlikely. The parties also agreed that at least half of the volatile chemicals would likely evaporate by the year 2000. To spend $9.3 million to protect non-existent dirt-eating children is what I mean by the problem of "the last 10 percent." (p. 12)

The problem is not that people want to be safe, but that their overreaction to many of these hazards means that funds are not available for other protective or constructive social programs. Each $9.3 million we spend on a useless cleanup will be $9.3 million less to spend on mitigating more important hazards.

2. There is a crossover point at about .20 on the objective probability dimension where, in many gambling situations (e.g., cards, dice, horse race-track betting), people are well-calibrated in terms of their sense of "objective" probabilities.

3. In most of the central portion of the curve, people are "regressive," the curve is "too flat," and substantial changes in objective probabilities produce small changes in decision weights. People are insensitive to differences in intermediate probabilities. This portion of the function implies that people will be *super-additive* for events associated with these objective probabilities: The sum of a set of decision weights will be smaller than the sum of the objective probabilities.

4. Finally, at the high end of the objective probability scale, the curve becomes steep again as a high probability changes to certainty. This phenomenon is sometimes called the *certainty effect.* It provides part of an explanation for the observed pattern of preferences between gambles in the Allais paradox (discussed in Section 11.4). It is important to people to be certain of getting the

big prize, so important that the shift from .99 to 1.00 is worth more to the experimental subject than the shift from .10 to .11. When choosing between the cleverly designed Allais paradox bets, for example, it leads people to violate the independence axiom of expected utility theory.

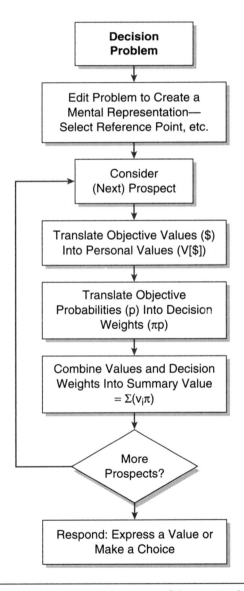

**Figure 12.3**    Flowchart summarizing the stages of decision making according to prospect theory

Figure 12.3 is a summary of the decision processes proposed by prospect theory. We have taken some liberties, by ordering the three preliminary sub-stages (editing, valuation, and decision weighting) in a temporal sequence. The theory itself is not explicit about the order of the computations. Furthermore, like most scientific theories, the formulation is revised to accommodate new empirical findings. The most recent version of the theory has a more complex "decumulative" weighting process than the one we describe here (Tversky & Kahneman, 1992). Let's take a look at some recent behavioral findings, especially those that discriminate between traditional expected utility theory and prospect theory.

## 12.2 Gain–Loss Framing Effects

The influence of the frame for the outcomes in a decision problem can be demonstrated by creating two versions of the problem—two different state-ments that describe identical decision situations in different words. When the two problem statements are presented to experimental participants and dif-ferent choices are made, the *framing effect* is demonstrated. We will consider examples in which alternate statements of a single problem affect the loca-tion of the chooser's reference point, but other violations of *invariance* have also been demonstrated. (Invariance is implied, for example, by Axiom 4 of subjective expected utility theory: A gamble that can be represented in an extensive tree format should be evaluated identically to the same gamble pre-sented in a collapsed "normal" format.) The reference point manipulation affects the perception of some of the component outcomes so that an iden-tical outcome seems like a gain when compared with a low reference point, but seems like a loss when compared with a high reference point.

Imagine that you have just been given $1,000. Which prospect would you prefer?

**Prospect A:** You receive $500 for sure.

**Prospect B:** A fair coin is tossed. Heads and you receive $1,000; tails and you receive nothing more.

Now imagine you have just been given $2,000. Which prospect would you prefer?

**Prospect C:** You must pay back $500 immediately.

**Prospect D:** A fair coin is tossed. Heads and you give back nothing; tails and you give back $1,000.

In the first pair, the status quo reference point is the money in your pocket including the $1,000 you were just given, and all outcomes are framed as gains. Accordingly, with the diminishing returns value function for gains, most people prefer the sure thing (Prospect A). But in the second pair, the reference point is your pocket money including your gift of $2,000 (imaginary, but the adaptation is remarkably fast. It works!), and all outcomes are framed as losses. Now the diminishing returns property of the value function for losses makes most people want to gamble, and they choose Prospect D. When all four prospects are written down next to each other, most people change their preference from Prospect C to Prospect D, although A and C are identical (certain gain of $1,500) and so are B and D (lottery with a .50 chance of gaining $1,000 and a .50 chance of gaining $2,000). This is irrational—an essential criterion of rationality being that choices be made on the basis of the consequences of behavior—yet with identical consequences people choose different courses of action. This result is problematic for traditional decision theories: How can we reliably change our preferences when making two formally identical choices? This result implies that it will be impossible to measure our utilities on a consistent numerical scale.

For the sake of precision, let's look at the prospect theory valuations of each prospect using numerical calculations based on the value function and decision weight equations presented in Section 12.1 above:

$$V_{PROSPECT\ A} = \Pi_{i1.00}(v_{+\$500}) = 237.19$$

$$V_{PROSPECT\ B} = \Pi_{i50}(v_{+\$1000}) + \Pi_{i.50}(v_0) = 198.18$$

$$V_{PROSPECT\ C} = \Pi_{i1.00}(v_{-\$500}) = -533.67$$

$$V_{PROSPECT\ D} = \Pi_{i.50}(v_0) + \Pi_{i50}(v_{-\$1000}) = -442.36$$

In the first pair, Prospect A has a larger total "gain" value; in the second pair, Prospect D has a smaller "loss" value. So people's choices are predicted to reverse from the first pair to the second, as they do for most individuals.

Another example of a gain–loss framing effect is from the consequential domain of medical decision making. When describing a medical procedure, which is more correct: to indicate its efficacy by presenting the survival rates or the mortality rates of those receiving the treatment? It shouldn't matter, but Barbara McNeil, Stephen Pauker, Harold Sox, and Amos Tversky (1982) found that it does, to physicians and their patients.

Suppose you have been diagnosed with a life-threatening medical condition. Which procedure do you prefer?

Surgery: Of 100 people having surgery for this condition, 90 live through the postoperative period, 68 are alive at the end of the first year, and 34 are alive at the end of 5 years.

Radiation Therapy: Of 100 people having radiation therapy for this condition, all live through the treatment, 77 are alive at the end of the first year, and 22 are alive at the end of 5 years.

You have been diagnosed with a life-threatening medical condition. Now which procedure do you prefer?

Surgery': Of 100 people having surgery for this condition, 10 die during surgery or in the postoperative period, 32 die by the end of the first year, and 66 die by the end of 5 years.

Radiation Therapy': Of 100 people having radiation therapy for this condition, none die during treatment, 23 die by the end of one year, and 78 die by the end of 5 years.

The first problem statements frame the treatments in terms of survival rates, and only 18% of respondents choose radiation. But in the second, mortality frame, 44% of the respondents chose radiation. Two identical uncertain prospects are treated differently merely because of the manner in which they are framed. Apparently, the reduction from 10 dead postoperatively for Surgery to zero dead for Radiation Therapy looms much larger in the mortality frame. The framing effect was clear for physicians, medical students, patients, and college students.

These discrepancies have become more important due to the increase in the medical practice of sharing with patients their diagnoses, prognosis, and likelihood of subsequent results given various possible treatments. The purpose of this practice is to allow patients themselves to decide which treatment option to choose, or at least to secure *informed consent* for choosing the one recommended by the doctor. Previously, doctors gave orders, and patients were often not even permitted to ask in hospitals about the content of the pills they were told to take; moreover, it was common practice not to tell the patients about potentially devastating diagnoses (e.g., of cancer), or about the likelihood of death, or when it is likely to occur—a practice that seems to be still common according to interviews conducted by Elizabeth Lamont and Nicholas Christakis (2000) with 258 physicians who were treating terminally ill cancer patients. Their conclusion was this: "We infer that direct, explicit, and frank verbal communication between physicians and terminally ill patients about prognosis probably occurs at most only one third of the time." We agree with Lamont and Christakis that this reluctance to be frank with patients is a barrier to patients' ending their lives in the manner they desire. But, in any case, the question arises about how prognoses and the likely results of various options should be shared with patients. Clearly, from a logical perspective, discussing such matters in terms of the probability of survival is equivalent to discussing them in terms of the probability of *not* surviving. But now it turns out that these two types of framing have different effects on decision making.

If the doctor is supposed to present information in the most neutral possible manner and allow the decision to be made by the patient, how should this information be presented? McNeil and her colleagues (1982) suggested presenting all this information in both survival and mortality frameworks. The problem there is that such presentation might be confusing, and some people may not even be able to understand the equivalence of the two frames. Another possibility is to present the information *visually*. For example, if a graph is constructed where the number of years is presented visually on the x-axis, then *both* the survival rate and the mortality rate can be presented in the same pictorial representation. In the current example, one such graph could be constructed for surgery and the other for radiation. Then, the potential patient can be asked to choose between these two procedures— and given that all the information is available in both graphs, any decision to focus on living or dying is made by the patients themselves, not by the physician supplying the information.

Now consider a choice, which is like the ones that social policy makers must make, posed to diverse samples of respondents by Tversky and Kahneman (1981):

Imagine that the United States is preparing for an outbreak of an unusual Asian disease that is expected to kill 600 people. Two alternative programs to combat the disease have been proposed. Scientific estimates of the consequences of the programs are as follows:

If Program A is adopted, 200 people will be saved.

If Program B is adopted, there is a 1/3 probability that 600 people will be saved and a 2/3 probability that no people will be saved.

Which program would you favor? Seventy-two percent of the original sample of college students chose Program A. The alternatives were presented in terms of gains—lives saved—and the subjects were risk-averse. A second group of respondents, however, was presented with the same situation but a different description of the alternative programs:

If Program C is adopted, 400 people will die.

If Program D is adopted, there is a 1/3 probability that nobody will die and a 2/3 probability that 600 will die.

Which program would you favor? Only 22% of the students chose Program C, while 78% chose Program D. Yet Program C is identical to Program A (400 people dying being exactly equivalent to 200 living—in both cases, 200 are alive and 400 are dead), and Program D is equivalent to Program B. This is again a matter of identical choices, between a sure thing and an uncertain prospect, being treated differently merely because of the conceptual frame. The difference in the way the programs were presented led to a whopping 50% difference in their endorsement.

Again, let's run the prospect theory calculations using the equations from Section 12.1:

$$V_{\text{PROGRAM A}} = \Pi_{i1.00}(v_{+200}) = 105.90$$

$$V_{\text{PROGRAM B}} = \Pi_{i.33}(v_{+600}) + \Pi_{i.67}(v_0) = 96.96$$

$$V_{\text{PROGRAM C}} = \Pi_{i1.00}(v_{-400}) = -438.53$$

$$V_{\text{PROGRAM D}} = \Pi_{i.33}(v_0) + \Pi_{i.67}(v_{-600}) = -349.55$$

The calculations predict that people will choose Program A in the first pair—its overall (gain) value is higher than that of Program B—but will choose Program D in the second pair, because its loss is less than that of Program C.

Psychologists have discovered that framing effects are particularly strong in matters regarding life and death. Why? Because the first life saved is the most important, just as is the first life lost. Thus, decision makers are risk-averse when questions are framed in terms of saving lives, but risk-seeking when the identical questions are framed in terms of losing lives. The number of lives lost plus the number of lives saved, however, must equal the number of people at risk for death—hence, the contradiction.

In fact, the contradiction concerning saving versus losing lives is even deeper than indicated by the inconsistent responses. Researchers such as Fischhoff, Lichtenstein, and Slovic have asked people not only to make such hypothetical choices, but also to enunciate general policies concerning death from various causes. In a typical study, members of the League of Women Voters were asked both to make hypothetical choices and to state their over-all philosophies. With great consistency, they opted for avoiding risk when questions were framed in terms of saving lives. However, when they were asked to state how serious it would be for various numbers of people in soci-ety to lose their lives, they consistently indicated that such seriousness *accel-erated* with the number of lives lost. Thus, a large airplane accident was seen as more than twice as serious as a smaller one with half the fatalities (which presumably would have less than half the disruptive effect on society). In a more extreme situation, it is probable that most of us would agree that a nuclear attack involving 80 million casualties would be more than twice as bad as one involving 40 million, and, at the greatest extreme, a nuclear war annihilating all life on earth would be more than twice as bad as one annihilating "only" half.

These *positively* accelerating concerns for loss of life are inconsistent with risk aversion for saving lives. For example, if 600 deaths is more than 3 times as bad as 200, then it is contradictory to opt for 200 of 600 people being saved for sure rather than a 1/3 chance of saving all 600. Nevertheless, people appear consistently risk-averse when presented with single choices in which the alternatives are phrased in terms of lives saved.

The same accelerating concern for possible deaths is implied by parents who fly on separate airplanes when their children are not with them. By doing so, they reduce the probability that both of them will be killed, while simultaneously increasing the probability that *at least one* of them will be— since the probability that 1 of 2 planes will crash is greater than the probability that either alone will crash. As was rigorously demonstrated in Section 11.5, this choice to fly on separate planes also implies, according to the von Neumann and Morgenstern theory, that the implicit *disutility* of both dying is more than twice as great as the disutility of one of them dying.

One place in which outcome frames are deliberately manipulated is in the courtroom when attorneys are arguing about the amounts that should be awarded to compensate a plaintiff for harm suffered as a result of the defendant's actions. Defense attorneys frame the award as a gain: "How much should the defendant pay to make the plaintiff whole again?" In contrast, plaintiffs' attorneys favor a loss frame: "How much would you have to be paid to suffer an injury like the harm done to my client?"

Is framing merely verbal trickery? The answer is "no," for two reasons. First, framing effects can be explained by simple psychological principles; they make sense in the context of a complex web of validated psychological concepts. And second, people who make such contradictory choices often stand by them when the inconsistency is pointed out. For example, Scott B. Lewis (unpublished work) took six pairs of questions that had been shown to produce framing effects, and he presented both frames of each pair to undergraduate subjects (although there were always at least two other intervening questions between each pair). His subjects, nevertheless, were inconsistent in the manner of the examples we have discussed: They were risk-averse when the alternatives were stated as gains, and risk-seeking when the alternatives were stated as losses. (When Lewis's subjects made contradictory choices, 75% of those choices were consistent with risk aversion for gains and risk-seeking for losses.) Lewis then pointed out these inconsistencies to his subjects, and almost all of them recognized that they had in fact been inconsistent. But when he gave them the opportunity to change their responses in order to achieve consistency, they did so only half of the time. Moreover, when they were presented with new pairs of logically equivalent questions framed to elicit different choices, the rate of inconsistency dropped only from 52% to 47%.

Dawes and colleagues (Hawkins, Dawes, & Johnson, 1987) replicated the result that framing effects can lead individuals to make such inconsistent choices. They found, for example, that over half of the subjects were inconsistent in the life-versus-death problems, and the sample of students was 4 times the size of Lewis's. Most important, the degree of inconsistency was as high within single subjects (who responded to identical questions framed in two different ways within 5 minutes of each other) as between subjects. Whereas verbal tricks lose their effectiveness once they are understood, framing effects are durable.

People buy insurance. Why? The easiest explanation is based on how people frame the situation. When considering insurance, they no longer view their status quo as neutral, but rather they view their possessions on the positive side of zero (and a good insurance salesperson encourages that view); hence, they are willing to take a small financial loss in order to avoid a risk of being wiped out. Again, the principle is that the expected utility of the gamble when dealing with positive amounts will always be less than the expected amount defined in monetary terms. But in fact, defined purely in monetary terms, individuals should expect to lose when they purchase insurance; after all, insurance companies make money.

Now consider people's unwillingness to use automobile seatbelts unless state or national legislation requires them to do so. According to prospect theory, people tend to adopt their status quo as the reference point. Due to the shape of the value function, small gains become very important. People believe that not wearing seatbelts yields a small gain in comfort. On the other hand, due to the diminishing returns shape of the value function for negative outcomes, the objective consequences of a catastrophic auto accident are undervalued. Hence, viewed in prospect theory terms, not wearing seatbelts appears to be a reasonable behavior.

The deeper point is that people's decisions may be changed by changing the reference level. As Norman Gutkin (personal communication to Dawes) has pointed out, people might be more willing to use seatbelts if their status quo was made positive. Instead of emphasizing all the terrible things that could result from an accident, seatbelt campaigns might better be framed in terms of how well off people are prior to the drive, in which case they would regard seatbelt use as a form of insurance—insurance that they remain in their happy state. Gutkin suggested that seatbelt advertising should not emphasize the terrible results of a serious automobile accident, but should rather show a happy and affluent young couple reminding themselves that they don't wish to lose their pleasant lives as a result of an avoidable injury.

Given our propensity to avoid sure losses, insurance sales pitches must be carefully framed. As one of our colleagues points out, a campaign advertising lower premiums that begins, "Reduce your sure loss," would not be likely to sell insurance. We speculate that at least some people buy insurance in part because they can imagine themselves to be "small winners" vis-à-vis the insurance company; if disaster does occur, they have won a low-stakes, low-probability-of-big-payoff bet against that company. Fully aware that the expected value of this bet is negative, they make it to assure peace of mind in contemplating what *might* happen: "At least my children will be able to make it through college if the wing falls off." The same prospective contemplation of possible outcomes may be one motive for buying lottery tickets with full knowledge of negative expectation.

Of course, sometimes insurance coverage pays off. Reuven Brenner (personal communication) notes that purchases of both insurance policies and lottery tickets may be explained when they are framed in terms of *relative* rather than *absolute* wealth, given that wealth relative to other people's wealth is generally not altered by the small amounts spent on the premiums and tickets. Brenner writes the following:

> They [people] perform both acts for the same reasons: in both cases individuals expect to lose relatively small amounts, either the price of the lottery ticket or the insurance premium. But these small amounts are worth losing since these are the only ways by which people can either change or avoid changing their relative position in the distribution of wealth. Thus people gamble in order to try to become richer and change their relative position in the distribution of wealth, and they insure themselves in order to prevent becoming poorer, thus avoiding a change in their relative position.

## 12.3 Loss Aversion

The basic concept of loss aversion is both intuitively appealing and well-supported empirically. Perhaps the most convincing evidence comes from transparently simple *endowment effect* demonstrations. Once people have possessed an object for even a minute, they act as though "losing it matters more than gaining it would have mattered if they didn't have it." Richard Thaler gave half the students in a class gift coffee mugs; the other half were then allowed to bid to purchase the mugs (e.g., Kahneman, Knetsch, &

Thaler, 1991). There were substantial differences between the dollar values placed on the mugs by those who were "endowed" with the mugs and those who were not. Students endowed with the mugs placed much higher selling prices on them compared with the nonowners' bids. This study has been repeated many times with various commodities and measures designed to more exactly elicit true, sincere valuations, always obtaining the same status quo bias.

The simple endowment effect has led to several further results extending our understanding of the role of cognitions and emotions in valuation processes. Elke Weber and Eric Johnson (2008) and their colleagues have demonstrated the crucial role of availability of thoughts concerning the value of the target object (e.g., Thaler's mugs) versus the value of money. They hypothesized that a person faced with the prospect of giving up a possession (for a price) would naturally focus his or her attention on the usefulness of the object. Thus, a research participant asked to consider selling her mug would find her thoughts dominated by (potential) uses for the mug. Just the reverse would apply to a participant asked to consider paying his money to acquire the mug; his thoughts would be dominated by alternate uses for the cash. In a series of intricate experiments, Johnson, Gerald Haubl, and Anat Keinan (2007) showed that buyers and sellers were thinking about very different aspects of the transaction and that when the contents of their thoughts were manipulated experimentally, their valuations changed systematically as predicted. Johnson and Weber propose a general cognitive account for valuation processes called *query theory,* referring to the manner in which consumers' thought contents are changed by internal or external "queries" to their memories, resulting in changed valuations of products and other objects of consumption.

Jennifer Lerner and her colleagues (Lerner, Small, & Loewenstein, 2004) demonstrated that another factor, *incidental emotional state,* changed the preferences expressed by sellers versus buyers in an endowment effect task. Lerner either endowed her experimental participants with a highlighter pen set or not, and then assessed selling versus buying prices. (Actually, for methodological reasons, she assessed selling versus a choice between a varying sum of money or the highlighters.) But before she assessed preferences, she put the college students into an emotional state, sad or disgusted or neutral, by showing them film clips (a poignant scene of a boy and his dying father from *The Champ,* a stomach-churning scene involving a filthy toilet from *Trainspotting,* or a nature scene of fish swimming in a coral reef). The sad mood increased buying prices and the disgusted mood decreased selling prices dramatically compared with the neutral emotional condition. Subsequent studies provided further demonstrations of sad mood effects on willingness-to-pay for commodities, now dubbed the "misery is not miserly effect" (Cryder, Lerner, Gross, & Dahl, 2008).

Lerner interpreted these results in terms of an *emotion appraisal theory framework* (Ellsworth & Scherer, 2002). The gist of this theory is that when a person is in an emotional state, the emotion activates certain action tendencies. Thus, when sad, a person is likely to attempt to change his or her situation (hence the willingness to pay more for an item that would "change the situation"), and when disgusted, a person is motivated to "expel" objects, hence the low willingness-to-sell price (see Han, Lerner, & Keltner, 2007, for a more complete exposition).

The query theory interpretation and emotional state findings do not diminish the importance of the basic endowment effect as evidence for the loss aversion principle. They are important because they provide insights into the cognitive-emotional mechanisms that produce the effect and into the range of conditions under which the effect will occur.

The loss aversion asymmetry is important in formal markets, where it predicts the common situation where a seller sincerely values his or her commodity more highly than a buyer. The endowment effect is surely part of the explanation for the malfunction of some markets in which trading occurs at inefficiently slow rates. The problem with this interpretation is that there are other plausible explanations for the predicted gap between buying price and selling price valuations. Obviously, it is strategically wise to bid low if you are a potential buyer (e.g., in an auction) and to start high if you are a seller. We all expect that there will be some negotiation, and we do not want to miss a bargain by offering too much or selling to cheaply. This is a reason why controlled experiments are important in order to rule out alternative explanations or to carefully assign credit to different causal factors in a complex situation.

There are uncertain outcome versions of the loss aversion phenomenon, too. Another illustration from Richard Thaler's research is this: Experimental participants were asked to put a price on their willingness to be exposed to a virus that would increase the chance they might contract an inevitably fatal disease from 0 to 0.001. The typical response was $10,000. Other participants were asked to imagine that they had the disease, and were then asked how much they would pay for a vaccine that would reduce their chance of actually contracting the disease from 0.001 to zero. Now the modal price for the vaccine was $200. The distance, in units of value from zero to .001, is not the same as the distance from .001 to zero.

What about some more subtle implications of loss aversion? Most of the examples are from the financial world (and are due, again, to Richard Thaler; see Barberis & Thaler, 2003, for many examples of financial anomalies and prospect theory interpretations). Why are so many markets "too sticky," inefficient in economic terms, because they "settle too slowly" and as a result support a low volume of trading? Part of the answer is surely that there is a psychological gap between willingness-to-sell and willingness-to-buy; people truly value a commodity that they possess more than they would the identical commodity when they were bidding to buy it. This phenomenon, surprisingly wide willingness-to-buy versus willingness-to-sell gaps, has been documented in many real and artificial markets.

In many universities, faculty members are offered some control over the form of their retirement fund investments. To simplify, they can allocate these funds between a relatively volatile stock investment and a relatively stable bond investment. For the most part (in laboratory and field studies of investment habits), people over-invest in the stable instruments like bonds and under-invest in volatile instruments like stocks. Thaler (Barberis & Thaler, 1993) calls this *myopic loss aversion* because, according to his analysis, the volatile investments are much more profitable over the long run. His interpretation is that the up-and-down roller-coaster experience of the volatile investment is very aversive. Every rise feels good but every fall hurts much more because the loss segment of the value function is much (2.25 times) steeper than the gain segment, and the more the price oscillates, the more pain accumulates relative to pleasure. In the real world, it is difficult to definitively show that the conservative investment is worse than the volatile investment, though Thaler provides convincing numbers on the returns from stock, treasury bill, and bond market investments. Certainly, the historical results from the academics' retirement funds support his contention that the volatile fund is under-invested. But Thaler has also conducted controlled demonstrations in which the only difference between experimental conditions is in the frequencies with which the current values of the investments are reported. (The investments simulated the behavior of bonds or stocks.) When reports were frequent (analogous to annual reports), people preferred the conservative, stable bonds—investing a majority of their funds accordingly. When reports were infrequent (analogous to 30-year return summaries), they invested 90% of their funds in the higher-paying, volatile stocks.

## 12.4 Look to the Future

Prospect theory is the best comprehensive description we can give of the risky decision process. It summarizes several centuries' worth of findings and insights concerning human decision behavior. Moreover, it has produced an unmatched yield of new insights and predictions of human behavior in laboratory and real-world decision-making tasks. The theory provides a useful catalog of irrational and anomalous behaviors and relates them to the traditional normative (rational) framework. In addition, it attributes many of these anomalies to underlying psychological processes. But the theory is not complete. There are phenomena that it does not predict or explain—for example, the preference reversals we described in Section 4.2: When presented with individual bets, people place higher prices on those that have high dollar payoffs, but when comparing pairs of bets, people tend to prefer bets that offer a high probability of winning some amount. Thus, their preferences are the reverse of their prices, contradicting traditional utility theories and also contrary to prospect theory.

While some of these anomalous behaviors—with reference to canons of rational decision making—can be justified by considerations of information search and decision costs, others, such as frames, depend on haphazard events and are arbitrary for any predictive purposes. Studying them can leave one with an uneasy feeling about the "course of history"—both personal and social—and the uneasiness is not diminished by considerations of the potential magnitude of the effects of choices in our technologically advanced (nuclear) world. Perhaps framing and other irregularities of the decision process partly explain the lack of predictability of human behavior—in the psychiatric clinic and on the street. People make choices every day, and many of these choices have important consequences (even ones that are considered trivial at the time—like whether to go to a party where you might happen to meet someone who will have a profound effect on your life). To the degree to which choices are influenced by factors other than considerations of their consequences, like arbitrary context and framing effects, they are arbitrary.

# References

Barberis, N., & Thaler, R. (2003). A survey of behavioral finance. In G. Constantinides, R. Stulz, & M. Harris (Eds.), *Handbook of the economics of finance* (pp. 1051–1121). Amsterdam: Elsevier North-Holland.

Breyer, S. (1993). *Breaking the vicious circle.* Cambridge, MA: Harvard University Press.

Cryder, C. E., Lerner, J. S., Gross, J. J., & Dahl, R. E. (2008). Misery is not miserly: Sad and self-focused individuals spend more. *Psychological Science, 19,* 525–530.

Ellsworth, P. C., & Scherer, K. R. (2002). Appraisal processes in emotion. In R. J. Davidson, K. R. Scherer, & H. H. Goldsmith (Eds.), *Handbook of the affective sciences* (pp. 572–595). New York: Oxford University Press.

Fox, C. R., & Tversky, A. (1998). A belief-based account of decision under uncertainty. *Management Science, 44,* 879–895.

Han, S., Lerner, J. S., & Keltner, D. (2007). Feelings and consumer decision making: The Appraisal-Tendency Framework. *Journal of Consumer Research, 17,* 158–168.

Hawkins, S. A., Dawes, R. M., & Johnson, E. J. (1987). *Intra-individual framing effects.* Unpublished working paper, Department of Social and Decision Sciences, Carnegie Mellon University, Pittsburgh, PA.

Johnson, E. J., Haubl, G., & Keinan, A. (2007). Aspects of endowment: A query theory of value construction. *Journal of Experimental Psychology: Learning, Memory, and Cognition, 33,* 461–474.

Kahneman, D., Knetsch, J. L., & Thaler, R. H. (1991). Anomalies: The endowment effect, loss aversion, and status-quo bias. *Journal of Economic Perspectives, 5,* 193–206.

Kahneman, D., & Tversky, A. (1979). Prospect theory: An analysis of decision under risk. *Econometrica, 47,* 263–291.

Kahneman, D., & Tversky, A. (1984). Choices, values, and frames. *American Psychologist, 39,* 341–350.

Lamont, E. B., & Christakis, N. A. (2000). *Physician's preferences for prognostic disclosure to cancer patients near the end of life.* Presented at the Annual Meeting of the American Society of Clinical Oncology (Abstract #1704), New Orleans.

Lerner, J. S., Small, D. A., & Loewenstein, G. (2004). Heart strings and purse strings: Carryover effects of emotions on economic decisions. *Psychological Science, 15,* 337–341.

Lopes, L. L. (1987). Between hope and fear: The psychology of risk. *Advances in Experimental Social Psychology, 20,* 255–295.

Lopes, L. L. (1995). Algebra and process in the modeling of risky choice. *Psychology of Learning and Motivation, 32,* 177–220.

Lopes, L. L., & Oden, G. C. (1999). The role of aspiration level in risky choice: A comparison of cumulative prospect theory and SP/A theory. *Journal of Mathematical Psychology, 43,* 286–313.

March, J. G., & Shapira, Z. (1987). Managerial perspectives on risk and risk taking. *Management Science, 33,* 1404–1418.

McNeil, B. J., Pauker, S., Sox, H., Jr., & Tversky, A. (1982). On the elicitation of preferences for alternative therapies. *New England Journal of Medicine, 306,* 216–221.

Simon, H. A. (1957). *Models of man: Social and rational: Mathematical essays on rational human behavior in a social setting.* New York: Wiley.

Thaler, R. H. (1999). Mental accounting matters. *Journal of Behavioral Decision Making, 12,* 183–206.

Tversky, A., & Kahneman, D. (1981). The framing of decisions and the psychology of choice. *Science, 211,* 453–458.

Tversky, A., & Kahneman, D. (1992). Advances in prospect theory: Cumulative representation of uncertainty. *Journal of Risk and Uncertainty, 5,* 297–323.

United States v. Ottatti & Goss, Inc., 900 F.2d 429 (1st Cir. 1990).

Weber, E. U., & Johnson, E. J. (2008). Mindful judgment and decision making. *Annual Review of Psychology, 60,* 53–85.

# 13

# What's Next?

## New Directions in Research on Judgment and Decision Making

*It's tough to make predictions, especially about the future.*

—Yogi Berra

It is impossible to predict the future course of an active field of science with much confidence. But we should be able to do better than a dull, "if we're doing a lot of it now, we'll be doing a lot of it tomorrow" persistence projection if we weight current trends by our assessment of how important and open-ended they are. With that in mind, we have mentioned several emerging lines of research in this book that we think are likely to produce important results in the next decade or so. But we must keep in mind that the cutting edge is also cluttered with more than the usual share of misleading and mistaken results, as we often cannot tell if a finding is reliable until it has been replicated. As the saying goes, the avant-garde of science involves going down a lot of alleys to make sure that they are "blind."

So, what's next in the behavioral decision sciences? Foremost is the trend to explore the neural substrates of judgment and decision behaviors, a subfield of cognitive neuroscience sometimes called *neuroeconomics*. This trend is a sure bet to continue, although specific projects are uncertain. But the general enterprise of connecting decision processes to the level of analysis at which cognitive causation actually occurs in the brain is a certain winner. Second are explorations of the roles of emotions in judgments and decisions. Excitement about this topic is spurred by the advances in our understanding of the nature of emotional processes through neuroscience investigations. We have already noted several intriguing findings on this subject in earlier sections of this book (e.g., mood-dependent availability effects on judgments, emotions as sources of fundamental values). Third, there is a new frontier of research on dynamic decision processes that was opened up by the popularity of dynamic decision tasks such as the Iowa Gambling Task in which participants make many choices and have to extract information about probabilities and payoffs from experience. Prior to 1990, there had been a few dynamic decision tasks in which a research participant was required to make many decisions, contingent on one another, across a span of time. But none of them caught on in the research world until Antonio Damasio and his colleagues introduced a gambling task in which the participants made 100 choices of cards from four face-down decks, winning and losing various amounts of money on each trial. Let's take a look at each of these interrelated research directions in turn.

# 13.1 The Neuroscience of Decisions

One of the breakthrough achievements in any field of science is to "reduce" phenomena at one level of analysis to another, more fundamental level by linking the theories and facts between the two levels. This has been achieved in many subfields in physics, chemistry, and biology, but it is still relatively new in the behavioral sciences. The clear examples in psychology are in fields concerned with vision and hearing, where it is now essential to have a solid background in the neuroscience of the senses to conduct productive behavioral studies. This enterprise of linking levels of analysis and fields of science is referred to with the label *consilience,* which was originally coined by the scientist and philosopher William Whewell (Whewell is also credited with coining the term *science*) and popularized by the great modern biologist Edward O. Wilson in a book with that title. We believe that identifying the relationships between levels of analysis is an extremely valuable form of progress in science.

In cognitive psychology, there is good reason to hope that some problems that seem intractable at one level of analysis may be solved by approaching them on more than one level simultaneously. This may mean that resources previously invested at one level (e.g., the behavioral level) are shifted as a problem is attacked from another angle (e.g., the neural, biological level), making some traditional researchers anxious. For example, the typical neuroscience study of decision processes today relies on well-established prior methods, results, and theoretical models to stabilize the behavioral side of the project, while breakthrough neuroscience results are sought. This means that if we ignore the neuroscience contributions from most of these studies, there is little new on the behavioral side. Furthermore, behavioral neuroscience draws research funds, scientists, and students away from the frontier of behavioral research. This means the development of a comprehensive neuroscience of decision making will compete with resources for cutting-edge behavioral studies. But we think that's okay because of the ultimate payoff from linking behavioral phenomena to their biological substrates. And, eventually, as in the study of vision and hearing, the two levels will interact congenially, in a true consilience.

The major impetus for the recent surge in behavioral neuroscience research is the advent of brain imaging techniques that allow researchers to "functionally" identify activity in the brain by measuring the flow of blood to neurons in various regions of interest. As we write, the most popular imaging technique is *functional Magnetic Resonance Imaging* (fMRI), which measures *blood oxygen level dependency* (BOLD) in *regions of interest* (ROIs) with a spatial resolution of 3mm × 3mm "voxels" and a temporal resolution window of about 2 seconds. The other currently popular technique for research on humans, electroencephalography (EEG), measures electrical activity, usually on the scalp, and is more precise temporally, but much less precise spatially. Similar research strategies are being pursued with non-human subjects, using measures of electrical activity inside the brain recorded by miniature electrodes surgically inserted into individual neurons, which provide even more precise localization in space and time.

Research tools and strategies are increasing in sophistication at a remarkable rate (so what we write will be a bit out of date by the time you read it). It is fair to say that most current research is aimed at localizing various functions relevant to well-defined cognitive processes, in parts of the brain that seem to "compute" them. Some conclusions about brain functions underlying decisions seem to be well-established. Cognitive processing that involves the deliberate consideration of gambles or consumer products seems to always include the *dorsolateral prefrontal cortex* (areas of the brain just behind the temples), which are generally assumed to be the residence of Working Memory (Figure 13.1). Valuation processes for hedonic consumption experiences, painful experiences, and money are associated with activity in central, motivational areas of the brain, sometimes called the *limbic system,* such as the striatum (including the nucleus accumbens), the amygdala, and the insula. The *orbitofrontal cortex* (a region of the brain just behind and above the eye sockets) seems to play a special role, integrating cognitive situation information and emotional valuations. Although claims about neural processing systems or "brain circuits" for decision making are highly speculative, the anatomy of the brain is consistent with the interpretation that the orbitofrontal cortex is an important "switchboard" linking cognitive (frontal cortex) and motivational (limbic region) subsystems.

Currently, many laboratories are attempting to localize various computations in the brain that could support the calculation of a *utility* or a prospect theory *summary value.* Starting in the 1980s, William Newsome trained monkeys to make discriminations between dots moving in different directions (up–down, right–left) (Sugrue, Corrado, & Newsome, 2005). The monkeys were rewarded with a sip of fruit juice when they correctly chose a direction of movement. The task is analogous to the gamble-choice tasks that we have described in laboratory research with human participants. On each trial, the monkeys choose between two uncertain prospects; they learn

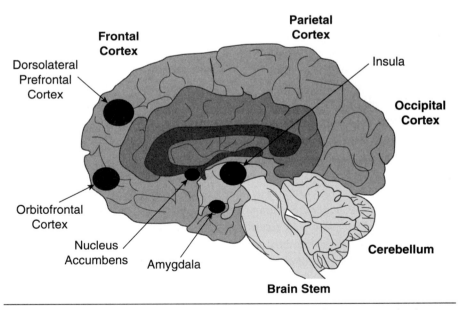

**Figure 13.1**    Major brain regions associated with cognitive functions involved in decision-making processes

the probabilities of receiving a reward (in their case, juice) from experience, and they receive their reward as an outcome of their decisions.

Newsome and his colleagues discovered systematic anticipatory activation of neurons in the lateral intraparietal area and the superior colliculus of the monkeys' brains. Neurons in these structures had elevated firing rates in the milliseconds just before the monkey indicated its decision by eye movements. Essentially, these researchers located "probability meters" inside their subjects' brains. It is important to notice two conditions on this method: First, the result was obtained on some test trials, distributed among regular trials, on which the dots moved in random directions. Thus, on those "random dot trials," the stimulus was unrelated to the outcome of the monkey's decision, verifying that the activity is truly a decision process and not a simple sensory process. Second, the relevant neurons are not located early in the visual perception part of the neural circuit, nor are they in a motor control segment of the circuit. They are right in the center, at a junction connecting perceptual to motor sub-systems. Most important, electrical *stimulation* of neurons in these locations biased the monkeys' decisions (Salzman, Britten, & Newsome, 1990), a result that virtually proves the causal role of these structures in the decision.

Researchers are also trying to discover how reward values are encoded. There is some suggestion that the *mesencephalic dopamine system* may play an important role in this. Again, researchers found linear relationships in anticipation of the reward, between the probability and magnitude of the reward and neural activity, suggesting that these areas function as "value meters" (Figure 13.2).

Analogous research with human participants has used neuroimaging methods to search for neural correlates of the calculation of uncertainty and utility. Several studies have found activation in the nucleus accumbens correlated with the prospect of monetary gains (Knutson & Peterson, 2005). Other researchers have observed activation of the nucleus accumbens, as well as of the amygdala, in anticipation of monetary gains and losses (Breiter, Aharon, Kahneman, Dale, & Shizgal, 2001). One especially interesting result is the observation that brains are responsive to the *relative*—not absolute—amounts to be gained or lost, as predicted by prospect theory. The key comparison is among three lotteries that all involve the potential outcome of $0 (on the surface, a neutral, null amount) with a probability of 1/3. Three variations of the basic lottery were created with the focal gamble, win $0 with probability 1/3, paired with two gains ($10, $2.50), with a mixture of a gain of $2.50 and a loss of $1.50, or with two losses (–$2.50, –$6.00). The finding was that the brain reaction, in the amygdala, to receiving $0 was either positive or negative depending on "what else might have happened." The brain registered "disappointment" when the alternative outcomes

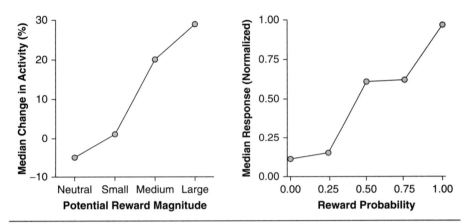

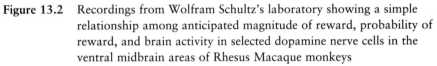

**Figure 13.2**    Recordings from Wolfram Schultz's laboratory showing a simple relationship among anticipated magnitude of reward, probability of reward, and brain activity in selected dopamine nerve cells in the ventral midbrain areas of Rhesus Macaque monkeys

*Source:* Based on Fiorillo, Tobler, & Schultz, 2003; Figures 2E, 4A.

were better than $0 and "elation" when $0 was the best of the three possible outcomes. Thus, there is accumulating evidence that the brain performs utility calculations like those prescribed by prospect theory.

Paul Glimcher has also been searching for neural mechanisms that might perform utility calculations like those described by the subjective expected utility equation. A monkey in Glimcher's experiments also learned to move its eyes to the right or left following a color signal and was rewarded with a sip of juice. The probability of receiving a sip and the amount of juice received were systematically varied. Single-cell recordings showed that individual neurons, again in the lateral intraparietal cortex, tracked the changes in *probability and reward magnitude* over a range of values *before* the outcomes were received (Platt & Glimcher, 1999).

Let's take a close look at one exemplary recent study of human brain responses to traditional gamble stimuli that was conducted in Colin Camerer's laboratory at Cal Tech (Hsu, Bhatt, Adolphs, Tranel, & Camerer, 2005). These researchers were interested in whether the brain distinguishes between crisp, well-defined probabilities and vague uncertainties—the risk-versus-ambiguity distinction expressed so clearly in Daniel Ellsberg's research (Section 11.4). This is an especially apt subject for neuroscience approaches, as the concept of ambiguity is abstract and there are several alternative cognitive interpretations of its psychological nature. Some have proposed that ambiguity is a form of mental uncertainty that is distinct from simple risk (well-defined probability) and that ambiguity-aversion is distinct from risk-aversion so that both can occur independently of one another. Others think it is a form of pessimism in the sense that, "If I don't know the probability for certain, the odds are likely to be against me." Still others have proposed it is a generalization of habits from competitive interpersonal interactions where when you don't know what the other party is up to, it's best to assume he or she has an advantage or has a hostile intention toward you.

Camerer and his colleagues set out to test if the brain treats probability risk differently from ambiguity. They conducted a study in which participants were presented choices between sure-thing payoffs and uncertain gambles. (We only describe a subset of the full experimental design here.) The following three types of risk-ambiguity comparisons, including an interpersonal situation, were presented as uncertain gambles to participants while their brains were scanned with an fMRI device:

1. Gambles in which the compositions of two card decks were precisely defined (10 red and 10 blue cards, and the player chooses the color to bet on, but with uncertainty about which card would be drawn) versus a gamble in which all that is known is that there is some mix of red and blue cards in the decks, and the player still chooses a color)

2. Gambles in which the outcome is determined by the temperature in New York City (risk) versus a gamble in which the outcome is determined by the temperature in Dushambe, Tajikistan (ambiguity)

3. Gambles in which the participant plays against an opponent who has no prior knowledge about the composition of the deck (risk) versus an opponent who has knowledge of the composition of a card deck (ambiguity)

The first question Camerer asked was whether the brain responds differently to ambiguity versus risk. We already know from Ellsberg's work that there is a behavioral difference, with most people strongly preferring well-defined risky prospects to murky ambiguous prospects. But are different regions of the brain engaged when a person contemplates risk versus ambiguity, and do the specific active regions give us some clues as to the nature of that reaction? This question was answered by comparing the recordings of brain activity when the participant was considering a risky gamble versus a sure-thing option versus the recordings when considering an ambiguous gamble versus a sure-thing option by literally "subtracting the two images."

Two brain areas showed reliably more activity when ambiguous gambles were considered: the amygdala and the orbitofrontal cortex.

At this point, the interpretation becomes speculative as we don't know exactly what those brain regions do, what computations they might perform. Furthermore, if cognitive or emotional functions can be assigned, they are likely to involve interactions among several regions—what are called *circuits* by neuroscientists. But, with those cautions in mind, the amygdala is frequently associated with emotional responses, most notably to fear-evoking stimuli, such as frightened faces, and the orbitofrontal cortex often appears to play a role in integrating cognitive and emotional information; patients with injuries to the orbitofrontal cortex often behave inappropriately in social situations, despite knowledge of the proper behavior. Conversely, the dorsal striatum (including the nucleus accumbens) was more active when risky (compared with ambiguous) prospects were considered. This area (see above) seems to play a role in predicting rewards (especially monetary rewards). These interpretations suggest that the brain treats ambiguous prospects as a bit scary and emotional, but treats risky prospects as something to think about in a "calculating" manner.

There is an important methodological subtlety we need to point out here. Many areas of the brain were active when the sure-thing-versus-gamble prospects were considered in this experiment. (In fact, one might say that all the brain is active all the time while we are alive.) What the comparative method tells us about is *relative activity* under different experimental conditions. Furthermore, to assist in data analysis and interpretation, statistical criteria are applied to declare a difference in brain activity in a local region significant and reliable—a "probability < .001" test in this experiment. This means that the differences reported above are worth interpreting and exploring, but it does not mean, for example, that the striatum was turned on when a risky prospect was considered and turned off when an ambiguous prospect was considered, only that the difference was larger for risky prospects than for ambiguous prospects—which is still important.

The analyses we have described so far tell us something about differential brain activity; Camerer's research team went further to examine the relationship between brain activity and overt gambling behavior. They computed separate behavioral indices of risk-aversion (based on the Utility Functions such as those displayed in Figures 9.3 and 12.1) and ambiguity-aversion (based on the Decision Weight Function in Figure 12.2) from the behavioral choices their participants made between the gambles they were presented. Then, they correlated those measures of *gambling behavior* with *brain activity* in the three regions of interest identified in the fMRI image analyses across participants. Is greater behavioral risk-aversion (ambiguity-aversion) correlated with differential activity in the striatum (amygdala and orbitofrontal cortex)? The answers were all affirmative: Brain activity in the previously identified regions of interest was related to the relevant behaviors, further confirming the entire analysis.

Camerer's results suggest that there are two brain systems—one associated with the amygdala and the orbitofrontal cortex, the other associated with the striatum—that respond to uncertainty in prospects presented for decisions. Both are active, but as uncertainty increases and becomes ambiguity, there is a shift toward relatively more activation of the amygdala-orbitofrontal system. Furthermore, the same shift in system activation was observed for uncertainty introduced by simple card-draw gambles and for increasing uncertainty produced by lack of expertise (i.e., your outcome depends on judging temperature in Tajikistan) and by the potential actions of a human opponent, implying that the systems are reacting to a very general sense of uncertainty-ambiguity.

We described this study in detail because it illustrates the state of the art in cognitive neuroscience investigations of decision making. At present, we see many efforts to localize computational functions in the brain—in this case, areas that systematically respond to degrees of uncertainty (we sometimes call them "uncertainty meters," "value meters," etc.). The computational functions are usually selected for study because they already play central roles in economic (e.g., expected utility theory) or psychological (e.g., prospect theory) models of the decision process. The first steps in the research involve measuring which brain regions of interest are differentially active when the relevant stimulus property (e.g., uncertainty) is high versus low. Second, activation in a ROI is correlated with the relevant behavior (e.g., choosing a risky or ambiguous gamble). Third, in Camerer's study, the time courses of activation of the various brain regions identified earlier were examined to see if anything could be inferred about the larger neural processing circuit for uncertain decisions. Finally, Camerer presented the same tasks to neurological patients with damage to the orbitofrontal cortex to see if their behavior (and brain activation) patterns were consistent with an interpretation that the orbitofrontal cortex function played a causal (and not just correlational) role in choices under risk and ambiguity. One important behavioral observation was that the patients' choices were both risk- and ambiguity-neutral, while non-brain-injured participants were mostly averse to risk and even more averse to ambiguity.

Camerer's study is just one of hundreds of studies being reported every year that help illuminate the mechanics of decision processes. It illustrates the systematic effort to localize functions in specific organs or regions in the brain, and anticipates the next generation of research that will combine temporal and spatial analyses to identify *processing circuits*. It also shows how observations of patients with brain damage can be compared with observations of uninjured participants to draw conclusions about the causal role of brain regions. This is an exciting, fast-moving program of research. Scientists from many disciplines—neuroscience, psychology, economics, and neurobiology—are collaborating in the study of the neural bases of decision making from their various perspectives, and the data that is emerging promises to increase greatly our understanding of how this essential behavioral achievement is carried out by our brains.

## 13.2 Emotions in Decision Making

Emotions have been neglected by cognitive researchers and decision researchers. Instead, researchers' attention has been captured by utility and prospect theory models that imply the deliberate calculation of consequences. Historically, in theories of decision making, emotions were usually viewed as an auxiliary phenomenon that operated to perturb the primary cognitive decision processes. This image of an impulsive emotional system that occasionally interferes with a more orderly rational system has been popular throughout the history of speculations about human nature. This dual-nature hypothesis has invoked many vivid metaphors. Plato used the image of a rational charioteer attempting to control two horses (one of which was wild and poorly trained) to illustrate his conception of competing sides of human nature. Several centuries later, Sigmund Freud used the image of a rider trying to control a spirited horse to describe the relationship between the rational, realistic ego and the hungry, desiring id. Moreover, practical thinkers from Isaac Newton to Thomas Jefferson have idealized a condition where "men can be governed by reason and reason alone" (Jefferson, 1905, Vol. 8, p. 124).

Although humans have a remarkable capacity for self-control, we all exhibit lapses and act contrary to our declared intentions to abstain, adhere, or save (Rachlin, 1989). One moment we behave like the prudent, hard-working ant in the fable, but the next we resemble the lazy, self-indulgent grasshopper. One method of studying how people resolve the conflict between immediate gratification and long-term welfare is to measure how much people value immediate versus delayed rewards. In a temporal discounting experiment, participants are offered choices between immediate outcomes and delayed outcomes. Their patterns of choices reveal the relative values of, for example, receiving $20 today versus $20 in 1 month. A specific type of apparent irrationality has emerged in these studies. Consider the following choice: Receive $20 immediately, today, versus receive $25 in 1 week. Most choose the $20 today and their reaction is almost visceral; they are already savoring the consumption of the $20. Now, consider the same amounts of money, but to be received in 5 weeks versus 6 weeks—$20 in 35 days versus $25 in 42 days. For most people, the delayed choice is also easy; they choose to wait for the $25. This type of preference reversal is called *dynamic inconsistency,* and it is contrary to standard economic models, which imply consistency—the rational models predict the value of $25 will drop with distance in time (*temporal discounting*), but in a manner so that there is no "crossover point" where an initially preferred outcome reverses with the non-preferred outcome (like our $20 versus $25 example).

One interpretation of the dynamic inconsistency result is that when an outcome is immediate, a visceral emotional system controls our behavior and chooses the immediately available gratification. However, when gratification is not immediately available, our cooler, rational system leads us to choose more wisely (Thaler & Shefrin, 1981). There are many examples where *visceral factors* reflected in emotions such as the cravings associated with drug addiction, sexual arousal, and intense hunger and thirst drive people to act directly against what they know at the time are their best interests (e.g., Loewenstein, 1996). This interpretation is consistent with our subjective experience when faced with a rich dessert, an opportunity for a sexual hookup, or the chance to make a quick buck. It also fits the common experience of being of two competing minds when choosing between temptation and a prudent course of action. Even the economic philosopher Adam Smith (1759/1892), renowned for his thoughtful discussions of enlightened self-interest, provides an introspective report that illustrates the point:

> At the very time of acting, at the moment in which passion mounts the highest, he hesitates and trembles at the thought of what he is about to do; he is secretly conscious to himself that he is breaking through those measures of conduct which in all his cool hours, he had resolved never to infringe. (p. 227)

Although the "two systems" account fits our intuitions well, it has been difficult to test with behavioral data. McClure, Laibson, Loewenstein, and Cohen (2005) have attempted a test that combines behavioral and neuroscientific measures. Participants in their research made choices between immediate and delayed money rewards while their brains were scanned. The hypothesis was that when both choice outcomes were delayed, only the cortical, deliberative brain system would be active—leading to a rational, prudent solution to the choice dilemma. However, when one of the outcomes was immediate, the emotional-visceral system would dominate the choice.

Their behavioral results confirmed the prior findings of dynamic inconsistency, with choice reversals occurring when identical pairs of choice options were presented at near versus distant time locations. The results from the brain scan data showed differential activation of four areas of the brain when immediate versus delayed rewards were compared: the ventral striatum, the medial orbitofrontal cortex, the medial prefrontal cortex, and the posterior cingulate cortex. When either immediate or delayed choices were contemplated, visual and motor areas were active (probably not central to the choice process), along with areas of the left and right intraparietal cortex, the right dorsolateral prefrontal cortex, the right ventrolateral prefrontal cortex, and the right lateral orbitofrontal cortex. Although the association is not perfect, immediate choices generally activated areas of the brain associated with emotional responses (limbic and orbitofrontal areas), while areas associated with deliberate reasoning (frontal and parietal) were active for both immediate- and delayed-choice pairs (but see Kable & Glimcher, 2007, for an alternate interpretation). It is also notable that two-system interpretations of moral decisions and consumer choices have been supported by similar differential activation patterns (Greene, Sommerville, Nystrom, Darley, & Cohen, 2001; McClure, Li, Tomlin, Cypert, Montague, & Montague, 2005). Distinctive limbic and cortical areas were activated when emotion played a central role in the decision.

Although it is a big inferential leap from controlled studies of individual decisions in laboratory experiments to macroeconomic phenomena, neuroeconomists and behavioral economists speculate that emotional responses like the ones measured by recordings of limbic system activity might explain some market anomalies and crashes (Akerlof & Shiller, 2009). Temporal myopia can explain some of the irrational exuberance of investors in bull markets, our willingness to rack up huge social debts today for the next generation to pay off, and our failure to heed the impact of today's polluting habits on the future environment of our planet.

Although emotions certainly lead us to act against our best interests under some conditions, there has been a shift to the view that emotions also play a positive adaptive role in behavior. One of the leaders in this shift was Robert Zajonc (1980), who established the importance of emotional reactions as useful guides to rapid evaluations and approach-avoid behavior. His classic aphorism, that "preferences need no inferences," referred to the fact that often emotions and emotion-based choices are inescapably evoked prior to any conscious analysis. We've all had experiences where we have simple "gut reactions" to people, situations, or products that we can't explain (and sometimes resist) at the conscious, deliberate level. And we've all started to recommend a movie or a book to someone else, and then paused because we realized we have no memory of the content or why we liked it so much. Zajonc moved beyond anecdotes and introduced a laboratory paradigm to study what he called the *mere exposure effect*. His method involved repeatedly presenting a research participant with an unfamiliar stimulus (a Chinese ideograph, a novel melody, an unfamiliar face) and subsequently asking for evaluative ratings of the item. The result was a fairly reliable increase in liking for the item as a function of the number of repetitions. But, more remarkably, when the original items were presented so briefly that the participants were not aware of the experience, or time had passed so they were forgotten, "mere exposure" still led to increased liking. It seemed that cognition (e.g., recognizing the item) was not necessary for preference (increased liking). The mere exposure effect is important because it represents a very pure form of preference formation, although it probably contributes only slightly to preferences for everyday objects (see Section 5.3 on fluency, which is now viewed as the primary mechanism underlying mere exposure effects).

Paul Slovic's research program studying the effects of emotions on judgments of risks develops the theme that emotions provide quick evaluations and guides to approach-avoid responses. In a classic study based on respondents' judgments of the similarities between different sources of societal risk, Slovic (1987) discovered that the "personality" of a risk could be more important in determining individual and societal efforts to manage that risk than rational considerations such as objective personal risk. What he discovered was a two-dimensional similarity space (Figure 13.3). One dimension was defined by the familiarity-knowability of the risk—Is the risky event highly visible, easy to understand?—and the other dimension was associated with the "dread" evoked by thinking about the risk—Is the risk hard to control, fatal, scary? His findings have had a major impact on national risk-communication and -management programs. They led Slovic to propose a more general *affect heuristic,* similar to the other heuristics we reviewed in Chapter 5 in the sense that one concept (affect, fluency, similarity) is substituted for another (dangerousness, frequency, probability). Slovic, Melissa Finucane, Ellen Peters, and Donald MacGregor (2007) manipulated the emotions associated with the potential risks of a technology like nuclear power and observed carryover of the positive (negative) mood to other aspects of the technology that had not been mentioned such as the benefits derived from the technology. The reverse also occurred: Affect associated with the benefits was "substituted" for missing information to make judgments of risk.

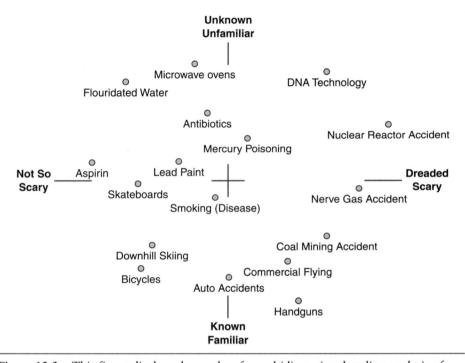

**Figure 13.3**    This figure displays the results of a multidimensional scaling analysis of citizens' judgments of the similarities between hazardous events and conditions that are of serious concern to our society. Two dimensions emerge from the analysis showing that people's responses to the "personalities" of threatening events can be summarized by knowing the familiarity and the "dreadfulness" of the event.

*Source:* Based on Slovic, 1987, Figure 1.

George Loewenstein and his colleagues Chris Hsee, Elke Weber, and Ned Welch (2001) have extended this theme by proposing a non-consequentialist "risk as feelings" framework that describes one mode of responding to threatening events. The risk-as-feelings hypothesis proposes that we respond based on the feelings evoked quickly and pre-analytically by a situation or experienced as a by-product of an analytic (consequentialist) decision process. Under some conditions, this mode of responding may replace the deliberate cost-benefit analysis assumed by classic rational or quasi-rational models. One implication of the claim that people respond emotionally is that more cognitive factors, such as probability, will be neglected. Yuval Rottenstreich and Hsee (2001) conducted a series of studies that demonstrated just this effect. They manipulated the emotionality of the outcomes in a pair of uncertain prospects: a 1% chance of winning $50 or a 1% chance of winning "a kiss from your favorite movie star." Under these conditions, 65% of the participants chose the kiss lottery. But when they changed the prospects to "sure things"—choose to receive the $50 or the kiss for sure—only one-quarter of the participants preferred the kiss. The results replicated with cash versus a European vacation and with cash versus a negative electric shock experience. The researchers' favored interpretation of these results is that people underweight probabilities when considering emotion-evoking outcomes. Emotions change the shape of the prospect theory decision weight function (see Figure 12.2) so that it is flatter in the central portions and steeper at the extremes when emotional outcomes are considered.

Current research exploring the role(s) of emotion in decision making is focusing on the question of emotion-specific responses. Can we account for most emotion-based responses with a simple one- (good-bad) or two- (good-bad, aroused-placid) type model of emotions (Russell, 1980), or are there notable differences between specific negative (angry, afraid) and positive (happy, serene) emotional types? The answer already seems to clearly be that it is important to distinguish between the action tendencies invoked by specific emotions (Ellsworth & Scherer, 2003; Lerner & Keltner, 2000). For example, Jennifer Lerner has demonstrated clear differences in the influence of distinct negative emotions—fear, anger, disgust—on decisions made in those emotional states (see Section 9.4). But there is plenty of work still to be done in spelling out the details of a comprehensive emotional-appraisal action theory.

The more fundamental scientific question behind the specific-emotion effects question is what is the nature of emotions and how should they be distinguished from cognitive processes. Most cultures agree on the dual nature of the internal processes that underlie behavior and describe a two-system, emotion-versus-cognition distinction. The scientific problem is that there are no clear boundaries between the two systems and no generally accepted operations to identify the workings of one or the other system. Neuroscience approaches are certain to help distinguish between the two systems and to describe their interplay—or to replace the dual-system concept with something more valid. We've noted that there are clear anatomical differences between the cortex, which is usually considered the primary seat of cognitive processes, and the limbic system, which includes organs like the striatum (including the nucleus accumbens), the amygdala, and the insular cortex (a bridge between cortex and limbic systems), which are associated with subjective reports of emotional experiences and operationalizations of emotional states in non-human animals like mice and cats. But no one yet can confidently point to neural signatures of emotional processes.

## 13.3 The Rise of Experimental Methods to Study Dynamic Decisions

Most of our current scientific understanding of decision making comes from studying behavior in highly controlled tasks in which participants make choices between well-defined options—between two gambles, among four apartments to rent—on independent, carefully demarcated decision trials. But in life, we usually don't encounter such well-defined choice options, and the choice process is often distributed across an interval of time and even composed of several component choice episodes. Metaphorically, it is as though we have studied people attempting to cross a stream in a single jump, but life is more like crossing the stream by making a sequence of jumps from one stone to the next until we are across. Although there has always been a trickle of studies of people's behavior in dynamic, multicomponent choice tasks, that trickle is turning into a flood of more realistic research tasks.

We date the beginning of this trend to study behavior in complex, dynamic tasks at the publication, by Antonio Damasio and colleagues (Bechara, Damasio, Tranel, & Damasio, 1997) at the University of Iowa, of an enormously influential study of the performance of brain-injured patients. Damasio's research was focused on the behavior of neurological patients who had sustained injuries to areas of the orbitofrontal cortex. The most famous patient of this type was Phineas Gage, a construction worker, who was injured in 1848 when a crowbar penetrated his prefrontal cortex in an explosion. The remarkable result, described as a "Wonderful Accident" in a newspaper headline, was that Gage seemed to be barely injured, was able to stand upright and walk unassisted a few hours after the accident, and then subsequently seemed to be fully competent intellectually. Gage's physician, John Harlow (1868), impressed by the apparently miraculous recovery, provided detailed descriptions of Gage's post-injury behavior. Although Gage was not physically disabled, his character and temperament changed: From a formerly temperate, model citizen, he became

fitful, irreverent, indulging at times in the grossest profanity which was not previously his custom, manifesting but little deference for his fellows, impatient of restraint or advice when it conflicts with his desires, at times pertinaciously obstinate, yet capricious and vacillating, devising many plans of future operation which are no sooner arranged than they are abandoned.

And, in Damasio's words,

> Gage had once known all he needed to know about making choices conducive to his betterment . . . [A]fter the accident, he no longer showed respect for social convention; ethics were violated; the decisions he made did not take into account his best interest . . . [and] there was no evidence of concern about his future, no sign of forethought. (p. 11)

In order to study the effects of injuries like Gage's, Damasio and his colleagues (Bechara et al., 1997) invented a gambling task, designed to mimic the conditions of everyday risky decision making more realistically than static "choose a gamble" tasks. In their Iowa Gambling Task, participants search for monetary payoffs in an uncertain environment composed of four card decks, A, B, C, and D. The participant's goal is to earn money by sampling repeatedly from the decks of cards, each of which is associated with gain and loss outcomes. On each trial, the participant chooses a card from one of the decks and receives the outcome printed on its hidden side. The participant has to learn the distribution of payoffs associated with each deck by experience through over 100 trials. The A and B decks are "disadvantageous" because both have negative expected values in the long run: A player who samples frequently from those decks will end up in the red. The C and D decks are "advantageous" because they have positive expected values, and repeated choices of those decks will win money over time.

As so often in life, it is far from obvious at first which decks are good and which are bad. Specifically, the cards in the disadvantageous decks (A, B) pay a positive gain of $100 on every trial, but some of the cards (1 or 5 out of every 10, depending on the deck) also include losses large enough to produce a net loss of $250 for every 10 cards sampled from those decks. Cards in the advantageous decks (C, D) also pay a constant gain on each choice—only $50, but the intermittent, unpredictable losses are also smaller in those decks, so that the balance for every 10 cards sampled is a gain of $250. Notice that the task was designed to be confusing: The losing decks had a consistent higher gain on every card ($100), and the winning decks had smaller gains. (The composition of each deck is summarized in Figure 13.4.)

The Iowa gambling studies focused on behavioral differences between orbitofrontal patients and uninjured control participants. Damasio (Bechara et al., 1997) found that all players were initially attracted to decks A and B with their consistent high gains. But after a while (typically 20 to 40 trials), the control participants shifted away from the A and B decks and chose instead from the advantageous C and D decks. The orbitofrontal patients, however, persisted

|                              | Deck A        | Deck B   | Deck C      | Deck D   |
|------------------------------|---------------|----------|-------------|----------|
| Reward on every card         | $100          | $100     | $50         | $50      |
| Punishment on some cards     | $150 – $350   | $1,250   | $25 – $75   | $250     |
| Probability of punishment    | .50           | .10      | .50         | .10      |
| First punishment on Card No. | Card 3        | Card 9   | Card 3      | Card 10  |
| Overall expected value per card | –$25       | –$25     | +$25        | +$25     |

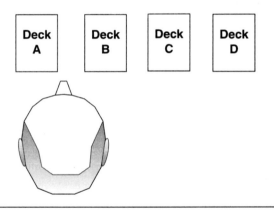

Figure 13.4    This figure depicts the situation facing a participant in the Iowa Gambling Task, an exemplar of the new wave of dynamic decision-making tasks, inspired by an interest in the neural substrates of everyday decision-making behaviors in normal and brain-injured individuals. On each trial of the experimental task, the participant samples a card from one of four decks and receives feedback, printed on the face-down side of the card, about the gains and losses earned by selecting that card.

in their preference for the disadvantageous decks. Damasio also tracked participants' emotional responses during the task by recording skin conductance levels (essentially a measure of sweaty palms) that indicate whether a person is experiencing anxiety or stress. The control participants quickly developed skin conductance reactions *in anticipation* of their choices from the disadvantageous decks, and notably, before they began to articulate specific beliefs about the losses associated with those decks. It was as though their bodies "knew" there was something wrong with the bad decks before they were able to state the problem. But the patients never learned to avoid the disadvantageous decks, and they did not show the anticipatory emotional responses.

Damasio drew a bold conclusion from these results, hypothesizing that normal adaptive decision making in complex, uncertain environments depends on *somatic markers,* emotional signals that warn us that important events (both good and bad) are about to occur. Thus, somatic markers warn us about exceptional threats or opportunities, or at least interrupt processing of other events and give a "heads up" signal that something important is about to occur. In routine decision making, somatic markers may help us winnow down large choice sets into manageable smaller sets. Extremely bad options are quickly eliminated from consideration because somatic marker signals tell us to avoid them, so that we can reason about the serious contenders with our deliberate, conscious thought processes. Consistent with this interpretation is the observation that one of the distinctive characteristics of orbitofrontal patients is that they can spend hours vacillating between two trivially different decision options—which pen to use to fill out a form, which topping to order on a hamburger, and so on.

The specifics of the *somatic marker hypothesis* have been restated over the course of a decade of vigorous, often critical, follow-up research. However, there is accumulating evidence that the orbitofrontal cortex plays a mediating role between cognitive (frontal cortex) and motivational (limbic system) neural systems (see Section 13.1 above). Furthermore, Damasio's basic insight seems valid and consistent with the behavioral findings by Zajonc and Slovic we described above in Section 13.2. When the deliberate, controlled strategies of our cognitive system are unable to make a decision, they will be overridden by more automatic, implicit, intuitive systems. Some intuitive, gut-level decisions seem to be based on a primitive approach-avoid mechanism that is relatively insensitive to the quantitative subtleties of expected utility theory's values and probabilities.

We want to emphasize the importance of the Iowa Gambling Task as a bellwether methodological innovation, which may have an even larger long-term effect on the study of behavioral decision making than the somatic marker hypothesis. Since its introduction, several other dynamic decision tasks have appeared and are increasing in popularity. Many of them, like the Iowa Gambling Task, were invented to facilitate the diagnosis and understanding of brain injuries or brain functions in decision-making situations. Others were simply introduced to provide more valid analogues to everyday decisions. The Balloon Analog Risk Task (BART) (Lejuez et al., 2002) encourages participants to skate on thin ice by inflating a cartoon balloon, one pump at a time. Each pump earns a small amount of money, encouraging the participant to keep inflating. But at some uncertain point in time, the balloon will explode, eliminating all the money earned. Robin Cubitt and Robert Sugden (2001) have invented an "accumulator gamble" task in which participants open a series of boxes to discover hidden payoffs, but as in the BART task, opening one box too many results in the loss of all winnings accumulated up to that point. The Angling Risk Task (ART) gives participants choices between risky and ambiguous options in a simulated fishing game (Pleskac, 2008). Tatsuya Kameda and his colleagues have pioneered the use of simulated primordial foraging tasks to study adaptive decision-making habits (e.g., Hastie & Kameda, 2005). And Camelia Kuhnen and Brian Knutson have a dynamic simulation of stock market investments called the Behavioral Investment Allocation Strategy task (BIAS).

Although this last new direction may seem like a mere methodological excursion, we believe it is very important. Already we can see several new lines of research moving up on the field's priority agenda. For example, there is heightened interest in studies of how probability information is extracted from experienced episodes, as in the dynamic tasks, versus when the information is presented in a declarative format, numbers, words, or graphs in traditional one-shot decision studies. This program of research is too new to report definitive conclusions, but there are hints that the relationship between objective and subjective (e.g., decision weights) is different for experienced versus stated probabilities (Hertwig, Barron, Weber, & Erev, 2004). Another set of questions is raised by the quest for individual consistencies in risk attitudes: Are people who are risk-averse (risk-seeking) on traditional task measures (those who choose to play uncertain gambles over equal-valued sure things) also risk-averse in dynamic tasks?

The new dynamic tasks encourage the development of new theoretical models for multiple, dynamic, interdependent decisions. These new models describe the decision process as a series of embedded choices that "move" through a decision space toward one ultimate decision or another. Unlike the classic decision models (utility theory, prospect theory), these models break the global process down into substages that can involve information sampling, a decision that terminates information acquisition, and then some mechanism that integrates the sampled information to select a course of action. It also turns out that these dynamic models are especially conducive to interpretations in terms of neural activity, and they are increasingly popular as a systematic framework to relate behavioral and neuroscience data (e.g., Busemeyer & Townsend, 1993; P. L. Smith & Ratcliff, 2004).

## 13.4 Do We Really Know Where We're Headed?

We are quite certain that neuroscience, emotion, and dynamic decision tasks will play an increasingly important role in the immediate future of decision research. It is interesting that these new directions are interrelated and reinforce one another, neuroscience contributing to our understanding of what emotion is and what it does. Much of what the brain does is reflected in emotional experience. The dynamic tasks and models for behavior in them help us relate non-laboratory decision behavior to its neural substrates. We expect that these developments will all lead to changes in our descriptive models for decision-making behavior. Indeed, the concept of rational, optimal behavior is also likely to be modified by a deeper understanding of the physical mechanisms that underlie the cognitive and emotional processes that are the primary subject of current theories, and by explorations of what it means to achieve behavioral goals in dynamic, temporally extended environments instead of on one-shot decision trials.

## References

Akerlof, G. A., & Shiller, R. J. (2009). *Animal spirits: How human psychology drives the economy, and why it matters for global capitalism*. Princeton, NJ: Princeton University Press.

Bechara, A., Damasio, H., Tranel, D., & Damasio, A. R. (1997). Deciding advantageously before knowing the advantageous strategy. *Science, 275*, 1293–1295.

Breiter, H. C., Aharon, I., Kahneman, D., Dale, A., & Shizgal, P. (2001). Functional imaging of neural responses to expectancy and experience of monetary gains and losses. *Neuron, 30*, 619–639.

Busemeyer, J. R., & Townsend, J. T. (1993). Decision field theory: A dynamic cognitive approach to decision making. *Psychological Review, 100*, 432–459.

Cubitt, R. P., & Sugden, R. (2001). Dynamic decision-making under uncertainty: An experimental investigation of choices between accumulator gambles. *Journal of Risk and Uncertainty, 22*, 103–128.

Damasio, A. R. (1994). *Descartes' error: Emotion, reason, and the human brain*. New York: Putnam.

Ellsworth, P. C., & Scherer, K. R. (2003). Appraisal processes in emotion. In R. J. Davidson, K. R. Scherer, & H. H. Goldsmith (Eds.), *Handbook of the affective sciences* (pp. 572–595). New York: Oxford University Press.

Fiorillo, C. D., Tobler, P. N., & Schultz, W. (2003). Discrete coding of reward probability and uncertainty in dopamine neurons. *Science, 299*, 1898–1902.

Glimcher, P. W. (2003). *Decisions, uncertainty, and the brain: The science of neuroeconomics*. Cambridge: MIT Press.

Greene, J. D., Sommerville, R. B., Nystrom, L. E., Darley, J. M, & Cohen, J. D. (2001). An fMRI investigation of emotional engagement in moral judgment. *Science, 293,* 2105–2108.

Harlow, J. H. (1868). Recovery of the passage of an iron bar through the head. *Publications of the Massachusetts Medical Society, 2,* 327–347.

Hastie, R., & Kameda, T. (2005). The robust beauty of majority rules. *Psychological Review, 112*(2), 494–508.

Hertwig, R., Barron, G., Weber, E. U., & Erev, I. (2004). Decisions from experience and the effect of rare events in risky choice. *Psychological Science, 15,* 534–539.

Hsu, M., Bhatt, M., Adolphs, R., Tranel, D., & Camerer, C. F. (2005). Neural systems responding to degrees of uncertainty in human decision-making. *Science, 310,* 1680–1683.

Jefferson, T. (1905). *The writings of Thomas Jefferson* (Vol. 8, p. 124). Washington, DC: Thomas Jefferson Memorial Association.

Kable, J. W., & Glimcher, P. W. (2007). The neural correlates of subjective value during intertemporal choice. *Nature Neuroscience, 10,* 1625–1633.

Knutson, B., & Peterson, R. (2005). Neurally reconstructing expected utility. *Games and Economic Behavior, 52,* 305–315.

Kuhnen, C. M., & Knutson, B. (2005). The neural basis of financial risk taking. *Neuron, 47,* 763–770.

Lejuez, C. W., Read, J. P., Kahler, C. W., Richards, J. B., Ramsey, S. E., Stuart, G. L., et al. (2002). Evaluation of a behavioral measure of risk taking: The Balloon Analogue Risk Task (BART). *Journal of Experimental Psychology: Applied, 8,* 75–84.

Lerner, J. S., & Keltner, D. (2000). Beyond valence: Toward a model of emotion-specific influences on judgment and choice. *Cognition and Emotion, 14,* 473–493.

Loewenstein, G. F. (1996). Out of control: Visceral influences on behavior. *Organizational Behavior and Human Decision Processes, 65,* 272–292.

Loewenstein, G. F., Weber, E. U., Hsee, C. K., & Welch, N. (2001). Risk as feelings. *Psychological Bulletin, 127,* 267–286.

McClure, S. M., Laibson, D. I., Loewenstein, G. F., & Cohen, J. D. (2005). Separate neural systems value immediate and delayed monetary rewards. *Science, 306,* 503–507.

McClure, S. M., Li, J., Tomlin, D., Cypert, K. S., Montague, L. M., & Montague, P. R. (2005). Neural correlates of behavioral preference for culturally familiar drinks. *Neuron, 44,* 379–387.

Platt, M. L., & Glimcher, P. W. (1999). Neural correlates of decision variables in parietal cortex. *Nature, 400,* 233–238.

Pleskac, T. J. (2008). Decision making and learning while taking sequential risks. *Journal of Experimental Psychology: Learning, Memory, and Cognition, 34,* 167–185.

Rachlin, H. (1989). *Judgment, decision, and choice.* New York: W. H. Freeman.

Rottenstreich, Y., & Hsee, C. K. (2001). Money, kisses, and electric shocks: On the affective psychology of risk. *Psychological Science, 12,* 185–190.

Russell, J. A. (1980). A circumplex model of affect. *Journal of Personality and Social Psychology, 39,* 1161–1178.

Salzman, C. D., Britten, K. H., & Newsome, W. T. (1990). Cortical microstimulation influences perceptual judgments of motion direction. *Nature, 346,* 174–177.

Schultz, W. (1998). Predictive reward signal of dopamine neurons. *Journal of Neurophysiology, 80,* 1–27.

Slovic, P. (1987). Perception of risk. *Science, 236,* 280–285.

Slovic, P., Finucane, M. L., Peters, E., & MacGregor, D. G. (2007). The affect heuristic. *European Journal of Operational Research, 177,* 1333–1352.

Smith, A. (1892). *A theory of moral sentiments.* London: George Bell. (Original work published 1759)

Smith, P. L., & Ratcliff, R. (2004). The psychology and neurobiology of simple decisions. *Trends in Neuroscience, 27,* 161–168.

Sugrue, L. P., Corrado, G. S., & Newsome, W. T. (2005). Choosing the greater of two goods: Neural currencies for valuation and decision making. *Nature Reviews: Neuroscience, 6,* 363–375.

Thaler, R., & Shefrin, H. M. (1981). An economic theory of self-control. *Journal of Political Economy, 89,* 392–406.

Wilson, E. O. (1999). *Consilience: The unity of knowledge.* New York: Vintage Press.

Zajonc, R. B. (1980). Feeling and thinking: Preferences need no inferences. *American Psychologist, 35,* 151–175.

# 14

# In Praise of Uncertainty

*To teach how to live without certainty, and yet without being paralyzed by hesitation.*

—Bertrand Russell

## 14.1 Uncertainty as Negative

People often abhor uncertainty. Our society spends billions of dollars to reduce it, often spending absurd amounts to abolish that last 10% of doubt (Breyer, 2006). The scariest kind of uncertainty arises from dread outcomes, especially what former Secretary of Defense Donald Rumsfeld called "the unknown unknowns" (Slovic, 1987)—the kinds of events that we are so ignorant about that we don't know how to think about them systematically. Unknown unknowns like terrorist attacks with hijacked airplanes or market crashes that result from a cataclysmic political event in Europe can be contrasted with events that we have systematically conceptualized as representatives of a known category of events—like ordinary airplane crashes and the daily up-and-down movements of stock prices in a normal market. In the extreme case, we have partly tamed the uncertainty by summarizing with the kinds of statistical models we have described throughout this book. Unknown unknowns are scariest of all when we think that a willful agent (terrorist, or man-eating shark) has the intention of harming us. (We submit that you will think more accurately about both unknown and known unknowns if you follow the advice to "take an outside view" presented in

Chapter 8; see Makridakis, Hogarth, & Gaba, 2009, for an engaging discussion of psychologically distinct types of uncertainty.)

A common way of dealing with our experience of the uncertainty in life is to ignore it completely, or to invent some "higher rationale" to explain it, often a rationale that makes it more apparent than real. A preacher in Ecclesiastes observed that "the race is not to the swift, nor the battle to the strong, neither yet bread to the wise, nor yet riches to men of understanding, nor yet favor to men of skills; but time and chance happeneth to them all." This sounds like an exhortation to expect and adapt to uncertainty. But his views are contradicted by most of the narratives in the remainder of the Old Testament, where people generally "get what they deserve," where there is a moral to every tale. The Old Testament Israelites, for example, lose battles when they turn away from Yahweh to worship graven images or to adopt the heathen practices of neighboring tribes; when they mend their ways, they win. False prophets are put to death; true ones triumph—although the heads of some of them end up on a platter first. The battle is to the morally superior—and not always to the strong; bread is supplied to the wise, and riches to men of understanding—although they may, as Job did, suffer first. Uncertainty and randomness are apparent, not real. (Admittedly, exactly what members of Job's first family—or the people of Jericho, other than the traitorous prostitute—did to deserve their fates is not entirely clear.)

Many who have abandoned traditional religion manifest the same dread of uncertainty in astrology, scientology, tarot cards, and innumerable other belief systems that help many people make sense of life's uncertainties, which are believed to be part of some deep underlying structure that they strive to understand. Fred Ayeroff and Bob Abelson (1976) conducted studies in which they searched for ESP (extrasensory perception) abilities in college students. They found no evidence for ESP at all in their careful experiments, but they did find plenty of evidence for ESB, extrasensory belief. (There is structure in the universe, but is it related to the course of an individual life?) Shaking off the dread of uncertainty in our lives and the need to deny its existence is extraordinarily difficult; even those who have a profound and compelling *intellectual* belief that the world is not constructed according to human needs cannot help but wonder what they "did wrong" when their children develop leukemia or their aging mother is hit, out of the blue, by a teenager joy-riding in a stolen car. Even intellectuals are prone to misconceptions concerning the behavior of random processes, unless they check themselves and analytically apply their school-learned probability theory calculations (see Chapter 8 and the Appendix).

We noted that people seem eager to interpret chance events in which they have some input (e.g., choosing a lottery ticket or picking numbers in Lotto) as if they involved an element of skill (see Section 7.2). Even in domains like sports and academic test taking, where Kunda and Nisbett (1986) have found that people's naive statistical intuitions are pretty good, the contributions of chance are underappreciated; people know that there is an element of inexplicable, even random influence in tests of human ability. So, for example, what percentage of variance in athletic outcomes can be attributed to the skill of players, as indexed by past performance records? Robert Abelson (1985) asked knowledgeable fans to consider whether a major-league baseball player would get a hit in a given turn at bat. He asked the fans to estimate the relative contributions of skill and chance to this outcome. (Actually, he asked them to estimate the squared correlation or "proportion of variance explained" by the player's batting averages—widely held to be the most useful summary of skill at batting.) The median estimate was around 25%, but the true answer is approximately 0.5%. Even in a familiar domain in which people appreciate chance factors, people overestimated the contribution of skill by a factor of about 50. As Abelson put it, "we as baseball fans are prone to regard a .330 hitter as a hero who will always come through in the clutch, and the .260 hitter as a practically certain out when the game is on the line." (This example has another important message: In many situations, small differences in skill and other biases of behavior add up when the behavior is repeated many times. What is the incremental impact of even tiny biases in judgment when amplified by hundreds of career success evaluations, hundreds of medical operations, or hundreds of prison sentences?)

This illusion of personal control and a hidden causal order is the basis of superstitious behavior. Superstitions are particularly likely to develop when the outcomes of behaviors involve components of both skill and chance (e.g., making a hit in a baseball game) because it is easy to confuse factors based on skill with those based on chance. In fact, if we were to evaluate these behaviors by simply noting what the person did and what outcome followed, there would be no way to distinguish between chance and skill components—short of deliberately varying our behavior in a systematic or random fashion and then conducting a statistical analysis to determine which behaviors are associated with success and which with failure. Neither people nor rats do that, however; instead, both have a strong tendency to adopt a "win-stay, lose-switch" strategy, repeating whatever behavior preceded success and changing whatever preceded failure (e.g., swinging the bat precisely 5 times while waiting in the on-deck circle for your turn at bat). Such a strategy has two *logical* consequences: First, it is impossible to evaluate the chance component in success versus failure, and second, the distinction between adaptive and superstitious behavior becomes meaningless. (One simply "did X," and "Y followed.") As pointed out in Sections 1.5 and 2.6, decisions based solely on the outcomes (reinforcements) of past behavior do not satisfy our criterion of rationality because they are not made with regard to probable future consequences.

A much-trumpeted success of Skinnerian behaviorism was its explanation of superstitious behavior (Skinner, 1948; see Staddon & Simmelhag, 1971, for a more detailed analysis). If the analysis just proposed is correct, this success is based on the fact that its principles do not distinguish between adaptive and superstitious behavior. Moreover, even a pigeon or rat (or a human) with expert statistical skills and training would tend to behave superstitiously when its total environment consisted of a Skinner box (operant conditioning chamber). Given that nothing can be done in such an environment other than to press a bar or refrain from doing so, and that the only environmental variability involves the appearance of food, a desperately hungry animal (the animals in Skinner's experiments were kept at 70% of their normal body weight) would experience an overwhelming temptation to adopt a "win-stay, lose-switch" strategy, and hence never learn. Moreover, the problem is confounded by the experimenter's deliberate reinforcement of superstitious behavior, thereby further blurring the distinction between superstition and adaptation.

Often, however, we even fail to understand the probabilistic nature of events in which we have no involvement whatsoever. For example, many psychological experiments were conducted in the late 1950s and early 1960s in which subjects were asked to predict the outcome of an event that had a random component but yet had base rate predictability; for example, subjects were asked to predict whether the next card the experimenter turned over would be red or blue in a task in which 70% of the cards were blue, but the sequence of red and blue cards was totally random (as the experimenter shuffled the deck before each experiment). In such a situation, the strategy that will yield the highest proportion of success is to predict the more common event on every trial. For example, if 70% of the cards are blue, then predicting blue on every trial yields a 70% success rate, the highest possible in this task. What subjects tended to do instead, however, was to *match probabilities*—that is, to predict the more probable event *on the proportion of trials on which it occurred.* For example, subjects tended to predict 70% of the time that the blue card would occur and 30% of the time that the red card would occur. Of course, their accuracy was unrelated to their strategies, and matched the prediction of a random probability model. Such a strategy yields a 58% success rate, because the subjects are correct 70% of the time when the blue card occurs (which happens with probability .70) and correct 30% of the time when the red card occurs (which happens with probability .30): (.70 × .70) + (.30 × .30) = .58. In fact, subjects predict the more frequent event with a slightly higher probability than that with which it occurs, but do not come close to predicting its occurrence 100% of the time, even when they are paid for the accuracy of their predictions. Despite feedback through 1,000 trials, even when the subjects are *explicitly told* that only the base rate prediction is relevant—"the sequence is random with no repetitive patterns"—subjects cannot bring themselves to believe that the situation is one in which they *cannot* predict (Tversky & Edwards, 1966, p. 680). Apparently, the uncertainty inherent in this experimental situation is unacceptable, even though failing to appreciate it results in reduced payoffs. (And, once again, it appears to be unacceptable to those of us who develop cancer or lose children.)

The well-known philosopher and behavioral researcher Patrick Suppes tells an instructive story from an unpublished experiment on the probability-matching task. In his experiment, subjects were told their prediction was correct, at random and independent of their responses, on either 10%, 50%, or 90% of the trials. Of course, the feedback was deceptive and no one was learning to predict anything. Then, at the end of the experiment, the subjects were asked to comment on what they had learned. Participants receiving the spurious 90% success feedback wrote brief answers with simple rules (perhaps like what the pigeons in Skinner's superstition experiment would have written if they had had language capacities). Participants receiving 50% success feedback did not provide a simple rule, but they instead provided complex rules and suggestions for how to refine those procedures with more feedback. Finally, the subjects who received 90% *failure* feedback (10% success) were still in the game, but they were methodologists. They had no rules to communicate, but they had methods for finding the rules, should they be allowed to continue learning. Very few subjects correctly stated that the task was an impossible contrivance of the experimenter. How many of us have been assigned, by accident, to the 90% success condition in life? To the 90% failure condition?

When there is a chance component in the outcomes of our own behavior, we tend to treat it *as if* it involves skill. In the probability-matching experiments, subjects responded to a purely probabilistic outcome beyond their control *as if* it were deterministic ("There *must* be some pattern here."). Hillel Einhorn (1986) has suggested that the crucial distinction between intuitive and statistical approaches to prediction and control is whether or not the predictor treats probabilistic events as if they were deterministic. Regarding probabilistic events as deterministic makes the rules of probability theory—such as the necessary consideration of base rates—irrelevant. For example, if the sequence of events in a probability-matching experiment really was deterministic, the prediction of the low-probability event would be neither counter-inductive nor silly. But it is precisely such counter-inductive judgments made by his colleagues that led Paul Meehl—a psychoanalyst as well as a leading researcher in the area of clinical judgment—to be critical of their reasoning capacities, recounted in his article "Why I Do Not Attend Case Conferences" (1973). A simple explanation is that, like subjects in probability-matching experiments, these colleagues do not regard the outcomes involving their clients as inherently probabilistic.

Einhorn (1986) goes on to argue that the statistical approach is *superior* to the clinical one, as evidenced, for example, in the studies conducted by Meehl and others summarized in Section 3.3. We concur. Even if the world has some underlying deterministic structure, we do not usually fully understand it, and in particular we do not comprehend it with respect to the events in everyday life about which we are most concerned. Moreover, subjects' inability to appreciate the probabilistic nature of the probability-matching experiments, even after as many as 1,000 trials, indicates that the tendency to reject uncertainty is a strong bias—not a consequence of adaptive learning from experience.

Could treating chance as skill be explained on a motivational basis? For example, does the belief that we cannot predict the outcome of coin tossing or batting somehow threaten our ability to cope with the world? Or is it that cognition itself is so inextricably bound with our attempts to predict and control, that our judgments about events in the world—no matter how clearly they are randomly determined—implicitly assume predictability? We do not know the answer.

Clearly, there are contexts in which lack of predictability involves threat. For example, Cable News Network presented an interview with three "experts" while the jury was deliberating during the New Bedford rape trial in 1984 (concerning a woman who was gang-raped in a tavern). One of these, a psychologist named Lee Salk, proclaimed that one of the worst aspects of such victimization is that the experience undermines the three beliefs on which our ability to cope with the world is based: the belief that we are superior, the belief that we are invulnerable, and the belief that the world is just; moreover, after victimization, "it takes several years to re-establish these beliefs." The entire American nation is struggling to recover from the experience of terrorist attacks on September 11, 2001, which threaten all three beliefs. But we need to remember the words of Lord Acton in 1887: "History provides neither compensation for suffering nor penalties for wrong."

## 14.2 The Illusion of Hedonic Certainty

We not only underappreciate uncertainty in the world outside of us; we are also prone to illusions of consistency, reliability, and certainty about the world inside our own heads. There can be little doubt that we think we are more logical, rational, and consistent than we really are. This book has cataloged dozens of examples of this kind of hubris; we even rewrite our personal biographies to reinforce our beliefs that we knew it all along and that we've "always felt this way." But the authors suspect we have a special blind spot when thinking about what we will want in the future—thinking about *decision utility* (Section 9.1).

Research on hedonic psychology, especially phenomena relevant to deliberate decision making, is in its early stages, but already there is a sizable catalog of errors and biases. Without repeating the many examples of bad judgments about hedonic consequences (see Section 9.1), we can state some summary premises concerning our capacities to predict our post-decision, experienced utilities: First, we are at best moderately accurate predictors of our evaluations and emotional reactions to future outcomes. Second, the outcomes themselves (which occur preceding our reactions) are often hard to predict and more complex than our anticipations of them. Third, even if we could predict our reactions to the outcomes, the impact of these outcomes on our long-term global well-being (and domain-specific happiness) is modest, much smaller than we think it is. There are at least two reasons for this overestimation error. First, we know that people are insensitive to regression toward the mean when they predict conditions based on only partly valid information. This means they will choose apparently best options, expecting they will be better on average than they are, and anticipate bad outcomes that are consistently a bit less bad than feared (see, for example, Harrison & March, 1984). Second, people do not seem to appreciate their own resiliency and adaptability. We recover from harm and loss much faster than we expect, but then we also become accustomed to good things faster than we expect—a condition that Dan Gilbert (2007) has called *immune neglect.*

This last point has been verified many times in research on personal well-being and happiness. The best current theory of well-being proposes that most people have *hedonic set points,* ambient levels of ebullience or depression that are consistent within an individual and that vary reliably across individuals (and that may even be genetically inherited, or perhaps set by early life experiences; Diener & Biswas-Diener, 2008). The image is of people bobbing up and down, as the day-to-day events perturb their hedonic levels, but with everyone returning to pretty much where they started on the up–down scale. Hedonically significant events (divorce, losing a job, winning the lottery, getting into your first choice college) move you up or down, but after 3 months (or at most, 6) you're back to normal. (David Lykken, 1999, argues that genetics may be an important determinant of your hedonic set point, just as heredity predicts your body weight.)

What does this mean for decision making? People have erroneous, self-aggrandizing beliefs that they can predict and control how happy they will be. People focus too much on decision utility, expending too much cognitive energy attempting to predict their future happiness when they make decisions. We are not advocating that people completely ignore what they want, or think they want, when they choose. But one useful tactic is to avoid focusing on global assessments of "how happy will it make me" when we are evaluating our prospects; rather, we should focus on predicting other important attributes of the consequences being considered (such as good health, productivity, variety of experience, helping others, and perhaps money) and on bad attributes that can be decreased (such as constraints on time or opportunities and risks of tangible losses). But perhaps that is what most of us do naturally. How often to you make choices by asking yourself, "Will this alternative make me happy?" Divorce is one of the few such decisions where the universal self-description is, "I got out of the marriage because it made me so unhappy." Usually we are focused on other, maybe more important attributes that are only probabilistically related to happiness—safety, health, durability, income, and other more tangible characteristics.

## 14.3 The Price of Denying Uncertainty

When Robyn Dawes was training to be a clinical psychologist, he met a patient we'll call Harold. Before his hospitalization, Harold had a shaky marriage held together by concern for his 2-year-old son, and he was doing badly at a job he disliked. One morning, he was fired from his job and he went home. When he arrived, the police were there and his wife was hysterical. His son had run into the street and been killed by an automobile. After his wife had been sedated, he wandered back to his former workplace, which was nearby, and into the canteen. An attractive woman motioned to him to join a group she was with for a cup of coffee. Drinking coffee was strictly forbidden by Harold's religion. He suddenly realized that this woman was trying to *liberate* him from his compulsive adherence to his religious teachings and that she might be trying to liberate him sexually as well. His boss had liberated him from his unpleasant job, and the motorist had liberated him from his bad marriage. He suddenly realized that all of these people had formed a conspiracy to *help* him! He ended up in the hospital when he mistook strangers for members of that conspiracy. His belief was unshakable; for example, protestations by the hospital staff members that they were trying to cure him from his delusions were simply met with a knowing smile.

Psychiatrist Silvano Arieti (1974) maintained that it is not uncertainty (or pain) per se that creates psychotic disorders, but rather the attempt to make sense out of it in a way that does not make sense to others—the "psychotic insight." Of course, not all attempts to reduce uncertainty are pathological. We all attempt to reduce uncertainty. Organizations do it; political decision makers do it. Uncertainty reduction is essential to science, if not all knowledge. It can become pathological, however, if it becomes too important. Such pathology is not limited to those of us socially designated as mentally ill.

There must, for example, be some explanation for a plague. "The Jews are poisoning the wells," some unenlightened people in the 13th century concluded. In fact, such explanations have been resurrected in the lifetime of many of us to explain such other phenomena as an economic depression, students running amok with automatic weapons in our high schools, or the global AIDS epidemic. It is *not* pathological to seek to reduce uncertainty. Such a quest may even lead to knowledge allowing us to understand things that puzzle us today. It *is* pathological to conclude that we *must know now* in situations containing irreducible uncertainty, at least when analyzed in terms of our present knowledge (see, for example, Hammond, 1996).

A belief that, "If I am successful, I must somehow have deserved it," can make a successful person into an arrogant ass. A belief that, "If I am not successful, I must have done something very bad in the past," can make a person into a depressed masochist. There is evidence, due mainly to the work of Bernard Weiner (1979), that most people ascribe their successes to their own characteristics and their failures to factors beyond their control, such as plain bad luck. Depressed people's thinking does not follow this pattern; if anything, it reverses it, as shown by Chris Peterson and Martin Seligman's (1984) research on explanatory style. Many of our colleagues have subsequently made the inferential leap that it is therefore mentally healthy to ascribe success to oneself and failure to circumstances—and that distressed people should be trained to make these self-aggrandizing but logically unjustifiable attributions. Of course, all outcomes are due to some combination of personal and situational factors, which are extraordinarily difficult to unravel, particularly for a single result.

Multi-cause, multi-effect situations, namely *all* situations, are seductively rich with explanations. On March 24, 1989, the *Exxon Valdez* oil tanker ran aground on Bligh Reef and spilled 11 million gallons of crude oil into Prince William Sound. It was America's worst oil spill. There were many ingredients available to construct causal narratives to explain the event: The ship's captain, Charles Hazelwood, had a history of drinking problems, including hospitalization for treatment; the Coast Guard had recently changed its policies, did not provide a local pilot, and had reduced its monitoring of ship passages; the crew of the *Exxon Valdez* had recently been reduced from 33 to 19; an unlicensed third mate was steering the ship when it hit the reef—he testified he had "spaced out" and missed the turn he had been instructed to make; the *Exxon Valdez* was behind schedule and the crew was short of sleep; Hazelwood consumed some amount of alcohol on the afternoon of the ship's sailing; there were seasonal ice floes in the normal tanker traffic lanes, and the *Exxon Valdez* had diverted its course to miss them; and much more. In such a situation it is easy—in fact, irresistible—retrospectively to construct a coherent causal narrative to account for the disaster.

If we were to do a prospective study to identify which of these factors predict the occurrence of tanker oil spills, we would surely find massive uncertainty. There are plenty of instances of each of these precursors being present, but without any oil spills: Many tankers were out of the shipping lanes that night; ice floes are a normal part of ocean environments at that time of year in Alaska; the practice of allowing unlicensed mates to pilot tankers was common. (The Exxon Corporation provided many examples as part of its defense in the resulting lawsuits.) The base rate incidence of oil spills is extremely low, impeding any systematic probabilistic analysis. But intuitive explanation processes usually produce high levels of hindsightful confidence. Dawes has argued that such explanations can only be trusted if there is prior or subsequent systematic, ideally experimental analysis that establishes *general* causal principles that can then be applied to the specific to-be-explained event. Many antecedents–many consequents situations invite spurious backward searches to find causes. (The details of Dawes's technical analysis are beyond the scope of this book, but see his essay, "Prediction of the Future Versus an Understanding of the Past: A Basic Asymmetry," 1993.) One inevitable by-product of our tendency to construct and tell causal stories is blindness to the extent of our ignorance and a derogation of the role of chance in life.

Again, while some phenomena that we now attribute to chance may eventually be predictable and controllable, they remain chance events from our current perspective. Many of us know people who have suffered some great misfortune who appear to prefer believing they did something to bring it about to believing that it was something that just happened. The price of our retreat from uncertainty is often paid by others. Some individuals believe that if people are poor, or are on the street or addicted or ill, they must somehow have done something to deserve that fate. In the face of such deservingness, it is believed, help is futile. Moreover, given the biasing effects of retrospective memory (see Section 6.7), these victims themselves may accept that judgment; for if they, too, believe in "just deserts," that could play a crucial role in determining their recall of what it is *they did wrong*.

A gross misunderstanding of the role of chance in evolution can lead to cruelty. Consider social Darwinism. Even the strongest adaptationists maintain that it is a *slight* genetic advantage that leads to a slight increase in the probability of success in the struggle for (gene) existence, which over *many* generations can lead to substantial genetic changes. But to claim, as some social Darwinists did, that a single individual's poor situation implies the lack of genetic capacity, viciously underestimates the role of chance in life— viciously because it leads to the conclusion that it is "nature's way" to let such people suffer and die, in order to let good genes multiply. While the threat of uncertainty may cause pain, its denial can be cruel.

Such costs of denying uncertainty are high—too high to justify any feeling of security that this denial may offer. In particular, the pathological consequences of believing in a *just world* are severe—both for others and for oneself (see Melvin J. Lerner, 1980). An essential part of wisdom is the ability to determine what is uncertain—that is, to appreciate the limits of our knowledge and to understand its probabilistic nature in many contexts. It follows that an essential part of bravery is eschewing a false sense of security—for example, not believing we are invulnerable or superior, or that the world is just.

Some psychologists, however, urge people to develop these beliefs—as part of a general effort to reinforce belief in personal control of outcomes, since belief in such control is supposed to be a motivator for desirable choice and putting forth effort. It is true that parents attempt to reward good behavior and punish bad so that their children learn to behave in ways that the parents wish; moreover, children who see little contingency between their own behavior and their rewards and punishments often behave badly— or at least, we can improve their behavior by increasing the contingency. In addition, employees who believe that they have control over the rewards they receive for their work are motivated to work hard and be productive.

Consequently, employers and supervisors are well-advised to establish within their organizations a contingency between employee accomplishments and rewards. Global, diffuse control is another matter. If we have "put away childish things" when we are no longer children, we should understand that we have more or less control over outcomes *depending on the particulars of the situation.* Illusory control can have the pernicious effects discussed above. Some control theorists, nevertheless, claim that belief in control, illusory or real, is a mentally healthy motivator.

Rationally, it often doesn't matter how much control we have over outcomes—so long as we have some. For example, various alternatives will still have the same ranking in expected value even if a large random component determines the actual outcome. Understanding the wisdom of Ecclesiastes should in no way inhibit us from choosing the best possible alternative and pursuing it with all our energy. To maintain that it is necessary or desirable to overestimate the amount of control we have is to maintain that we can function only as children or agents of someone else, not as autonomous adults. Unfortunately, some of our colleagues treat their adult clients as if they really were children, and give advice to the entire population on the same basis. (Striking examples of treating the adults as adults may be found in some of the rhetoric of John F. Kennedy. In one speech, he stated bluntly that life is not fair—and gave the example that during wartime some people are shot on battlefields while others sit at desks. In his famous American University speech shortly before his assassination, he proclaimed that this country, comprising 6% of the world's population, cannot control everything that happens on the globe, and that it would be a tragic mistake to equate national security with such control.)

Shelley Taylor (1983), who refers to herself as a "control theorist," has argued that belief in control is adaptive to coping in threatening situations. Taylor presents the following anecdote about a woman with breast cancer—which we interpret, contrary to Taylor, as an example of overestimation of degree of personal control:

> One of the women I interviewed told me that after detection of her breast tumor she believed that she could prevent future recurrences by controlling her diet. She had, among other things, consumed huge quantities of Vitamin A through the singularly unappetizing medium of mashed asparagus. A year and a half later, she developed a second malignancy. This, of course, is precisely the situation all control researchers are interested in: a dramatic disconfirmation of efforts to control. I asked her how she felt when that happened. She shrugged and said she guessed she'd been wrong. She then decided to quit her dull job and use her remaining time to write short stories—something she had always wanted to do. Having lost control in one area of her life, she turned to another area, her life work, that *was* controllable. (p. 1170)

Taylor presents no evidence that her subjects who attempted to achieve illusory control over the recurrence of breast cancer were better off than those who did not, although the article itself implies that attempting such control is psychologically valuable. Her anecdote, however, can be interpreted as an example of how *giving up* the attempt to control is valuable. The woman's shrug was clearly an acknowledgment that she *did not* have control. Perhaps if the shrug had occurred a year and a half earlier, a year and a half of the woman's life would have been devoted to the work she desired rather than to a dull job and mashed asparagus.

## 14.4 Two Cheers for Uncertainty

Imagine a life without uncertainty. Hope, according to Aeschylus, comes from the lack of certainty of fate; perhaps hope is inherently blind. Imagine how dull life would be if variables assessed for admission to a professional school, graduate program, or executive training program really *did* predict with great accuracy who would succeed and who would fail. Life would be intolerable—no hope, no challenge.

Thus, we have a paradox. While we all strive to reduce the uncertainties of our existence and of the environment, ultimate success—that is, a total elimination of uncertainty—would be horrific. In fact, it may be that such procedures as testing for AIDS antibodies and predicting the recurrence of breast cancer on the basis of hormonal and now genetic analyses are the results of long medical marches that have taken us to a place we do not wish to be. Imagine the horror of being notified that you possess a gene that invariably leads to Alzheimer's disease. Would that be worse than learning you have a terminal illness? At least in the latter situation, most people already feel sick. As we write this, genetic testing is developing at an amazing pace. But in many such situations, people choose *not* to receive the feedback (at least probabilistic feedback) about the implications of their genetic constitution. (Even the psychologist Steven Pinker, one of the most inquisitive people the authors know, says that there are aspects of his genetic endowment that he does not want to know about—for example, the genotype that might dispose him to early Alzheimer's disease; Pinker, 2009.) Another example, some people who have a parent with Huntington's disease (due to a single dominant gene) choose not to be tested to determine whether or not they have that gene—which inevitably leads to horrible debilitating and irreversible neurological degeneration.

On the other hand, some people do wish to find out. The results of such discovery (Sieff, Dawes, & Loewenstein, 1999) were quite interesting. Many doctors and health professionals were opposed to a test for Huntington's disease that usually led to a conclusion with high probability that people either did or did not have the gene; a third result was also possible—the test could be inconclusive. (Today, there are tests available that are never inconclusive.) The rationale for their opposition to the test was that they feared people who found out they probably had the gene might become suicidal. The counterargument was that such people might also choose not to have children, in which case the problem would disappear over a few generations. Both predictions turned out to be wrong (Sieff, Dawes, & Loewenstein, 1999). Among those people wishing to find out, those who were told that the results of the test were inconclusive were the most distressed. Among those who found out they had the gene, they adapted to the bad news—just as pointed out in our discussion of "The Illusion of Hedonic Certainty" (Section 14.2 above). Moreover, they did not decide to refrain from having children, which they appeared to regard as equivalent to a wish that they themselves had never been born (and recall that most do not commit suicide). Conversely, those who received the good news that they most probably did not have the gene did not lapse into dysfunctional euphoria. People adapt.

But consistent with the illusion of hedonic certainty, a study of people who tested HIV positive or negative indicated that they grossly exaggerated how the news of their HIV status would affect them. These people were asked to predict how they would fill out a standard mood score 5 weeks after finding out their test results. They were then contacted (as much as possible, given that the experiment was done under conditions of anonymity rather than confidentiality) to fill out these mood questionnaires roughly 5 weeks after they did, in fact, find out their test results. In addition, people who claimed to have found out they were HIV positive or negative roughly 5 weeks earlier also filled out these questionnaires. Compared with the anticipation of very negative feelings or very positive ones, the actual feelings were much more neutral. Again, people adapt. The major finding of the HIV study was that people failed to anticipate how much they'd adapt. (For a review of the Huntington's results and a presentation of the HIV testing results, see Sieff et al., 1999.)

It should be pointed out that these results are valid only for people who had indicated a very clear preference for finding out whether or not they have a condition that leads to extremely negative outcomes. Because these experiments and surveys were conducted in a predominantly free society, it was not possible to sample people at random and simply force information on them about their medical status. Thus, it is not possible to determine whether the results concerning Huntington's and HIV status are applicable to the general population at large, or only to people who already want to find out whether or not they have a devastating medical condition. Moreover, it is not possible on the basis of sampling such people to determine how large a proportion of the general population they constitute. Because the surveys and experiments can be conducted only on people who volunteer, these surveys and experiments themselves do not lead to an estimate of how prevalent people who wish to know such information really are. Of course, it would be possible to supplement the work already done by asking the general population whether they would want to find out, but that has the problem of equating actual behavior with people's hypothetical statements of how they would wish to behave—and the original problem stems from the question of whether people can anticipate their future feelings very well, and it is their feelings when facing the possibility of taking an actual test that are important.

Knowing *pleasant* outcomes with certainty would also detract from life's joy. An essential part of knowledge is to shrink the domain of the unpredictable. But while we pursue this goal, its ultimate attainment would not be at all desirable.

## 14.5 Living With Uncertainty

Without uncertainty, there would be no hope, no ethics, and no freedom of choice. It is only because we do not know what the future holds for us (e.g., the exact time and manner of our own deaths) that we can have hope. It is only because we do not know exactly the future results of our choices that our choice can be free, and can pose a true ethical dilemma. Moreover, there is much uncertainty in the world, and one of our most basic choices is whether we will accept that uncertainty as a fact or try to run away from it. Those who choose to deny uncertainty invent a stable world of their own. Such people's natural desire to reduce uncertainty, which may be basic to the whole cognitive enterprise of understanding the world, is taken to the extreme point where they believe uncertainty does not exist. The statistician's definition that an optimist is "someone who believes that the future is uncertain" is not as cynical as it may first appear to be.

We are optimistic about the contributions to general social welfare from research that will follow the studies and theories reported on in this book. There are many constructive lessons from the body of scientific knowledge that is amassing on judgment and decision making. We know much about important limits on our abilities to make accurate judgments and rational decisions. The reader will recognize many problematic habits and potential pitfalls from the insights provided by the collection of examples described here. We have several genuinely useful technologies for assessing, aiding, and replacing human decision makers. The key insight is to apply statistics and probability theory whenever you can—if not to calculate numerical solutions, then to structure and guide your decision-making process. When people deliberately scrutinize their decisions, they are able to identify and correct their own biases and inconsistencies. Finally, our advice is to strive for systematic external representations of the judgment and decision situations you encounter: Think graphically, symbolically, and distributionally. If we can make ourselves think analytically, and take the time to acquire the correct intellectual tools, we have the capability to think rationally. But, like Benjamin Franklin, we have not tried to tell you what to decide, but rather how to decide.

# References

Abelson, R. P. (1985). A variance explanation paradox: When a little is a lot. *Psychological Bulletin, 97,* 128–132.

Arieti, S. (1974). *Interpretation of schizophrenia* (2nd ed.). New York: Basic Books.

Ayeroff, F., & Abelson, R. P. (1976). ESP and ESB: Belief in personal success at mental telepathy. *Journal of Personality and Social Psychology, 34,* 240–247.

Breyer, S. (2006). *Breaking the vicious circle: Toward effective risk regulation.* Cambridge, MA: Harvard University Press.

Dawes, R. M. (1993). Prediction of the future versus an understanding of the past: A basic asymmetry. *American Journal of Psychology, 106,* 1–24.

Diener, E., & Biswas-Diener, R. (2008). *Happiness: Unlocking the mysteries of psychological wealth.* New York: Wiley-Blackwell.

Einhorn, H. J. (1986). Accepting error to make less error. *Journal of Personality Assessment, 50,* 387–395.

Gilbert, D. (2007). *Stumbling on happiness.* New York: Vintage Press.

Hammond, K. R. (1996). *Human judgment and social policy: Irreducible uncertainty, inevitable error, unavoidable injustice.* Oxford, UK: Oxford University Press.

Harrison, J. R., & March, J. G. (1984). Decision making and postdecision surprises. *Administrative Science Quarterly, 29,* 26–42.

Kunda, Z., & Nisbett, R. E. (1986). The psychometrics of everyday life. *Cognitive Psychology, 18,* 195–224.

Lerner, M. J. (1980). *Belief in a just world: A fundamental delusion.* New York: Plenum Press.

Lykken, D. (1999). *Happiness: What studies on twins show us about nature-nurture, and the happiness set-point.* New York: Golden Books.

Makridakis, S., Hogarth, R., & Gaba, A. (2009). *Dance with chance: Making luck work for you.* Oxford, UK: Oneworld Publications.

Meehl, P. E. (1973). Why I do not attend case conferences. In P. E. Meehl (Ed.), *Psychodiagnosis: Selected papers* (pp. 225–302). New York: Norton.

Peterson, C., & Seligman, M. E. P. (1984). Causal explanations as a risk factor for depression: Theory and evidence. *Psychological Review, 91,* 347–374.

Pinker, S. (2009, January 11). My genome, my self. *New York Times Magazine,* pp. 24–46.

Sieff, E. M., Dawes, R. M., & Loewenstein, G. (1999). Anticipated versus actual reaction to HIV test results. *American Journal of Psychology, 112,* 297–311.

Skinner, B. F. (1948). "Superstition" in the pigeon. *Journal of Experimental Psychology, 38,* 168–172.

Slovic, P. (1987). The perception of risk. *Science, 236,* 280–285.

Staddon, J. E. R., & Simmelhag, V. L. (1971). The "superstition" experiment: A reexamination of its implications for the principles of adaptive behavior. *Psychological Review, 78,* 3–43.

Taylor, S. E. (1983). Adjustment to threatening events: A theory of cognitive adaptation. *American Psychologist, 38,* 1161–1173.

Tversky, A., & Edwards, W. (1966). Information versus reward in binary choice. *Journal of Experimental Psychology, 71,* 680–683.

Weiner, B. (1979). A theory of motivation for some classroom experiences. *Journal of Educational Psychology, 71,* 3–25.

# Appendix

## Basic Principles
## of Probability Theory

### A.1 The Concept of Probability

The bulk of this book deals with the evaluation of the likelihood, or probability, of consequences of choice. All such future consequences are viewed as uncertain. Moreover, there is empirical evidence that even those of us who believe in the uncertainty of the future underestimate it. Thus, an absolute essential of rational decision making is to deal constructively with this uncertainty. Irrationality is not constructive; at least, the conclusions that follow from it cannot be true of the world. Thus, the bottom line is that likelihoods and probabilities must be assessed rationally.

Uncertainty is commonly expressed in terms of probabilities, or odds. The odds of an event equal the probability of its occurrence divided by 1 minus the probability; for example, a probability of 2/3 equals odds of 2 to 1, that is, (2/3)/(1/3). A set of probabilities (or odds) is consistent if and only if it satisfies four broad algebraic rules. Otherwise, it is contradictory. These rules, which are quite simple, are formally termed the principles of probability, or of *probability theory*. This appendix will explain each of these principles. The method of presentation is first to discuss probabilities relevant to each principle in the context of equally likely outcomes (most commonly illustrated by coin tosses and dice rolls), then to present the principles both algebraically and verbally, and finally to discuss them in more general contexts.

Because we evaluate and discuss uncertainty in terms of probabilities, it follows that our view of uncertainty is rational if and only if the probabilities we assign to possible events satisfy the four rules. If the rules are satisfied, our view of uncertainty is termed *coherent*; otherwise, it is *incoherent* (read: "irrational").

Before proceeding, however, four caveats are in order. First, our discussion of probability will be limited to numerical (or vaguely numerical) judgments about future events. For the decision maker, events in the past either have occurred—and thus are not uncertain—or have not occurred, in which case they cannot have probabilities assigned to them. We speak loosely, of course, of the probability of past events. For example, we might speak of the probability that Lee Harvey Oswald was the assassin of John F. Kennedy (or the lone assassin), the probability that a defendant "actually" committed a crime, or even the probability that a hypothetical coin has rolled off a table and landed heads up. For the purposes of this book, however, such statements about the probability of past events can be interpreted as the probability that we would reach certain conclusions were we to learn the truth, which of course is a possible future event. Sometimes probabilities are interpreted as *"degree of belief"*—or as objective frequencies over a large number of repetitions. Nevertheless, all students (and developers) of probability theory agree that the four basic rules must be satisfied. (In fact, the abstract branch of mathematics dealing with probabilities defines them as numbers that follow these rules, and concrete interpretations and other meanings assigned to probabilities are not considered.)

This appendix also considers beliefs about probabilities that order them or categorize them. Such beliefs, as well, may or may not reflect coherent judgment because such beliefs can in fact either satisfy or violate the principles. For example, the belief that the world's best tennis player is more likely to lose the first set of a championship match and win the match than he is to lose the first set alone (a purely ordinal belief) contradicts the principles of probability theory—as does the belief that the probability of a disease given a symptom is necessarily equal to the probability of the symptom given the disease (a belief of equivalence with no specific number proposed).

Only sets of two or more probabilistic beliefs may be irrational (except for the trivial constraint that a probability less than 0 or greater than 1 is irrational). Probabilities cannot be evaluated for rationality in isolation. For example, it is not necessarily irrational to believe that the sun will not rise tomorrow with a probability of .9. It *would* be irrational, however, to hold that belief and the belief that you will go to work tomorrow with probability .8 and the belief that you will go to work only if the sun rises—all simultaneously. (One explanation for irrationality in assessing probabilities—and in decision making in general—is that people fluctuate between different states of mind when viewing different parts of a problem, and that conclusions reached in one state are not compared with those reached in another—the same concern that led economists to assume that preferences, or the utilities underlying them, are stable. Although technically it might not be correct to call someone whose values or expectations are fluctuating rapidly "irrational," it would not be sensible to call them rational or adaptive, either.)

## A.2 From Gods to Numbers

How did probability theory begin? It began by evaluating gambles (we recommend Leonard Mlodinow's *The Drunkard's Walk: How Randomness Rules Our Lives* [2008], for an engaging introduction to the history of probability theory).

In Robert Graves's *I, Claudius* (1943), Caligula and Claudius are playing dice prior to Caligula's assassination (and watching bloody games with just enough attention so that Caligula could order losers—and occasionally winners—to be put to death). The four dice they used (termed *astragali*) were made from ankle bones of dogs or sheep and had four faces, each with a different number: 1, 3, 4, and 6. The winning throw is a *Venus roll*, a roll in which four different numbers are face up. Claudius is winning—a possibly mortal situation for him given Caligula's outbursts of pathological anger. Fearful, Claudius hands Caligula a set of beautiful new astragali that are loaded to yield Venus rolls. When Caligula wins back his money, he is especially delighted because he interprets his success as a sign that the goddess Venus is favorably disposed toward him that day. In his euphoria, he fails to take the usual precautions departing from the games and is assassinated.

(Most of us today would regard Caligula as superstitious and silly. There is, however, the alternative interpretation. By giving Caligula loaded dice, Claudius deceived him into believing Venus was favorably disposed when in fact she wished him ill—as demonstrated by Caligula's earlier losses. Thus, Claudius's deception made him partially responsible for the assassination and his own ascension to the throne.)

How would we determine the probability of a Venus roll? Consider the order of the astragali reading from left to right (from any perspective) and assume for purposes of this example that any of the 4 numbers on one die is equally likely to occur. The "1" may be in any of the four positions, the "3" in any of the remaining three, the "4" in any of the remaining two, and the "6" in a position then determined. Hence, there are $4 \times 3 \times 2 \times 1 = 24$ possible ways of obtaining a Venus roll. The total number of possible rolls, however, is $4^4$ (or 256), because any of the four numbers can occur in the first position, in the second, and so on. Thus, we conclude that the probability of a Venus roll is 24/256, or approximately .094.

There is another way of reaching the same conclusion. Consider the four positions in sequence. Any number face up in the first position is compatible with a Venus roll. Given the number appearing in the first position, the number in the second can be any of the three remaining; the probability of that is 3/4. Given that the numbers in the first two positions are different, the number in the third position must be one of the two remaining; the probability of that is $2/4 = 1/2$. Finally, if the numbers in the first three positions are all different, the probability that the number in the last position is the remaining one is 1/4. "Chaining" these probabilities yields $1 \times (3/4) \times (2/4) \times (1/4) = 6/64 = 24/256$, or approximately .094. (Because not all outcomes are equally likely, the actual probability is lower, approximately .04.)

According to historian Florence N. David (1962), belief that the outcome of games was due to the influence of gods or goddesses, or of supernatural forces ("destiny"), was common in the ancient Egyptian, Greek, and Roman civilizations (and, in its implicit form, may still be common today among compulsive gamblers). Moreover, different gambling outcomes were often associated with different gods. In fact, these beliefs about gambling apparently were one reason for it being outlawed by the Roman Catholic Church in the Middle Ages. A monotheistic God did not "play at dice"—and gambling was a catalyst to polytheism.

Of course, not all ancient Greeks and Romans believed that gambling outcomes were influenced by the gods. In Book II of *De Devinatione*, Cicero wrote the following:

> Nothing is so unpredictable as a throw of the dice [modern translation], and yet every man who plays often will at some time or other make a Venus-cast; now and then indeed he will make it twice and even thrice in succession. Are we going to be so feeble-minded then as to aver that such a thing happened by the personal intervention of Venus rather than by pure luck?

Cicero believed "luck" determined the success of gambling with essentially random devices. He also apparently understood that there was a relationship between the luck (odds) on a particular throw or set of throws and long-term frequencies. But Cicero was later executed, illustrating that rationality does not guarantee success; it only increases its likelihood. In fact, as pointed out earlier, opting for rationality when others do not can lead to social ostracism.

The major modern development that was not foreseen by Cicero is that of determining the odds by counting. And counting was possible only after the development of arithmetic procedures that made complex computation possible; despite the Greeks' skill in geometry and logic, arithmetic was not developed in the Western world until the Renaissance. Such counting was first systematically proposed by Cardano (1501–1576). Here is how counting leads to the principles of probability theory:

Tossing a coin results in 1 of 2 possible outcomes: heads (H) or tails (T).

Tossing a coin twice results in 1 of 4 possible outcomes: HH (two heads), HT (a head followed by a tail), TH, or TT (see Figures A.1 and A.2).

Tossing a coin three times results in 1 of 8 possible outcomes: HHH, HHT, HTH, HTT, THH, THT, TTH, or TTT.

And so on.

*Outcome* is a technical term in probability theory. It refers to a specific result of an experiment such as tossing a coin a certain number of times. An *event* is a collection of outcomes. This concept is crucial to probability theory, and the term is used throughout this book—even when less stilted English would require another word. *Collection* in this definition does not necessarily mean more than one outcome; that is, an event may consist of a single outcome. Moreover, a collection may consist of all outcomes; that is, the event consisting of all outcomes is a well-defined one. It is symbolized *S*.

Tossing a coin twice results in one of a number of possible events. For example,

A. The event *two heads* consists of the single outcome HH. (It is equivalent to the event *no tails*.)

B. The event *exactly one head* consists of the outcomes HT and TH. (It is equivalent to the event *exactly one tail*.)

C. The event *at least one head* consists of the outcomes HH, HT, and TH. (It is equivalent to the events *at most one tail* and *not two tails*.)

And so on.

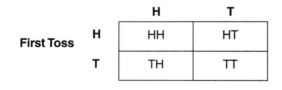

**Figure A.1**    Possible outcomes of two coin tosses

In fact, there are 15 (= $2^4 - 1$) events consisting of at least one outcome:

Events consisting of a single outcome,

HH

HT

TH

TT

Events consisting of pairs of outcomes,

HH, HT

HH, TH

HH, TT

HT, TH

HT, TT

TH, TT

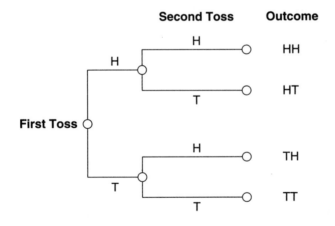

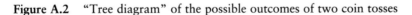

**Figure A.2**    "Tree diagram" of the possible outcomes of two coin tosses

Events consisting of triples of outcomes,

HH, HT, TH

HH, HT, TT

HH, TH, TT

HT, TH, TT

And the event consisting of all four outcomes,

HH, HT, TH, TT

A verbal description may be given to each event. (Try it.)

Note that as a result of tossing a coin twice, there are 4 possible outcomes and 15 possible events consisting of 1 or more outcomes. Actually, mathematicians define 16 possible events, because for the sake of completeness, they also consider the event consisting of no outcomes. It is termed the *null event* ("nothing happened"), and it is symbolized ∅. Is the null event nothing but the (null) result of an obsessive-compulsive frame of mind? No. The concept of the null event has had the same salutary effect on the development of probability theory that the concept of *zero* had on the development of our number system. The concept zero was not introduced into computation in Western culture until about 900 ACE. Prior to that, there was one Roman symbol for 10 (X), another for 20 (XX), and so on, with the result that it was much more difficult to add and subtract than it is using zeros—for example, X + XXX = XL, rather than 10 + 30 = 40, which is obtained in part by adding 0 to 0 to obtain 0.

Let's illustrate how probabilities are assigned to events by considering equally likely outcomes, and then generalize to other events. Consider two tosses of a fair coin. By fair, we mean that both of the following hold true:

1. Heads or tails are equally likely on each toss.

2. There is no relationship between the results of successive tosses.

Fairness resides in both the coin and the coin tosser. The first condition states that the coin has no bias and that the coin tosser cannot or does not control the outcome. The second condition states that the coin "has no memory," and once again that the coin tosser cannot or does not control it. (Many "subjectivist" statisticians allege that fairness resides in the beliefs of the observer that the coin and coin tosser satisfy these conditions.) Under these conditions, there are four equally likely outcomes: HH, HT, TH, and TT.

The probability of an event when outcomes are equally likely is equal to the number of outcomes in the event divided by the number of possible outcomes. The number of outcomes is 4 when a coin is tossed twice.

A. The event two heads consists of only the outcome HH; therefore, its probability is 1/4.

B. The event exactly one head consists of the outcomes HT and TH; therefore, its probability is (1 + 1)/4 = 1/2.

C. The event at least one head consists of the outcomes HH, HT, and TH; therefore, its probability is $(1 + 1 + 1)/4 = 3/4$.

And so on.

Following standard notation, events are symbolized by capital letters and their probability by $p$. For example, if $A$ is the event *all heads* or *all tails*, it consists of the outcomes HH and TT; hence, $p(A) = (1 + 1)/4 = 1/2$.

## A.3 The Principles of Probability Theory

It should be clear now that probabilities are numbers between 0 and 1. Moreover, $p(\varnothing) = 0$, because there are no outcomes in the null set. Thus, the following principles are true for probabilities assigned to events consisting of equally likely outcomes:

Principle I: $0 \leq p(A) \leq 1$

Principle IIa: $p(S) = 1$

Principle IIb: $p(\varnothing) = 0$

Events can also be combined. The event *A and B*, termed their *intersection* or *conjunction,* consists of all outcomes common to both. For example, the event *at least one head* consists of the outcomes HH, HT, and TH, while the event *at least one tail* consists of the outcomes HT, TH, and TT. Thus, the event *at least one head and at least one tail* consists of the outcomes HT and TH. (Note that this event is equivalent to the event *one head and one tail.*) Such an event is termed a *compound event,* and the probability of such an event is termed a *compound probability.* (Note that any one event may be considered to be a compound event; for starters, each event is equivalent to the intersection of itself and S.)

Another type of combination involves outcomes in either of two events. The event *A or B*, termed their *union* or *conjunction,* consists of all the outcomes in either. (Any overlapping outcomes are included; logically, *or* means "in either singly or in both.") For example, the event *at least one head* consists of the outcomes HH, HT, and TH, while the event *at least one tail* consists of the outcomes HT, TH, and TT. The event *at least one head or at least one tail* consists of HH, HT, TH, and TT; that is, it is S (because there must be at least one head or at least one tail in any "experiment" or toss).

In these examples, the two events of the intersection or union were partially overlapping. That need not be so—as was indicated, for example, by taking the intersection of an event with S, or its union with ∅. We may take the intersection or union of totally disjointed events—those that have no outcomes in common. Or one event may be a distinct part of another—all the outcomes comprising the first are in the second as well, or the events are identical. An event is a set of outcomes. Linking any two events by *and* or *or* defines a new set of outcomes, an event.

When two events have no outcome in common, they are mutually exclusive. For example, the event *two tails* and the event *at least one head* are mutually exclusive.

Mathematicians and statisticians make use of the null set to express the fact that two events are mutually exclusive—that is, they have no outcomes in common. Briefly, when two events A and B are mutually exclusive, the compound event consisting of their intersection is the null set (is devoid of outcomes). Thus, A and B are mutually exclusive whenever

$$(A \ and \ B) = \varnothing,$$

which by Principle II means that

$$p(A \ and \ B) = 0.$$

Again, consider tossing a fair coin twice. Let A be the event *two tails* and B be the event *exactly one head*. These events are mutually exclusive, the first consisting of the outcome TT and the second of the outcomes HT and TH. Moreover, the probability of A is 1/4 while that of B is 2/4 = 1/2. The probability of (A or B) is 3/4 because there are three outcomes in A or B, namely TT, HT, and TH. Thus, $p(A \ or \ B) = p(A) + p(B)$.

Whenever any two events A and B are mutually exclusive, the number of outcomes in (A or B) must equal the sum of the number of outcomes in each. If there are $n$ equally likely outcomes in S, $m$ in A and $m'$ in B, then if A and B are mutually exclusive,

$$p(A \ or \ B) = \frac{m + m'}{n} = \frac{m}{n} + \frac{m'}{n}$$
$$= p(A) + p(B).$$

This observation yields a third general principle of probability theory:

Principle III: If $p(A \text{ and } B) = \varnothing$ (equivalently, $p(A \text{ and } B) = 0$),

then $p(A \text{ or } B) = p(A) + p(B)$.

Does this principle work backward? That is, if $p(A \text{ or } B) = p(A) + p(B)$, does it necessarily follow that $(A \text{ and } B) = \varnothing$? This question may be answered by noting that if $A$ and $B$ have at least one outcome in common, $p(A \text{ or } B)$ is less than $p(A) + p(B)$.

The introduction of two more concepts completes this sketch of probability theory. The first is that of the *complement* of an event. Specifically, the complement of an event $A$ consists of all the outcomes in $S$ that are not in $A$. The complement of $A$ is often symbolized $-A$ or $\bar{A}$. For example, consider a coin tossed twice:

If $A$ is the event *two heads* (consisting of HH), then the complement of $A$ is the event consisting of HT, TH, and TT—the event *at least one tail*.

If $A$ is the event *exactly one head* (consisting of HT and TH), then the complement of $A$ is the event consisting of HH and TT—the event *all heads or all tails*.

If $A$ is the event *at least one head*, then $\bar{A}$ is the event *all tails*.

And so on.

Relationship I: If $\bar{A}$ is the complement of $A$, then $p(\bar{A}) + p(A) = 1$.

This relationship is established by noting that $A$ and $\bar{A}$ are mutually exclusive; hence, by Principle III, $p(A \text{ or } \bar{A}) = p(A) + p(\bar{A})$. But $(A \text{ or } \bar{A})$ is equal to $S$ because $\bar{A}$ by definition consists of all those outcomes in $S$ not in $A$. Therefore, $p(A) + p(\bar{A}) = p(S)$, which equals 1 by Principle IIa.

Note that Principle IIb, $p(\varnothing) = 0$, was not used in establishing Relationship I; it was established entirely from Principles IIa and III. In fact, Principle IIb itself can be shown to follow from Principles IIa and III via Relationship I. For since $\varnothing$ is the complement of $S$, $p(\varnothing) + p(S) = 1$, but since $p(S) = 1$ from Principle IIa, it follows that $p(\varnothing) = 0$. (This is a rigorous proof that the probability of nothing is nothing—zero.)

Finally, it should be noted that the implication in Relationship I cannot be reversed, unlike that in Principle III. It does not follow that if the sum of the probabilities of two events is 1, they are complements of each other. For example, the event *exactly one head* resulting from two coin tosses has probability 1/2 when outcomes are equally likely, as does the event *exactly one tail*. But the probability of *exactly one head or exactly one tail* does not equal

1 (1/2 + 1/2); they are not complementary events. In fact, they are identical, both consisting of the outcomes HT and TH.

The final concept is that of *conditional probability*. It can be easily defined by a formula, but that can wait. The essential idea is that the probability of an event *A* is assessed differently, conditional upon knowledge of whether another event has or has not occurred. For example, if the events *A* and *B* are mutually exclusive, then an outcome in *A* cannot be in *B*; thus, the probability of *A* given *B*'s occurrence is 0. At the other extreme, if all the outcomes in *B* are also in *A*, then the probability of *A* *given B* is 1.

The conditional probability of *A* *given B* is symbolized $p(A|B)$; it can be expressed verbally in a variety of ways:

1.  The probability of *A* *conditional upon* *B*'s occurrence

2.  The probability of *A* *conditional upon B*

3.  The probability of *A* *given B*

4.  The probability of *A* *if B* occurs

If outcomes are equally likely, the probability of *A* *given B* is equal to the number of outcomes in both events (their intersection) divided by the number of outcomes in *B*. In effect, having been "given" *B*, we know that the actual outcome must be selected from it, and the probability that an outcome from *A* occurs is therefore equal to the relative number of outcomes in *B* that are also in *A*. The event *B* now defines the number of possible outcomes; it has, in effect, replaced *S*.

Let $m'$ be the number of outcomes in *A and B* (their intersection), and let $m$ be the number of outcomes in *B*. Then, given equally likely outcomes,

$$p(A|B) = m'/m.$$

Now divide the numerator and denominator of the fraction $m'/m$ by $n$ to obtain

$$p(A|B) = \frac{m'/n}{m/n}.$$

But since $p(A \text{ and } B) = $ while $p(A) = m/n$, we conclude the following:

$$\text{Principle IV}: p(A|B) = \frac{p(A \text{ and } B)}{p(B)}$$

This principle constitutes the formal definition of conditional probability.

Now let's look at some examples of conditional probabilities resulting from tossing a fair coin twice. The probability of the event *two heads* given the event *at least one head* is 1/3. (HH is the only outcome in the event *two heads,* while the event *at least one head* consists of the outcomes HH, HT, and TH.) Occasionally, this probability is mistakenly believed to be 1/2 rather than 1/3; for example, some people think the probability of a two-child family having two daughters when at least one child is a daughter is 1/2.

In contrast, probability of the event *two heads* given the event the first toss is a head is 1/2. The common event is again HH, but here the event that is given has only the two outcomes, HH and HT. The probability that a two-child family consists of two daughters when *the first* is a daughter is 1/2, because boys (B) and girls (G) have (roughly) equal probabilities of being born. In contrast, there are three ways to have *at least one girl:* GG, GB, BG; in only one of these (GG) is the other child a girl. Thus, the probability of two girls given at least one girl is 1/3, not 1/2.

Principle IV may be reformulated by "multiplying through" by $p(B)$. That is,

$$p(A|B)p(B) = p(A \text{ and } B), \text{ or}$$

Principle IV': $p(A \text{ and } B) = p(A|B)p(B)$.

When expressed in the manner of Principle IV', the conditional probability definition constitutes a *chaining principle* for obtaining the probability of compound events. (Remember the Venus roll example.) For example, the probability that both coin tosses are heads (the event *both heads*) is equal to the probability that the first one is a head multiplied by the probability that the second one is a head given the first one is a head. The reader should verify that both these latter probabilities are 1/2, so that the desired probability of the compound event is 1/4. The probability of drawing two spades randomly without replacement from a deck of cards is equal to the probability that the first draw is a spade (13/52, because there are 52 cards in the deck, 13 of which are spades) multiplied by the probability that the second is a spade given the first is a spade (12/51, because there are 51 cards left of which 12 are spades). The desired probability of this compound event is $(13/52)(12/51) = 3/51$. We could also derive this probability by dividing the number of pairs of spades (78) by the number of pairs of cards (1,346), again obtaining 3/51.

Chaining may take place in either direction: $p(A \text{ and } B)$ equals both $p(A|B)p(B)$ and $p(B|A)p(A)$. Sometimes it is more convenient to chain in one direction than in the other—such as when there is a natural sequence from earlier to later in time.

Finally, *independence* between events can now be defined. The intuitive definition is that $A$ and $B$ are independent if $p(A|B) = p(A)$. Accepting this definition, we can multiply both sides by $p(B)$ to obtain the following:

Independence (definition): $p(A \text{ and } B) = p(A)p(B)$

(since $p(A|B)p(B) = p(A \text{ and } B)$ by Principle IV′).

Moreover, dividing by $p(A)$, we can infer that $p(B|A) = p(B)$; hence, independence is symmetrical. The definition that $p(A \text{ and } B) = p(A)p(B)$ is the one used by mathematicians, because the concept should also be valid if $p(A)$ or $p(B)$ equals 0, in which case division and multiplication would be inappropriate.

Probability theory is now applied in much broader contexts than just to gambling games. For example, the designs of dikes and dams are based on estimates of the probability that rivers will reach certain flood levels. Engineers clearly don't believe that all flood levels are equally likely; rather, they reference the frequencies with which certain water levels have occurred in the past. We also may speak of the probability that the Chicago Cubs will defeat the Chicago White Sox in the World Series, or the probability of an atomic holocaust prior to the year 3000. In such cases, there is no relative frequency to use, but instead an estimate based on knowledge of baseball, politics, technology—or perhaps on our level of pessimism. When there are neither equally likely outcomes nor frequencies on which to rely, probabilities are often related to "fair" betting odds. For example, if you believe that the probability is 1/3 that the Cubs defeat the White Sox, you should be barely willing to bet $2 on the White Sox against $1 on the Cubs; that is, you should be willing to accept all bets in which you must bet less than $2 to $1 and reject all those in which you must bet more than $2 to $1. That's an assessment of your personal probabilistic belief, and in fact a school of philosophers of probability known as *personalists* or *subjectivists* have argued that all probability is ultimately based on personal belief and willingness to bet. (Isn't, for example, the fundamental assertion that all elementary outcomes are "equally likely" in a probability analysis one of belief?)

Actually, there has been considerable debate throughout the centuries about whether probability statements refer to facts, individual beliefs about the world, or logical relationships between evidence and belief—or between different beliefs. It is not clear how important this debate is to probabilistic reasoning; however, it is clear that people with different understandings about the meaning of the term *probability* reach the same conclusions about particular probabilities. For example, consider an experiment in which one of two dice is drawn at random from a bag. One of them has four green and two red faces and the other has four red and two green faces. Without examining the die drawn, the experimenter rolls it. What is the probability of a red face showing as a result? All in the experiment agree it is 1/2. And all agree that the reason is that the probability of drawing each particular die is 1/2.

Some people argue that this latter conclusion follows because we have no reason to believe that we have drawn one particular die or the other; some argue that 1/2 reflects their belief that each die is equally likely; some argue that the concept of *randomness* logically entails a probability of 1/2 that we have drawn either; and still others argue that the equal probability of drawing either is based on a hypothesis about an objective fact whose validity could be assessed by repeated draws. It is even possible to argue that the "real" probability of drawing whichever is actually drawn is 1, because nothing ever really occurs at random in the world, but that in our ignorance of all the factors involved and their interaction we must opt for 1/2. All in the experiment concluded, however, that the probability of drawing either die is 1/2. Then, the probability that a red face shows is the sum of the probabilities that the predominantly red-faced die is drawn and that a red face shows, plus the probability that the predominantly green-faced die is drawn and that a red face shows (by Principle III). The first probability is $(1/2) \times (2/3)$, and the second is $(1/2) \times (1/3)$—both by Principle IV'. Hence, the probability of a red face is $2/6 + 1/6 = 1/2$. Agreed.

So what, in general, is a probability? First, probabilities refer to numbers assigned to well-defined events. A "well-defined event" is one that can be unambiguously interpreted as occurring or not occurring in the future. Second, probabilities must satisfy the four basic principles, reiterated here:

I.  $0 \leq p(A) \leq 1$

II.  $p(S) = 1$

III.  If the intersection $(A \text{ and } B) = \varnothing$, then $p(A \text{ or } B) = p(A) + p(B)$

IV.  $p(A|B) = p(A \text{ and } B)/p(B)$

Without demeaning the philosophers who attempt to find an additional meaning for *probability,* we can accept the structural, formal meaning of probability as numbers that satisfy these four principles. For the purposes of this book, we have added the additional condition that events shall be in the future.

Note that a single probability cannot violate the principles unless it falls outside the interval between 0 and 1. Thus, probabilities refer to sets of numbers describing relationships between sets of events. Of course, people may assert probabilities that violate the principles and insist that they are discussing "probabilities" in the usual sense of the term. But rational or coherent probabilities must satisfy the principles, and this is the only type of probability a mathematician or statistician would accept.

## A.4 Beliefs That Violate the Principles of Probability Theory

What is an example of a common *probabilistic* belief that violates these principles? Consider these sequences of events:

1. A star athlete becomes a drug addict, enters a treatment program, and wins a championship.

2. A star athlete becomes a drug addict and wins a championship.

When one or another such sequence of events is presented to people, many judge the first to be more probable than the second. But by the principles of probability, it cannot be. To understand why, break the sequences into their constituent events:

A. The athlete becomes an addict.

B. The athlete becomes a champion.

C. The athlete enters a treatment program.

(It is not necessary to label events in the order in which they occur in time.) Now the belief is that

$$p(A \text{ and } B \text{ and } C) > p(A \text{ and } B).$$

But that is not rational or coherent according to the principles, which we can demonstrate in two ways:

First demonstration: By the chaining principle (IV′) and because the intersection ($A$ and $B$) is just another event, it follows that
$p(A \text{ and } B \text{ and } C) = p(C|A \text{ and } B)p(A \text{ and } B)$.
But since $p(C|[A \text{ and } B]) \leq 1$ by Principle I,
$p(A \text{ and } B \text{ and } C) \leq p(A \text{ and } B)$.

This is a logical contradiction, proving that the original assertion is invalid.

Second demonstration: (*A and B*) = (*A and B and C*) joined with (*A and B and $\bar{C}$* ). But (*A and B and C*) and (*A and B and $\bar{C}$* ) are mutually exclusive. Therefore, by Principle III,

$$p(A \text{ } and \text{ } B) = p(A \text{ } and \text{ } B \text{ } and \text{ } C) + p(A \text{ } and \text{ } B \text{ } and \text{ } \bar{C}).$$

This means $p(A \text{ } and \text{ } B)$ must be greater than or equal to the first term—another contradiction. The point is that the athlete could have won the championship by some route other than entering a treatment program. The athlete could have quit drugs for other reasons, he or she could have been so extremely talented and lucky that it didn't matter, the championship could have been rigged, and so on.

The belief that the likelihood of an unlikely event, or combination of events, is enhanced by adding plausible events to it, is termed the *scenario effect;* such effects have been extensively investigated by Amos Tversky and Daniel Kahneman (1983). These added events can yield a "good story," even though they in fact restrict the number of possibilities that can lead to the original event, or combination. For example, when anthropologists reconstruct from a few bones the nature of a particular prehistoric culture, their reconstructions often seem more believable when they supply details about which they couldn't possibly have any knowledge, as pointed out by Paul Washburn (personal communication to Dawes). And we all know that telling people only known facts is not as persuasive as embellishing our story (for example, in courtroom summations). It is well documented by cognitive psychologists that the scenario effect results in irrational probability judgments (see Chapters 6 and 7).

Here are two probabilistic beliefs that are wrong, but not irrational. Their combination, however, is irrational.

**The gambler's fallacy:** The more often a coin falls heads (tails), the more likely it will be to fall tails (heads) on the next toss. Thus, HT is more likely than HH, HHT is more likely than HHH, and so on. (As noted earlier, such a belief would be correct only if the coin had a memory—or if the person tossing it could control it.)

This fallacy also occurs in contexts other than coin tossing. Consider the example in the letter to "Dear Abby" reprinted in Section 7.3: "My husband and I just had our eighth child. Another girl, and I am really one disappointed woman. . . . Abby, this one was supposed to have been a boy." The probability of bearing 8 consecutive daughters is (roughly) $1/2^8 = 1/256$, but the probability of bearing a daughter after 7 other daughters have been born is about 1/2. Like coins, sperm have no memories, especially not for past conceptions of which they know nothing. The principle is the same as that in the solution to the game of balla referred to in Section 2.6.

**Distribution of ignorance fallacy (distributing ignorance equally across verbally defined categories, rather than across concrete, equally likely outcomes):** Since a coin tossed twice can yield 0, 1, or 2 heads, this pseudo-principle states that each such result occurs with the probability 1/3.

Suppose that someone believes in both the gambler's fallacy and the distribution of ignorance. By the gambler's fallacy,

$$p(HT) \geq p(HH).$$

But by the distribution of ignorance fallacy,

$$p(HH) = 1/3.$$

Therefore, $p(HT) \geq 1/3$, and by a similar argument, $p(TH) \geq 1/3$. Hence, their sum is greater than or equal to 2/3, but their sum must simultaneously equal 1/3 by the distribution of ignorance fallacy (i.e., "a coin tossed twice can yield 0, 1, or 2 heads").

Such combinations of belief are irrational, yet people hold them. Choices based on such incoherent probabilistic assessments must themselves be incoherent—and may lead to personal and social harm. The inverse conclusion, that probabilities satisfying Principles I through IV cannot lead to a contradiction, is also true, but proving it lies beyond the scope of this book.

# A.5 The Bayes' Theorem

Let us suppose that we have two bookbags containing black and red poker chips. Bookbag A contains 70% red poker chips, while bookbag B contains 40% red poker chips. Someone rolls a die. If it comes up 1 or 2, he hands us bookbag B; otherwise, he hands us bookbag A. We are not allowed to observe the outcome of the roll of the die, but we are allowed to sample 10 poker chips from the bag presented. After each observation, we are required to replace the poker chip before drawing again. Our task is to make a probabilistic inference about which bag we are sampling from.

Suppose that we draw 6 black chips and 4 red ones. That would certainly be more "representative" of bag B than of bag A, but on the other hand, we know that as the result of the roll of the die, it is twice as likely that we have been handed bag A. How can we combine the evidence from our sample with our prior belief based on the roll of the die? And, more generally, how should we rationally update our beliefs about a hypothesis (e.g., that we are drawing from Bag B), given some relevant evidence?

One way is to use Bayes' theorem, a one-step derivation from the fourth principle of probability theory, commonly attributed to the Reverend Thomas Bayes. Apparently, the Reverend Bayes discovered the principle in his quest for a rational method to evaluate the manifest evidence for the existence of God (a Christian God, we suppose). But he was unconfident enough in his derivation that his discovery was communicated only to a friend who published it after Bayes's death in 1761. (We can recommend Dennis V. Lindley's fine introduction, *Understanding Uncertainty* [2006], to those who want to explore Bayesian analysis further.)

Let *d* stand for the data we have collected—6 blacks and 4 reds. Let *A* and *B* refer to the two bags. It is easy enough to determine the conditional probability of the data, given that we are sampling from either bag A or bag B. We can then infer the conditional probability that we are sampling from a particular one of the bags, given the data, if we know both the probability that we are sampling from that bag at the outset (which we do) and the probability of obtaining the data, which can be computed. Specifically,

$$p(A \text{ and } d) = p(d \text{ and } A).$$

From the fourth principle of probability, we can infer that

$$p(A|d)p(d) = p(d|A)p(A), \text{ or}$$

$$p(A|d) = \frac{p(d|A)p(A)}{p(d)}.$$

Actually, it is simpler to use the ratio rule presented in Section 5.10. To recapitulate in this context,

$$\frac{p(A|d)}{p(d|A)} = \frac{p(A)}{p(d)}.$$

Similarly,

$$\frac{p(B|d)}{p(d|B)} = \frac{p(B)}{p(d)}.$$

Dividing, we obtain

$$\frac{p(A|d)}{p(B|d)} = \frac{p(A)p(d|A)}{p(B)p(d|B)}.$$

As a result of division, we eliminated the troublesome term $p(d)$; our result, in the last equation, is the ratio of $p(A|d)$ divided by $p(B|d)$. Knowing this ratio and that the sum of the two probabilities must equal 1 (we are sampling from just one bag, so by Principle III, the probabilities sum to 1), we can easily compute both.

In the example, $p(A) = 2/3$, and the probability of obtaining the sample of 6 blacks and 4 reds in the particular order we drew them *given we are drawing from bag A* is $.3^6 \times .7^4$. Similarly, $p(B) = 1/3$, and the probability of getting the sample in that same order *given we are drawing from bag B* is $.6^6 \times .4^4$. Thus, $p(A|d)$ divided by $p(B|d) = .0001167/.0003981$, or .29. Hence, the probability we are drawing from bag A is .22, and from bag B is .78. Note that the evidence in this hypothetical experiment has strongly outweighed the *prior odds* of 2:1 that we were drawing chips from bag A.

In general, Bayesian analysis consists of specifying prior beliefs, by which we mean beliefs that exist prior to the time we sample. In the example, the roll of the die leads to such prior beliefs. Evidence sampled is then combined with prior beliefs according to Bayes' theorem, and they are updated by the rules of probability theory.

## A.6 The Post Hoc Analysis of Coincidence

Everyday life is full of coincidences. Robyn Dawes's older daughter was born on the same day of the year that his mother died, and his younger daughter was born on the same day of the year that his mother was born. What a remarkable coincidence! A totally naive analyst might conclude that the probability of that was $(1/365)^2$, or .0000075. But, of course, the coincidence could have been reversed, and it would be equally remarkable—so perhaps a more appropriate figure is .000015. And, of course, they both could have been born on the same day of the year their grandmother was, or both born on the same day of the year she died, so perhaps that figure should be doubled to yield .00003. Then again, the older daughter has visual artistic talent and the younger one writes short stories—and their birthdays could, of course, be the same as those of well-known persons in those respective fields. And then there are the birthdays of people we all know such as George Washington, Abraham Lincoln, Grover Cleveland, John F. Kennedy—not to mention Omar Khayam, Mahatma Gandhi, Bertrand Russell, and whoever it was that wrote Ecclesiastes. The point is that we could go on and on, although in retrospect a particular coincidence—such as common birthdays—may appear to be very improbable. However, it is also very probable that many coincidences will occur.

To understand this principle, consider the probability of death. We will make the simplifying assumption that it is equally probable each day. Then, given a life expectancy of 70 years (25,568 days), the probability of dying on a particular day is .00004, but the probability of dying on *some particular* day is 1.00. Or consider another example. Let us select, totally at random, a number between 1 and 10,000; the probability that any particular number is chosen is .0001, yet the probability that some number is chosen is, again, 1.00. Interestingly, some philosophers in the 18th century, when probability theory was being developed, equated a probability of .9999 with a "moral certainty." In the death example, that would imply that it is morally certain that we will live through every next day. (Therefore, don't buy insurance? Or at least, don't buy it on any particular day?)

These first two paragraphs of this section are meant to illustrate an important principle: Although the probability that a particular event will occur may be close to 0, the probability that nothing at all will happen is exactly 0.

How do we decide, therefore, whether a coincidence is really evidence of ESP? Or whether the finding in a particular study of helping behavior on a subway, that tall people are more helpful than short people, indicates that there is a correlation between height and altruism? Or whether the fact that between 1900 and 1968 inclusive, the taller candidate always won the presidency indicates that American voters prefer taller men?

The answer to such questions is not easy, but a simplified example might help. Consider, again, drawing a number at random from the numbers 1 through 10,000. If a friend who claims to have ESP says in advance that you will sample the number 973 and you do, you are impressed. If, on the other hand, he or she asks you to draw a number and then explains its extrasensory significance after you have announced it is 973, you are not the least bit impressed. Now, it's the same number. Your awe or lack of it, however, is determined by the procedures leading to the claim that 973 has some special significance—specifically, the decision-making procedures employed by your friend, and consequently by you. By announcing the number in advance, he or she would have led you to consider only the number 973 as a "success." You can specify that decision prior to drawing the number. When the significance is explained to you after the number is drawn, however, you are sufficiently leery of your friend to realize that there are a great many such numbers to which he or she could ascribe some "significance." This principle is illustrated in Figure A.3. The figure presents 16 patterns of heads and tails that can result from six tosses of a coin to which some significance could be ascribed post hoc (all heads, all tails, alternation, alternation by pairs, mirror images, etc.). Once the coin has been tossed six times, however, the probability of one of these uniquely interesting patterns occurring is not 1/64, but rather 16/64.

Do people make such post hoc judgments? And do people believe such patterns are *significant,* not only in the everyday sense of that word but in the technical, statistical sense as well? Consider the remarks of an astrologer encountered by Dawes:

> Isn't it remarkable? Among the five of us here there are three Leos and two Cancers, and President Jerry Ford is a Cancer, which makes three Leos and three Cancers. I bet the probability of that is almost zero. Is that the sort of thing you people could figure out?

One method of inflating the apparent significance of such events is the *optional ending point* maneuver described in detail by statistician (and professional magician) Persi Diaconis (1978). This technique, used by many psychics, involves keeping the naive observer in the dark about exactly what is to be accomplished until it is done. For example, the psychic B. D., whom Diaconis analyzed in some detail, would ask a volunteer to name two cards and then ask two other volunteers to pick small numbers "at random." He would then place two shuffled decks of cards on a table and start turning over the cards in each deck one by one until he reached the larger of the two numbers selected. Of course, if the two cards happened to appear before he turned over the larger of the two numbers, it was a "successful demonstration." If both cards appeared simultaneously, it was clearly a success. If one of the cards named appeared with the larger number, the demonstration was considered a success, also. If nothing "unusual" happened, then the cards of one deck were turned over one by one until the smaller of the two numbers selected was reached. By that time, all sorts of outcomes could have occurred. And so on, and so on. The *optional stopping trick* is not to tell people in advance how you will manifest your psychic powers. The probability of a coincidence then becomes remarkably large. It helps also to proclaim, as the psychic Uri Geller does, that your powers come and go for reasons that are inexplicable to you, or that interference is created by skeptical test procedures. Then, *not* finding some striking coincidence in a number of attempts— or even in half of your attempts—is readily understood by the observers.

Would "scientists" engage in such nonsense? Unfortunately, the answer is "yes." (Some analysts have even speculated that scientists, with their capacity to entertain as yet unproven hypotheses, may even be especially susceptible to belief in ESP or quasi-sensory communication.) A recent president of

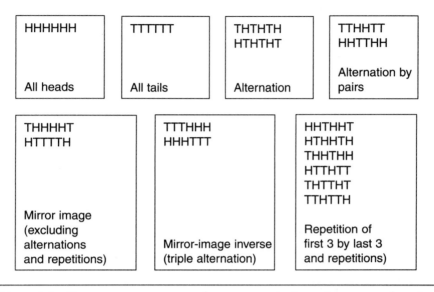

**Figure A.3**  Sixteen apparent patterns that can occur in six random tosses of a coin

the American Psychological Association gave as his presidential address a talk on "torque and schizophrenic viability." In it, he presented some absolutely striking data. Of 52 children who had seen him 10 years earlier who drew circles clockwise, 11 were later diagnosed as schizophrenic; of the 54 who drew circles counterclockwise, only 1 had been diagnosed schizophrenic. This relationship reached the ".01 level of statistical significance." He related his finding to the fact that "the world turns in a counterclockwise direction with respect to the north–south axis" and that "with some exceptions, this 'left-turning' is characteristic of living cells."

Certainly, a finding of this magnitude—particularly when it is related to fundamental properties of the earth and of the very unit of life—should have set the psychological world on its ear. At the least, it might have contributed to our understanding of schizophrenia, which is one of the two most prevalent mental health problems in the United States (along with depression). The average citations by other scientists to that article hovered around three per year in the subsequent 8 years, until it vanished from the charts. Why so few citations? Perhaps the researcher will be neglected for 50 years, only to be rediscovered as the founder of a modern theory of schizophrenia. A more likely explanation is found in part of his talk: "Subjects for this study were 155 children first seen for psychological evaluation at my private psychological clinic." Children seen for such evaluations are given many tests, each of which can be evaluated on a multiplicity of variables. The researcher reported his findings on only one of these tests in his presidential address. Our educated guess is that it was 1 out of approximately 200 that he could have easily related to later diagnoses of schizophrenia. (It is important to what follows to note that this guess is based on the authors' knowledge of clinical practice, not on the plausibility that he looked at many tests. But imagine a scenario in which a child enters a psychologist's office, is asked to draw a circle, and is then told to go away.)

How does one evaluate whether one of these very unusual findings might be important? The best answer, of course, is to determine whether it can be repeated. Attempts to replicate such "psychic power" findings have had a dismal history. Absent the possibility of prediction, control, and replication, the best approach is to precisely specify the hypothesis of interest in advance, to specify the conceptual sample space of possible relevant events, and then to systematically collect data—even anecdotes—to describe the *entire space* of possible outcomes. Persi Diaconis and Fred Mosteller (1989) have outlined such a strategy and illustrate it with an application to the common experience of encountering coincidental "clusters" of newly learned words in everyday life.

If we look hard enough, we're bound to find something. After all, the probability that exactly nothing will happen is indeed exactly zero. And, as Diaconis and Mosteller (1989) note, "When enormous numbers of events and people and their interactions cumulate over time, almost any outrageous event is bound to occur" (p. 853). Both classical and Bayesian analyses of statistical significance and informativeness are addressed to *questions asked beforehand*. In evaluating research findings in order to reach rational decisions, it is crucial to determine whether they were hypothesized in advance or simply picked out post hoc—from the imagination of the person purporting to have discovered them.

# References

David, F. N. (1962). *Games, gods, and gambling: The origins and history of probability and statistical ideas from the earliest times to the Newtonian era.* New York: Hafner.

Diaconis, P. (1978). Statistical problems in ESP research. *Science, 201,* 131–136.

Diaconis, P., & Mosteller, F. (1989). Methods for studying coincidences. *Journal of the American Statistical Association, 84,* 853–861.

Graves, R. (1943). *I, Claudius.* New York: Penguin.

Lindley, D. V. (2006). *Understanding uncertainty.* New York: Wiley-Interscience.

Mlodinow, L. (2008). *The drunkard's walk: How randomness rules our lives.* New York: Pantheon.

Tversky, A., & Kahneman, D. (1983). Extensional versus intuitive reasoning: The conjunction fallacy in probability judgment. *Psychological Bulletin, 90,* 293–315.

# Index

# About the Authors

**Reid Hastie** completed a conventional course of study at the University of California at San Diego and Yale University, finishing with doctoral research studying human memory for lists of words and geometric shapes. But, after starting his first academic job at Harvard University, he vigorously worked to get "off campus," studying medical and legal decision making in hospitals and courtrooms. His interest in applications of cognitive psychology methods and theories to understand judgment and decision-making processes and achievements in important outside-the-laboratory and off-campus settings has been a lifelong habit that includes studies of medical decisions, legal decisions, meteorological forecasting, and now many consumer, business, and finance decisions.

Somewhere along the way, Hastie became interested in small-group and team decision making and problem solving and has moved up from the individual cognitive level of analysis to study social, interpersonal phenomena in decision-making situations. Hastie is probably best known for his research on legal decision making (*Social Psychology in Court* [with Michael Saks]; *Inside the Jury* [with Steven Penrod and Nancy Pennington]; and *Inside the Juror* [edited]) and on social memory and judgment processes (*Person Memory: The Cognitive Basis of Social Perception* [edited]). He has served on review panels for the National Science Foundation and the Office of Naval Research, and on the National Institute of Mental Health, the National Academy of Sciences, and the National Research Center, and on 15 professional journal editorial boards.

Hastie is extremely proud of his 30-year record of teaching and advising at the college and graduate level on many topics in judgment and decision making. In a sense, *Rational Choice in an Uncertain World* (originally authored solely by Robyn M. Dawes) is the culmination of his years of communicating fundamental principles and observations about rational and human decision-making behavior. He is currently on the faculty of the University of Chicago Booth School of Business.

**Robyn M. Dawes** (BA in philosophy, Harvard, 1958), entered clinical psychology at University of Michigan. Two years later, he entered mathematical psychology, with content interests in behavioral decision making, social interaction, and attitude measurement (PhD, 1963), and graduate training in mathematics. For 5 years he served as a researcher psychologist at the local VA hospital and a member of the University Psychology Department, moving to Oregon in 1967, where he became a professor in 1971 and served 6 years as a department head (acting 1972–1973, 1979–1980; regular, 1981–1985). He also worked part-time at the Oregon Research Institute, where he was a vice president in 1973–1974 and fired for insubordination. He moved to Carnegie Mellon University (CMU) in the fall of 1985 as a professor of psychology in the department of Social and Decision Sciences and served as that department's head for a 5-year term. He also served as acting department head for a 1-year term in 1996. He is now the Charles J. Queenan, Jr., University Professor.

Dawes is the author of more than 150 articles and 6 books (including *House of Cards: Psychology and Psychotherapy Built on Myth* [1994]; *Everyday Irrationality: How Pseudo-Scientists, Lunatics, and the Rest of Us Systematically Fail to Think Rationally* [2001]; and *Judging Merit* [2008]). He was author of the first edition of *Rational Choice in an Uncertain World* (1988), for which he won the William James Award, Division of General Psychology of the American Psychological Association. Dawes has served as president of the Oregon Psychological Association (1983–1984), as president of the Society for Judgment and Decision Making Research (JDM) (1988–1989), as a member of the APA's national Ethics Committee (1985–1988), and on executive boards of The Society for the Advancement of Socio-Economics (SASE) and The American Association of Applied and Preventive Psychology (AAAPP). In addition, he has served on the National Research Council's AIDS Research and the Behavioral, Social, and Statistical Sciences Committee and has contributed to its reports—*AIDS, Sexual Behavior, and Intravenous Drug Use* (1989) and *AIDS: The Second Decade* (1990).

He has also led a life that might politely be described as "interesting."

# Supporting researchers for more than 40 years

**Research methods have always been at the core of SAGE's publishing program.** Founder Sara Miller McCune published SAGE's first methods book, *Public Policy Evaluation*, in 1970. Soon after, she launched the *Quantitative Applications in the Social Sciences* series—affectionately known as the "little green books."

Always at the forefront of developing and supporting new approaches in methods, SAGE published early groundbreaking texts and journals in the fields of qualitative methods and evaluation.

Today, more than 40 years and two million little green books later, SAGE continues to push the boundaries with a growing list of more than 1,200 research methods books, journals, and reference works across the social, behavioral, and health sciences. Its imprints—Pine Forge Press, home of innovative textbooks in sociology, and Corwin, publisher of PreK–12 resources for teachers and administrators—broaden SAGE's range of offerings in methods. SAGE further extended its impact in 2008 when it acquired CQ Press and its best-selling and highly respected political science research methods list.

From qualitative, quantitative, and mixed methods to evaluation, SAGE is the essential resource for academics and practitioners looking for the latest methods by leading scholars.

For more information, visit **www.sagepub.com**.

# NURSING MALPRACTICE

## Liability and Risk Management

CHARLES C. SHARPE

**AUBURN HOUSE**
Westport, Connecticut • London

**Library of Congress Cataloging-in-Publication Data**

Sharpe, Charles C., 1935–
　　Nursing malpractice : liability and risk management / Charles C.
　Sharpe.
　　　　p.　　cm.
　　Includes bibliographical references and index.
　　ISBN 0–86569–280–7 (alk. paper). —ISBN 0–86569–286–6 (pbk. :
　alk. paper)
　　　1. Nurses—Malpractice—United States.　2. Nursing—Law and
　legislation—United States.　3. Nursing errors.　4. Risk management.
　I. Title.
　　[DNLM: 1. Malpractice nurses' instruction.　2. Liability, Legal
　nurses' instruction.　3. Risk Management nurses' instruction.
　W44.1 S532n 1999]
　RT85.6.S53　1999
　344.73'0414—dc21
　DNLM/DLC
　for Library of Congress　　　　98–31027

British Library Cataloguing in Publication Data is available.

Library of Congress Catalog Card Number: 98–31027

ISBN: 0–86569–280–7
　　　0–86569–286–6 (pbk.)

First published in 1999

Auburn House, 88 Post Road West, Westport, CT 06881
An imprint of Greenwood Publishing Group, Inc.
www.greenwood.com

Printed in the United States of America

∞™

The paper used in this book complies with the
Permanent Paper Standard issued by the National
Information Standards Organization (Z39.48–1984).

10 9 8 7 6 5 4 3 2 1

**Copyright Acknowledgment**

The author and publisher gratefully acknowledge permission for use of the following
material:

Excerpts from "State-by-State Survey of Legal Provisions" in Diann Johnson and Sidney M.
Wolfe, *Medical Records: Getting Yours* (Public Citizen's Health Research Group, 1995),
p. 39. Reprinted by permission of Public Citizen's Health Research Group.

# Contents

# Tables

# Preface

As the practice of nursing continues to evolve, expanding clinical roles and applications of new technology have brought additional responsibilities and, concomitantly, increased risks of legal liability for the profession. This book was written to provide the nursing student, the professional nurse at any level of clinical practice—and collaborating health care providers—with an introduction to basic legal concepts and principles of malpractice, liability, and risk management. I believe that their more extensive incorporation into nursing education curriculums and application in clinical practice will enhance the professional growth, accountability, and recognition of the nursing profession. This is not a textbook on law, and I disclaim any intent to provide legal advice. That is the sole prerogative of an attorney.

In our litigious society, an increasing number of nurses are being named in malpractice lawsuits by patients turned plaintiffs. It is my hope that the knowledge and understanding of malpractice liability and risk management strategies will help to dispel many of the unwarranted fears and uncertainties prevalent in the nursing profession and mitigate the incidence and repercussions of malpractice lawsuits. For their own protection, and certainly for that of their patients, all nurses must be aware of their legal rights and responsibilities. Promoting such an awareness and its application in professional practice is the primary purpose of this book.

# Abbreviations

| | |
|---|---|
| ADR | Alternative dispute resolution |
| AMA | Against medical advice |
| ANA | American Nurses Association |
| APN | Advanced practice nurse |
| CE | Consulting expert |
| CNS | Clinical nurse specialist |
| DNR | Do not resuscitate |
| HMOs | Health maintenance organizations |
| JCAHO | Joint Commission on Accreditation of Healthcare Organizations |
| NCSBN | National Council of State Boards of Nursing |
| NLN | National League for Nursing |
| NP | Nurse practitioner |
| NPDB | National Practitioner Data Bank |
| PSDA | Patient Self-Determination Act |
| TE | Testifying expert |
| UAP | Unlicensed assistive personnel |

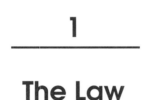

# The Law

## DEFINITION OF LAW

The English word "law" derives from the Anglo-Saxon word "lagu"; this in turn comes from the Old Norse "lag", which means layer or stratum. Law is "That which is laid down, ordained, or established; a body of rules of action or conduct prescribed by controlling authority and having a binding legal force" (Black 1990, 884). It is the body of rules, regulations, or principles that have been prescribed by authority or established by custom; and which a society, nation, state, or community recognizes and enforces as legally binding on each of its members; and which must be obeyed and followed by all citizens subject to sanctions. These rules of conduct are embodied in the sources of our law in the United States.

For the professional nurse, laws provide a basis for nursing intervention in the provision of care to patients; they act to distinguish the roles and responsibilities of the nurse from those of other health care providers; and they define the boundaries of dependent or autonomous practice in various roles and clinical settings.

## SOURCES OF LAW

There are four sources of law in the United States.

1. Constitutional law, which defines the structure and power of the federal government and the rights of all citizens under it.
2. Statutory law, which evolves from statutes enacted by federal, state, or local legislative bodies.
3. Administrative law, which deals with the enactment, implementation, and enforcement of laws, rules, and regulations by departments, bureaus, and other agencies established and maintained by a federal or state government entity.
4. Common law, which has largely evolved from case decisions made by federal and state courts.

### Common Law

Common law, also called case law, is that body of law that has derived from custom or from the prior decisions of courts (precedents) rather than from legislation. Where no written statute exists, a court of proper jurisdiction is charged with resolving legal disputes in cases, and gradually such judicial decisions have formed our common law. It is the usual source of law in malpractice issues.

#### Stare Decisis

The concept of precedent forms the basis of the legal doctrine of *stare decisis*, which translates from Latin as "to stand on that which has been decided." This practice of permitting lower courts in a given jurisdiction to decide new cases with reference to prior higher court decisions in cases with the same or very similar legal issues is a cornerstone of the American judicial system. Judges are, as a general rule, required to follow precedents established in prior cases, but are not absolutely bound by them. They do, albeit reluctantly, at times depart from them as the unique circumstances and issues of a case before them may dictate. In complying with the doctrine of *stare decisis*, however, judges provide consistency, stability, and continuity in the law. In establishing new precedents, the courts replenish the law with dynamic innovation in response to an inconstant, ever evolving, society.

### THE TWO PRINCIPAL SUBDIVISIONS OF LAW

In violation of order and logic, we must discuss the two principal subdivisions of law prior to a discussion of the two principal divisions. This, because the subdivisions of (1) substantive law and (2) procedural law can co-mingle with each of the two principal divisions, (1) criminal and (2) tort law—as the reader will see.

## Substantive Law

Substantive law is that area of law that defines and regulates the rights of individuals with respect to one another and those specific wrongs, harms, duties, or obligations that can provide one person cause for an action in law against another.

## Procedural Law

Procedural law prescribes the rules of conduct and the measures to be implemented in enforcing those rights and duties and in seeking redress. It defines the course of action that the parties in a lawsuit are required to follow at all stages of litigation. Procedural law directs and controls the legal process.

In a malpractice lawsuit both substantive and procedural law will apply. The elements of malpractice will be prescribed by substantive law. Procedural law will define such factors as the sequence of steps in the litigation process, the statute of limitations, and the matters of evidence.

## THE TWO PRINCIPAL DIVISIONS OF LAW

The body of all United States law is composed of two principal divisions: (1) criminal law and (2) civil law. The subcategories of substantive and procedural law are incorporated into each of these two primary categories.

## Criminal Law

A crime is an intentional wrong committed against the state—against society as a whole—as well as against individual victims. Criminal statutes define various crimes and prescribe the punishments to be imposed by the state on persons convicted of such crimes. In a criminal case, an official representing the state will prosecute and will endeavor to effect the penalty prescribed by criminal law. For such crimes as first degree murder, a defendant must be found *guilty* on the basis of proof *beyond a reasonable doubt*.

Criminal charges are rarely filed against health care providers. However, in March 1997, five nurses in New Jersey were indicted on charges of endangering the welfare of a patient who bled to death. In April 1997, three nurses in Colorado were indicted of criminally negligent homicide in the death of newborn. In January 1998, an emergency room physician in Elem Indian Colony, California, was awaiting trial for a charge of second degree murder in the death of an eleven-month-old boy. These cases have raised new concerns among physicians and nurses who now must be concerned with the possibility of criminal prosecution in addition to civil litigation when their care is deemed to have fallen to the level of criminal negligence.

### Civil Law

Civil law addresses the duties that exist between individual citizens or between citizens and the state. This excludes the duty not to commit a crime. Tort law, which addresses the infringement by one individual on the legally recognized rights of another, is a principal area of civil law. Malpractice is litigated in the area of tort law. Tort law and criminal law can converge in some instances. In such cases there can be an action by the state and also a separate civil action by an individual. In a civil case, a plaintiff must meet the burden of proof by a *preponderance of evidence*. That is, the evidence presented by the plaintiff must be more convincing to the trier than that presented by the defendant. A defendant in a civil action is found *liable*, rather than guilty.

## THE LAW OF TORTS

The law of torts addresses personal, private transgressions, as well as fault and blame. Every person is responsible, or has a duty, to conduct himself or herself in an expected manner or according to defined standards; and, by failing to do so, may not cause another person to suffer. Should a person fail in that duty, he or she could be liable under tort law.

Most tort law is founded in common law—court-decided law (*stare decisis*). The substantive law of torts is concerned with those actions or omissions that constitute a breach of an established legal duty owed by one person to another and the harm to another person or his or her property caused by such breach.

### Definition of Tort

A tort is a civil wrong that is committed by any entity against a person and that results in injury to that person, property, economic status, emotional well-being, or personal relationships. "Civil" in this case pertains to a citizen in his or her ordinary capacity, life, and affairs. It is a "private" offense, as distinguished from a crime that is a public offense.

The injured party (the plaintiff) may sue the *tortfeasor* (the defendant) for some form of compensation and pursues his or her lawsuit in a civil court. The redress sought in the civil lawsuit is usually monetary compensation in the form of "damages" awarded to the victim. The primary purpose of tort law is to compensate individuals for losses suffered from the tortious actions of others.

## TYPES OF TORT

There are two types of tort: (1) unintentional and (2) intentional.

### Unintentional Tort

An unintentional tort is an unintended, careless, or accidental but wrongful act or failure to act that causes injury or harm to another person. This substantive area of tort law is known as negligence law. Negligence is defined as a failure to use that degree of care that any reasonable and prudent person would use under the same or similar circumstances. Its focus is on injury or harm that may result from carelessness on the part of another or by accident. An unintentional tort may arise from an act of commission or from one of omission. In either event the harm derives from some failure in caution or due care.

Malpractice is a distinct form of negligence—that which is committed by a professional while acting, and only while acting, in his or her capacity as a professional. There are four common elements usually found in unintentional torts of negligence:

1. a legal duty owed by one individual to another;
2. an act or a failure to act that breaches that duty;
3. an injury or harm to another; and
4. the injury or harm was the direct result of the act or omission.

To recover damages, the plaintiff has the burden of proving *each* of these four elements by a preponderance of evidence. Malpractice and each of these elements will be discussed in detail in chapter 2.

### Intentional Tort

By definition intentional tort is an intentional, deliberate, willful, wrongful action that directly invades or violates the rights or property of another person. It is the purposeful commission of some act that is prohibited by law or the purposeful failure to act in conformance with the law or with acceptable standards of practice. Relatively few malpractice lawsuits brought against nurses derive from intentional torts. "The ethical concept of non-maleficence—the obligation to 'do no harm' to a patient is the underlying principle involved in the legal issue of intentional torts. If the principle of nonmaleficence were never violated, then no harm would ever come to patients, and there would be no grounds for lawsuits based on intentional torts" (Aiken and Catalano 1994, 136).

## INTENTIONAL TORTS

In tort law, intent is the conscious decision to commit an act and intend the consequences. This is demonstrated by any statement of intent or by circumstantial evidence. The requirement of intent does not necessarily mean that the actor desired to do harm; it means that he or she intended to commit, or omit, an action and, by implication, also intended the consequences, whether or not they caused harm or injury. It is a general assumption in law that an individual intends the normal or expected consequences of his or her purposeful actions or behavior.

The intentional tort differs from negligence in that the action complained of must have been intended—the action was done voluntarily. Negligence can arise without intent. There may not be the breach of duty that is relevant only in negligence. In an intentional tort it is not required to prove the four elements of malpractice. Injuries are not at issue. The plaintiff is not required to show that actual injuries were sustained. The harm suffered lies in the invasion of the plaintiff's rights rather than any specific injuries as required in negligence.

A wrongful action that does not result in harm or injury cannot be grounds for a suit at law. If an alleged act of malpractice results in no harm or injury to a patient, the practitioner will not be culpable. However, in those instances where there is patent evidence of intrusion on a plaintiff's legal rights, the law can presume a degree of injury sufficient to sustain a lawsuit and the awarding of damages. The amount of damages—the amount of monetary compensation—which might be awarded to the plaintiff will be derived from the jury's subjective judgment of the extent of encroachment on the plaintiff's rights. Punitive (exemplary) damages can also be awarded in intentional torts. Such damages are rare in malpractice cases.

### Elements of Intentional Tort

All intentional torts have three common elements:

1. an action that is offensive to another; the act constitutes an infringement on the rights of another; the motive may not necessarily be hostile; such an infringe-

ment was a consequence that should have reasonably been foreseen by the defendant;

2. the intent to commit such an act; the action or omission involved must be voluntary, deliberate—the individual carrying out the act must intend the consequences or present the appearance of such an intent; and

3. the consequences must be the direct result of the intended action or omission—there must be what the law defines as "causation".

## INTENTIONAL TORTS AGAINST PERSONS

There are several intentional torts against persons that nurses might be charged with. These include assault, battery, intentional infliction of emotional distress, false imprisonment, defamation, and invasion of privacy.

### Assault

Assault is a wrongful, intentional, statement or action performed by one person that causes another person immediate and actual fear, or reasonable apprehension, of being touched against his or her will in an injurious or offensive manner. The action can be an attempt or a threat to inflict injury or harm. It can be *any* action that generates apprehension or fear in another. Words and/or gestures could be sufficient depending on the circumstances. No actual physical injury or contact need occur.

Assault is any credible, reasonably believable threat. It is *threatened battery*. If there is any actual contact or touching, battery has been committed. An essential element in assault is the apprehension of being touched, and that is the only thing needed to prove a claim for assault. There must be an awareness, an anticipation, a knowledge, and a fear of immediate physical harm on the part of the victim. An unconscious or comatose patient could not be a victim of assault.

### Battery

Battery is the intentional physical contact with another person in an injurious or offensive manner without that person's explicit or implied consent. It is any act of physical contact that is unapproved and unwarranted. It is the actual performance of an act of contact or personal physical touching that is only threatened in assault. The victim need not have any fear of immediate harm for the act to be considered battery.

Battery is the most common allegation involving nurses and intentional torts. There are several aspects of battery that the nurse must be aware of.

- First, if the requisite elements of battery are otherwise present, a single touch no matter how brief or how light constitutes battery.

- Second, no actual injury need occur. The patient does not have to suffer physical harm or experience pain of any kind.

- Third, there need be no fear, apprehension, or awareness of immediate harm on the part of the patient. An unconscious person can be the victim of battery.

- Fourth, the unpermitted touching of a individual's personal effects or of any such objects on that person or in his or her hand constitutes battery. Under the law, any personal item that is connected to an individual in any way is treated as an extension of that individual.

- Fifth, the contact required can be direct or indirect. The victim does not have to be touched personally. If a patient is struck, even inadvertently, by an object in the hands of a nurse, or by one that is set in motion by any action of a nurse, while in the act of a battery, that nurse may be liable.

Treatment without consent is the most frequently alleged act of battery involving nurses. If any health care provider conducts physical examinations, performs diagnostic procedures, or initiates treatments without first obtaining the consent of the patient (when this is necessary, appropriate, and possible) the health care provider can be liable for charges of battery.

For a plaintiff to prove the charge, he or she must provide evidence that he or she did not give consent for the treatment or procedure carried out by the defendant or that the defendant's conduct went beyond the limits defined by the consent that the plaintiff had given. Or it must be shown that he or she had withdrawn consent prior to the treatment or procedure that was then carried out with disregard of that withdrawal.

Often an allegation of assault and battery will be presented rather than one of negligence. When such a charge constitutes the basis of a lawsuit, negligence need not be proven. The very nature of—the action of—assault and battery provides the basis for a claim. As noted previously, the plaintiff is primarily charged with proving a lack of consent. Expert witnesses are not required in such proceedings. State criminal laws and tort laws provide for legal action in cases of assault and battery.

### Intentional Infliction of Emotional Distress

This intentional tort is any extreme and outrageous conduct that is intended to cause, or effectively causes, another person to suffer *inordinate* mental distress and anxiety. It is a willful infliction of an emotional assault on another person's peace of mind. The conduct of the perpetrator must be such that it exceeds the acceptable bounds of civilized behavior and human decency. It is an offense to the conscience.

Because it is often difficult to prove emotional distress, some jurisdictions may require evidence of a presenting physical illness as corroboration and/or that the distress be manifested for a significant period of time and require psychiatric or psychological intervention and treatment.

As offensive as they may be, epithets, invective, insults, humiliation, ridicule, and derision may not be enough to prove this tort in many jurisdictions. However, such intemperate displays could lead to charges of harassment. Under some state statutes, family members who witness such reprehensible behavior can also file suit and attempt to recover damages.

There are three conditions required to prove this tort: (1) the offensive conduct was egregious, outrageous, abhorrent, and beyond all decency; (2) the calculated intent of the act was to inflict inordinate mental distress; (3) the wanton behavior caused extreme, manifest, emotional distress to the victim.

## False Imprisonment

False imprisonment is the intentional, unlawful detention of a person against his or her will where there is no valid justification or legal sanction for such confinement. The law of torts protects a person from such unlawful constraints on his or her liberty. The tort itself involves some form of restraint or confinement either by some physical or other means or by a threat of such. This may include a threatened use of force and also the apparent intent to carry out the action. (Kidnapping is a crime of abduction, unlawful imprisonment, and extortion involving the use of force and violence.)

Actual physical effort or action, including force, need not be involved. Any actions or speech that create a reasonable fear in the mind of a person that force might be implemented are sufficient to create false imprisonment. Words can restrain as effectively as walls. Generally, the victim must be aware of false imprisonment to claim injury from it. The duration of false imprisonment is not relevant in law. If the plaintiff can prove the imprisonment, the defendant must prove that it was lawful and justified and, therefore, not false imprisonment.

A nurse can be accused of false imprisonment when he or she restrains, secludes, or confines a patient in such a way as to deprive that patient of the right not to be so detained. This includes the improper use of restraint devices or confinement of a patient to a bed, a room, or to another defined area.

There are circumstances where detention of a patient is legally justified, if not in fact mandated. These include violent, mentally ill, or psychotic patients who are a threat to themselves and others; those persons who are confused, disoriented, or otherwise incompetent; and, by law, those exhibiting defined communicable diseases that threaten society-at-large. Institutions are required to detain such individuals by due process of law. Should forcible restraint be required by the circumstances at any time, only that degree of force that is reasonably necessary may be used.

### Restraints as a Form of False Imprisonment

The use of restraints and their implications for charges of false imprisonment continues to be controversial. "Federal regulations now mandate strict procedures for using restraints in long-term care facilities, and many of these institutions are adopting restraint-free policies. So far, however, few hospitals have joined this trend—most still use safety devices and medications to limit patient movement under certain circumstances" (Calfee 1991, 36).

The Nursing Home Reform Act of 1987, which was to have been implemented in stages beginning in 1990, stipulates that physical restraints can be used only under certain circumstances. The statutes provide that competent residents have the right to refuse restraints. In addition, medications must have a medical justification and not be prescribed for purposes of control and sedation only.

In most states, a physician's written order, placed in the medical record, is required before restraints may be used. Such an order does not mitigate a nurse's responsibilities. On the contrary, it increases both the responsibilities and the risks. Standing orders, protocols, and policies and procedures are usually in place to be effected at the nursing staff's discretion. These may include pharmacological measures such as sedatives and tranquilizers and any mechanical apparatus such as vests, wrist or ankle restraints, and bed rails.

Nurses who restrain or seclude a patient without justification leave themselves open to a variety of charges, including false imprisonment, battery, negligence, and malpractice. In implementing these interventions, it must be demonstrated that they were necessary to protect the patient from personal injury or to protect others from injury by that patient. It must also be shown that this was the only feasible course of action at the time when other measures were evaluated and viewed as insufficient. Nurses must verify that, in their professional judgment, there was a valid reason for their action. If this cannot be proven they risk a lawsuit for battery and/or false imprisonment. If a patient, while competent, confirms an informed decision to refuse restraints, a signed release must be obtained to protect the institution and staff from liability.

If a patient's status indicates the need for some form of protective constraint, a physician should be contacted to personally assess the individual and write appropriate orders. In the event that a patient becomes markedly agitated, violent, or combative and must be subdued immediately, the nurse must do so immediately! A physician's order should be obtained as soon as possible afterward. This is a nursing responsibility, and failure to act promptly in this instance could leave a nurse open to charges of negligence or reckless endangerment. "As a general rule, in the acute care setting, the nurse is more likely to be held liable for failing to restrain a patient who should be restrained than for restraining one who should not be" (Fiesta 1994, 4). The circumstances surrounding the events must be thoroughly documented.

Seclusion or restraint may never be utilized as a punitive measure or for the convenience of the institution's staff, particularly when a short-staffing situation exists. Devices or drugs cannot be an expedient alternative for more appropriate intervention and management. They must not be forms of discipline or domination. A patient's age, in itself, is not sufficient justification for the indiscriminate use of such measures—particularly maintaining side rails elevated where such confinement may not be necessary. "There is no absolute liability for falls that occur in hospitals. There must be proof that the nurse had reason to foresee that a patient could be harmed by falling before the duty to protect the patient arises" (Aiken and Catalano 1994, 124).

Family members will, out of genuine concern or unreasonable fear, suggest or demand that a loved one be restrained or that restraints be removed (they may even attempt to do so). The nurse must use his or her own best judgment and not submit to such demands when such action is not justifiable. He or she must explore the family's concerns with them but not allow them to usurp the nurse's responsibilities.

It is a dangerous breach in standards of care for a nurse to agree to a family member assuming responsibility for an at-risk patient in lieu of appropriate restraining measures. The nurse has no legal justification for delegating his or her duties to anyone other than another qualified member of the institution's staff. All discussions with family members regarding the need and rationale for restraining a patient should be thoroughly documented.

### Guidelines for Implementation of Restraints

Under the "least restrictive" doctrine in most states, when such measures must be taken they must be applied to the least extent as is possible—only to that degree that will effectively and adequately protect the patient or others from injury—only what is necessary and appropriate under the circumstances.

The individual applying a physical restraint device must know exactly how it is to be done for maximum effectiveness and patient safety. If the apparatus is applied incorrectly and the patient is injured as a result, the nurse could be held liable for all or a part of the injuries. Certain forms of restraints may be forbidden by law in any given jurisdiction or may be proscribed by the policies and procedures of the institution. A nurse could face liability for failure to remove restraints in a timely manner or from premature removal.

Care must be taken to avoid the use of undue force or even threats of such force. Such behavior could give rise to charges of assault and/or battery. Only a "reasonable" degree of force may be utilized in such efforts. If the patient is out of control, reasonable force is whatever it takes to check a potentially lethal rampage. If he or she is armed, deadly force may be the only recourse. Guidelines for documenting the use of restraints are shown in Table 1.1.

**Table 1.1**
**Documenting the Use of Restraints**

- A complete and accurate assessment of the patient's physical and mental status, and behavior, at the time of the decision
- The rationale, the determination of need—based on the assessment—evidence of clinical necessity—justification
- Alternatives, if any, that had been attempted beforehand and found to be ineffective
- A reference to the policy and procedure manual
- A citation of the physician's order
- The specific type of physical device utilized
- The site(s) of application of the apparatus
- The date and time the measures were implemented, and the intended duration
- A schedule indicating the times and by whom the patient was monitored and an assessment to include vital signs, level of consciousness, circulatory status, skin integrity, and other parameters.
- The patient's response and tolerance

- Effectiveness of the intervention as a safety measure
- A schedule of the times physical restraints were removed or loosened in accordance with policies and procedures
- The type of care, if any, required as a result of restraint
- Rationale and patient's status when the restraints are discontinued and removed
- A confirmation that restraints were, or should be, maintained longer than anticipated, and the rationale

### Defamation

Defamation is the intentional publication, communication, or dissemination of false information that injures the good name, character, or reputation of the person who is the subject of such false statements. "Publication" as used in this context means that the defamatory statements are communicated in some way to third parties. Such material need not be presented to the public-at-large. Disclosure to a third party or several parties may be sufficient provided that they understand or interpret the statements to be defamatory. Disclosure to the subject, and to the subject only, does not constitute defamation.

If the defamatory information is made public orally, or in some cases by gestures, it is *slander*. If it is presented graphically, pictorially, in writing, or in any permanent format, it is *libel*. For this reason, libel is considered to be more serious than slander. No actual damage must be proven for slander but such must be proven for libel.

There are several rules or principles of defamation law.

- The information published is false and defamatory.
- It was made known to a third party or parties.
- The statements were not made only in jest.
- The subject was a living person; there can be no action in tort if the subject is dead.
- The individual harmed must be readily identifiable.
- The plaintiff must show that he or she was the subject of the defamation.
- The perpetrator intended to communicate false information.
- The information harmed the reputation of the plaintiff in some way.
- The individual who published the information is the cause of the harm.

### Invasion of Privacy

Invasion of privacy involves four distinct rights:

1. the right to the exclusive use of one's own name and likeness;
2. the right not to be placed in a false or humiliating light in the public eye;
3. the right to be free from intrusion upon one's person or private affairs—the inherent right to be left alone; and
4. the right against unauthorized or unwarranted publicity of personal, private affairs or facts.

There are several elements that define invasion of privacy.

- The action complained of infringed on the plaintiff's right to privacy.
- Such an infringement was effected without the plaintiff's consent.
- The action and its consequences were offensive to the plaintiff.
- Information or facts divulged were very private and personal in nature.
- There was a disclosure of such information or facts to a party or parties who had no right to know or need to know.

Generally, any damages awarded in a case of invasion of privacy will be for the mental distress and emotional suffering that any normal, sensible person would be likely to suffer under the same or similar circumstances. Truth, a defense in libel and defamation, is not a defense in the tort of invasion of privacy.

### Breach of Confidentiality

Breach of confidentiality is a failure on the part of a *professional* to keep all privileged, confidential information private. It is the unlawful publication of certain private facts about a person without that person's consent. Nurses are particularly vulnerable to claims of breach of confidentiality. Most often the breach occurs when a patient's name and/or other private information is discussed in a public area of the institution such as at the nurses' station, in an elevator, in the patient's room in the presence of visitors, or in the cafeteria. Indiscrete disclosure to a relative or any visitor of confidential information regarding a patient is another common basis of a claim.

Telephone calls are a major potential problem area for nurses who must be extremely cautious when divulging any information to a caller. They should be absolutely certain of the identity of the caller and the legitimacy of the inquiry—the need to know, the right to know. All such calls should be referred to a proper resource if there are any doubts or questions.

The nurse is especially cautioned in revealing any patient information to the news media. There are circumstances when the general public's right to know may take precedence over another's privacy. Media reports on the status of the president's health, the hospitalization of a prominent public figure, the names of patients involved in major breakthroughs in medicine are some examples of this. Such persons must still be allowed their dignity and, to whatever extent possible, some degree of their privacy. A staff nurse, in the course of his or her routine duties, should not have the occasion, need, or urge to present himself or herself to the media.

Under certain circumstances the law permits the public disclosure of information to preclude possible danger or harm to the welfare of an individual or the general public. When the nurse, in his or her best professional judgment, and after careful consideration, determines that there is in fact a duty to disclose he or she might then divulge confidential information. If the information concerns a patient in a hospital, the initial revelation should be made to a nursing supervisor. A nurse's direct public disclosure would usually be done only if the nurse has been authorized to do so, and then the disclosure should be made in accordance with the employing institution's policies and procedures. In clinical practice, it is unlikely that a nurse would find himself or herself in a situation where personal initiative in direct disclosure would be indicated or appropriate. In a personal off-duty encounter, the duty would exist and the law would protect the nurse if he or she acted in good faith.

Statutes dealing with confidentiality vary by state. Virtually all of these disclosure laws provide for immunity from civil lawsuits against those required to report if the disclosure has been made in good faith. Common reportable information includes elder or child abuse, births and deaths, certain communicable diseases, and injuries suffered in the act of committing or attempting to commit a crime. Several states allow for the release of otherwise confidential information in criminal cases where such information is deemed relevant to prosecution of the case. A nurse is also protected by law when the information disclosed is essential to the proper and continuing care of a patient.

Each of the fifty states and the District of Columbia have implemented laws requiring the reporting of child abuse by certain professionals. These include nurses in all instances. Failure to report can incur punishment under criminal laws.

## PATIENTS' BILLS OF RIGHTS

Unless defined by federal or state statutes, patients' bills of rights have no force in law. Such declarations by health care institutions or professional organizations have only as much authority as their source. Only those rights that have been incorporated into laws or regulations carry meaningful legal authority because they define sanctions and specific recourse in law for the patient seeking redress when these rights are deemed to have been violated.

All statements of patients' rights are, however, professionally and ethically binding. They carry the highest moral and ethical weight for each member of the nursing profession. Nurses have always incorporated patients' rights in nursing care. The first such bill of rights was prepared by the National League for Nursing in 1959. It was followed by statements issued by the American Civil Liberties Union, the American Hospital Association, and several other professional organizations.

A copy of a patient's bill of rights, derived from one source or another, is usually given to every patient at the time of admission. It is likely to be a compilation developed by the institution itself, and framed copies may be displayed prominently throughout the premises. Nurses and all other caregivers are expected to ensure these rights regardless of their source.

The patients' bill of rights has at times been characterized as unnecessary, even redundant. One writer laments: "Somehow it seems a sad commentary that patients' bills of rights needed to be written at all or that they had to be given statutory enactment to be enforced. The rights contained therein should be self-evident. All persons, whether patients or not, are entitled to dignity, consideration, and self-determination" (Guido 1988, 201).

From a legal aspect, perhaps the most significant purpose of patients' bills of rights is that they serve to inform patients as consumers of health care of the options available to them if and when such rights are perceived as having been violated or denied.

## REFERENCES

Aiken, Tonia, and Joseph Catalano. 1994. *Legal, Ethical and Political Issues in Nursing*. F. A. Davis.

Black, Henry C. 1990. *Black's Law Dictionary*. 6th ed. West Publishing.

Calfee, Barbara E. 1991. Protecting yourself from allegations of nursing negligence. *Nursing91* 21 (12) (December): 34–39.

Fiesta, Janine. 1994. *20 Legal Pitfalls for Nurses to Avoid*. Delmar Publishers.

Guido, Ginny W. 1988. *Legal Issues in Nursing: A Source Book for Practice*. Appleton & Lange.

# 2

# Malpractice

## DEFINITION OF MALPRACTICE

Malpractice is *negligence* on the part of a *professional only while he or she is acting in the course of professional duties.* This unintentional tort involves acts of negligence by an individual employed in a position where defined levels of knowledge, technical skills, and professional standards are prescribed for anyone assuming that position. It is a failure on the part of a professional to act according to such defined standards or a failure to foresee the consequences that a person having the same or similar knowledge, education, and skills should have foreseen. A "professional" includes a nurse, physician, clergyman, educator, and attorney among others.

## NEGLIGENCE

A tort of negligence results when an individual fails to fulfill a required duty of care and that failure results in an injury to another individual. Negligence is carelessness. The negligent individual neither intends the consequences nor believes they will occur. This is the distinction between negligence and an intentional tort. Many of the acts previously discussed in the section on intentional torts would constitute negligence if there were no element of intent. Negligence is generally defined as a deviation from those standards that a reasonable, prudent person should or would apply in the same or a similar situation. The hypothetical "reasonable person" is ubiquitous in the law.

Gross negligence (a consideration in an award of punitive damages) involves the determination of a reckless disregard for the rights or well-being of another, even when an injury to the person is highly likely, if not certain, to result from the act or failure to act. It is a deliberate and wanton indifference that is apparent in the act itself, let alone its consequences.

Malpractice, therefore, is a very specific form of negligence that takes into account the status of the individual as a professional and the standards defined for that particular profession. It is a violation of a duty to act in good faith and with reasonable care. As a general rule, lawsuits for negligence and for malpractice will involve the same elements. Any one can be liable for negligence, but only a professional can be liable and can be sued for malpractice.

## REQUIRED ELEMENTS OF MALPRACTICE

In an alleged case of malpractice there are four elements, *each* of which must be proven by the plaintiff in order to find the nurse-defendant liable. These are the same elements which, as we have seen previously, must be proven in any tort of negligence. The plaintiff must present to the jury a preponderance of evidence that demonstrates unequivocally that all the allegations are more probably true than not. If successful, a judgment against the defendant will likely be made. These four required elements of malpractice are: (1) duty, (2) breach of duty, (3) injury, and (4) causation.

### Duty

Duty is the obligation of due care owed by one person to another as appropriate for the circumstances and as may be dictated by law. In a malpractice lawsuit against a nurse, the patient must claim, and prove, that the nurse owed him or her a professional duty of care. At the time of the alleged incident there must have existed a nurse-patient relationship that created duty.

Duty incorporates the fundamental legal concept of personal accountability for our actions or omissions. Every human being, regardless of his or her occupation or status, has an inherent obligation not to injure or harm another person by a negligent act or omission. We are free to act provided that our actions do not in some way intrude upon or violate the rights of another. Duty dictates appropriate conduct in society and prescribes that each of us act as a prudent, reasonable, individual who will exercise all possible care in avoiding any unreasonable risk to another.

In a nurse-patient relationship, duty involves the defined standards of nursing care that direct each nurse's conduct in his or her clinical practice. Duty is usually not an issue in a nursing malpractice case. The fact that a patient has been admitted to a hospital, and that a nurse who is an employee of that hospital has accepted an assignment to care for that patient (has created a nurse-patient relationship) usually establishes duty. It is not merely the nurse's employment status that creates the relationship, but also the establishment of a degree of reliance, of dependence, upon the nurse as a provider of care. This concept of reliance is the basis of duty and of the nursing process.

### Foreseeability

Another common factor in nursing malpractice lawsuits is foreseeability. This concept is inherent in the required elements of duty and causation. It suggests that a reasonable, prudent person of average intelligence should realize and anticipate the nature and extent of the consequences of his or her actions or omissions. A given action or course of action can be expected to produce given results. A *predictable* harm that resulted from the absence of due care should have been foreseen.

In law, foreseeability holds every person responsible for the consequences of negligent actions that cause harm to another person to whom some form of duty is owing. Proving this element requires the patient-plaintiff to show that the nurse should have reasonably foreseen the outcome of his or her actions, given the circumstances surrounding the alleged incident at that time. The merits of the lawsuit will be judged on those facts. Proof cannot come from hindsight; it must be based on the nurse's perspective then, not the plaintiff's retrospective now. The general rule is that if the consequences were not foreseeable, there is no liability.

### Breach of Duty

The second element that must be proven in a case of malpractice is breach of duty. This is defined as a failure to carry out the responsibilities of a particular position in a manner appropriate to that position. The nurse liable for breach of duty has failed in providing the required standards of nursing care defined for the profession. These incorporate all of the standards that should be applied by any professional nurse, with comparable experience and education, in the same or similar circumstances. In the courtroom these standards and the scope of nursing practice will be interpreted (not defined) by *nurse* expert witnesses and compared to those applied by the defendant. At issue will be what the standards of care were *at the time* of the alleged incident and if, and how, they might have been breached by the nurse-defendant. This will be a critical factor in a judgment of liability or innocence. Nursing standards of care are discussed more fully in chapter 4.

### Injury

The third required element is that of injury ("injury in fact"), which is an *actual* harm of any kind that the plaintiff has experienced. The plaintiff must prove that he or she has suffered physical, emotional, or economic wrong. The primary purpose of tort law is to provide some form of compensation to an individual who has been harmed by a wrongful act of another. *Injury is the key element* in malpractice. The harm sustained by the plaintiff must be "compensable"—it must be a *legally recognizable* injury. If there is no injury, there is nothing to compensate for, and there is no malpractice; therefore, there can be no liability. The mere fact of an injury does not necessarily create liability. Liability arises when the injury is the result of a nurse's failure in the standards of care.

Claims for emotional injury are generally not sustainable where there has been no physical injury, and the courts may not allow such suits. The exception is where there is evidence that the actions of the nurse-defendant were extreme, outrageous, or grossly negligent. Patients can and do sue for mental anguish and psychological injury; however, courts in many jurisdictions have usually been disinclined in awarding monetary compensation for such claims. In a recent court case in Pennsylvania, the judge commented that the legal system is not charged with compensating for "every minor psychic shock incurred in the course of everyday life; the law is not the guarantor of an emotionally peaceful life and cannot protect any of us from the emotional slings and arrows of daily living" (*Pennsylvania Jury Verdicts* 1993, 17).

The question arises as to what should be done in that instance where negligence has occurred, but the patient was not harmed in any way and is unaware of the event. Is there a *legal* duty to disclose the incident of negligence to the patient? Since the patient was not the victim of any injury, there is no legal duty to disclose. No injury means no liability under the law. From a professional, ethical, or moral perspective, however, imposing such ignorance on the patient could be tantamount to victimization. When appropriate, a direct and honest revelation of human error by a nurse will serve better than an inadvertent discovery by the patient or his or her family. Established trust, honesty, and mutual respect can be major factors in a plaintiff's decision to sue should any incident of nursing malpractice warrant.

## Causation

To prove causation, the fourth element in malpractice, the plaintiff must establish a *causal connection* between the breach of duty that is claimed and the injury that is alleged to have resulted from that breach. It is the concept of cause and effect seen in the physical sciences, in cosmology, and in law. It proposes that a given action or combination of actions will produce a given result. In litigation it is known as the "but for" criterion. But for the action (or omission) of the defendant, the injury could not have been sustained by the plaintiff. *Causation in fact* will be established. The defendant's conduct was the *proximate* and *substantial* cause of the resulting harm done to the plaintiff. The claim made is that the nurse's breach of duty is the most likely and probable cause of an injury that otherwise could not have occurred—there was "cause in fact".

Proximate cause (legal cause) will be determined if it can be shown that the action of the defendant was the substantial cause, the "next" cause, of the plaintiff's injury. The injury was the natural, continuous result of the defendant's negligence. The doctrine of foreseeability is the standard test for proximate cause, and a plaintiff will recover damages if it can be shown that the defendant should reasonably have foreseen that, as a consequence of his or her action, the plaintiff was at risk for injury. Proximate cause requires consideration of foreseeable consequences.

## THE LEGAL DOCTRINE OF *RES IPSA LOQUITUR*

*Res ipsa loquitur* is an exception to the requirement that a plaintiff must prove all four elements of malpractice. The *inference* of the defendant's negligence is known as *res ipsa loquitur*, which translates from Latin as: "The thing speaks for itself." It is a legal principle, a rule of evidence, that proposes that negligence on the part of the defendant can be inferred from the very fact that there was an incident which caused harm to the plaintiff. The rule affirms that the obvious nature and extent of the plaintiff's injury may *infer* negligence by the defendant and, therefore, liability. The injury itself speaks, it accuses.

This doctrine is applied only when the injury is such that it could ordinarily not occur unless negligence was the causative factor. In the instance where a professional duty of care existed, the nurse-defendant's negligence was the most likely cause of the patient's injury, and the nurse had *exclusive control* over the action, the doctrine of *res ipsa loquitur* will most likely be invoked. The burden of proof then shifts to the defendant who must then show that the plaintiff's injury was the result of a cause other than the alleged negligence of the defendant.

Causation can be the most problematic element in a case of malpractice. A plaintiff may be unable to prove a claim of negligence by, or ascribe blame for the harm sustained to, any one of a number of individuals named as defendants. In this instance, a court may apply the doctrine of *res ipsa loquitur* to assist the plaintiff in sustaining a claim. In effecting this rule, the court imparts a measure of equality to the plaintiff's position where this may have been lacking due to an unwarranted disadvantage imposed on the plaintiff. What the court has done is to permit the plaintiff to attempt to prove negligence by presenting circumstantial evidence against a defendant who, alone, may have full knowledge of the exact cause of the plaintiff's injury.

The court will require that three conditions be met before invocation of the rule of *res ipsa loquitur*:

1. Given the circumstances surrounding the alleged incident, there is reasonable cause to believe that the injury could not have otherwise occurred had there been no negligence on the part of the defendant. Such an injury is one that would not ordinarily occur except in a concurrent incident of negligence.
2. The instrumentality, the agency, of the injury was under the exclusive control and direction of the defendant.
3. The plaintiff did not contribute in any way to his or her injury.

When *res ipsa loquitur* is applied it usually obviates the need for the plaintiff to present testimony of expert witnesses. It also removes from the plaintiff the burden of proving all four of the required elements of malpractice; only injury and causation need be proven.

## THE LEGAL DOCTRINE OF VICARIOUS LIABILITY

The legal doctrine of vicarious liability imposes and imputes liability on one person for a tort committed by another acting as agent or employee. In a suit for malpractice, the institution itself is invariably named as a defendant because it is seen to have "deep pockets". The institution as an employer is included in a suit under the doctrine of vicarious liability ("substitute liability"), which holds an employer responsible for the acts of employees. In the search for the deep pocket, the plaintiff's attorney might include as defendants any number of staff who may have had no direct involvement in or responsibility for the alleged incident of malpractice. No matter how remote their contact with the plaintiff, they can be initially embraced by the claim under vicarious liability. Most will be "unsuited" later. In legal theory, vicarious liability is addressed in four concepts: (1) ostensible authority, (2) corporate liability, (3) *respondeat superior*, and (4) borrowed servant.

### Ostensible Authority

This legal doctrine affirms that a hospital, or any such institution, can be held liable for any negligence on the part of an independent contractor providing care or treatment for a patient if and when the patient can reasonably assume that the contractor is an employee of the hospital. The patient is the hospital's patient first, and the independent contractor's patient second. It is the hospital that may be held ultimately responsible for such contractors even though they are not employees—as a patient might assume. Independent contractors might include physician groups operating specialty services such as an emergency room, radiology department, or pathology laboratory. Advanced practice nurses including nurse practitioners and clinical nurse specialists can also provide various services as independent contractors.

### Corporate Liability

The focus of this doctrine is on the institution as an incorporated entity. Under the law a corporation is a "person" with clearly defined legal responsibilities. These corporate liabilities are over and above those inherent in the concept of vicarious liability and include such areas as safety and security for patients, employees, and visitors, maintenance and condition of the hospital's physical plant and all equipment utilized, organizational and management policies and procedures. The institution is held responsible to monitor all aspects of its day-to-day operation, and each of the personnel involved in those functions, in a reasonable effort to identify all foreseeable risks. It is these foreseeable risks that may be the measure of its liability. Certain aspects of professional staffing also come under this doctrine such as a failure to carry out appropriate employment prescreening to confirm the background and credentials of prospective medical or nursing staff applying for clinical privileges.

Janine Fiesta confirms that: "More recent court decisions have expanded the hospital's direct obligation to ensure not only a proper level of hospital management and operations and the appropriate conduct of employees and agents, but also the clinical competence and performance of all practitioners granted clinical privileges. . . . This developing doctrine of corporate liability has major consequences for the nursing profession. It is now the nurse's responsibility to communicate significant management information such as physician, staffing, and equipment problems" (Fiesta 1994, 142).

Virtually every hospital has a risk management department whose primary functions are to identify, analyze, reduce, and eliminate those factors that represent actual or potential hazards, and in so doing diminish the risk for lawsuits and possible financial losses. The objective is to assure the maximum safety of patients, employees, and visitors by preventing the preventible accident before it occurs or reoccurs. Whenever an untoward incident is reported, risk managers will examine the circumstances to determine the likelihood of a lawsuit or the potential for a claim and plan appropriate strategies and future preventive measures.

### Respondeat Superior

Under the legal doctrine of *respondeat superior* a principal-employer is liable for any injury or harm to a third party that is caused by the agent-employee while acting in the scope of employment. It is vicarious liability. This is a very ancient concept in common law that has it origins in the relationship of a servant to the master in the very earliest civilizations and social orders. It translates as: "Let the master respond." Every person is responsible for the management of his or her own affairs whether this is done personally or through servants or agents. In a malpractice suit against a nurse, a master-servant relationship is defined. The hospital is the "master"—employer; the nurse is the "servant"—employee—and the master must answer for the conduct of it servants.

A hospital can be held indirectly liable for a nurse's negligent acts carried out in the scope and course of his or her employment and which may cause injury to a patient of the hospital. The doctrine applies to acts of commission or omission. Both parties can be held liable on the basis of an employer-employee relationship. The hospital may be named as a defendant, and the nurse may not be.

For the hospital to be held liable under *respondeat superior* it must be shown that, as an employer, it directed and controlled the actions of its employee, and that the alleged malpractice occurred while the nurse, as employee, was acting while on duty and within the scope and course of his or her employment. In such instances the nurse must have carried out an act of negligence while on the hospital's premises, during a time he or she was actually assigned for and on duty, and while performing nursing duties defined by the job description. The principle of foreseeability is usually applied here, and many court decisions confirm that an employer should be able to foresee that an employee might be able to act in any given way and what the consequences might be.

There are several other elements that are considered in applying this doctrine. These questions include:

- Was the unit or site one to which the nurse was normally assigned for duty, or was he or she working in an unfamiliar area?
- Did the nurse act in any way primarily to benefit the interests of the hospital—his or her employer?
- To what extent did the nurse's actions conform to or deviate from those defined by the scope of practice?
- Could an employer have anticipated such actions and their outcomes?

An employer may claim that the nurse was, in fact, not on duty or acting outside the scope of employment and thus attempt to avoid liability. If the actions by the nurse can be demonstrated to have been outside the defined scope of practice the hospital may be absolved. In this event, the accused nurse may stand alone in defending the allegations.

The concept of *respondeat superior* is applied much more readily in the litigious climate of today in an increasing number of nursing malpractice suits. Prior to the last decade or two, the physician and/or the hospital were required to answer for the conduct of nurses, and as the "masters" they were usually named exclusively as defendants in claims of malpractice. The nurse, as "servant," was merely carrying out the binding orders of the master (physician) and was usually viewed as not culpable. That tradition was swept aside as nursing came to be recognized as a science and as a profession with concomitant legal liabilities. Nurses must now also answer for themselves.

### Borrowed Servant Doctrine

This is another doctrine based on vicarious liability. It is also known as "the captain of the ship" doctrine and is very similar to *respondeat superior*. This addresses negligence on the part of a nurse while he or she is working under the control or direction of an acting superior or supervisor—the "captain"—who is not the nurse's ordinary supervisor or manager. This temporary captain may be an independent contractor to whom the nurse is assigned or "loaned". The nurse is then a borrowed servant under the control and direction of the master and should not have to bear the entire burden of blame or liability that might result from carrying out the captain's orders.

Application of this doctrine in malpractice cases appears to have waned somewhat over the years, due in part to the increasing complexity of medical and nursing care and technological procedures. In today's health care setting and practice, it can be extremely difficult to assign individual blame when a number of disciplines and practitioners participate in the care of an individual patient. In such collaborative endeavors the principle of joint liability may be the only feasible recourse in defining defendants in malpractice litigation.

## REFERENCES

Fiesta, Janine. 1994. *20 Legal Pitfalls for Nurses to Avoid*. Delmar Publishers.
Morelaw, Inc. *Pennsylvania Jury Verdicts*. October 4, 1993.

# Defenses in Malpractice

## PRINCIPAL TYPES OF LEGAL DEFENSE

Under the law, an attorney can offer two principal types of defense on behalf of the nurse who has been named as a defendant in a suit for malpractice. The first is "defense of fact" which will contend that there was, in fact, no breach of duty; or there was a breach of duty, but that it was not the cause of the patient's alleged injury. The attorney will then attempt to provide a variety of alternative facts, causes, or circumstances, which, the attorney will contend, led to the injury. In those instances where a suit is seen to be clearly indefensible, an offer of a settlement may be the only feasible recourse. The second type of defense is "defense of law." An example of this is a statute of limitations in a given state.

### Defense of Fact

Specific defenses will be offered based on the type of tort that forms the basis of the lawsuit. These include *affirmative defenses* that are defined in substantive law. Affirmative defenses will be presented in an effort to show that there were certain facts or circumstances that obviate the claims of the plaintiff. They are not denials of the truth or facts of the plaintiff's claims.

Rather, they are assertions of reasons why the defendant is not liable. They are a challenge to the plaintiff's legal right to bring the action. Affirmative defenses can be presented in cases of intentional and unintentional tort.

### Defenses in Intentional Tort

There are four defenses in intentional tort.

- Absolute need: The action taken was imperative given the circumstances. There was no feasible alternative.
- Self-protection or the defense of another: Such situations permit the use of *reasonable* force if an individual believes he or she is going to be harmed and there is no possible option. The degree of force must be reasonable under the circumstances.
- Consent: The plaintiff had consented to the defendant's action.
- Authority of law: The defendant's action was required by law.

### Defenses in Unintentional Tort

Defenses in unintentional tort include the following.

- Contributory negligence: Most states have abolished this defense; however, the concept is particularly relevant to nursing practice. In this defense, the patient-plaintiff is implicated in the incident that caused his or her injury. If it can be shown that the patient contributed to the alleged injury in any way, the patient may not be allowed to recover full damages. This can be very difficult to prove in the circumstances of an ill or injured person and may not be proven in the case of the patient who is disoriented, confused, or irrational.
- Comparative negligence: This is now the law in a majority of states. There will be an attempt to prove that *both* the patient and the nurse contributed to the injury. Under this doctrine, a plaintiff who was contributively negligent can recover damages; however, the amount awarded will be reduced in proportion to the plaintiff's degree of negligence.
- Assumption of risk: This legal doctrine provides that a plaintiff may not recover damages if the patient willingly and knowingly accepted the risk of a medical procedure. The risk can be assumed by an expressed agreement or implied by the patient's knowledge of the risk and actions based on this knowledge. This doctrine is directly related to the issues of informed consent, which will be discussed in chapter 11. This defense will maintain that the patient knew and fully understood all of the risks involved in the procedure; willingly consented to it; and in so doing, accepted any and all consequences, including the alleged injury.
- Unavoidable accident: An inevitable event or set of circumstances was the cause of the injury. The cause was accidental—and only that.

- False claims: The charges and allegations being made by the plaintiff lack sufficient credibility or proof to sustain the claim that the nurse is liable for malpractice. If the court finds in the defendant's favor the case will be dismissed. The plaintiff may have exposed him- or herself to counter charges by the defendant.

- Sovereign immunity: Historically this doctrine precluded lawsuits against the federal or state governments. Plaintiffs were thwarted in any attempts to sue such political entities for negligence. Under the Federal Tort Claims Act, the federal government is now amenable to such suits, and most of the states are no longer immune from tort liability.

- Consent: Voluntary, which can be written, oral, or implied. This may come from the patient or from one authorized to give it.

- Truth: A defense in a suit for defamation if the defamatory statement is true in its entirety.

- Privilege: Another defense in defamation that allows the divulgence of privileged information where required by law. If such disclosure is made without malice and in good faith, there is no liability.

### Defense of Law

The two principal defenses of law are (1) statutes of limitations and (2) Good Samaritan laws. These vary by state.

#### Statutes of Limitations

A statute of limitations is an example of a procedural law that was defined in chapter 1. A statute of limitations delimits the period of time within which a plaintiff is allowed to bring an action in law for malpractice. In most states the lawsuit must be initiated within a prescribed time frame beginning on the specific date on which the plaintiff knew, *should have known*, or *discovered* that an act of malpractice was the cause of the alleged injury. If the plaintiff fails to file his or her petition for damages (complaint) within the time frame mandated by the law, the plaintiff may forfeit the right to sue.

In law, the statute of limitations is an example of an affirmative defense. It is the defendant who must show that the statute has, in fact, run out. If the court concurs in this assertion the plaintiff cannot pursue the lawsuit against the defendant. When the specific date on which the statute commences becomes an issue, the attorney for the plaintiff will pursue any possible extenuating circumstances and petition the court to extend the statute based on any credible cause.

Each state has incorporated a provision for a statute of limitations in the medical malpractice laws that have been enacted. As a result there are many variations in the period of time allowed and in the guidelines for determining it. When the statute of limitations becomes a point of disputation, the court will look to the definition framed by the state in determining an appropriate and applicable interpretation. Statutes dealing with the general laws on personal injuries may be applied in a malpractice suit. There are several procedural rules involved in these laws. These have been implemented to assist in fixing the precise date on which a statute of limitations begins to run. Examples of these procedural rules are shown in Table 3.1.

**Table 3.1**
**Procedural Rules in the Statute of Limitations**

- Occurrence Rule: The statute begins to run at the moment of, on the date of, the injury.

- Discovery Rule: The statute begins to run on the day the plaintiff actually *discovers* that he or she has been injured by an act of malpractice. In applying this rule the court will consider whether or not the plaintiff *could have*, or *should have*, discovered the alleged injury at any preceding time. That is, would this injury have been apparent to any reasonable person? "Discovery" can be interpreted in several ways: (1) the date the plaintiff determined that an act of malpractice actually occurred, (2) the date on which the plaintiff learned that the injury was the result of such an act, (3) the date on which it is determined that the injury sustained is of a degree and nature to warrant a malpractice suit to recover damages.

- Termination-of-Treatment Rule: The statute begins to run on the date of the plaintiff's last treatment. This rule is applied when a plaintiff's injury is alleged to have been the result of, and occurred during, an ongoing treatment regimen. During that time it might not be possible to identify a specific date or incident when the plaintiff might have sustained the alleged injury.

- Minors: The laws regarding minors vary by state. Some states define the statute of limitations according to the age of a minor on the date of his or her injury. In some statutes there may be no specific provision for minors. The rights of parents or legal guardians also varies. Most states provide for an extension of the time period within which a minor, or the parents or legal representatives of a minor, may act to initiate a lawsuit. This is usually one to two years beyond the legal age of majority—eighteen or twenty-one—as defined by the particular jurisdiction.

- Incompetency: This discovery rule will usually be applied in the case of an incompetent patient or in the event that such a patient recovers competency and/or is declared competent.

- Wrongful death: Wrongful death rules permit survivors to file lawsuits based on negligence or intentional acts. In this event the court may determine that the statute begins to run on the date of the patient's death; survivors, as plaintiffs, must file suit accordingly.

- Fraud: A proven allegation of deliberate fraud, concealment, or deceit perpetrated by any parties to the defense could extend the statute of limitations for an *indefinite* period of time.

### Good Samaritan Laws

Each state has a Good Samaritan law. These special negligence statutes have been enacted to provide protection from liability for negligence for anyone who endeavors to assist a victim at the scene of an accident, disaster, or other emergency situation. Individual state laws define those who are covered including professionals and nonprofessionals. Usually, only those personnel with a legal "duty to rescue" as defined by a state law are obliged to render aid in emergencies. These might include fire fighters, paramedics, emergency medical technicians, and law officers. Every nurse should know the provisions of the Good Samaritan law as it applies to the scope of nursing practice in his or her state.

Any person who does intervene may be sued, regardless; but the Good Samaritan law presents a formidable defense unless one's efforts have been wantonly careless or grossly negligent. The law will not provide protection for intentional harm or recklessness. Because of the protection these statutes provide, health care professionals and laypersons alike should be more willing to offer their help when and where needed, knowing that the law provides a measure of protection from lawsuits arising from allegations of negligence. Their first obligation is to do no harm. If they give their best in an effort to aid they should have no cause to fear legal reprisal.

As a general rule, unless required by a specific state statute, there is *no legal mandate* requiring a nurse or anyone else to render assistance to a victim in an emergency situation. The ethical or moral mandate to assist is one that the individual must define personally. Nurses who believe themselves inadequate or lacking in the proper clinical knowledge or skills demanded in the particular situation may have reasonable cause not to intervene.

Unless a nurse stops at the scene of an accident or presents him- or herself at the site of a disaster or any type of emergency with the intent to render assistance, he or she is under *no legal duty* to any victim. No one can lay claim to a nurse's professional skills or knowledge, and a nurse has the full right to withhold or deny services. The nurse's legal duty is created at the moment he or she initiates care and establishes a nurse-patient relationship. At that instant duty is established, and the individual will be held to the defined standards of nursing care. The legal duty, therefore, is one of reasonable care, and the law will protect only the nurse who provides such care. The Good Samaritan law cannot be invoked if one is grossly negligent.

Once the nurse initiates intervention, the victim becomes his or her "patient," and the nurse is then required to remain with the patient until one of the following events releases him or her from this duty:

- The victim refuses intervention or directs the effort cease.
- It is readily apparent that the victim is in no imminent danger.
- Qualified medical personnel arrive and assume care.
- His or her personal safety or life becomes at risk.
- He or she is directed to leave the scene by proper authority.
- The nurse is exhausted and cannot continue his or her efforts.
- Their intervention is to no avail. Despite all reasonable rescue efforts on the nurse's part, it is readily apparent that the victim is going to die and intervention will not prevent it.

At the time of this writing, only two states have a duty-to-rescue law; these are Vermont and Minnesota. In Vermont, any individual who recognizes that another person is at grave risk or whose life is threatened as a result of an injury is required to assist provided that one's efforts do not place him or her at similar risk. The law in Minnesota is similar. In all other states a nurse is not required to intervene. The general exception is when a nurse (or any other citizen) is in any way responsible for an accident and the victim's injuries. All state laws require individuals to stop at an accident in which they are involved. A nurse may be required not only to stop, but to assist any victims as well.

In most instances these laws are applicable only to such events that are encountered beyond the health care provider's place of employment. The Good Samaritan statutes do not cover allegations of negligence that occur in the scope of employment. When nurses are traveling to or from a job site or are engaged in personal activities at home or elsewhere, they are solely responsible for the legal consequences of their actions. This is one of several reasons that it is essential for a professional nurse to maintain a personal malpractice insurance policy.

A final point is that the nurse who accepts monetary compensation for the intervention he or she may have provided to a victim could forfeit his or her right of protection under a Good Samaritan law. By soliciting and/or accepting such payment, the nurse could establish a "fee-for-service" situation which, in effect, is a business arrangement, and which may prevent the nurse from invoking the Good Samaritan defense.

# 4

## Standards of Nursing Care

### DEFINITION OF STANDARD OF CARE

The American Nurses Association defines "standard" as an: "[A]uthoritative statement enunciated and promulgated by the profession by which the quality of practice, service, or education can be judged" (ANA 1991, 22). Nursing standards of care define the levels of skill and knowledge and the quality of patient care required and expected of any member of the profession carrying out the nursing process in a similar setting and under similar circumstances. It is that degree of care that is considered minimally adequate for, and acceptable from, each member of the nursing profession possessing a common body of skills and knowledge.

Nurses often express concern regarding their responsibilities for various ethical issues, and they should be aware that their legal and ethical responsibilities are not identical. . . . In the absence of a [legal standard], the nurse must be guided by the ethics of the profession and by personal moral standards. . . . [T]he law requires a basic minimum standard, whereas the ethical standards of the health care professional may require a higher standard of care in a particular situation. (Fiesta 1994, 179)

The fundamental premise of all such standards is that nurses must protect their patients. Standards have been created to provide practitioners with those guidelines necessary to accomplish this objective. By defining the acceptable and appropriate level of quality care, they facilitate the protective duty of the nurse in clinical practice. They are the bases for competent, therapeutic, and safe nursing care. They represent the duty each nurse undertakes to exercise that degree of ordinary and reasonable care that will assure that no preventable harm comes to his or her patient.

## APPLICATION OF STANDARDS OF CARE IN NURSING MALPRACTICE

In a nursing malpractice suit, it is these standards of care that will be the criteria used to determine if the nurse-defendant is liable for negligence. The courts will look to current, national, minimum standards, and they will also consider all relevant internal standards of the employing institution. These will provide the evidence that will prove or disprove that the nurse did or did not breach his or her duty. Duty may be defined as the applicable standard of care. The verdict will be dictated by a consideration and judgment of what any reasonable and prudent nurse with the same or similar experience and education would have done under the same or similar circumstances.

The plaintiff will be obliged to demonstrate that:

- published standards of care were in existence, disseminated, and readily available to the defendant;
- the standards that the plaintiff presents to the court were applicable and appropriate to the circumstances;
- the defendant should have known those standards;
- the defendant should have applied them;
- the defendant failed to apply them;
- the nature and extent of the defendant's breach of duty is evident; and
- the defendant's breach of duty caused the plaintiff's injuries.

Whether or not standards may be admitted in any given malpractice proceeding will depend on applicable principles and theories of law, the nature of the proceeding, the court of jurisdiction, and the relevancy of the standards themselves. No standard is guaranteed admission as evidence. If it is to be introduced as such, it must be shown to be germane to the issues and must overcome any objections to its validity. It must be authoritative, pertinent, and specific to the facts of the case.

Compliance to a standard will be gauged by the degree of conformity, incompetency, negligence, or gross negligence alleged of, or demonstrated by, the defendant. Ideally, presentation of standards of care will facilitate the determination of liability. To protect the rights of all parties, however, these must be legitimate interpretations of the care that was reasonable, appropriate, and expected given the circumstances surrounding the alleged incident. In every malpractice suit against a nurse, there will be the allegation that the nurse has breached his or her duty—has failed in the standards of care. Most often these standards are *the* criteria used in civil law in torts of professional negligence.

Standards of care may also be considered in a determination of a nurse's liability for violation of a state's nurse practice act or in proceedings involving charges under criminal statutes. The nurse practice act of any state may or may not incorporate standards of practice. There may be no reference to them in the statutes or in rules and regulations promulgated under the statutes. If they are not embodied in a statute they are not law—they are merely guidelines. However, they are guidelines that have the utmost legal significance for every nurse. Nurse practice acts are discussed in more detail in chapter 15.

## EXPERT WITNESSES AND STANDARDS OF CARE

In cases of negligence (unintentional torts) standards of care are relevant. They are not relevant in intentional torts. Expert witnesses are usually required in malpractice suits to interpret the appropriate standards. Predefined nursing standards should be and typically are elucidated by nurses employed as expert witnesses. The role of the nurse in this capacity is to present to the court the accepted standards of care that would have been expected and required in the circumstances of the alleged incident of nursing malpractice and to present an *opinion* that the defendant met or did not meet those standards. The defense attorney for a nurse accused of malpractice would likely protest a physician testifying as to the standards of nursing care unless the procedure under consideration involves a skill or function that either a physician or a nurse may routinely perform.

## SOURCES OF STANDARDS OF CARE

There are a number of variations in standards of care. They can be based on the nature of care to be provided, the setting for and the level of that care, and the competencies and required credentials of the subject caregivers. Standards can be very general and couched in language and provisions that apply to a very broad group, or they can be quite specific and applicable primarily to a defined group or subgroup within a profession and thus "profession specific". There are two basic sources of standards of care and the criteria upon which compliance will be evaluated. These are (1) external sources and (2) internal sources.

### External Sources

The primary external sources of standards of nursing care include the following:

- The Joint Commission on Accreditation of Healthcare Organizations: The JCAHO publishes the *Accreditation Manual for Hospitals* annually. The manual defines, in general terms, the standards for each department in a hospital including the nursing department. The hospital's policies and procedures are derived or revised using these. (JCAHO 1993, 79–84)
- State statutes (nurse practice acts): These, together with various rules and regulations issued under the statutes, define the requirements for licensure, grounds for actions against licensure, and the scope of practice. State boards of nursing may publish standards in the nurse practice acts or in the rules and regulations enforcing the acts. These may guide the court in a determination of nursing malpractice.
- American Nurses Association (ANA): The publications catalog of the ANA lists a number of generic standards applicable to various nursing clinical practice settings and specializations.
- National League for Nursing (NLN): The NLN defines the standards of nursing education at all levels. Ultimately these should be transferred to standards of care as high standards of teaching should engender high standards in professional practice.
- Nursing textbooks and professional journals (*not* nursing magazines): These must be accepted as authoritative publications whose authors are considered experts in their field. Many of the journals are published by the various national nursing specialty organizations and associations.
- Professional nursing organizations and accrediting agencies: Most of the nursing specialty organizations publish and distribute standards applicable to their members. It is an inherent right of any profession to define the credentials for admission to, and continuing association with, the group and the conduct required of each member.
- Federal and state statutes: Relevant laws include those applicable to Medicare, Medicaid, and Social Security.

### Internal Sources

Internal sources of the standards of nursing care include the policy and procedure manual of the institution and a nurse's particular job description.

## Policies and Procedures of the Institution

A policy is a general statement of a goal or a purpose. Procedures are the steps defined to attain goals or desired outcomes. A policy and procedure manual is not necessarily the definitive source for standards of care. It may merely be an accumulation of protocols, standards, and guidelines that have been in place since the last accreditation visit by the JCAHO. These may not reflect revisions and updates directed by the annual *Accreditation Manual*.

Not all policies need be in writing to be accepted as such. An unwritten policy with which all nursing staff is familiar is a valid policy. The problem of potential liability arises when the hospital fails to confirm such awareness among all staff members. For maximum protection of all concerned, all policies and procedures should be in writing, disseminated, and available to all personnel.

It is essential that a policy and procedure manual be updated constantly so that the professional nursing staff utilizing it is functioning at all times under the most currently defined standards of practice. All policies and procedures need to be consistent with both national and state standards. The nurse who relies on the content of an outdated manual incurs an unwarranted liability. Nurses should demand that administration provide them with current standards where and when deficiencies are identified.

Every nurse must have a thorough knowledge of the institution's policies and procedures, particularly those that bear directly on a particular position. In cases of nursing malpractice, courts have usually permitted introduction of a policy and procedure manual in defining applicable standards of care. The nurse who acts in compliance with the hospital's policies and procedures can affirm in his or her own defense that these standards have been met. Employee handbooks provided to nurses, and which may include rules, regulations, and selected standards, may be equally binding and could be used to demonstrate deviations by a nurse that can be considered failure to meet a standard of care.

The merits of the hospital's policies and procedures and the content of their standards of care will, to some extent, be dictated by the level of care provided by the hospital, its location, and its affiliations—if any. A university medical center may be held to higher standards than those expected of a rural community facility. However, this is no guarantee of a higher caliber of patient care. A hospital may draft and implement standards of care that are superior to those it has considered as prevalent in its general area of service. The nursing staff of that institution will be held to those standards, as high and as demanding as they may be. Every effort should be made to assure that all standards of care are realistic and attainable. The minimum standards of the institution should be reasonable and not impose undue onus—professional or legal. If a hospital prescribes standards that are inferior to those prevailing, the nurse will be held to those that have been defined as acceptable by and for the profession—those in prevalent use.

A policy and procedure manual may contain a statement condoning the use of independent judgment by the nurse in certain situations. When such discretion is allowed the nurse need be especially cautious and aware of the heightened potential for liability. Every nurse should be thoroughly familiar with the section of the manual that presents the institution's chain of command.

### Job Descriptions

A nurse's job description may or may not include a definition of the standards of care applicable to his or her particular position and duties.

## APPLICATION OF STANDARDS OF CARE IN NURSING PRACTICE

Standards of nursing practice enhance the professional standing of nursing. They are the criteria, the touchstone, that validate professional nursing practice. However, the number and variety of nursing standards confound and confuse nurses. The ideal would be a formulation of a body of national standards that might provide a more cohesive, systematic, and consistent approach to patient care. An embodiment of generic standards could serve to improve standards of care generally, patient care directly, and the status of the profession inevitably. Efforts must continue to coalesce local, state, institutional, and organizational standards into a useful, manageable, and universally applicable and acceptable resource. Specialization presents the most formidable challenge.

It has been said that: "[S]tandards of care are what everyone would like to see rather than objective statements of how things really are. . . . A common concern has been that standards often have no basis in sound scientific research. They are more often than not based on the 'textbook' patient and case studies" (Moniz 1992, 59). In short, they can be overly generalized statements of ideals with questionable relevancy to the fluid realities of clinical practice and limited applicability to the dynamics of the experiences and exigencies encountered moment by moment.

Those same standards, which have served to distinguish the nursing profession and enhance public awareness and appreciation, will also increasingly expose nurses to closer scrutiny, greater expectations, and greater liability. As court decisions during the past two decades show, an ominous trend of inclusion is likely to continue as increasing numbers of nurses will be called upon to defend themselves in malpractice litigation.

## REFERENCES

American Nurses Association. 1991. *Standards for Clinical Nursing Practice*.

Fiesta, Janine. 1994. *20 Legal Pitfalls for Nurses to Avoid*. Delmar Publishers.

Joint Commission on Accreditation of Healthcare Organizations. 1993. *Accreditation Manual for Hospitals*.

Moniz, Donna M. 1992. The legal danger of written protocols and standards of practice. *Nurse Practitioner* 17 (9) (September): 58–60.

# 5

## The Nurse at Risk for a Malpractice Lawsuit

### COMMON BASES OF NURSING MALPRACTICE LAWSUITS

There are a number of common bases that have been consistently identified as giving rise to malpractice lawsuits against nurses. These can be grouped into seven principal categories:

1. Safety: Failure to ensure patient safety and make this a priority—incidents of patient falls continue to be a major cause of malpractice suits against nurses who did not recognize possible risk factors and/or failed to take appropriate preventive measures.
2. Medication administration errors: Most such errors are the result of failure to follow the basic techniques and guidelines of medication preparation and administration. Parenteral medications are a primary risk. One or more of the six "rights" had not been observed: the right (1) patient, (2) medication, (3) dose, (4) route, (5) time, and (6) technique.
3. Assessment and monitoring: Failure to properly monitor, assess, and report a patient's status—this has been identified in a majority of malpractice lawsuits.
4. Procedures and treatments: Improper or inadequate nursing intervention—not following the institution's policies and procedures, including risk management principles.

5. Equipment misuse, defect, or failure: Using equipment without proper training; failure to test equipment before use, and to read instructions, specifications, and warnings; attempting to repair, adapt, or modify equipment—the increasing use, complexity, and sophistication of medical devices have created innumerable possibilities for injury and liability.

6. Communication: Breakdown between nurse and physician or among other members of the health care team, not listening to the patient—the nurse can be liable for failure to report the errors or impairment of others responsible for patient care.

7. Documentation: Inadequate documentation in nurses' notes is a *principal* factor in adverse court decisions in malpractice lawsuits.

A failure in any one of these seven general categories can turn the best practitioner into a defendant. It is a common misconception that injuries occur principally in the high-tech, high-stress, and fast-paced setting of emergency rooms or intensive care units. In actuality, the more "mundane" setting of a medical-surgical unit and the routine tasks of basic patient care have been identified in a predominant number of patient injuries and negligence suits.

## THE NURSE MOST LIKELY TO BE SUED

The nurse who may be at greatest risk of being sued is one who appears oblivious or unresponsive to the needs of his or her patients. The nurse may fail completely in identifying and/or responding to the needs of either the patient, the family, or both. This individual may be rigid, autocratic, and peremptory in his or her interpersonal relationships with both patients and peers. This is the nurse who is perceived to *give* care, but not *to* care.

The practitioner who attempts to care too much is also at risk. The conscientious, dedicated nurse who oversteps the limits of his or her clinical skills, training, and professional knowledge in providing what may well be meticulous care, places him- or herself and the patient in jeopardy. No matter how well-intentioned, the nurse who accepts an assignment, or has an assignment imposed on him or her for which he or she is not prepared by education, training, or experience may be inviting a malpractice lawsuit.

## THE PATIENT MOST LIKELY TO SUE

There are several traits or behaviors that have been consistently identified in the litigious patient. If a patient (or a family member) exhibits any responses to nursing or medical interventions that appear unwarranted or irrational, and that persist in spite of sincere efforts to resolve them, such an individual may be predisposed to filing a lawsuit. The nurse can expect to hear suggestions, hints, or outright threats and warnings of an intent to sue. These must be documented in detail and risk management staff should be advised.

Before this patient leaves the hospital, he or she may have asked for, and written down, the name of every caregiver that patient has encountered. Just prior to discharge, the patient, or a family member, will demand to review the medical record—if he or she has not already made such demands during the course of his or her stay. Throughout their hospitalization such individuals will constantly criticize or question the staff regarding every detail of the care they are being given. They may be observed taking notes of conversations or events. These patients may be angry, hostile, abusive, even combative. Nothing will mollify them. They will overreact to every perceived deficiency, criticism, or slight, no matter how trivial. As any nurse knows, this may be an unwitting attempt to project their fear, anger, and stress onto others.

The opposite of the angry, violent, verbally or physically abusive patient is the inordinately passive one. This is the individual who displays constant and excessive dependency on his or her caregivers. The caregiver is challenged to persuade this person to assume some responsibility for his or her own care and recovery. An even greater challenge is presented by the patient who is determined to assume full responsibility for, and direction of, the medical and nursing regimen. This individual will participate selectively or not at all. At any given moment this patient may decide to discharge him- or herself regardless of all efforts of dissuasion. *Document* such behaviors!

## PREVENTING A LAWSUIT

Having identified the type of nurse who is likely to be sued and the type of patient who is likely to sue, there are several strategies for health care providers that may help keep both parties out of court.

- Be a *patient advocate* at all times.
- Carry out the nursing process meticulously.
- *Document* that care meticulously. This may be *the* most important factor in personal risk management.
- Know and apply the standards of nursing care.
- Know and utilize the institution's policies and procedures.
- Recognize the limits of your knowledge and skills.
- Constantly strive to improve your knowledge and skills.

- Nurture professional growth in yourself and others.

- Assume professional accountability for your own actions, those of your peers, and those of your subordinates.

- Cultivate an awareness of the legal and ethical issues surrounding nursing practice.

- Listen to your patients. Address their fears, needs, and anger.

- Approach each patient with sincerity and concern.

- As difficult as it may be, try to treat the "difficult" patient as you would the pleasant, cooperative patient—as a professional should.

- Above all, protect your *patient first*, then yourself. Identify all risks—in your patients, yourself, your peers, and your environment.

## OTHER INSTANCES OF POTENTIAL LIABILITY

There are several other situations that can involve nurses—particularly those in any supervisory capacity—in potential liability for malpractice.

### Unlicensed Assistive Personnel (UAP)

At a congressional hearing in Washington on October 19, 1994, several nursing associations, including the American Nurses Association (ANA), addressed the profession's concerns with the growing trend in the American health care system directed at reducing hospital costs by cutting registered nurse staff and replacing these professionals with Unlicensed Assistive Personnel (UAP). The nurses who testified affirmed that such efforts are short-sighted and in the long run will prove ineffective in achieving the goal of cost reduction. The legal risks and implications of these measures to the nursing profession have just begun to be examined and could open a whole new field of legal questions, cases, and precedents.

Changes in the health care industry, particularly the trend toward managed care, will continue to place cost-cutting pressures on institutions. This, in turn, is likely to result in increased utilization of UAP for direct, hands-on patient care in selected clinical nursing settings. These may be called "care support associates", "multiskilled technicians", "patient care technicians", "patient care associates", or simply, "technicians". This national trend began in California in the latter part of the 1980s, and has become widespread. The traditional role of the professional nurse is being reevaluated as concepts of patient care and staffing change and evolve. A number of nursing schools are now training UAP.

The ANA has been monitoring the educational preparation and the utilization of UAP for four decades and has continued to do so in response to widespread deficiencies or differences in state nurse practice acts regarding the education, training, utilization, and legal status of such personnel. The delegation of patient care, and the registered, licensed nurse's legal accountability is defined in most acts. At the time this book was being prepared, only the state of Oklahoma had a certification procedure for UAP. Other states have been considering legislation that would place education and licensure of UAP under the jurisdiction of a state's board of nursing.

In its 1994 report on this topic (*Registered Nurses and Assistive Personnel*) the ANA affirmed that the registered nurse is responsible, legally and clinically, for the actions of those UAP assigned to them and under their supervision in the provision of patient care. The ANA's position on the replacement of licensed professionals with unlicensed staff confirms their belief that:

Patient care and safety are at risk due to decreased levels of registered nursing staff in health care institutions across the country.... Many hospitals, as part of their process of restructuring the workforce, have established new staffing patterns that have diminished the quality of care and may put patients' and providers' safety at risk.... [The] ANA believes that safety and quality of health care services are the highest priority and an obligation for health care institutions.... Regrettably, many health care institutions appear to be losing sight of this fundamental mission and instead are focussing on saving money by cutting the nursing staff. (American Nurses Association 1994, 11)

The increasing use of UAP has raised serious and legitimate questions and concerns among professional nurses regarding patient safety and well-being and the quality of care being provided by such personnel. Nurses have protested the decreasing numbers of professional nursing staff being utilized in patient care together with the increasing responsibilities, legal liability, and risks inherent in supervising the UAP who are *displacing* them. Their fears are grounded in a perception that UAP are *replacing* them.

The registered nurse, or any other health care provider, who delegates patient-care tasks to such personnel must be aware of the implications of legal liability under the doctrine of vicarious liability. In delegating responsibility, the nurse becomes a *supervisor* (as discussed later in this chapter). Supervision is defined as assigning, guiding, directing, monitoring, and evaluating a subordinate. This imputes responsibility and potential liability whether or not the nurse is physically present at all times. The nurse becomes liable if he or she failed to assure that the patient received proper care—that is, the same degree of care that would have been given by the nurse, personally. The UAP must function as a *supplement, not as a substitute* for the licensed professional!

A practitioner increases exposure to legal liability when he or she fails to follow certain guidelines in delegating patient care. Such oversight could leave that individual open to a charge of breach of duty. Examples of such failures are outlined in Table 5.1.

**Table 5.1**
**Potential Failures in Delegating Patient Care to UAP**

- Fails to assess a patient personally and thoroughly before delegating care of that patient to UAP
- Fails to personally monitor the patient's ongoing status
- Assigns UAP to patients whose status or complexity of care demand a licensed professional nurse as primary caregiver
- Delegates tasks or procedures to UAP that are the exclusive prerogative of a registered nurse—by law or by the policies of the institution
- Delegates tasks or procedures to UAP without confirming that such staff have the proper training or experience for the assignment
- Fails to supervise UAP adequately; the nurse at risk is the nurse who assumes that someone else will do his or her job
- Fails to document the details of the assignment and the patient's response

### Supervisor Liability

Nurses, by education, training, and tradition, are sometimes imbued with a conviction that they are personally responsible for *every* minute detail of patient care and, consequently, *every* mishap. This perception is misguided and can be self-destructive. Liability in the law demands individual responsibility from the individual in whom that responsibility is invested.

The nurse responsible for supervising, delegating, or assigning professional and nonprofessional staff faces a gamut of legal risks and liability exposure. As a practitioner moves away from the bedside and into a management position, the risks of malpractice in patient direct-care decisions declines but is supplanted by the risks inherent in managerial and supervisory decisions—any of which could ultimately involve a claim of malpractice.

On May 23, 1994, the United States Supreme Court, in a five-to-four decision (written by Justice Kennedy) found that a professional nurse who, using independent judgment, directs the actions of others as a duty of his or her position can be considered a *supervisor*. A statutory definition of a nursing supervisor, therefore, is any nurse engaged in assigning, overseeing, and providing "responsible direction" for the performance and actions of licensed staff or unlicensed assistive personnel. Justice Ginsberg, in a dissenting opinion, maintained that staff nurses, as professionals, should not be considered supervisors while carrying out their routine duties which, by their nature, involve independent judgment in assigning, directing and, supervising other staff. The justice opined that the definition of the majority was far too broad and its implications too sweeping (Furmidge and Barter 1994, 10).

A supervisor, in delegating assignments, transfers responsibility for the performance of the assignment but retains ultimate accountability for the consequences. Assignment is a delegation downward; co-assignment is delegation laterally. Ultimately, *responsibility* does not shift and situate in either direction. It simply extends and encompasses. A nurse as supervisor will be legally liable only for personal acts or omissions while acting in the capacity as a supervisor. His or her liability can arise when he or she fails to assign and/or supervise properly. A supervisor can be found negligent in assigning *any* staff member to a patient or a unit for which the individual—by declared or demonstrated lack of education, training, or experience—is clearly unsuitable. It is a generally accepted principle that control is concomitant with accountability. The individual who creates and controls the assignment of a subordinate is responsible for the consequences.

### Inadequate Staffing

The administrators (including nursing) of an institution are charged with providing and maintaining levels of staffing that will ensure a reasonable degree of patient safety and quality of care. This obligation has been confirmed in numerous court decisions and is addressed in the legal doctrine of corporate liability that was discussed previously in chapter 2. Under this doctrine an institution can incur liability for any harm to a patient that occurs as a result of deficiencies in staffing—including number and caliber of staff.

### Floating

An inevitable outcome of institutional downsizing will be short staffing. It follows that nurses will increasingly be required to train for and float to various units. A reluctant nurse who responds too rashly to a short-staffing situation may be at risk for a lawsuit. As professionals, nurses are responsible for cooperating in the institution's, and in their own, duty to provide a reasonable level of patient care and to maintain patient safety. Individuals who refuse to accept a float assignment do so at their own peril. If the hospital has a clearly defined policy on such alternative assignments, and these contingencies are included in a job description, the nurse who refuses to float may find him- or herself sunk! The exception is the individual who has a *written* contract, policy, or agreement of some kind that specifies those units to which he or she will be assigned exclusively.

Refusing to float simply because of uncertainty, anxiety, or fear is not a legally or professionally tenable argument. There are times when nurses are professionally, ethically, and legally obligated to decline an assignment. In these instances the nurse's right to refuse must be based on a demonstrated, *documented* lack of training, education, or experience required for the proposed assignment. If an individual sincerely believes that he or she is lacking in these, the nurse should not accede. In the event that disciplinary action is taken against the nurse or he or she is discharged, legal recourse could be possible.

In these situations the nurse must advise the appropriate supervisor of his or her convictions and concerns. These should be communicated in writing if possible and a personal copy retained. The nurse should not be intimidated and should not talk him- or herself into a false sense of confidence and capability. Convictions should be expressed and reservations affirmed. If protests are refuted, the nurse can proceed on one of two courses: (1) take a stand, refuse, and open oneself to disciplinary action or (2) concede, accept, make a best effort to prepare and report for duty. The latter choice, made under duress, should be documented in the nurse's personal anecdotal records.

There will inevitably be times when inadequate numbers of professional nursing staff can potentially compromise the quality of patient care and jeopardize patient safety. In such instances the patient with *a nurse lacking in certain skills and experience is preferable to the patient lacking a nurse*. If there are no other viable options for the patient, the nurse should accept the assignment. The law will expect nothing more than that degree of care that any reasonable and prudent individual would provide under the circumstances. It recognizes that every professional nurse should be able to function to some degree in any clinical setting with a basic repertoire of nursing skills. It will not expect or demand perfection. However, that individual will be expected to seek all appropriate and available supervision and guidance. Constantly weigh the risks and remember that the safety of the patient is the paramount concern.

### Abandonment

Abandonment is a nurse's failure to act as circumstances dictate. It is breach of duty. It is a wrongful act of omission and, under the law, a form of negligence. A nurse who fails to assess and monitor his or her patients in a continuous, timely manner could be guilty of abandonment. The individual who refuses to work overtime when overriding needs of patient care demand such effort might be charged with abandonment. So also the nurse who leaves an assigned unit without proper permission or without adequate notification. Refusing to float could be construed as an act of insubordination and/or abandonment unless the individual can show that a contract, a hospital policy, or a documented lack of required competencies precluded acceptance of an assignment.

### Giving Advice

Nurses are frequently called upon for advice and assistance in other than clinical situations. Before responding to any requests for advice, or services as a volunteer, one should consider several questions:

- Am I covered under my personal malpractice insurance policy for any potential liability?
- Is my action within the scope of nursing practice as defined by the nurse practice act of my state?
- Am I qualified by training, experience, and education?
- Is my advice or action consistent with defined standards of nursing care and appropriate to the situation?
- Will I be able to defend or justify my action if necessary?
- Am I the appropriate source of advice or intervention, or must I decline and provide a referral to an alternate source?
- Will I create the impression that what I propose is the most feasible or the only course of action?
- What would another nurse do in this situation?

A nurse should *never*, under any circumstances, offer any advice that could be construed as *medical* in nature. This is tantamount to *practicing medicine without a license*. This is a *crime*! A nurse should never speculate or offer opinions regarding the signs or symptoms of illness in others. Medical diagnosis is the sole prerogative of the physician, and the nurse is obliged to refer the individual with such questions to a physician.

It is very unlikely that a relative, friend, or neighbor of a nurse would consider the act of approaching him or her with casual or serious health questions or concerns to be the initiation of a nurse-patient relationship or the establishment of duty. However, if the well-meaning nurse receives such requests willingly and perpetuates a dependency relationship by continuing indiscriminate advice or intervention, he or she may be creating and cultivating duty and, consequently, liability. The *best advice* about giving advice is *don't give advice*!

### Volunteering Services

The same considerations in providing advice apply in the volunteering of one's services. The nurse-volunteer should first confirm that such activities are covered under a personal malpractice policy. He or she should also inquire about the insurance coverage of the organization with whom he or she will be affiliated during the volunteer experience. The nurse-volunteer will be held to the same standards of professional care in this setting as in a clinical setting. It is advisable that the nurse who provides such services personally document these in as much detail as possible without compromising confidentiality.

If any procedures, treatments, or medications are to be given, the nurse should request and review all appropriate physicians' standing orders or protocols before initiating these. When acting as a volunteer the nurse should never request or accept any form of compensation that could be interpreted as establishing a fee-for-service relationship.

### LIABILITY RISKS IN ADVANCED PRACTICE NURSING

The evolution of nursing science and the expansion of the scope of nursing practice has produced an increased body of knowledge as well as multiple levels of nursing. These are most exemplified by the emerging role of the advanced practice nurse (APN). The professional designation "advanced practice nurse" is an umbrella term, which includes primarily nurse practitioners, nurse anesthetists, nurse midwives, and clinical nurse specialists. There are some who might assert that this distinction represents a fragmentation rather than an advancement.

The need for APNs is expected to increase by 300 percent by the year 2000. This growing trend reflects a combination of health care consumer demand, a vigorous campaign by the nursing profession, and our evolving health care system with its increasing emphasis on cost containment. "The demand for nurses practicing in advanced rules with greater autonomy has increased. Federal regulations requiring statutory recognition of advanced nursing for third party reimbursement have been a catalyst in many jurisdictions for the regulation of advanced nursing practice" (National Council of State Boards of Nursing 1993a, 1).

There has been an increasing incidence and recognition of the merging and duplication of many facets of medical practice and those of other health care providers—particularly APNs. Many physicians consider this encroachment and usurpation rather than extension and enhancement. Increasingly APNs are functioning independently in primary care settings, autonomous from the direct or indirect supervision of a physician. Health maintenance organizations, Medicare, Medicaid, and other insurers are beginning to expand the accreditation and utilization of nurses in roles traditionally reserved for physicians. The medical establishment has vehemently opposed the concept.

All fifty state boards of nursing have language that addresses APN practice (National Council of State Boards of Nursing 1993b, 1). In recent years, twenty-six states have passed laws permitting nurse practitioners to provide health care services without subservience to a physician. A number of others, including New York and California, still require oversight by a physician. In every state except Illinois, APNs are permitted prescriptive privileges with varying restrictions.

At this time, the trend is a nascent one. As the federal government and the various states enact new laws, the roles and responsibilities of the APN will continue to evolve and expand as will increased risks for legal liability. The nursing profession and the legal system are just beginning to address the issues involved in advanced practice nursing. There have been malpractice lawsuits involving APNs and there will be many more. There have been many lawsuits initiated by physicians alleging that APNs were engaging in the unlawful practice of medicine, and there will be many more. It is hoped that future nursing research will address the implications of the role and the concomitant issues of legal liability.

"The public has a right to the access to health care, and to make informed choices regarding selection of health care options through knowledge of the area of expertise, qualifications and credentials of individuals who provide health care" (National Council of State Boards of Nursing 1993a, 3). The public has a right to seek redress in law if their choices prove injurious.

## REFERENCES

American Nurses Association. 1994. *Registered Professional Nurses and Assistive Personnel.*

Furmidge, Marva L., and Marjorie Barter. 1994. Supreme Court decision affects bargaining rights of nurses. *Journal of Nursing Administration* 24 (7/8) (July-August): 9–11.

# 6

# The Legal Process

## STEPS IN THE LEGAL PROCESS

Malpractice lawsuits against health care providers can vary widely in the bases, issues, questions of law, and complexity of a particular case. There are certain procedural requirements common to all such cases. These are defined in the applicable rules of the court (state or federal) that will have jurisdiction in the lawsuit. Most civil cases are tried in state courts. Each lawsuit begins with an event that gives rise to a claim of malpractice—the basis for legal action—and ends with either a settlement by the parties or a judgment by a court. From beginning to end, a variety of legal maneuvers intervene. The legal process is outlined in Table 6.1. Each step in the process will be discussed in further detail.

**Table 6.1**
**Steps in the Legal Process**

Incident of alleged malpractice and alleged injury

↓

Injured party retains an attorney

↓

Pretrial activity: retrieval and review of the medical record, interviews—
patient, witnesses—informal investigation

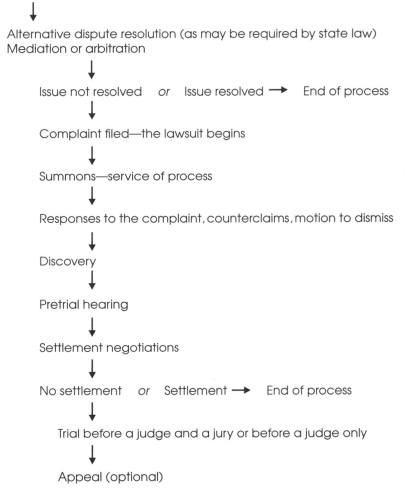

Alternative dispute resolution (as may be required by state law)
Mediation or arbitration

Issue not resolved    *or*    Issue resolved  ➞    End of process

Complaint filed—the lawsuit begins

Summons—service of process

Responses to the complaint, counterclaims, motion to dismiss

Discovery

Pretrial hearing

Settlement negotiations

No settlement    *or*    Settlement  ➞    End of process

Trial before a judge and a jury or before a judge only

Appeal (optional)

## INITIATION OF A MALPRACTICE LAWSUIT

Most states have clearly defined rules, procedures, or protocols that all
members of the legal profession are expected to adhere to under threat of
censure, revocation of a license to practice, and disbarment. These include a
requirement that an attorney must present a legitimate rationale for the filing of a lawsuit, including the intent of filing in good faith. The attorney
who initiates a suit that is deemed frivolous, or that lacks any inherent merit,
can be subject to censure or disciplinary action by the appropriate bar association.

The *parties* in a lawsuit are the plaintiffs and the defendants. The plaintiff is the party who initiates the lawsuit. A malpractice lawsuit can begin when a patient perceives himself or herself to have suffered an injury of some kind at the hands of a health care provider. If the patient has died, the next-of-kin might make the decision to sue, particularly in a claim of wrongful death. If the patient has been adjudicated to be incompetent, a legal guardian might initiate the suit.

The patient, now plaintiff, will then contact an attorney—ideally a reputable trial lawyer with extensive experience in malpractice litigation. It is at this time that many potential litigants are rebuffed in their efforts. A very large percentage of suits are turned away by lawyers because they are specious, the claims are tenuous at best, no serious injuries have been sustained, or the amount of damages that could be recoverable are minimal.

Pursuing a case of malpractice can represent a significant commitment of time and money on the part of an attorney whose anticipated fee is usually contingent on the amount of damages awarded by a court or the amount of compensation offered in any settlement. If the anticipated amount is considered insufficient to cover desired fees and projected expenses, an attorney might decline the case. It is the attorney's prerogative. However, there are many lawyers who will accept a case on its merits alone and provide their time and talents to ensure a client's welfare. They will serve *pro bono*—that is, without consideration of personal financial compensation. If the plaintiff's assertions and claims are considered to have merit, the attorney can elect to accept and pursue the case and the legal process formally begins.

## PRETRIAL ACTIVITY

Prior to the beginning of any eventual trial, there are a number of processes and procedures that are undertaken by both parties in the lawsuit. The following are descriptions of these several activities.

### Informal Investigation

At this stage, the patient-plaintiff and any witnesses are interviewed; medical records and other relevant documents are obtained and reviewed. Expert witnesses or consultants will be retained to review the medical records and prepare their opinions. The objective of the investigation is to identify and locate any and all factual evidence that could be used by either side to support his or her case and impeach the parties, evidence, or witnesses of the opposing side, or which could be the basis of a settlement offer.

It is estimated that 90 to 95 percent of malpractice suits are settled out of court, most after the lawsuit has been filed but before a trial begins. In these instances, pretrial investigations, informal or formal, provide each side with the opportunity to assess the issues, the merits of the claims, and the strengths and weaknesses of their case, and come to a much quicker, less expensive, and less adversarial resolution of the case.

### Prelitigation Panel

Before a malpractice lawsuit reaches the trial stage the plaintiff may be required by state law to submit his or her case for review by a prelitigation panel that can be an arbitration panel, a medical review board, or a medical tribunal. Such requirements vary by state. A prelitigation panel may be made up of physicians, nurses, dentists, or other health care professionals, and usually includes lawyers as well. The attorney for the plaintiff submits the claim and all evidence forming the basis of the claim to the designated panel for review. Unless arbitration has been directed, or other requirements are defined, the suit proceeds to trial following this review procedure. These proceedings can add six months to one year to a legal process that normally can go on for three to five years. Many critics consider this a needless, expensive delay that works to the disadvantage of a plaintiff. To defendants they represent a means of discharging nuisance suits and frivolous claims.

### Alternative Dispute Resolution

Once a plaintiff files the lawsuit, the court system takes over and the process and timing of events is determined by the formal rules of the system. The process, by its nature, is structured, adversarial, and time consuming—very time consuming! More and more cases that have traditionally been decided within the judicial system are now being settled by alternative dispute resolution (ADR). A court trial is no longer the only option in settling civil suits. A trial is generally the last resort desired by parties in the legal process because of the time, costs, and uncertainties involved in pursuing a lawsuit in which there may be no significant damages or issues.

For these reasons, many civil lawsuits are referred to alternative dispute resolution that could include: (1) negotiation—the parties in the suit meet informally to resolve the matter and consider terms of a settlement agreement, (2) mediation—a neutral third party acts as an intermediary who *proposes*, but does not *impose*, solutions on the parties, and (3) arbitration—a neutral third party (or a panel) makes a decision that may or may not be legally binding on the parties.

Alternative dispute resolution invests control of the dispute process in the parties themselves. Each side is permitted to reach a mutual agreement on when, where, and how long they will meet, what will be discussed, who will be present, and whether the final decision will be binding or nonbinding on the parties. The final decision can be arrived at in a matter of hours, days, or perhaps months.

In some instances, judges who are overburdened with case loads are ordering the parties in certain lawsuits to attempt ADR. Cost containment efforts in the health care industry have motivated hospitals and health maintenance organizations (HMOs) to resort to ADR in efforts to resolve disputes.

### Negotiation

The parties themselves and/or their attorneys, meet privately in an effort to resolve the issues and come to a settlement agreement without outside intervention.

### Mediation

In mediation, the mediator, an independent third party, endeavors to bring both sides together to negotiate an agreement. An effort is made to make the proceeding a meeting of minds rather than a confrontation of wills. If an agreement is reached, it is a contract that is then legally binding on both sides. If either side fails to comply with the terms, either side could be liable for breach of contract. If no agreement can be reached in spite of the mediator's efforts, the dispute can be pursued further by a lawsuit or by arbitration.

### Arbitration

Arbitration is a more formal process. There is some semblance of a court proceeding here. There are opening statements, presentation of evidence, examination and cross-examination of witnesses. As in mediation, a neutral third party—individual or a panel—considers the argument of both sides in the dispute and is then charged with deciding in favor of one side or the other. That decision is final, binding, and enforceable on both sides if both have previously agreed that the decision would be so. An appeal to a court of proper jurisdiction is possible. However, the courts have shown some reluctance to overturn decisions in arbitration and in some cases have not accepted jurisdiction over such matters.

### Filing of a Lawsuit and Service of Process

These next steps are magisterial rather than maneuvering. They are the setting out of one's position rather than the jockeying for it.

#### Filing of a Lawsuit

Filing the lawsuit is the first formal step in the process of litigation. It establishes the date on which the suit officially begins, and it informs the court of jurisdiction of the suit, which now becomes a matter of public record.

The first step is the filing of the *complaint*. The complaint is a list of the claims that are being made by a plaintiff against a defendant. It identifies the parties and states the cause of action. The purpose of the complaint is to introduce the cause of the action that has been filed, invoke the jurisdiction of the court in which the action is being filed, present the claims, and advise a defendant of why and by whom he or she is being sued, and for what form of damages. It is a formal declaration of all the general allegations of injury that the plaintiff will endeavor to prove were caused by the defendant.

The complaint will also contain a statement of the court's jurisdiction, ("jurisdictional allegations") in the matter. It also constitutes a formal request to the court for redress under the law in the form of a judgment for the plaintiff ("prayer for relief"). There will be a demand for remedy, usually money damages in a specific amount, if this is permitted by law. The complaint must be filed within that period of time prescribed by procedural law—the statute of limitations. These statutes vary by jurisdiction and type of case.

#### Summons

A summons identifies all parties in the lawsuit and indicates the court of jurisdiction in which the case will be tried. It also directs a defendant to respond to the complaint within a specified time period. It "summons" the defendant to appear and defend him- or herself.

#### Service of Process

A copy of the complaint and the summons is "served on", delivered to, the defendant. This is *service of process*. Before a court can exercise its jurisdiction over a defendant—before a lawsuit can formally begin—the court must have proof that the defendant has been officially and legally notified of the lawsuit and the defendant's need to respond to it. Service of process also gives the court personal jurisdiction over a named defendant; this is necessary to enable the court to impose any legally binding judgment on the defendant. Collectively, the formal documents filed in a lawsuit in which both plaintiff and defendant state facts, claims, issues, and defenses in the case are called *pleadings*.

### Discovery

The formal investigation that involves the exchange of information and documents between attorneys for opposing sides is called *discovery*. This process of exchange is governed by court rules of procedure and sanctions. Generally all information that is not privileged, that is relevant to the lawsuit, or that might lead to additional admissible evidence is discoverable. It is at this stage of the legal process that both sides make every conceivable effort to "discover" all the evidence, facts, circumstances, events, and details that may be relevant to the alleged instance of malpractice. In addition to such information, facts, and data, the process will also assist the plaintiff's attorney in identifying any additional possible defendants; and either side may identify witnesses to facts of the case. Discovery will preserve all of the information derived for possible use at a trial.

The purpose of the discovery process is to assure that all of the parties in the lawsuit are fully informed of all of the facts and of all the contending claims regarding the facts. These include both the evidence and the witnesses to be presented by either side. The objective is, ideally, to provide both sides with an equal advantage in the overall preparation of their case and the strategies and tactics they will pursue in prosecuting or defending it. The case can then be tried on the merits, the evidence, of the case. Ideally it eliminates any untoward surprises and trial by "ambush".

The process of discovery serves to define the primary issues of dispute in the case so that in the event of a trial the focus will be on these, resulting in a more expedient trial. If all parties agree on the facts and issues, discovery can facilitate an out-of-court settlement or possibly a summary judgment. If the process reveals that there is, in fact, no basis for the lawsuit, it can result in a summary judgment or dismissal of the case. Discovery is the longest and most arduous step in the legal process. Under certain conditions, the courts can impose limits on the discovery process.

### MECHANISMS OF DISCOVERY

There are various methods used in obtaining information and facts relevant to the alleged incident of malpractice. Which means of discovery and the extent to which employed will be directed by the nature and complexity of the case and the amount of damages claimed. The mechanisms of discovery include:

- interrogatories: written questions submitted to any party;
- requests for production of documents and things;
- motion for an order to submit to medical examination of a party;
- request for admission of facts;
- reports and opinions of experts; and
- deposition: oral statements of a witness or party questioned under oath.

### Interrogatories

Interrogatories consist of a series of written questions submitted by each side in the lawsuit to the parties on the opposing side. These questions may request very specific information and detailed answers, or they may be very general in nature. The total number of questions permitted under procedural rules can vary by state as can the time allowed for responding to the questions. The usual time permitted is thirty to sixty days.

Interrogatories may request answers the content of which can be considered confidential or privileged by either side, and they can refuse to answer such questions. In this case, an attorney can file a motion requesting a court to direct the answering of any questions that are demonstrated to be relevant to the case.

Each side must submit its written answers to the questions under oath. Under no circumstances should a nurse-defendant attempt to formulate answers and respond to the interrogatories without the direction and supervision of an attorney. The attorney will review each question with the nurse and collaborate on an appropriate, consistent response. The nurse-defendant may be requested to prepare preliminary drafts of answers. The final phrasing of the answers must be done very carefully to avoid any ambiguity or any suggestion or actual admission of liability. Neither side will wish to provide any more information in a response than is absolutely necessary.

It is in responding to the interrogatories that the patient-plaintiff is initially confronted with the duty of accurately and honestly presenting the details of the injuries alleged. In answering, he or she is challenged to define the nature and extent of those injuries—physical and/or emotional—which form the basis of the lawsuit. The assertion of blame for these will be found in the complaint.

The interrogatories directed to the plaintiff will attempt to elicit extensive and detailed facts regarding past medical history, occupational status—past and present—and any history of prior suits or insurance claims. They may attempt to explore the plaintiff's economic, social, educational, and family background. The questions could delve into very personal aspects of the respondent's past and present lifestyle.

A primary focus for the questions by the defense will be the plaintiff's medical history. The responses to these questions will be compared with the medical records and may also provide a resource for locating other medical records that can then be obtained and reviewed for possible relevancy. Such a review and comparison should reveal any attempt to hide any facts such as prior medical conditions, hospitalizations, treatments, and evidence of prior noncompliance with a medical regimen.

The medical records will be examined for evidence of any contributing or alternative causes of the plaintiff's alleged injury—particularly his or her own acts or omissions. Should any discrepancies or contradictions be identified in comparing past medical records with the present ones or with information in the interrogatories or the deposition, the defense will use these in an attempt to impeach the credibility of the plaintiff.

The details of the allegations will be compared with past and present medical records to determine if the injuries now claimed are new, or if they are a recurrence or exacerbation of a prior condition that in some way may have contributed to the present complaint. The objective is to place the plaintiff in the position of having to prove that the injuries claimed were the result of, and caused by, the defendant's act of malpractice. A review and analysis of the medical record may demonstrate that the patient was not injured or, if an injury actually occurred, the nurse-defendant is not liable.

Interrogatories directed to the nurse-defendant will include the nurse's education, professional credentials, past and present employment history, any prior incidents of malpractice suits, actions by state boards, criminal history, certain personal data, and clinical knowledge and details specific to the alleged incident.

### Reports and Opinions of Expert Witnesses

In the interrogatories, each side will require the name, address, and title of every expert witness who is expected to be called at the trial. The particular subject they will address and a report of the general nature and substance of the facts and opinions to be expected in their testimony is also requested, together with a summary of the bases, the authoritative sources, for their opinions.

In nursing malpractice cases, nurse expert witnesses are usually retained by attorneys for both plaintiff and defendant. The standards of nursing care are *interpreted* (not established) by the testimony of a nurse as expert witness. His or her duty is to give an opinion on breaches in the accepted standards of nursing care, if any, the nature and extent of any injury, and causation. Note that the *opinions* of an expert witness are admissible in a trial. He or she does not serve as witnesses to facts. Professional nurses also function as *consulting* experts in cases of nursing malpractice. In this capacity, their opinions and reports are considered "attorney's work product" and are generally not discoverable. The roles of the testifying and consulting expert are discussed in detail in chapter 16.

### Requests for Production of Documents and Things

The second procedure in discovery may be the request for production of documents and things. Each side requests the opposing side to provide any and all items in any form that would be relevant to the conduct of the case, the issues, the allegations, and which might be used as evidence. Certain information may be considered nondiscoverable and protected from disclosure or release. Many states, by statute, close certain files to public scrutiny, including that of attorneys involved in litigation.

### Motion for an Order to Submit to Medical Examination of a Party

For the order to submit to medical examination of a party method of discovery, the defendant's attorney may file a motion requiring a party to be examined by a physician of the defendant's choice or by a physician mutually agreed on. This is in effect a second medical opinion. The objective is to confirm and define the nature and extent of the injuries claimed by the plaintiff and to determine his or her present status both physical and emotional. Another purpose is to identify the plaintiff as a possible malingerer.

### Request for Admission of Facts

The request for admission of facts tactic of discovery consists of written requests presented by each side to the other. These ask that certain facts relevant to issues in the suit be admitted or denied. These could be such things as dates, times, locales, or other basic facts or details on which both sides can readily agree or disagree. The purpose of this request is to have the opposing side admit certain facts that will then not have to be proven or contested at a trial by separate evidence. Limiting the number of facts or issues in dispute can facilitate an expeditious trial.

## Deposition

A deposition is the questioning—the examination and cross-examination—of a party, a material witness, an expert witness, or any other individual who has been placed under oath. The individual being interviewed under oath (deposed) is called the "deponent." The questions are presented to the deponent by the attorney for each side in the action. The questions may be in writing ("depositions on written questions"), but the answers must be given orally under oath. The most commonly used procedure is oral questioning ("depositions on oral examination"). In either type, the oral testimony of a deponent is recorded by a court reporter, a stenographer, or other individual legally authorized to administer an oath. An official transcript of all testimony is prepared, and a copy is given to both sides for review of content and accuracy. Unlike the respondents to interrogatories, the individual deponent is expected to answer an appropriate question spontaneously and in his or her own words. The purposes of the deposition are shown in the Table 6.2.

**Table 6.2**
**Purposes of the Deposition**

- Discover any and all relevant facts, documents, or other evidence
- Determine each deponent's knowledge and/or version of the facts, any evidence in support of that version, and the location of such evidence
- Identify any and all other individuals who may have evidence
- Assess the strengths and weaknesses of the opposing side
- Prescreen and evaluate all potential witnesses
- Establish the course of action, tactics, and strategies to be pursued
- Elicit evidence that might facilitate a settlement
- Define the nature, extent, and possible causes of the injuries claimed
- Determine the defendant's financial resources—including any insurance
- Prepare a transcription of all testimony given for later use at a trial
- Possibly impeach the trial testimony of a deponent

Deposition is the primary method of discovery. It is typically the most prolonged and most arduous stage in the discovery process. Unlike interrogatories, the deposition provides a pretrial opportunity for attorneys to question individuals other than the parties. A deposition on oral examination is a dress rehearsal for a trial. Because the deposition is that component of the legal process that a nurse, as defendant or testifying expert, is most likely to encounter personally, its protocols will be discussed in some detail in chapter 8. This will include a number of tips and strategies for the nurse in preparing for and surviving a deposition.


## SETTLEMENT

At any time in the legal process—prior to or even during a trial—the parties may agree on an out-of-court settlement. It is usually in the best interests of the parties to settle a case out of court, and attorneys will make every effort to assist their clients in reaching a settlement. Ordinarily it is proposed and agreed upon during pretrial negotiations as an alternative dispute resolution. It is estimated that only 5 to 10 percent of all malpractice suits that are filed progress to a trial; and of those that do reach this stage, only 10 percent actually end in a verdict by a jury.

Such a settlement is *not an admission of liability* by a defendant. It is very often the most expedient way to dispose of the case, and, significantly, may be the least expensive way in the long run. A malpractice insurance carrier will weigh the cost of a settlement against the cost of defending the suit, particularly legal fees, for the prolonged duration of the pretrial proceedings, a trial, and any subsequent appeals. This is a business decision. If the defense determines that their case is very weak or virtually indefensible, they may seek an early settlement as the most feasible alternative when faced with the possibility of a large award in damages to the plaintiff.

Under the terms of his or her malpractice insurance policy, a nurse named as a defendant in a case may play no part in an out-of-court settlement. It might be negotiated, decided, and effected without any prior knowledge on his or her part. The nurse-defendant's consent may not be sought or even necessary. The terms of the insurance policy will define rights, if any, in this decision. For this reason every nurse should read his or her malpractice policy very carefully and understand its provisions completely. (For a detailed discussion of malpractice insurance see chapter 13.)

The compensatory damages (money award) acceded to in a settlement are usually not disclosed to the public. This can be mutually agreed upon by private agreement among the parties, or nondisclosure may be directed by a judge under penalty of contempt of court. However, any and all amounts paid out in damages on behalf of a defendant, either by jury award or in a settlement must, by law, be reported to the National Practitioner Data Bank. (The Data Bank is discussed in chapter 14.) Various states also require the reporting of such payments to appropriate state agencies such as boards of medicine or nursing.

## THE TRIAL

A trial can be held with or without a jury, that is, before a judge only. The constitutional right to a jury trial need not be exercised. In most states and in the federal courts, one of the parties must request a jury trial or the right to such a trial is presumed to be waived. The trial is the final stage in the legal process—unless an appeal from a trial verdict is made. It comes after all the proceedings of the discovery process have been completed. The entire process from complaint to trial can take anywhere from three to five years. As previously noted, relatively few malpractice lawsuits ever reach the point of a trial. The greatest majority are settled out of court and well before the attorneys and parties are prepared to enter a courtroom to plead the case. The stages in a typical trial are shown in Table 6.3.

**Table 6.3**
**Stages in a Trial**

1. Calling, questioning, and selection of a jury (*voir dire*)
2. Opening statements, introductory remarks, by the opposing attorneys
3. Presentation of the plaintiff's case by examination of witnesses
4. Cross-examination of the plaintiff's witnesses by the defendant's attorney
5. Presentation of the defendant's case by examination of witnesses
6. Cross-examination of the defendant's witnesses by the plaintiff's attorney
7. Plaintiff's rebuttal
8. Defendant's rejoinder, rebuttal
9. Closing arguments, statements
10. Instructions to the jury (if a jury trial)
11. Verdict—by a judge or by a jury

## DAMAGES

The complaint filed in the court of jurisdiction contained a "prayer for relief"—a demand for judgment for the plaintiff and for some form of relief. Usually this is in the form of *damages*. The terms "injuries" and "damages" are frequently used interchangeably; however, in the context of malpractice there is a distinct difference in meaning for these two terms. Patients sustain damage. They sue for damages. Damages is the amount of monetary compensation that the plaintiff claims from a defendant for injuries (damage) received at the hands of the defendant. It is the amount of money that the court awards when a judgment is entered for the plaintiff or which is received in an out-of-court settlement. The primary purpose of awarding damages is to compensate the injured party, to attempt to restore him or her to his or her original status or condition insofar as is possible. There is no intent to punish the defendant by awarding compensatory (*general* and *special*) damages. That is the purpose of *punitive* damages.

## Types of Damages

There are three types of damages that may be awarded in malpractice cases. These are (1) general, (2) special, and (3) punitive.

### General

Also called "soft" damages, general damages are inherent in the injury per se. They are the natural and direct result of the defendant's negligence. These include physical pain and suffering—past, present, and future—and any permanent disability and/or disfigurement deriving from the injury.

### Special

Also called "hard" damages, special damages actually have been, or are most likely to be incurred but not necessarily *directly* from the defendant's negligence. These may represent financial or economic losses and include such costs as medical bills, charges for hospitalization, treatments, rehabilitation, and medications. Included here are loss of income—past, present, and future—and funeral expenses.

### Punitive

Punitive or "exemplary" damages may be sought to *punish* the defendant for the egregious nature of an act that the court has deemed malicious, grossly negligent, or wanton. The defendant's act will be the primary focal point in a consideration of such an award, and the plaintiff will be charged with demonstrating that the defendant's conduct warrants punitive damages. A nurse may be seen to have committed very serious errors in judgment or to have failed very badly in the standard of care; however, it is rare that a charge of nursing malpractice would result from gross negligence—a willful, reckless, and malicious act that would warrant an award of punitive damages.

Punitive damages are typically awarded in amounts double or treble those of other damages already imposed. Although they have been relatively uncommon in malpractice cases, there has been an evident increase in the number of such awards over the past several years. Punitive damages have particular significance to a nurse because they are virtually *never covered* by a malpractice insurance policy.

The practitioner should not be surprised to find direct correlation between the amount of damages claimed and the limits of his or her malpractice insurance coverage. Any claims for damages beyond the amount of coverage typically requires the patient's attorney to prove justification for punitive damages. This is rare, as most damage claims fall well within policy limits. If punitive damages are awarded, they are not covered by malpractice insurance and must be paid out of personal funds. Claims for punitive damages often include allegations of fraud or malicious intent to harm. (Lobb, Riley, and Clemens 1994, 4)

In March 1998, the United States Supreme Court (in *Kawaauhau et vir. v. Geiger* [97–115] 113 F3d848, affirmed) eased the way for physicians and others (including nurses) who lose malpractice or personal injury lawsuits to escape damage judgments by filing for bankruptcy. In a unanimous decision, written by Justice Ginsburg, the Court affirmed that malpractice damage judgments can be discharged through bankruptcy unless the defendant intentionally caused an injury. The decision resolved diverging opinions among lower courts where, in some instances, a claimant was allowed to collect from a bankrupt debtor who intended to perform some negligent act that resulted in injury, even if the debtor did not intend to cause a specific injury.

Justice Ginsburg wrote:

The word "willful" . . . modifies the word "injury," indicating that nondischargeabilty takes a deliberate or intentional injury, not merely a deliberate or intentional act that leads to injury. Had Congress meant to exempt debts resulting from unintentionally inflicted injuries, it might have described instead "willful acts that cause injury." Or, Congress might have selected an additional word or words, i.e., "reckless" or "negligent," to modify "injury." Moreover, as the Eighth Circuit observed, the (a)(6) formulation triggers in the lawyer's mind the category "intentional torts," as distinguished from negligent or reckless torts. Intentional torts generally require that actor intend "the consequences of an act," not simply "the act itself." (Restatement [Second] of Torts §8A, comment a, p.15 [1964])

## REFERENCE

Lobb, Michael L., Gary C. Riley, and April M. Clemens. 1994. The legal nurse consultant's role on the defense team in a medical malpractice lawsuit. *Network* 5 (4) (April): 3–7.

# 7

# Surviving Notification of a Nursing Malpractice Lawsuit

## THE NURSE AND THE LEGAL PROCESS

A nurse can be involved in the legal process in several different ways—as:

- defendant;
- expert witness for either side;
- consulting expert for either side;
- witness to facts;
- plaintiff;
- member of a jury;
- nurse-attorney; and
- nurse paralegal.

## THE NURSE AS DEFENDANT

Practitioners who have an understanding of the basic principles and doctrines of law, the legal process, and what will be expected of them in the event that they are named as defendants in a malpractice suit will be much better prepared for the anxiety involved in what can be a long, frustrating, and tedious experience. Being named as a defendant in a lawsuit can be a very stressful experience; the uncertainties of being led into and through the labyrinth of the legal system can compound the stress.

The nurse-defendant's attorney will define the direction and course of the proceedings from the outset. Knowing precisely where you are at any given time and what lies ahead on the route—the detours and the obstacles—will make the journey much easier. Make your lawyer your team partner, your collaborator, and your guide.

The defense attorney you may be required to retain personally, or who will be appointed by your malpractice insurance company, is called your "attorney of record". You have a right to review the qualifications and experience of any attorney assigned to you. You should demand an attorney who is most competent, experienced, and qualified to handle your case.

An insurance company has a great deal at stake in any malpractice claim, and it is to the company's advantage to employ only those attorneys whose credentials and litigation experience will protect them from exposure to financial loss or minimize such loss. That attorney has a legal duty to act in your best interests as well as those of the insurer. Your interests, however, should be his or her priority. If you feel that the attorney has not defined that priority, you have the right to request another attorney. If it would ultimately be shown that the attorney failed to represent you adequately, or in some way was deficient in protecting your interests, you could have legal recourse in a malpractice lawsuit against that attorney.

The attorney should contact you within several weeks to set up an appointment for an initial conference. Make the appointment as soon as possible. At the initial meeting, ask the attorney to review your mutual expectations and duties and outline what you may expect to happen. Request an overview of the applicable law, the proposed case strategy, and a tentative timetable. At that time, you should be given an opportunity to review and discuss the complaint so that you may identify any claims that you consider false or inaccurate.

From the outset, you must provide your attorney with your full cooperation. It is essential that he or she be apprised of *all* facts relevant to the charges against you. It is essential that he or she know everything that could be of value in preparing a defense for your case. From your initial meeting to the final resolution of the case you must be completely honest with your counsel. This includes any and all relevant personal facts about yourself, including any prior criminal convictions or civil judgments against you. All potentially damaging information must be divulged before it is discovered by the opposing side and used against you. You can lie to your physician, you can lie to your clergyman, but *never lie to your attorney*!

You must have no hesitancy about revealing the most intimate, or even damning, information to your attorney if it is in any way relevant to the charges against you. All such communication with your lawyer is considered by law as *privileged*; and, therefore, *not discoverable* by the opposing side. Never try to second-guess your attorney!

You may not be able to remember any or all of the details surrounding the alleged incident of malpractice, but a review of the medical record will refresh your memory on these. All other relevant information you can provide to your attorney must be as complete and accurate as possible. Propose any other possible causes of the alleged injury other than your alleged negligence. Suggest possible expert witnesses who may be able to support your defense.

An integral part of preparation is an assessment of the strengths and weaknesses of the case as a means of planning an appropriate defense strategy. Under no circumstances can you or your attorney permit the opposition the advantage of knowing more than you do. You are an integral part of your defense team. You will be required to—expected to—play an active role in your defense. A deliberate failure to do so could immediately void your malpractice insurance coverage and remove your appointed attorney from your case!

## The Role of the Nurse as a Defendant

The nurse-defendant must effectively assume the role of defendant and not completely relinquish his or her interests to the attorney. Defending yourself against a malpractice lawsuit requires a collaborative, informed, and dedicated effort on your part, and vigorous ongoing participation in your defense team. The role and responsibilities of the nurse as a defendant are shown in Table 7.1.

**Table 7.1**
**The Role and Responsibilities of the Nurse-Defendant**

- Become *your own best* defense, resource, and advocate
- Assume your role as an active member of a defense *team*
- Participate in, monitor, and understand the process
- Make your efforts and contributions valuable—and valued
- Confirm that you are interested and cooperative
- Keep informed of all facts, issues, and events
- Ask relevant questions and insist on intelligible answers
- Make yourself accessible to your attorney at all times

- Request that your attorney be accessible to you as necessary
- Check on the progress of the lawsuit at reasonable intervals
- Verify that your case is proceeding as expeditiously as possible
- Confirm that your defense is in the hands of a competent attorney
- Verify that your attorney is aggressively pursuing your best interests
- Educate your attorney about nursing standards and procedures
- Prepare a list of authoritative references relevant to the case
- Copy articles, prepare a read file, do your homework
- Review the medical record in detail
- Prepare and provide your notes, your memories, of the alleged event and provide your written or dictated notes to your attorney *only*
- Compile a list of possible expert witnesses to support your case
- Be receptive to any overtures regarding an out-of-court settlement

## WHAT TO DO IF YOU ARE SUED

In the event that you notified that a lawsuit has been filed naming you as a defendant, you should take certain steps immediately.

- If you are covered by a personal malpractice insurance policy, notify your insurance carrier *immediately*.
- Document this notification in some way (e.g., certified mail).
- Read your insurance policy for specific instructions and follow these *precisely* regarding defined time frames and procedures of notification. Failure to do so could *void* your policy.
- If applicable, notify your employer immediately. Contact the risk manager *only*.
- Set up your own personal file. Secure this file, and *never* reveal its existence to anyone but your attorney.
- Meet with your attorney as soon as possible. Insist on this!

## WHAT *NOT* TO DO IF YOU ARE SUED

The news that a lawsuit has been filed against you is likely to be a very stressful experience. In a stage of confusion, frustration, and anger, a defendant can become immobilized or take various irrational and self-damaging actions. The following suggestions are made to help avoid making things worse than they might appear to be.

- Do *not* attempt to avoid service of process. This could prove very detrimental to your case.
- Do not ignore the lawsuit. A *judgment by default* might be entered against you.

- As a general rule, *do not discuss the matter with anyone* other than your attorney.
- *Never* discuss the lawsuit with your co-workers. (Anything you say could be used against you later.)
- *Never contact the plaintiff*, the plaintiff's family, or the plaintiff's attorney. Do not accept any overtures for such contacts and inform your attorney of any attempts.
- Without the knowledge and consent of your attorney, do not surrender any notes, documents, or records of any kind to the plaintiff or to the plaintiff's attorney.
- As a general rule, it should not be necessary for you to consult your personal, family attorney. This will incur a needless expense. His or her services should not be necessary if an attorney of record has or will be appointed for you. Your personal attorney may be of some help in pointing you in the right direction at the outset but will not be included in the proceedings unless you elect to retain (and pay) him or her yourself.
- Do not let the allegations and their implications immobilize you in what may be a time of crisis mentality.
- Do *not not do* anything.

# 8

# Preparing for and Surviving a Deposition and a Trial

## DEPOSITION PROCEDURES AND PROTOCOLS

Prior to the actual deposition date, a nurse-defendant (or nurse expert witness) should meet with the attorney to begin preparing for the experience. There are several points that should be reviewed.

- Exactly what will be your role in the proceedings?
- What will be expected of you?
- What can you expect?
- Who will participate in the deposition?
- Will the plaintiff be present?
- What types of questions can be asked?
- Who will ask the questions?
- What is the examining attorney like?
- Where will the deposition take place?
- How long might it last?
- In testifying, what should you be wary of; what can cause problems?
- Will the attorney be able to coach or help you in any way during the deposition?

Witnesses other than adverse parties in a suit must, as a general rule, be subpoenaed. Parties usually attend after some form of notice and without service of subpoena. A nurse who is requested to testify at a deposition as a fact (material) witness is not required to do so and has the right to demand a subpoena, which is the only legal recourse to force compliance with such a request. If a subpoena is issued, the prospective witness is then required, under penalty of law, to appear for the deposition.

At a deposition the individual who presents testimony (the deponent) can represent either side. This individual may be a defendant, a witness to the facts (material witness), an expert witness, or the custodian of relevant documents. The proceedings are basically a very structured process of examination and cross-examination. The ground rules will be presented to each witness at the outset of the proceedings. Everyone present will be identified for the record.

The deponent is placed under oath, and all statements made are recorded by an official court reporter or other stenographer, or by any individual legally authorized to administer an oath and take such testimony. The locale is usually the office of the attorney who requested the deposition. The procedure is the same for parties, witnesses to facts, and expert witnesses.

Well in advance of the actual date of the deposition, the plaintiff's attorney will have subpoenaed all records and materials relevant to the lawsuit, including any materials in the hands of the defendant. It is essential, therefore, that a nurse named as defendant does not take any personal notes, memos, diaries, or any such written or taped information to the deposition. This would make them discoverable by the plaintiff's attorney, and they could be used as evidence against the nurse. All documents or other materials in the nurse's hands must be prescreened to identify any privilege that might apply to them. Any such materials should have been given directly to the attorney as soon as possible, thus making them attorney's work product and nondiscoverable. At the deposition the examining attorney may ask you if you have kept any personal journals, diaries, or anecdotal records. Under oath, you must confirm that you have or have not done so.

With the approval of your attorney, you can take anything to the deposition that you both agree will be helpful; however, anything you do bring might be identified by the examining attorney as an exhibit and retained for possible later use in court. If you are directed to bring documents of any kind and refer to them in answering questions, copies must be given to the opposing attorney.

Each side will have a copy of the plaintiff's medical record at hand. When questioned about a specific fact contained in the medical record, the nurse should refer directly to the record and not attempt to answer from memory. The necessity of the defendant reviewing the medical record thoroughly before deposition and again before trial cannot be overemphasized.

The procedures of the deposition anticipate those of a trial. As a general rule, the attorney who requested the deposition will begin the examination and will propose most of the questions to the deponent, whose own attorney will object as necessary. The lawyers for each side will conduct a direct examination of the deponent, and each side will have the opportunity to cross-examine.

The questions that can be asked of the deponent may be very specific, very personal, or very general. At times the questions may seem completely irrelevant to the issues. Much wider latitude is allowed in a deposition than in a courtroom, and the scope and intensity of the questions can be much broader. The questions asked at a deposition are not limited by the same rules of admissibility of evidence as those in testimony at a trial. Therefore, virtually any relevant question may be asked, including any that might lead to additional discoverable evidence. A nurse-defendant may be asked to assist in preparing questions for the plaintiff.

A deponent is not required to answer each and every question. However, any question that is deemed relevant to the issues in the case should be answered. These can include questions that might not be admissible in a trial. You can invoke the Fifth Amendment and refuse to answer any question that you consider self-incriminating. Should you have already answered a question pertaining to the same topic, you may have forfeited the right to claim the Fifth Amendment when succeeding, relevant, questions are presented to you.

Your attorney will be present to advise you and to object to any questions that he or she considers self-incriminating, ambiguous, vague, confusing, or irrelevant. Attorneys are required by law to preserve your legal rights and maintain your best interests. A deponent can invoke lawyer-client privilege and cannot be required to answer any questions that derive from communications with his or her attorney. These are considered privileged and confidential and the content or nature of these communications is not discoverable. Ultimately a judge and only a judge, in a court of law, can direct that a witness must answer a question.

The deposition can be an adversarial encounter for all participants. The attorneys endeavor to learn if there is anything a deponent is trying to cover up or hold back. In this effort they may resort to browbeating, insinuation, derision, accusation, and insult. Any tactic may be attempted in an effort to reduce a deponent to a state of confusion and contradiction. There is no personal motive in this behavior. The attorney is simply doing what is required to obtain information. He or she has the right to examine or cross-examine a deponent. A deponent may not like the attorney, the line of questions, or the tactics used, but this is no reason to become overtly hostile toward the attorney. Evoking such behavior by a deponent simply makes the attorney's task easier.

The lawyer for either side is going to probe and press each deponent in an attempt to find weaknesses. If the individual can be controlled in a deposition, he or she might be controlled to advantage in a courtroom to make or break a case.

### The Deposition Transcript

Each deponent has the opportunity to review the transcript of his or her testimony and clarify, correct, or expand on any of the answers. The recorder of the deposition testimony will forward a copy of the complete transcript to each attorney who in turn should provide the appropriate deponents with a copy. Read it very carefully making separate notes as you go. Rules vary by state regarding changes and/or additions that can be made to a transcript. You cannot change an answer, but you may correct any portions of the transcript that you believe to have been misunderstood or mistranscribed by the recorder. Your comments or corrections must not be made anywhere on the transcript; convey your thoughts to your attorney verbally or by confidential memo. Any corrections must be made on the forms that may accompany the transcript. When you and your attorney have agreed that the transcript is accurate, you will sign it and remit it and the accompanying forms with comments and corrections to the deposition recorder.

You should retain a copy of these documents for your personal file. If the lawsuit should proceed to trial, you can expect to be asked many of the very same questions that are detailed in the transcript of your deposition. You can also expect to be presented with any number of additional questions that may have been derived from the transcript—from what was asked and from what was not asked. A competent trial lawyer will carefully review the transcript both to develop and to anticipate answering such questions. You should have advance knowledge and preparation for such surprises.

### THE EXPERT WITNESS AT A DEPOSITION

The nurse who testifies at a deposition or a trial as an expert witness can expect the opposing counsel to ask questions that are designed to discredit the "expert" credentials of the witness or to confirm that the nurse is truly an expert, and then weigh his or her expertise and credibility against his or her own testifying experts. Questions will be rephrased or repeated to elicit inconsistencies or contradictions. An attempt will be made to show that the *expert* witness is an expert *witness*, a *professional witness*. It is the testifying expert's role to educate the attorneys, the judge, and the jury while not sounding pompous, condescending, or overly pedantic. An expert witness should *never* address a subject or issue that is outside his or her area of experience and expertise. The role of the expert witness will be discussed in more detail in chapter 15. The topics of the questions the expert witness can expect are shown in Table 8.1.

**Table 8.1**
**Questions That May Be Addressed to an Expert Witness**

- General personal information
- Educational background
- Employment history
- Professional clinical nursing experience, particularly in the area of the alleged malpractice
- Membership in professional organizations
- Experience in presenting lectures, seminars, and workshops
- Authorship of published or unpublished works
- Prior experience testifying as an expert witness
- Fees that have been received for such services
- Authoritative sources that witness will cite
- Standards of nursing care
- Opinions on breaches in standards of nursing care
- Opinions on cause of alleged injury
- Various hypothetical questions, situations, scenarios
- History of any adverse action by a state board of nursing
- Defendant in civil or criminal lawsuit
- Prior judgments or convictions

## PREPARING FOR A DEPOSITION

Knowing what to expect is the best preparation for a deposition. Proper preparation will give the witness the necessary confidence to survive the ordeal. An experienced malpractice litigation attorney will be invaluable in this respect. Trial lawyers who specialize in malpractice frequently find themselves sitting across the table from a familiar professional opponent, and they remember his or her temperament, tactics, abilities, and successes. Your attorney, in formatting the best possible case, should allow some time to provide you with a coaching session. The attorney can do this personally, or it can be done by a nurse litigation consultant collaborating with the attorney on the case.

He or she will be able to anticipate the nature and generally the content of the questions that could be asked by the opposing side and be best able to educate and prepare you. These are the same or similar questions they would want to ask and are likely to have asked in numerous cases in the past. The attorney may propose a mock deposition in which he or she assumes the role of the opposing counsel who will examine you. Some attorneys feel that an extensive predeposition review of case materials may not be helpful to a deponent, or that a mock deposition may make their client's responses sound overly rehearsed.

Begin to prepare yourself by carefully reading a copy of the medical record and making your own chronological summation and interpretive notes. As you do this, try to anticipate any possible questions. Unless you are given a working copy, do not write any notes or comments in the record itself. Any such information included in the record in any way could make it discoverable and your own notations could be used against you. Any such annotations or comments should be labeled as attorney's work product and should be retained by your attorney to prevent discovery.

## THE DEPOSITION

The nurse-defendant's experiences, responses, expectations, and the impressions made at a deposition can be described in four scenarios: (1) answering questions, (2) interacting with the examining attorney, (3) collaborating with his or her own attorney, and (4) his or her personal deportment and appearance.

Remember, your attorney will be present. He or she will guide and support you. Your attorney cannot answer for you, but can tell you when you should not answer by objecting to any question deemed inappropriate. It is your right to consult your attorney at any time for direction, explanation, or clarification. This must be a team effort.

## SURVIVAL TACTICS FOR THE DEPONENT

For a deponent to survive a deposition, he or she should follow the ABCs and a D.

## A. Answering

- Tell the *truth* and convey that idea in each response.
- *Never lie*! Remember that you are under oath. *Lying under oath is perjury*—a felony, a *crime*.
- Each answer must be as truthful and as accurate as possible.
- Do not attempt to distort or hide the facts; this could impeach your credibility and severely compromise your defense.
- Be sincere, open, and forthright at all times.
- Do not equivocate or try to manipulate the facts in such a way as to present yourself or your case in a more favorable light.
- *Never admit any liability or blame*!
- *Never mention that an incident report was prepared.*
- Make no attempt to justify your actions or decisions, or propose your rationale for them.
- Offer no excuses for any of your actions.
- Unless asked, do not mention the names of any other persons.
- Never blame or accuse others.
- Do not make denigrating remarks about others.
- Do not make prejudicial comments of any kind.
- Do not try to evade a question or change the subject.
- Make each answer as positive as possible.
- Do not state dates, times, or any other facts or data unequivocally if you are not absolutely certain of them. Avoid such words as "always" and "never".
- *Do not give an opinion* in answer to a question unless you have been deposed as an expert witness.
- If specific facts are requested, answer only to the extent of your direct knowledge of such facts.
- Do not substantially change an answer without good reason.
- Qualify, explain, or expand an answer only if it is absolutely necessary.
- Avoid such qualifying statements as "maybe", "possibly", "if", "perhaps", "to tell the truth", "honestly", "I think", "might have", and other such vague phrases.
- Do not speculate, theorize, or hypothesize.
- *Never make assumptions.*
- *Never guess!*

- If you are asked to approximate, estimate, or guess, phrase your response so that it is clearly qualified as such.

- State directly if you do not know an answer or that you do not remember. Say: "I do not know" or "I do not remember". These are acceptable, truthful, and appropriate answers.

- Never say *what* you do *not* know.

- Answer the question asked and only that question.

- Do not give the opposing attorney more information than is required by the question. Doing so could provide ideas for a new line of questioning.

- Do not volunteer any information. The whole purpose of the deposition is to make the examining attorney "discover" the facts.

- Make the examining attorney ask questions.

- You are not there to educate the examining attorney or present him or her with any advantage.

- Do not fall into the "pregnant pause" trap. If the examining attorney reacts to your answer with a long expectant silence, ignore it.

- Answer each question in as few words as possible. The best answer is the briefest, most direct. A succinct "yes" or "no" is usually adequate and always advisable.

- Be direct and to the point in answering each question.

- Each answer should be as concise and as unambiguous as possible.

- Do not respond to a question with any information or data of which you do not have firsthand knowledge.

- You can provide hearsay information if this is requested but only if it is clearly identified as such.

- Do not attempt to answer until the attorney has finished the question.

- Confirm to yourself that you fully understand the question before attempting to answer it.

- Do not allow yourself to be pressured or rushed in answering.

- Do not let the examining attorney force a "yes" or "no" answer; say what you must say to answer the question completely.

- Take as much time as you need to formulate your response.

- Pause for a moment or two before answering. This provides your attorney time to object to a question that may be inappropriate.

- An objection is your signal to immediately stop answering a question.

- If a question is ambiguous or unclear, ask that it be clarified, repeated, or rephrased. You do not have to say why.

- If the question is long, convoluted, complex, or compound, request that it be simplified. You do not have to say why.

- Do not anticipate questions. You may be reasonably certain of what is going to be asked next. Wait until it is asked.

- If the examining attorney attempts to cut you off, affirm that you have not finished speaking, and continue your answer.

- If he or she persists, remain silent and wait for your own attorney to present the question to you again in their examination.

- Correct what you believe to be any errors in facts stated by opposing counsel.

- Respectfully challenge any erroneous assumptions.

- Be alert for a series of leading questions in quick succession.

- Be alert for hypothetical questions; these are for the expert witness only, not the fact witness.

- Do not answer questions by gestures or by nodding or shaking your head. All responses must be oral, audible, and clear so that they can be accurately recorded in the transcript.

- Avoid the use of slang, jargon, idioms; use proper grammar.

- Do not rely on your memory; it may lead to errors or contradictions.

- Utilize the medical record and any other resources as necessary.

- Take your time in finding any document you need.

- If you must use medical or scientific terms, be sure you use the correct term in the correct context.

- You may be asked to spell such terms—be prepared.

- Ask to examine any document that opposing counsel refers to in framing a question.

- If you are given documents or other items to examine or identify, do so very carefully before answering any questions.

- If you have been deposed and are testifying as a nurse expert witness, do not readily accept the opposition's cited authors as the sole authorities on the subject.

## B. Bandying, Badgering, and Browbeating

- Do not be intimidated. Take control!

- Keep your wits about you.

- Do your best to maintain your self-control.

- Do not get excited or upset.

- Try very hard not to loose your temper and become visibly angry.

- Do not let yourself become sarcastic, testy, or irritable.
- The opposing attorney may do his or her utmost to rattle you and provoke you. This is a test to see how well you will stand up in a courtroom before a jury.
- Stay calm.
- You will be challenged; do not react in kind.
- Maintain your composure, even when being blatantly provoked.
- Be assertive but not aggressive.
- Do not take an overly offensive or defensive stance.
- Defend yourself, your dignity, and your rights.
- Confirm that you will not be bullied or intimidated.
- Be extremely cautious of overly agreeing with the examining attorney.
- Do not become inordinately friendly with the opposing attorney. Remember this person is an adversary. He or she is not your personal enemy but is not your friend.
- Be polite, courteous, and respectful.
- Look directly at the attorney when you are being asked a question and when answering.
- *Never argue.* You can not win. You can challenge, dispute, or disregard, but do not allow yourself to be drawn into an argument. The deposition must not turn into a battle of wits or egos. Remember, this is not a platform for debate. The experienced trial attorney has an undeniable edge here.
- Play to beat the attorney at his or her own game.
- Do not make it easy for him or her!

### C.  Collaboration and Communication

- As a general rule, never sit beside your attorney when being questioned.
- Request that you be seated so that your attorney is directly in your view.
- Do not turn and look to your attorney for help in answering a question. He or she cannot do this in a deposition or a trial.
- A deponent is expected to answer each question spontaneously as best as he or she can, and in his or her own words.
- Constantly looking toward your attorney may prompt a criticism or a challenge from the examining attorney, who may accuse you of uncertainty, lack of conviction, lack of self-confidence, or of hiding something.
- Stop speaking immediately whenever your attorney interjects.
- Listen very carefully to any objection being made by your attorney. It may provide clues to an appropriate answer.

- As necessary, you can write notes to your attorney, or quietly ask questions while sitting at the table.

- Do not communicate with your attorney when someone else—attorney or deponent—is speaking.

- It is not advisable to ask your attorney questions or make any statements regarding the case that could be overheard by opposing counsel or by any one else.

## D.  Deportment

- Maintain your self-control at all times.

- Remember: It is *your* deposition!

- Be honest and credible.

- Be positive.

- Present yourself as a professional at all times.

- Look and act confident.

- Exude competence.

- Be cordial, polite, and civil throughout the proceedings.

- Try to be as relaxed as possible.

- Do not embellish or exaggerate.

- Do not emote—no hyperbole, theatrics, histrionics.

- Never allow yourself to appear weak, apologetic, repentant.

- Do not play for sympathy. You will get none of it here.

- Do not whine or complain.

- Do not appear cavalier, blasé, or overly casual.

- Do not surrender under a salvo of interrogation.

- Be organized, come prepared.

- Be knowledgeable, but do not be pedantic. Unless you are an expert witness, you are not there to teach.

- Try not to sound "rehearsed", "coached", or "canned".

- Speak only when spoken to during your examination.

- As a general rule, do not interrupt another.

- Speak slowly, clearly, and loud enough for all present to hear you.

- Stop speaking when your attorney or opposing counsel begins speaking (unless the latter is interrupting you).

- Your body language will speak volumes about you. Always be aware of your posture, movements, and facial expressions. Do not testify with your arms crossed. This could indicate a defensive, hostile posture.

- Make yourself as comfortable as possible before you start.
- Sit up straight; sit still.
- You may hold something in your hand, but hold it still.
- Avoid touching yourself or your clothing unnecessarily or too frequently.
- Do not look at your watch; this can convey the impression of impatience.
- Do not try to be amusing, tell jokes, or quip. This is not the time for it.
- Make a best effort to appear very interested even when the proceedings may become very boring.
- Remain alert and attentive, particularly when you are being questioned or when another deponent is testifying.
- You may look around during pauses but always keep your gaze up.
- Do not sit staring abjectly at the table or at the floor.
- Do not allow yourself to be intimidated by the presence of the plaintiff and/or the plaintiff's family. They may have been instructed to sit in your line of sight and stare hostilely at you.

### Deponent's Personal Appearance

How a witness presents him- or herself can make a favorable or unfavorable impression in a videotaped deposition or live—before a jury. The witness should:

- Appear neat and well groomed;
- dress for and act the role of a professional;
- wear conservative, comfortable clothing;
- not wear excess or oversized jewelry; and
- not reek of perfume or aftershave lotion.

## THE TRIAL

In the absence of a settlement, the day might eventually come when the nurse-defendant may be faced with the demands of appearing and testifying at a trial. This is the final personal step in what may have been a long ordeal. This day may never come, or if it comes it may end very abruptly. However, the nurse must be prepared.

### Preparation for a Trial

The prospect of a trial presents some new challenges and new learning needs. Prior to the actual date of the trial, there are a number of things you, as a defendant, should do. Some of these you can do alone, others you will do in collaboration with your attorney.

Request that you have an opportunity to meet with your attorney at a convenient time, and for a reasonable number of times, to discuss the case to that point and the implications of the impending trial. Discuss the strategy and any possible defenses he or she proposes to use in your behalf. To prevent inadvertent disclosure, the attorney may decline to reveal a plan to you. Ask for an honest appraisal of your situation—the weaknesses as well as the strengths of your case. During the meeting, ask for a brief outline of the court proceedings—what you can expect, what will be expected of you. This is also a good time to discuss the possibility of a settlement.

Much of this preparation will be a review of documents and records that you should have examined previously in preparation for the deposition. Re-examine the complaint, the medical record, and all other documents relevant to the case. Refresh your memory on the details, the facts, and the allegations. Make copious notes, but be sure that only you and your attorney have access to them. If you have not already done so, prepare a detailed, chronological summary of all the events surrounding the alleged incident. If this has already been done, review it carefully and add any additional information as necessary.

Read the transcript of the deposition, particularly your testimony. Review a videotape of the mock deposition and/or trial that your attorney may have conducted. Study your performance, and critique yourself objectively. Identify those mannerisms or speech patterns that might be considered distracting should you have to take the stand in court. Make an effort to correct these. Rehearse, but try not to show it. Your testimony should not sound memorized or "canned".

### Conduct of a Witness During a Trial

Virtually all of the suggestions and cautions that have been made previously regarding a deposition apply to the conduct of a witness in a courtroom. If you have survived the deposition and learned from it, you are reasonably prepared to face the trial. The protocols and procedures of a trial are different from those of a deposition. The examining attorney may be more constrained by courtroom etiquette, rules of evidence, and other procedural laws, and may appear less aggressive here.

There are several other differences you need be aware of in testifying in a courtroom.

- You should have carefully reviewed your deposition transcript to confirm your answers to previous questions and avoid contradictions.

- Listen very carefully to the opening statements of each attorney.

- When answering a question in the courtroom, direct your response to the jury or, if it is not a jury trial, to the judge.

- Look at each member of the panel as you speak.

- Try to observe any subtle clues as to which jurors may be sympathetic. Focus on them. Win them over.

- During the times you are not testifying, maintain your appearance of interest, alertness, and confidence.

- When other witnesses are testifying, study them and the jury's reaction to their testimony.

- You may speak quietly to your lawyer, but do not do so when another witness or attorney is speaking, and *never* do so when the judge is speaking.

- *Under no circumstances should you or any of the parties speak to a member of the jury outside of the courtroom.* This is immediate cause for a *mistrial*.

- As a general rule, do not discuss the case with anyone beyond the confines of the courtroom.

# 9

# Defensive Documentation

## NURSING DOCUMENTATION AS A RISK MANAGEMENT STRATEGY

Defensive charting is one of the best ways to protect any health care provider from exposure to legal liability. *Chart with a jury in mind*! Careful and complete documentation of nurses' progress notes is a principal method of reducing the risk of liability in nursing malpractice lawsuits. They may sustain or preclude a suit for negligence from the outset. They may support or undermine the nurse-defendant before a jury in the event of a trial. In a negligence suit, nursing documentation will be as critical a factor as the nursing care itself. A nurse's notes should provide answers to questions at issue in a lawsuit. They should not prompt more questions or raise additional issues. Poorly written notes can be a veritable gold mine for the patient-plaintiff's attorney.

The presumption in law may be that if an event is not documented, it did not take place, and if it is not written in the record, the nurse did not do it (or even consider doing it). The maxim familiar to every student nurse and practicing nurse is: "If it was not charted, it was not done." This is frequently a contentious issue in malpractice litigation. It is a misconception that should be rejected as unrealistic—as an unattainable performance or unreasonable demand made on a nurse. In a deposition, or in court, however, the plaintiff's attorney (and their *nurse* expert witnesses) may make every possible attempt to convince a jury of the literal truth of this assertion. The defendant's attorney will endeavor to show that, although there may be an apparent omission, the action in question was the nurse's "usual practice", which routinely need not be documented.

Nurses cannot possibly function as court reporters or stenographers, transcribing the minute details of every event or conversation. However, if a nurse-defendant's notes do not corroborate his or her testimony, the nurse-defendant will be challenged to persuade the jury to accept as credible his or her version of the events surrounding the alleged negligence. Regardless of the sworn testimony, the written entries in the medical record will serve as the definitive statement of what actually transpired.

### Objectives of Documentation

There are two principal objectives for documentation of patient care. The first is to communicate to all members of the health care team essential information regarding the patient's history, present status, response to care, prognosis, and the nature and extent of care required, provided, and anticipated. The increasing trend in specialization has created opportunities for assessment, treatment, and care by a variety of nurses, physicians, and other professionals. It is essential that each health care provider be aware of the findings, opinions, actions, and recommendations of others.

The second objective is to protect each of these many team members from the risk of legal liability or mitigate that risk as far as possible.

### NURSES' NOTES

To accomplish defensive documentation, each nurse's note should incorporate certain objectives and elements, follow a generally prescribed format, and utilize an acceptable quality and style of writing. When corrections or addenda are necessary, certain guidelines should be followed consistently.

### Objectives of Nurses' Notes

Nurses' notes should incorporate as many of the following objectives as possible.

- Confirmation of the type, extent, and quality of care that is provided in each patient care assignment—the nursing process

- Evaluation and verification of patient responses to, and outcomes of, nursing interventions
- Affirmation that such care meets the acceptable standards of nursing care and that the nurse's interventions were safe and therapeutic
- Demonstration of legal and professional responsibility and accountability and conformity with all applicable statutes, rules, and regulations
- Protection of the rights of all parties involved
- Interdisciplinary communication of all significant information in order to coordinate and facilitate continuity of care
- Compilation of data for continuing application in risk management, quality assurance, research, care planning, case management, discharge planning, fiscal administration, and the education of students and peers

### Essential Elements of Nurses' Notes

An acceptable nurse's note should include several essential elements.

- Current, complete, and accurate information that reflects a continuing assessment of the patient's status and progress
- Pertinent and significant data; exclusion of trivia
- Identification of actual and potential needs and concerns of the patient—physical, psychological, social, and spiritual
- A description of nursing interventions addressing those needs
- The patient's response to the nursing interventions
- Confirmation of continuity of care
- Patient teaching

The exact content of patient teaching during the course of hospitalization is highly variable, and would be prescribed by the individual's diagnosis, medical and nursing regimens, constant changes in status, identified learning needs, and many other factors. Discharge teaching can be more significant from a legal aspect, and is detailed later, in Table 9.2.

### General Format of Nurses' Notes

In addition to the essential elements outlined previously, a nurse's note should include several other characteristics and components that can add to its clarity, utility, and effectiveness as a defense in any potential liability. Every note should be as descriptive as possible and include complete, accurate, and appropriate patient data. This information must be as objective as possible. There should be little or no subjective commentary. Where a subjective statement is indicated it should be supported by observed facts, direct quotes, or accurately paraphrased statements of the patient or another reliable source.

The nurse must be cautious in making unfounded conclusions or assumptions, or in offering personal opinions. Conclusory statements such as "normal", "fine", "good", "well", "assume", "seems to", "appears to be", or the cliché "in no acute distress" should be avoided. Such statements are vague and ambiguous. Any such judgments must be accompanied by supporting facts or data present elsewhere in the medical record. The language of the notes must be as concise and clear as possible. Brevity is ideal. Clarity is essential.

There must be no attempt to keep any secrets. Include all of the facts, and let them speak for themselves. Do not attempt to put any "spin" on them, downplay them, or manipulate them in a self-serving way. The nurse must chart everything that is relevant and significant—including errors and omissions. As discussed previously, if it should be determined that a nurse has deliberately attempted a cover-up, this in itself could be the basis for a lawsuit. And if such efforts could be proven to be an attempt at fraud or deliberate deceit, this could have very serious criminal implications, and may extend the statute of limitations indefinitely. There have been many malpractice lawsuits arising from accusations of what a nurse did *not* do. What is *not* in the medical record may be as critical as what is in it. What is omitted, deliberately or inadvertently, can have serious connotations in the event of a malpractice claim.

There must *never* be any language in a note indicating or admitting *liability*—on the writer's part or on anybody's part. No attempt should be made to rationalize or justify one's actions. Do not include such wording as "accident", "accidentally", "incident", "mishap", "error", "unexplained", or "somehow". State the facts as you know them and *only* the facts!

The patient's chart is not a forum for debate. Its primary function is to record the care that the patient received and identify those who provided it. This is not the place to criticize or characterize other members of the health care team. Derogatory remarks, personal comments, unflattering observations, and all other unprofessional language do not belong here. This it not a medium to assign or infer blame, accuse, or incriminate. Personal conflicts, disputes, or petty vendettas must not be aired in the medical record. This is not the proper arena for "chart wars". The chart is not the appropriate means to catalog complaints about short staffing, overwork, or inadequate conditions. A plaintiff's attorney will find a cloth-of-gold among any dirty laundry. When interpersonal conflicts or work-related problems arise, as they surely will, discuss them privately. Do not document them publicly.

## Generally Acceptable Writing Style

Nurses are required to document in accordance with defined standards—for example, those of the ANA, the JCAHO, and the institution itself. Each nurse should endeavor to develop his or her own style of documentation and use it consistently to facilitate quick and accurate charting that can be individualized to each patient. A properly written note, no matter its length, should reflect proper grammar, syntax, and spelling. Slang or jargon should be excluded. If the nurse intends to use medical terminology, it must be the correct terminology.

The events described should be presented in some logical and chronological order. Each new topic should be started on a new line. Each note must be dated and the correct time indicated. Times can be noted under the date or, if a summary note is being written, the progress of events can be shown within the body of the note by indicating the time of each event. A new line for each time and event is preferable. Military time should be used in all medical records where this is permitted by the institution's policy and procedure manual. All dates and times must agree—among documents and throughout the record. Nurses should never chart before the fact. Charting in advance could compromise credibility. Notes should never be backdated.

Ambiguous abbreviations or symbols have been identified as a consistent problem in documentation. Misinterpretation of these has been the cause of many patient injuries and deaths, and the basis for numerous allegations of negligence. All abbreviations must conform to those listed in the institution's policy and procedure manual or, in the absence of such a list, to those included in any authoritative medical dictionary. Any symbol or abbreviation that could possibly be misinterpreted should be eliminated. The general rule is: "When in doubt, write it out."

Handwriting must be legible. Sloppy writing can convey the idea of sloppy patient care. Such apparent laxity will be exploited by the plaintiff's attorney in front of a jury. A nurse-defendant's illegible scrawl will be projected on a screen before a jury and he or she will be asked to decipher it for the benefit of the viewers. If the nurse is not able to read his or her own handwriting or persuade the court of his or her interpretation of it, a question of tidiness of intellect or habits of work may arise in the minds of the jurors.

Every note, flow sheet, medication administration record, or any other document that requires a signature with an entry must have that signature. A nurse should sign legibly with his or her full name and title. Some institutions permit the use of initials for a first name; this is acceptable. However, a full signature is preferable. Initials are acceptable in restricted spaces in the columns of sign-off blocks when a corresponding signature is indicated elsewhere on the document to identify the owner of initials.

There should be no blank spaces, lines, or pages in a progress note. Such spaces can invite "refinements" or "sanitization" in previously written notes. A single line should be drawn through such spaces or large areas can be hatched off. A common practice of nurses is to leave empty lines before their own notes to accommodate another provider's note and preserve the time sequence. This practice should be eliminated. A late entry is much more acceptable and can defuse any questions of manipulating the record. Late entries are discussed in a following section.

### Correcting Entries

It is inevitable that an individual will make a minor error in writing a note or in recording data. It may be the wrong spelling or choice of word or the wrong selection of a chart. Check the name on the chart before opening it and beginning to write anything in it. A common error is pulling a chart according to the patient's room number—a number that can change abruptly during a shift. The nurse must always be aware that even well-intentioned attempts to correct errors could, in the hands of a plaintiff's attorney, damage his or her credibility and impugn all of his or her documentation. From a legal aspect the nurse should observe certain precautions in correcting entries. A number of these are shown in Table 9.1.

**Table 9.1**
**Correcting Entries—Cautions**

- Avoid using the words "error" or "mistake". These might convey the idea of faults in clinical procedures or skills. Use such words as "delete", "void"," disregard", "mistaken entry", "incorrect entry", or "erroneous entry".

- *Never* attempt to erase an entry.

- Do not use correction fluids to provide a new substrate for an entry.

- *Do not obliterate* an entry in any way. Any entry that must be corrected must remain readable and legible.

- Draw a *single line* through an incorrect word or phrase and write the correct information *next* to it on the same line if this is possible. This confirms to the reader that the correction was made at that instant. Otherwise write the correction above the line.

- Revised text placed *above* a lined-out entry might raise a question as to exactly when that modification was inserted into the record. Include the date, time, and your initials.
- A later clarification within the body or at the end of the note, or an addendum in a later progress note, will suffice if there is inadequate space on the line to reflect an afterthought.
- Write any addendum indicating the correct information with a specific reference to the site of the incorrect entry.
- Do not attempt to squeeze lengthy corrections onto or between lines of previously written text.
- Write nothing in the margins.
- It may be necessary to recopy pages of progress notes. Each copy must be identified as such, and all original copies must be identified as such, and *retained* in the medical record.
- Once any document can be considered as an official part of a patient's medical record, it cannot be removed or discarded. In the event of a malpractice lawsuit, a suspicion, and certainly a confirmation, of any missing documents will severely prejudice the defendant's case and may leave him or her open to charges of fraud.

## Late Entries

Nurses should make every effort to avoid unnecessarily long intervals between their entries in the progress notes during a shift. There should be no substantial gaps in the chronology. These could infer neglect or even abandonment. In those many instances when the demands of the day prevent even the most efficient nurse from writing notes coincident with events, or when some significant detail is forgotten, a late entry is acceptable. Provided that the information is clear, complete, and accurate, the fact that it is not recorded contemporaneously with care should not present a problem.

A late entry or one that is not in proper sequence will not come under suspicion unless there is a discernible ulterior motive. Any significant prior omissions phrased and presented as concurrent or new entries could impeach all of the nurse's notes. Late charting could be suspect if there is a pattern evident. If certain individuals habitually write such notes, a question of their competency, integrity, and efficiency might be raised in the event of a lawsuit.

A late entry may be inserted in the medical record within a reasonable time provided a full explanation for the entry is included. Any such entry should be written as soon as possible after the fact and in the first available space in the progress note with a precise reference to the previous place in the notes where it properly belongs. It must include the exact date and times of the events described. It must be clearly identified as a late entry.

### Writing or Signing Notes for Others

The general rule regarding writing a note for another is: *Do not* write a note for another! It is a very risky practice that could leave all parties exposed to legal liability. There may come a time when a nurse inadvertently omits a significant comment from the progress notes to which he or she now has no immediate access. In such an instance, the individual may telephone another staff nurse and request that the dictated note be incorporated into the record as a late entry. The recipient of the request may make the entry provided he or she makes absolutely clear that the recipient did not perform, participate in, or witness the actions described; that the information was dictated, and by whom. The note must be countersigned by the originator as soon as possible thereafter. If a staff nurse is required to chart the care given by an ancillary staff member the notes must provide specific details. Any such notes must make it very clear as to who performed the duties described.

Signing or countersigning a progress note written by another, or a verbal order, attests that the signer read the entry and is verifying that the content is correct. If what they are attesting to is incorrect, they could be held liable in a claim of malpractice. If a nurse has no direct knowledge of the veracity of a note, he or she should not countersign it. If a nurse does sign a note that is seriously deficient or erroneous, he or she could share liability in the event of litigation. Countersigning a note does not necessarily imply that the individual personally performed or witnessed the actions described therein. However, it does affirm that he or she reviewed the content of the note and, by a signature, approved the actions indicated, affirmed that the procedures were carried out and that they were appropriate.

Only those staff authorized by the policy and procedure manual to chart in a medical record should be permitted to do so. The manual may require that a nurse countersign any notes written by ancillary staff (e.g., UAP) where this practice is permitted. Before signing, the staff nurse should read the subordinate's notes very carefully, direct any corrections, revisions, or additions, and then sign it. A countersignature also confirms that the actions of the individual who wrote the note were, in fact, within the scope of practice and that he or she has the proper training and degree of competence required.

## NURSING DIAGNOSES: LEGAL ASPECTS

Nursing diagnoses are defined as those health problems that have the *potential* for resolution by means of *nursing* actions. Patients' nursing problems are defined in terms of nursing diagnoses. They are *not* medical diagnoses, medical treatments, or diagnostic studies. They may not be the problems that a nurse experiences while delivering patient care. They are clinical judgments of those problems that have the potential to be resolved by means of nursing intervention.

From a legal aspect, many nurse practice acts do not address the matter of nurses making such diagnoses. Those that do often fail to define what the term means. For example, the Pennsylvania Nurse Practice Act defines the practice of professional nursing as: "diagnosing and treating human responses to actual or potential health problems. . . . [The] foregoing shall not be deemed to include acts of medical diagnosis or prescription of medical therapy".

*Nursing diagnosis* is a term that has come into use in recent years through nursing education. It has physicians confused and some health care attorneys concerned. For the most part, making a diagnosis is an act of medical judgment that may be done only by a licensed physician. From the risk management standpoint, it may be wise not to use the term. There are some types of diagnosis that a nurse may do independently—for example, wound care. A nurse does not need the authorization of a physician to diagnose a superficial abrasion of the knee. The nurse is doing the same thing a physician would be doing, and it is not necessary to qualify the term as a nursing diagnosis.

The term and the concept of nursing diagnosis have no place in an outpatient medical record. Typically, chart entries are made by physicians and nurses in the same set of progress notes. Any use of the term *diagnosis* will be perceived as a true diagnosis in the medical sense. A nurse making a diagnosis must be working under strict protocol or direct supervision of a physician. Any other diagnosis made by a nurse constitutes the unauthorized practice of medicine.

The term *nursing diagnosis* is often used as the title of a nursing care plan. This is confusing but legally acceptable if the nurse is not making a diagnosis or ordering care. Problems arise when the nurse fails to understand the difference and writes a medical diagnosis on a patient. (Richards and Rathbun 1993, 433)

From the perspective of many in the nursing profession, nursing diagnoses have been described as redundant terminology that clouds communication; as statements of the obvious; as so much doublespeak to describe medical clinical symptoms and diagnoses. Anything is acceptable as long as it is not used by physicians. This is perceived by many nurses as creating pretentious barriers with others in the health care profession and as just another way to confuse the patient.

Telenursing presents a particular dilemma for the champions of nursing diagnoses.

The challenge to nursing is to organize this material in terms of ease of access, confidentiality of usage, accuracy and contextual relevance, and ease of comprehension. . . . Telenursing, because of its communicative nature, is forced to use modern idiom, if not the vernacular, to communicate effectively. This disallows much of the specious nursing jargon and private use of language to which nursing has been exposed in recent years [nursing diagnoses]. The bottom line seems to be that if one wishes to make oneself understood, one had better use language that can be understood. (Yensen 1996, 213)

## DOCUMENTING DISCHARGE TEACHING AND PLANNING

Changes in the health care delivery system and increased efforts at cost control have resulted in increasingly abbreviated hospital stays. It is inevitable that an increasing number of lawsuits alleging premature discharge as a cause of injury or even death will be initiated. This is an area of litigation that will present entirely new issues and challenges for the professional nurse charged with preparing patients and families for a physician-ordered discharge that the nurse may consider inappropriate.

It will be the patient's physician who will ultimately be responsible for documenting in the medical record that the patient's status and prognosis warranted discharge at that time. The patient's nurses will be the ones assigned the task of preparing the patient and the family for the event and documenting their teaching and supportive efforts in detail. Proper discharge planning and teaching may play a critical role in the recovery process. Deficiencies in this professional responsibility can leave the practitioner open to liability.

### Discharge Teaching Guidelines

There are a number of guidelines and suggestions for the nurse involved in discharging a patient who may be relatively ill and for relatives who may be ill-prepared. These are shown in Table 9.2.

**Table 9.2**
**Discharge Teaching Guidelines**

- Ascertain the needs and knowledge of the parties before beginning.
- Do not assume that the patient or the family can "manage", or take them for granted.

- Begin with the simplest instructions and basic ideas and gradually introduce more complicated procedures and concepts. They may be overwhelmed at this time.
- Proceed very slowly. Teach in several short sessions, or, if appropriate, arrange for at-home follow-up teaching when they are settled in.
- Provide as much written material as possible—preprinted brochures, pamphlets, instruction sheets, videotapes, or any other instructional material. Ask that these be prepared if they are not available. Prepare them if necessary. Have the patient or family member sign a list of all materials provided to confirm receipt.
- Include this list in the progress notes.
- Explain everything in terms that they can understand. Confirm their understanding. Ask questions. Answer questions.
- Provide opportunities for return demonstrations of all procedures.
- Document in detail who was taught, what was taught, how it was taught, and by whom it was taught.
- Document the degree of understanding and how this was determined.
- Confirm availability for any further questions or ongoing support.

## INCIDENT REPORTS

"An incident report is a written description, factual and nonjudgmental, of an event that caused an injury (or had the potential to cause an injury). It doesn't belong in the patient's medical record, nor does any mention that it's been filled out" (Cournoyer 1995, 21). The incident report, the "unusual occurrence report", or whatever it may be called, is the proper place to document untoward events or compromised care. Any extraordinary event (one that is a *marked deviation* from the routine) usually requires the filing of a report *whether or not there has been any injury* involved.

The departure from the routine may be any occurrence that is considered inconsistent with the institution's normal operation or with the care of patients in the institution—including the incompetence of any caregiver. This would always describe any occurrence that could possibly impute liability on the part of the institution. A report may outline the circumstances of an incident that caused an injury or it may present factors *predictive* of a possible injury. The preferred and widely used format is a check-off list arranged by categories of circumstances or factors. This (by design) may present limited space for any personal narrative description of the circumstances of the event.

### Purpose of the Incident Report

To maintain accreditation, a hospital is required by the JCAHO to set up and maintain some internal system of incident reporting according to defined standards and guidelines. Such a system functions as an integral part of the total risk management and quality assurance program maintained by every hospital. The primary purpose is to provide the institution with a means to review and evaluate patient care in order to effect improvements in the overall quality of that care and to forewarn appropriate administrative staff of potential exposure to liability. By tracking specific facts and circumstances surrounding all untoward events, the institution can identify patterns and develop strategies of identification and prevention that will serve to decrease the risk of similar incidents or injuries reoccurring. Ultimately such a system should protect patients, staff, and the institution itself.

In addition to identifying actual and potential problems, the incident report may identitfy potential litigants and assist the institution's counsel in preparing for a possible or likely lawsuit. With the knowledge of those events that might precipitate a suit, the hospital's attorney can begin planning defense strategies or proposals for a settlement offer in lieu of a trial. An incident report may also serve in apportioning blame. See Table 9.3 for guidelines for preparing this report.

**Table 9.3**
**Guidelines for Preparing an Incident Report**

- Prepare only one copy.

- Prepare it as soon as possible.

- The person preparing the report should be the one who actually saw what happened or who has complete and accurate knowledge of the facts.

- Do not describe other than what you have seen or what you have been told by *reliable*, impartial witnesses.

- If you include the statements of witnesses, confirm that they are not merely hearsay. Name the source and indicate how they know of the circumstances. Quote them.

- Describe precisely what transpired, what actions were taken at the time, and by whom.

- Be accurate, concise, and, above all, *objective*.

- Be honest. Tell the *truth* as best you know it even if this could compromise you or another. Regardless of your involvement, document completely and factually. This could eventually prove to be your best defense.

- Present *facts only*. No conclusions, assumptions, opinions, or unfounded statements of any kind should be offered.

- Do not include any recommendations, suggestions, or advice—this will be done by the staff member who will investigate the incident.

- You can and should name names. Include the addresses of family, visitors, or any other such witnesses. The names of all parties involved, including staff, must be included in the incident report but *never* in the chart.
- *Never* admit liability, culpability, or error. Be very careful of your choice of words. Avoid words that might convey the slightest suggestion of fault or blame.
- Do not attempt to assign blame, or suggest, or infer who is or could have been responsible.
- Include the patient's statements and his or her version of the events. Quote or paraphrase the patient's statements.
- If equipment malfunction is involved, describe the failure. Note the specific type of device, the manufacturer, the product number and any serial number, the name of the technician who last inspected it, and the date. Ideally such items should be secured as is until proper documentation of any defects can be done.
- If a medication error is involved, include all details.

In the event of an incident involving injury to a patient, the appropriate physician should be advised as soon as possible. If the patient and/or family is not already aware, they also should be informed. It can be argued that this should be done in any incident regardless of whether or not the patient has suffered any harm. Should the patient and/or family discover the facts on their own, it could set up a climate of suspicion, mistrust, and anger—the usual motivating factors of a lawsuit. "If the result of an injury is unexpected or a complication has occurred, whether a lawsuit follows often depends on the perception of events and the degree of rapport between the health care provider and the patient" (Fiesta 1994, 5). Competency is the first malpractice preventive measure in nursing practice. Honesty follows close behind.

## Discoverability of the Incident Report

An incident report should *never* be mentioned in a nurse's notes. If this is done, the legal doctrine of "incorporation by reference" can be claimed by the plaintiff's attorney. If a nurse states in his or her notes that an incident report has been prepared and filed, this reference incorporates that report into the medical record and thus makes it discoverable. The events involving compromised patient care should be documented but not identified as "incidents". Any information in the chart can be included in the incident report. However, do not include something in a note just because it is in the incident report—for example, names of staff or witnesses.

In many states an incident report is considered to be confidential—a privileged communication between the institution and its counsel. As noted, however, any reference to the report in the record can strip away this veil of secrecy and provide the plaintiff's lawyer with a view of a potentially damaging piece of evidence.

The courts in various states have examined the matter of the discoverability of the incident report and its admissibility as evidence in malpractice litigation. Rulings have varied, and there have been no consistent decisions. There has been an increasing number of rulings that permit plaintiffs the right of discovery provided they can demonstrate a licit need. More and more courts are opening incident reports to discovery and scrutiny. Many insurance companies and agencies of federal and state government are exercising rights to secure and review them in their fiduciary and regulatory capacities.

An incident report may pass through many hands and be seen by many eyes—some appropriate, some just curious, inquisitive staff, whether they were involved or not. Incident reports are likely to be reviewed by nursing supervisors and administrators, the hospital's administration, counsel, and its insurance carrier. Various governmental agencies including the JCAHO may examine them. And, eventually, the attorney for the plaintiff may succeed in obtaining the report and presenting it in open court for public scrutiny.

A nurse should always prepare an incident report as if it were discoverable. But prepare it without any inordinate fear of its being discovered. If the report is complete, accurate, and truthful, it should hold no peril for the preparer. If it is riddled with inconsistencies, hearsay, accusations, unfounded conclusions, or any implication of culpability, it may become a valuable weapon in the hands of a prosecuting attorney.

## COMPUTERIZED CHARTING

As more and more hospitals adopt systems of computerized documentation, nurses have reacted with varying attitudes and degrees of enthusiasm and acceptance. Ideally, computerized charting will provide a medium for more complete, accurate, and timely charting. It will facilitate immediate access to clinical data together with interpretations and implications of that data for patient care. All members of the health care team will have the means for comprehensive review, analysis, consultation, and communication of data on the patient's status, prognosis, and needs. All such information will be instantly retrievable, manageable, and legible. And all such information will be worthless (if not dangerous) unless it was complete and accurate when entered into the database.

It will be every nurse's responsibility to assure the accuracy of each datum they enter. The same responsibility is involved in reviewing all data retrieved and presented on the screen or in a printout. Even if the individual nurse was not responsible for an input error, he or she could be held liable for failure to detect and correct the error. Checking the accuracy of a computer printout, detecting errors, and comparing the information to that already in the chart will be an area of increasing potential liability for nurses. Another area of risk is the ease with which patient files might be retrieved and copied, altered, or even deleted from data banks. Computerized charting may make an onerous task easier, but it will not remove the onus of complete, accurate, and timely documentation. It is a technology that will present new challenges and liability risks for nurses.

### Confidentiality in Computerized Medical Records

In addition to generating and managing information, computerized charting presents another major concern for nurses—that of confidentiality and the breach of it through inadvertent or deliberate disclosure of information to unauthorized persons. Nurses who are careless with their access code or password, allowing it to be revealed to unauthorized persons or sharing it indiscriminately, place themselves at serious risk for liability if patient confidentiality is breached as a result. After a patient record has been displayed on a monitor and the required information noted, the record should be removed from the screen and not left available for unauthorized viewing.

The quantity and sophistication of information contained in computerized patient records—quick access to data, the ability to combine and cross-match information from divergent sources, and the ease of transmitting large amounts of data—pose increased patient confidentiality risks and raise the stakes for hospitals and nurses in case of breach. Moreover, because the legal status of computerized medical records still is ill-defined, these records are vulnerable to legal challenge, especially regarding their admissibility in court. (Gobis 1994, 15)

### REFERENCES

Cournoyer, Carmelle P. 1995. How to protect yourself legally after a patient is injured. *Nursing95 Career Directory* (January): 18–23.

Fiesta, Janine. 1994. *20 Legal Pitfalls for Nurses to Avoid*. Delmar Publishers.

Gobis, Linda J. 1994. Computerized patient records: Start preparing now. *Journal of Nursing Administration* 24 (9) (September): 15–16, 60.

# 10

# The Medical Record As Evidence in Nursing Malpractice

## THE MEDICAL RECORD

The medical record, in its entirety, is a written chronicle of the medical and nursing care that a patient has received, or is expected to receive, over a period of time, and a record of those who provided that care. This includes care prior to admission to an institution, care while in the institution, or an anticipated course of treatment after discharge. It is first and foremost a medical document and second a legal document. As a legal document it will provide evidence of the type and quality of care that a patient received at the hands of those caregivers whose orders, progress notes, and various reports are included in it (Sharpe 1999).

### Standards and Purposes of the Medical Record

In the *Accreditation Manual for Hospitals*, the JCAHO defines the standards and purposes of a medical record. These are applicable in all patient care settings.

#### Standards

- The record will confirm that the patient has been properly identified, assessed, and admitted to the institution

- The record will reflect timely and proper medical and nursing intervention and treatment based on medical diagnoses
- Such intervention and treatment will be completely and accurately documented
- The documentation in the medical record will conform to the standards defined by the JCAHO and the U.S. Department of Health and Human Services
- All such documentation will be retained and protected by the institution for the prescribed period of time

### Purposes

- Directs and documents the medical regimen
- Directs and documents the nursing process
- Documents patient care management and the patient's response to, and effectiveness of, medical and nursing interventions
- Provides a central repository of data to be communicated to all members of the health care team
- Provides a business record for the institution
- Establishes a legal record to protect the rights and interests of the patient, the institution, and the providers of care
- Contributes data for scientific research and continuing education in relevant fields

The principal function of the record is to facilitate continuity in patient care. It is the primary means of communication among all members of the health care team. Thorough documentation demonstrates thorough care. Deficient documentation may demonstrate deficient care. The nursing staff's record of the nursing process must be as exact as the process itself. Complete and accurate documentation is an inherent part of competent care.

### Legal Significance of the Medical Record

The significance of the contents of a medical record in a malpractice lawsuit is of paramount importance. The adequacy of the record can make or break a case. If it demonstrates deficiencies in care—breach of duty—it will severely hinder a defense to charges of malpractice. If it is complete, accurate, and factual, it may serve to repudiate allegations of negligence.

The patient-plaintiff's medical record provides his or her attorney with the single most effective weapon in assailing the defendant's credibility and competency. It will be the primary source of the facts and circumstances surrounding the incident at issue and will invariably be presented in the courtroom as evidence in a malpractice trial. When presented as evidence at a trial the content of the record is presumed to be true. If any significant element in the record can be shown to be missing, inaccurate, or untruthful, the credibility of the entire record could be compromised. The attorney for each side will scrutinize the record to weigh its merits and its utility in supporting his or her respective cases. If the record is tight, the plaintiff's case may not be. "[A]s many as one out of four malpractice suits are decided from the patient's chart" (Edelstein 1990, 40).

### Ownership of the Medical Record

"It is generally held that the hospital or medical provider generating the record is the owner of the original document. However, all states recognize the right of patients to have access to the information contained in their medical record and to make copies at their expense" (Appleby and Tarver 1994, 128). The institution maintains legal ownership of a patient's medical record, and physicians own patients' records that are maintained in their offices. In each setting, these are business records that are necessary to the proper administration of the institution or conduct of a practice.

Although the institution or physician has control over the physical record, the question of ownership of the information contained in it is debatable. "The plain fact is that patients have a proprietary interest in their own medical records. At the very least the *information* contained in medical records is the property of the patient. But for the patient, the information would not exist! To require the assistance of counsel to get such records unfairly and unnecessarily burdens a patient who is trying to obtain what is rightfully his" (Wecht 1978, 9).

The American Medical Association considers the content of the record to be the property of the physician. The AMA has stated that: "[N]otes made in treating a patient are primarily for the physician's own use and constitute his personal property. . . . [O]n request of the patient a physician should provide a copy or a summary of the record to the patient . . . an attorney or other person designated by the patient" (AMA 1992, 32).

### Access to the Medical Record

As noted previously, the collection of documents is the property of the institution. The collected data belongs to the patient. The right of physical possession, of ownership, does not mean that access to the content of the record can be completely denied to any one outside the institution. As a general rule, under common law, a patient has the right to review the content of his or her record and submit appropriate additions and corrections for inclusion. An individual may not alter or remove any document. At the time of this writing, one-half of the states have laws in effect that grant patients access to their medical records in the possession of hospitals or physicians. The laws vary considerably by state (Johnson and Wolfe 1995, 35, 39). Most define the criteria and procedures for access. Even those states that grant access may impose a variety of restrictive limitations. For example:

- The law may apply differently to hospitals, physicians, or mental health institutions.
- The individual(s) granted access may specify the patient only and/or the patient's attorney or other legal representative.
- The nature of access may permit only a review of the record or also the right to have a copy of it.
- The patient may be permitted access to the entire record or only a summary.
- Release of the record may be only at the custodian's discretion.
- In a number of states, attending physicians may retain the right to withhold or release a record.
- There may be certain predefined conditions such as demonstrated relevancy to litigation. A court order may be required. "Good cause" may have to be shown. (For a listing of access laws by state, see appendix I.)

Certain documents contained in a medical record may not, by law, be released without proper authority. These usually include records relating to psychiatric diagnoses and treatment, and certain information that would be considered privileged and confidential. Twenty-seven states and the District of Columbia do permit patients direct access to their mental health records (Johnson and Wolfe 1995, 39).

In 1977, the Privacy Protection Study Commission, which had been created under the 1974 Federal Privacy Act, prepared a report that defined a number of recommendations regarding the rights of patients to access their medical records. In the report, the commission recommended that both federal and state statutes be implemented or adapted to provide an individual who is the subject of a medical record maintained by a health care provider the right to access the record, including the right to read and copy its contents (Privacy Protection Study Commission 1977, 298).

The various state statutes may include specific disclosure laws that permit access without the consent or the knowledge of the patient. It is incumbent upon the institution to identify those individuals or agencies that have a

legitimate need to know this information. A competent person can author-
ize access to his or her medical record by an attorney, a third-party payer, or
any other legal representative on his or her behalf. If the individual lacks the
legal capacity for such authorization, a parent or a legal guardian may represent the rights to access. A court subpoena will open any record to legally
sanctioned inquiry.

Any individual, in any jurisdiction, can request a subpoena to gain access
to his or her records. Several states provide a right of direct access; a patient
does not have to initiate a formal legal procedure, or a lawsuit, to obtain his
or her records. In some jurisdictions, there may be a requirement that only
the patient's attorney can initiate such a request. Frequently, the procedure
involved is daunting—this to discourage frivolous inquiries. There is no
evidence to support contentions that providing a patient with access to his or
her medical record will give impetus to a lawsuit.

The institution may reserve the right to define the time, place, participants, and supervision of the patient's examination of his or her file. The patient is entitled to a copy of this record, and the institution should provide it
for a reasonable processing fee. There have been recent incidents of institutions assessing unreasonable, exorbitant fees to provide copies of medical
records to patients and attorneys involved in cases of malpractice. Several
states have now outlawed these excesses by imposing a maximum per-page
charge.

Some statutes may require that the record be complete before it may be
released and define a period of time within which this must be accomplished. This may be several weeks following the patient's discharge or de-
mise—if the latter occurs during his or her hospital stay.

Access laws should be the concern of the nurse. A staff nurse or a nurse
manager should not routinely provide a file to a patient or to any one not
authorized to see the medical record. All such requests should be directed to
the appropriate administrative staff. If a patient persists in requesting to see
his or her record, the nurse must refer the demand to the nursing supervisor
for further action. If the nurse is given permission to release the record or
any part of it, he or she should request that this approval be in writing. Ideally the institution's policies and procedures should forbid the staff nurse
any direct involvement in these matters.

A patient's medical record is open to any member of the health care team
involved in that patient's care. Quality assurance and risk management staff
routinely review charts as part of their role. Insurance company representatives will visit nursing units or medical records departments and examine
the charts of those patients who are their business clients. Representatives

of governmental agencies and programs such as Medicare or Medicaid also have access.

Appropriate staff members of the institution usually have free access. Student nurses are permitted to examine charts in preparation for and during clinical assignments; the consent of the patient is usually not required in these instances. Records can be the source of research data. A request by an outside individual or agency is normally submitted to a review panel for evaluation of the merits of the proposed research and a guarantee of patient-subject confidentiality.

When the medical records department of a hospital receives a letter from an attorney (or a subpoena) requesting the records of a patient, this is usually a red flag. The risk management department and the institution's counsel are alerted to the request and the possibility of a lawsuit. The attorney representing the institution will call for a medical record at the first hint of a lawsuit. The original record is usually secured to eliminate the possibility of tampering. A copy will be prepared and forwarded to the patient's attorney making the request.

The request may set in motion a review of the record by the hospital's quality assurance, risk management, and legal counsel to predetermine the likely cause of a claim of negligence and preevaluate the merits of any potential claim. An effort will be made to define the degree of exposure to liability, the possible damages to be claimed, and the strengths and weakness of their position. Contingent on the findings of the review, strategies for a possible defense in an anticipated lawsuit may be defined and implemented. Terms of a settlement proposal may be formulated.

## LEGAL IMPLICATIONS OF TAMPERING WITH THE MEDICAL RECORD

A corrected note is an altered note. However, an altered note is not necessarily a corrected note. The writer's intent may not be to amend and clarify but to deceive and conceal. Any attempt at deliberate falsification of a record can be evidence in law of the concept of "consciousness of negligence." The inference that could be drawn is that the individual who altered the record was fully aware of his or her own negligence, and this action was an attempt to conceal it. In such instances, a judge may instruct a jury that negligence on the part of the defendant can be assumed from the defendant's apparent attempt to cloak it—even though no other evidence of negligence is apparent. Tampering is illicit altering. It is wrongfully adding to or changing information or data that is already contained in a medical record. Additions might be made to complete or clarify. But no matter the intent, any such alterations could be interpreted as tampering unless fully documented reasons accompany the changes.

The deliberate *omission* of significant facts is another form of tampering. A nurse should never succumb to temptation, suggestion, or pressure to delete relevant and crucial facts no matter how potentially damaging these might be. Unsanctioned removal and/or destruction of any documents in the record is equally reckless. If a document must be rewritten the original must not be discarded. A jury might suspect that the document that was destroyed could have been incriminating and might consider such an action to have been an attempt to conceal evidence. If this was in fact the intent, the individual has perpetrated a fraud.

A physician or a nurse should never arbitrarily add to, change, or rewrite another's notes. If a nurse determines that this has occurred he or she should refer the matter to nursing administration. Inevitably alterations to a medical record must be made. These can be as routine as correcting spelling, grammar, or mistranscribed data; or they can involve substantive errors such as missing orders, omitted assessments, or absent progress notes. If any *significant* alteration must be made in a patient's record, the practitioner must advise the institution's administration in writing of the need and intent. When and if approved, the physician or nurse must proceed with the addendum according to the direction of the institution's risk management department and/or counsel. Any other person who might have relied on the original record must be advised of the revision.

Under no circumstances should a nurse retrieve a record from the medical record department files and attempt to make any significant alterations on his or her own. It must be remembered that long before a lawsuit is actually filed the plaintiff's attorney may have already obtained a copy of the complete record, and this has been reviewed in detail by the attorney and/or a nurse litigation consultant. Any discrepancies that are later identified (especially before a skeptical jury) may impeach the entire record and certainly the credibility of the defendant.

"When key records are altered or destroyed, the plaintiff's ability to make a prima facie case for negligence is greatly hampered or disappears altogether" (Appleby and Tarver 1997, 66). If the plaintiff's attorney can demonstrate that the patient-plaintiff's record was tampered with, he or she can claim fraud and conspiracy to commit fraud. The accused nurse might face additional charges of aggravated and outrageous conduct. Any attempt to conceal or manipulate facts with a deliberate, willful intent to impede a legitimate inquiry, evade blame, misinform, mislead, or deceive constitutes fraud. Under such circumstances it is a *criminal* offense—a *felony*. Otherwise, inappropriate alteration of a medical record may be treated as misdemeanor crime in most states.

A nurse, or any one else, should *never* attempt to tamper with a medical record. Any competent forensic document examiner will be able to detect an effort to subvert a record. Any compromised record will be the *kiss of death* for the defendant's case and perhaps for the career of the party responsible. Inevitably the consequences of misguided efforts to conceal or mislead can be far more devastating that a frank admission of the truth.

## REFERENCES

American Medical Association, Council on Ethical and Judicial Affairs. 1992. *Code of Medical Ethics: Current Opinions.*

Appleby, Kristyn S., and Joanne Tarver. 1997. *Medical Records Review.* 2d ed. *Cumulative Supplement.* John Wiley & Sons, Inc.

Appleby, Kristyn S., and Joanne Tarver. 1994. *Medical Records Review.* 2d ed. John Wiley & Sons, Inc.

Edelstein, Jacqueline. 1990. A study of nursing documentation. *Nursing Management* 21 (11) (November): 40–46.

Johnson, Diann, and Sidney M. Wolfe. 1995. *Medical Records: Getting Yours.* Public Citizen Publications.

Joint Commission on Accreditation of Healthcare Organizations. 1993. *Accreditation Manual for Hospitals.*

Privacy Protection Study Commission. 1977. *Record-keeping in the Medical-care Relationship: Personal Privacy in an Information Society.* U.S. Government Printing Office.

Sharpe, Charles C. 1999. *Medical Records Review and Analysis.* Auburn House.

Wecht, C. H. 1978. Patient access to medical records: Yea or nay? *Legal Aspects of Medical Practice* (October): 8–10.

# 11

# Legal Implications of Informed Consent

## CONSENT

In 1914, Justice Benjamin Cardozo opined: "Every human being of adult years and sound mind has a right to determine what shall be done with his own body." (*Schloendorff v. Society of New York Hospital*, 105 N.E. 92 [1914], 17). The patient's act of consent imparts to a health care provider the right to treat and demands of that practitioner the right treatment. There are two fundamental moral and ethical principles inherent in this process. First is the right of free choice affirmed by Justice Cardozo, and second is the concept of nonmaleficence embodied in the Hippocratic Oath, which demands that the practitioner swear that: "[T]he regimen I adopt shall be for the benefit of my patients according to my ability and judgment and not for their hurt or for any wrong."

### Forms of Consent

There are two forms of consent: (1) expressed and (2) implied.

### *Expressed Consent*

Expressed consent may be written or oral. Either is considered valid in most jurisdictions. However, in the event of a lawsuit where consent, or alleged lack of it, becomes an issue in dispute, proving oral (or implied) consent could be a challenge for the defense. Obviously, written consent is the most desirable form from a risk management view. If at all possible, a witness should be present for an oral consent. In all situations, the circumstances should be documented in detail.

### Implied Consent

Consent may also be implied. It is that consent that may be inferred from a patient's actions such as a nod of the head, a wave of a hand, or other gesture to express assent, or by the patient's inaction or inability to act. In an emergency situation where a person is unable to give consent for treatment the law presumes implied consent.

## CONSENT IN NURSING PRACTICE

Clinical nursing practice may involve either form of consent, and a nurse must actively and routinely affirm a patient's consent by informing the patient of and explaining an intended action and confirming the patient's understanding and agreement. For the nurse, consent is usually verbal, but a patient's resigned shrug of the shoulders or the absence of any words or actions of protest can signify implied consent. If a competent patient offers no apparent objection, this can be interpreted as implied consent. When in doubt as to the patient's intent, the nurse should document what was actually involved in the exchange, including both the patient's verbal and/or body language.

In the event that a consent must be obtained by telephone, it is advisable that the practitioner accept the consent while another person listening confirms that it has been given and by whom. If an interpreter is needed, it is important to confirm that the interpreter is fluent in the patient's language, fully understands the information being presented, can accurately convey the information, and can verify the patient's understanding and approval. The interpreter's name and relationship to the patient should be documented.

The patient's permission for routine, basic, nursing and medical procedures is implied by his or her admission to, and very presence in, the hospital. During the admission process each patient is routinely asked to sign a consent form that is applicable to those procedures required to provide basic assessments and the initiation and continuation of routine care. Subsequently, the individual's ongoing cooperation in the medical and nursing regimen attests to consent. For other than such routine procedures and treatments, *informed* consent is required for those involving a higher degree of risk for injury, serious complications and side effects, or death. The patient participating in any experimental treatment or medical trials must give informed consent, which, under federal laws and regulations, has specific and rigid guidelines. A person may not be tested for certain diseases or conditions without his or her knowledge and consent—HIV/AIDS is an example.

Any medical or nursing intervention or attempts at such intervention without a competent patient's expressed or implied consent, informed or otherwise, could result in a claim of battery or of negligence in failure to obtain such consent. Battery is normally a tort but can also escalate to a criminal charge. Malpractice litigation, which may include a claim of lack of consent, is most likely to revolve around a principal issue of professional negligence rather than a minor issue of battery.

"Technical battery" occurs when a nurse, physician, or other health care provider exceeds the scope of the consent given by a patient. Should the patient rescind his or her consent and the practitioner proceeds in disregard of this recision, a lawsuit for battery could be initiated. The exception could be that such a withdrawal of consent constitutes an immediate and unwarranted risk to the patient's health, well-being, or very life. Otherwise, the legal right to refuse, and that decision by the patient, must be respected. Should a patient refuse or revoke a consent, particularly an informed, signed consent, the nurse must advise the physician immediately and document the event fully. The patient or the patient's legal representative should be apprised by the *physician* of the consequences of that decision.

The right to refuse or to revoke includes a competent patient's election to leave the institution at any time, for whatever reason, against medical advice (AMA). The nurse dealing with this patient must follow the policies and procedures of the institution. If possible, the patient should be persuaded to sign the appropriate release form indicating discharge AMA. However, the right of self-discharge AMA is not absolute. If such an individual is deemed to be incompetent or a threat to society or to him- or herself, he or she can be legally detained by the use of such reasonable force as is necessary to prevent elopement.

In addition to direct implications for the person's health, a decision to withdraw consent could have economic repercussions. The individual's health insurance carrier may refuse reimbursement or rescind coverage to the client who refuses to accept a course of treatment that is considered appropriate and essential to prevention, diagnosis, and management of his or her illness—routine or catastrophic. What a patient may perceive as a reasonable, personal choice, an insurance company may construe as the unilateral imposition or continuance of an unreasonable insurance risk that warrants the cancellation of a policy.

## INFORMED CONSENT

Informed consent is that permission, given freely and willingly, by a person, or by that person's legally appointed surrogate, which enables a provider of health care, in mutual agreement, to render service to that person as his or her patient. Such mutual consent imparts to a practitioner the right to treat a patient: to do something, which is intended to be therapeutic, to or for that person.

There have been an increasing number of malpractice cases in which the patient-plaintiff has alleged that his or her "informed" consent was not given for the procedure or course of treatment that caused the injury claimed. It is very likely that, at some time in the course of clinical practice, a nurse will become involved in obtaining and/or witnessing a patient's informed consent for surgery or some other treatment or procedure where this is required. The nurse should be aware of his or her responsibilities in these instances and the legal implications of participating in this process. Informed consent, or lack thereof, is primarily a liability risk for physicians, dentists, or other autonomous health care providers, such as nurse practitioners. Various states have enacted both substantive and procedural laws that provide definitions of informed consent, define claims and defenses that will be allowable, and specify the elements of a claim for a tort of negligent nondisclosure.

## REQUIRED ELEMENTS OF INFORMED CONSENT

There are two intrinsic elements required to validate informed consent: (1) the patient must have the legal capacity to give such consent, and (2) the duty of full disclosure. These are the legal elements that are defined by virtually all states. However, what a plaintiff may be required to demonstrate in a claim of malpractice may differ from jurisdiction to jurisdiction.

### Legal Capacity

The law recognizes that only that person who has legal capacity can consent to or refuse medical treatment. Capacity is defined as the person's ability to comprehend all of the significant implications and consequences of his or her actions or a refusal to act. A basic concept in the law is that of the "reasonable person" test. Should a plaintiff in a lawsuit claim a lack of informed consent, he or she must prove that a reasonable person under the same or similar circumstances would not have given consent on the basis of the information that he or she had been given.

Only a patient deemed fully capacitated may give valid informed consent. A capacitated patient is one who fully comprehends the facts being presented and realizes the implications of whatever choice he or she makes based on those facts. The individual who is unconscious, severely impaired as a result of drugs or alcohol, insane, mentally retarded, or otherwise mentally impaired cannot acquiesce in an act of informed consent. Any alert, fully oriented adult is normally viewed as manifesting legal capacity.

In obtaining informed consent, the patient's *physician* is legally responsible for confirming that the patient is competent and has the legal capacity to give it. For that person who has been adjudicated as incompetent, a court-appointed surrogate or guardian can act in his or her behalf. If such a guardian has not been named, the circumstances may require a petition to a court to appoint one immediately.

In some jurisdictions, designated members of an incompetent or incapacitated patient's family or even a friend may give consent. In the order of priority, and contingent on availability, the patient's spouse would normally be consulted first, then adult children, and last, parents. Virtually all states now empower their citizens to formalize such designations by documents such as living wills, powers of attorney, or other legally appropriate directives. These will be discussed in chapter 12.

Another essential element is that the consent must be *freely given* by the patient. There can be no coercion or duress of any kind. This includes physical force or psychological pressure in the form of intimidation or threats. Once given, consent may be withdrawn at any time. The right of refusal is not necessarily an absolute right. The state may supersede that right in several instances. These might include:

- the refusal of consent by a parent or guardian that jeopardizes the life or well-being of a minor (including a fetus);
- the individual, by their refusal, is unjustifiably jeopardizing his or her own life; in such instances, honoring the refusal could be viewed as participation in an assisted suicide; and
- preservation and protection of public health and safety is involved.

### Full Disclosure

A duty to disclose goes to the very heart of informed consent. That duty is the mandated requirement that *all significant and material facts* be presented to a patient, in language that the patient can fully understand, in order that the individual may make what can be accurately construed as an informed decision to accept or refuse a proposed course of action. *Not every conceivable risk* or side effect need be included. This presentation must also include *all possible alternative courses of action*—including taking no action at all—and the consequences of these.

Two standards have evolved from court decisions that are recognized as guidelines for the quantity and quality of information to be included. The first is that of the "reasonable physician" who must include all of those facts that any other reasonable medical practitioner would provide under the same or similar circumstances. The second standard is that of the "reasonable patient" who is entitled to information which, in content and format, is necessary for any reasonable person to make a rational choice. The patient must be given a quantity and a quality of information such that he or she can make an intelligent, judicious decision in accepting or rejecting the treatment or procedure proposed. In most jurisdictions, an objective test will be applied that will attempt to confirm whether or not the risks presented would be considered material to any reasonable individual in the same or similar circumstances; and would such an individual consider those material risks of such significance as to prompt him or her to refuse consent.

A malpractice lawsuit might not involve any claim by a plaintiff that he or she did not give an informed consent for the treatment rendered, or such an assertion can be a peripheral issue. If the lawsuit has its basis in an asserted lack of informed consent, the plaintiff must demonstrate that the physician or other health care professional—by a failure in full disclosure—breached his or her duty to the plaintiff and in so doing caused the plaintiff to decide on a course of action that he or she would not have elected otherwise. In effect, the patient must prove that the alleged breach of duty was the cause of the injury claimed.

### Required Elements in Full Disclosure

There is continuing debate on what constitutes "material risk". However, it is generally agreed that full disclosure must include certain essential components. These are:

- the patient's present clinical status and/or current prognosis;
- pertinent details regarding the proposed treatment or procedure—*in a layperson's language*;
- inherent, *significant* risks and usually expected adverse side effects;
- anticipated therapeutic outcomes as they can best be defined;

- alternative treatments or procedures, if any, and their risks and benefits;
- the patient's right to refuse and right to retract consent at any time; and
- possible or expected developments should the patient refuse.

A practitioner's inadvertent deficiency in the requirements of full disclosure may not invalidate the patient's informed consent, but it may become a factor in sustaining a liability claim for negligence. The multitude of laws and the infinite subtleties in interpretation of constituent disclosure factors in informed consent have given rise to many lawsuits.

### Exceptions to the Duty of Full Disclosure

There are several exceptions to the duty of full disclosure.

- Emergency: Life-saving intervention is required immediately. The patient's condition precludes obtaining informed consent. Consent is implied. There may be a state statute defining procedures for obtaining consent and who may give it. In some instances, a court order may be required.
- Waiver: Any competent adult can refuse consent or waive consent. A patient can waive his or her right to full disclosure yet still consent to the proposed treatment or procedure.
- Obvious risk: The inherent risks of the treatment or procedure are apparent to any reasonable person. They have been widely publicized and are known to the population-at-large. Or the patient knows the risks because he or she had previously undergone the same course of treatment for which informed consent had been given.
- Therapeutic privilege: The practitioner who intends to perform the procedure may assert that certain information that he or she considers potentially detrimental to the patient's health or well-being can and should be withheld in obtaining the patient's informed consent. The practitioner may deem that full disclosure could jeopardize the patient's physical or mental status, interfere with treatment, impede recovery, or impair prognosis. When invoking therapeutic privilege, the practitioner is required to justify the decision by complete documentation of the rationale.

Related to exceptions to full disclosure is the "extension doctrine" that permits a practitioner to initiate a course of action not specifically discussed or consented to previously, but that is now required by exigencies arising during the procedure. In effect, a life-threatening situation arises that warrants an extension of the scope of the patient's consent and at that instance, the patient is not able to concur. An example would be more extended surgery determined to be immediately necessary for the unconscious patient present on the operating table.

## MINORS AND CONSENT

The statutes of each state generally prohibit any health care practitioner from providing services to a minor without the consent of a parent or legal guardian. The exception to this is an emergency where the minor's well-being or life may be at risk. In the case of an unemancipated minor, consent would normally be given by a parent or a legal guardian. Where the parents are divorced or separated, the parent with primary custody would usually be responsible. The adoptive parents of a child enjoy the same rights as natural parents. A stepmother or stepfather may not have the right of consent. The prerogatives of foster parents will be determined by applicable statutes and regulations governing the placement agency involved. With few exceptions, a court-appointed guardian is endowed with such a legal right.

According to the statutes in any given state, a minor who is self-supporting and living in a residence that he or she maintains, or a minor on active duty in the armed services, may be considered an emancipated minor and, therefore, has the legal capacity for informed consent and to enter into certain contracts. As a general rule, however, an unemancipated minor is considered to be lacking in the legal capacity for informed consent. There are a number of exceptions that various state laws may allow or that define specific guidelines.

- Treatment for substance abuse or addiction
- Treatment for mental health problems
- Care and management of specified communicable diseases, including sexually transmitted diseases
- Reproductive health services including birth control and abortion

## CONSENT FORMS

The standard consent form that patients are asked to sign upon admission to a hospital is usually adequate for routine procedures. However, presenting a patient with a preprinted form that he or she is asked to read and sign does not constitute true, legal informed consent. Informed consent is a process of instruction, education, and revelation. It is not a cursory reading and signing of a document. To be legally acceptable, informed consent should incorporate the elements described previously.

If the statutes of a state define the content of a consent form, and if the language of the form that a patient signs conforms to the statutes, there can be a presumption in law that informed consent was, in fact, given. In the event of a malpractice lawsuit in which informed consent becomes an issue, a signed form that is couched in very general terms or that merely affirms that the content has been presented to the patient may not suffice. In several states a signed consent form may provide a defendant with strong, but not conclusive, incontrovertible evidence. A plaintiff may still be permitted to challenge the document in court and claim its inadequacy of content, his or her lack of understanding, incapacity, duress, or irrationality under stress.

Many state statutes do not define a requirement for a signed consent form. If a physician has thoroughly documented that he or she has verbally presented to the patient all of the required elements of full disclosure, and that the patient understood and assented, the progress notes of the practitioner may serve as evidence in lieu of a signed form. The physician may also have obtained the patient's signed consent in the office at some time before an actual admission date. This form may be forwarded to the hospital, and, assuming no significant change in the patient's medical status or contraindications for the proposed procedure, could be legally acceptable. Such authorization forms should be examined for an expiration date.

A consent form may not include any language that precludes the patient from revoking authorization at any time. Unless withdrawn, a signed form remains in effect until such time as a change in the patient's status introduces a significant alteration in the parameters of risk and intervention that mandate review, revision, or recision—or until a specified expiration date has passed. In this event, the process of full disclosure in informed consent must be repeated as necessary. A periodic review and renewal, regardless of the patient's condition, may also be required by the policies and procedures of the institution as defined by the JCAHO.

## RESPONSIBILITY FOR OBTAINING INFORMED CONSENT

It is the primary, legal responsibility of the *practitioner* (usually a physician) who has ordered, or who will perform, a procedure or administer a treatment to affirm to his or her satisfaction that the information they presented to their patient was completely understood, and to obtain that patient's informed consent. The staff nurse, in the usual course of his or her duties, should have no direct responsibility in providing full disclosure or obtaining informed consent. A practitioner may legally delegate this responsibility to a nurse, but assumes the inherent risks of this action. This includes a risk of joint liability for a claim of negligent nondisclosure. A nurse may then act as the agent of the practitioner and assumes the role of the delegator—and the liability. If a nurse assumes this role, the institution also incurs increased exposure to liability under the doctrine of *respondeat superior*.

Informed consent obtained by a nurse has been considered acceptable in a case in which the court ruled that the information which the nurse provided was within that particular nurse's scope of practice. A nurse practitioner may be allowed and/or required to obtain informed consent before carrying out certain procedures. Generally, the law directs that a nurse is permitted to attempt full disclosure only if that responsibility has been delegated to him or her by a physician and in accordance with the policies and procedures of the employing institution. Regardless of the source, the information must be provided to the patient by the individual most qualified by education and experience to do so.

If the practitioner fails to or refuses to carry out full disclosure, a nurse must report this to a nursing supervisor for further action. If the nurse is reasonably certain that any requisite element of the full disclosure process has been omitted, he or she must present his or her concerns to the physician; and, if not satisfied, refer the matter to nursing administration for further action. The nurse's failure to do so could present a risk of liability. If a patient has not been fully informed for any reason, the nurse must document the circumstances in detail, including attempts to resolve the matter.

## THE NURSE AS A WITNESS TO INFORMED CONSENT

Depending on the jurisdiction, a witness may not be required to validate informed consent. A nurse's signature as a witness could provide some degree of additional protection from liability for the physician. Some institutions have a policy that requires a nurse witness a consent form. The primary function of the nurse who witnesses this document is to attest that the patient was competent and had the legal capacity to sign, signed voluntarily, and the signature affixed is, in fact, authentic—it is that of the person giving the consent. The signature of the witness should not attest to the degree of comprehension by the patient of the information that he or she has been given by the physician.

The nurse who signs as a witness is not obtaining the patient's informed consent. Ideally, the signature of the nurse-witness should come after he or she actually *heard* the verbal exchange between the physician and the patient—the physician informing the patient and requesting the patient's signature. Legally, if the nurse is reasonably certain that full disclosure has taken place, he or she can request that the patient sign the consent form and also witness the signature. Otherwise, unless the nurse is actually present to observe and hear the physician's presentation of information, he or she cannot verify the content of the discussion. Know and follow the applicable policies and procedures of the institution.

Signing the form only as a witness does not present the nurse with any liability for failure to obtain informed consent. However, he or she should confirm the fact of informed consent before witnessing the signature of the patient. If the patient, or perhaps a family member, states to the nurse that he or she (the patient) does not understand any portion of the information presented, the nurse should instruct the patient not to sign the form and notify the physician. If the nurse permits such a patient to sign the form without taking appropriate action, he or she could be held liable.

The nurse should not attempt to answer a patient's questions regarding the medical aspects of the treatment or procedure after the physician has provided the disclosure information. Any such questions should be referred to the physician. The nurse has no professional duty or authority to answer such questions. In electing to act as witness, the nurse incurs no responsibility for providing information or clarification. A nurse may elect to reinforce selected information previously given, but is cautioned not to usurp the practitioner's legal duty to inform. Should the nurse choose to answer questions or provide clarification on any matter, he or she must address only those aspects of the procedure that are clearly within the scope of nursing practice. Should he or she step beyond this line, he or she may incur the risk of an accusation of practicing medicine.

## WITNESSING OTHER LEGAL DOCUMENTS

In witnessing a document such as a will, power of attorney, or bill of sale, the nurse simply attests to the authenticity of the signature that he or she actually saw being affixed to the document. The nurse should examine the document to confirm that what he or she is signing is, in fact, what it is purported to be. Each time a nurse agrees to participate is such nonprofessional business, he or she should note the details in any personal anecdotal records. *Before* a patient signs any legal document, the nurse, as witness, should do an assessment of the patient's mental status and later note this in the chart.

If the nurse has any reservations as to the competency or the legal capacity of the person signing, he or she should not witness the person's signature. The nurse should refuse to participate if he or she suspects or observes any evidence of coercion, fraud, or undue influence. The nurse could be held liable if he or she witnesses a document knowing, or having reasonable cause to suspect, that the person who is signing it is legally incapable of doing so.

What a nurse elects to do in these circumstances can have very serious legal implications. In the event of litigation revolving around the document in question, the nurse could be subpoenaed and required to recount the circumstances of the event and his or her impressions of the participants' behaviors. Under no circumstances should a nurse request or accept compensation of any kind for acting as a witness while on duty.

There may be a time when a nurse could be witness to statements made by a patient in anticipation of impending death. It is very common for a patient to elect to dictate a last will and testament after admission to a hospital. Many institutions have standardized forms available that have been prepared by their legal departments. When the request is made, the staff nurse should refer it to a nursing supervisor for appropriate action. If the urgency of the situation requires immediate action, and an oral will is expressed by the patient as testator, ideally two persons should be present for the dictation and transcription, and to witness the patient's signature on the transcription—if he or she is able to sign. In some jurisdictions, witnesses are not required. The provisions of this oral last will and testament should be recorded in the medical record and the notation signed by both witnesses. If such an oral will is valid under the state's statutes, it is a legally binding document. A declaration such as deathbed confession of a past crime should be taken down verbatim and placed in the medical record. The appropriate law enforcement authorities should be notified immediately; it could be a critical element in criminal proceedings—including exoneration of another.

# 12

# Legal Implications of Advance Directives and No-Code Orders

## ADVANCE DIRECTIVES

"Advances in medical knowledge and the development of life-sustaining technologies have changed the very nature of death. No longer a 'moment', dying may now be viewed as a process or continuum, the duration of which can be prolonged indefinitely. This technological potential has given rise to an unprecedented array of professional, moral, and legal questions within the health care delivery system" (Schwarz 1992, 92). The nursing profession has now become intimately involved in the protocols of death. There is even a nursing diagnosis for it: "Dying Process".

The rights of a terminally ill person to refuse medical intervention of any kind have not always been clear. Two legal landmark cases (*Quinlan* in 1976 and *Cruzan* in 1990) focused widespread interest on the legal and ethical implications of the "right to die" issue. On December 1, 1991, the Patient Self-Determination Act of 1990 (PSDA, the Act) went into effect in the United States. This statute confirmed the immemorial common law principle that every competent human being who has reached majority has an inherent right to accept or refuse medical treatment—the concept affirmed by Justice Cardozo over eight decades ago. It is in dealing with the incapacitated or incompetent adult in need of medical intervention that at times confounds the courts. Who will make the decision when the person whose sole prerogative it may have been, can no longer do so? The PSDA did not address this question and, in effect, relinquished such decisions to courts of the various states.

In 1990 the U.S. Supreme Court [in deciding the *Cruzan* case] . . . acknowledged that a competent adult has a constitutionally protected right to refuse unwanted medical treatment. However, it found that for an incompetent patient, in order to protect the state's interests, the court may require 'clear and convincing' evidence of what the patient, if competent, would want. The Court did not define 'clear and convincing' but it did acknowledge that a proper living will, a legal document stating what health care a patient will accept or refuse, would have satisfied this higher standard. (Aiken and Catalano 1994, 108)

The Court prescribed that such clear and convincing evidence of an individual's desires regarding medical treatment be present before a decision can be made to withhold life-sustaining interventions. It was left to the individual states to determine the quality of proof required. Clarification and affirmation of these desires is the objective of advance directives.

Each state now has differing laws on its books that permit any adult having legal capacity to effect some form of legal document prescribing the desired course and preferences of his or her medical care in the event that the adult becomes unable to define his or her wishes. These enactments are variously called "right-to die", "natural death", or "living will" laws. They incorporate the self-determination concept presented previously, and recognize a person's right to decline any and all extraordinary, heroic, life-saving measures when there is no reasonable expectation of survival. Certain elements are seen in most of the statutes. There is usually a requirement that the patient has been determined to be incompetent or incapacitated before the advance directive is implemented. The statute may also require that a terminal illness with no possibility of recovery be evident, that the patient be in an intractable coma, persistent vegetative state, or so profoundly debilitated as to show no promise of response to treatment. The language of several statutes is sufficiently broad as to include those individuals in a state of dementia, including those with Alzheimer's disease.

Generally, the laws prescribe that the advance directive will go into effect only when a physician makes a determination of one or more of the above conditions. In some instances the statutes require that a second physician concur in this determination. Such a diagnosis and decision may have to be made only after the individual is actually admitted to a hospital.

A potential problem exists with the "portability" of advance directives—the situation that arises should an individual relocate or travel to another state whose statutes may not recognize certain provisions of an advance directive created in another jurisdiction. In some states, a directive is valid only if it complies with the statutes of the state in which it was created. In others, the document is valid only if it is in compliance with the statutes of the state in which it is to be implemented. In the event of establishing permanent residence in another state, an attorney should be consulted in that state to review the documents and bring them into compliance.

Advance directives generally are binding on all health care providers. They are drawn up while the actor is capacitated and go into effect only when he or she is incapacitated. "The term *incapacity* should not be confused with the term *incompetence*, although they are frequently used interchangeably in the clinical setting. Incompetency requires a judicial determination; it is a finding by a court that an individual lacks the ability to make *all* decisions, including health care decisions" (Schwarz 1992, 94). Since the Act affirms that a particular state's law will control any such directives permitted under an enacted statute, the language of a directive must conform to the prerequisites of that statute. Health care providers must know the provisions of the law in their locale.

## TYPES OF ADVANCE DIRECTIVES

There are three principal types of advance directives: (1) the living will, (2) medical directives, and (3) durable power of attorney.

### Living Will

The living will is a written, witnessed declaration of a person's specific desires and intentions concerning the nature and extent of medical care he or she wishes to receive—or not receive—in the event that he or she is personally unable to affirm such desires or intentions. It is an expression of a person's hope that the terminally ill patient will be allowed to die a natural, dignified death when that is the only, final option. It will direct decisions regarding the course of treatment when a terminally ill patient, with no reasonable possibility of recovery, can no longer make such decisions.

Unfortunately living wills are often couched in very broad, vague, comparatively simple terms that deal primarily with extraordinary interventions—when there is "no hope". They may include such language as no "heroic" or "extraordinary" efforts, but fail to address such basic measures of life support as nutrition and hydration. Despite a consensus among medical, ethics, and legal experts that hydration and nutrition, via one route or another, are recognized as medical interventions and should be recognized as such in an advance directive, there is still much controversy surrounding decisions to withhold such efforts.

With few exceptions, each state provides a different written format for a living will. In some, patients are required to use the prescribed form; in others, they are not. However, the language of any form utilized, particularly on "standard" forms, must conform to the state's law. This may leave wide latitude for a variety of individual interpretation and selective implementation. Frequently a preprinted form for a living will may incorporate specific patient directives that may not be allowed under the statute of a particular state. Such forms are readily available in various publications and on many Web sites. An attorney who is knowledgeable regarding the provisions of the state of jurisdiction should be retained to prepare a living will that will not only be a "legal" document but a legally binding document.

Oral living wills are usually not legally binding; although, it must be remembered that a patient's statements regarding his or her election to refuse treatment are binding. If a patient expresses his or her wishes to a nurse about the course of treatment, the nurse should record such statements in the progress notes, quoting the patient as accurately as possible. An oral living will should, however, be respected; any documented living will, written or oral, will likely be accepted by a court as definitive evidence of a patient's wishes. More specific medical directives can supplement or replace such deficient documents.

### Medical Directives

Medical directives may also be called "physician directives"; they are a more specific and comprehensive embodiment of the living will. An array of specific clinical circumstances is presented together with the patient's election in each situation. The patient defines the medical regimen he or she desires and expects in each scenario. These attempt to provide specific guidelines for the provision of or withholding of life-sustaining medical intervention. They cannot possibly include an option for every conceivable scenario.

### Durable Power of Attorney

A durable power of attorney, also called a "medical power of attorney" or a "durable power of attorney for health care" is an instrument which appoints a surrogate—an individual who, by proxy, is charged with making decisions relevant to an incompetent grantor's medical care, treatment, and termination of care and treatment when appropriate. A durable power of attorney takes effect immediately if the principal or grantor has legal capacity. The grantor can revoke the power of the attorney at any time. This power of attorney is "durable" in that it survives the grantor's incapacity; it does not survive the grantor. It terminates upon the death of the grantor. Many state laws now assume that any power of attorney may be durable unless stated otherwise. Durable powers of attorney can be recorded with the appropriate officer of a court. The process of recording such legal documents can make them (and their private details) a part of the public record. In some states, the individual must have both a terminal illness and a lack of legal capacity for a durable power of attorney for health care to be effected.

## INFORMING THE PATIENT REGARDING ADVANCE DIRECTIVES

The PSDA requires hospitals and nursing homes that receive federal funds such as from Medicare and/or Medicaid to inform each patient of his or her right, under the applicable state statute, to forego medical intervention should he or she become incapacitated. These institutions are required to determine, and document, if the patient has prepared any advance directives. They are mandated to provide *written* information about them to every patient at the time of admission. The admissions office of the institution usually presents each patient and/or family members with a brochure or pamphlet that summarizes the provisions of the state law, and defines and explains the patient's rights and the various forms of advance directives permitted under their state's statute. It was the original intent of the PSDA to encourage every individual to prepare advance directives in anticipation of a time when incapacity or terminal illness precipitates a need—a time when the individual is unable to do so.

## NURSES' ROLES IN ADVANCE DIRECTIVES

Nurses are expected to assume an active, supportive, and key role based on a thorough understanding of the statutes applicable in their state and the implications of the provisions of those laws for nursing practice. As patient advocates, nurses are charged with a degree of professional responsibility in educating the health care consumer regarding informed consent and decision making—including advance directives. In 1992, the American Nurses Association recommended that the subject of advance directives be included routinely in every nurse's admission assessment.

The PSDA requires that each institution have a policy and procedure in place regarding advance directives. Nurses should become educated in the appropriate procedures, timing, and techniques to be used in eliciting this information. "For patients (and proxies or surrogates) who wish to complete advance directives, nurses have a responsibility to ensure that patients: (1) have access to the knowledge on which to base a treatment decision, (2) have clearly expressed their decision and desires, and (3) receive treatment in accord with their expressed preferences. . . . There is evidence that nurses are the health care providers most likely to implement the PSDA" (Mezey et al. 1994, 31).

A nurse may be the first health care provider to become aware of the existence of a directive. This may be elicited during the course of the admission assessment of the patient. When this is determined, the information should be documented in the nurse's assessment notes and confirmed to the physician and all others involved in the patient's care as directed by the institution's policies and procedures.

As a result of intimate and ongoing involvement with the patient, a nurse may ascertain facts that could warrant a revision, or even recision, of a directive. The patient may express uncertainty, lack of conviction, or reluctance to let a directive stand; the nurse may be the first and only one privy to such confidences. When such sentiments are expressed or suggested, the nurse should discuss the matter with the patient's physician who may then confirm the patient's feelings and intentions and mutually reevaluate the course of action. Nurses should encourage patients to express their concerns, misgivings, and intentions, and, in a continuing process of support, assist them in confirming and defining these most personal decisions—this while validating the individual's decision-making capacity and using all appropriate procedures and personnel.

## DOCUMENTING ADVANCE DIRECTIVES IN THE MEDICAL RECORD

The Patient Self-Determination Act also mandates that a notation regarding a patient's written directive be entered into his or her medical record. The Act does not require that a copy of the document be included. If the patient has not brought the documents with him or her at the time of admission, the nurse should ask an individual who has access to them to send valid copies of them to the institution as soon as possible for review, validation, inclusion into the record, and communication to all appropriate personnel. Should the patient decide to execute or revise an advance directive after admission, the nurse is advised not to become directly involved in the procedure. He or she should refer the matter to a supervisor who may request that a social services or risk management staff member assist the patient. Nurses are not required (or even allowed in some states) to witness the patient's signature on these documents. Should they do so, they could ultimately be called on to defend their assessment of the patient's legal capacity at that time.

## COMPLIANCE WITH ADVANCE DIRECTIVES

The patient's *physician* will be primarily responsible for the interpretation and implementation of an advance directive since it deals with the medical regimen and the course of medical intervention. The physician, nurse, or other health care provider who makes every reasonable effort to carry out a directive should, as a general rule, be immune from civil or criminal liability.

The laws of each state have not only sanctioned advance directives, but have also established legal procedures to guarantee that these will be carried out by those health care professionals charged with that duty. It may not be a physician's sole and final prerogative to elect not to honor an advance directive. Such a decision is the sole and final prerogative of a court. If a physician decides not to honor a directive on the basis of personal, religious, ethical, or moral convictions, he or she must initiate a transfer of the patient to another physician or institution that is willing to do so. If the physician or the institution persists in providing intervention clearly contraindicated by a legitimate advance directive, the patient's family or a legally appointed designate may seek a court order to force compliance with the patient's wishes.

Conflicts are bound to arise with persons who have a direct interest in the patient's welfare (or estate). There usually are criminal penalties imposed on individuals for any attempt to tamper with an advance directive or make false statements regarding one's existence or nonexistence without the knowledge or consent of the grantor. These can apply no matter how well intentioned their efforts may be. Many physicians fear a lawsuit from family members who insist on compliance or, conversely, demand noncompliance. Many state statutes do provide immunity from liability for physicians who make good-faith decisions about life-sustaining interventions initiated in some circumstances.

Several articles of the ANA Code for Nurses (ANA 1985) affirm that nurses have a moral and professional responsibility to act as patient advocates, especially in those instances where a professional colleague is perceived to be in violation of the standards of practice—medical or nursing. When a nurse suspects or confirms that an advance directive is being disregarded, he or she has a legal and professional duty, as patient advocate, to intervene. Failure to do so could expose the nurse to a share of liability.

## ORGAN DONATION AND ADVANCE DIRECTIVES

In the event that the patient has been properly identified as an organ donor, life-sustaining measures may be initiated despite the existence of an advance directive that contraindicates them. This may be done in order to maintain the designated organs in a viable state until they can be harvested. There can be a number of complex issues introduced in such situations. Anyone who intends to be an organ donor should consult with both their physician and an attorney regarding the relevant provisions of any advance directive they may have signed or intend to prepare. The eventual, complying act of euthanasia to recover the donated organs at the most opportune time is, in effect, a deferred compliance with the directive and would not appear to contravene the expressed or implied wishes of the dying or clinically dead donor.

## NO-CODE ORDERS

In the absence of a written appropriate advance directive, any competent individual has the right to request that his or her physician write a "no-code" order when circumstances warrant it. This affirms the patient's personal decision that neither medical nor nursing staff attempt resuscitation in the event of cardiac and/or respiratory failure. The patient may also elect to refuse other life-sustaining procedures and define the criteria to be considered. All discussions with the patient or appropriate family members regarding the decision should be documented thoroughly by the physician involved. Any patient or family discussions with a nurse regarding the matter must also be documented and referred to the physician so that he or she can evaluate the patient's intentions and write the order accordingly. A nurse should never agree to an inappropriate request from a family member or any other person, unless the individual is acting under a documented advance directive that has been implemented based on the patient's status.

This so-called slow code is *the* order that most often does not appear in the physician's written orders or notes but is most frequently given orally. A verbal "do not resuscitate" (DNR) order presents an unacceptable risk to the nursing staff. As a general rule, nurses should not accept and/or act on a verbal DNR order. Should there be any question of the propriety of a nurse's action in the event of a code, a physician could disclaim a verbal order by denying he or she gave it or by refusing to countersign it. If a nurse is required by the urgency or mitigating circumstances of the situation to accept a verbal DNR order, it is advisable to have a witness who can confirm the subject, date, time, originator, and the verbatim content of the order.

In the absence of a written DNR order (or physician-activated advance directive) a nurse must initiate full-code protocols and begin resuscitative efforts immediately—even if the patient is terminally ill. If a DNR order has in fact been written, the nurse should, of course, not call a code. To do so could expose the nurse to a charge of insubordination, breach of duty, battery, or even criminal negligence. Failure to take appropriate action, with or without a written order, could be construed as an independent medical judgment, tantamount to practicing medicine without a license. Such an action could expose a nurse to censure and possible loss of licensure. Without a documented no-code order, the nurse must behave as if the order simply does not exist. Failure to take what a court might eventually deem appropriate action may be cause for a claim of malpractice. Defending such a claim could be very difficult in the absence of a written DNR order.

Every hospital accredited by the JCAHO is required to have a written policy regarding withholding or termination of life-sustaining measures. Every staff nurse must know what that policy prescribes and act accordingly. A typical directive on this matter states that any no-code order must be *written*—by the appropriate physician—in the patient's medical record. It is a legal and professional responsibility of the physician. The policy may include a procedure for periodic review of a DNR order and criteria for continuance or cessation contingent on the patient's status.

## REFERENCES

Aiken, Tonia, and Joseph Catalano. 1994. *Legal, Ethical and Political Issues in Nursing*. F. A. Davis.

American Nurses Association. 1992. *Position Statement on Nursing and the Patient Self-Determination Act.*

American Nurses Association. 1985. *Code for Nurses with Interpretive Statements.*

Mezey, Mathy, Lois K. Evans, Zola D. Golub, Elizabeth Murphy, and Gladys B. White. 1994. The patient Self-Determination Act: Sources of concern for nurses. *Nursing Outlook* 42 (1) (January): 30–38.

Schwarz, Judith K. 1992. Living wills and health care proxies: Nurse practice implications. *Nursing and Health Care* 13 (3) (March): 92–96.

# 13

## Malpractice Insurance

### PROFESSIONAL RESPONSIBILITY FOR COVERAGE

Anyone involved in the provision of health care in any capacity should have professional liability insurance. It is every nurse's professional duty to be responsible in all matters of practice. This includes competency in nursing skills and also fiscal accountability. Although there may be no legal requirement for a nurse to have malpractice insurance coverage, there is a moral and ethical imperative in this responsibility. It is a reasonable expectation on the part of every patient that a nurse will provide safe and therapeutic care; and, in the event that the nurse fails in this duty, that a financial remedy will be available to compensate the patient for any injuries. The injured patient can seek this remedy in restitution from an insurance company and/or in seizure and conversion of the nurse-defendant's personal assets and future wages. Malpractice insurance is a logical requirement in our litigious society. It should be a practice requirement in the professional community. It has been suggested that proof of such coverage be a criterion for professional licensure.

### THE NEED FOR MALPRACTICE INSURANCE

Any nurse, in any practice setting, at any time, can be named in a nursing malpractice claim or lawsuit. This includes the student aspiring to the profession, the staff nurse or administrator in active practice, the nurse who is temporarily away from practice, or the individual who has enjoyed active retirement for some time. None is exempt from potential litigation or immune from the risk. If any one of these does not now have, or has never had, the appropriate type of malpractice insurance coverage, this risk could perpetuate itself. Know the type of coverage you have, and take immediate remedial steps if it is deficient in any way.

The days when a nurse did not have to worry about or even need malpractice insurance are long gone. In the litigious climate of today's health care, the nurse who does not recognize the constant peril of being sued, and who does not take appropriate steps to mitigate such risk, is naïve, reckless, and fiscally and professionally irresponsible. It is the foolish nurse who does not appreciate the reality that he or she can be the victim of a lawsuit by any one at any time (even long after his or her retirement from active practice) and that the suit may be based on the flimsiest pretext or the remotest connection to a long-passed event.

Malpractice, as defined previously, is professional negligence. It is not synonymous with incompetence. Even the most competent nurse can be sued for an action or omission that harms a patient. Insurance coverage will not eliminate the risk of being sued; but it will go a long way in easing the fear of being sued and provide a reasonable sense of security and some degree of peace of mind. It will never provide immunity for the incompetent.

A nurse's malpractice insurance policy should not be another liability, an additional risk to manage, in his or her practice. It could be argued that it has no actual relevancy to clinical practice. It cannot enhance a practitioner's skills or prevent negligence. It does not directly protect the hospital, a clinical nursing instructor, an academic institution employing that instructor, or the nurse's fellow staff or supervisors. It certainly does not protect the patient. Essentially, it protects only the policy holder.

## GOING NAKED

A reasonable question then is: If a nurse has no substantial assets that could be taken in an adverse judgment, why incur the expense, why incur the cost of coverage? Why not "go naked"? If the individual has no material wealth, what is at risk? They do not have the deep pockets of a physician or the deeper pockets of the hospital. Without significant resources, they may think they are, in effect, "lawsuit-proof" or "judgment-proof". There is a very serious flaw in this logic. The laws applicable to damages awarded in judgments vary according to the jurisdiction. In many jurisdictions the judgment remains open, or the plaintiff can file, and refile it, until it is satisfied or until they elect to forego it. During the time the judgment remains open, liens may be placed on property. Any assets that the defendant might acquire, including inheritances, could be seized in satisfaction. Wages could be garnisheed. His or her estate could be sued.

State laws vary on the nature and amount of personal assets that can be seized in satisfaction of a judgment. However, in most states, jointly owned assets are not subject to attachment. In the event that a nursing malpractice lawsuit actually goes to trial, an adverse judgment awarded by a jury could force a defendant into bankruptcy and an ongoing state of insolvency. A negotiated settlement could have equally devastating financial consequences. This can happen to the nurse who is insured when the amount of damages exceeds the policy limits, or to the nurse who is uninsured—where there is no policy and no limits.

A legal defense must be mounted against a malpractice action. Every nurse should carry a personal policy if for no other reason than it will provide, and compensate, an attorney to defend the nurse in any malpractice claim. Damage awards aside, attorney's fees could bankrupt a defendant without coverage. This alone dictates a personal policy as a sound investment at modest expense. Once a complaint or lawsuit has been filed against a defendant, he or she will not be able to obtain insurance coverage after-the-fact. Efforts to protect assets will likely be to no avail.

## MISTAKEN PERCEPTIONS OF MALPRACTICE INSURANCE

A prevalent and mistaken belief is that malpractice coverage actually invites lawsuits against nurses and physicians or markedly increases the risk of malpractice litigation. Research shows that there is no substantive evidence for this notion. Neither the plaintiff nor his or her attorney can verify a prospective defendant's insurance coverage until a lawsuit has actually been filed and the discovery process is initiated.

Another fallacy is that a sympathetic jury will be more inclined to award damages, or to be more generous in such awards, when they believe that a bountiful supply of an insurance company's money is available for distribution to the injured victim. In fact, the jury is likely to be ignorant of existing coverage, let alone the amount. In some jurisdictions this knowledge is forbidden to a jury by law. Of course, it would be a reasonable supposition by a patient-plaintiff and by any or all members of a jury, that an intelligent and prudent practitioner would carry malpractice insurance and that the coverage involves substantial sums.

## TYPES OF MALPRACTICE INSURANCE POLICIES

There are two types of malpractice insurance policies. It is absolutely necessary for every nursing student, for every nurse in clinical practice of any kind, and for the nurse who is no longer practicing—even long retired—to know which type of policy he or she now carries or *has ever carried*. The two types of policies are "occurrence" and "claims-made". They cover either medical or nursing malpractice.

### Occurrence

An occurrence malpractice insurance policy covers all events (injuries or alleged injuries) that occur *during the period in which the policy was in effect. This would include all claims that might be made after the policy has expired or been terminated.* Most personal policies are occurrence, and it is the most advantageous type to have, even though premiums might be higher. The advantage lies in the fact that once the policy goes into effect, *a suit arising from any incident while it is in effect will be covered regardless of how long afterward it may be brought.* Because of the vagaries in the statutes of limitations, the occurrence policy offers the best and most long-lasting protection. Look for language in the policy such as "any injury arising out of . . . during the period of coverage of this policy"—this denotes an occurrence-based policy.

### Claims-made

A claims-made policy *covers any claims made while the policy is actually in effect.* Under this type of coverage, even if the alleged injury occurs during the policy period, but the lawsuit is not filed until after the policy has lapsed, the insurer has no obligation. *If this policy is terminated or is allowed to expire, all coverage ceases.* The *claim must be made within the policy period* and must be promptly reported to the insurance carrier during the policy period or during the "tail". Once this type of policy is purchased, *it must be maintained continuously and uninterrupted in order to provide adequate protection. Under such a policy, the individual is also covered for any claim that might arise from an event that occurred before the policy went into effect.*

The majority of institutional coverage is claims-made. Since these policies cover only claims filed while the policy is actually in effect, the nurse who has left the employment of the institution, and does not have, or has never had, appropriate personal coverage, could incur the sole responsibility for defending himself or herself against a claim for malpractice arising many years after terminating employment by a particular institution. The individual who changes jobs frequently or has several different employers (such as agencies) at one time, can lose track of malpractice insurance status and create potentially dangerous deficiencies in coverage. Acquisition and maintenance of an appropriate personal policy substantially reduces such risks.

### "Tail" Coverage

"Tail" coverage is added coverage that provides an uninterrupted extension of a policy period. It is also known as an "extending reporting endorsement". It extends the coverage provided under a claims-made policy and provides protection to a health care provider against any claims filed for events that might have occurred during the period of the preexisting claims-made policy, which is no longer in force. The availability of such supplemental coverage may be limited. It can be an expensive option for the purchaser of a claims-made policy.

## READING AND UNDERSTANDING A POLICY

A malpractice insurance policy that practitioners purchase represents a business contract between them and the insurance company. The promotional materials that they may have received will not contain every detail and provision of the policy. In deciding if a policy is adequate or appropriate for their circumstances, they should review the various terms and conditions of the proposal with a representative of the carrier. Prospective purchasers should be prepared to ask pertinent questions and insist on clear, intelligible answers. If they have already acquired coverage, they should examine their policy in detail to confirm their understanding of the language and terms.

Every policy will contain certain sections and provisions. These elements are common to all policies but may vary in the degree of comprehension allowed the reader. If the language of the policy is not clear, the insured should contact a representative of the insurance company, preferably the agent who sold the policy, and ask for an explanation. If not satisfied, he or she should write directly to the company's chief executive officer and state a complaint politely, firmly, and succinctly.

### Elements of a Policy

The elements in any given malpractice insurance policy may vary by arrangement within the body of the policy but generally include the following.

### Insuring Agreement

This is the part of the contract that defines the rights and obligations of each party. The insurer promises to provide, and pay for, legal representation to defend the policy holder against a lawuit for malpractice regardless of the merits of the claim. In return, the insured agrees to pay the premiums (the "consideration" of the contract) and agrees to accept and abide by the terms of the policy—*each and every one of them*! The insured is required (possibly under oath) to provide complete and accurate information on an insurance application form. It must be remembered that a falsified application, if discovered by the carrier, can nullify the policy at *any* time.

Of particular significance to a defendant will be any statement regarding the insurance company's right to settle any and all claims against them *without* their prior consent or knowledge. A policy may or may not require the insured's consent before a settlement agreement can be reached. If the insured withholds such consent without reasonable cause, the carrier could rescind coverage. The insured should know and understand what, if any, part he or she will play in discussions or agreements regarding a settlement of the claim. It must be remembered that *a settlement is not an admission of liability*; however, it denies a defendant the opportunity to present his or her side of the story to a jury and it could leave him or her with a feeling of betrayal. Settlement does not provide vindication.

Generally, a malpractice insurance policy will prohibit the insured from incurring any expenses or obligations, or making any payments, unless these are voluntary, and at the personal expense of the insured. The terms of the contract may also provide that unless the insured has fully complied with each of the terms of the policy, he or she cannot initiate an action against the carrier.

If a nurse elects for ADR in any claim of malpractice, he or she may be required to retain an attorney personally. Malpractice insurance carriers, as a general rule, do not provide legal counsel for a client in the event of ADR proceedings unless a *lawsuit* has actually been *filed*.

You must notify your insurance carrier that you intend to use ADR in a lawsuit. Although the company may be amenable to the less costly alternative to litigation, it may still retain the right to decide how the claim against you (and, in effect—them) will be disposed of. If the insured fails to notify the carrier that he or she has elected ADR, the insured could risk forfeiture of coverage for any settlement of the suit agreed on without the carrier's consent or knowledge.

### Coverage Agreement

This section will specify the particular individual insured and define those areas of nursing practice that are covered by the policy. This will usually be an individually named practitioner, properly licensed by a state board, who provides professional services within the scope of nursing practice defined by a state's nurse practice act. The term "professional services" may have different meanings to the parties, and a dispute could arise in the event of a suit.

There may be language in this portion of the policy that refers to "such professional services that may be personally provided by the individual named as the insured". This covers the individual nurse in the course of his or her own personal nursing duties and actions. Any nurse whose duties might routinely include supervision of other nurses, ancillary staff, nursing students, or any one providing patient care should examine the policy for language referring to "services which are provided by any individual acting under the personal supervision, control, or direction of the insured". Inclusion of this statement offers protection for the nurse, as a supervisor, in the event that a claim based on improper supervision would arise. As previously discussed, the Supreme Court has recently expanded the definition of "supervisor".

### Conditions

This section of the policy bears close scrutiny and thorough understanding. It is here that the obligations of the insured and the insurer in the event of a claim or lawsuit are set forth. The rights of the insurer to cancel the policy and the applicable criteria will be defined here. There will be a requirement that the insured notify the carrier within a specified time period in the event of any claim or suit that could give rise to a payment of damages. The method of notification may or may not be specified. The insured may be required to forward certain relevant documents to the insurer. The insured must follow these conditions exactly. Any failure in following the defined notification procedures could be cause for *immediate voiding* of the policy. An employer's policy may also specify precise procedures for notification of the employer in the event that a nurse becomes aware of a possible claim or suit. Failure here could result in selective voiding of that nurse's coverage under the employer's policy.

In the event of litigation, the insured defendant will be obliged to cooperate with and to assist the attorney assigned by the insurance company in every possible way in the preparation of a defense. This includes a full and truthful disclosure of all relevant facts. Any attempts to withhold or falsify pertinent information could be cause for the carrier to void coverage and withdraw the assigned attorney's services. The now uninsured individual would be obliged to retain an attorney at his or her own expense.

The defendant will be expected to appear and testify at depositions and at a trial. Failure to cooperate with the insurance company or its representatives could cause cancellation of the policy. If during the course of the lawsuit, the attorney retained by the carrier determines that the insured has attempted a cover-up, is not cooperating, or has violated any of the terms and conditions of the policy, the attorney is obliged to report the circumstances to the insurance company that has retained his or her services. The company could then elect to refuse to further defend the insured, leaving the insured to his or her own devices.

An insurance company may permit policy holders to select counsel of their choice in the event of a suit for nursing malpractice. Usually the carrier will provide a defense attorney to represent the insured. The nurse has a right to know and evaluate the credentials and experience of any attorney retained on his or her behalf and should demand a trial lawyer who has extensive experience in litigation involving medical and/or nursing malpractice.

### Exclusions

Exclusions are the specified actions or circumstance that are *not covered* under the terms of the policy. Under a "reservation of rights", the carrier reserves the right to deny coverage if it determines that the claim involves any alleged action or circumstance that is defined as excluded. The company will not pay the costs of defending a nurse in these circumstances. If it were to be determined at some future time that a defense had been provided for an action which, in fact, was excluded, the insurer may demand and/or sue for reimbursement from the insured (to include attorney's fees and any damages paid out!). There are some carriers who might require that the defendant be responsible for a certain portion of expenses involved in the litigation until such time as it is demonstrated that an activity was *not* excluded.

An individual liability policy usually provides rather broad coverage, and for purposes of exclusion, would focus on those actions that would be usually defined as beyond a practitioner's scope of practice. The scope of nursing practice includes any and all skills, procedures, and knowledge included in any curriculum of nursing education and/or defined and authorized by a state's nurse practice act. Nurses employed in advanced practice and expanded roles such as midwives, practitioners, consultants, or as entrepreneurs should confirm any exclusionary provisions of their policy applicable to their positions, practice, and professional services.

Other specific exclusions may include any claims resulting from actions of a nurse on duty while he or she was impaired as a result of substance abuse. *Criminal acts are universally excluded.* These include fraud and various forms of patient abuse, including assault and battery. Actions considered to be gross negligence may be listed. A more recent exclusion is the transmission of HIV/AIDS by a nurse to a patient. *Punitive damages* that might be awarded by a court are *virtually always excluded.* The costs of legal representation required in a hearing before a state board of nursing are generally not covered.

### Subrogation

In an institution's policy, the conditions may also include the insurance company's statement of subrogation of rights. In a situation where the institution is named as the sole defendant in a malpractice lawsuit in which a practitioner (physician or nurse) was directly involved but not named as a co-defendant, the insurance company will pay damages in a settlement or in an awarded judgment. The insurer could retain the right to sue (cross-file against) that practitioner deemed negligent in the original action and, therefore, responsible for the loss. Under the common law of some states, the nurse or physician could be held liable. Without a personal malpractice policy, the individual would incur all costs of defending the suit and any damages awarded.

### Policy Limits

"Limits" is a policy's predetermined maximum amount that the insurance carrier will pay out in the event of a settlement or judgment in a lawsuit. The "double limits" of coverage specify the amount that will be paid for each individual claim and an aggregate amount. The first is identified as the "per incident" or "per occurrence" limit. This delimits the monetary amount that the insurance company will pay out for a *single* claim. The second, the "aggregate" limit, is the total amount the insurer will pay out *in any given policy year.* The aggregate of claims that might arise from a single occurrence are treated as a single claim for the purposes of coverage under the policy.

The amount of coverage that a practitioner decides to commit for may be determined by the cost. The largest amount for the least cost is the ideal. The individual should shop for malpractice insurance and explore the market as he or she would for life, health, or property insurance. A practitioner's particular specialty area of practice and the nature of that practice should be a factor in determining the appropriate amount of coverage. Self-employed, advanced practice nurses, and those practicing in high-risk nursing specialties should commit for the maximum amount available and affordable. Staff nurses should also acquire maximum coverage that is usually available for a modest investment.

### Supplementary Payments

Certain policies may provide for stipends to the insured to supplement reduced earnings resulting from their involvement in litigation. There may also be reimbursement for reasonable expenses relating to the suit. This optional additional coverage is usually available at a modest cost. It is worth the added expense. An employer's policy is not likely to provide for such supplementary coverage, and the individual who does not have this provision in a personal policy runs the risk of any financial losses incurred as a result of missed work and incidental expenses related to the lawsuit.

### EMPLOYER COVERAGE

A recurring question for nurses is whether or not they should purchase individual malpractice insurance or practice under their employer's policy. A prevalent delusion is that they are fully covered under the employer's policy. An employer's policy may not provide blanket protection. There may be limits to the scope, length, and amount of coverage provided. Typically, the employee will be covered under a group contract, but not as an individual. The nurse who believes that he or she is covered under such a policy (which is usually quite comprehensive) may elect to forego the purchase of a personal policy. As far as the institution's coverage goes, it should benefit an employee to some degree. However, it goes only as far as the limits of the premises—while the nurse is actually on duty, as an employee—and only when acting within the scope of nursing practice.

The nurse-employee may not be covered for any actions that are not defined in the job description, not in conformance with the institution's policies and procedures, or in violation of the state's nurse practice act. In the event of a lawsuit, if the employer can demonstrate that the nurse's action was, in fact, outside of the scope of his or her practice, the individual without a personal policy may find it necessary to retain a defense attorney at his or her *own expense.* Even if covered personally, it is likely that his or her own insurer would refuse defense under the conditions of the policy relating to such actions. Most employer policies do not include any form of supplementary payments for an employee's lost wages or other expenses incurred during a lawsuit. These will be the employee's personal responsibility.

If a nurse and the employer are named as co-defendants in a lawsuit and found liable for damages, the employer will take priority in coverage, the nurse secondary. If the limits of the policy are expended on behalf of the institution, the nurse will be on his or her own unless he or she has a personal malpractice policy. It must remembered that the insurance carrier's obligation is first and foremost to protect the interests of its institutional client—whose employees may be secondary. The policy coverage will be structured to meet the needs of the institution and not necessarily those of its employees.

A second deficiency in employer coverage could be in the legal representation provided to the nurse by the institution's insurance carrier. As noted, the institution is the attorney's primary client, and the interests of that client may take precedence. The institution may elect to settle a lawsuit in order to avoid the expense and adverse publicity that a trial might engender. The nurse will likely have no say in this decision—a decision that could have a more adverse effect than a trial that might ultimately have been to the nurse's advantage. For this reason, every prudent nurse is encouraged to acquire and maintain a personal policy to protect his or her personal interests. With such a policy, the carrier's first allegiance will be to the nurse. He or she should be the sole priority of the attorney assigned as defense counsel.

Even when a nurse is covered by an employer's policy, he or she still could be at risk from the insurance company's subrogation rights as previously described or from the employing institution itself. Based on a nurse's proven malpractice, the employer (or former employer) could elect to file an indemnity countersuit against the nurse to recover its costs and any monetary losses incurred in the lawsuit when the amount of damages awarded is in excess of the coverage limit. This is very rare. It can be very demoralizing to staff. It may be prohibited by terms of the institution's policy. Of course, the institution's policy will not cover the nurse in this unlikely instance; a personal policy may or may not. If an individual does not have the benefit of this type of coverage under a personal policy, the costs will be the individual's and the individual's alone.

In the past, institutions paid additional premiums for coverage of nursing staff and other health care providers. There has been a trend identified in which staff nurses are not being included in an institution's blanket liability insurance policy. In an ongoing effort to cut operating costs, many institutions now recommend, or require, that their employees personally contract and pay for coverage. In some instances premiums may be reimbursed as a part of a benefits package. If the institution remits the premiums for personal policies in a lump sum to a carrier, there is a risk that a nurse could default in his or her personal responsibilities under this arrangement. In the event of a malpractice lawsuit filed against the nurse personally, he or she might assume that the matter will be handled by the institution and fail to take the prompt and direct notification steps required by a personal policy. This failure could result in a forfeiture of coverage.

### Learning about Your Employer's Coverage

The nurse is entitled to know the extent of coverage (if any) under an employer's policy. He or she should request an opportunity to meet with an appropriate risk management or human resources administrator to review the provisions of the employer's insurance policy and their implications for that nurse in their particular practice setting. Having done this, the nurse should review his or her own personal policy to identify any deficiencies and needs for augmented coverage. The elements to look for in an employer's policy are shown in Table 13.1.

**Table 13.1**
**What to Look for in an Employer's Policy**

- Is the individual specifically named in the institution's policy? This is essential to prove to an insurer that he or she is/was an employee of the institution.

- Is his or her title, position, or job description listed as covered?

- What language indicates that he or she is, in fact, covered?

- What type of policy is in effect—claims-made or occurrence?

- Does the policy provide the individual with personal liability coverage?

- What are the applicable limits of that coverage? What are the limits of liability? Will the individual share in a specified limit that includes other staff and the hospital itself?

- Is there a subrogation provision?

- Which, if any, exclusionary clauses pertain to the individual?

- Is there a deductible? If so, what is the amount?

- Is the individual covered only while on duty or also off the job?

- Will a copy of the policy be made available to the individual? This is essential. Without it, the individual has no guarantee that he or she is, in fact, covered.

# 14

# The National Practitioner Data Bank

## THE CREATION OF THE NATIONAL PRACTITIONER DATA BANK

The National Practitioner Data Bank (NPDB, Data Bank) was established through Title IV of Public Law 99–660, the *Health Care Quality Improvement Act of 1986*, as amended (the Act). The intent of Title IV was to improve the quality of health care by encouraging hospitals, state licensing boards, and other health care entities, including professional societies, to identify and discipline those who engage in unprofessional behavior; and to restrict the ability of incompetent physicians, dentists, and other health care practitioners to move from state to state without disclosure or discovery of previous damaging or incompetent performance. At the same time, it is charged with protecting the rights of the practitioner.

In 1987, Section 5 of the Medicare and Medicaid Patient and Program Protection Act (PL 100–93) expanded certain provisions of the 1986 law. The expanded scope included provisions for licensure actions taken against certain health care practitioners. Final regulations governing the Data Bank were published in the *Federal Register* on October 17, 1989, and are codified at 45 DFR Part 60. On September 1, 1990, the NPDB was formally inaugurated. There were no retroactive reporting requirements for events prior to September 1, 1990. Copies of the Act and the final regulations are provided in the *National Practitioner Data Bank Guidebook*, which is available through the Data Bank Help Line. (See appendix II for the NPDB's Web site.)

## DEFINITION OF "HEALTH CARE PRACTITIONER"

Initially the focus was primarily on the medical and dental professions, but when eventually implemented, and as amended, the scope of the law included all licensed health care practitioners. These other health care practitioners are defined as individuals other than physicians or dentists who are licensed or otherwise authorized (certified or registered) by a state to provide some form of health care services. There is no requirement to query or report on laypersons who are not licensed or otherwise authorized by a state

**Table 14.1**
**Examples of Other Health Care Practitioners**

"The following list is provided solely for illustration. The inclusion or exclusion of any health care occupational group should not be interpreted as a mandate or a waiver of compliance to Data Bank reporting requirements, since licensure and certification requirements vary from state to state."

| | |
|---|---|
| Acupuncturists | Occupational Therapy Assistants |
| Audiologists | Ocularists |
| Chiropractors | Opticians |
| Dental Hygienists | Optometrists |
| Denturists | Orthotics/Prosthetics Fitters |
| Dietitians | Pharmacists |
| Emergency Medical Technicians | Pharmacists, Nuclear |
| Homeopaths | Physical Therapy Assistants |
| Medical Assistants | Physical Therapists |
| Medical Technologists | Physician Assistants |
| Mental Health Counselors | Professional Counselors |
| Nuclear Medicine Technologists | Psychiatric Technicians |
| Nurse's Aides | Radiation Therapy Technologists |
| Nurse Anesthetists | Radiologic Technologists |
| Nurse Midwives | Rehabilitation Therapists |
| Nurse Practitioners | Respiratory Therapists |
| Nurse, Registered | Respiratory Therapy Technician |
| Nutritionists | Social Workers, Clinical |
| Occupational Therapists | Speech/Language Pathologists |

*Source*: National Practitioner Data Bank 1996, C–2.

to provide their legitimate services. Examples of these practitioners are shown in Table 14.1.

## CONFIDENTIALITY OF DATA BANK INFORMATION

Information reported to the Data Bank is considered confidential and can not be disclosed except as specified in the regulations at 45 CFR Part 60. A comprehensive security system has been designed to prevent access to and manipulation of the data by any unauthorized persons. Persons or entities that receive information from the NPDB either directly or indirectly are subject to the confidentiality provisions and the imposition of a penalty if they violate those provisions. Federal statutes subject individuals or entities who knowingly and willfully report to or query the Data Bank under false pretenses, or who fraudulently access the Data Bank computer databases, to criminal penalties, including fines and imprisonment.

### The Privacy Act of 1974

The *Privacy Act*, 5 USC, Section 552a, protects the contents of federal systems of records on individuals, such as those contained in the Data Bank, from disclosure without the subject's consent, unless the disclosure is for a routine use of the system of records as published annually in the *Federal Register*. The published routine uses of Data Bank information do not allow disclosure to the general public. The limited access provision of the *Health Care Quality Improvement Act of 1986*, as amended, supersedes the disclosure requirements of the *Freedom of Information Act* (FOIA), 5 USC Section 552, as amended.

## WHAT MUST BE REPORTED TO THE DATA BANK

The NPDB is charged with collecting and maintaining three types of information:

- Reports of medical or nursing malpractice payments of damages resulting from:
    1. a *written* claim;
    2. a negotiated settlement of a claim;
    3. the awarding of a judgment in a court; or
    4. any decision in formal arbitration.
- Reports of adverse licensure actions taken by state boards of medicine or nursing.

- Reports of professional review actions taken by hospitals and other health care entities that adversely affect clinical privileges for a period longer than thirty days; or the voluntary surrender or restriction of clinical privileges while under, or in return for not conducting, an investigation relating to possible incompetence or improper professional conduct; and reports of review actions taken by professional societies that adversely affect the subject's membership in the society.

### Payments of Claims

Only those payments made for the benefit of a named practitioner as a result of suits or claims are reportable. The subject of the report may be any health care practitioner. The fact that such an individual may not have been named as a defendant is not material.

Any health care entity or insurance company that pays out money on behalf of a licensed practitioner as a result of a *written* malpractice claim or action in law is required to report such payment within thirty days. If the party making the payment fails to report any such disbursement, the statues provide for civil penalties, including a fine of up to $10,000 for each act of omission in reporting.

The payment can be one resulting from a negotiated settlement of a claim, the awarding of a judgment in a court, or any decision in formal arbitration. Any and all such payments, *regardless of the amount*, made as a result of a written claim, or a lawsuit for malpractice, which names an individual health care provider, and which demanded monetary compensation, whether such payment is made as an award in a judgment or in a negotiated settlement, must be reported. These payments include all those the terms of which may have been stipulated as confidential by a court. If a claim, lawsuit, settlement, or trial does not involve or require cash disbursements for other than legal expenses, no report is necessary.

Reports must be submitted to the Data Bank when medical malpractice payments are made for the benefit of residents or interns. Medical malpractice payments made for the benefit of house staff insured by their employers are also reportable.

Payments made for the benefit of medical, dental, or nursing students are *not* reportable. Unlicensed student providers provide health care services exclusively under the supervision of licensed health care professionals in a training environment, for example, a clinical nursing instructor. Students do not fall into the "other health care practitioner" category. These latter are licensed by a state and/or meet state registration or certification requirements.

The filing of a lawsuit or claim is *not*, in itself, reportable. *There is no requirement that the claim actually be filed in any court of law.* The NPDB makes no evaluations or presumptions as to the merits of any claims of malpractice upon which a payment may have been based. The NPDB is primarily concerned with the accuracy of the data reported and its mandate under the federal laws in the compilation and proper dissemination of the data.

### Report Format

The report must include the name of the practitioner, and other specific data regarding him or her, the amount of the payment made, and all relevant details surrounding the circumstances of the claim—*including the name of the claimant*. Reporting entities are required to provide a detailed narrative that describes the acts or omissions and the injuries upon which the medical malpractice action or claim was based.

Narrative descriptions must include seven general categories of information:

1. Age: The patient's age at the time of the initial event.
2. Sex: Male, female, and disputed; disputed may be used in claims involving individuals whose sex has been physically altered or who are physically one sex but live outwardly as the other.
3. Patient Type: Generally an indication of inpatient or outpatient status. This category is useful when the event might occur in a variety of clinical settings.
4. Initial Event (Procedure/Diagnosis): Usually the event on which the claim is predicated. It should reflect a generic diagnosis and procedure, if applicable.
5. Subsequent Event: Usually an occurrence that precipitated the claim. The time sequence in relation to the initial event is relevant.
6. Damages (Medical and/or Legal): A description of damages resulting from the initial and subsequent events.
7. Standard of Care Determination: If a determination was made by the payer whether or not standards of care were met, the determination is to be included. (National Practitioner Data Bank 1996, E–7)

### WHO MUST REPORT TO THE DATA BANK

The federal statute prescribed mandatory reporting of specified data on selected health care professionals and defines those entities that are required to report. These entities are shown in Table 14.2.

**Table 14.2**
**Reporting Requirements Affecting Physicians, Dentists, and Other Health Care Practitioners**

| Entity | Reporting to the Data Bank |
|---|---|
| Hospitals and other health care entities: | *Must* report: (1) professional review actions related to professional competence or conduct that adversely affect clinical privileges of a physician or dentist for more than thirty days; (2) a physician's or dentist's voluntary surrender or restriction of clinical privileges while under investigation for professional competence or conduct or in return for not conducting an investigation; and (3) revisions to such actions. May report on other health care practitioners. |
| State medical and dental boards: | *Must* report certain adverse licensure actions related to professional competence or professional conduct and revisions to such actions for physicians and dentists. |
| Professional societies: | *Must* report professional review actions that adversely affect professional memberships and revisions to such actions for physicians and dentists. May report on other health care practitioners. |
| Medical malpractice insurers: | *Must* report payments made on behalf of physicians. dentists, and other health care practitioners in settlement of or in satisfaction in whole or in part of a claim or judgment against such practitioner. |
| Health care practitioners: | Are not required to report on their own behalf. |

*Source*: National Practitioner Data Bank 1996, C–1.

## WHO CAN AND WHO MUST QUERY THE DATA BANK

An entity may be required by law to query the NPDB in certain instances, and in others, may have an option to do so. Only health care institutions and entities, professional organizations, and state licensing boards have access to the database. Any individual practitioner may access the data bank only on his or her own behalf. State boards of medicine and nursing have access.

Insurance companies offering medical malpractice policies are prohibited access even though they are required to report payments.

Information in the files of the NPDB is prohibited to the public-at-large. There have been several bills introduced in Congress to permit public access, but these have been vehemently objected to by the American Medical Association and failed to become law. A plaintiff or a plaintiff's attorney who has actually filed a claim or suit for malpractice against a hospital may have limited access. Attorney access is discussed in detail in a following section. A *Fact Sheet for the General Public* and a *Fact Sheet for Attorneys* is available from the NPDB. Query requirements are shown in Table 14.3.

**Table 14.3**
**Title IV Querying Requirements**

| Entity | Requirement |
| --- | --- |
| *Hospitals*: Screening applicants for medical staff appointment or granting of clinical privileges; every two years for physicians, dentists, or other health care practitioners on the medical staff or granted clinical privileges | *Must* query |
| At such times as they deem necessary | May query |
| *Other health care entities*: Screening applicants for medical staff appointments or granting of clinical privileges; supporting professional review activities | May query |
| *State licensing boards*: At such times as they deem necessary | May query |
| *Professional societies*: Screening applicants for membership or affiliation; supporting professional review activities | May query |
| *Plaintiffs' attorneys*: Plaintiff's attorney or plaintiff representing himself or herself who has filed a medical malpractice action or claim in a state or federal court or other adjudicative body against | May query |

a hospital when evidence is submitted
which reveals the hospital failed
to make a required query of the Data Bank
on the practitioner(s) also named
in the action or claim

*Physicians, dentists, or other health care*
*practitioners*:
Regarding their own files                                    May query

*Medical malpractice insurers*:                              May *not* query

*Source*: National Practitioner Data Bank 1996, D–4.

Health care facilities other than hospitals may submit a request for information on any licensed practitioner who is employed or being considered for employment. A hospital is not required to query more than once every two years regarding a practitioner who is continuously on staff. Hospitals with annual reappointment are not required to query annually. Hospitals *may* query at any time in conjunction with professional review procedures.

Hospitals are not required to query the Data Bank regarding medical and dental residents, interns, or staff fellows even though these may be licensed. They are considered trainees in a structured program of supervised graduate medical education rather than members of the medical staff. A hospital is required to query the Data Bank regarding residents or interns when such individuals are appointed to the medical staff or granted clinical privileges to practice outside the parameters of the formal educational education program (e.g., moonlighting in an ICU or emergency room).

### Queries Regarding Staff Nurses

A hospital has the *option* to query the data bank regarding a registered, professional nurse who is being considered for a *staff* nursing position that does not involve the granting of clinical privileges. However, the regulations refer to a health care practitioner as an individual "on the medical staff"; therefore, most nurses would be excluded. Such privileges usually are granted only to advanced practice nurses such as nurse practitioners, clinical nurse specialists, nurse midwives, or nurse anesthetists. In any instances where clinical privileges are being granted to a nurse, a query is mandatory.

### LEGAL IMPLICATIONS OF A HOSPITAL'S FAILURE TO QUERY
### THE DATA BANK

As shown in Table 14.3, *hospitals are the only health care entities with mandatory requirements for querying* the Data Bank. If a hospital fails in the inquiry protocol, as mandated by law, which could have revealed information that would have given cause for the hospital to deny or revoke clinical privileges, the hospital could be held liable in a malpractice claim against the practitioner. It could be presumed that the hospital might have had knowledge of any information reported to the Data Bank concerning that individual and was aware of what the Data Bank could have revealed about the practitioner who is the subject of a malpractice claim.

What the attorney for the plaintiff will attempt to prove is that the hospital was negligent in:

1. hiring and granting clinical privileges to the defendant practitioner;
2. failing to adequately investigate the practitioner's background by accessing the NPDB as required by law;
3. failing to verify the truth and accuracy of the practitioner's professional education and experience as shown on an application before employment and granting of clinical privileges; and
4. failing to establish and/or follow written policies and procedures regarding employment and the granting of clinical privileges.

## ATTORNEY ACCESS TO THE DATA BANK

A plaintiff's attorney who has actually filed a claim or suit for malpractice against a hospital may have limited access. He or she is permitted to obtain information from the NPDB only under certain conditions (National Practitioner Data Bank 1996, D5–D6.)

If a hospital is named as a defendant together with individual practitioners, the plaintiff's attorney must demonstrate that the hospital failed in its statutory obligation to query the Data Bank as described previously. If this can be proven, the NPDB may disclose the information; however, the attorney can utilize any information derived only in that specific case and involving only that specific hospital. *It may not be used to assail the individual practitioner.*

The conditions and limitations for attorney access are defined in the Act and in the Rules and Regulations as follows:

§60.11 Requesting information from the National Practitioner Data Bank.
(a) *Who may request information and what information may be available.* Information in the Data Bank will be available, upon request, to the persons or entities, or their authorized agents, as described below:

. . .

(5) An attorney, or individual representing himself or herself, who has filed a medical malpractice action or claim in a State or Federal court or other adjudicative body against a hospital, and who requests information regarding a specific physician, dentist, or other health care practitioner who is also named in the action or claim. Provided, that this information will be disclosed only upon the submission of evidence that the hospital failed to request information from the Data Bank as required by § 60.10(a), and may be used solely with respect to litigation resulting from the action or claim against the hospital. (Federal Register 1989, 13)

### Defense Attorney Access

Defense attorneys are *not* permitted to access the Data Bank under Title IV because the defendant practitioner is permitted to self-query the Data Bank. If the attorney is representing the practitioner as defendant, the easiest and most direct way to access the Data Bank is, of course, to assist the client in making the request directly on his or her own behalf.

## OTHER DATA BANKS

The NPDB database is the latest of its kind but certainly not the only one. What is unique is that it was established and functions under federal laws that provide for mandatory reporting and inquiry. The scope of information required, and now retained, exceeds that of all other data banks; however, there was no provision for retroactive inclusion of the data that had been amassed by its predecessors. These include:

- The American Medical Association: The AMA has maintained a file on each of its members since 1905. AMA Physician Select Information, including the AMA Physician Masterfile, is available through the AMA Website. (See appendix II.)

- State boards of licensure—medical and nursing: These have long maintained data on individual practitioners licensed in their jurisdiction. Generally, any adverse action taken against a licensee is a matter of public record. This may not include complaints filed or investigations in process. Some states require reporting of any claims, settlements, or judgments based on malpractice.

- The National Council of State Boards of Nursing (NCSBN): The NCSBN has maintained a data bank since 1980. Participation by each state is discretionary. Access to this data bank can be through a state board only.

- The Federation of State Medical Boards: A central repository for data gathered from the various state medical boards on physicians whom they have disciplined.

- The National Nurses Claims Data Base: Created by professional nursing organizations to monitor liability claims and incidents for the entire profession and provide a resource for nurses involved in lawsuits. Insurance companies and employers do not have access. Nurses are expected to provide information *voluntarily*.

## REFERENCES

*Federal Register*. 1989. 54 (199) (Tuesday, October 17): 1–14.
National Practitioner Data Bank. 1996. *National Practitioner Data Bank Guidebook*. U.S. Department of Health and Human Services.

# 15

# Disciplinary Actions by State Boards of Nursing under Nurse Practice Acts

## HISTORY OF NURSE PRACTICE ACTS

By the end of the first two decades of the twentieth century, a number of states had enacted laws requiring that nurses register with an appropriate state agency in order to be permitted to practice. These states included New Jersey, New York, North Carolina, and Virginia. By 1923, each state had enacted a registration act. It is from these requirements that the designation "registered" nurse derives. Any nurse who filed the proper forms and paid the required fee was registered—no license per se was issued. However, it is from these early laws that mandatory licensing in each state also derives.

The first state to require that nurses be licensed as well as registered was New York, which passed the first licensing act in 1938. This represented the first formal amalgamation of law and nursing which recognized nursing, as a profession with concomitant legal rights and privileges granted, obligations and liabilities imposed, and sanctions and penalties prescribed. The stature of nursing was now enhanced by a statute of law. By 1952, every state had enacted a nurse practice act.

## CONTENT AND PURPOSE OF A NURSE PRACTICE ACT

The nurse practice act of each state defines the practice of nursing and, in varying detail, the standards of that practice. The act itself, together with the various rules and regulations promulgated under the act that effect the implementation and enforcement of the statute, constitute the primary regulatory mechanism for nursing practice in any state. The structure, content, and scope of an act will vary by state. In very broad language, the acts define nursing, the scope of nursing practice, the prerequisites of nursing licensure, and the requisites of continuing licensure. The various acts are embodied in such a way as to provide nursing practice with maximum latitude as the profession evolves and grows. Many of the preexisting state nurse practice acts embody a model act proposed by the American Nurses Association in 1980.

An act usually empowers a state's board of nursing to draft and publish various rules and regulations. It is in these specific directives that nurses will learn the details of the law as it affects day-to-day practice. These are not laws per se, but are recognized as having the force of law. These are the mechanisms by which the general provisions of the statute are implemented and enforced. A state board, in response to formal inquiries, may also issue rulings relevant to the scope of nursing practice. These do not carry the force of law. From time to time, as circumstances dictate, a board may seek an opinion from other state agencies, particularly the office of the attorney general. These opinions, although not law, will carry great weight in a court of law.

### Content of an Act

The content of a typical state nurse practice act includes the following:

- a definition of nursing;
- a statement of the scope of nursing practice;
- the basic requirements for the issuance of a license to practice as a registered nurse;
- standards for curricula of nursing education and for examination for licensure;
- a description of matters that must be reported to the board;
- policies and procedures regarding disciplinary actions to be taken against a license; and
- the organization of the state's board of nursing—the composition of its governing body, bylaws, responsibilities, and duties.

## Purpose of an Act

The paramount objective of every nurse practice act is to protect the public-at-large—the consumer of health care. It does this by defining the scope and standards of nursing practice and the credentials required of those permitted to that practice. The board of nursing is charged with the responsibility of fully investigating any and all charges against a licensed practitioner and, where indicated, taking appropriate disciplinary action. This regulatory effort is essential for the protection of the health, welfare, and safety of society. It is the duty of each state's board of nursing to carry out this mandate. It is the professional duty of each licensed, registered nurse to know and understand the applicable act and its implications for professional practice.

## DEFINING NURSING

Virtually every state nurse practice act defines "nursing". The ANA prepared a model definition in 1955, which was to act as a guideline for each state. This was revised in 1970 when nursing diagnoses began widespread use, and again in 1979 to include the expanding roles of nurses. These definitions have generally been broad enough to include nurses practicing in various clinical settings and roles. It would be very difficult, if not impossible, to formulate a precise yet comprehensive definition that would satisfy all state regulators (and all nurses). Any definition need be acceptable as a reasonably comprehensive guideline for competent practice by any nurse in a variety of clinical settings.

The constantly changing and evolving role of the professional nurse, together with advances in practice and increased autonomy, continually challenge traditional definitions of nursing. States have been required to redefine this element of their nurse practice acts to accommodate the increasing numbers of advanced practice nurses including clinical nurse specialists, nurse practitioners, and nurse midwives.

## SCOPE OF NURSING PRACTICE

The scope of practice embodies the permitted actions and duties of a profession. It is a legal demarcation of the boundaries of nursing practice drawn according to the nurse practice act and all subsequent rules and regulations evolving from the act. As nurses have expanded their roles and attained semi-independence in certain clinical procedures and settings, challenges to the propriety, to the legality, of these roles have inevitably followed.

Where nurses have been permitted to practice in expanded roles, new issues in standards of care have concomitantly arisen. When nurses assume clinical duties and procedures traditionally reserved to physicians, courts may impart higher standards and a more rigorous duty. Nurses must be willing and able to accept these implications for practice and realize that with increased autonomy comes increased accountability and liability. To provide the maximum protection from liability for the nurse in an expanded role, nurse practice acts must include language that is as broad as possible yet as specific in intent as attainable.

The policies and procedures of an institution define the scope of nursing practice in that institution. This definition may or may not agree with that presented in an applicable state nurse practice act. It may be more restrictive and definitive, but it cannot be more comprehensive. The institution cannot arbitrarily expand the definition of a state's nurse practice act by developing and implementing policies and procedures proscribed by law. The statute will always take precedent. Every nurse is legally bound to act within the scope of practice as defined by statute and will incur sanctions if he or she ventures beyond those boundaries.

## THE BOARD OF NURSING

Each state licensing board is charged under the applicable act with all aspects of licensure and nursing practice. Any given state board of nursing is usually composed of nurses (including LPNs) from various areas of a state. This provides not only geographical diversity but also professional, social, and cultural variety. A board may also have one or more representatives from the public-at-large; these may come from a variety of backgrounds not involved with health care. The governor of a state may have the prerogative of appointing a given number of members of the board for terms of three to six years. (See appendix III for a list of state boards of nursing.)

## LICENSURE

A license is a formal permission granted by a legally constituted authority to an individual that gives that individual authoritative permission to do something or to practice some profession which, without such legal permit, would otherwise be considered unlawful. Licensure is the process by which a governmental agency grants such authority under law. The authority of the state to draft and enforce various professional practice acts derives from common law, which charges the state with protection of the health and well-being (the "commonweal") of its citizens.

Licensure defines the standards expected, and the credentials demanded, for admission to a profession, and the criteria for continuance in that profession. It identifies the individual professional's scope of practice and predicts the consequences of failure in compliance to be imposed by appropriate disciplinary action.

## Types of Licensure

There are two types of licensure. The first is "permissive", which concerns the use of a specific title conveyed to an individual by the license. If the individual intends to display this title and present it as a credential in professional practice, he or she is required to comply with the applicable statute.

The second type is "mandatory", which involves the selected profession itself. If an individual intends to practice in medicine or nursing, for example, he or she must meet all of the requirements for admission to the profession and to engage in its practice as these are defined by the profession itself and the state licensing authority.

## VIOLATIONS OF A NURSE PRACTICE ACT

A formal complaint against a nurse can be filed with a board of nursing by a patient, a nursing colleague, a physician, a professional organization, an administrator of an institution, by the state board itself—by anyone. Many acts require that nurses report violations that they *themselves* have committed as well as violations that they have identified on the part of other health care providers. These actions include any "unprofessional" conduct, including negligence, malpractice, moral turpitude, fraud, various criminal acts, incompetence, and any actions considered outside the defined scope of practice. Unprofessional conduct is the prevailing basis for such actions. Application of the statutes in accusations of it can be challenging to a board of review that will consider each case individually The term *unprofessional conduct* is somewhat vague and can encompass a great number of actions or omissions on the part of a nurse.

Unprofessional conduct includes a failure to report, within a reasonable time, any violations of the nurse practice act, including any of the rules and regulations that have been promulgated under the act. Failure to report such violations is in itself a breach of the law. Every effort should be made to protect the rights of the individual making the disclosure. This includes not revealing his or her identity and some provision for immunity from retaliation. If the individual who files the report does so in good faith and without malicious intent, he or she will not likely incur liability for a charge of defamation in any eventual lawsuit.

Should the violation alleged have occurred in an institution, the reporting process would begin there. The policies and procedures of the institution will direct the process and define the protocol. Typically these would require that a report be in writing; that it be factual, complete, and accurate in all assertions; that it include the names of all parties involved; and that it be made in good faith. If the nurse who initiates a report determines that the institution has failed to take what would be considered appropriate action, he or she is required to report the situation to the state board, which may pursue the matter further.

## BASES FOR DISCIPLINARY ACTIONS BY A STATE BOARD

As noted previously, unprofessional conduct is the most common allegation involved in disciplinary actions under the various nurse practice acts. This conduct includes, but is not limited to:

- negligence, even in the absence of injury to a patient;
- incompetence;
- moral turpitude;
- substance abuse;
- conviction for a criminal act—a felony or certain misdemeanors;
- fraudulent application for licensure;
- failure to report the denial, suspension, or revocation of a license in another jurisdiction;
- failure to report a physical or mental impairment that could render a nurse unable or unfit to practice and that might require intervention by the board;
- violations of any specific provision of the act and/or any of the rules and regulations promulgated under the act; and
- aiding or abetting another in any violation of the act.

## TYPES OF DISCIPLINARY ACTIONS BY A STATE BOARD

Not every claim or incident of nursing malpractice will be grounds for adverse action against a nurse's professional license. The action of the state board will depend on the circumstances of the alleged incident, the degree of injury to the patient, and the nurse's professional record. Even that nurse who has been found liable for malpractice by a jury will emerge from the courtroom with his or her license intact. The courts have no jurisdiction in initiating actions against licensure. This is the sole prerogative of the state board. A nurse may have entered the courtroom already deprived of his or her license as a consequence of prior action by the board's "court"—the disciplinary review panel.

Following the required procedures, a state board may initiate one or more adverse actions against the nurse named in a complaint. These include:

- Censure: A statement of disapproval recorded in the official minutes of the board. This then becomes a matter of public record.

- Reprimand: This written advisory is usually given to the individual personally and becomes part of his or her file. It may also be disseminated publicly, usually in the board's official publications.

- Probation: This may be for a period of varying duration.

- Suspension of a license: This may be for a prescribed period of time.

- Revocation of license: This can preclude issuance of a license to practice by any other state.

A board may demand that certain conditions be met before an action of probation or suspension be lifted and the nurse's license is reinstated. He or she may be obliged to undergo a period of supervised clinical experience during which he or she may be required to demonstrate clinical competency in selected areas. There may be a requirement for attendance at selected seminars, inservice presentations, or successful completion of specific educational programs or academic courses. Retesting and recertification in certain relevant competencies and skills may be ordered.

Substance abuse has become *the* major cause of disciplinary actions against nurses, and more and more state boards are reporting proceedings involving impaired nurses. If impairment due to substance abuse has been identified, participation in a counseling or rehabilitation program may be required; and reinstatement will be contingent on successful completion of the program. Any other form of counseling or intervention considered appropriate to the circumstances may also be directed. The nurse's reinstatement to professional practice will be determined to a great degree by the nurse's personal commitment and cooperation.

## DISCIPLINARY PROCEEDINGS

A number of states require that a report be filed with the board of nursing whenever a nurse is named as a defendant in a malpractice lawsuit. This does not necessarily initiate any disciplinary proceedings by a state board.

The report may merely be received and reviewed by the board and filed in the nurse's dossier. There may be no action against the practitioner's license at that time. Such action could be considered and effected as the circumstances of the plaintiff's complaint are fully presented or in the event that an adverse judgment is decided in court—after the nurse-defendant has been found liable. A number of states require reporting of any amounts paid out in damages awarded against a physician or nurse.

If the nurse's file contains previous substantiated records of negligence or criminal behavior, the board may elect to initiate action against the defendant's license, and set the disciplinary proceedings in motion immediately—compounding the defendant's problem of civil litigation. Each state board has outlined the process involved in handling disciplinary actions initiated under the act. These generally follow the same format as shown in Table 15.1.

**Table 15.1**
**State Board Disciplinary Proceedings**

- Formal filing of a complaint according to the policies and procedures defined by the board
- Written notification of the complaint sent to the health care provider who is named in the report
- Preliminary review and evaluation of the complaint by a panel
- Preliminary investigation of the allegations by a state attorney
- Preliminary conference to discuss findings of the investigation
- Formal hearing before the full board
- Board review of the testimony in the hearing
- A decision on the form of disciplinary action proposed
- An appeal, to a court of proper jurisdiction, of any adverse action taken by the board

### The Preliminary Investigation

Investigators for the board will contact all possible witnesses to obtain facts and statements regarding the complaint. Relevant medical records will be subpoenaed and the institution's policy and procedures will be obtained. When the board's investigation is completed, the attorney for the state will schedule a conference to include the subject of the complaint and his or her attorney. At this conference, the state's attorney, or possibly a panel of board members, will review the report of the investigation and advise the nurse of what formal charges could be filed with the board. A consent agreement may be offered after this preliminary conference. This usually provides for sanctions that are less severe than those that *could* be imposed at a full hearing. If this is declined, the matter proceeds to the full hearing.

## The Formal Hearing before the Board

When the board decides to hold a hearing on the allegations presented in the preliminary report, the subject of that report will be notified. He or she will receive a letter that will define the specific allegations that have been made. The subject will be advised of the hearing date, the time, and the place in which it will be held. This notice will also include various procedural instructions for the recipient. When the nurse receives such notice, he or she should immediately retain the services of an attorney who is familiar with such licensure proceedings. A professional malpractice liability insurance policy does *not* cover the nurse in responding to actions by a state board.

The purpose of the hearing is to ascertain the validity of the complaint and determine what formal action, if any, the board might be required to take. Witnesses may be presented. Attorneys should be present. The nurse who has been called should not expect the same dynamics that take place in a deposition or trial. This is a formal fact-finding effort and not necessarily an adversarial confrontation. The interests of the individual nurse and those of the profession are of prime concern.

The proceedings will be transcribed by a stenographer (in the event of a court appeal a transcript will be necessary). The findings of the investigation will be presented. The nurse will be questioned by the attorney representing the board (usually an assistant state attorney general) and his or her own attorney regarding the allegations. Members of the hearing panel may also pose questions. When all testimony has been heard, the members of the board will consider its content and deliberate as to what action will be taken. Their decision may be announced immediately, but is more likely to come down at a later date. The subject of the hearing will be sent a formal written advice of the findings and the board's decision.

In the event that the decision is adverse, the nurse may initiate an appeal to an appropriate civil court within the time period defined—usually two to three weeks. The court will consider only the propriety of the action and decision of the board and *not* the merits of the nurse's conduct that gave cause to that action and decision. The court may affirm the decision, reverse it, remand it, or modify it in some way. Where indicated, continuing appeals to higher courts may be pursued. An appeal process can be a very tedious and very expensive endeavor. By the time the appeal wends its way through the jural maze, sufficient time may elapse for the nurse to reapply for licensure or reinstatement under any applicable provisions of the nurse practice act or other state laws.

## CYBERCARE
### Telemedicine

There has been increasing discussion in both the general and professional media about telecommunications technology and its applications to the rapidly developing concept of "telemedicine". This term, which is used most frequently, actually refers to a subset of the more inclusive "telehealth", which is becoming the preferred terminology because it more accurately represents the current model of health care delivery with its focus on health maintenance, wellness, and disease prevention. As a health care mode, telehealth has been available in one form or another since the 1960s. The more comprehensive "telehealth" also incorporates the concept of "telenursing".

### Telehealth

[A]s telecommunications technology becomes more accessible and more widely used by different health care professionals, "telehealth" is a more inclusive and descriptive term for what is being done and what is possible. . . . Telehealth is a broader, more inclusive term and is more reflective of current views that health care is more than treatment of illness or injury; that it involves teaching, learning, lifestyle alterations, understanding of the impact of culture, ethnicity and other factors on the individual and the health care professional. . . . Different terms may lead to confusion among the public, promote an impression of divisiveness and competition among users of telehealth. (Milholland 1995, 13)

Telehealth is the linking of two or more discrete end-users by any interactive electronic means for the purpose of transmission and/or exchange of information and data in any health-related application. It is remote, electronic, clinical consultation, assessment, and monitoring of consumers of any form of health care. Telehealth is the utilization of telecommunications technology in the dissemination of health information, expertise, and intervention across varying distances to a disparate population most often in greastest need of such access.

## Telenursing

Telenursing is defined as the practice of nursing over distance using telecommunications technology. The nurse engages in the practice of nursing by interacting with the client at a remote site to electronically receive the client's health status data, initiate and transmit therapeutic interventions and regimens, and monitor and record the client's response and nursing care outcomes. The value of telenursing to the client is increased access to skilled, empathetic and effective nursing delivered by means of telecommunications technology. (National Council of State Boards of Nursing 1997, 1)

As noted previously, telenursing is merely another subset of telehealth. It is the application of the art and science of nursing mediated in whole or part through any electronic means. The two key dimensions of telenursing are distance and electronic mediation. It is the nurse's electronic presence at a patient's bedside providing personal care by means of an impersonal medium.

Technology in one form or another has always been viewed with discomfort, disdain, or dread, by a large number of nurses (the "nurseosaurus"). Telenursing is no exception. "Many fear that rapid implementation of computerized telecommunications in managed care health plans and in home health agencies will lead to replacement of direct in-person registered nurse care, weakening the therapeutic nurse-patient relationship" (Helmlinger and Milholland 1997, 61). The ANA has affirmed that telenursing will not replace the direct, hands-on interventions of a nurse; rather it will serve to enhance both the nursing process and the profession (American Nurses Association 1996, 2). The emerging role of nurses presents unique professional and economic opportunities as well as unique questions and problems. "Telecommunications is advancing at such a rapid rate that its application to health care delivery and nursing practice will continue to emerge and evolve" (National Council of State Boards of Nursing 1997, 2).

Telenursing is now being utilized in all four fields of professional nursing: (1) clinical practice, (2) education, (3) administration, and (4) research. It is to its applications in clinical practice that the focus of policy makers, regulators, HMOs and other payers, health care institutions, and nursing and medical practitioners has been primarily directed. Telenursing enhances the roles of advanced practice nurses in the initiation and management of both nursing and medical regimens by electronic implementation of standing orders, protocols, and guidelines.

Telenursing has been in existence in one form or another for quite some time. However, a review of the nursing literature derives relatively few references. Despite the growing interest in telecommunications as a health care delivery medium, research on the actual and potential contributions of the nursing profession has been markedly absent. In fact, little to no information—with the exception of brief anecdotal comments—has been available on the role of nurses in telehealth (Horton 1997, 1).

Virtually all nurses in advanced practice, and many nurses in any clinical setting, will inevitably be required to utilize this next wave in the provision of health care. The electronic age has changed the ways in which health care is being delivered—by whom—and to whom. Nurses in the most distant clinical settings can now collaborate with other providers—nurses and physicians—in real-time, interactive video consultation. The patient can be seen, heard, assessed, and treated by a team of experts dispersed among many sites.

"The challenge to nursing is to organize this material in terms of ease of access, confidentiality of usage, accuracy and contextual relevance, and ease of comprehension. . . . Telenursing, because of its communicative nature, is forced to use modern idiom, if not the vernacular, to communicate effectively. This disallows much of the specious nursing jargon and private use of language to which nursing has been exposed in recent years. The bottom line seems to be that if one wishes to make oneself understood, one had better use language that can be understood" (Yensen 1996, 213).

### Legal Issues in Telehealth

The problem that telehealth presents is that the revolution in science and technology has run ahead of the devolution of law. The legal system has not yet caught up. A key issue that has just begun to be addressed by state boards of medicine and nursing is of the legality of providing health care across state lines, an inherent aspect of telemedicine and telenursing. Are nurses and physicians practicing "modem medicine" violating the laws of the states in which they are licensed to practice by, in effect, practicing across state lines? Are they violating the laws of those states in which their remote patients reside—and in which they are not licensed? (Gobis 1996; Kjervik 1997)?

Telecommunications has created, and certainly will continue to create, new questions, problems, and challenges to the nursing profession and its regulators. The most germane question is: Is telenursing nursing practice? The consensus is that if nursing services are delivered by any means, it constitutes nursing practice. This has been affirmed by the National Council of State Boards of Nursing and the American Nurses Association.

There are many more issues involved in telenursing, including patient confidentiality, informed consent, and the relinquishment of personal, physical contact with the patient. The concept and all of its professional and legal implications are the subjects of much further legal and nursing research.

## REFERENCES

American Nurses Association. 1996. *Action Report: Telenursing and Telehealth.*

Gobis, Linda J. 1996. Telenursing: Nursing by telephone across state lines. *Journal of Nursing Law* 3 (3) (March): 7–17.

Helmlinger, Connie, and Kathy Milholland. 1997. Telehealth discussions focus on licensure. *American Journal of Nursing* 97 (6) (June): 61–62.

Horton, Maria C. 1997. The Role of Nursing in Telemedicine. (January): 1–7. Article retrieved from: http://www.matmo.org/pages/library/papers/ nurse-rol/nursrol.html

Kjervik, D. K. 1997. Telenursing—Licensure and communication challenges. *Journal of Professional Nursing* 13 (2) (March-April): 65.

Milholland, D. Kathy. 1995. Telehealth, telenursing, telewhat? *American Nurse* 27 (6) (September): 13.

National Council of State Boards of Nursing. 1997. *Position Paper on Telenursing: A Challenge to Regulation*: 1–2.

Yensen, Jack. 1996. Telenursing, virtual nursing and beyond. *Computers in Nursing* 14 (4) (July-August): 213–14.

# 16

# Roles of the Professional Nurse in the Legal Process

## NURSES' ROLES IN THE LEGAL PROCESS

In the course of his or her nursing career, a nurse may find him- or herself on one side of the law as defendant, on another side as plaintiff, or amidst the law—between either side as a nurse attorney, a testifying expert (TE), or as a consulting expert (CE). These last two roles represent relatively new, emerging, and very rewarding alternative careers for the professional nurse. In these expanded roles, the nurse is not confined to cases of malpractice only, but can become involved in other forms of personal injury, toxic torts and environmental issues, product liability, workers' compensation; and even criminal actions as a forensic witness in such cases as rape or child and elder abuse. Opportunities for nurses are limited only by their knowledge, their creativity, and their initiative in persuading the legal community of their valuable contributions and cost saving effectiveness.

## WHY NURSES ELECT TO FUNCTION IN THESE ROLES

A nurse may be motivated to undertake these roles for several reasons.

- He or she can enhance the image and status of nursing by presenting nurses in a legitimate role in the legal arena

- The roles present an opportunity for the professional nurse to define and maintain the standards of nursing care
- A nurse can be instrumental in identifying unsafe practitioners and removing them from clinical practice, thus protecting the public as consumers of health care
- The roles provide an opportunity to protect and defend peers from unjust accusations and nonmeritorious suits that can impugn the individual nurse and the profession
- A nurse seeks the challenges and learning experiences these new and expanding roles present
- He or she enjoys independence and autonomy in an entrepreneurial role
- A nurse recognizes and appreciates the monetary rewards that his or her efforts will bring

## THE NURSE ATTORNEY

The nurse attorney is yet another distinguished role for the professional nurse. He or she may function in independent practice, as a member of a law firm, on the staff of an insurance company, or as nursing-legal scholar and author.

## THE NURSE AS A TESTIFYING EXPERT

Since the landmark decision in 1985 in *Tripp v. Humana* (474, So.2d 88, 1985) more courts have been directing that nurse experts testify in trials involving nurses and standards of nursing care. This acknowledgment that nursing, as a profession, involves a distinct body of scientific knowledge has been a hard-won concession from the legal system that has traditionally failed to recognize and accept this concept, and has consistently called upon physicians to testify to the propriety of nursing care. This has long served only to denigrate the nursing profession, and engender and sustain the misconception that nurses lack professional status, autonomy, responsibility, and credibility.

As a general rule, a physician may be permitted to testify in the courts of every state regarding the standards of nursing care. Conversely, it is highly unlikely, and equally inappropriate, that a nurse would be allowed to address the standards of the practice of medicine except in those instances where certain skills and procedures might be shared by each discipline. The roles of the nurse practitioner or the nurse anesthetist are examples. In other matters not exclusively within the scope of professional nursing, the courts have permitted physicians or other appropriate health care providers to testify in cases of nursing malpractice.

Typically, a physician has no knowledge of nursing practice other than that derived from transient and cursory observation, confirmation that his or her orders have been carried out, and critical interrogation when a nurse is seen to have failed in "subservient" duties. A physician's education in medicine provides little, if any, knowledge of the formal standards, policies, and procedures that define and direct nursing care. The physician is trained in the science of medicine, the nurse in the art and science of nursing. It is appropriate that this academic dichotomy be sustained in the setting of litigation, but not maintained in collaborative efforts in patient care. Neither profession is served well when one usurps the prerogatives of the other—in court or in clinic.

The TE is not what is known in law as a "witness to the facts". The fact witness will testify from the perspective of one who actually saw the alleged incident or participated in the event directly or indirectly. The TE does not attest to the occurrence of facts, but rather provides opinions and interpretations of the alleged facts. The role of the expert witness is to define what would have been the reasonable care that would have been appropriate and expected under the circumstances surrounding the event of alleged nursing malpractice. The TE will be called upon to address two primary issues: (1) the standards of nursing care and (2) any deviations from the standards of care as a causative factor in the plaintiff's alleged injury.

Presentation of the testimony of a TE constitutes the principal difference between a suit for ordinary negligence and one of malpractice. During the deposition, and in the event of a trial, the nurse expert witness will define the standards of nursing care, and present his or her own (and other) expert opinions on the perceived deviations from those standards. A TE does not establish them. His or her duty is to educate the court regarding standards already defined, established, and accepted by the nursing profession.

He or she may be asked to provide answers to a number of hypothetical questions posed by either side. However, testimony will address one fundamental question: What would any reasonable nurse with the same education, knowledge, skills, and experience have done under the same or similar circumstances? Therefore, much of what an expert witness will be expected to provide will be his or her own opinions and judgments on the issues at hand. These opinions and judgments will be derived from his or her personal credentials, including education, experience, and recognized expertise.

An expert witness' testimony presented in a court of law, incorporated in a transcript of the legal proceedings, and possibly available through citation of the case, could conceivably serve to establish legal and nursing precedents and further define the standards and practice of professional nursing.

The nurse as expert witness will be well advised to confine his or her opinions on the issues exclusively to nursing practice. Opposing attorneys will announce vigorous objections in court if a nurse presumes to stray over the line. A favorite tactic of the attorney is to propose a series of questions, hypothetical or otherwise, which might elicit from the nurse opinions or comments on matters that are exclusively in the realm of medical practice. If a TE falls into the lawyer's trap, his or her "expertise" in such matters will be challenged, professionalism ridiculed, and credibility called into question.

In accepting nurses as expert witnesses, the courts have come to acknowledge that much of what constitutes the present scope of nursing practice is now beyond the knowledge of the average layperson who might sit in judgment. In matters of highly technical, complex, or specialized skills, procedures, and language, the advanced education, training, informed opinions, and critical judgments of the expert nurse are essential. It is the TE who presents the definitive standards to the jury who must then decide if those standards were breached. When the opinions of the experts conflict or contradict, the jury will be left to decide the credibility of one or the other. In those instances where the issues and evidence are not too esoteric, the jurors may be left to their own instincts, knowledge, and common sense in deciding the case, and expert witnesses may not be permitted by the court.

The TE may also be consulted by the client or employing attorney during the trial preparation phase of the suit. As a witness for the plaintiff, he or she may be asked to participate in defining the complaint to be filed. As a witness for the defense, the TE may assist in preparing refutations to the complaint. He or she will also review the transcripts of depositions given by his or her counterparts. Frequently the opinions of the expert will be a determining factor in a negotiated settlement. Ideally, the TE (and the CE) approach their assignments as impartial professionals. Inevitably, the attorney who engages their services expects that their findings will corroborate the allegations and claims of his or her client exclusively. Questions put to one's own expert witness will attempt to elicit answers that refute the position of the opposition. Questions put to the opposing side's witness will attempt to elicit those positions and opinions that might eventually be presented in court and that may suggest possible strategies of the opposition and appropriate countermeasures.

## Qualifications of the Testifying Expert

The TE is a professional, expert nurse—not a professional, expert witness. As a nurse, the first duty is to serve the profession. Providing a service to the legal system is secondary. Any nurse who is considering this role must be able to demonstrate the expertise and integrity demanded of both masters.

Inevitably, there will be the same conflict and disagreement between the parties in a lawsuit as to what constitutes an "expert" witness and over the credibility and merits of each expert's testimony and opinions. There is invariably a scenario of dueling experts, some of dubious merit. The courts are filled with experts who propound educated guesses as profound opinions. The most highly qualified are often reluctant to enter into the adversarial, confrontational, and demeaning arena of trial testimony where an attorney will likely attempt to discredit the credentials of the opposition's TE by disparaging his or her education, experience, expertise, or motives. A common innuendo is that the individual is a "hired gun", a "professional witness", a mercenary with opinions for sale.

The nurse may be questioned extensively regarding his or her prior services as a TE, the time that is devoted to providing this service, and the total amount of remuneration received in the past and expect to receive in the present case. In this instance, the witness will be challenged to assert that he or she is being compensated appropriately for his or her expertise and valuable time in testifying and not being "paid" to testify. The objective of this whole demeaning exercise is to demonstrate that the individual is not an expert, and is, therefore, not suitable to serve as such in the matters at issue and should be disqualified. In addition to the qualifications listed, the person who intends this career must have a very thick hide.

The TE cannot have any direct relationship or connection with any of the parties in the case. There can be no hint of conflict of interest; otherwise, the TE's credibility could be impeached. In accepting a case, the expert witness must be willing to determine, and judge, the merits of the case, and withdraw or continue according to his or her convictions. Agreeing to testify is tantamount to endorsement of the case and the client's position.

An attorney, in a misguided effort to promote the best case for a client, may assume that any nurse should know all there is about nursing and attempt to exert some pressure or offer an attractive incentive to a prospective expert witness. The nurse in this situation would be obliged to refuse any case involving issues beyond his or her area of expertise. However, he or she can still serve the attorney and the profession effectively by assisting the attorney in locating a suitable nurse expert. Many nurses (and physicians) elect to reject cases in their immediate geographical area when they are asked to testify for a plaintiff. Testifying for a defendant in their own locale is usually more palatable.

The credentials of a testifying expert must be at least equal to, if not superior to, those of the nurse against whom he or she is testifying. Ultimately a judge may determine if a TE is qualified to testify in court.

The qualifications of a nurse expert witness are:

- Appropriate nursing education—an attorney, or a judge, may require a BSN as a minimum level of academic preparation. Many demand a master's degree. (The higher the degree, the more impressed the jury might be!)
- Sufficient clinical experience, past and current—this could be a minimum of five years in the specialty area that the TE or CE is addressing in the case.
- Certification in a specialty area of nursing—a clinical nurse specialist (CNS), nurse practitioner (NP), or other advanced practice nurse is a most suitable expert witness.
- Other professional credentials—these might include faculty in nursing education, publication, public speaking, honors and awards, and membership in appropriate professional organizations.
- Understanding of the legal system and the legal issues in nursing practice—many TEs and CEs are also paralegals.
- He or she should have a reasonably thorough familiarity of the state nurse practice act and its rules and regulations.

## THE NURSE AS A CONSULTING EXPERT

The nurse as litigation consultant provides support services to an attorney throughout the trial preparation process and during a trial. As a consulting expert to either plaintiff or defense attorney, he or she acts as a collaborator and strategist. Utilization of a nurse CE represents a very cost effective way for a lawyer to prepare a well-organized and effective case and anticipate the strategies of the opposition. Since fewer than 10 percent of all malpractice lawsuits ever go to trial, the CE's value is in helping to prepare a sound case, the merits of which could induce an offer of prompt and reasonable settlement by the opposition and thus reduce the costs of a prolonged suit.

### Comparison of the Roles of the Testifying and Consulting Expert

Unlike the TE, the CE *does not testify*, he or she only consults, as the title indicates. This service may be provided for either side in a lawsuit. The testifying expert may have a high and visible profile while presenting testimony during a deposition or a trial. The consulting expert is "invisible", working behind the scenes in a "clandestine" collaboration with the attorney from the initial phases of the case right on through any eventual trial where, if the client-attorney is amenable, he or she might be allowed to sit at the table in the courtroom. This could be the first time that the opposition becomes aware of this covert collaborator.

Any report generated by the CE is considered "attorney's work product", and as such is considered privileged and confidential. Unless a TE incorporates any or all of a report generated by a CE into his or her own discoverable testimony, a CE's work is generally not discoverable. The CE's thoughts and opinions are protected from scrutiny by the cloak of anonymity that the role imparts.

The focus of the nurse expert witness is much narrower, and his or her testimony will be confined to the area of his or her nursing expertise or clinical specialty. He or she may be provided only limited access to the medical record. The nurse litigation consultant can take a much broader approach to a case and should have unlimited access to the medical record and all other pertinent materials. In this capacity, the CE can review and assess the actions of any health care provider (including physicians) involved in the patient's care and address any one of a large number of cogent and peripheral issues. The CE's approach to a case is global rather than regional.

## Services Provided by the Consulting Expert

Among the services that the CE may provide are:

- liaison between parties, physicians, and attorneys;
- identify and locate potential witnesses and defendants;
- interview clients, witnesses, and other parties;
- assist in the preparation of witnesses;
- aid in preparing questions and responses in depositions and trial;
- assist in the preparation of interrogatories, complaints, and other documents, and responses to them;
- assessment of plaintiff's alleged injuries;
- identify and obtain all pertinent records and documents;
- organize, review, and analyze medical records;
- prepare summaries, chronologies, and reports;
- review, analyze, and summarize transcripts of depositions;

- identify and evaluate expert witnesses and negotiate for their services;
- prepare or obtain exhibits and/or demonstrative evidence;
- educate attorneys and other parties on facts and issues relating to nursing care or validate their knowledge;
- define standards of nursing care and any deviations from them;
- research—locate, obtain, and summarize pertinent literature;
- present the client with the most current information available; and
- assist the client in setting up or improving his or her medical/nursing reference library.

### Advantages in Using the Consulting Expert

Nurses as consultants bring several advantages to the prosecution or defense of a case of nursing malpractice:

- they are experts in nursing practice;
- they know the standards of nursing care; and
- they have the superior advantage of hindsight.

### Qualifications of the Consulting Expert

Like the expert witness, the litigation consultant's credentials, ethical standards, and integrity must be above reproach for the sake both plaintiff and defendant in a case. However, the CE may work on any type of case regardless of the nursing specialty involved, performing a variety of services. The issues may involve injury, illness, or health. In reviewing the medical records, the nurse can draw on his or her own knowledge, skills, experience and education in identifying and reporting the issues involved. However, nurse experts in any given specialty should be consulted as the need arises. It would be reckless and presumptuous for any nurse to present him- or herself as an expert in all areas of nursing practice. No one can know, or credibly pretend to know, everything about the profession and all of its specialties and subspecialties.

### BECOMING A TESTIFYING EXPERT AND/OR A CONSULTING EXPERT

The nurse who is considering either or both of the challenging roles of becoming a testifying agent and/or a consulting expert may elect to focus on only one side—plaintiff or defense. It is recommended, however, that accepting assignments from either plaintiff or defense attorneys will provide valuable insights into how opposing parties think and plan. Any nurse considering these roles should first examine his or her own credentials—personal and professional. As an expert witness, can he or she legitimately claim to be an expert, or is he or she merely a dilettante who will attempt to convince an attorney-client that a nurse is a nurse is a nurse? Is he or she primarily motivated by monetary rewards in what can be a very lucrative occupation, or is he or she committed to maintaining and improving the standards and image of the nursing profession? Does he or she have the work habits, communication skills, and the physical and emotional stamina that these high-stress roles demand?

## IMPLICATIONS FOR THE NURSING PROFESSION

It is likely that the number of malpractice suits against nurses will continue to increase, and, concomitantly, the opportunities and the need for nurses to participate in such litigation as expert witnesses or as consultants. Nurses in these roles can enhance the understanding of all parties regarding professional nursing and its essential involvement in the health care delivery system. They can present a comprehensive view of the entire spectrum of health care, including current and future needs and a definition of how nursing expertise can and will respond to those needs.

Nurses have the right to demand that only members of their own profession be allowed to testify in matters of nursing malpractice and that this be a consistent convention. Nursing has a right and a duty to participate in the legal process. It is incumbent upon the appropriate members of the profession to assert this right and make every effort to educate the members of the legal profession and the public-at-large regarding the unique and valuable contributions that the nursing profession can make in a litigious society. Nursing must become politically active in initiating and pressing for enactment of statutes prescribing that nurses be permitted the prerogative in testifying in those malpractice lawsuits naming nurses as defendants.

Remember, however, that in the unlikely event that you are sued for nursing malpractice, a professional *nurse—one of your peers—might be at work on the case for you—or against you.* A plaintiff or an attorney may be naïve or uninformed about nursing practice, but the nurse testifying experts and consulting experts who will collaborate with him or her in preparing a lawsuit are not. These nurses will be the true "jury of your peers" who may condemn you or acquit you long before you encounter the other in a courtroom.

# Appendix I

## State Laws on Patient Access to Medical Records

| State | Physician | Hospital | Mental Health Records |
|---|---|---|---|
| Alabama | No | No | No[1] |
| Alaska | Yes | Yes | Yes |
| Arizona | Yes | No | Yes |
| Arkansas | Yes[2] | Yes[2] | No |
| California | Yes | Yes | Yes |
| Colorado | Yes | Yes | Yes |
| Connecticut | Yes | Yes | Yes |
| Delaware | No | No | No[3] |
| Dist. of Columbia | No | No | Yes |
| Florida | Yes | Yes | No[4] |
| Georgia | Yes | Yes | Yes |
| Hawaii | Yes | Yes | Yes |
| Idaho | No | No | Yes |
| Illinois | No[3] | Yes | Yes |
| Indiana | Yes | Yes | Yes |

| State | Physician | Hospital | Mental Health Records |
|-------|-----------|----------|-----------------------|
| Iowa | No | No | No |
| Kansas | No | No | No[5] |
| Kentucky | No | No | Yes |
| Louisiana | Yes | Yes | No[3] |
| Maine | No[6] | Yes | No |
| Maryland | Yes | Yes | Yes |
| Massachusetts | No[6] | Yes | No[3] |
| Michigan | Yes | Yes | Yes |
| Minnesota | Yes | Yes | Yes |
| Mississippi | No | No[7] | Yes |
| Missouri | Yes | No | No[3] |
| Montana | Yes | Yes | Yes |
| Nebraska | No | Yes | No[8] |
| Nevada | Yes | Yes | Yes |
| New Hampshire | Yes | Yes | Yes |
| New Jersey | Yes | Yes | No[3] |
| New Mexico | No | No | No |
| New York | Yes | Yes | Yes |
| North Carolina | No | No | No[9] |
| North Dakota | No | No | No[3] |
| Ohio | No | Yes | Yes |
| Oklahoma | Yes | Yes | No[10] |
| Oregon | No[11] | No[11] | Yes |
| Pennsylvania | No | Yes | No |
| Rhode Island | No | No | No |
| South Carolina | Yes | No | Yes |
| South Dakota | Yes | Yes | Yes |
| Tennessee | No | No[7] | No[3] |
| Texas | No[6] | No[6] | Yes |
| Utah | No[3] | No[3] | No |
| Vermont | No | No | No |
| Virginia | Yes | Yes | Yes |
| Washington | Yes | Yes | Yes |

| State | Physician | Hospital | Mental Health Records |
|-------|-----------|----------|----------------------|
| West Virginia | Yes | Yes | No[3] |
| Wisconsin | Yes | Yes | Yes |
| Wyoming | No | Yes | No |

*Source*: Johnson and Wolfe, 1995. Used with permission.

## NOTES

1. Records may be released by a court order only.

2. Records may be released to the subject patient if a lawsuit is being prepared or has been filed.

3. Records will be released to the subject's attorney only.

4. The physician may provide a summary report of the record in lieu of the record itself.

5. Records may be released to patients in community or state mental health institutions.

6. The physician is required to provide either a summary of the record or the record itself.

7. "Good cause" must be demonstrated by a patient in order to obtain his or her record.

8. Records can be released to patients in state mental institutions.

9. Access is permitted to any individual who is or has been a patient of a mental health, substance abuse, or developmental disability treatment center.

10. Records may be released by court order, or with consent of the treating physician(s).

11. State, community, or other nonprivate institutions are required to release records. Private institutions and physicians are not required, but are encouraged to do so.

# Appendix II

# List of Web Sites

American Bar Association
http://www.abanet.org/

American Institute of Medical Law (The)
http://www.aimlaw.com/

American Medical Association
http://www.ama-assn.org/

American Nurses Association
http://www.nursingworld.org/

CounselQuest
http://www.counselquest.com/index.html

Emory University Law Library: Reference
http://www.law.emory.edu/LAW/refdesk/toc.html

FindLaw
http://www.findlaw.com/

Galaxy
http://www.einet.net/

Hardin MetaDirectory of Internet Health Sources: Nursing
http://www.arcade.uiowa.edu/hardin-www/md-nurs.html

Internet Legal Resource Guide
http://www.ilrg.com/

Internet Resources in Health Law
http://lawlib.slu.edu/centers/HLTHLAW/HLTHLINK.htm

Internet's Nursing Index
http://www.wwnurse.com/

Law Links: Legal Resources
http://lawlinks.com/

'Lectric Law Library's Medicine and Law (The)
http://www.lectlaw.com/tmed.html

'Lectric Law Library: Reference
http://www.lectlaw.com/ref.html

Legal Information Institute
http://www.law.cornell.edu/

Medical and Public Health Law Site (The)
Online: Richards, Edward, and Katharine Rathbun,
*Law and the Physician: A Practical Guide*
http://www.plague.law.umkc.edu/

Medical Law: Martindale
http://www-scilib.uci.edu/HSG/Legal.html

Medical Malpractice Resource Page
http://www.helpquick.com/medmal.htm

Mining Co. (The): Nursing
http://azlist.miningco.com/

Multimedia Medical Reference Library
http://www.med-library.com/medlibrary/

National Council of State Boards of Nursing (NCSBN)
http://www.ncsbn.org/

National League for Nursing
http://www.nln.org/

National Library of Medicine: MEDLINE search
http://www.ncbi.nlm.nih.gov/PubMed/

National Practitioner Data Bank
http://www.npdb.com/

Nightingale: Nursing information and links
http://nightingale.con.utk.edu/

Nursing Internet Resources
http://www.slackinc.com/allied/allnet.html

NursingNet
http://www.nursingnet.org/

Nursing Resource (The)
http://www.intersurf.com/~jesse/index.html#medref

Nursing Sites on the WWW
http://ublib.buffalo.edu/libraries/units/hsl/internet/nsgsites.html

Springnet: Nursing
http://www.nursingmanagement.com/

"Virtual" Medical Law Center: Martindale
http://www-sci.lib.uci.edu/HSG/Legal.html

"Virtual" Nursing Center: Martindale
http://www-scilib.uci.edu/~martindale/Nursing.html

WWW Virtual Law Library
http://www.law.indiana.edu/law/v~lib/lawindex.html

WWW Virtual Library: Bioscience
http://milkman.cac.psu.edu/~dxm12/wwwlibng.html

Yahoo: Health: Nursing
http://www.yahoo.com/Health/Nursing/

# Appendix III

# List of State Boards of Nursing

**ALABAMA**

Alabama Board of Nursing
P.O. Box 303900
Montgomery, AL 36130
Phone: (334) 242–4060

**ALASKA**

Alaska Board of Nursing
Department of Commerce & Economic Development
Division of Occupational Licensing
13601 C Street, Suite 722
Anchorage, AK 99503
Phone: (907) 269–8163, FAX: (907) 269–8156

**AMERICAN SAMOA**

American Samoa Health Services
Regulatory Board
LBJ Tropical Medical Center
1869 Executive Drive

Pago Pago, AS 96799
Phone: (684) 633–1222

## ARIZONA

Arizona State Board of Nursing
1651 E. Morten Avenue, Suite 150
Phoenix, AZ 85020
Phone: (602) 255–5092, FAX: (602) 906–9365

## ARKANSAS

Arkansas State Board of Nursing
University Tower Building
1123 S. University, Suite 800
Little Rock, AR 72204
Phone: (501) 686–2700, FAX: (501) 686–2714

## CALIFORNIA

California Board of Registered Nursing
P.O. Box 944210
Sacramento, CA 94244
Phone: (916) 322–3350, FAX: (916) 327–4402

California Board of Vocational Nurse and Psychiatric Technician Examiners
2535 Capitol Oaks Drive, Suite 205
Sacramento, CA 95833
Phone: (916) 263–7800, FAX: (916) 263–7859

## COLORADO

Colorado Board of Nursing
1560 Broadway, Suite 670
Denver, CO 80202
Phone: (303) 894–2430, FAX: (303) 894–2821

## CONNECTICUT

Connecticut Board of Examiners for Nursing
Division of Health Systems Regulation
410 Capitol Avenue, MS# 12HSR
Hartford, CT 06134
Phone: (860) 509–7624, FAX: (860) 509–7286

## DELAWARE

Delaware Board of Nursing
Cannon Building, Suite 203
P.O. Box 1401
Dover, DE 19903
Phone: (302) 739–4522, FAX: (302) 739–2711

## DISTRICT OF COLUMBIA

District of Columbia Board of Nursing
614 H Street, N.W.
Washington, DC 20001
Phone: (202) 727–7468, FAX: (202) 727–7662

## FLORIDA

Florida Board of Nursing
4080 Woodcock Drive, Suite 202
Jacksonville, FL 32207
Phone: (904) 858–6940, FAX: (904) 858–6964

## GEORGIA

Georgia Board of Nursing
166 Pryor Street, S.W.
Atlanta, GA 30303
Phone: (404) 656–3943, FAX: (404) 657–7489

Georgia State Board of Licensed Practical Nurses
166 Pryor Street, S.W.
Atlanta, GA 30303
Phone: (404) 656–3921, FAX: (404) 651–9532

## GUAM

Guam Board of Nurse Examiners
P.O. Box 2816
Agana, GU 96910
Phone: (671) 475–0251, FAX: (671) 477–4733

## HAWAII

Hawaii Board of Nursing
Professional and Vocational Licensing Division
P.O. Box 3469
Honolulu, HI 96801
Phone: (808) 586–2695, FAX: (808) 586–2689

## IDAHO

Idaho Board of Nursing
P.O. Box 83720
Boise, ID 83720-0061
Phone: (208) 334–3110, FAX: (208) 334–3262

## ILLINOIS

Illinois Department of Professional Regulation
James R. Thompson Center
100 W. Randolph, Suite 9–300
Chicago, IL 60601
Phone: (312) 814–2715, FAX: (312) 814–3145

## INDIANA

Indiana State Board of Nursing
Health Professions Bureau
402 W. Washington Street, Suite 041
Indianapolis, IN 46204
Phone: (317) 232–2960, FAX: (317) 233–4236

## IOWA

Iowa Board of Nursing
State Capitol Complex
E. Court Avenue
Des Moines, IA 50319
Phone: (515) 281–3255, FAX: (515) 281–4825

## KANSAS

Kansas State Board of Nursing
Landon State Office Building
900 S.W. Jackson, Suite 551–S
Topeka, KS 66612
Phone: (913) 296–4929, FAX: (913) 296–3929

## KENTUCKY

Kentucky Board of Nursing
312 Whittington Parkway, Suite 300
Louisville, KY 40222
Phone: (502) 329–7006, FAX: (502) 329–7011

## LOUISIANA

Louisiana State Board of Nursing
3510 N. Causeway Boulevard, Suite 501
Metairie, LA 70002
Phone: (504) 838–5332, FAX: (504) 838–5349

Louisiana State Board of Practical Nurse Examiners
3421 N. Causeway Boulevard, Suite 203
Metairie, LA 70002
Phone: (504) 838–5791, FAX: (504) 838–5279

## MAINE

Maine State Board of Nursing
158 State House Station
Augusta, ME 04333
Phone: (207) 287–1133, FAX: (207) 287–1149

## MARYLAND

Maryland Board of Nursing
4140 Patterson Avenue
Baltimore, MD 21215
Phone: (410) 764–5124, FAX: (410) 358–3530

## MASSACHUSETTS

Massachusetts Board of Registration in Nursing
Leverett Saltonstall Building
1100 Cambridge Street, Room 1519
Boston, MA 02202
Phone: (617) 727–9961, FAX: (617) 727–2197

## MICHIGAN

State of Michigan
CIS/Office of Health Services
Ottawa Towers North
611 W. Ottawa, 4th Floor
Lansing, MI 48933
Phone: (517) 373–9102, FAX: (517) 373–2179

## MINNESOTA

Minnesota Board of Nursing
2829 University Avenue S.E., Suite 500

Minneapolis, MN 55414
Phone: (612) 617–2270, FAX: (612) 617–2190

## MISSISSIPPI

Mississippi Board of Nursing
239 N. Lamar Street, Suite 401
Jackson, MS 39201
Phone: (601) 359–6170, FAX: (601) 359–6185

## MISSOURI

Missouri State Board of Nursing
P.O. Box 656
Jefferson City, MO 65102
Phone: (573) 751–0681, FAX: (573) 751–0075

## MONTANA

Montana State Board of Nursing
111 N. Jackson
Helena, MT 59620
Phone: (406) 444–2071, FAX: (406) 444–7759

## NEBRASKA

Department of Health and Human Services
Regulation and Licensure Credentialing Division—
Nursing/Nursing Support Section
P.O. Box 94986
Lincoln, NE 68509
Phone: (402) 471–4376, FAX: (402) 471–3577

## NEVADA

Nevada State Board of Nursing
1755 E. Plumb Lane, Suite 260
Reno, NV 89502
Phone: (702) 786–2778, FAX: (702) 322–6993

## NEW HAMPSHIRE

New Hampshire Board of Nursing
Health & Welfare Building
6 Hazen Drive
Concord, NH 03301
Phone: (603) 271–2323, FAX: (603) 271–6605

## NEW JERSEY

New Jersey Board of Nursing
P.O. Box 45010
Newark, NJ 07101
Phone: (201) 504–6586, FAX: (201) 648–3481

## NEW MEXICO

New Mexico Board of Nursing
4206 Louisiana Boulevard, N.E., Suite A
Albuquerque, NM 87109
Phone: (505) 841–8340, FAX: (505) 841–8347

## NEW YORK

New York State Board of Nursing
State Education Department
Cultural Education Center, Room 3023
Albany, NY 12230
Phone: (518) 474–3845, FAX: (518) 473–0578

## NORTH CAROLINA

North Carolina Board of Nursing
3724 National Drive
Raleigh, NC 27602
Phone: (919) 782–3211, FAX: (919) 781–9461

## NORTH DAKOTA

North Dakota Board of Nursing
919 S. 7th Street, Suite 504
Bismarck, ND 58504
Phone: (701) 328–9777, FAX: (701) 328–9785

## NORTHERN MARIANA ISLANDS

Commonwealth Board of Nurse Examiners
Public Health Center
P.O. Box 1458
Saipan, Marianas Protectorate 96950
Phone: (670) 234–8950, FAX: (670) 234–8930

## OHIO

Ohio Board of Nursing
77 S. High Street, 17th Floor

Columbus, OH 43215
Phone: (614) 466–3947, FAX: (614) 466–0388

## OKLAHOMA
Oklahoma Board of Nursing
2915 N. Classen Boulevard, Suite 524
Oklahoma City, OK 73106
Phone: (405) 525–2076, FAX: (405) 521–6089

## OREGON
Oregon State Board of Nursing
800 NE Oregon Street, Suite 465
Box 25
Portland, OR 97232
Phone: (503) 731–4745, FAX: (503) 731–4755

## PENNSYLVANIA
Pennsylvania State Board of Nursing
P.O. Box 2649
Harrisburg, PA 17105
Phone: (717) 783–7142, FAX: (717) 783–0822

## PUERTO RICO
Commonwealth of Puerto Rico
Board of Nurse Examiners
Call Box 10200
Santurce, PR 00908
Phone: (787) 725–8161, FAX: (787) 725–7903

## RHODE ISLAND
Rhode Island Board of Nurse Registration and Nursing Education
Cannon Health Building
Three Capitol Hill, Room 104
Providence, RI 02908
Phone: (401) 277–2827, FAX: (401) 277–1272

## SOUTH CAROLINA
South Carolina State Board of Nursing
110 Centerview Drive, Suite 202
Columbia, SC 29210
Phone: (803) 896–4550, FAX: (803) 896–4525

## SOUTH DAKOTA

South Dakota Board of Nursing
3307 S. Lincoln Avenue
Sioux Falls, SD 57105
Phone: (605) 367–5940, FAX: (605) 367–5945

## TENNESSEE

Tennessee State Board of Nursing
426 Fifth Avenue North
1st Floor, Cordell Hull Building
Nashville, TN 37247
Phone: (615) 532–5166, FAX: (615) 741–7899

## TEXAS

Texas Board of Nurse Examiners
P.O. Box 430
Austin, TX 78767
Phone: (512) 305–7400, FAX: (512) 305–7401

Texas Board of Vocational Nurse Examiners
William P. Hobby Building, Tower 3
333 Guadalupe Street, Suite 3–400
Austin, TX 78701
Phone: (512) 305–8100, FAX: (512) 305–8101

## UTAH

Utah State Board of Nursing
Division of Occupational and Professional Licensing
160 E. 300 South, 4th Floor
Salt Lake City, UT 84145
Phone: (801) 530–6628, FAX: (801) 530–6511

## VERMONT

Vermont State Board of Nursing
109 State Street
Montpelier, VT 05609
Phone: (802) 828–2396, FAX: (802) 828–2484

## VIRGIN ISLANDS

Virgin Islands Board of Nurse Licensure
Veterans Drive Station

St. Thomas, VI 00803
Phone: (340) 776–7397, FAX: (340) 777–4003

## VIRGINIA

Virginia Board of Nursing
6606 W. Broad Street, 4th Floor
Richmond, VA 23230
Phone: (804) 662–9909, FAX: (804) 662–9943

## WASHINGTON

Washington State Nursing Care Quality Assurance Commission
Department of Health
Olympia, WA 98504
Phone: (360) 753–2686, FAX: (360) 586–2165

## WEST VIRGINIA

West Virginia Board of Examiners for Registered Professional Nurses
101 Dee Drive
Charleston, WV 25311
Phone: (304) 558–3596, FAX: (304) 558–3666

West Virginia State Board of Examiners for Practical Nurses
101 Dee Drive
Charleston, WV 25311
Phone: (304) 558–3572, FAX: (304) 558–4367

## WISCONSIN

Wisconsin Department of Regulation and Licensing
1400 E. Washington Avenue
Madison, WI 53708
Phone: (608) 266–2112, FAX: (608) 267–0644

## WYOMING

Wyoming State Board of Nursing
2020 Carey Avenue, Suite 110
Cheyenne, WY 82002
Phone: (307) 777–7601, FAX: (307) 777–3519

# Glossary

*Abandonment*: The abrupt, unjustified dissolution by a health care provider of a duty to a patient without the patient's consent or foreknowledge.

*Absolute privilege*: The protection, granted under law, to the confidentiality of communications between an attorney and the attorney's client.

*Action*: Lawsuit.

*Administrative agency*: A department of government that promulgates, administers, and enforces the statutory laws enacted by that government.

*Administrative laws*: Those rules and regulations created and enforced by administrative agencies in order to enforce statutory laws.

*Admissions of fact*: Written requests by both sides asking each other to admit to, or deny, certain facts concerning the issues presented in a lawsuit.

*Advance directive*: A written, signed, legal document that defines a competent individual's wishes regarding life-sustaining medical intervention on his or her behalf in the event that he or she would become incompetent.

*Affidavit*: A declaration or written statement of facts made voluntarily and while under an oath administered by an officer of a court or by a notary.

*Affirmative defense*: A challenge by the defendant to the plaintiff's legal right to bring a lawsuit rather than a challenge to the veracity of the plaintiff's claims.

*Amended pleadings*: Those that in some way alter pleadings previously entered in the lawsuit.

*Assault*: Any attempt or threat made by one person to use force upon, to inflict injury upon, or to touch another person in an offensive way without his or her consent. It is any willful action or statement that creates fear or apprehension of being touched in an injurious or abhorrent manner. Actual touching need not occur. A threatened battery.

*Battery*: The intentional, unpermitted, and wrongful touching of another person, or that person's possessions, in an injurious or offensive manner.

*Borrowed servant/employee doctrine*: Also known as the "captain of the ship doctrine." The temporary assignment of vicarious liability from a principal employer to a designated employer who then becomes legally responsible for any employee who, voluntarily, is "borrowed" from the primary employer.

*Breach of duty*: Any failure in a defined legal, moral, or ethical duty owed. Negligence in the proper performance or fulfillment of the duties inherent in a position, office, or profession.

*Burden of proof* (Onus probandi): Under the laws of evidence, this is the requirement that either party in a lawsuit is obligated to prove, by a preponderance of evidence, the allegations he or she makes. This burden usually falls upon the plaintiff.

*Capacity*: The intellectual capability to understand the nature, the purpose, and the consequences of one's actions.

*Captain of the ship doctrine*: Synonymous with the borrowed servant doctrine.

*Causation*: Any antecedent action or situation that can define a consequent effect.

*Cause in fact*: The specific action or situation that defines a consequent effect and, without which, the effect could not have come about.

*Cause of action*: Those alleged facts that give an individual sufficient legal right to initiate a claim in law for redress, relief, or other form of judicial remedy in his or her own behalf.

Caveat: Lit. "beware," or "take heed". A caution or warning.

Caveat emptor: "Let the buyer beware".

Caveat lector: "Let the reader beware".

*Civil law*: That body of law that addresses noncriminal litigation, for example, the rights and duties of parties involved in contracts, torts, and patents.

*Civil penalty*: Monetary compensation (damages) or other form of retribution prescribed and imposed as a penalty for violation of a civil law.

*Claims-made policy*: That form of a malpractice insurance policy that provides coverage only for claims made, and reported, to the insurer during the period in which the policy is in effect, or during the "tail".

*Comparative negligence*: The degree of relative negligence and liability is measured in proportion to the percentage of shared fault for, or relative contribution to, the plaintiff's injuries on the part of the plaintiff and/or one or more defendants. Damages claimed are then apportioned accordingly as determined by the jury.

*Compensatory damages*: An amount awarded to an injured party to compensate for the injury by indemnification for any loss caused by the injury.

*Competency*: Legal capacity. An affirmation of competency may be sought from, and declared by, a court.

*Complaint*: The document in which the plaintiff, under oath, presents allegations of injury and a formal plea to a civil court for relief under the law in a claim for damages. Also called a petition. It is a statement of cause for judicial action against a named defendant.

*Consent*: A voluntary acquiescence, approval, agreement, or permission conveyed by one person to another and which allows the other to do something to or for the person consenting.

*Contributory negligence*: A negligent action or omission on the part of a plaintiff which, together with a like action or omission on the part of a defendant, constitutes a proximate cause of the injuries claimed by the plaintiff.

*Corporate negligence*: Legal principle under which a corporate entity is held liable for the actions or omissions of employees while those employees are on the job and acting within the scope of their job descriptions.

*Counterclaim*: A claim made by a defendant that disputes, denies, opposes, contradicts, or refutes the claims made by the plaintiff and that attempts to show cause for action in favor of the defendant.

*Damage*: The injury, harm, or loss sustained by one person as a result of the tortious action of another.

*Damages*: The amount of money claimed and/or awarded as compensation for damage.

*Defamation*: The intentional publication of false information that injures the reputation of another; includes slander and libel.

*Default judgment*: A judgment made by the court in favor of a plaintiff when a defendant fails to respond to a lawsuit or appear at the trial in his or her own defense.

*Defendant*: The accused; the person or entity who is being sued. The one against whom a lawsuit is brought and who is charged with defending against the allegations and the claims of the plaintiff for relief under the law.

*Defense*: That which is offered and alleged by the defendant in response to the action or suit by a plaintiff and which attempts to show as a reason in law, or in fact, why the plaintiff should not recover damages.

*Deponent*: The individual who is called upon to testify under oath to the truth of certain facts presented orally or in writing.

*Deposition*: The procedure of deriving pretrial testimony from a deponent.

*Discovery*: The pretrial procedures and methods used to obtain all relevant information from opposing parties in a lawsuit.

*Discovery rule*: Under this rule, the statute of limitations in malpractice does not commence until the actual date of discovery of the malpractice by the plaintiff, or that date on which any reasonable person could have, or should have, discovered that an injury was the result of malpractice.

*Dual servant doctrine*: The legal concept that recognizes shared liability on the part of both a principal and a secondary employer for the actions of a shared employee.

*Durable power of attorney*: A form of an advance directive that appoints another to act as proxy decision maker should the grantor become incompetent. Revocable; it is nullified when the grantor dies.

*Duty*: A legal or moral obligation owed by one person to another to conform to defined, acceptable standards of conduct in order to protect others from unreasonable risks.

*Emancipated minor*: Any individual under the legal age of majority who is totally self-supporting, and no longer under the control of, or dependent on, the care of a parent or guardian.

*Exclusions*: The provisions in any insurance policy that define the conditions, occurrences, or circumstances that are not covered under the terms of the policy.

*Expert witness*: An individual who, by reason of specialized education, training, and experience, possesses a superior degree of knowledge regarding specific subjects which, ordinarily, another person would not possess.

*Fact witness*: An individual who has direct knowledge of, and testifies to, the factual circumstances and issues involved in a lawsuit; a material witness.

*False imprisonment*: The unlawful, unjustified, and intentional restraint, detention, or confinement of a person without consent, and/or without legal warrant, so that the person so confined is conscious of the confinement and threatened or harmed by it.

*Foreseeability*: The perception and understanding expected of any reasonable and prudent person of the liability for, and the consequences of, his or her actions or omissions—particularly regarding the inherent risks to others.

*General damages*: Monetary compensation awarded to a plaintiff for pain, suffering, and other abstract injuries caused by the negligence of a defendant.

*Gross negligence*: The willful failure to perform a manifest duty with reckless disregard for the possible or probable consequences of that failure regarding the well-being of another. It may be an action or an omission.

Guardian-ad-litem: An individual appointed by a court to act as a special and impartial guardian to represent an unborn, an infant, a ward, or any person adjudicated as incompetent. The appointment exists only for the duration of the particular litigation involved.

*Guidelines*: A defined or recommended course of action or series of procedures which, if followed, will enable effective implementaion of a policy or attainment of a goal.

*Hard damages*: Monetary compensation awarded to a plaintiff for the specific amounts of expenses and financial losses incurred, and claimed to have resulted, from the defendant's negligence.

*Hearsay evidence*: That testimony of a witness who presents not what he or she knows directly and personally, but what he or she has heard or been told. A statement made by other than the declarent, which is offered as evidence but not generally admissible.

*Incompetence*: The lack of legal or professional qualifications, knowledge, ability, or suitability to discharge a duty. A determination of competency may be a matter for a court.

*Informed consent*: Consent given only after a full disclosure and confirmed understanding of all pertinent facts necessary for the individual to make an intelligent, reasonable, and voluntary choice.

*Intent*: The desire, design, determination, or resolve with which a person acts to accomplish a given purpose through a deliberate course of action.

*Intentional infliction of emotional distress*: The egregious and willful invasion of another's peace of mind in a manner that is wanton, outrageous, and beyond all acceptable standards of decency and morality.

*Intentional tort*: A civil wrong resulting from an intentional act by the tortfeasor and that causes injury or harm to another's person or property.

*Interrogatories*: A pretrial discovery procedure in which a series of written questions are presented to the opposing parties named in a lawsuit. The answers are presented under oath.

*Invasion of privacy*: The unwarranted publication of another person's private affairs, or the intrusion into another's private activities in such a way as to violate his or her intrinsic rights and cause personal harm in some way.

*Judgment*: The adjudicated decision of a court that defines the rights and duties of the parties in a lawsuit.

*Judicial law*: Rules of law established by courts or the judiciary; decisional law.

*Jury*: "Twelve persons selected to decide who has the best lawyer." (Robert Frost)

*Law*: That which is laid down and established as the embodiment of those rules of conduct defined by a legal authority and having binding legal force on the members of a society.

*Lay witness*: An individual who is called upon to give testimony on matters regarding the lawsuit but who possesses no special knowledge or expertise regarding the issues or facts about which he or she testifies.

*Liability*: Legal duty, responsibility, or obligation each person is bound to in law or justice to perform. Legal accountability and responsibility for one's personal actions or conduct.

*Libel*: Defamation that is expressed in writing or pictorially.

*Licensure*: The procedures by which an agency of government conveys the right, permission, and authority to a person or entity to engage legally in an activity, practice, or professional occupation.

*Living will*: A form of advance directive. A written, signed, and witnessed legal document that defines a person's wishes regarding life-sustaining measures of medical intervention to be implemented on his or her behalf in the event that the person becomes incompetent.

*Locality rule*: Refers to those standards of care that prevail in a community or a defined geographical area. National standards have largely displaced these in malpractice lawsuits.

*Malice*: The state of mind that motivates an individual to willfully commit a wrongful act with the deliberate intent to injure another or with wanton disregard of the likelihood of such injury as a consequence of his or her action.

*Malpractice*: Negligence or misconduct on the part of a professional while acting in the capacity of a professional. A failure in professional duties or standards that causes harm or injury to another.

*Mandatory licensure*: A statutory requirement that permits the practice of certain professions or activities only to those who have received a license to engage legally in such practice.

*Material risk*: An apparent and significant danger that any reasonable person should recognize as a likely consequence of an action or omission.

*Motion*: A formal application made to a court in order to obtain a ruling or order that directs an action in favor of the applicant.

*Motion for a directed verdict*: A formal request that a lawsuit be concluded by a verdict in favor of the defendant because the plaintiff has not met the burden of proof, or the defendant has presented a sufficient, irrefutable defense.

*Motion to dismiss*: Application to the court requesting the court to set aside the case because there is no valid cause of action or form of relief.

*Negligence*: Ordinary negligence. The failure to act with that degree of care that any ordinary, prudent, and reasonable person would exercise in the same or similar circumstances.

Non compos mentis: Lit. "not of sound mind." Incompetent, insane, afflicted with some form of debilitating mental impairment.

*Nonmaleficence*: The legal and moral principle that enjoins health care providers to do no harm to a patient—intentionally or otherwise.

*Nonsuit*: The adverse judgment of the court when the plaintiff fails to properly proceed to a trial, leaving the allegations unresolved, or is unable to sustain the burden of proof during a trial. Also used to indicate a defendant who is discharged from a lawsuit.

*Occurrence-basis, occurrence policy*: The category of professional liability insurance that protects the insured for acts of malpractice that occur while the policy is in effect, regardless of when a claim is made afterward.

*Ordinary negligence*: *See* Negligence.

*Ostensible authority*: The doctrine of law whereby an institution is liable for the negligence of an independent contractor if a patient has a reasonable basis to assume that such a contractor is an employee of the institution. (See Borrowed servant/employee doctrine).

Parens patriae: Lit. "parent of the nation." Refers to the role of the state in its sovereign capacity as legal guardian of an adjudicated incompetent person or a person having some form of legal disability that prevents him or her from acting on his or her own behalf.

*Party*: A person or entity that is designated in a lawsuit as either a plaintiff or a defendant of record.

*Personal liability*: The legal and moral doctrine that holds the individual solely responsible, and fully accountable, for his or her own actions or omissions.

*Petition*: A formal written application to a court requesting judicial intervention in the matter presented, and a presentation of allegations and facts that have given rise to the cause of action. *See* Complaint.

*Plaintiff*: The party who brings an action, who sues in a civil court, seeking damages or other form of relief under the law for alleged damage, loss, or harm caused by the defendant.

*Pleadings*: The formal presentation to the court of claims and defenses by the respective parties in a lawsuit. A statement of the plaintiff's cause for action, and the defendant's defense and/or refutation of that cause.

*Precedent*: A case that has been decided or adjudicated by a court, and which is afterward accepted and cited as authoritative in the adjudication of a similar case or like matters or questions of law. Also known as the doctrine of *stare decisis*.

Prima facie: Lit. "at first sight," on primary appearance, on the face of it. A fact or matter that can be judged at its first disclosure and presumed to be true unless, or until, it can be proven untrue by evidence to the contrary.

*Privileged communication*: The transmission of information or facts between or among those individuals who, in a professional relationship, are protected by law or custom from compelled divulgence of such confidences.

*Procedural law*: That body of law that defines the processes, methods, and procedures to be used in enforcing legal rights and obtaining relief or redress when they are violated.

*Proximate cause*: That continuous sequence of actions or natural happenings which, without any other identifiable intervening factors, produces an effect which, otherwise, would not have occurred.

*Prudent patient standard*: Takes into consideration the principal risks and the likely consequences that would be apparent to, and understandable by, any reasonable, prudent person in a decision to accept or reject medical treatment.

*Punitive damages*: Exemplary damages. Those that are awarded, in addition to ordinary or general damages, against a defendant as punishment for the egregious nature of the tort.

*Qualified privilege*: Defense to a *prima faciae* case of defamation when it can be shown that there was no malicious intent on the part of the defendant. That is, the statements were made in duty or good faith, in a reasonable manner, for a valid reason, and directed to another person with a legitimate right to know.

*Question of fact*: A disputed fact, claim, or issue that is usually left to the jury to decide and resolve.

*Question of law*: A disputed legal contention that is usually left to the court or the judge to decide. This involves the application or intepretation of the law itself, and, therefore, is appropriately within the purview of the court rather than a jury.

*Release*: A statement, written or oral, which declares the maker's intent to discharge another person from an existing or asserted duty, or the abandonment or relinquishment of a present and/or future claim or right.

*Requests for production of documents and things*: A step in the discovery process. Formal requisition made by parties in a lawsuit to each side for any and all items that might provide discoverable facts pertinent to the issues.

Res ipsa loquitur: Lit. "let the thing speak for itself." The negligence of the defendant can be inferred or presumed, based on proof that the instrumentality that caused the plaintiff's injury was under the exclusive control of the defendant, and that the injury is such that it otherwise could have not have occurred except in negligence.

Respondeat superior: Lit. "Let the master answer." The master is responsible for the acts of the servant. An employer is indirectly liable, under certain circumstances, for the wrongful acts of an employee while the employee is acting within the course of employment. This includes negligence that causes harm or injury to another.

*Scope of practice*: Those limits, duties, and responsibilities of any given profession that are defined by statutes, rules, and regulations.

*Service*: Service of process, a summons. The delivery of an official notice to the defendant that a lawsuit, claim, or a charge has been filed against him or her.

*Settlement*: The private agreement and transactions between the parties to a pending lawsuit to effect a resolution of all claims and issues involved.

*Slander*: Oral defamation.

*Soft damages*: Monetary compensation awarded to a plaintiff for such things as loss of consortium, pain and suffering, emotional distress, disfigurement.

*Special damages*: Damages based on the plaintiff's actual or anticipated, direct or indirect, monetary losses or expenses, which are directly attributable to the defendant's negligence.

*Standard*: An established, authoritative, and generally accepted rule, model, or criterion that serves as a basis of evaluation, comparison, or validation.

*Standard of care*: In tort law, that average, acceptable degree of skill, care, and diligence that a reasonable and prudent person in the same profession, would, or should, exercise in the same or similar circumstances.

Stare decisis: Lit. "let the decision stand." *See* Precedent.

*Statute of limitations*: The procedural law that defines the maximum duration of time within which certain legal actions can be brought by a plaintiff.

*Substantive law*: That body of law that creates, defines, directs, and controls individual rights and duties and that identifies specific causes for action regarding such rights and duties.

*Substitute judgment*: A subjective assessment or decision by one person as to how another person would decide, if that other person were, in fact, competent to do so.

*Supplemental pleadings*: *See* Amended pleadings.

*Tail*: An uninterrupted extension of the coverage period of a malpractice insurance policy; also known as the extended reporting endorsement.

*Testimony*: Statements of evidence given by a competent witness under oath.

*Therapeutic privilege*: The legal concept that sanctions the withholding of information by a health care provider when such information is deemed likely to jeopardize the health and well-being of a patient.

*Tort*: A civil wrong, other than that involved in a contract, that results from a breach of duty, and which produces harm or injury to the person or property of another.

*Tortfeasor*: One who commits or is guilty of a tort.

*Unintentional tort*: A civil wrong resulting from an unintentional act by the tortfeasor and that causes injury or harm to another's person or property.

*Vicarious liability*: The imputing of liability on one person for the wrongful actions of another based on a direct relationship between the two persons. Also known as substituted liability.

Voir dire: A judicial process. A requirement "to speak the truth."

*Waiver*: Voluntary relinquishment of a right.

*Writ of* certiorari: A formal written petition to the Supreme Court, made by the losing party, that the Court review the case.

*Writ of* habeas corpus: Lit. "you have the body." A legal procedure to determine the legality of a individual's custody or confinement by having the person brought before court at his or her request or on order of the court itself (the writ).

# Bibliography

Aiken, Tonia, and Joseph Catalano. *Legal, Ethical and Political Issues in Nursing*. F. A. Davis, 1994.

American Medical Association, Council on Ethical and Judicial Affairs. *Code of Medical Ethics: Current Opinions*. 1992.

American Nurses Association. *Action Report: Telenursing and Telehealth*. 1996.

American Nurses Association. *Registered Professional Nurses and Assistive Personnel*. 1994.

American Nurses Association. *Position Statement on Nursing and the Patient Self-Determination Act*. 1992.

American Nurses Association. *Standards for Clinical Nursing Practice*. 1991.

American Nurses Association. *Code for Nurses with Interpretive Statements*. 1985.

Appleby, Kristyn S., and Joanne Tarver. *Medical Records Review*. 2d ed. *Cumulative Supplement*. John Wiley & Sons, 1997.

Appleby, Kristyn S., and Joanne Tarver. *Medical Records Review*. 2d ed. John Wiley & Sons, 1994.

Beckman, Janet. *Nursing Negligence: Analyzing Malpractice in the Hospital Setting*. Sage Publications, 1996.

———. *Nursing Malpractice: Implications for Clinical and Nursing Education*. University of Washington Press, 1994.

Bernzweig, Eli P. *The Nurse's Liability for Malpractice: A Programmed Instruction.* 6th ed. C.V. Mosby, 1995.

Black, Henry C. *Black's Law Dictionary.* 6th ed. West Publishing, 1990.

Brent, Nancy J. *Nurses and the Law.* W. B. Saunders, 1997.

Bullough, Barbara, et al. *Nursing Issues for the Nineties and Beyond.* Springer Publishing, 1994.

Calfee, Barbara E. Protecting yourself from allegations of nursing negligence. *Nursing91* 21 (December 1991): 34–39.

Catalano, Joseph. *Ethical and Legal Aspects of Nursing.* Springhouse Corp., 1991.

Cournoyer, Carmelle P. How to protect yourself legally after a patient is injured. *Nursing95 Career Directory* (January 1995): 18–23.

———. *The Nurse Manager and the Law.* Aspen Publishers, 1989.

Creighton, Helen. *Law Every Nurse Should Know.* 5th ed. W. B. Saunders, 1986.

Cushing, Maureen. *Nursing Jurisprudence.* Appleton & Lange, 1988.

Edelstein, Jacqueline. A study of nursing documentation. *Nursing Management* 21 (November 1990): 40–46.

Eichorst, Patricia, ed. *Medicolegal Issues for Nurses.* Eastwind Publishing, 1993.

Eskreis, Tina R. Seven common legal pitfalls in nursing. *American Journal of Nursing* 98 (April 1998): 34–40.

*Federal Register* 54 (199) (Tuesday, October 17, 1989): 1–14.

Feutz-Harter, Sheryl. *Nursing and the Law.* 4th ed. Professional Education Systems, 1991.

Fiesta, Janine. *Legal Issues for Long Term Care.* Delmar Publishers, 1996.

———. *20 Legal Pitfalls for Nurses to Avoid.* Delmar Publishers, 1994.

———. *The Law and Liability: A Guide for Nurses.* 2d ed. John Wiley & Sons, 1988.

Fletcher, Nina, and Janet Holt. *Ethics, Law, & Nursing.* St. Martin's Press, 1995.

Furmidge, Marva L., and Marjorie Barter. Supreme Court decision affects bargaining rights of nurses. *Journal of Nursing Administration* 24 (July-August 1994): 9–11.

Gardner, Sandra. *Legal Aspects of Maternal Child Nursing Practice.* Addison-Wesley Longman, 1997.

Gobis, Linda J. Telenursing: Nursing by telephone across state lines. *Journal of Nursing Law* 3 (March 1996): 7–17.

———. Computerized patient records: Start preparing now. *Journal of Nursing Administration* 24 (September 1994): 15–16, 60.

Goldstein, A., S. Perdew, and S. Pruitt. *The Nurse's Legal Advisor.* Lippincott, 1989.

Guido, Ginny W. *Legal Issues in Nursing.* 2d ed. Appleton & Lange, 1996.

———. *Legal Issues in Nursing: A Source Book for Practice.* Appleton & Lange, 1988.

Helmlinger, Connie, and Kathy Milholland. Telehealth discussions focus on li-
    censure. *American Journal of Nursing* 97 (June 1997): 61–62.

Horton, Maria C. The Role of Nursing in Telemedicine. January 1997: 1–7 re-
    trieved from: http://www.matmo.org/pages/library/papers/nurse-
    rol/nursrol.html

Iyer, Patricia. *Nurse Malpractice*. Lawyers & Judges Publishing Company, 1996.

Johnson, Diann, and Sidney M. Wolfe. *Medical Records: Getting Yours*. Public
    Citizen's Health Research Group, 1995.

Joint Commission on Accreditation of Healthcare Organizations. *Accreditation
    Manual for Hospitals*. 1993.

Kjervik, D. K. Telenursing—Licensure and communication challenges. *Journal
    of Professional Nursing* 13 (2) (March-April, 1997): 65.

Lobb, Michael L., Gary C. Riley, and April M. Clemens. The legal nurse con-
    sultant's role on the defense team in a medical malpractice lawsuit. *Net-
    work* 5 (April 1994): 3–7.

McHale, Jean V. *Law and Nursing*. Butterworth-Heinemann, 1998.

McManamen, L., and L. Hendrickx. Telemedicine: Tuning in critical care's fu-
    ture? *Critical Care Nurse* 16 (March 1996): 102–7.

Mezey, Mathy, Lois K. Evans, Zola D. Golub, Elizabeth Murphy, and Gladys B.
    White. The patient Self-Determination Act: Sources of concern for
    nurses. *Nursing Outlook* 42 (January 1994): 30–38.

Milholland, D. K. Telehealth, telenursing, telewhat? *American Nurse* 27 (6) (Sep-
    tember 1995): 13.

Moniz, Donna M. The legal danger of written protocols and standards of practice.
    *Nurse Practitioner* 17 (September 1992): 58–60.

Morelaw, Inc. *Pennsylvania Jury Verdicts*. October 4, 1993.

National Council of State Boards of Nursing. *Position Paper on Telenursing: A
    Challenge to Regulation*. 1997.

National Council of State Boards of Nursing. *National Council Position Paper on
    the Regulation of Advanced Practice Nursing*. 1993a.

National Council of State Boards of Nursing. *National Council Position Paper
    (8/93): Facts About Advanced Nursing Practice Regulation*. 1993b.

National Practitioner Data Bank. *National Practitioner Data Bank Guidebook*.
    U.S. Department of Health and Human Services, 1996.

Northrop, Cynthia, and Mary Kelly. *Legal Issues in Nursing*. Mosby Year Book,
    1987.

Privacy Protection Study Commission. *Record-keeping in the Medical-care Re-
    lationship: Personal Privacy in an Information Society*. U.S. Govern-
    ment Printing Office, 1977.

Richards, Edward, and Katharine Rathbun. *Law and the Physician: A Practical
    Guide*. Little Brown and Co., 1993. (An electronic book, online. See ap-
    pendix II: List of Web Sites, Medical and Public Health Law Site [The].)

Rozovsky, Fay, and Lorne Rozovsky. *Home Health Care Law: Liability and Risk Management.* Little Brown and Co., 1993.

Schwarz, Judith K. Living wills and health care proxies: Nurse practice implications. *Nursing and Health Care* 13 (March 1992): 92–96.

Sharpe, Charles C. *Medical Records Review and Analysis.* Auburn House, 1999.

Sloan, Gale. *Nursing and Malpractice Risks: Understanding the Law.* Western Schools, 1993.

Springhouse Corporation. *Nurse's Handbook of Law and Ethics.* Springhouse Corporation, 1992.

Wecht, C. H. Patient access to medical records: Yea or nay? *Legal Aspects of Medical Practice* (October 9, 1978): 8–10.

Yensen, Jack. Telenursing, virtual nursing and beyond. *Computers in Nursing* 14 (4) (July-August 1996): 213–14.

Youngberg, Barbara, and Becky Colgen. *Nursing & Malpractice: Understanding the Law.* 3d ed. Western Schools, 1996.

# Index

## About the Author

CHARLES C. SHARPE is a retired pediatric clinical nurse specialist. In addition to his many years of experience in clinical nursing practice, he has been a faculty member of the departments of nursing and paralegal studies at several colleges in Pennsylvania. He is also the author of *Medical Records Review and Analysis* (Auburn House, 1999).